DATA VISUALIZATION FOR SUCCESS

Interviews with
40 Experienced Designers

DATA VISUALIZATION FOR SUCCESS

Interviews with 40 Experienced Designers

Edited by Steven Braun

images
Publishing

Published in Australia in 2017 by
The Images Publishing Group Pty Ltd
Shanghai Office
ABN 89 059 734 431
6 Bastow Place, Mulgrave, Victoria 3170, Australia
Tel: +61 3 9561 5544 Fax: +61 3 9561 4860
books@imagespublishing.com
www.imagespublishing.com

Copyright © The Images Publishing Group Pty Ltd 2017
The Images Publishing Group Reference Number: 1363

All rights reserved. Apart from any fair dealing for the purposes of private study, research, criticism or review as permitted under the Copyright Act, no part of this publication may be reproduced, stored in a retrieval system or transmitted in any form by any means, electronic, mechanical, photocopying, recording or otherwise, without the written permission of the publisher.

Title: Data Visualization for Success: Interviews with 40 Experienced Designers
Author: Steven Braun (ed.)
ISBN: 9781864707205

For Catalogue-in-Publication data, please see the National Library of Australia entry

Printed by Everbest Printing Investment Limited., Hong Kong/China

IMAGES has included on its website a page for special notices in relation to this and our other publications. Please visit www.imagespublishing.com

Every effort has been made to trace the original source of copyright material contained in this book. The publishers would be pleased to hear from copyright holders to rectify any errors or omissions. The information and illustrations in this publication have been prepared and supplied by the author and the contributors. While all reasonable efforts have been made to ensure accuracy, the publishers do not, under any circumstances, accept responsibility for errors, omissions and representations, express or implied.

Contents

- **6** — **Data Visualization in the World Around Us**
  - 6 — The Definition of Data Visualization
  - 7 — Key Principles of Design
  - 8 — Visualization and the Quest for Objectivity in Medium and Message
  - 10 — Future Trends
  - 11 — References

- 12 — Kim Albrecht
- 18 — RJ Andrews
- 22 — Adriano Attus
- 28 — Steven Braun
- 36 — Nadieh Bremer
- 44 — Luis Carli
- 50 — Chelsea Carlson
- 54 — Sabina Castagnaviz
- 60 — Meng Chih Chiang
- 66 — Cloudred
- 70 — Dataveyes
- 76 — Marcelo Duhalde
- 80 — Antonio Farach
- 84 — Artur Galocha
- 90 — Manuela Garreton
- 96 — Stefania Guerra
- 102 — Hahn+Zimmermann
- 112 — Heyday
- 118 — Interactive Things
- 126 — JESS3

- 130 — LaTigre
- 138 — Susana Lopes
- 144 — Massimiliano Mauro
- 148 — Santiago Ortiz
- 158 — Valerio Pellegrini
- 166 — Periscopic
- 172 — Sara Piccolomini
- 182 — Pitch Interactive
- 188 — Raconteur Media
- 192 — Matthew Rowett
- 198 — Signal Noise
- 206 — South China Morning Post
- 212 — Moritz Stefaner
- 224 — Duncan Swain
- 230 — The Design Surgery
- 234 — Roxana Torre
- 240 — Jan Willem Tulp
- 246 — Gemma Warriner
- 250 — Krist Wongsuphasawat
- 256 — Carlo Zapponi

- 262 — Index

Data Visualization in the World Around Us

Steven Braun

The Definition of Data Visualization

In recent years, an explosion of interest in information visualization has resulted in a proliferation of products, tools, and resources for expert and novice alike to quantify and visually communicate the world around us in stunningly beautiful ways. Increasingly the poster child of interdisciplinarity, visualization has made great strides in breaking down walls that once divided the arts and humanities, social sciences, and natural sciences, showing that cross-fertilization across fields can produce insights that may have been out of reach before. By pulling together paradigms and knowledge from design, psychology, philosophy, cognitive science, and countless other fields of inquiry, information visualization has become a critical catalyst of technological and disciplinary equalization in the creative maker culture; anyone can lift compelling narratives out of their data with the right tools, regardless of background or training. Visualization has played a critical role in digital humanities as well, inspiring humanists to think about their data in new digital ways and offering novel pathways of inquiry through texts, images, and maps. The designers and works featured in this volume demonstrate these myriad ways in which data visualization has been developed as a medium for communicating information and interrogating the world around us.

Although few may argue that its impact has been significant and far-reaching in social, cultural, and academic domains, the same cannot always be said when it comes to agreement about even the most basic definitions in the field. In practice, defining what is and is not data visualization can yield varying responses. Some definitions focus on aesthetics, emphasizing the intrinsically visual and communicative nature of data visualization; for example, Helen Kennedy define visualizations as 'visual representations of data and datasets which communicate precise information and values'. Meanwhile, Stuart K. Card and Jock Mackinlay offer a definition that emphasizes function, identifying visualization by its reference to 'the use of computer-supported, interactive, visual representations of abstract data to amplify cognition'. In *Design for Information*, too, Isabel Meirelles emphasizes this functional significance and identifies several key ways in which that function is manifest: to record information, convey meaning, facilitate discovery, and support perceptual inference, to name just a few of them. Andy Kirk echoes this sentiment in his own definition, whereby he refers to data visualization as 'the representation and presentation of data to facilitate understanding,' where facilitating understanding is the key function in motion. Jacques Bertin, in his seminal work *Semiology of Graphics*, defines graphical displays in semiological terms as cognitive artifacts of the relationship between image and cognition, stating, 'Graphic representation constitutes one of the basic sign-systems conceived by the human mind for the purposes of storing, understanding, and communicating essential information. As a "language" for the eye, graphics benefits from the ubiquitous properties of visual perception'. And any discussion of data visualization would be incomplete without reference to the work of Edward R. Tufte, who offers a prescriptive definition based on both aesthetics and function in referring to visualizations as graphical displays that should do several things: 'show the data', 'avoid distorting what the data have to say', and 'reveal the data at several levels of detail, from a broad overview to the fine structure'.

This range of definitions offered by different designers and theorists collectively illustrates practical differences in how we may engage with data visualization. And those differences are further nuanced by additional forms of language we use to describe other visual expressions of information: information design, a broader term that refers to general forms of design that aim to communicate information that may be expressed in manifestations beyond data alone, and infographics, which may be regarded as particular persuasive manifestations of visualized data. At the same time, however, this range of definitions also demonstrates that there are regions of overlap among them suggestive of common ground. In all of them, that common ground is the centrality and significance of narrative, broadly understood, which offers a new framing for collectively explaining what data visualization is or is not regardless of the specific language used. In this framing, information visualization and design are the transformation of data into a visual narrative and medium that can be expressed and interpreted in different ways. When designers create a visualization, they construct a narrative about the data that underlay it, and that narrative becomes the focus of the interpretative act that connects the designer of the visualization with the user. Thus, we can conceive of data visualization as a reference to two complementary understandings of the term: first, the creative process that transforms data into visual expression, and second, the products of that process, including the charts, graphs, and other representations we produce in that act of translation into visual media. In these framings, there is space for all of the variable definitions that have come before because the emphasis on visual narrative takes center stage.

One of the consequences of this broad definition is that visualizations themselves manifest in many different forms across different media, disciplines, and designers. A static visualization showing protein abundance from a mass spectrometry experiment will differ significantly in form and function from an interactive visualization showing relationships between Oscar nominees, for example, and thus the principles by which each is produced may differ significantly. And visualization itself is not limited to conventional media, as designers have shown that even food and basket weaving can be valuable media for visualizing information in their own right. Far from a destabilizing force, however, this apparent multimodality of information design as discipline and practice does much more to demonstrate its vitality as a highly interdisciplinary and dynamic field, one that can take on diverse challenges and tackle them with deftness. The designers showcased in this volume demonstrate that diversity as well, as their examples are cross-disciplinary and multimodal in their form. Perhaps the greatest lesson to be learnt from the collection showcased here is that data visualization, and information design more broadly, is not so easily confined to singular definitions, and to localize a definition of data visualization is to deny the intellectual and creative richness at its core.

This diversity means that data visualizations can be found all around us, and sometimes in places we may not immediately recognize or notice. Those manifestations can be found in any place that data has a story to tell, which includes practically everywhere in our world. History has shown that there are no restrictions as to what can or cannot be visualized, and new approaches to visualizing data are constantly being invented and engineered by practitioners in the field. The only limit is human imagination, which the field of information design itself seeks to challenge. In this way, visualization touches our social, cultural, political, and physical lives, affecting how we engage with information in subtle ways. The nutrition labels on the back of food packages guide our diets and food purchase habits, while maps of crime incidents influence where we buy our homes. We are exposed to charts and graphs in the news media, which with varying degrees of truthfulness and accuracy affect our perceptions of current events and political issues. In business, we may use visualization to demonstrate profits or losses in company sales, while in the scientific community, we may use visualization to communicate the findings from our experiments. Whether or not one is an active practitioner or designer, it is clear that visualization shapes our understanding of the world in countless capacities. To raise one's alertness of those many presences is to become a critical consumer of visualization, with an awareness of the ways in which visualization shapes our beliefs and behaviors.

Key Principles of Design

What makes a good visualization? Much like the act of defining what does and does not constitute data visualization itself, this question is often met with many different responses. For as many different opinions there are of what is a visualization, there are just as many or more opinions of what determines whether or not a visualization is designed effectively. Although many designers may have different criteria for effectiveness or quality, there are some general principles that tend to guide most design thinking today.

Perhaps the most foundational and classic of these come from Edward R. Tufte, an information designer who is well known for his oft-cited principles of design. In *The Visual Display of Quantitative Information*, Tufte outlines several ideas that have formed the cornerstone of visualization excellence and graphical integrity. Tufte's work is also often cited for his beliefs about the data–ink ratio, which he defines as the ratio of ink used to represent data in a visualization to the total ink used to print the graphic. Tufte is known for stating 'Above all else show the data', which can be accomplished through two simple tasks: maximize the data–ink ratio, erase what is not data–ink, and redundant data–ink, all within reason. Because of their universality, Tufte's principles of design are often the entry point for new practitioners navigating the field of information design for the first time.

Beyond the works of Tufte, however, principles of 'good' visualization design span the whole spectrum of design across many different levels of resolution. For instance, at the level of visualization mechanics, designers often rely heavily on gestalt principles of perceptual organization to guide specific choices they make in visualization design. These principles describe basic laws by which we tend to group objects in visual space, including proximity, similarity, continuity, and figure/ground. In this way, basic principles of art and design have made their way into the work of visualization more specifically. Meanwhile, principles of cognitive science have also made their way into visualization design, including scientists' knowledge of how certain visual attributes are processed differentially in the brain. For instance, Colin Ware speaks of 'preattentive attributes', like color, size, and length, which are properties of visual cues that are processed very quickly in the brain, and suggests that paying particular attention to design choices made with respect to these features and how they unfold in visual working memory can greatly enhance the quality of a good visualization. Yet other frameworks capitalize on a range of both mechanics and practical effects in considering what makes good visualization. Nathan Yau in *Visualize This: The Flowing Data Guide to Design, Visualization, and Statistics*, for example, identifies several key tasks that are essential to designing good visualizations, urging the reader to explain encodings, label axes, use appropriately scaled and proportional geometries, include sources, and consider their audience. Such a framework combines facets of both practical use and aesthetic design to assess the effectiveness of a visualization.

As with the variable definitions of 'data visualization' offered above, the varying approaches that designers take in assessing the quality of a data visualization demonstrate practical differences as well as the opportunity for common ground. In this case, that common ground can be found around a few key responsibilities that visualizations are expected to uphold in their role as medium of communication. The first of these is that good data visualization should tell a story. It is not enough to simply state the facts of a set of data; instead, those facts should be organized around a cohesive narrative. From this flows an additional responsibility, which is that a visualization should be accurate. In building a narrative around data, it is essential for that narrative to be an accurate portrayal of the data upon which it is built. A visualization should also be intuitive, empowering the user; a well-designed visualization should not require significant amounts of effort to be understood by the user and should provide the user with new information or knowledge that can be used or extrapolated in other contexts. Finally, a good visualization must gracefully fulfill its core functions of explaining data, exploring data, and discovering knowledge. These functions are explored more in the next section.

Visualization and the Quest for Objectivity in Medium and Message

Visualizations are ubiquitous in our world, and in their prevalence, they serve several different core functions. The first and perhaps most basic of these is to explain data, or communicate information in a way that is visual. A visualization in its most general capacity provides a medium of expression through which information may be presented or stated, in the process guiding our attention to specific issues or ideas. After this, a visualization functions as a medium to explore data; as a visual form of analysis, visualization makes it possible for us to dissect, engage, and interact with a set of data in ways that may not be possible through other non-visual media. Finally, visualization helps the user discover knowledge. Through visualization, new insights or knowledge may be discovered that would have not been discoverable in other expressions. To 'do good with data', as states information design firm Periscopic's mission statement, is to recognize visualization as a medium of empowerment for consumers and practitioners alike over these functions, where visualization becomes both a communicative medium and the message delivered over that medium that connects users to new ideas, facts, realities, or insights.

The first two functions of data visualization operate in predictable ways in our daily lives. We expect a visualization to first and foremost explain data to us, and any visualization that fails to meet this most basic goal fails to serve as an effective visualization. This function spans a range of effectiveness, and as we become exposed to many different types of visualizations with increasing frequency, we become trained to identify when a visualization has or has not explained the data behind it effectively. The same may be said about visualization's second core function, which is to explore data, and indeed, we have likewise been conditioned to understand and engage with visualizations as forms of dialogue and discourse rather than static products. A visualization is effective when it enables us to touch, move, or otherwise engage with data in ways that would be impossible in other forms.

The ways in which visualizations function in this third capacity—translating information into knowledge—are not always as simple, however. As Helen Kennedy and other members of the Seeing Data project demonstrate, the reality is that visualization and data as practice and discipline are complex in their own right, challenging our conceptions of authority, knowledge, and their practical manifestations in ways we may have not imagined even a decade ago. Where data has become inextricably bound to our contemporary notions of knowledge and its validation, visualization has brought about a new era of its representation, along the way raising the question of what data itself means for how we formulate our claims of truth. While we may revere data as objective and complete, it is in many cases constructed just as much as the visualizations that represent it. In their pursuit of objectivity, visualizations can sometimes give us the impression that knowledge is absolute if interrogated and framed in the rightly phrased way.

How well a visualization serves this final function is both integral to its success as a medium for communication as well as highly contingent upon the theoretical implications that visualization as discipline poses for our representations of knowledge. The relationship between the function of representation and how we construct knowledge thus cannot be neglected in any study of information design and poses special interdisciplinary challenges in the work of designing for visualization. Many different fields or approaches of inquiry can tell us different things about how we practically engage with visualization, and generating a holistic understanding of visualization and its effects requires a collective consideration of them all in tandem. Cognitive scientists, for example, assert that visualization helps illuminate new knowledge in data or information by presenting it in a way that makes it easier to see patterns with the human eye, given our natural strength in recognizing and distinguishing visual expressions of patterns. As Colin Ware states in *Visual Thinking for Design*, 'visual thinking consists of a series of acts of attention, driving eye movements and turning our pattern-finding circuits. These acts of attention are called visual queries, and understanding how visual queries work can make us better designers.' In this framing, the challenge of effective information design, then, is to maximize the extent to which basic facets of visual design interact synergistically with both human perception as well as patterns and observations intrinsic to a set of data, thereby positioning a viewer to easily make connections and generate new knowledge. Alternatively, a specialist in user experience may shift that framing slightly to consider effective visualization as a challenge in responding to human behavioral tendencies in interacting with interfaces and modalities, emphasizing the importance of prior behavioral experience in the function of a given visualization.

Designing a visualization effectively in this way is a major challenge to nearly all work in visualization. The design of a visualization is rarely a neutral act, nor is its interpretation an act free from bias or suggestion, making the process of designing a visualization in a way that is neutral to what new knowledge may be discovered a difficult endeavor. As the design process includes a series of choices about representation that are often made by a single person or group of people, there is always some element of bias that may be introduced, regardless of one's best intentions. Preserving the knowledge discovery capacity of visualization requires the designer to have an awareness of how bias may manifest through particular design choices and to be able to compensate accordingly. In successfully doing so, designers endeavor to use visualization to 'do good by data', that is, to use visualization as a neutral medium for communication.

What does this kind of compensation look like in design? One way of striving for neutrality is considering how design choices relate to different conceptualizations (epistemologies) of what knowledge is and how knowledge is generated. Visualization practitioners are often confronted with a wide range of questions when designing a visualization, including the following:

- What patterns are intrinsic to a set of data?
- What conclusions emerge naturally from those patterns?
- How do we validate those conclusions, with and without visualization?
- What knowledge do those conclusions impart?
- How does a viewer reach conclusions based on visual observation?
- How does a viewer translate conclusions into knowledge?
- How do particular design choices provide a scaffold for translating patterns intrinsic to data into knowledge that is faithful to the data itself?

These questions are challenging in two broad ways. First, each inevitably lacks a clear, singular answer, one that does not shift with the contexts in which they are asked. Indeed, the framing of any of these questions can often be informed by both explicit and implicit factors ranging from the requests and needs of a client to the ideological leanings of the designer. Second, any answers that are provided inherently carry with them the biases of the individual asking them, whether designer or user. Importantly, how both designer and user characterize the nature and generation of knowledge has a critical effect on how each relates to a particular form of visual representation, especially when those characterizations differ in irreconcilable ways.

Increasingly, different frameworks have emerged to facilitate a more critical understanding of data and its visualization and the ways in which we engage with both. One of these frameworks, for example, is feminist studies, which adopts the feminist theory perspective that all knowledge is socially situated. Catherine D'Ignazio, research affiliate with the MIT Center for Civic Media, notes that feminist studies offers the unique advantages of providing a platform for examining power structures manifest in visualizations and inventing new ways to represent uncertainty and ambiguity, represent the material economy behind data, and make dissent possible. From this perspective, knowledge is a constructed product, and visualization becomes a constructed space in which the terms of expression are negotiated between designer and user. Frameworks like these in which visualization is critically assessed as a medium of objective (or subjective) communication and inquiry point to significant ways that visualization as a discipline has the potential to challenge our understanding of information, data, and knowledge in new ways. Certainly, as the field of information design continues to develop and mature, more practitioners and consumers of visualization alike will learn to assess the message behind visualizations through a more critical lens in these ways.

Future Trends

As we look to the future, it seems clear that visualization will continue to have a lasting impact on not only scholarly academic but also cultural, social, and political spheres. And it is also clear that the future of data visualization rests on the future of data and our engagement with it as much as it does on the future of visualization and design itself. As institutes like Harvard's Berkman Klein Center for Internet and Society and MIT's Center for Civic Media emerge and develop, new directions of critical inquiry will continue to shape the field of data visualization as a whole. This is particularly true in social and political realms, as data visualization continues to play an increasingly dominant role in shaping the ways in which we engage with data about phenomena that affect our social lives. Research at both the Berkman Klein Center and Center for Civic Media push understandings of data in these directions, offering a useful framework for understanding the ways in which data and visualization may affect our lives in the future.

One important expression of this is the pivotal role that data and visualization have begun to play in civic life and social justice. The wide availability of data about many different aspects of society has made it possible for advocates of social justice to demand accountability of individuals, political groups, social institutions, and the government, inspiring new movements for and expectations of openness. Practitioners in the field of data visualization, too, have begun to respond to these movements. The information design agency Periscopic, for example, identifies itself as a 'socially-conscious data visualization firm that helps companies and organizations promote information transparency and public awareness', emphasizing the important work that visualization can play in serving the public good. Indeed, Periscopic seeks out work with organizations on environmental issues, human rights, peace and equality, education, and the arts, incorporating its philosophy of practice into its work with clients. An interesting byproduct of the increased visibility of visualization in public affairs has been the gradual elevation of societal information literacy and transliteracy, both of which pose challenges that visualization has the capacity to confront.

Another important trend in the world of data is the quantified self, especially within the context of the Internet of Things. In this domain as well, visualization will likely play an increased role. As more and more devices track data about our daily behaviors, including our physical activity, our locations, and our spending habits, there has been an increased appetite for ways to visualize the immense quantities of data that are produced in the process. More broadly, big data will continue to pose new challenges to data visualization, requiring new approaches to visualizing vast quantities of data to illuminate patterns that may be buried within them. Here too, trends in data visualization will be pushed more by trends in data than by the work of practitioners in the field alone.

Data visualization has enormous potential to challenge our understandings of the world and our place in it. Multimodal and interdisciplinary in nature, it holds the potential to change our conceptions of perceived divisions between disciplines, methodologies, and ways of knowing. The major challenge to the field in this respect, however, is to leverage visualization effectively as a medium for change. As the field of data visualization has historically been driven by the ingenuity and creativity of the designers behind it, the works and designers in this volume demonstrate that there will continue to be many opportunities for that change to occur in new, exciting, and unprecedented directions.

References

Bertin, Jacques (2010), *Semiology of Graphics*, Esri Press

Card, Stuart K. and Mackinlay, Jock (1999), *Readings in Information Visualization: Using Vision to Think*, Morgan Kaufmann

Kennedy, Helen (2016), "The work that visualisation conventions do", *Information, Communication & Society*, Taylor & Francis Online

Kirk, Andy (2016), *Data Visualization: A Handbook for Data Driven Design*, SAGE Publications Ltd.

Meirelles, Isabel (2013), *Design for Information*, Rockport Publishers

Tufte, Edward R. (2001), *The Visual Display of Quantitative Information*, Graphics Pr

Ware, Colin (2008), *Visual Thinking for Design*, Morgan Kaufmann

Yau, Nathan (2011), *Visualize This: The Flowing Data Guide to Design, Visualization, and Statistics*, Wiley

Kim Albrecht

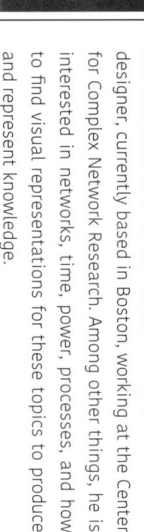

Kim Albrecht is a visual researcher and information designer, currently based in Boston, working at the Center for Complex Network Research. Among other things, he is interested in networks, time, power, processes, and how to find visual representations for these topics to produce and represent knowledge.

[Q] What do you think about data visualization/infographics?

[A] Over the last five years, my work has become influenced by the idea of design as 'drawing things together', a connection between art, science, and technology. Before the Renaissance, art and science were not seen as two separate disciplines. Today they coexist in our cultural realm but intersect only seldom. I am trying to bring these disciplines closer together through the artifacts I create. My work is done collaboratively with scientists, and once created, my projects are able to reach various audiences.

[Q] What kind of design methods do you commonly use?

[A] The basic question I'm always asking is: how can visualization help us understand the world surrounding us? That is the basic underlying question that comes up in all projects that I have worked on throughout the last years. This theme sees design as something different from communication or decoration. It is not about a style, a trend or a fashion anymore. The design process becomes a tool to create insights and knowledge. But once we investigate these created technological artifacts in more depth, all the cultural formations forming the graphics come into focus, demonstrating the subjectivity of visualization.

[Q] What kind of design elements do you commonly use?

[A] Points, lines, and areas.

[Q] Where are your works applied?

[A] Scientific investigation and scientific communication.

[Q] How do you turn boring and complex data into something interesting and understandable?

[A] Visualization is a medium between data and the viewer. If a data set is boring, the visualization will be boring. But that is where my job comes in. I'm not just taking data sets randomly and visualizing them. It is as much about researching, finding, filtering, sorting, and analyzing data as it is about visualizing it. I'm more concerned about finding the right data set than finding the right representation. I'm not enhancing or adding features to a visual representation to make it look more interesting. The 'gestalt' of the visualization should come from the data and its manipulation in the first place, and not from some outside enhancement.

Complex data sets are different. Visualization in opposition to statistical analysis can humanize complexity by revealing it, making it visible to the viewer. Here the medium of visualization manifests itself. What we can show and the way we can show it are very specific. Points, lines, areas, colors, etc. all have specific properties that restrict the communication between data and the viewer. This is the research field I'm working in, pushing the usage of the medium visualization to represent complexity.

[Q] What is your suggestion for beginners?

[A] Love what you do to an extent that your work is not work anymore, but pleasure.

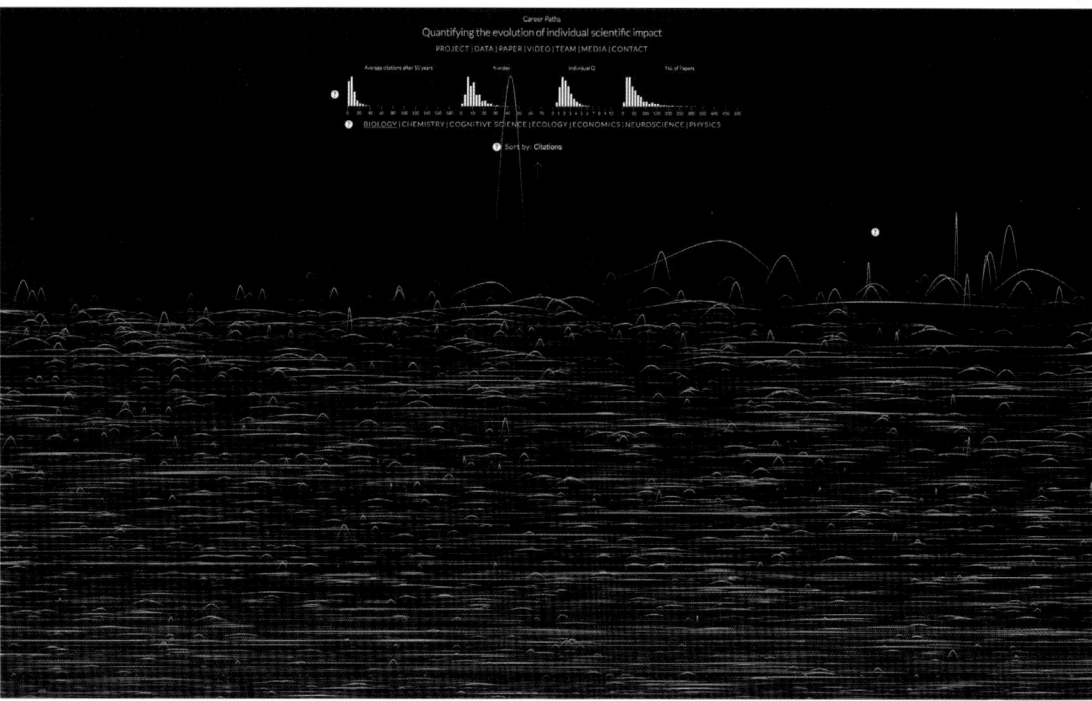

1

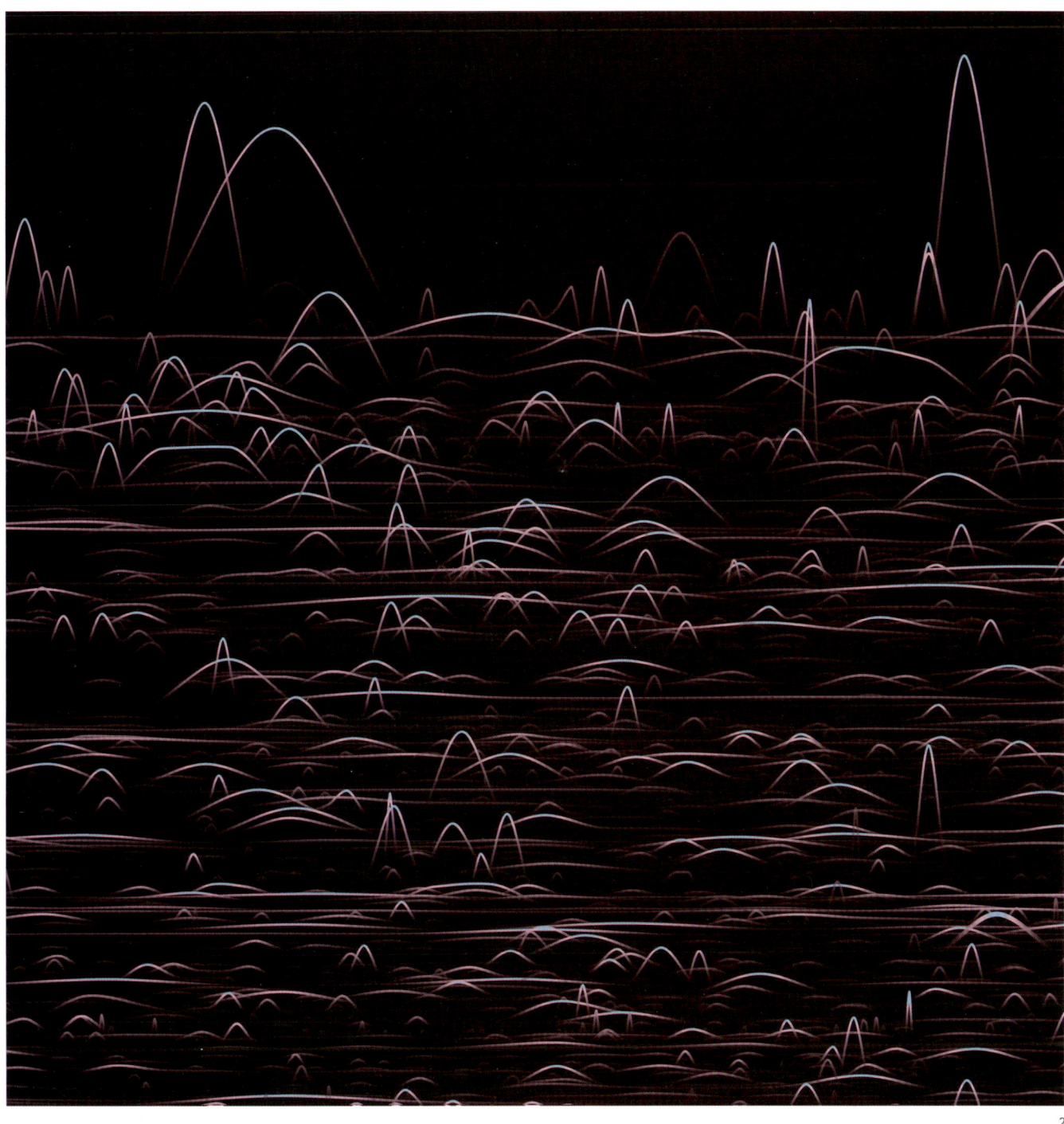

[1–2] Science Path

Credits: Roberta Sinatra (science), Dashun Wang (science), Pierre Deville (science), Chaoming Song (science), Albert-László Barabási (science), Kim Albrecht (visualization)
Completion: 2016
Interactive link: kimalbrecht.com/project/science-paths

How does impact change over a scientific career? Does impact, arguably the most relevant performance measure, follow predictable patterns? Can we predict the timing of a scientist's outstanding achievement? Driven by these questions, the designers studied the evolution of productivity and impact throughout thousands of scientific careers. They reconstructed the publication record of scientists from seven disciplines, connecting each paper with its long-term impact on the scientific community as quantified by citation metrics. It is found that the highest impact work in a scientist's career is randomly distributed within the body of work. That is, the highest impact work has the same probability of falling anywhere in the sequence of papers published by a scientist. It could be the first publication, midcareer, or last. This result is known as the random impact rule.

This visualization shows the random impact rule in all its power. You can explore careers in different disciplines, rank scientists according to different career parameters, or select a subset of them. You will always find the impact peaks occurring all over the place, from the beginning of a career on the left to the end of a career on the right.

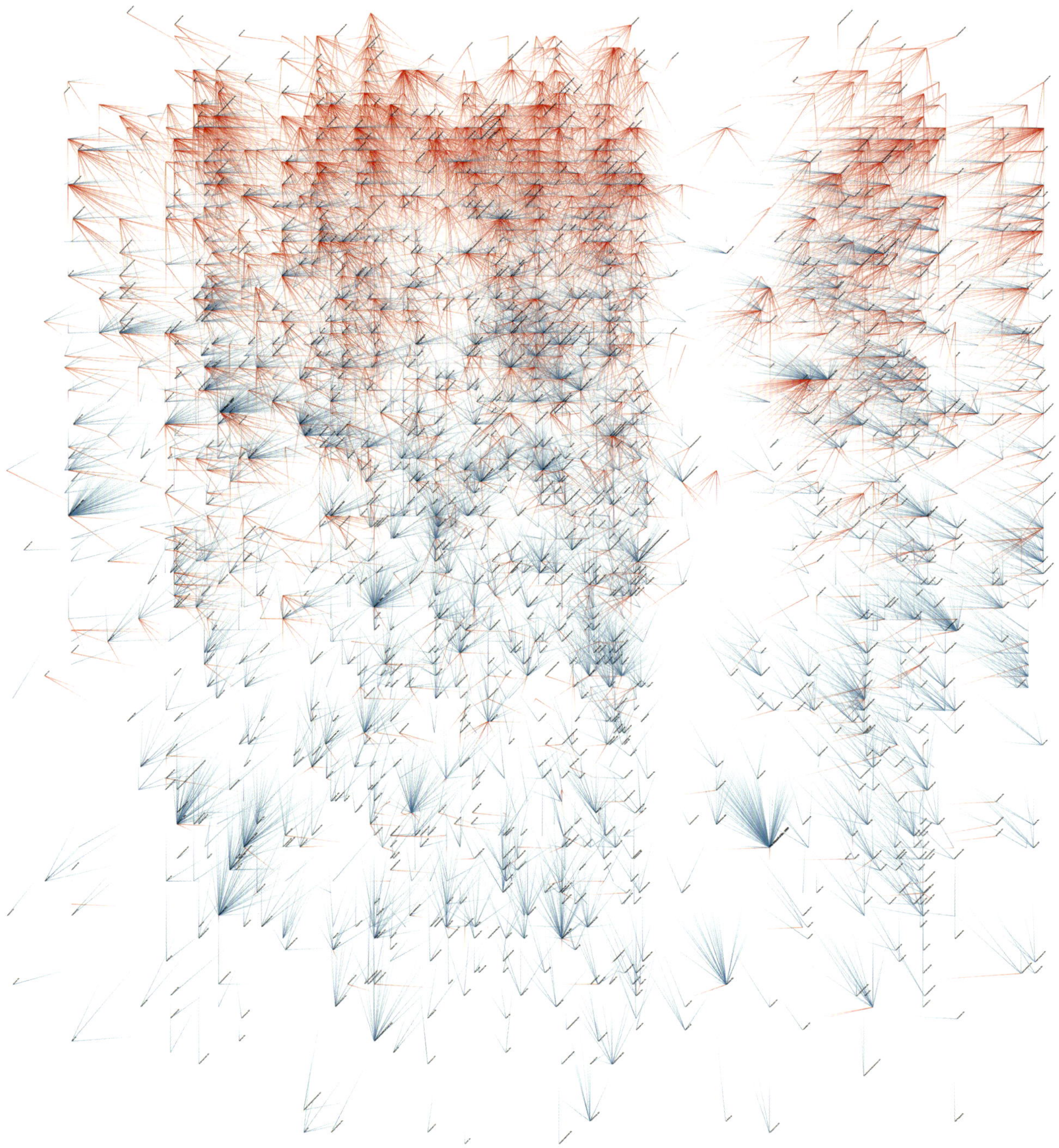

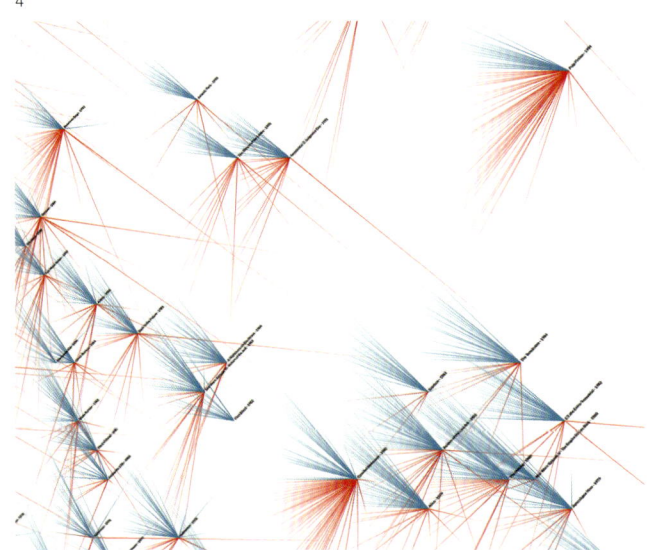

[3–6] Culturegraphy

Credit: Kim Albrecht
Completion: 2014
Interactive link: kimalbrecht.com/project/culturegraphy

Culturegraphy investigates cultural information exchange over time also known as 'memes'. Treating cultural works as nodes and influences as directed edges, the visualization of these cultural networks can provide new insights into the rich interconnections of cultural development. The graphics represent complex relationships of movie references by combining macro views summarizing 100 years of movie influences with micro views providing a close-up look at the embedding of individual movies. The macro view shows the rise of the self-referential character of postmodern cinema, while the micro level illustrates differences between individual movies, when they were referenced and by whom. The visualizations provide views that are closer to the real complexity of the relationships than aggregated views or rankings could do.

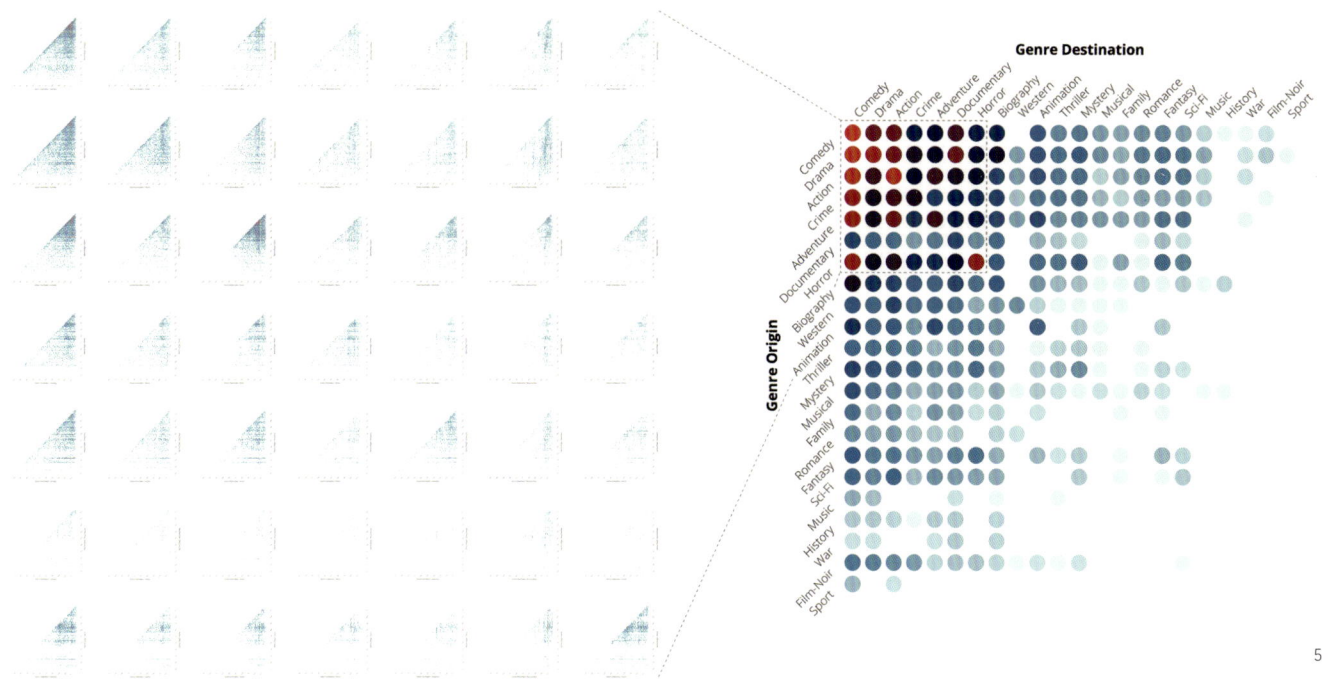

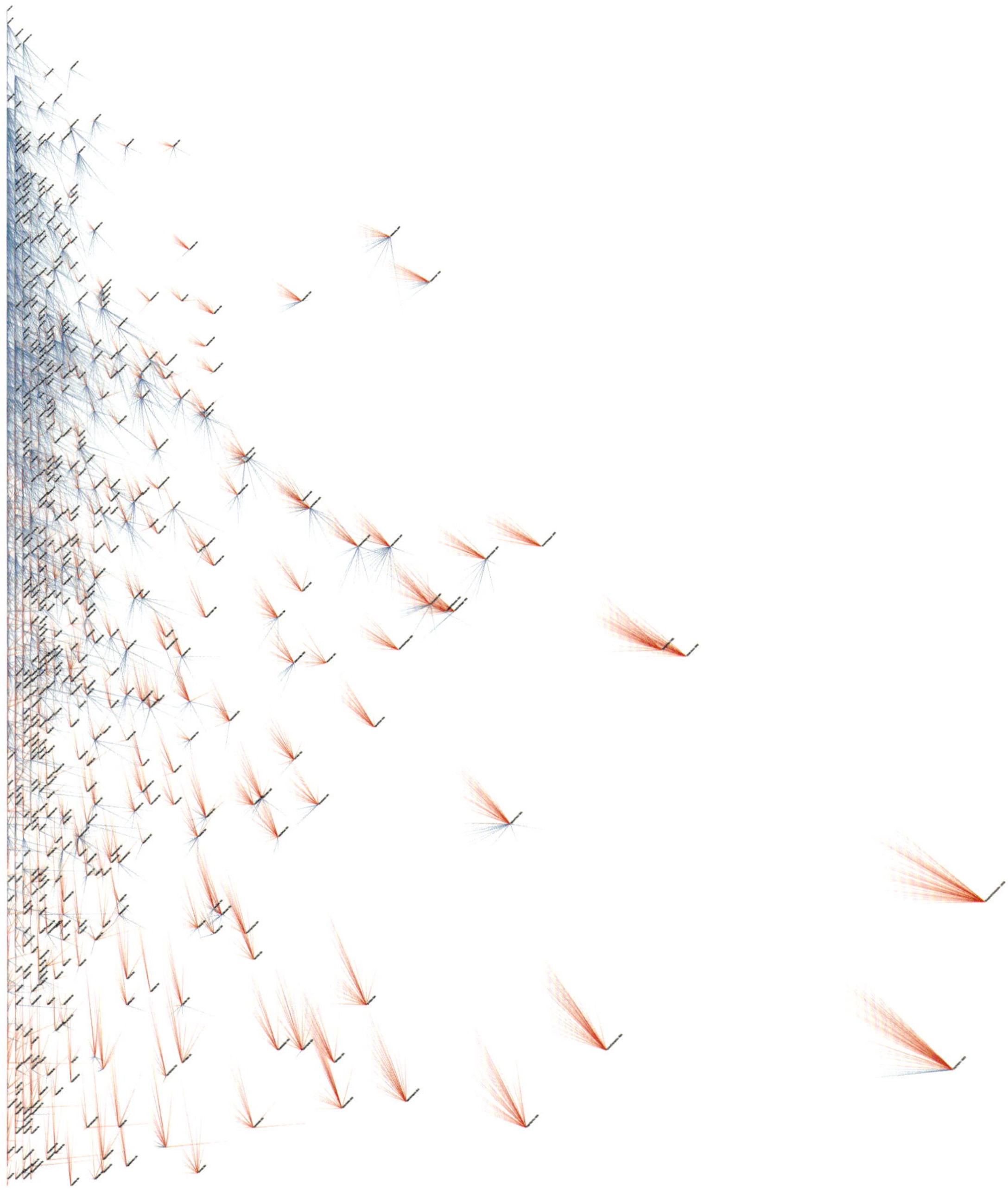

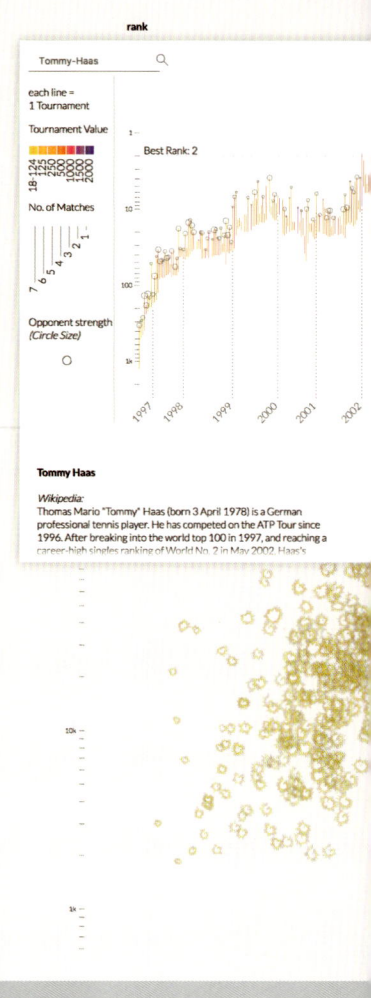
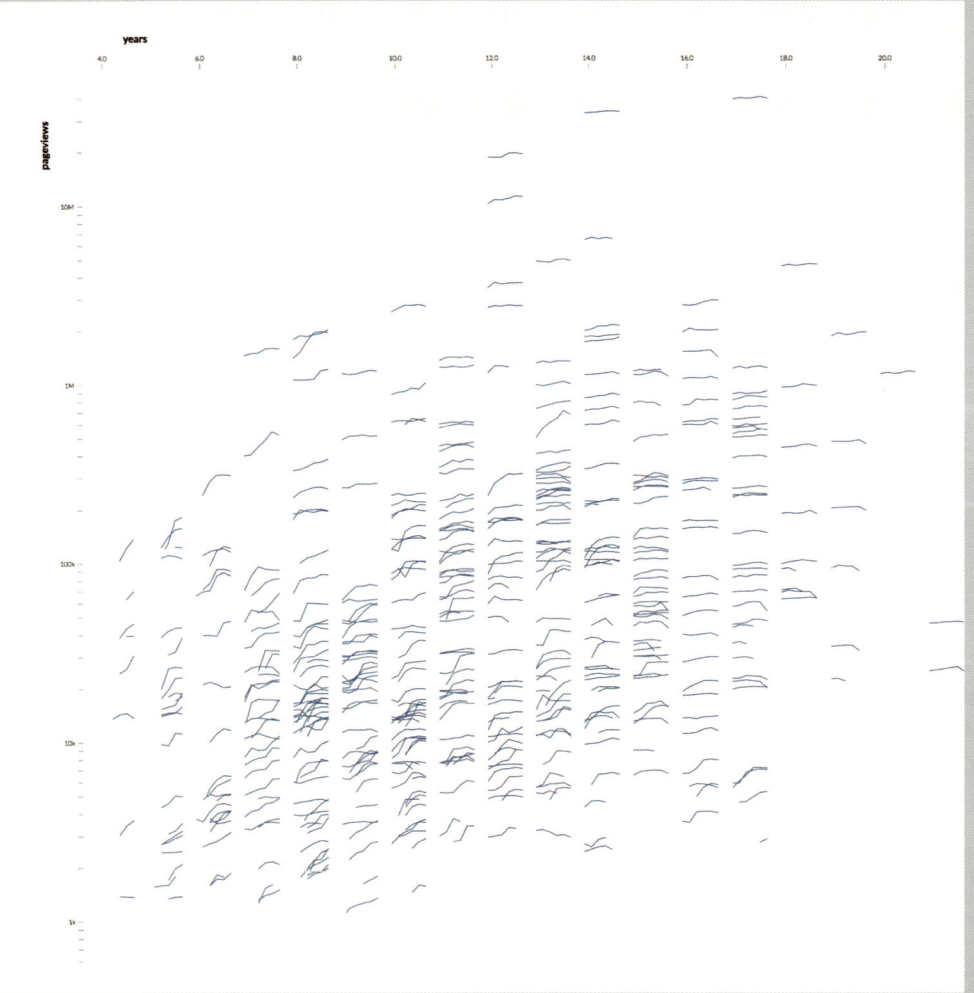
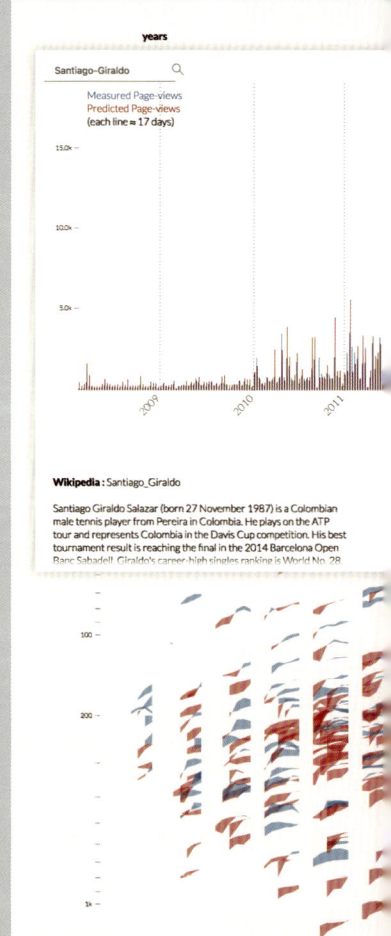

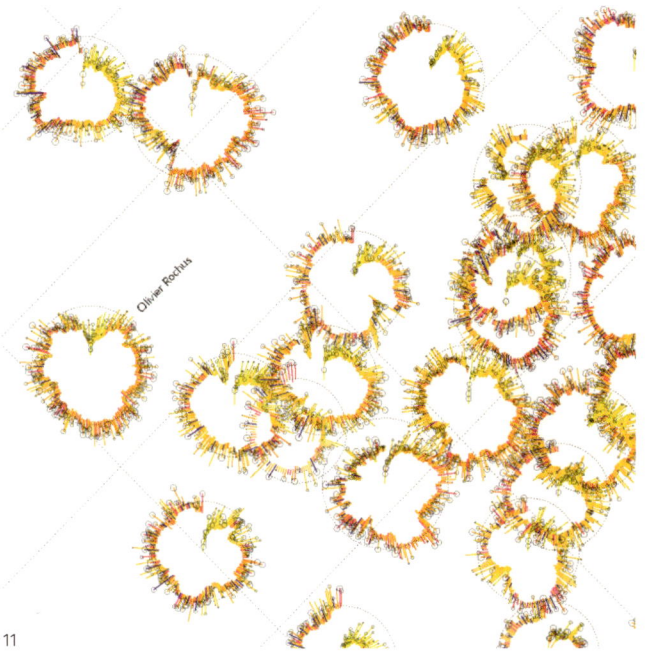

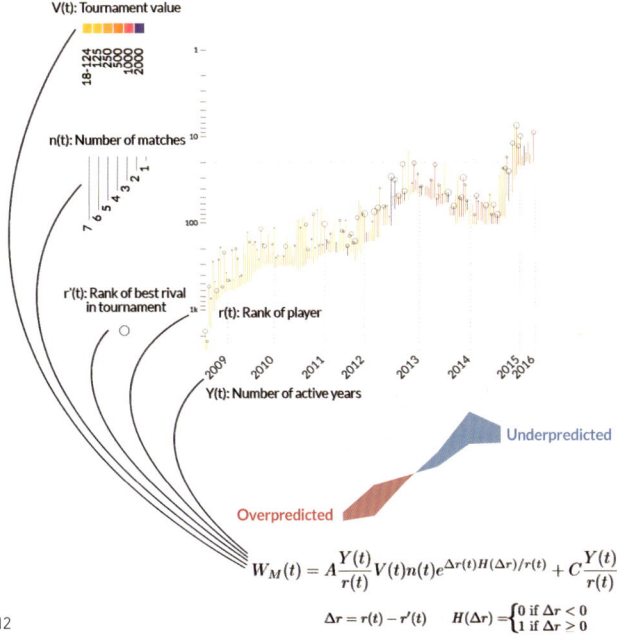

[7–12] Untangling Tennis

Credits: Burcu Yucesoy (science), Albert-László Barabási (science), Kim Albrecht (visualization)
Completion: 2015
Interactive link: kimalbrecht.com/project/untangling-tennis

This is a visual and data analytic exploration of success in tennis, uncovering the relationship between performance and popularity. The life of a professional athlete is not a smooth ride, but is full of ups and downs, life-changing victories and crushing defeats, serious injuries, and awe-inspiring recovery. It is also glamorous, as athletes are cherished, admired, and often criticized as celebrities. Succeeding in the world of tennis means both excelling in the game and being popular enough to attract good endorsement deals. Here the work delves deeply into how success is achieved, both in regards to performance and popularity, and how those two relate to each other.

RJ Andrews

info we trust.

RJ Andrews founded the award-winning agency Info We Trust to explore how to better humanize information, and has enjoyed publishing a variety of data stories about a broad spectrum of topics he finds fascinating. Professionally, he has worked with clients across many industries to put their data to work in strategy, product, marketing, and fundraising. His formal training is in engineering (BS/MS Mechanical Engineer) and business (MBA).

[Q] What do you think about data visualization/infographics?

[A] By encoding information visually, data visualization enables access to complex information by harnessing our pattern-recognizing visual cortex. Data visualization can also be used to power data storytelling in order to engage and communicate insights to others.

[Q] What kind of design methods do you commonly use?

[A] My design process is to first saturate myself with the data (which usually requires learning from many experts) and then, once I have an opinion about what is interesting, I will decide how to move it from my head to my audience so that others can share my perspective. I have a multi-disciplinary toolkit that I use to produce my work. Each new data story is a chance for me to learn new techniques that help me bring data to life, so I endeavor to be constantly expanding my toolkit.

[Q] What kind of design elements do you commonly use?

[A] The most powerful and useful charts are bar and line graphs, because they enable effortless comparison of values and often reveal interesting patterns. Sometimes I have deviated from these charts for storytelling and engagement purposes. For example, I used animal silhouettes for Endangered Safari.

[Q] Where are your works applied?

[A] My public data stories can usually be found online and have been reprinted and translated in newspapers, posters, and books worldwide.

[Q] How do you turn boring and complex data into something interesting and understandable?

[A] I have rarely found data to be boring, and get most excited when I find data whose stories have not been unmasked yet. Complexity can be navigated as long as access points, such as simple patterns or comparisons, are provided as a means of introduction and the proper framing allows the audience to investigate the complexity.

[Q] What is your suggestion for beginners?

[A] Data visualization is a multi-disciplinary craft. Read as much as you can (both online and books), not only about what people are doing in the industry, but in many other fields so that you can bring a unique perspective. Find a simple workflow that allows you to engage with data quickly and expand your toolkit incrementally from there. Do not wait to dive in!

1

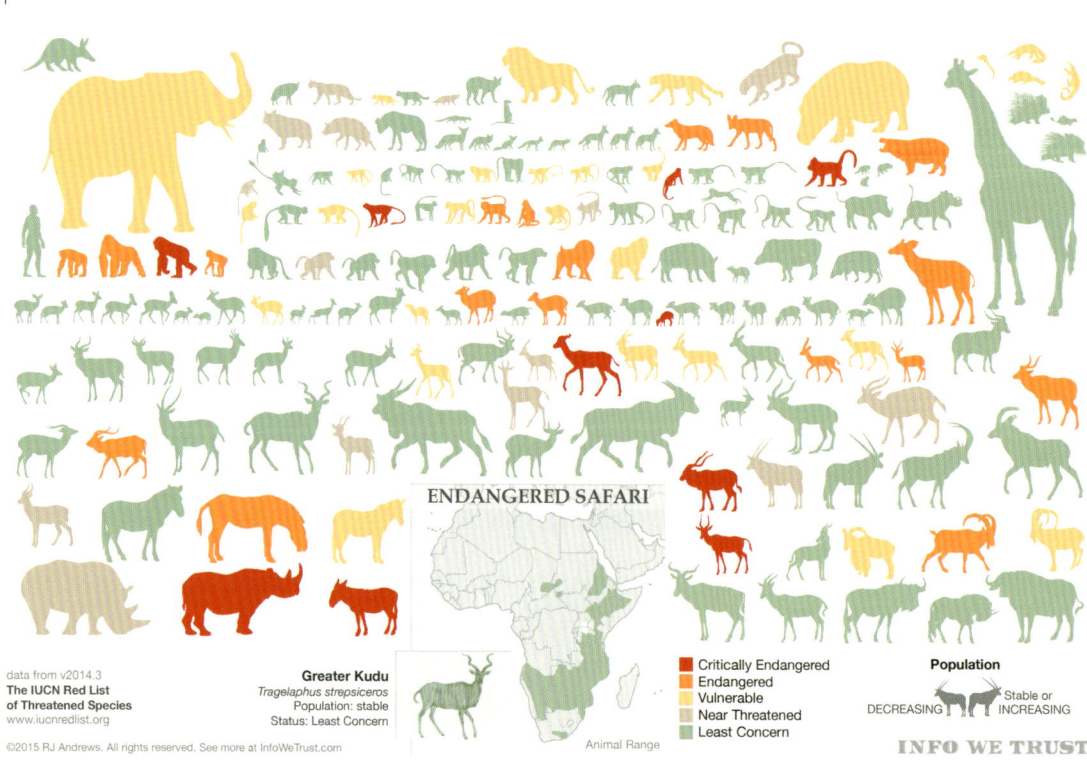

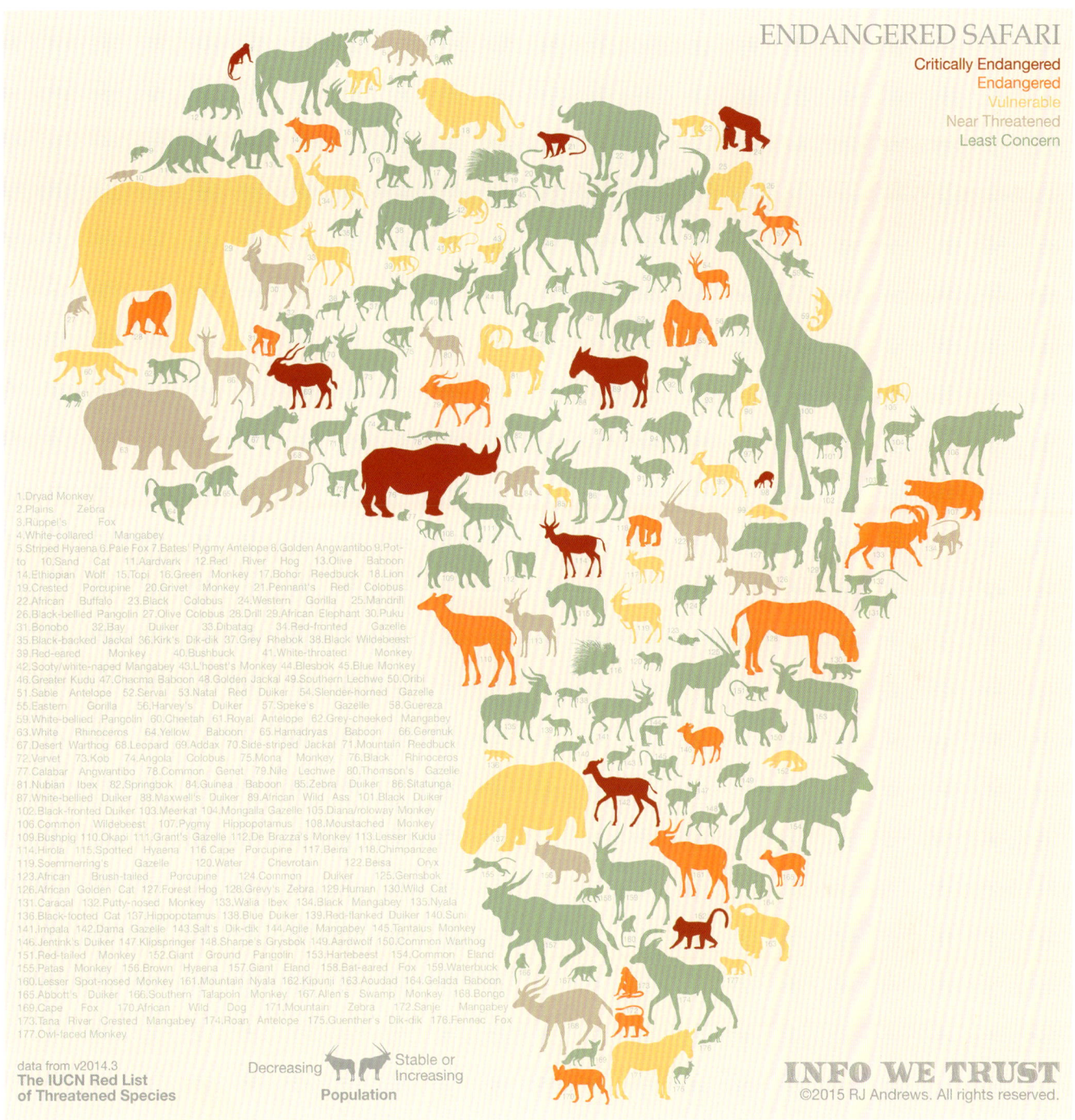

[1–2] Endangered Safari

Credits: RJ Andrews, Info We Trust
Completion: 2015
Interactive link: www.infowetrust.com/endangeredsafari

This project contains all of the large African mammals along with juicy info such as animal size, family, population trend, range, and IUCN threatened-species status. To play with the data, including individual animal range maps, the visualization is activated by hovering over each animal. Endangered Safari was named a Tableau Public Viz of the Week and selected for the 2015 Kantar Information is Beautiful awards interactive longlist.

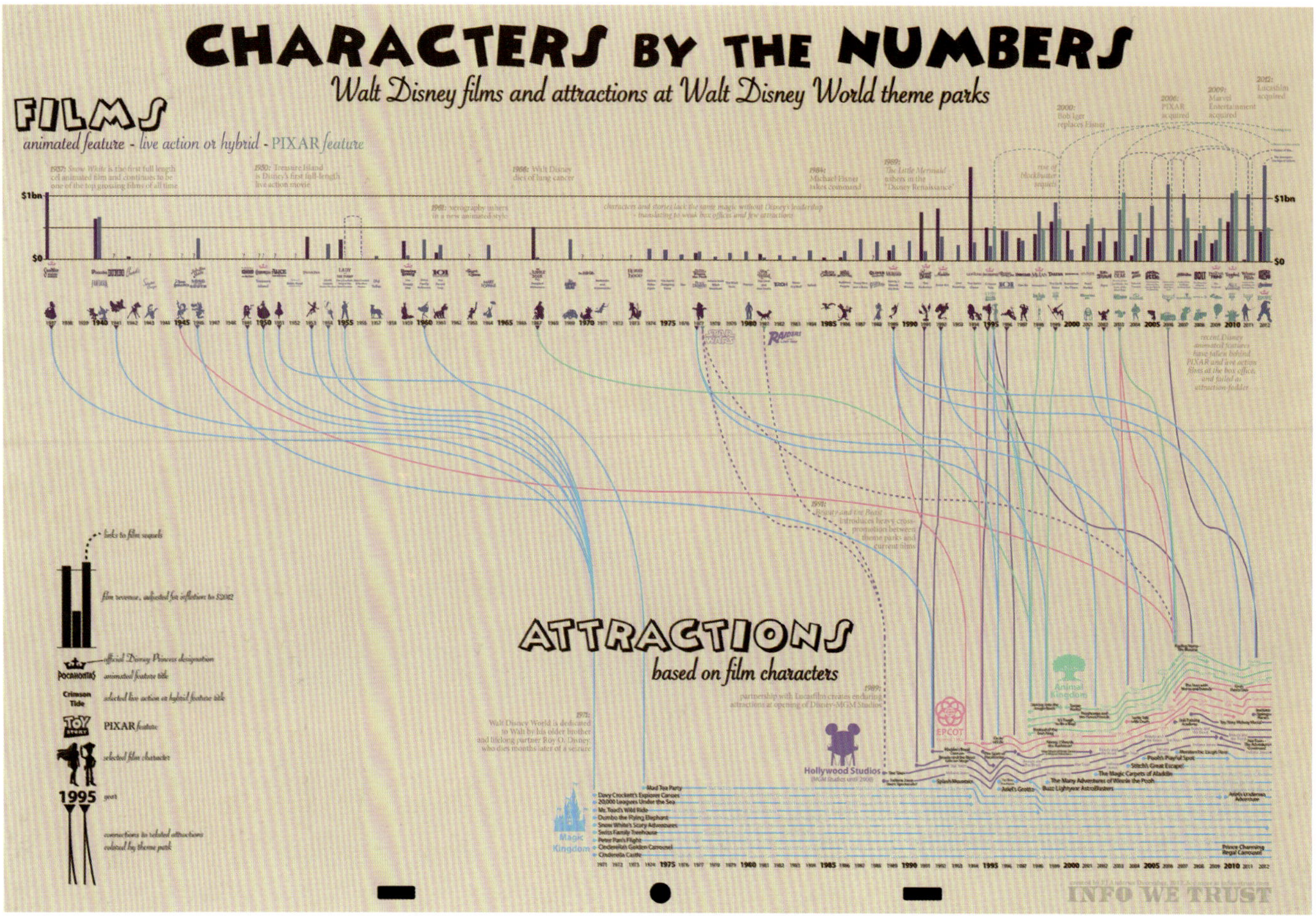

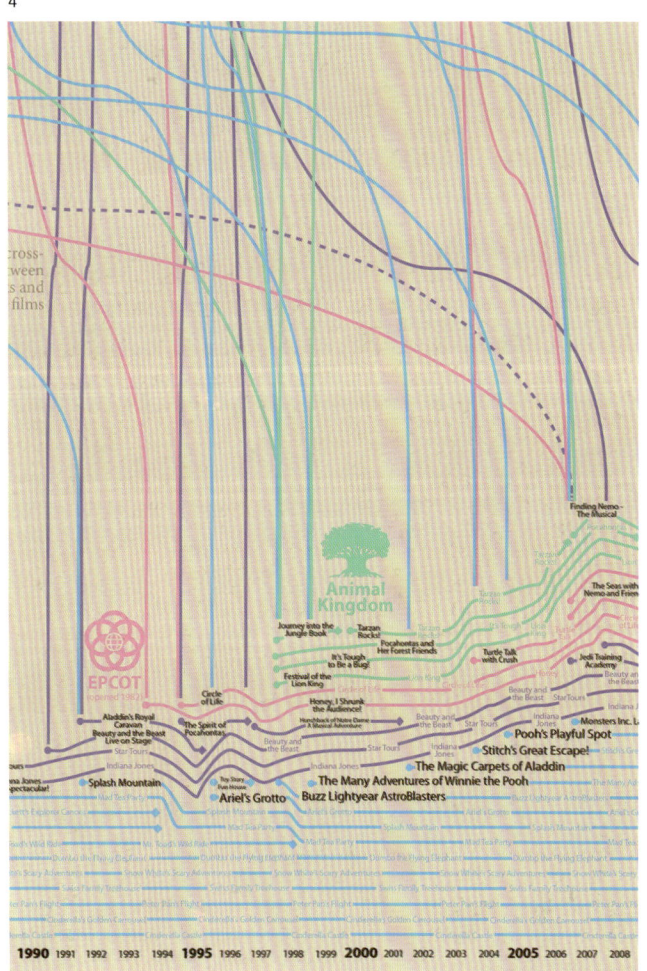

[3–4] Characters by the Numbers

Credits: RJ Andrews, Info We Trust
Completion: 2013

Steve Jobs counseled Disney CEO Bob Iger to think in terms of brand deposits and brand withdrawals. Since 1937's *Snow White and the Seven Dwarfs*, enduring film characters have been Disney's biggest brand deposits, and their success is most fantastically expressed with a dedicated theme park attraction in Florida at Walt Disney World. Several points about Disney's evolution can be inferred from the chart (some of which are labeled in the piece): creative vacuum that occurred after Walt Disney's death in 1966, rise of cross-promotion between films and attractions in the 1990s (attractions are no longer reactive to successful films, but are rather proactively opened in the same year of the film's release), rise of mechanized annual new releases (including reliance on sequels), impact of PIXAR and live animation in the 21st century—both at the box office and in the parks.

---

[5] Creative Routines

Credits: RJ Andrews, Info We Trust
Completion: 2014

How do creatives—composers, painters, writers, scientists, philosophers—find the time to produce their opus? Mason Currey investigated the rigid daily rituals that hundreds of creatives practiced in order to carve out time, every day, to work on their craft. Some kept to the same disciplined regimen for decades while others locked in patterns only while working on specific projects. Creative Routines won the 2014 Kantar Information is Beautiful award for best infographic.

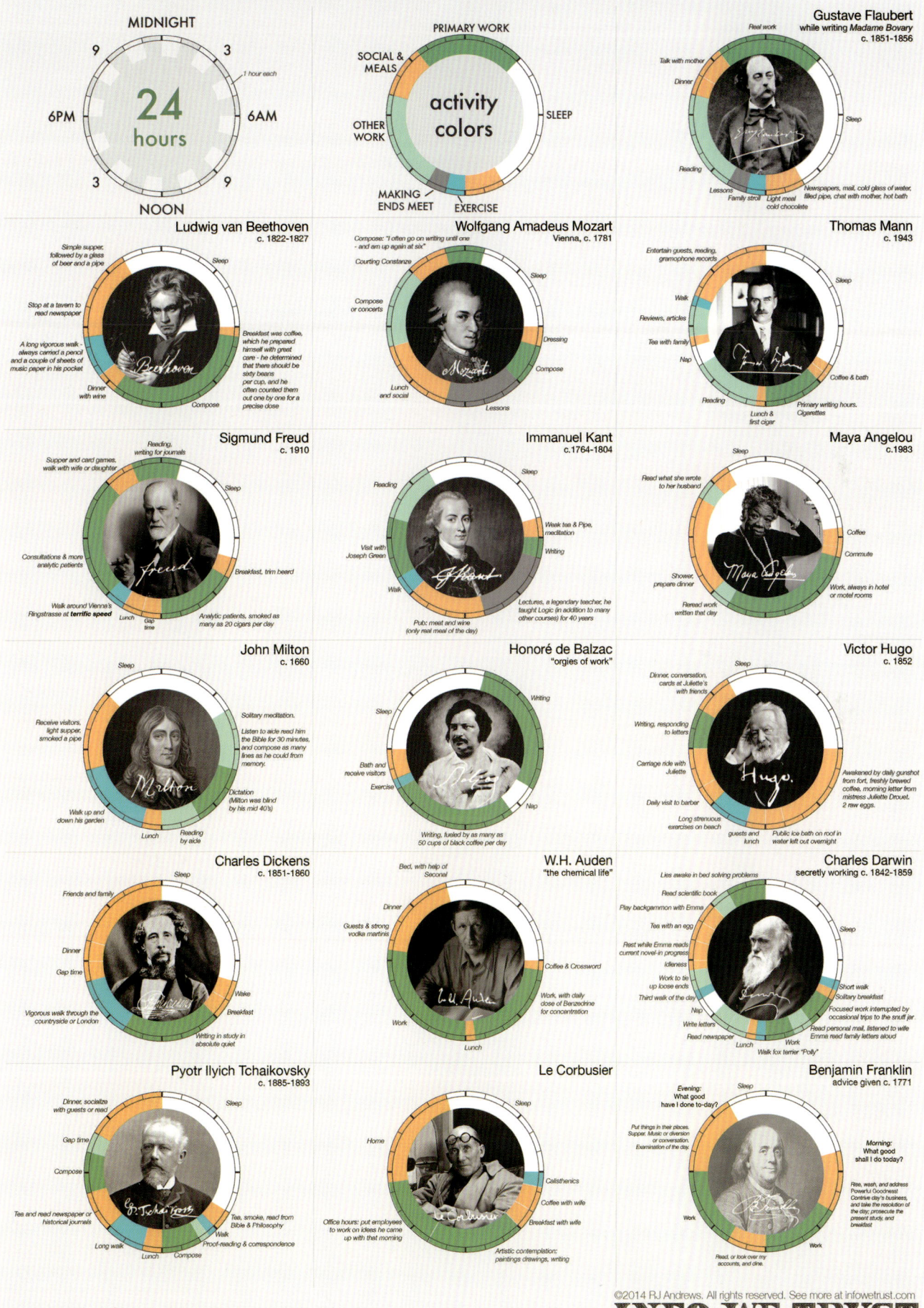

Adriano Attus

Adriano Attus is the creative director of *Il Sole 24 Ore* (Italy's leading financial newspaper). He has been working as a designer for more than 20 years for a variety magazines published by some of the major Italian publishing houses. He also worked as a contributor for Eni, Enel, Bmw, and Bloomberg, and he's currently a data visualization consultant for IMT Istituto Alti Studi in Lucca, and an infographics teacher at MIMaster in Milan.

[Q] What do you think about data visualization/infographics?

[A] Data visualization or infographics is a valid instrument to give information to consumers and readers. I think it should improve and potentially increase the supply of information without replacing the written text, but rather emphasizing its effects. The most effective representation of the available data must be used to help the reader to comprehend the event.

[Q] What kind of design methods do you commonly use?

[A] First of all, we try to talk to the colleagues who retrieve the data in order to understand their inspiration or the facts that hide behind the story being told. Then we use the most suitable means to communicate the message that we want to spread by organizing the information we have. In that moment, we start to sketch with paper and pencil to give order and structure to various aspects, surfing between the trends of time variations, studying the comparisons among subjects, analyzing methods of behavior (connections, exceptions, flows, hierarchies, etc.), and evaluating the complex information.

At the same time, when numbers allow it, we analyze the data in an electronic spreadsheet before selecting the appropriate parameters in the visualization software. We finally try to spot excellence and/or anomalies, choosing the best type of table or diagram to show the data in the best way. Then we use the most suitable or effective composition to strengthen the story behind the numbers.

[Q] What kind of design elements do you commonly use?

[A] We usually choose the most appropriate graphic for representing a given set of data and information. Normally we try to use basic elements to create our views, with points, lines, and bars. We can cover almost all of the requirements while maintaining a large amount of material, guiding the reader to understand the data. So we separate, sort, and organize the materials to simplify the exposure.

But when we consider merging the data to enhance our research, or emphasize visually some characteristics, we turn inevitably to some standard geometric shapes, mainly circles and squares, to represent the values and ensure good retention for the reader. We are very scrupulous with the surface dimension to ensure clarity. To this end we try to avoid three-dimensional figures of varying sizes, as these can be misleading in comparisons and complex management.

[Q] Where are your works applied?

[A] Newspaper and website.

[Q] How do you turn boring and complex data into something interesting and understandable?

[A] Once we have collected, analyzed, and organized the data, we try to find visualizations that could provide the reader with structured and functional knowledge. Our goal is to help the user to understand the events, and we are aware that an attractive visualization has more chance of catching the audience and being remembered. The stylistic choice of *Il Sole 24 Ore* strengthens the group identity of our readers, in order to attract client loyalty.

[Q] What is your suggestion for beginners?

[A] Usually I suggest that students start with the fundamental guidelines of infographics. Many of the basic rules, from colors to typography, from shapes to proportions, are essential for clear communication. Even if most of the present visualizations are considered unique pieces, the basic elements are standard and universal.

[1] Greece's Economic Challenges

Credits: Adriano Attus (designer), Federico Barbara (designer), Alice Calvi (designer), Luca Galimberti (designer), Michela Finizio (text and data), Andrea Gianotti, Luca Tremolada
Completion: 2015

Data sets show the challenges Greece is facing in a wide array of fields: from household conditions to companies' performances, the comparison with the past highlights a series of defeats. The notable exception is tourism, which accounts for 17.3 percent of GDP.

Infodata del Lunedì
CONTI D'EUROPA

Su Info Data Blog potrebbe interessarti anche:
Classifiche. I Paesi più felici del mondo: crolla il Sud
Timeline. La crisi ellenica, da Papandreou a Tsipras

Grecia, i numeri di un'economia all'angolo

PAGINA A CURA DI
Chiara Bussi
Michela Finizio

Il verdetto dei mercati è atteso per oggi, ma la performance economica della Grecia è già ben visibile. Tutto è cominciato nell'autunno 2009, quando l'allora ministro socialista George Papandreou ha rivelato che le statistiche inviate a Bruxelles erano state falsate per poter entrare nell'Eurozona. Da allora Ue e Fmi hanno aperto due paracaduti per 240 miliardi in cambio di un pesante programma di austerity sotto la regia della troika. Cinque anni dopo la gloria dell'antica Olimpia è un ricordo lontano: il Paese e i suoi abitanti appaiono sempre più come un atleta stinito che ha spanellato una serie di sconfitte. Il Pil pro capite è crollato del 25% e rappresenta il 45% in meno rispetto alla media dell'Eurozona. La spesa per i consumi è sempre più ridotta al lumicino, così come gli investimenti, scesi di oltre il 9% dal 2010 e con una quota inferiore di 8 punti rispetto alla media europea. I primati collezionati sono in negativo: il debito pubblico al 177% del Pil mette in ombra persino l'Italia, ferma al 132% e vale più del doppio della media della zona euro. Ma anche la disoccupazione, quasi triplicata in cinque anni, oggi è più alta del 14% rispetto a quella italiana e il 16% più alta della media europea. Sul fronte delle imprese il confronto con il nostro Paese è impari: la maggior parte degli indicatori ne certifica la perdita di competitività. Soffrono anche le famiglie che hanno visto calare la spesa media del 26% e sono state costrette a rinunciare al superfluo destinando un quarto delle uscite solo al cibo. Anche se il 7% non riesce a garantire ai figli un pasto al giorno con carne o pesce. Persino il riscaldamento non è più essenziale: solo il 38% delle case ha un impianto, rispetto al 73,5% di 5 anni fa. L'unica risorsa che ha resistito agli scossoni è il turismo, che vale il 17,3% del Pil contro il 10,1% del nostro Paese. L'ultima spiaggia che potrebbe rappresentare il nuovo approdo per la rinascita.

I NUMERI DELLA CRISI ELLENICA www.infodata.ilsole24ore.com

Timeline della crisi. Dall'arrivo al potere di Papandreou il 4 ottobre 2009 alla vittoria di Tsipras, online le tappe della lunga crisi greca e del debito sovrano dell'eurozona non ancora finita

Timeline del debito. Debito greco, sono quasi 16 i miliardi che Atene dovrà restituire entro il 21 settembre: su internet il cronoprogramma delle scadenze verso i creditori e i prossimi appuntamenti

Data visualization Infografici Il Sole 24 Ore

LE SFIDE ECONOMICHE

Una serie di statistiche settoriali mettono in luce le sfide che la Grecia si trova ad affrontare su diversi campi da gioco: dalle condizioni di vita delle famiglie, alle performance delle imprese, il confronto con qualche anno racconta una serie di sconfitte. A fare eccezione è il turismo, che in Grecia vale il 17,3% del Pil contro il 10,1% del nostro Paese

● Grecia ● Italia ○ 2009 ● Ultimo dato disponibile

POPOLAZIONE
Milioni di abitanti
- 11,2
- 10,9
- 59,0
- 60,8

	Emigranti	Immigrati
2009	119.985	119.070
ULTIMO DATO	117.094	47.058
2009	78.771	458.856
ULTIMO DATO	125.735	307.454

SPESA DELLE FAMIGLIE
	2009	ULTIMO DATO
Media mensile	2.065,18	1.509,39
In % sul totale		
Cibo	17,3%	20,4%
Alcol e tabacco	3,3%	4,2%
Abbigliamento	7,9%	5,8%
Casa	11,2%	13,7%
Beni durevoli	6,7%	5,6%
Salute	6,5%	6,9%
Trasporti	13,3%	12,5%
Comunicazioni	4,3%	4,1%
Tempo libero	4,9%	4,6%
Istruzione	3,2%	3,4%
Hotel e ristoranti	11%	9,6%
Altro	10,3%	9,3%

CONDIZIONI DI VITA
Percentuale di famiglie

	Tv a colori	Pc	Cellulare	Seconda casa
2009	98,7%	46,4%	86%	17,8%
ULTIMO DATO	99,3%	59,5%	89,2%	16,5%

	Riscaldamento	Auto	Connessione a internet	Ecommerce, ultimi tre mesi
2009	73,5%	66,6%	33%	8%
ULTIMO DATO	38,1%	64,6%	65%	20%

	Persone a rischio di povertà	Peso del welfare sul reddito	Impossibilità di partecipare a eventi scolastici a pagamento	Impossibilità di far mangiare frutta e verdura una volta al giorno
2009	19,7%	28,1%	7,6%	1,1%
ULTIMO DATO	23,1%	44%	25,4%	4,4%

	Impossibilità di garantire ai figli un pasto con carne o pesce	Impossibilità di invitare gli amici a cena	Lavastoviglie	Linea telefonica fissa
2009	4%	4,7%	37%	85,5%
ULTIMO DATO	7,4%	9,2%	36,5%	81,6%

IMPRESE

	Numero di imprese	Valore aggiunto, in miliardi	Importazioni, in milioni	Esportazioni, in milioni
2009	814.000	55	52.087	17.674
ULTIMO DATO	740.000	34	47.773	27.157
2009	4.470.000	482	297.609	291.733
ULTIMO DATO	4.400.000	422	355.115	397.996

TURISMO

	Spesa turistica, ricevute emesse	Spesa media per notte	Peso rispetto al Pil %	Occupati
2009	10.400	27,27	15,9	798.600
ULTIMO DATO	12.115	25,58	17,3	688.800
2009	28.856	69,88	9,6	1.200.000
ULTIMO DATO	33.063	52,78	10,1	2.600.000

LE OLIMPIADI DELLA CRISI

Sono diversi gli indicatori macroeconomici che raccontano la crisi ellenica: lungo la pista olimpica si possono vedere le performance della Grecia rispetto a quelle dell'Eurozona e dell'Italia. Dall'incidenza percentuale del debito pubblico sul Pil, al reddito pro capite, passando per la disoccupazione, il Paese si classifica sempre più sul fondo e negli ultimi anni (dal 2009 all'ultimo dato disponibile) ha perso ulteriormente terreno. Elaborazione Sole 24 Ore su dati Ameco, Eurostat, Ufficio di statistica greco, Banca centrale greca e Wttc

● Grecia ● Eurozona ● Italia
○ 2009
● Ultimo dato disponibile

PIL PRO CAPITE In euro
- 16.300
- 29.800
- 26.600

SPESA PUBBLICA In % rispetto al Pil
- Grecia: 49,3 / 54
- Eurozona: 50,6 / 51,1
- Italia: 49 / 51,1

INVESTIMENTI PUBBLICI LORDI In % sul Pil
- Grecia: 11,6 / 16,8
- Eurozona: 20,9 / 19,5
- Italia: 21,1 / 20

ENTRATE FISCALI In % sul Pil
- Grecia: 33,7 / 32,9
- Eurozona: 43,4 / 44
- Italia: 40,4 / 40,4

SPESA PENSIONI In % sul Pil
- Grecia: 14,4 / 13,9
- Eurozona: 13,5 / 10,9
- Italia: 14 / 14,1

DEBITO PUBBLICO In % sul Pil
- Grecia: 129,7 / 177,1
- Eurozona: 79,9 / 94,2
- Italia: 116,4 / 132,1

SPESA PRO CAPITE PER I CONSUMI In euro
- 16.200 / 11.700
- 16.600 / 14.700
- 15.600 / 16.200

DISOCCUPATI In %
- Grecia: 9,5% / 26,5%
- Eurozona: 7,8% / 11,6%
- Italia: 12,7% / 18,0%

REDDITO LORDO PRO CAPITE In euro
- Grecia: 16.200 / 14
- Eurozona: 26.500 / 30.000
- Italia: 26.400 / 20.700

Obviously, 'modern' infographics cannot be limited to bars and Excel-style pie charts; instead, they require further development to be appealing, as well as accurate and reliable. An essential step is to organize the elements, the structure, and the visual story, just like a well-written plot visualization should have an introduction (title with explanation) and a development with a possible ending. To study the 'masters' and analyze their works is an excellent exercise to improve one's own work: wire framing the structure of the best layouts and understanding the dynamics could easily lead to creating a personal style.

Never forget that a complex data visualization production requires a team where everyone contributes to a continuous exchange to reach the best possible result; beyond graphics, it is fundamental to consider the journalistic side, statistics, and technology to realize static, dynamic or interactive diagrams. Every medium has its characteristics, its limits, and its qualities, but the final goal is always to find the clearest and best expressions of the six Ws of modern journalism: what, who, when, where, why, and wow!

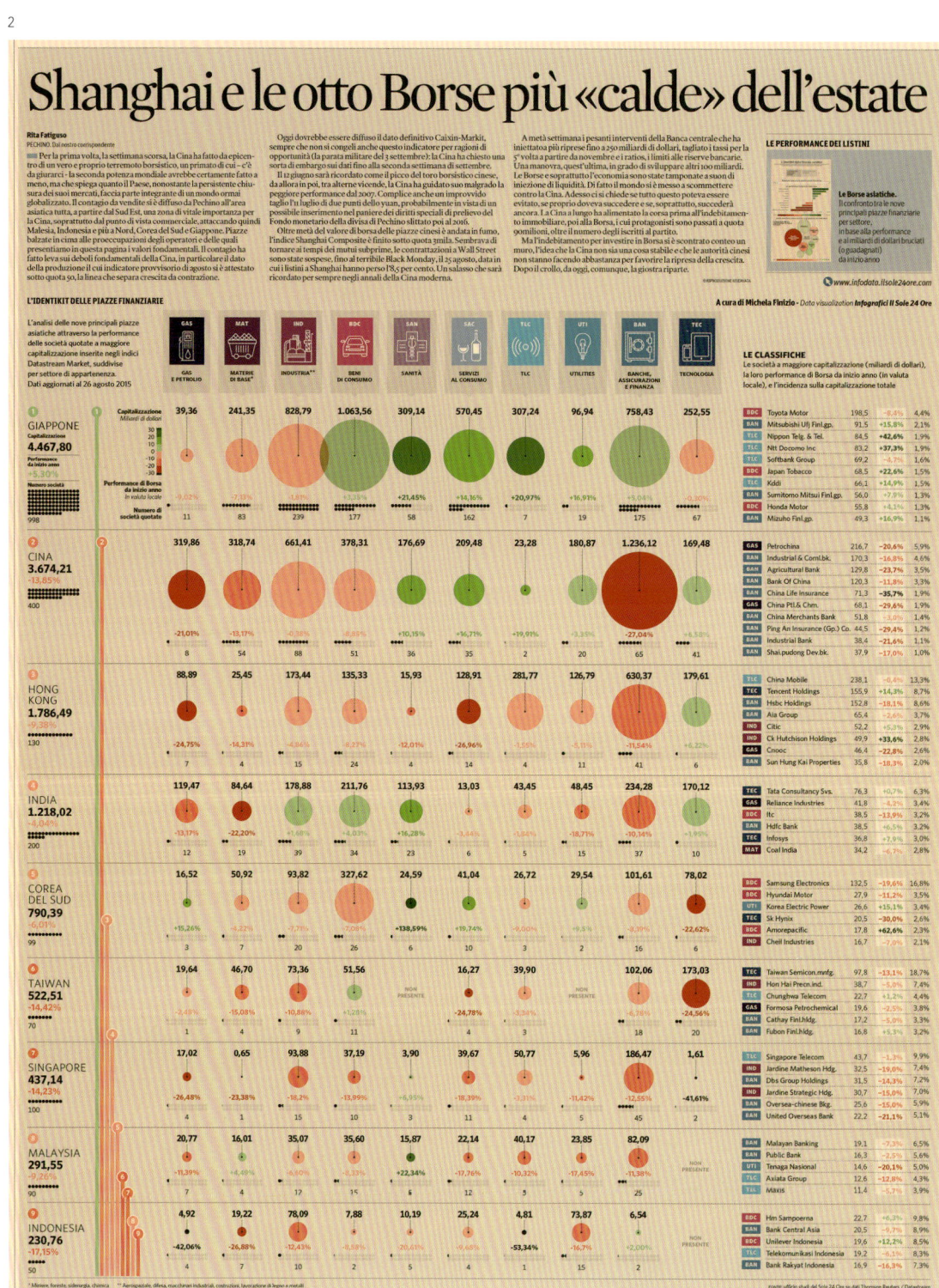

2

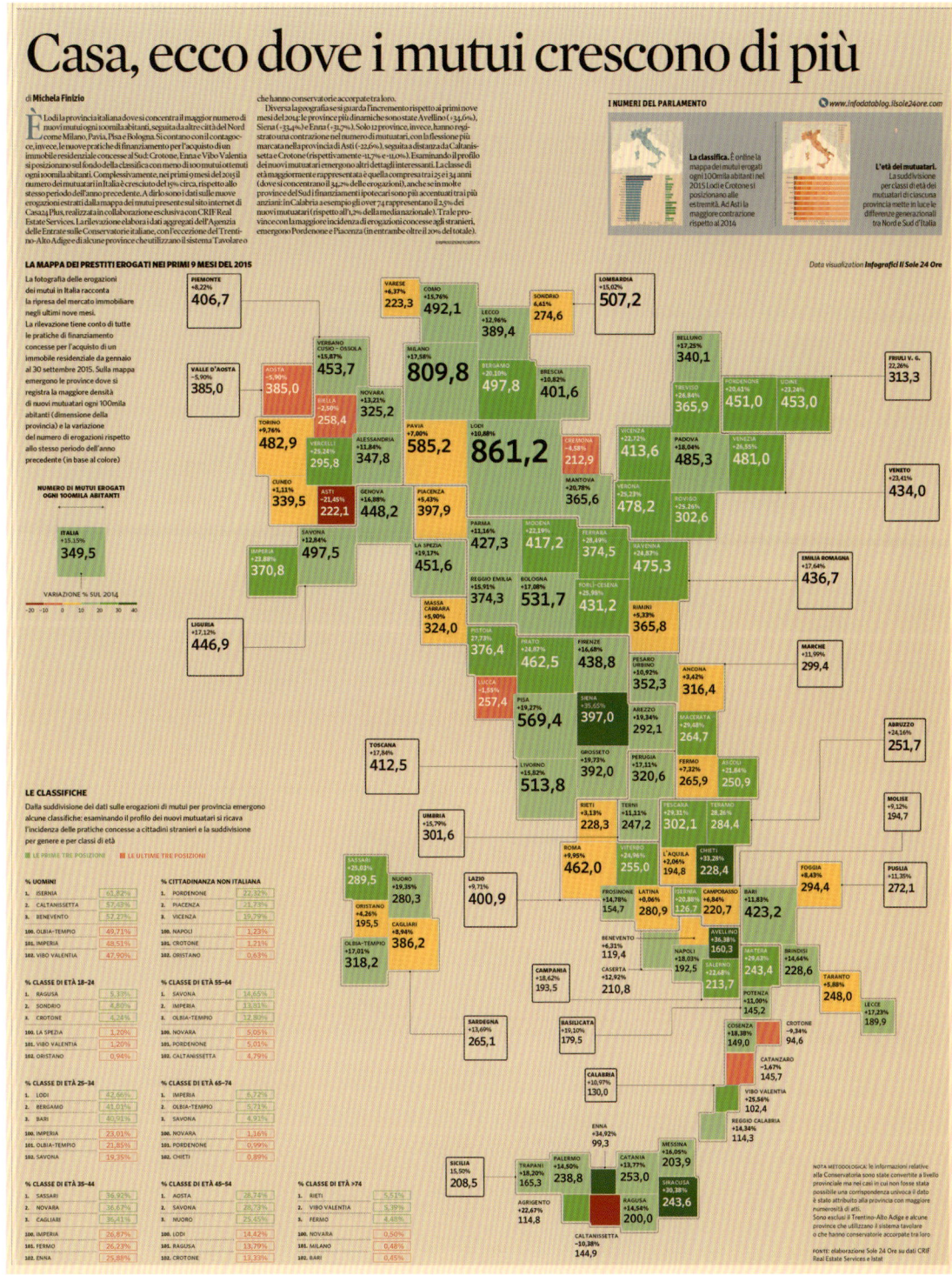

[2] Shanghai Stock Exchange

Credits: Adriano Attus (designer), Federico Barbara (designer), Alice Calvi (designer), Luca Galimberti (designer), Michela Finizio (text and data), Andrea Gianotti, Luca Tremolada
Completion: 2015

The turbulence in China's financial markets in August 2015, which began at the financial epicenter in Shanghai, has spread throughout all major Asian markets. An analysis of nine major Asian stock-exchange lists of the highest capitalization, broken down by business sector, allows better understanding of the impact of the crisis. The identikit by sector shows that one-third of China's market capitalization is represented by banks, and insurance and finance companies, which suffered the most in 2015.

[3] A Map of Mortgages in the First Nine Months of 2015

Credits: Adriano Attus (designer), Federico Barbara (designer), Alice Calvi (designer), Luca Galimberti (designer), Michela Finizio (text and data), Andrea Gianotti, Luca Tremolada
Completion: 2015

A map of new mortgages issued by Italian banks shows a recovery of the real estate market in the January–October 2015 period. The map highlights the provinces where the ratio of new mortgages to every 100,000 citizens is the highest (size of the province), and the increase in the number of new mortgages compared with the same period of 2014 (marked by different colors).

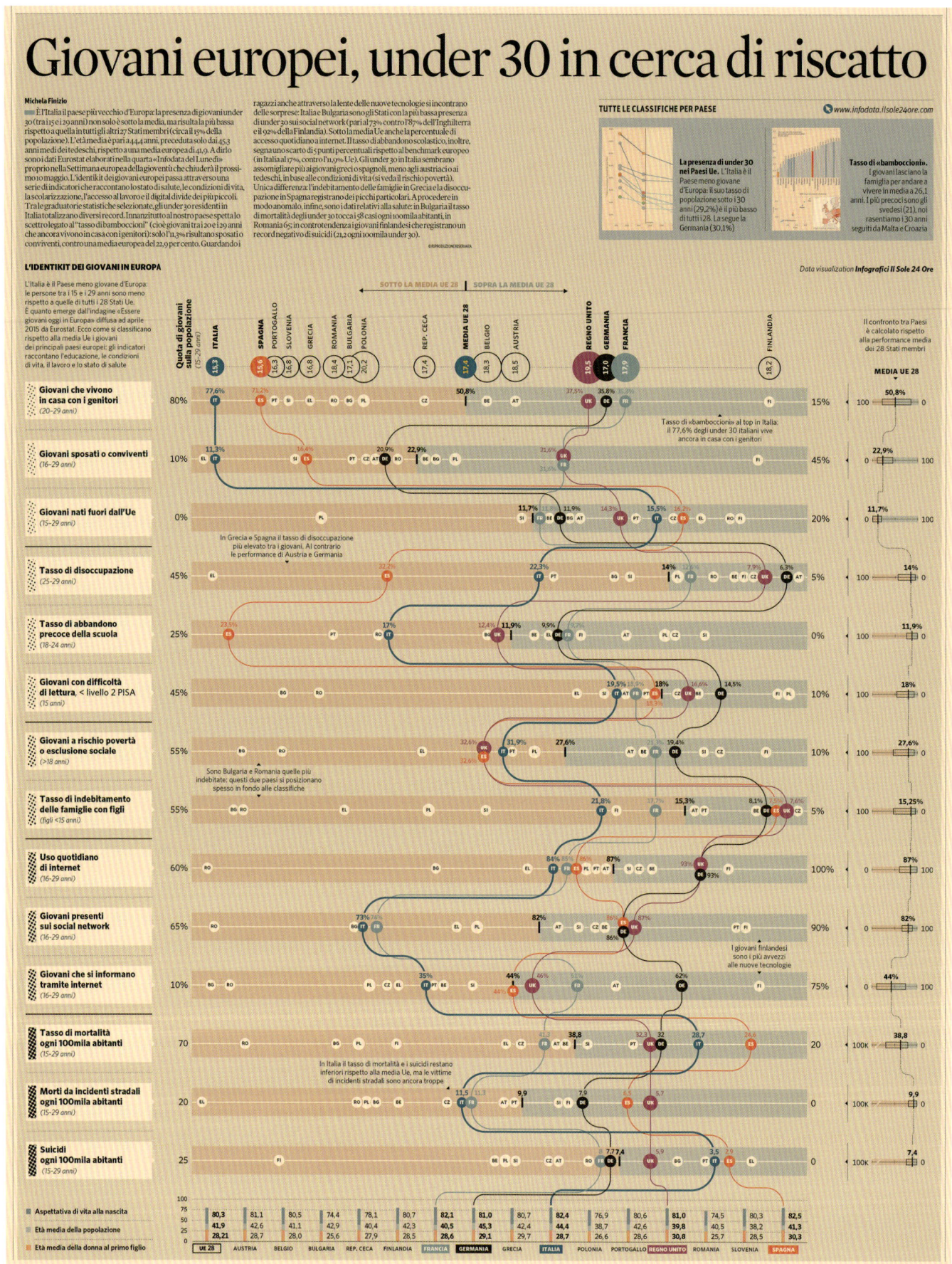

[4] The Identity Card of Young Europeans

Credits: Adriano Attus (designer), Federico Barbara (designer), Alice Calvi (designer), Luca Galimberti (designer), Michela Finizio (text and data), Andrea Gianotti, Luca Tremolada
Completion: 2015

Italy is Europe's oldest country. The ratio of people aged between 15 and 29 is lower than in each of the other 27 countries belonging to the EU (Eurostat figures, 2015). Here's how youngsters living in the major European countries fare compared with the European average in terms of education, life conditions, work, and health.

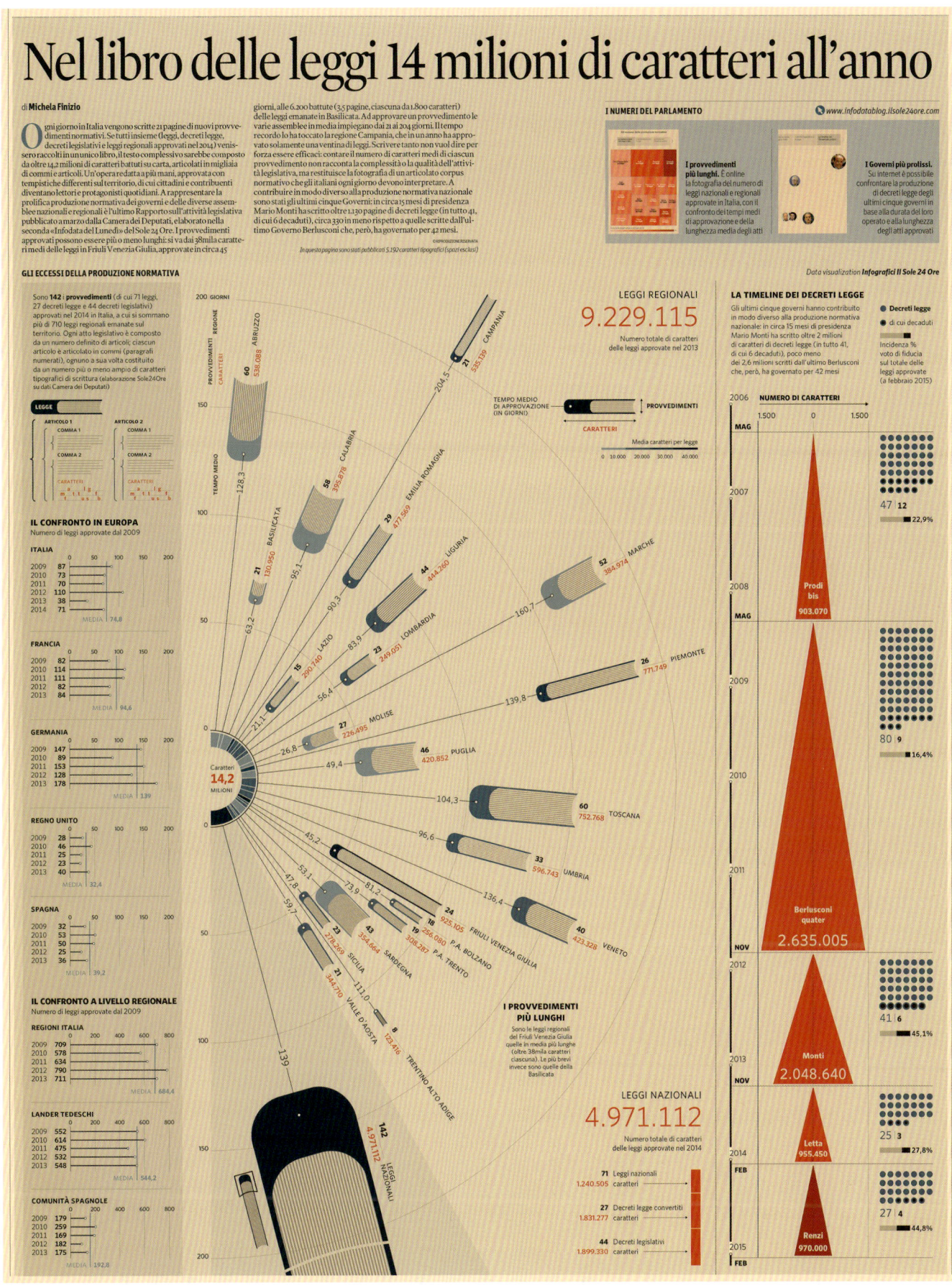

[5] Law-making Activity in Italy

Credits: Adriano Attus (designer), Federico Barbara (designer), Alice Calvi (designer), Luca Galimberti (designer), Michela Finizio (text and data), Andrea Gianotti, Luca Tremolada
Completion: 2015

In 2014, the Italian parliament approved 142 laws, of which 71 were promoted by one of the two branches of parliament, 27 by the government on its own initiative, and 44 by the government after being requested to do so by the parliament. A further 710 were approved at a regional level. Every bill is made up of a certain number of articles; each article is divided into so-called *commi* or numbered paragraphs, and each of them is made up of a certain number of typographic letters.

Steven Braun

Steven Braun holds a BA in chemistry and Asian studies from St Olaf College in Northfield, Minnesota, USA, and earned his MS in molecular biophysics and biochemistry at Yale University. He has been the data analytics and visualization specialist with the Digital Scholarship Group in the Northeastern University Libraries (Boston, Massachusetts, USA) since November 2015. His experiences living and studying in Japan have deeply informed his general philosophy about data visualization: visualization is constructed space, where data are manifold and our choices in design directly inform how those data are interpreted and used.

[Q] What do you think about data visualization/infographics?

[A] Perhaps even more than its practical aspects, I am deeply interested in the philosophical and theoretical implications of data visualization and how they relate to conceptions of self and the human condition. I believe that data visualization can be a powerful mirror for not only reflecting upon ourselves, our beliefs, and our biases, but also those of others around us. Through data visualization, it is possible to facilitate dialogue that cultivates understanding between people with different conceptions of the world. We come to better understand why we have the beliefs we do, and through visualization, we build compassion for perspectives that are not our own as we are reminded of the constructedness of perception.

People come to data visualization for a variety of reasons. Some of those are purely aesthetic; like others, I am fascinated by visualization from a strict design angle, and I think visualization can be beautiful, poignant, and striking when designed well. Other reasons are more technical, with people gravitating toward visualization because of the intellectual stimulation it can provide; there is something satisfying in the ability to successfully take a large and complicated set of data and elegantly extract emergent trends within them through visual representation. These reasons align with my own, and to be sure, the creative, aesthetic, and intellectual satisfaction that visualization offers are all important parts of its appeal. That being said, however, they are also only very small parts of the bigger picture. More deeply, my work in visualization is important to me because it is an exercise in perspectives. It is a lens for dissecting the philosophical, ethical, epistemological, and theological yearnings of ourselves and how they intersect to form the complex landscape of human experience that we live each day. It is a mechanism for getting people to look in places they might not ordinarily look, to encourage them to broaden their understanding of the world by showing them that other

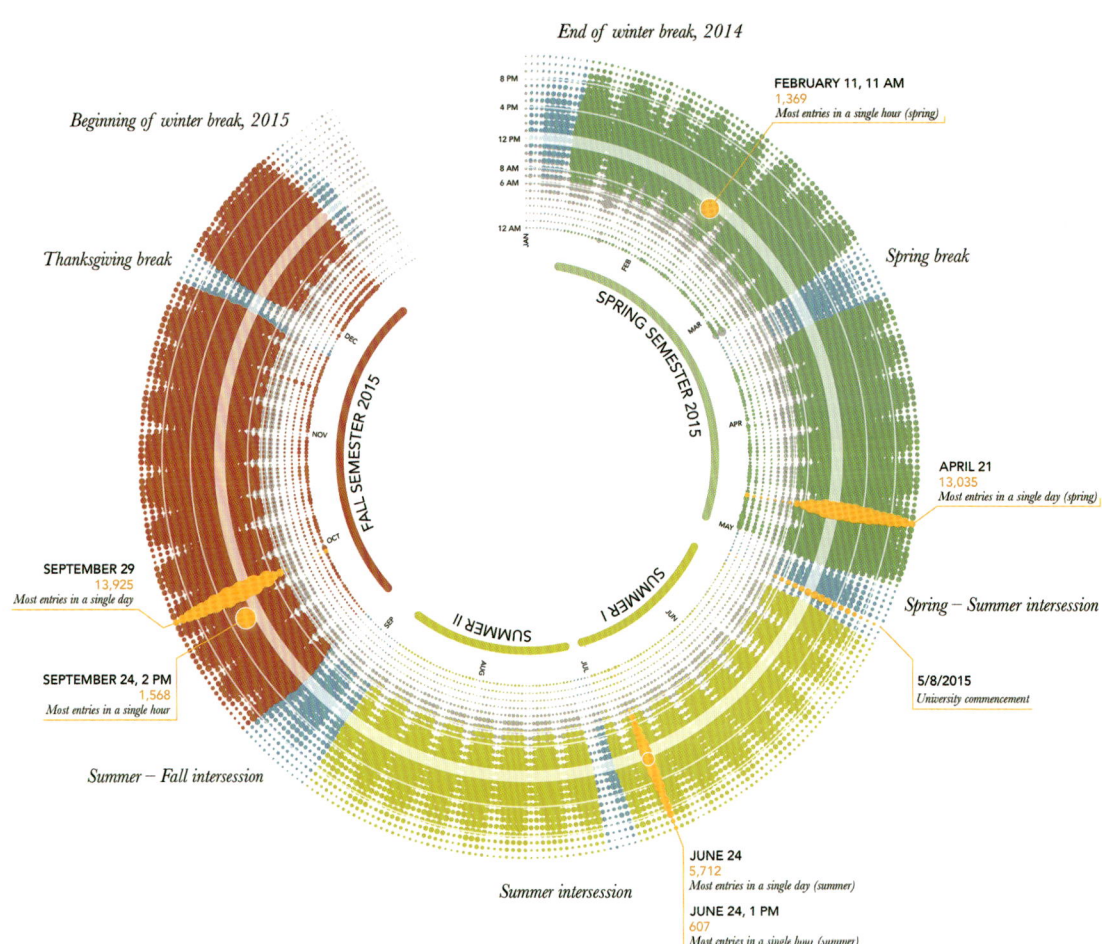

1

frames of reference and perspectives exist. It is an opportunity to demonstrate that humility and ignorance are nothing to be ashamed of when a visualization exposes us to new knowledge, wisdom, or information that lies well outside our comfort zone. It demands of us intentionality, the capacity to think critically about authority and bias when we form our own values and judgments around tricky issues. And, ultimately, it is about being human, about seeing the self in its nakedness—because interpreting a visualization is just as much an act of construction of the self as the process of design is an act of constructing any visual narrative.

[Q] **What kind of design methods do you commonly use?**

[A] I create mostly interactive web-based visualizations. Generally, in the process of creating any visualization, I generate ideas first and then prototype those ideas. Doing so helps me better define my ideas about a visualization's design, which in turn can inform how I formulate the project as a whole. As I prototype, I try my best to find inspiration in real-world contexts in which a visualization might be read. For example, for my Throat Tones project, I wanted to create a visualization that was inspired by the shape of the throat as someone sings. In this way, I attempt to link a visualization with the organic environment from which it might emerge.

I also make sure to carry a sketchbook around with me wherever I go. The idea for a new visualization project can strike at any moment, and when that happens, I make an effort to record the idea and outline a sketch of what it might look like. Usually, these ideas emerge in the most ordinary places, but I find that the ordinary is often where the most interesting projects are born.

[1–2] IN/EFFLUX: Visualizing Snell Library Statistics

Credit: Steven Braun
Completion: 2016

In this visualization, created for Snell Library at Northeastern University, Steven seeks to portray the library as a living, breathing ecosystem. Using data about card swipes of patrons entering Snell Library and Google Analytics data about user sessions on the library website for the calendar year 2015, Steven highlights the ways in which the library pulses with the rhythm of the campus, both in the physical realm as well as the digital.

The visualization is designed as a radial plot, with time represented around the circle, showing patron entries to the library and online user sessions on the library's website for each hour of every day in the 2015 calendar year. Each individual circle corresponds to a total number of card swipes throughout a given hour of the day. Each row of circles along the arc of the diagram represents a single day in a month, and each circle in that row represents a single hour of the day. The relative size of a circle corresponds to the total number of recorded ID card swipes for that time: a larger circle means a relatively greater number of swipes and thus more entries into Snell Library. Circles are colored to show semesters and breaks, from the beginning of the spring semester 2015 through the end of the following fall semester. Gray circles show relative numbers of user sessions on the library website. Finally, the data is also broken out into smaller plots showing only web sessions, entries by graduate students, entries by undergraduate students, and entries by students in the College of Professional Studies.

[Q] **What kind of design elements do you commonly use?**

[A] I generally like to integrate some form of interactivity into most of my visualizations, so the ability of the user to hover, click, and toggle elements in order to explore the data in greater detail tends to make appearances in my work. I also pay significant attention to the role of color in my work, so wide-ranging color palettes are also common elements. Beyond that, I typically rely upon basic geometries such as circles and squares as visual encodings for data.

[Q] **Where are your works applied?**

[A] Most of the visualizations I create are designed for interactivity, and thus they most often appear on my personal portfolio website. I also have experience creating visualizations for print media, however, including a large-format poster print of my visualization, IN/EFFLUX: Visualizing Snell Library Statistics, which was displayed in Snell Library at Northeastern University. For me, the web and print are ideal media for my work as they give me the flexibility to experiment with new design ideas that push me to explore interactivity in new ways.

[Q] **How do you turn boring and complex data into something interesting and understandable?**

[A] Data that is 'boring' and data that is 'complex' have different needs when it comes to visualization. While boring data may need to be made more interesting to increase its appeal, this has to be done with caution as it is worse to construct a false narrative about a set of data than it is to tell a narrative that might not be

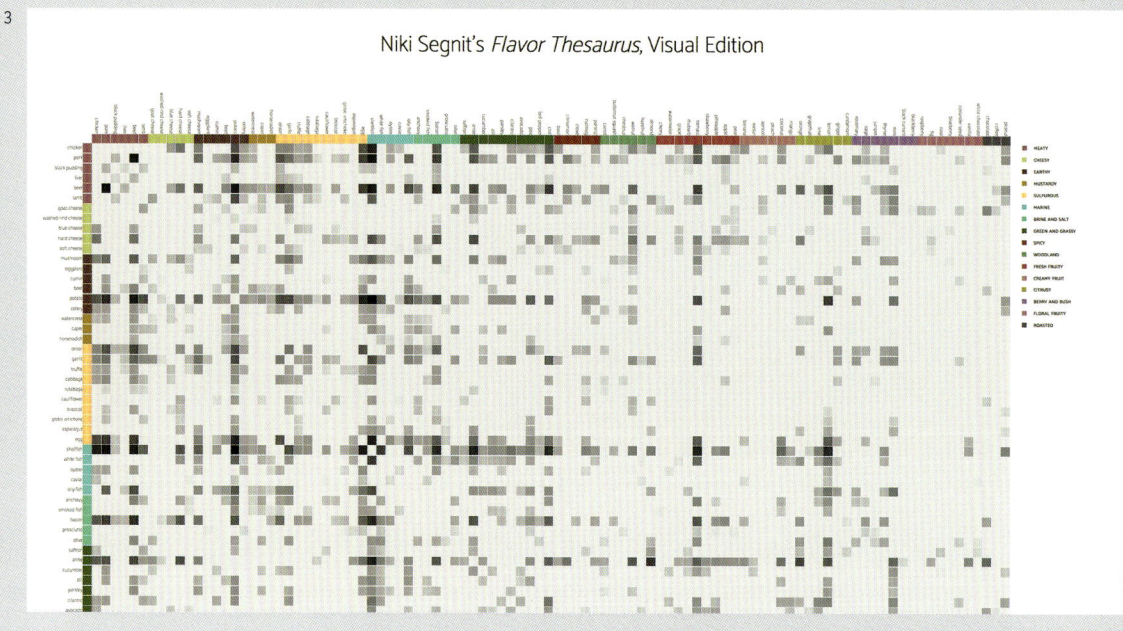

3

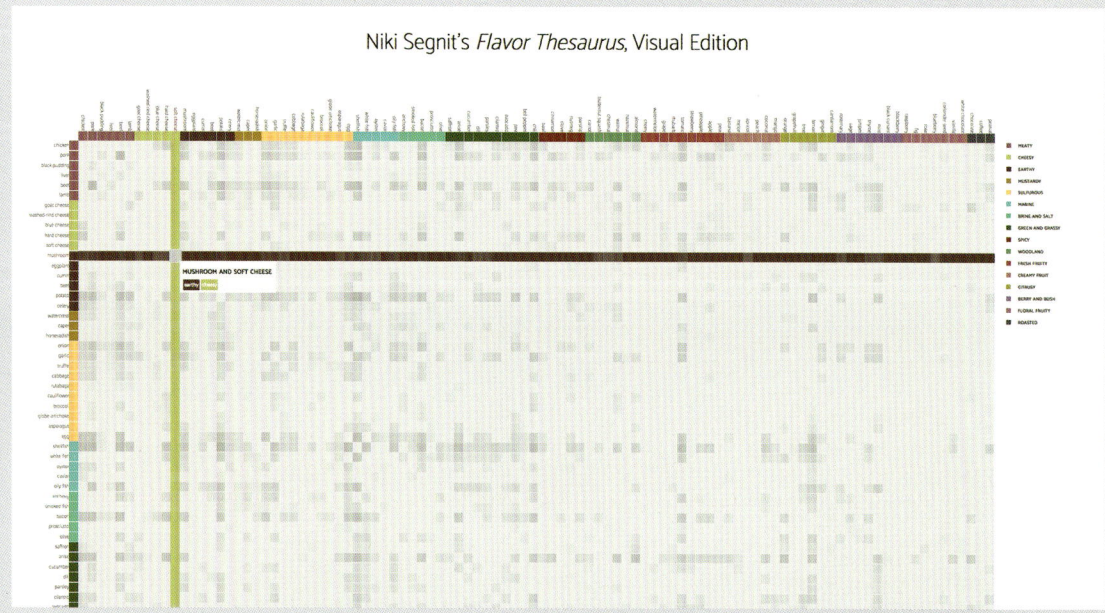

4

interesting. Meanwhile, complex data suffers from the opposite problem; amid that complexity there may be countless interesting narratives, and the challenge is determining how to communicate those narratives simply while remaining faithful to the value of its complexity.

However, I would also argue that there is no such thing as 'boring' data, because all data has something to say. Data is only boring if its expression is boring, which means it is incumbent upon the designer to lift those narratives up effectively. In my own work, I also look for the fundamentally human angle present in data. By making data and its visualization relatable to the human condition, more people can come to it and find something about themselves reflected in it, which is much more powerful than the data or visualization itself. A visualization should be the medium and the data should be the message, and as long as those roles are honored, I find that any data can become exciting.

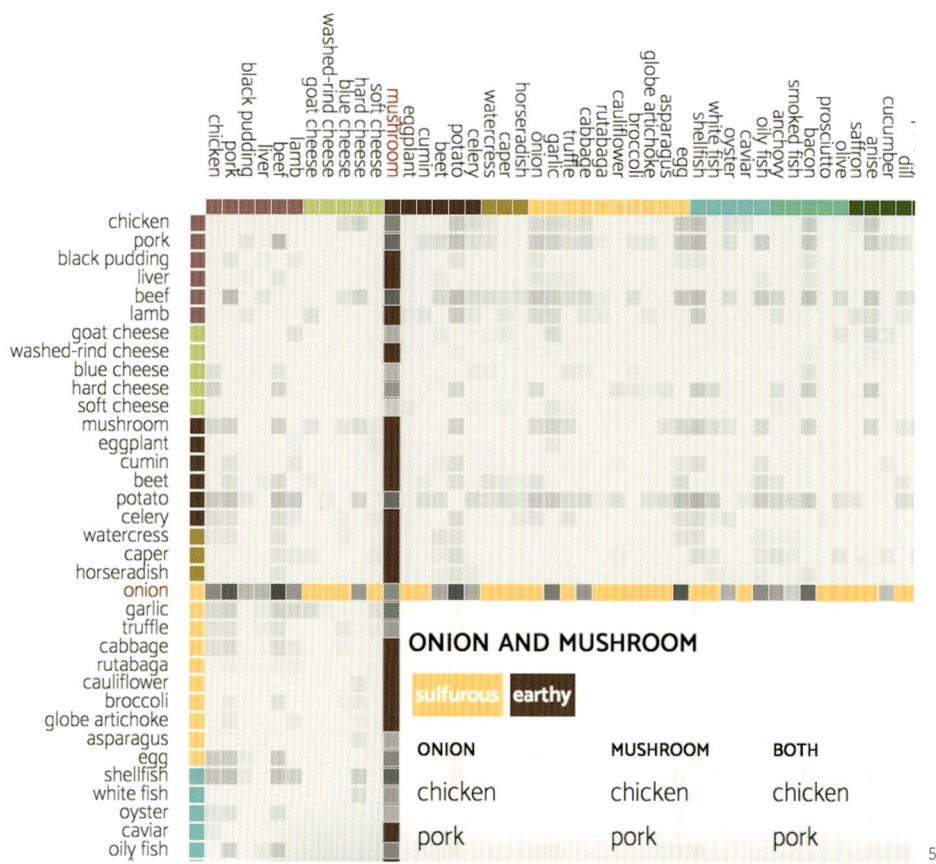

[3–5] Niki Segnit's *The Flavor Thesaurus*

Credits: Steven Braun (analysis and design), Niki Segnit (author of *The Flavor Thesaurus*)
Completion: 2016
Interactive link: www.stevengbraun.com/dev/flavor-thesaurus/index.html

Niki Segnit's book *The Flavor Thesaurus* is a handbook for connoisseurs of flavor everywhere. Written in the style of an index of ingredients and flavors, the book provides interesting, unique, and unusual pairing suggestions for flavors and recommended recipes for trying them out. In this project, Steven has collected all of the flavor pairings recommended in the book and visualized them in an adjacency matrix. The user can explore the matrix, discover new flavor pairings, and build their own.

In this visualization, flavor pairings are represented by a cross-tabulated matrix with rows and columns corresponding to individual flavors or ingredients. This particular matrix is an adjacency matrix, meaning that column and row headers are redundant, giving the visualization diagonal symmetry. Each individual flavor is assigned to a specific flavor class in *The Flavor Thesaurus* (i.e. meaty, fruity, or roasted), and each column or row header is colored according to these classes, using the same color scheme provided in the book. Look up individual flavors or ingredients by column or row, and hover over labels, flavor classes, and pairings to explore more. Each two-flavor pairing—that is, each square inside the matrix—is colored in proportion to the number of three-flavor pairings that are possible with the given two flavors; darker squares indicate more possible pairings and triplets. When the user clicks on any square/flavor pairing, a list of additional suggested pairings for each component flavor as well as for both flavors together is provided so they can explore and build their own.

[Q] What is your suggestion for beginners?

[A] It is easy to feed into the misconception that the best visualizations are created instantaneously with a clear vision from the beginning. The reality is that the exact opposite is true. The best visualizations are those that cycle through iteration after iteration; for many of my own visualizations, I have experimented with countless versions that have neared completion before being scrapped entirely. Creating a good visualization takes time, energy, and the willingness to take risks in design even when those designs may be thrown away in the end. The best designers that I look up to know this reality quite intimately—do not be afraid to ask designers about their failures, because they will often tell you that it is from those failures they learnt the most.

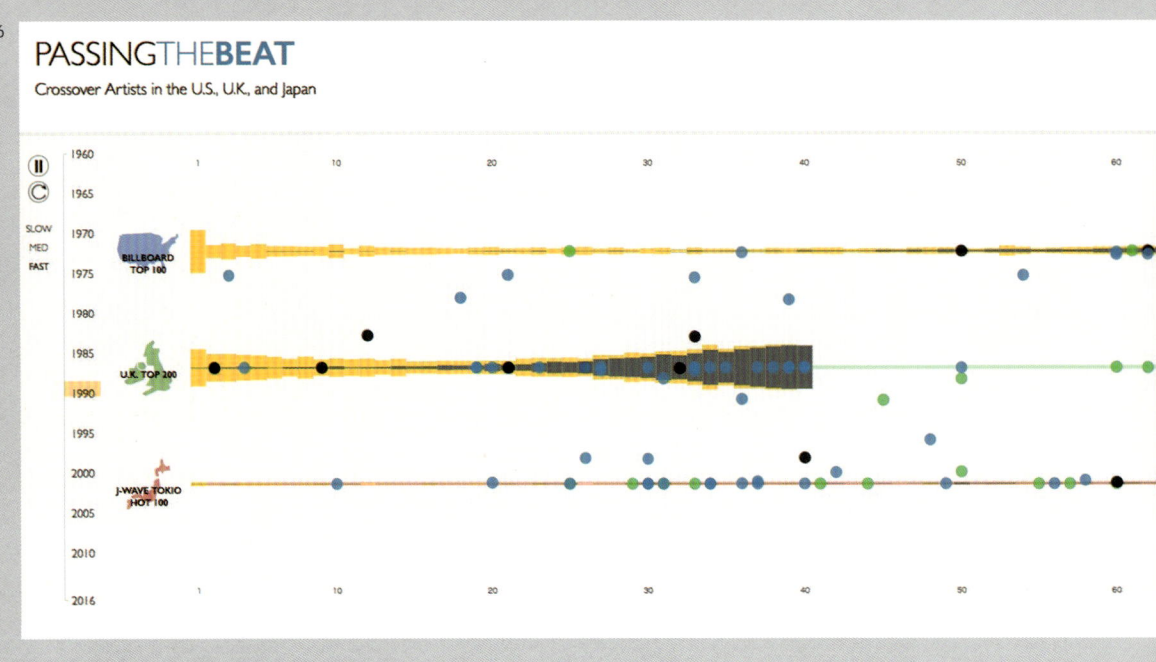

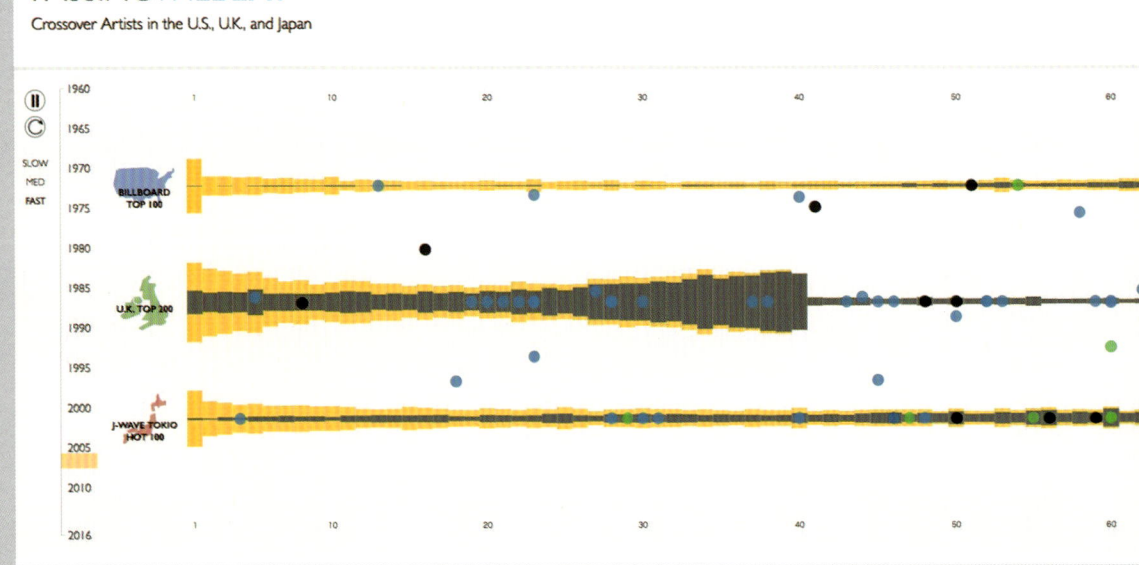

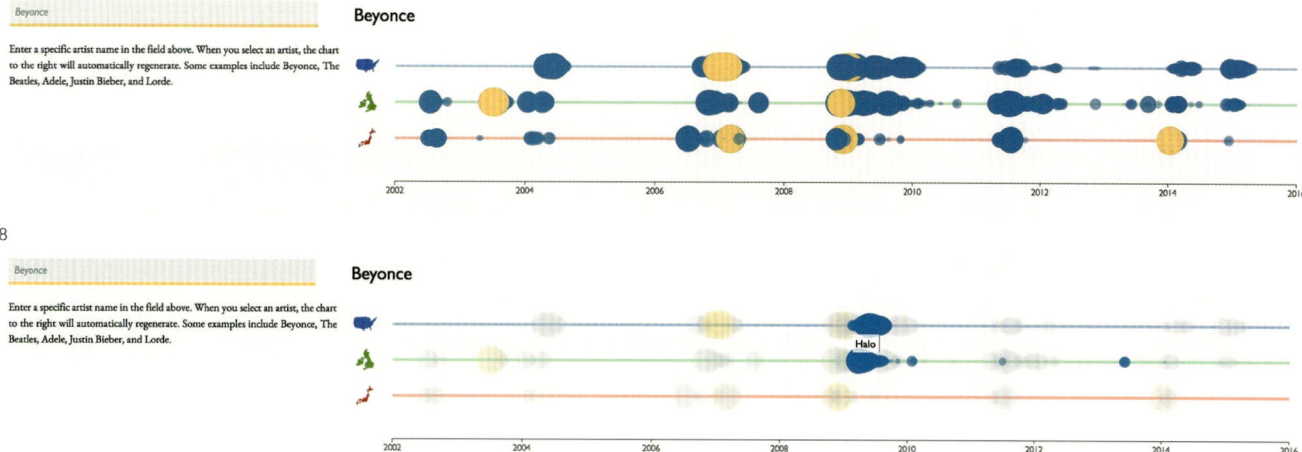

[6–9] Passing the Beat: Crossover Artists in the US, UK, and Japan

Credits: Steven Braun (analysis and design), Roger Press (data), Academic Rights Press (data)
Completion: 2016
Interactive link: www.stevengbraun.com/dev/passing-the-beat

In this visualization, historical single rankings from the Billboard Top 100 (the United States), the UK Top 200 (the United Kingdom), and J-Wave Tokio Hot 100 (Japan) are aggregated to show the frequency with which artists from these three countries (and around the world) attain success with their music across the Pacific and the Atlantic.

In the animation, each horizontal axis corresponds to the top music charts of these three countries, shown in order from top to bottom. When a circle appears on one of these axes, this means a single by an artist from another country has made an appearance on the chart represented by the axis. The color of the circle indicates the artist's country of origin (blue for the United States, green for the United Kingdom, red for Japan, and black for all other countries), and a marker's movement indicates that the single has jumped from one other country's chart to the one indicated. The horizontal position of each marker indicates the single's rank position in the given chart, with position 1 at the far left and position 100 at the far right.

As the animation progresses, it keeps a tally of how many singles by foreign artists have held each given rank position on each chart over time. As this grows, a horizontally arranged bar chart is created on each axis; the gold bars represent the peak chart position reached by a given single, and the dark gray bars indicate the position into which a foreign single first makes its appearance on the given chart. As the width of these rectangles grows in proportion to the number of singles obtained at each position, it becomes possible to see, for instance, the proportion of foreign artists' singles that enter a country's music charts at the #1 position.

The user can hover over a circle to see international ranking trends for each given single. When one circle is hovered over, the rest of the circles corresponding to the same single are highlighted as a group. In some interesting instances, a single that makes an appearance on one of the top music charts may make additional appearances decades after its first release.

THROAT TONES
Vowels and Pitch in the Music of Sia and Adele

The timbre of a singer's voice is determined by many psychoacoustic factors. Some of these are created in the mind via the process of perception, such as the loudness or texture of a sound. But others are physical features that can be measured directly, independent of any psychoacoustic correlates. Trained singers are able to manipulate the timbre of their voice by changing these physical features, achieved primarily through changing the shape of their vocal tract. In this visualization, timbre is imagined as a product of two measurable features in particular: formant frequency, correlating with vowel and throat openness, and pitch frequency. Have you ever heard of a "close" vowel or an "open" one? Have you ever paid attention to the position of your tongue when you speak or sing? **Read more and click the labels for tracks below to see clusters in pitch and formants in the music of Sia and Adele.** (Data may take a few seconds to finish loading.)

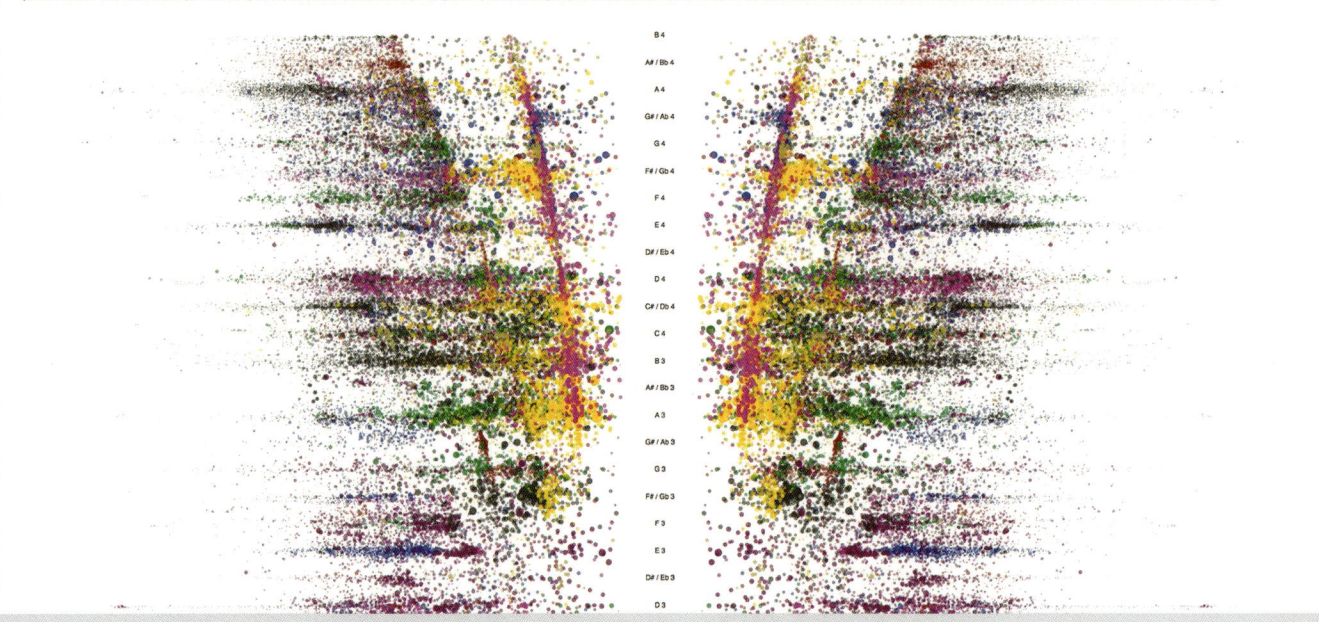

10

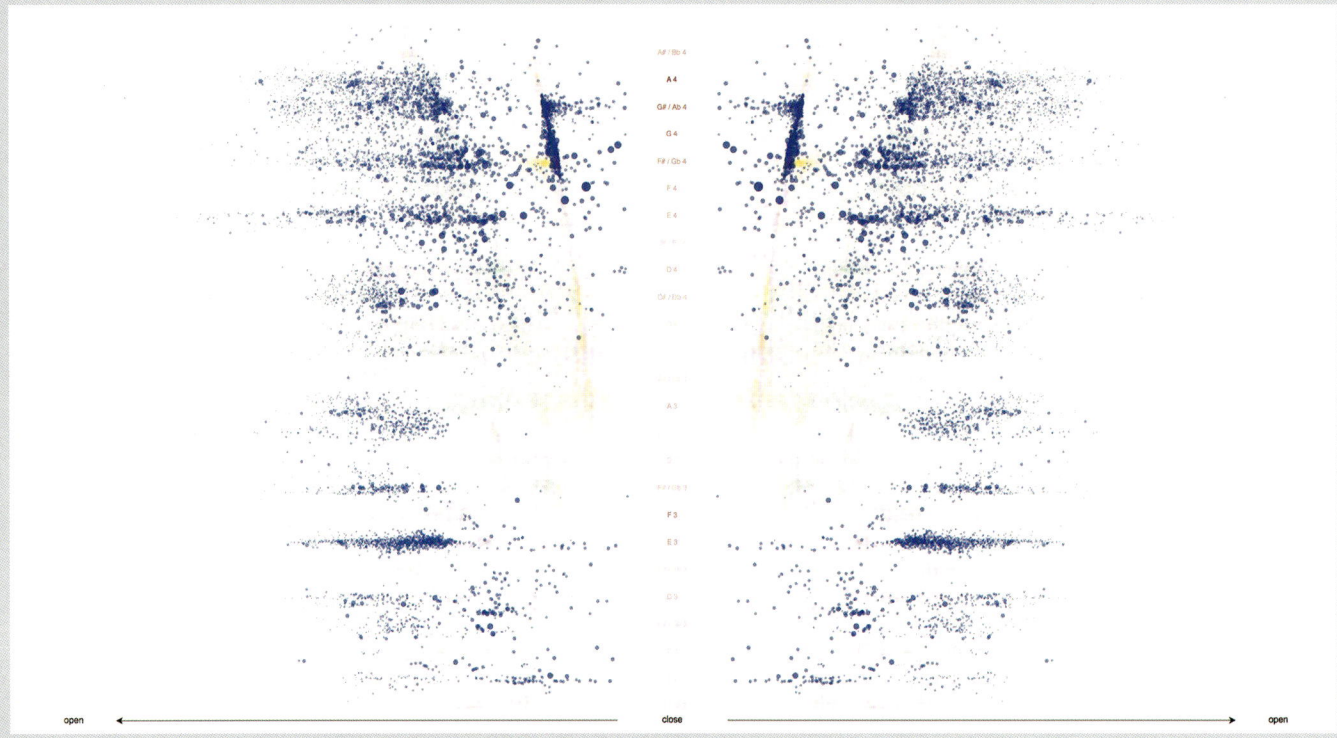

11

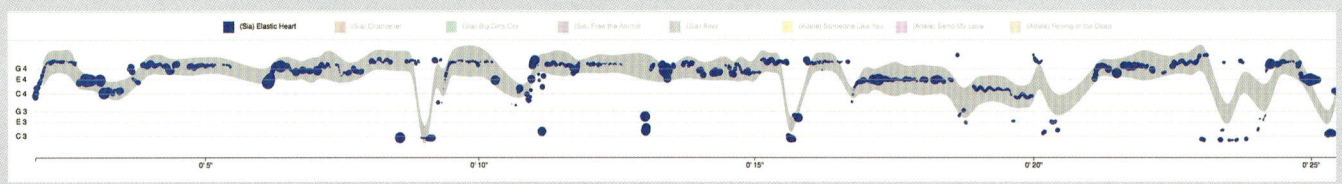

12

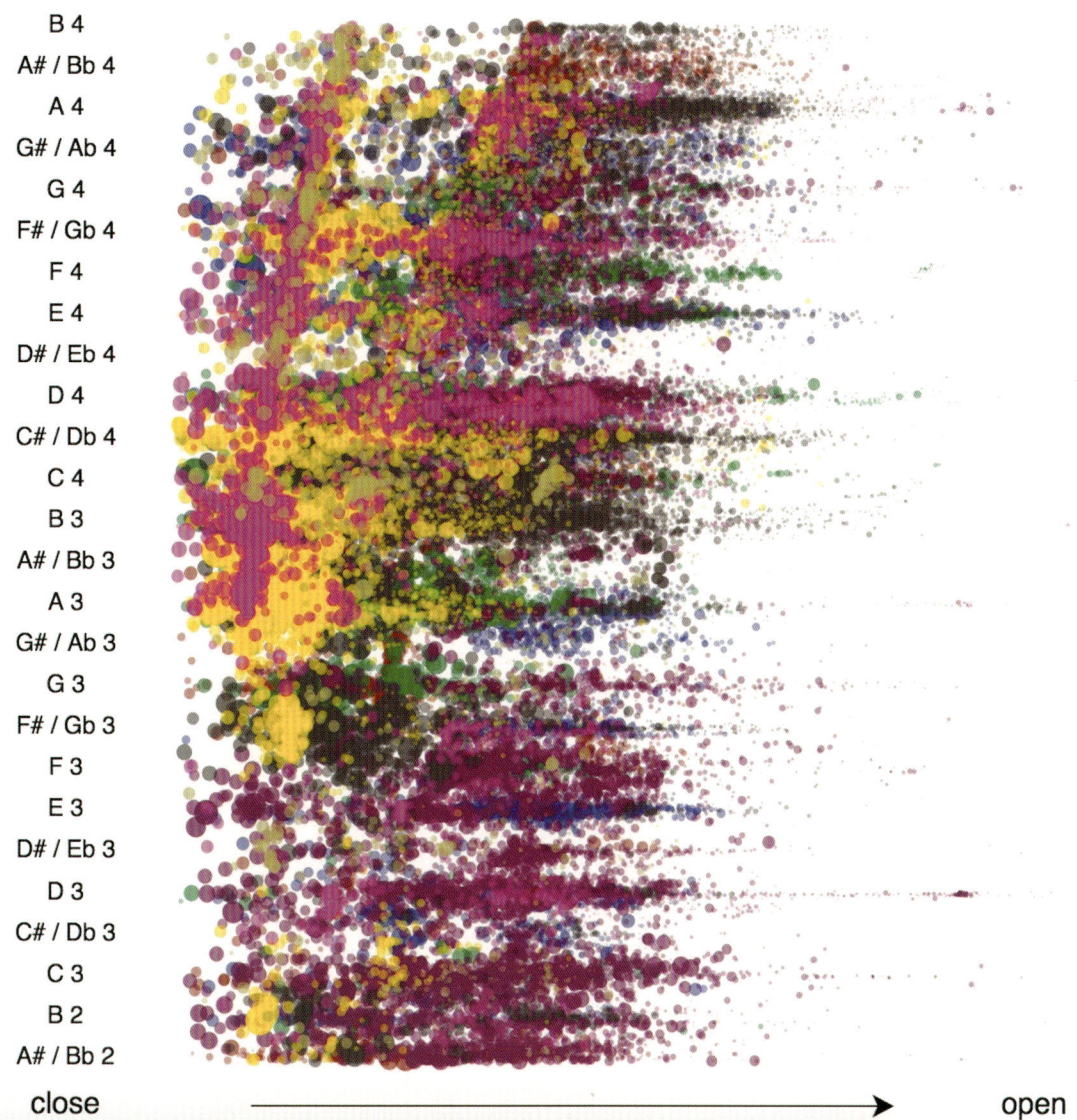

[10–13] Throat Tones: Vowels and Pitch in the Music of Sia and Adele

Credits: Steven Braun (analysis and design), Sia (music), Adele (music)
Completion: 2016
Interactive link: www.stevengbraun.com/dev/throat-tones/index.html

The timbre of a singer's voice is determined by many psychoacoustic factors. In this visualization, timbre is imagined as a product of two measurable features in particular: formant frequency, correlating with vowel and throat openness, and pitch frequency.

In this project, data about formant and pitch frequency were sampled at 0.05-second intervals for five songs performed by Sia and three performed by Adele. These songs are separated into color categories; within each color category, a single circle (point) represents the measured first formant (on the horizontal axis) and approximate pitch (on the vertical axis) for a given 0.05-second slice of the respective song. Points that are further up vertically in the chart are higher in pitch, and points corresponding to sounds are positioned closer to the center. The data is mirrored on each side to mimic this effect: more closed voicings are represented by data points that are closer to the central axis, showing a constriction of the vocal tract, and more open voicings are represented by data points that are further away from the central axis, showing a more open vocal tract. There are also differences in circle sizes, which correspond to subtractive differences in the first two formants for each continuously sampled sound.

The bottom visualization shows the same data about formant and pitch frequencies for individual songs but in a different format. Here, pitch and formant frequencies are spread out horizontally along a time axis that spans the duration of each song. Each circle represents a data point, oriented horizontally by time in the song and vertically by pitch. The size of each circle indicates the relative subtractive difference between the first two formants of the respective sound slice.

Nadieh Bremer

[Q] **What do you think about data visualization/infographics?**

[A] Being a data visualization designer, I'm of course biased in my opinion, but I truly believe in an adaptation of a well-known saying: 'A data visualization is worth more than a thousand (or even million) data points'. People are very visual people, and although the developed world these days might work on numbers, people understand it through visualizations of these numbers, in whatever form that might be. People can see trends in a simple line chart within a fraction of a second and remember this, even days later, which cannot be done if the numbers from the line chart were presented in a table. It seems that more and more companies are beginning to understand the power of good data visualization and how it can explain complex concepts and engage non-experts, which is a development that I'm very happy to see.

[Q] **What kind of design methods do you commonly use?**

[A] I don't follow any 'official' methods; being self-taught in design I follow what has worked best for me in the past. When I create something personal, I always start with a question: 'How have the most popular baby names risen and fallen from fame in the past?', for example. For my work-related projects, I start with interviews of the eventual users of the visualization/dashboard to try and understand their goals. What information are they trying to get from the data? I then dive into the data, think about what is available out there or within the company, and make some quick and dirty statistical charts to get a feeling of what's in there. With those two elements, question/goals and data, I then use pen and paper to design the basic structure and chart forms.

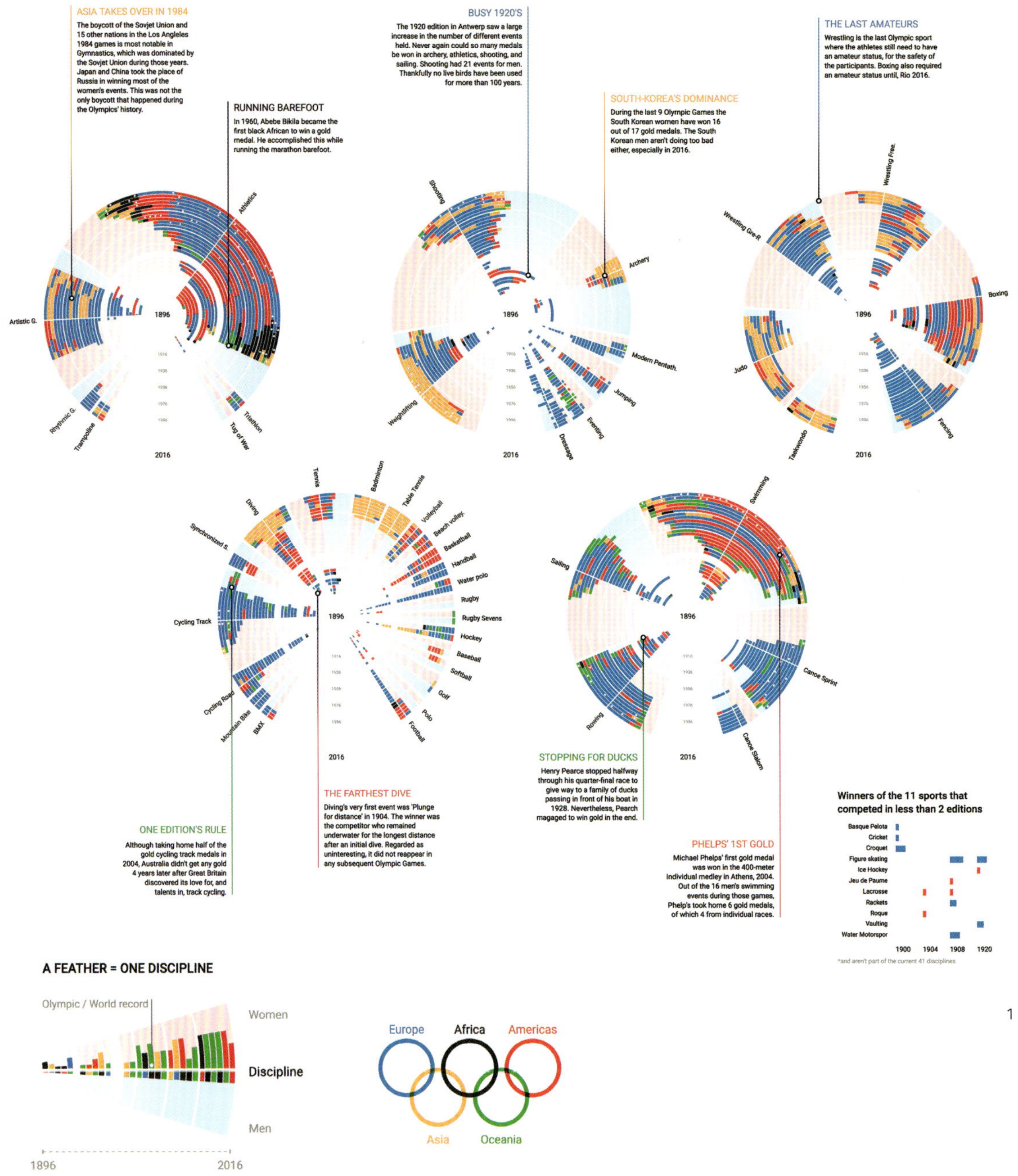

Nadieh Bremer has been spending most evenings and weekends reading about best practices, creating (interactive) data visualization projects, and sharing lessons learnt on her personal blog, www.visualcinnamon.com. Several of her works were nominated in the 2015 Kantar Information is Beautiful awards, and she has won the Rising Star award in 2016. And she also won a data visualization competition organized by the World Bank & Visualizing in March 2015.

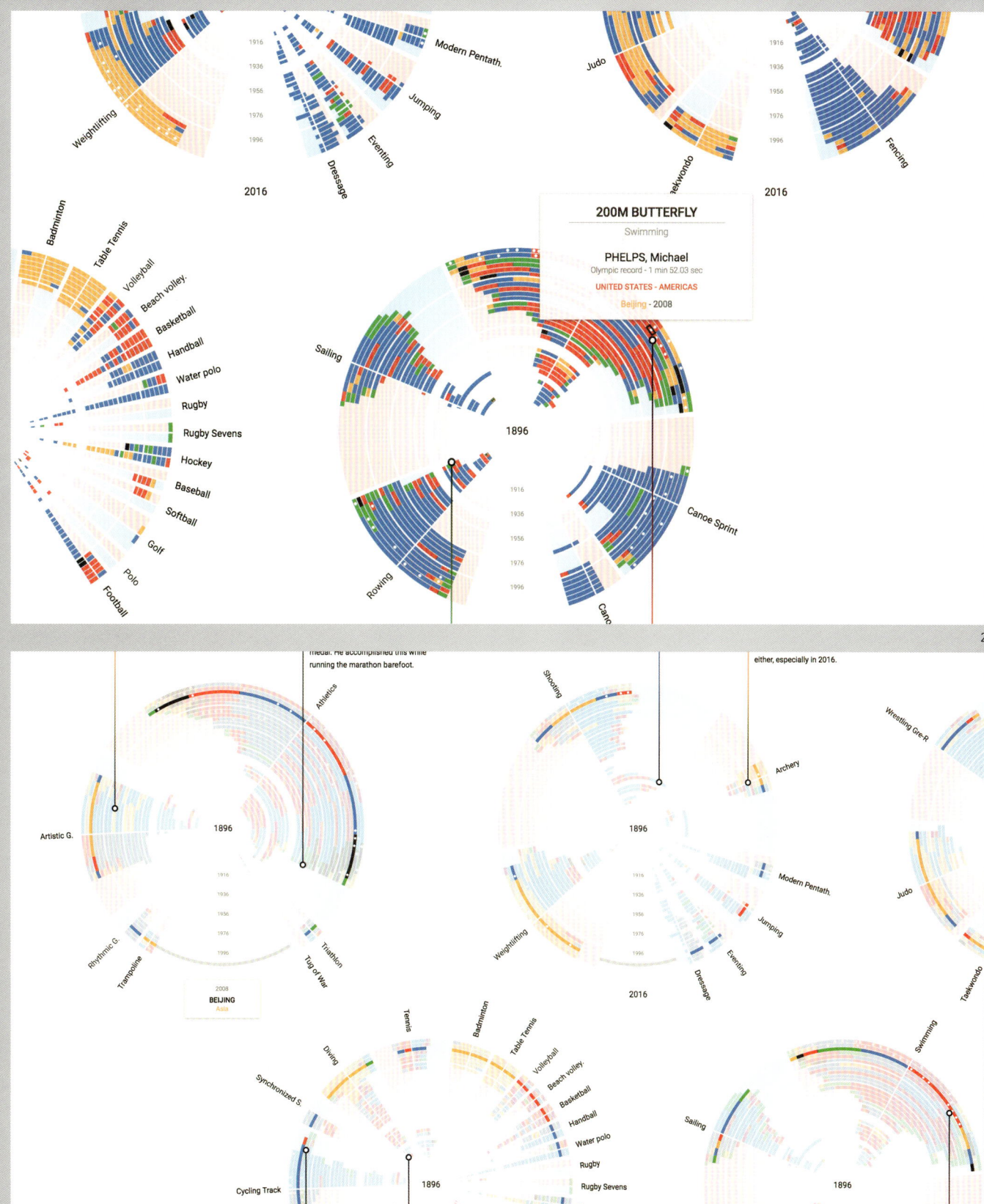

[1–3] Olympic Feathers

Credit: Nadieh Bremer
Completion: 2016
Interactive link: nbremer.github.io/olympicfeathers

This interactive data visualization shows all of the 5100 Olympic gold-medal winners since the first modern Olympic Games in 1896. As an extra level of detail, it also marks the current Olympic Records. The medals are ordered by sport, edition, gender, and continent. The medals have been placed in circles on purpose to make sure that the more recent editions of the games have more emphasis, due to the increasing size of the ring. By hovering over the medals, you can see which person or team won the gold, and by hovering over the timeline at the bottom of each circle you can see one particular Olympic Games highlighted to help you find your own interesting stories.

For personal projects, these forms can be more artistic or far-fetched. I tend to skip the static mock part (I only do that if I have to pass the design on to a team member to build it) and go straight from paper to program the design and tweak it further in the browser. I guess I just prefer to design with code. But another advantage of going straight to the coding is that I can easily use the actual data to build the visualization. There have been enough times that I had to make changes to an initial design, because it just didn't fit the typical data quite right or didn't bring out the insights well enough. Adding the interaction is the last big leg, which can be an extremely important factor, even though not much is changing visually on the screen anymore.

[Q] What kind of design elements do you commonly use?

[A] I often use elements in different ways to create new forms or charts. Even for my work-related projects, I make enough line and bar charts, since these are very powerful and flexible.

[Q] Where are your works applied?

[A] My personal projects all appear on my website, but some have later been featured in online media, such as the *Scientific American*. Although most are interactive and meant for the online world, sometimes I do create static visualizations as well that take more of a poster form.

[Q] How do you turn boring and complex data into something interesting and understandable?

[A] For me, boring data is data that cannot answer any interesting question. You can't turn this into something interesting with visualization. However, many people see data as being boring in general, but for me personally, when I get my hands on a new data set, I just can't wait to find the insights that are hidden beneath the nicely structured rows of numbers. You just need to figure out how to restructure it to show your answers. Finding a compelling insight or being driven by some question, I think, is the most important element to making data interesting. Be curious. Even a simple bar chart can be fascinating if it reveals some wonderful fact that was hidden in the numbers before.

For visualizing more complex data, it is the way you present it to the audience. Don't present it all at once, but slowly build it up. Having a good introduction is the key then. Start small and tell the viewer what the data is about in general. I feel text is somewhat underappreciated in data visualization, but not everything has to be understood from visual marks and icons alone. Pick an interesting example from the total data set that is contained and explain this in full detail with annotations or animations if needed. Finally, slowly reveal the total data set in all its complexity while still pointing out interesting insights. Hopefully the viewer will understand how to read the chart by the end of the introduction without having been intimidated by it.

[4] Traffic Accidents vs Influential Factors

Credit: Nadieh Bremer
Completion: 2015

Every day, traffic accidents happen, but this number differs each day because there are factors that influence it. This visualization displays all traffic accidents that occurred in the Netherlands in 2013 and combines it with several factors that might have an influence on traffic accidents and for which the data is freely available: amount of rain, snow days, school holidays, and number of daylight hours. It leaves it to the viewer to discover and see the trends that arise.

TRAFFIC ACCIDENTS

COMPARING THE NUMBER OF TRAFFIC ACCIDENTS TO WEATHER, HOLIDAYS AND DAYLIGHT HOUR PATTERNS

NETHERLANDS | 2013

One year of traffic accidents, about 100.000 or 280 per day on average, according to BRON in 2013

The chart combines a few indicators that can result in a higher than average number of accidents, such as official snow days, amount of precipitation, school holidays and the number of daylight hours

The overall trend shows that fall was the worst time of the year, whereas holidays provided a small dip in the trends throughout the year

The absolute numbers also reflect the weekend pattern of significantly less accidents

The 5 worst days have been annotated, with January 15th ranking on top with 602 accidents. As can be expected, all these days had very bad weather conditions with snow, frost, severe rain or extreme winds

Jan 15th snow during morning rush hour results in the biggest traffic jams ever reported in the Netherlands

Jan 21st snow and frost created dangerous road conditions

Valentines day snow and melting snow freezing again caused many accidents

Oct 10 & 11th a weather alarm was in effect due to severe winds and rain

Sep 10th the first fall storm with an amount of rain that usually falls in an entire month and strong winds

Number of traffic accidents — 600, 400, 200

Precipitation [mm] — 40, 20

Hours of Daylight — 9, 12, 15

fall holiday · spring holiday · may holiday · summer holiday period

absolute number of accidents
LOESS curve to show trend

❄ weekday snow
❄ weekend snow
❄ weekday & weekend snow

created by Nadieh Bremer | VisualCinnamon.com
data | weather - KNMI
data | traffic accidents - BRON (Bestand geRegistreerde Ongevallen in Nederland)

[Q] **What is your suggestion for beginners?**

[A] Start creating! There's no better way to start learning how to do data visualization than by making your own projects and sharing these with the world. Try to think of a question that interests you personally, and see if there's data online (or gather it yourself) that can answer it. Then start thinking of the design with pen and paper, don't go straight to the computer. With the pen, you can draw whatever you want without being constrained by the options of your drawing program (or programming language). If you've drawn something, and this doesn't have to be beautiful but merely some schematic sketch of what you have in your mind, and you come across some technical issues while you actually create it, you'll be much more motivated to try and think of innovative ways to make that image in your mind appear on the screen. During each project you'll learn new things, which you can reuse for your next project. It's all about experience. Reading a few books on visualization best practices is a good thing to do on the side as well.

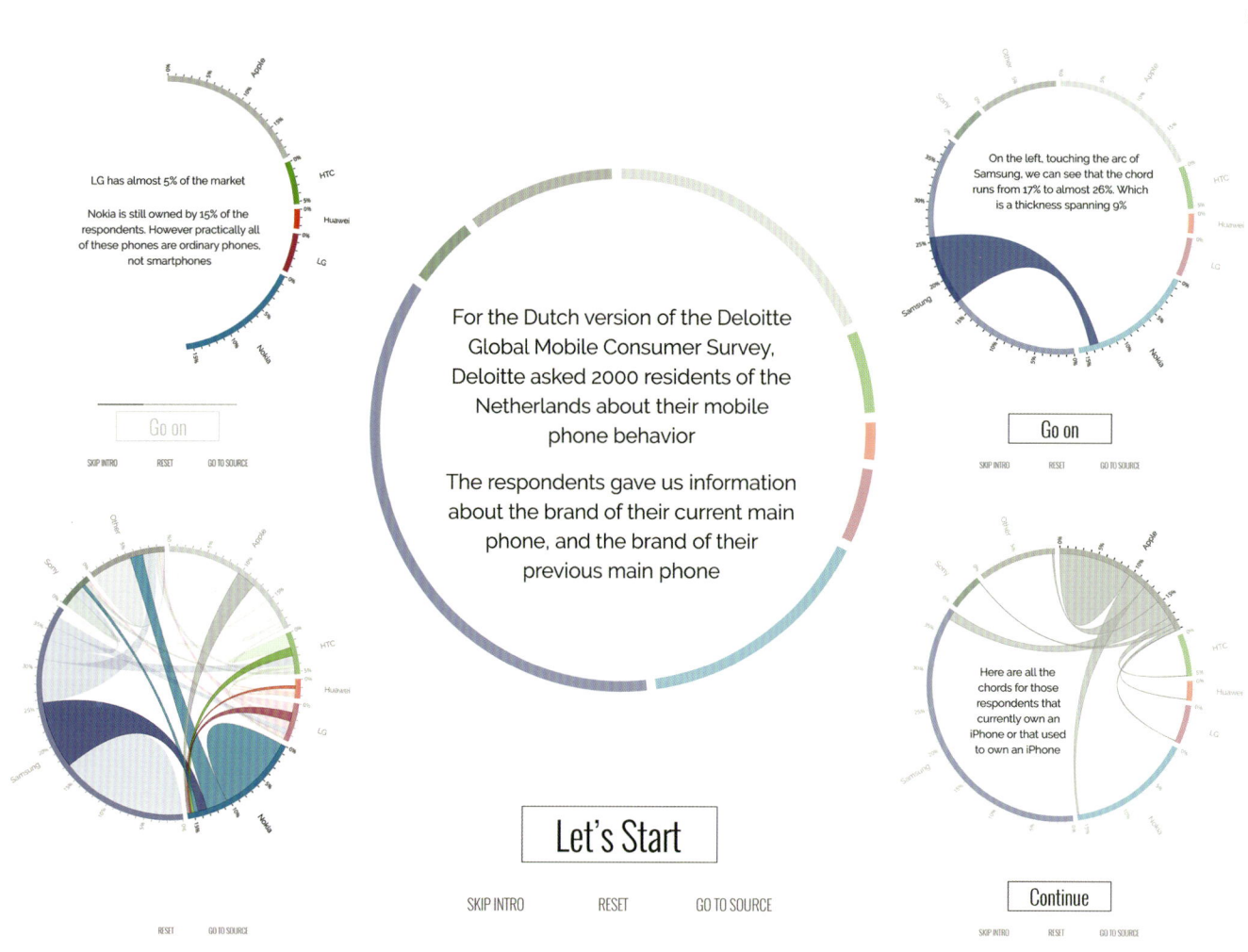

[5–8] Switching Between Phone Brands

Credits: Nadieh Bremer, Deloitte Netherlands
Completion: 2014
Interactive link: nbremer.github.io/Chord-Diagram-Storytelling

For the Dutch version of the Deloitte Global Mobile Consumer Survey, Deloitte asked 2000 residents of the Netherlands about their mobile-phone behavior. The respondents gave information about the brands of their current main phones, and the brands of their previous main phones. The resulting flows between the top five phone brands are compactly visualized in a Chord diagram layout. Due to the unusual display of the Chord diagram, the approach of data storytelling is used to slowly introduce the viewer to the insights that can be found.

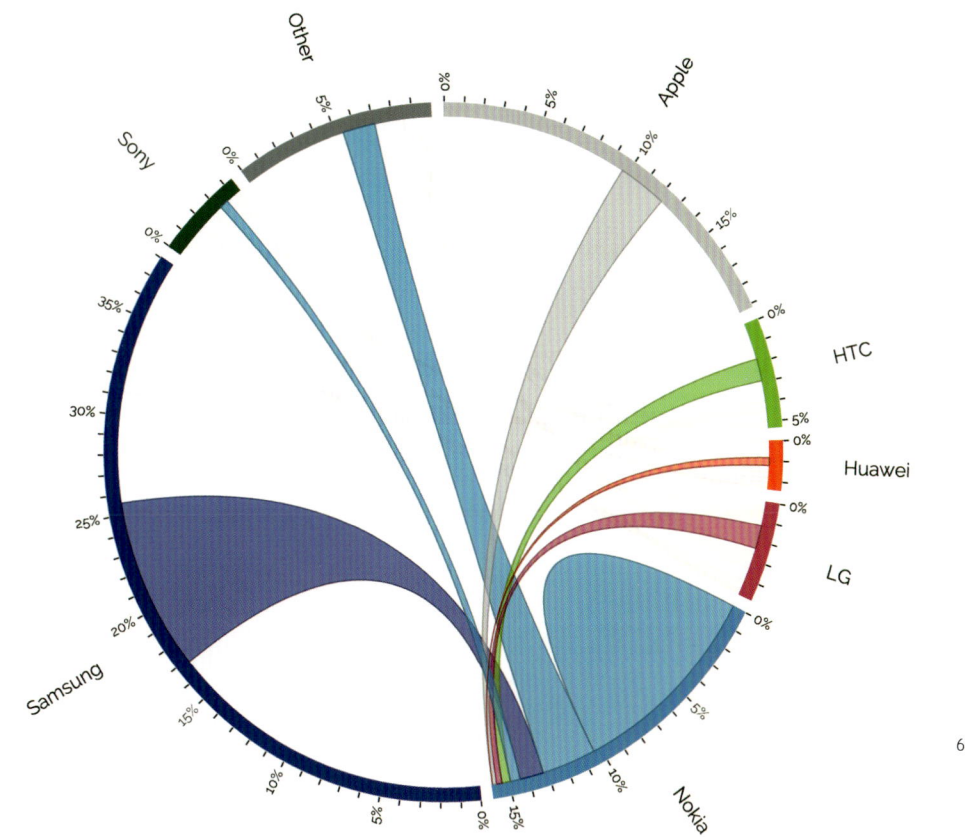

There are also people that stay loyal and did not switch brands between their previous and current phone

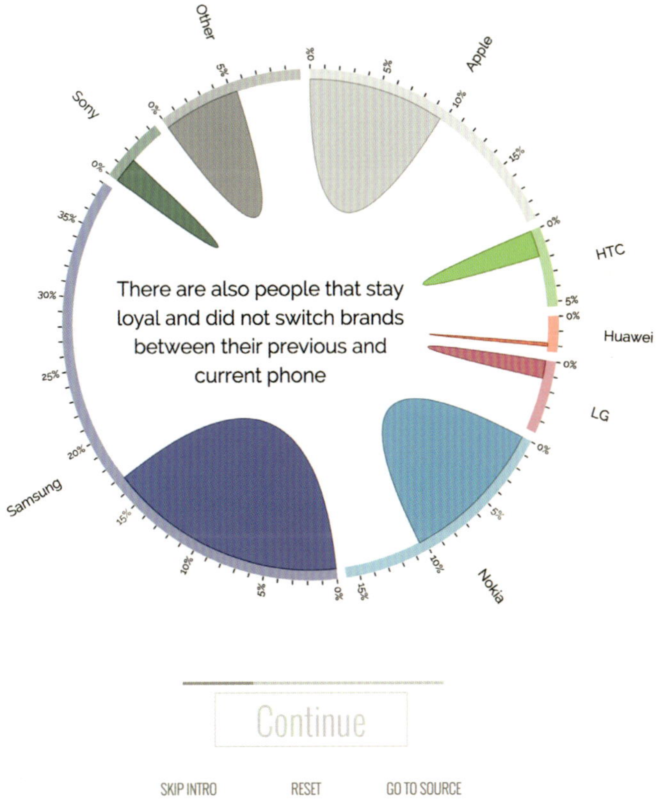

Thank you for staying with me so far! After these examples I think you're absolutely ready to face the full impact of all chords simultaneously

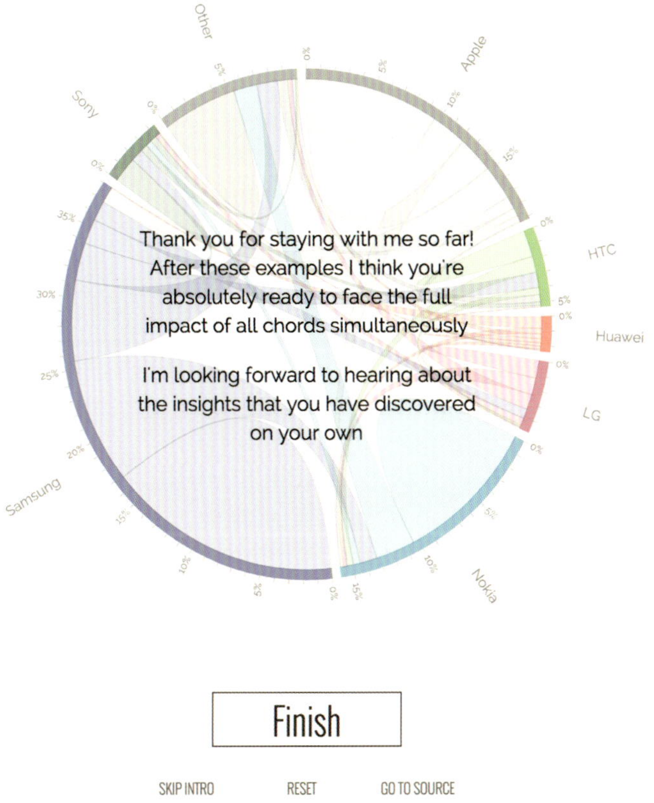

I'm looking forward to hearing about the insights that you have discovered on your own

Continue

Finish

SKIP INTRO   RESET   GO TO SOURCE

SKIP INTRO   RESET   GO TO SOURCE

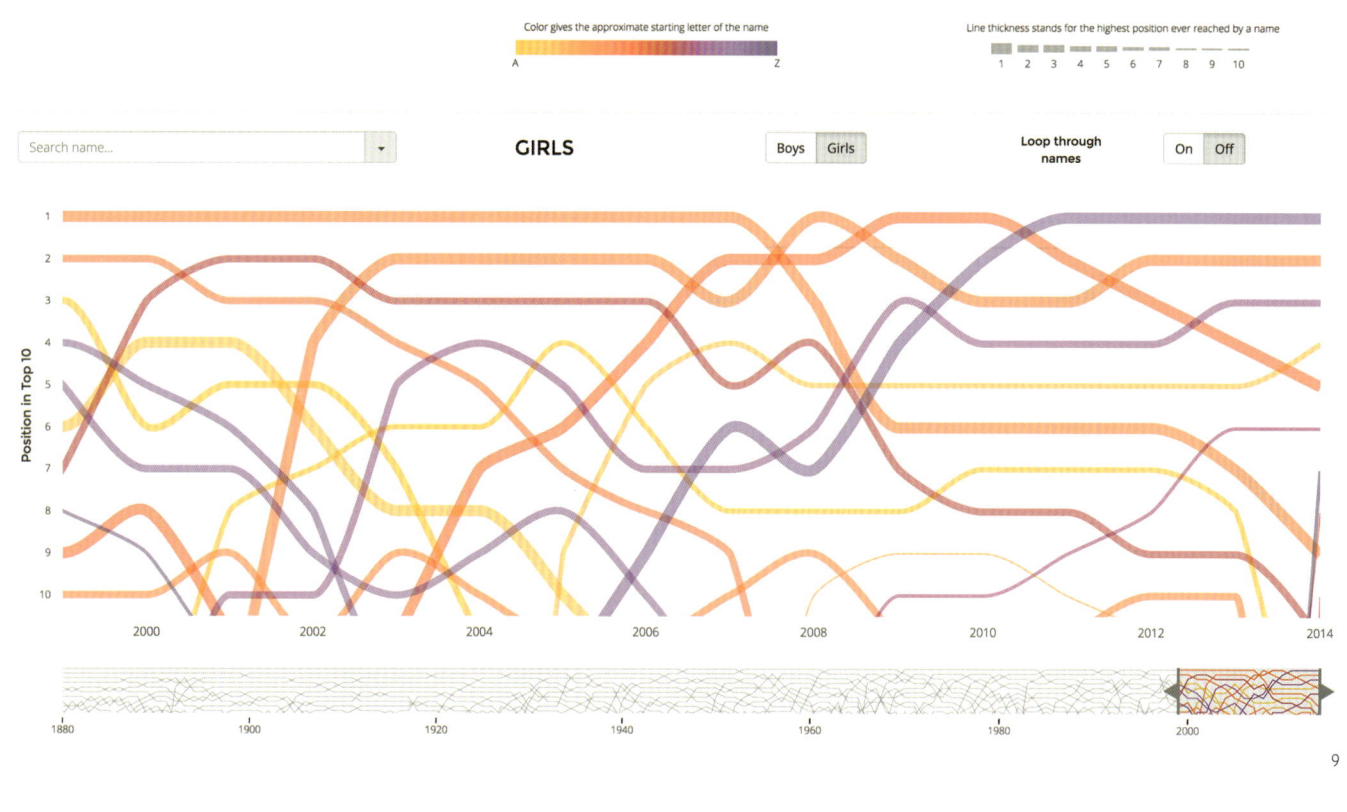

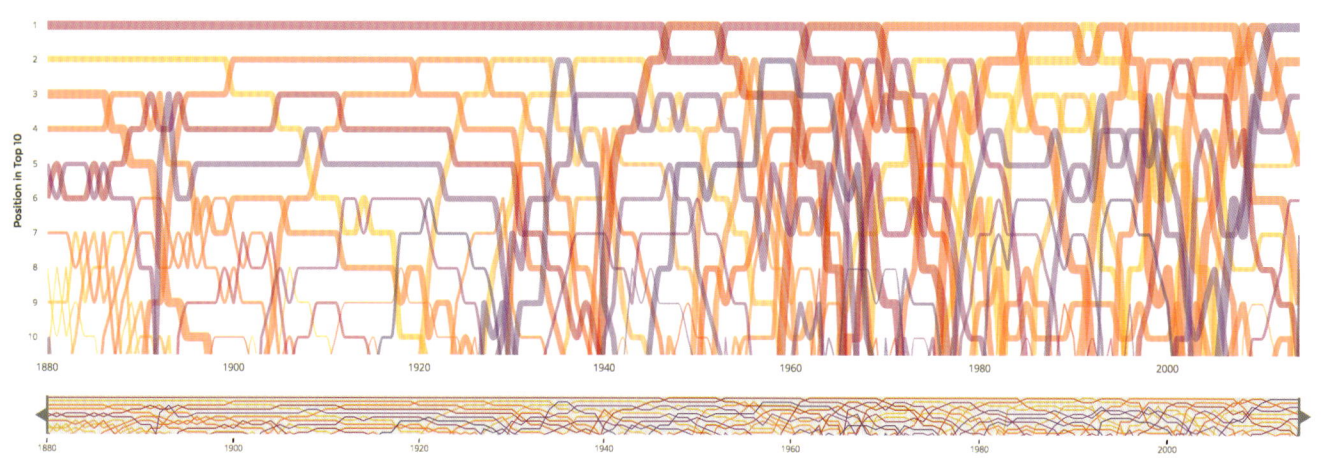

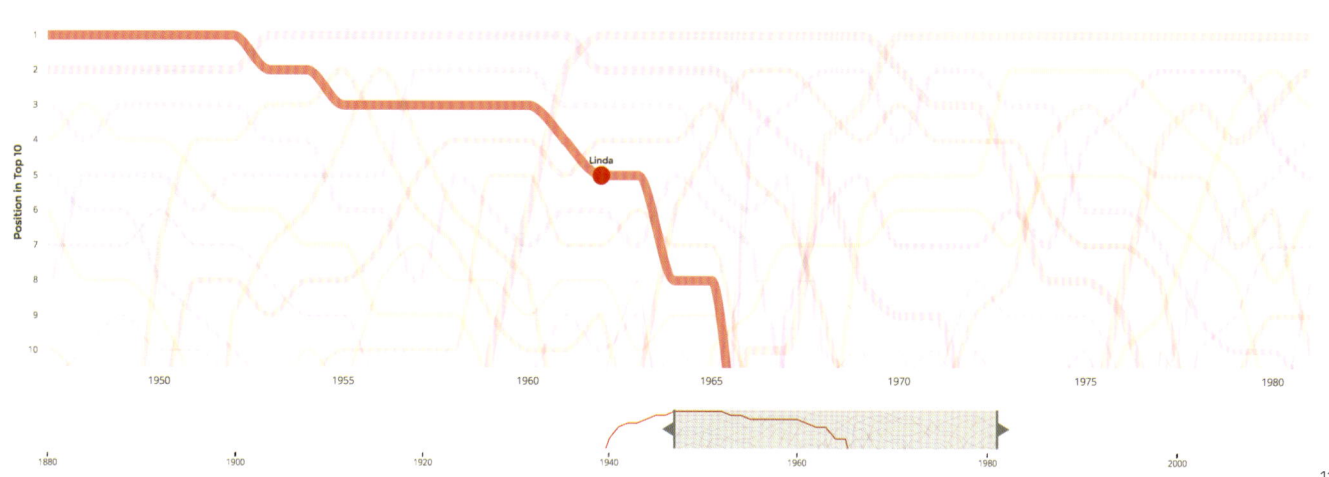

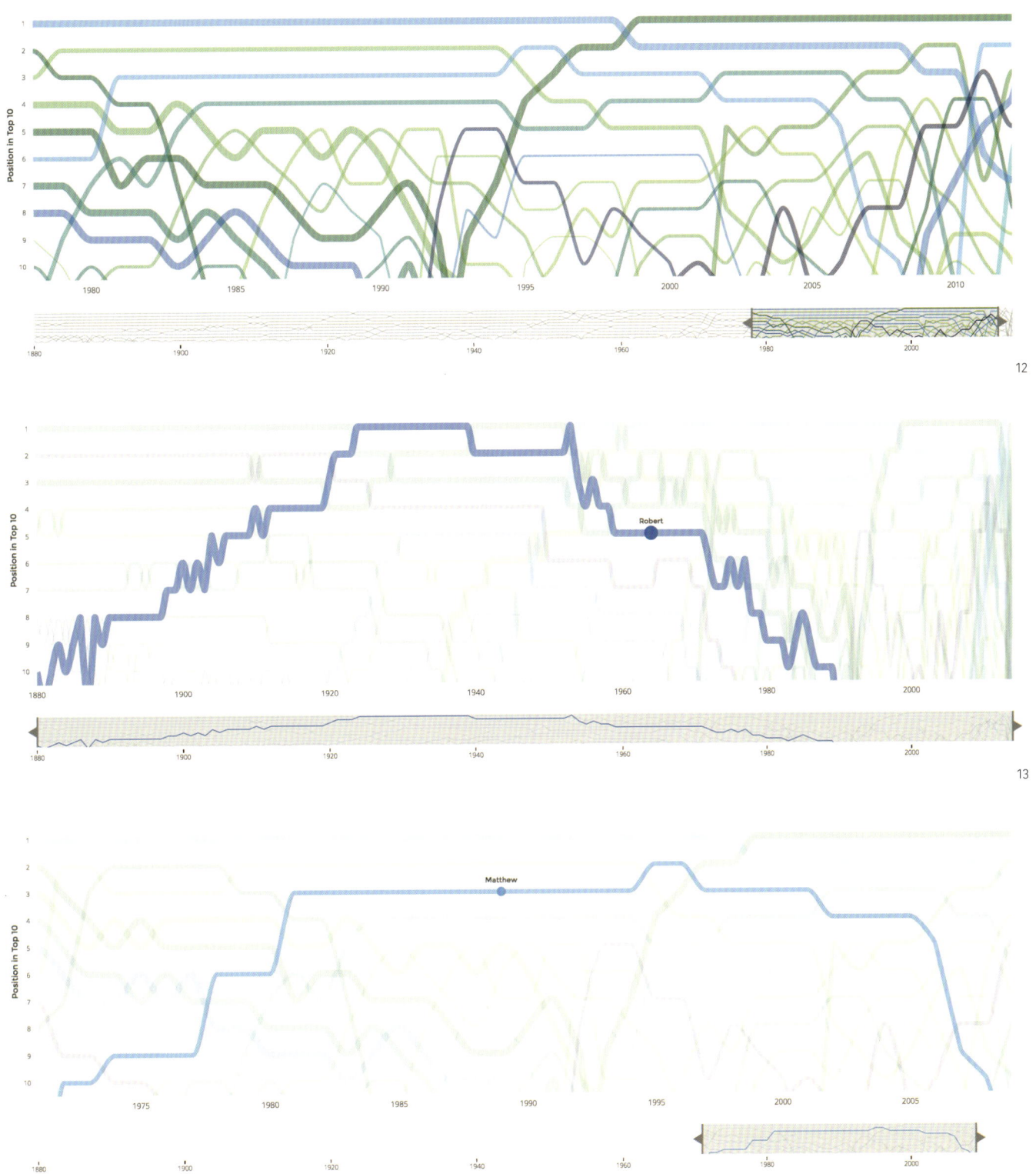

[9–14] The Top 10 Baby Names in the US Since 1880

Credit: Nadieh Bremer
Completion: 2015
Interactive link: www.visualcinnamon.com/babynamesus

Last year, almost four million babies were born in the US. Although thinking of four million unique names is pretty difficult, theoretically it is not impossible. Nonetheless, there are always many babies given the same name. This visualization shows the top 10 names per year and per gender since 1880. You can search for any of about 50 boy names and 90 unique girl names that have entered the top 10 in the last 135 years, and see their rise and fall.

Luis Carli

Luis Carli is a design technologist and a data visualization specialist. He has a degree in architecture and a doctoral degree in architecture and design, both from the University of São Paulo. He has worked with newspapers, research labs, and several companies around the world, developing visualization systems to help people understand, present, and act on data.

[Q] What do you think about data visualization/infographics?

[A] Data visualization is a unique activity that can leverage the cognitive system to help humans parse and understand large amounts of data. The breadth of information that can be consumed by a good visualization is incomparable to any other available technique. Data visualization is a study of transformation from data to visual representations in order to facilitate effective and efficient cognitive processes in performing tasks involving data.

[Q] What kind of design methods do you commonly use?

[A] It's often good to start a data visualization design by understanding the domain of the problem, talking with specialists and users who have knowledge about the data I'm trying to visualize. From there I begin doing sketches, mocks, and prototypes, using real data whenever possible. I often do quick throwaway code for plotting multiple dimensions of the data and send these plots to a vector program, so I can more loosely play with the layout and information architecture of the product. When the design starts to get more stable, I move to a more production-ready code, in which more technical aspects of the product are taken into account, like performance, database access, and deployment. Because design is a non-linear process of trying to find solutions to ill-defined problems, the described process is often messy, and I normally keep moving back and forward between domain discussions, mocks, and code.

[Q] What kinds of design elements do you commonly use?

[A] I use any possible mappings between data and visual channels and marks. Often this can result in well-known graphs such as line charts and scatterplots, but can sometimes result in new hybrids. The best way to make something beautiful and understandable is to have a good knowledge of visual theories, concepts, and techniques available, and apply those by continuously iterating and generating new ideas.

[Q] Where are your works applied?

[A] I have done works for newspapers, posters, websites, and apps. Recently I've been developing data visualization systems to help bring fast and powerful insights to the biggest banks in the world.

[Q] How do you turn boring and complex data into something interesting and understandable?

[A] Elegant design solutions are a consequence of iteratively exploring a problem or solution space. Design is the creative process of searching through a vast space of possibilities to select one of many possible good

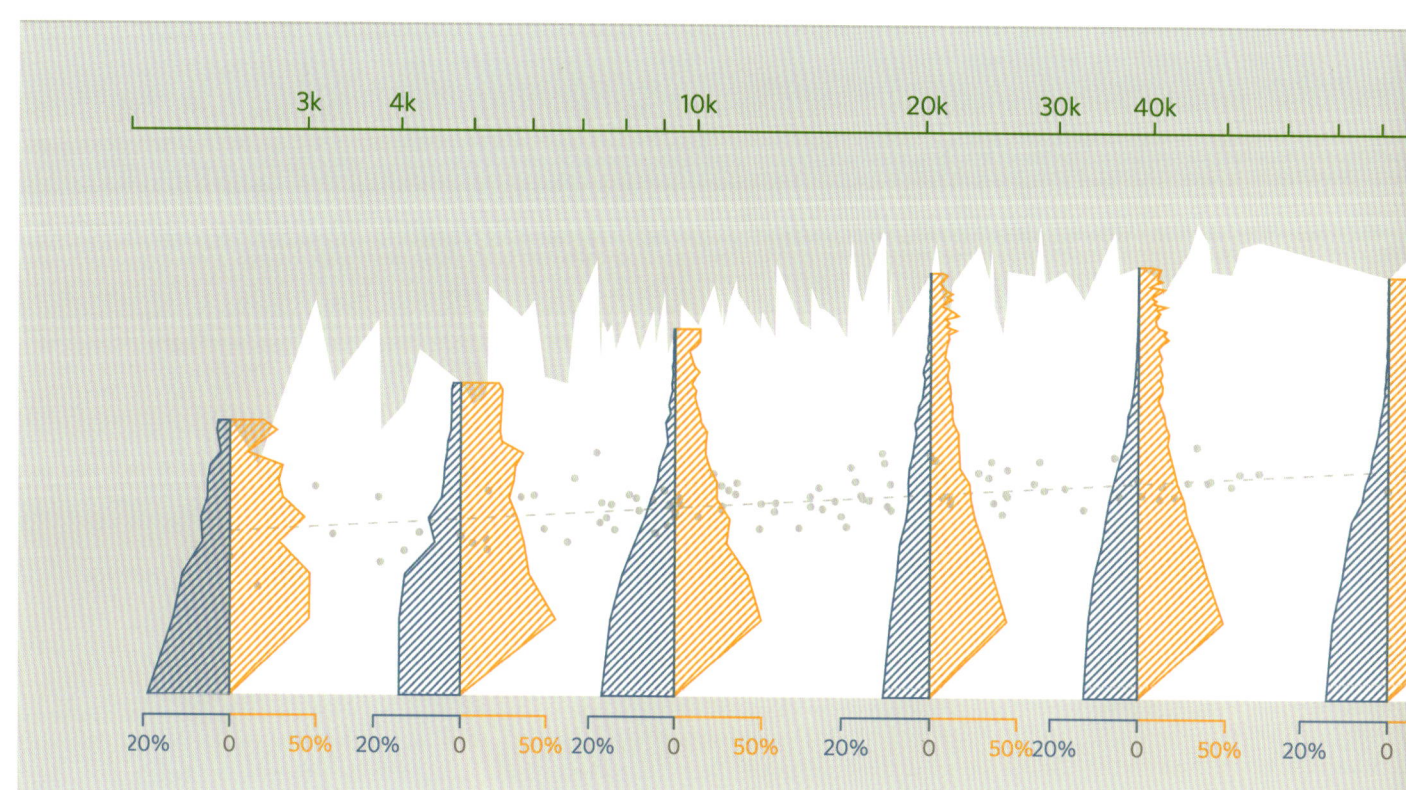

choices from the backdrop of the far larger set of bad choices. Successful design typically requires the explicit consideration of multiple alternatives and a thorough knowledge of the space of possibilities.

[Q] **What is your suggestion for beginners?**

[A] Read, sketch, code, and prototype new projects as much as you can.

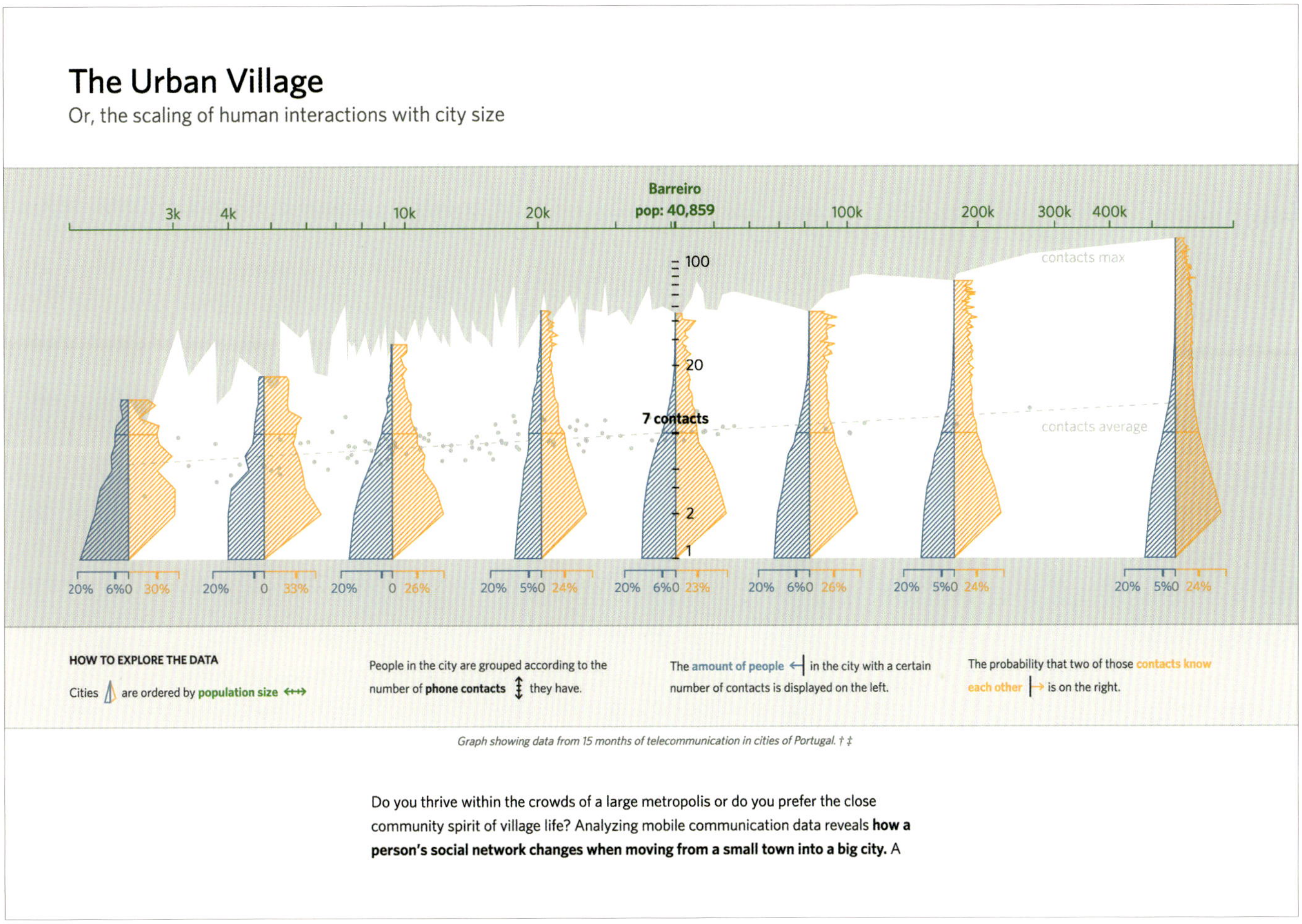

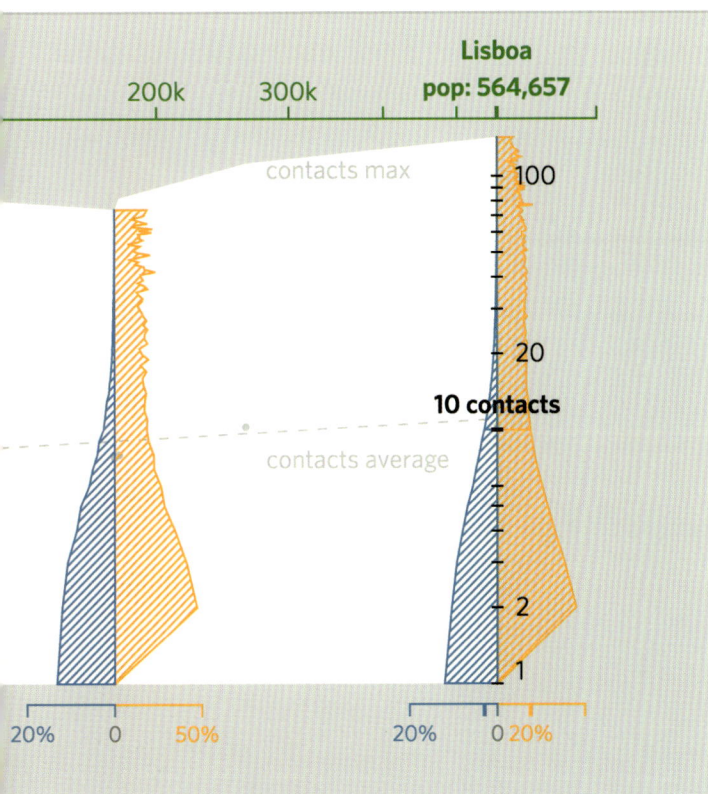

[1–2] Urban Villages

Credit: Luis Carli
Completion: 2014
Interactive link: senseable.mit.edu/urbanvillages

The objective of this work was to show the relationship between the population of a city and the number of contacts their habitants have. The data had several interesting dimensions, and the designer wanted to find a way to show and compare multiple dimensions in the same image. He explored several ways of aggregating and slicing the data before arriving at the solution shown here. The solution started with the concept of using violin plots for each city, but instead of mirroring the data, each side displays different values. Also, instead of just displaying the individual plots side by side, they are positioned according to an X scale that represents another dimension of the data (the size of the city). For that to work, only some of the cities are initially displayed; the user can then explore the hidden ones through interaction. As the user hovers over the visualization, the chart for the city is displayed and the charts that would overlap are hidden.

On this piece, the colors are used to represent each one of the specific dimensions of the data, which created not only an interesting aesthetic but also helped connect the legend with the visualization.

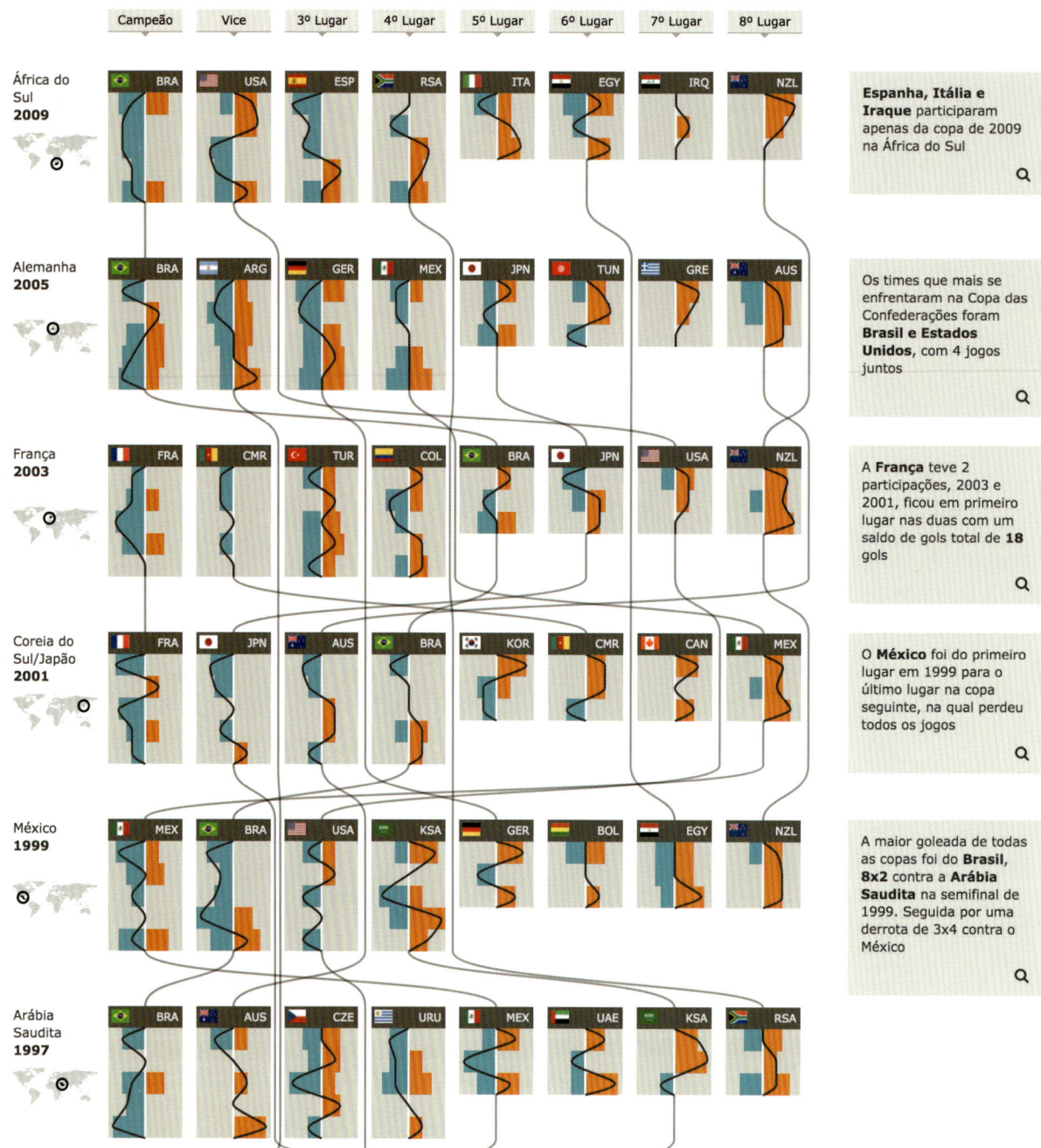

[3–5] Confederations Cup

Credit: Luis Carli
Completion: 2013
Interactive link: www.luiscarli.com/copa

The objective of this piece was to visually show the data for all the games that happened in all Confederation Cups. There was also an exploration of how to display multiple dimensions of the data in the same visualization. This kind of exploration often creates unique pieces, because it's heavily tied to the specificities of the data used. It also allows more comparisons to be drawn from the result, because several dimensions of the data are cohesively displayed.

Each of the main rows shows the data for a specific cup, ordered by the date that they happened. Inside each cup, we have the countries displayed as columns and ordered by their final result in the cup. For each country, we have all the games that the team played in the cup displayed as rows. On each row, there are two bars, a blue and an orange one, which represent the number of goals scored and taken by the team during the game. Those bars start on middle of the row; the bigger they are the more goals they represent. The last representation of data here is the gray line that passes through each one of the games, and this line represents the final score of the game, the difference of goals scored, and goals taken. If the line is on the left, the team scored more goals and consequently won the game. The line also has a second use of visually connecting the same team between cups.

When a user hovers over one of the games (see image 4), the score of the game is displayed with numbers and both teams that played that game are highlighted. This makes it possible to see how their performance was across the cups. The line that connects the team is really useful here, wiggling left and right to show not only the scoring performance of each game, but also the team performance on each cup.

One interesting detail of this project is that the positions of all the lines were done algorithmically by code, which was necessary to generate all the interactions that the visualization has. But it also posed very specific problems, for example, not all the teams played in all the cups, so sometimes one or more lines needed to pass between the boxes. The algorithm needed to be able to consider and correctly display those cases.

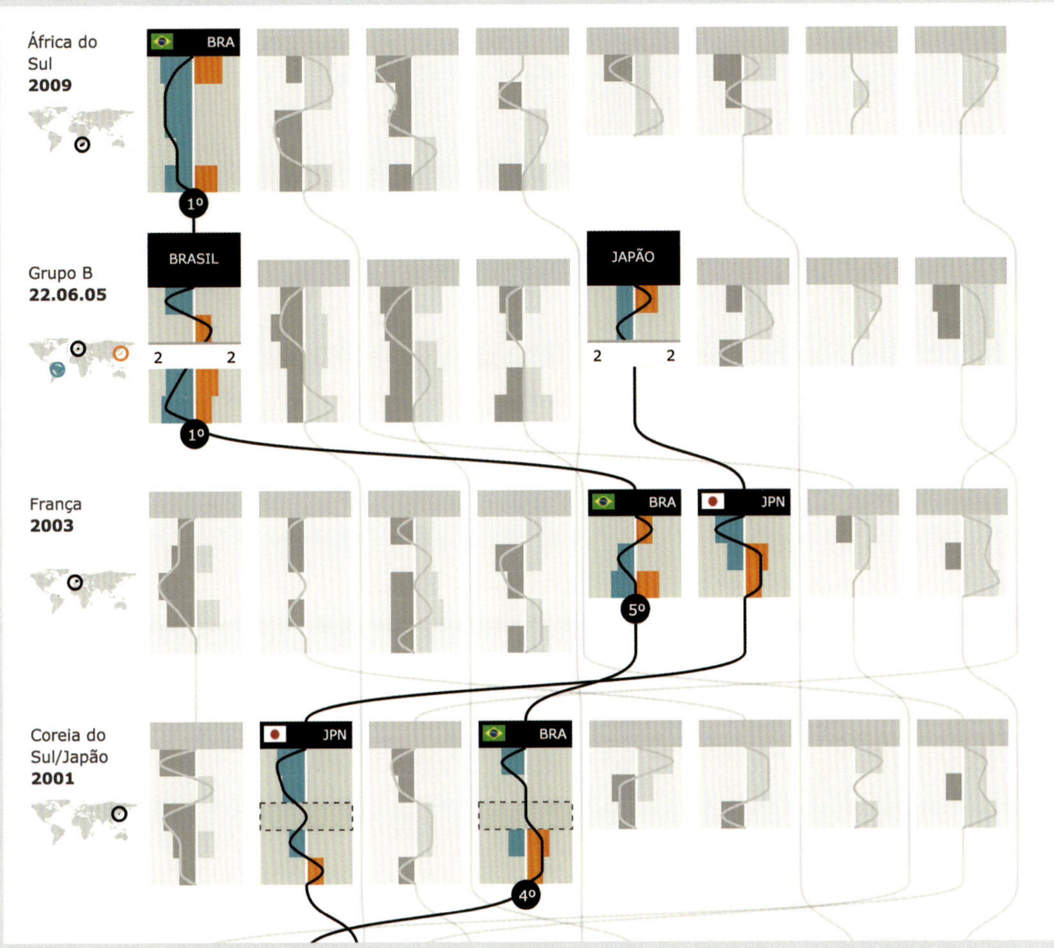

África do Sul
2009

Grupo B
22.06.05

França
2003

Coreia do Sul/Japão
2001

Espanha, Itália e Iraque participaram apenas da copa de 2009 na África do Sul

Os times que mais se enfrentaram na Copa das Confederações foram **Brasil e Estados Unidos**, com 4 jogos juntos

A **França** teve 2 participações, 2003 e 2001, ficou em primeiro lugar nas duas com um saldo de gols total de **18** gols

O **México** foi do primeiro lugar em 1999 para o último lugar na copa seguinte, na qual perdeu todos os jogos

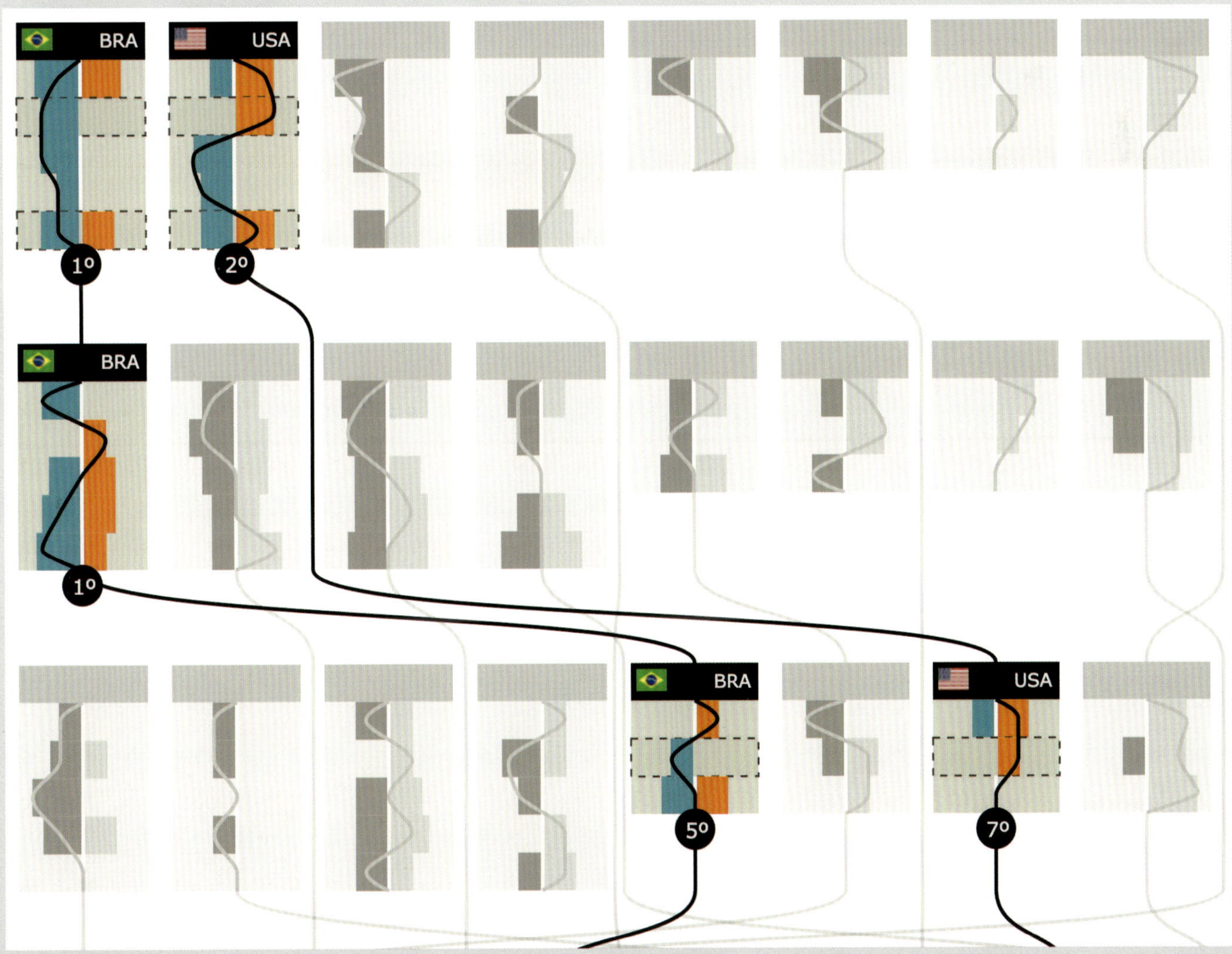

Temperature, Humidity and Moisture Content (MC)

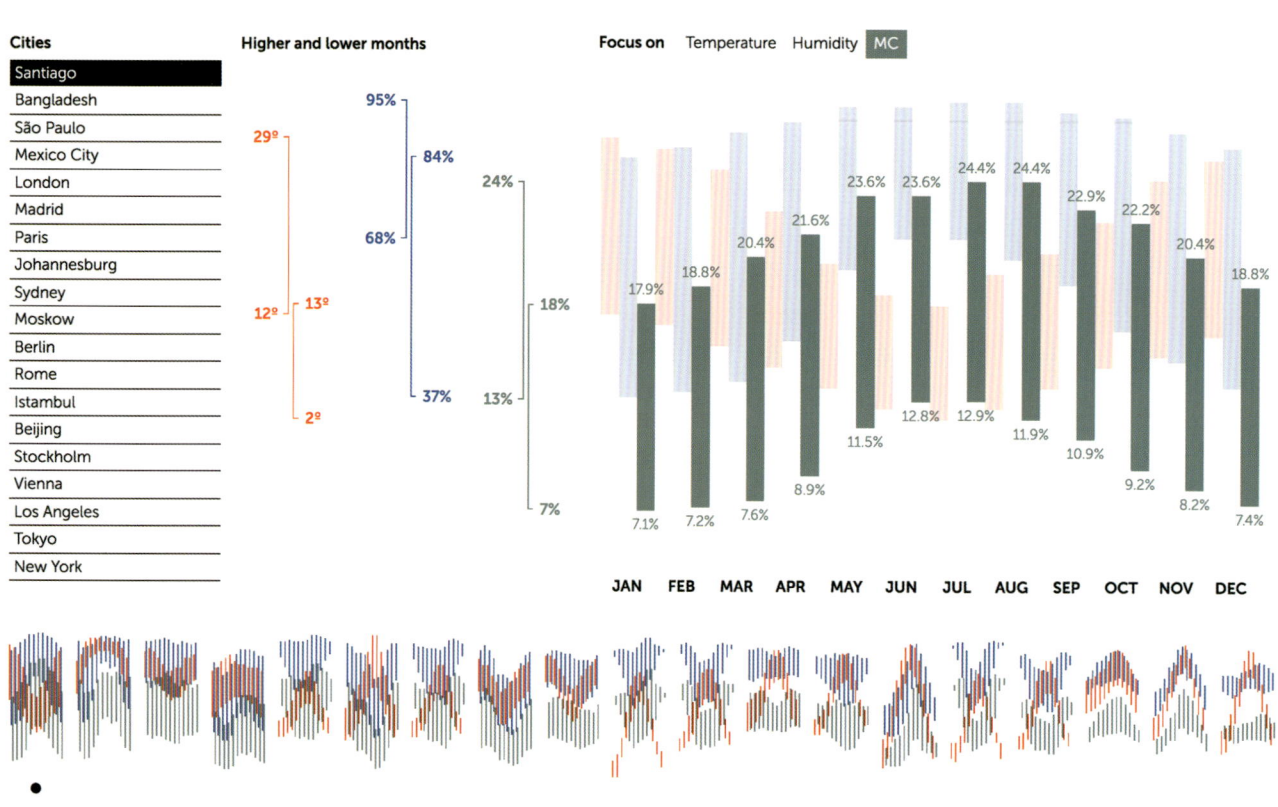

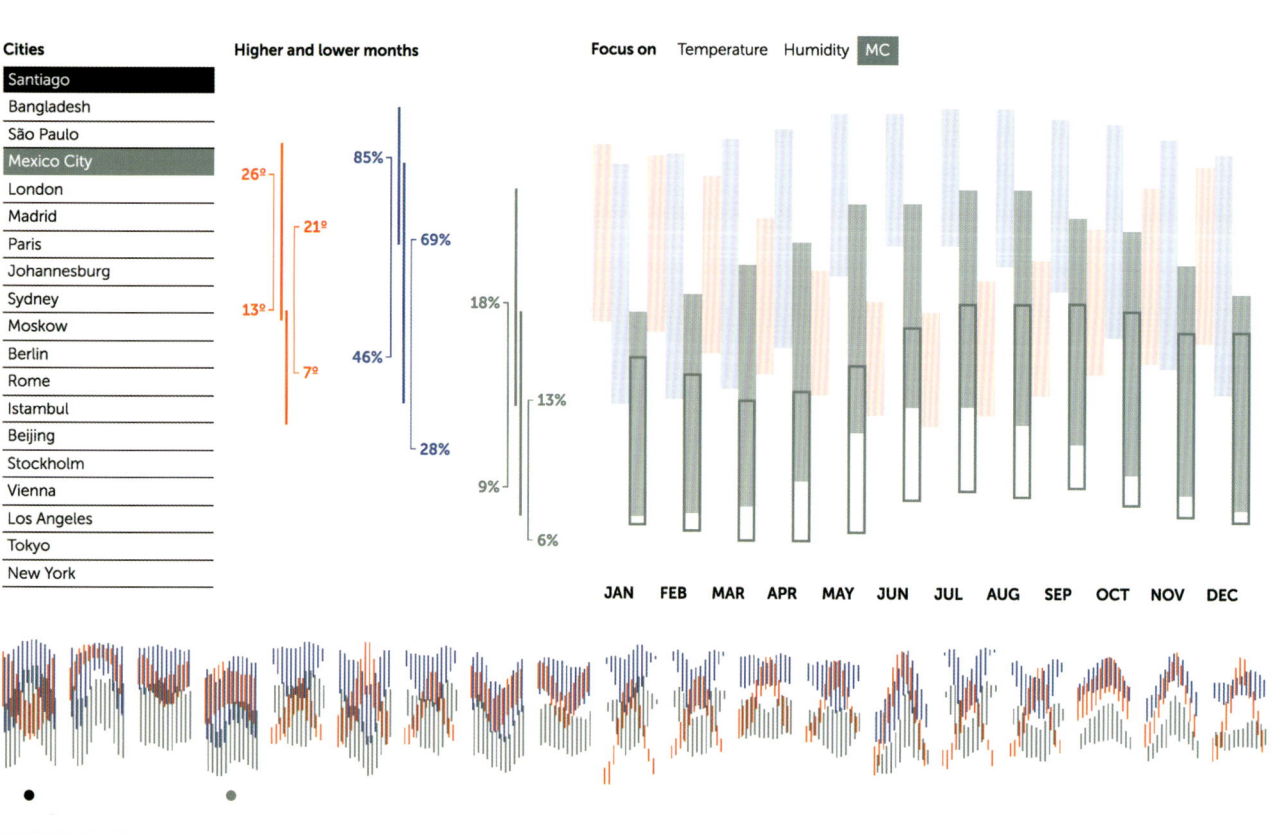

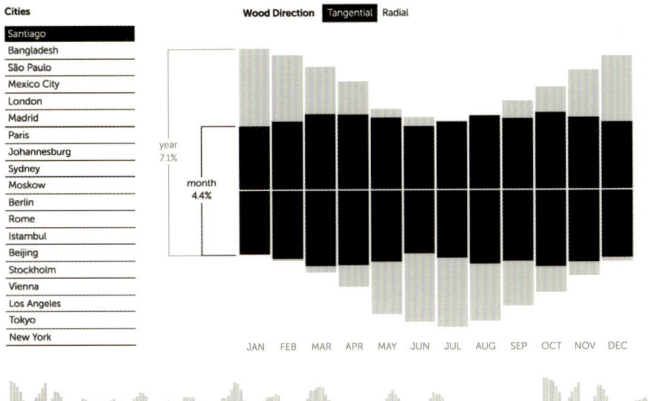

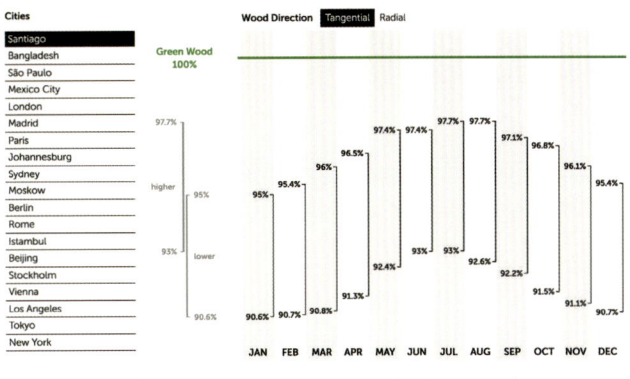

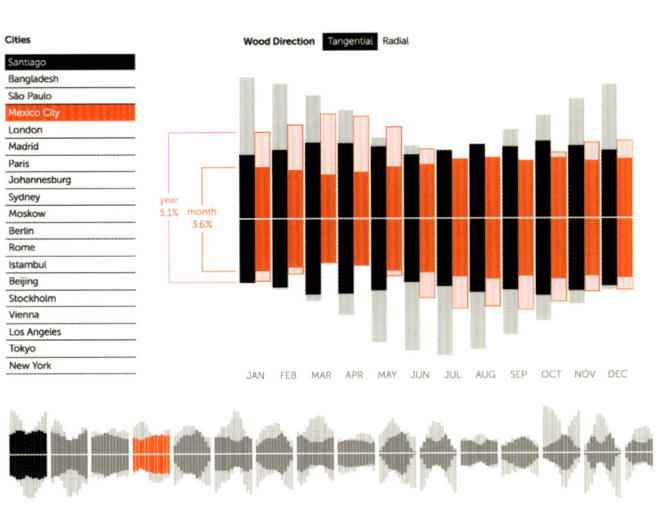

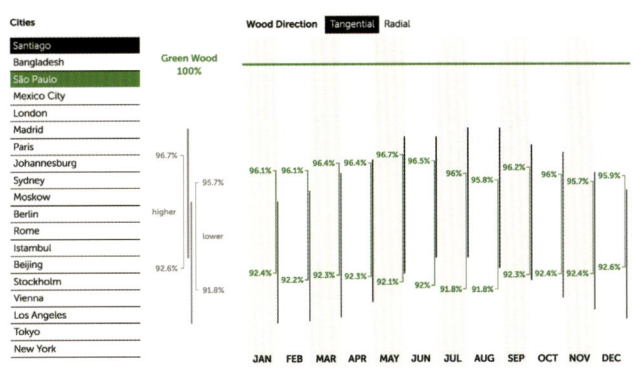

7

8

[6–8] Wood Changes

Credits: Luis Carli, Rafael Passarelli
Completion: 2012
Interactive link: www.woodchanges.com

The objective of this work was to compare the size changes that wood goes through according to the type of wood and the weather of different cities. This is very important when designing products or buildings that use wood, because this change needs to be taken into account during the design phase.

This project had a focus on allowing quick comparison between any of the possible selections. In image 6, it's possible to see two of the project visualizations with the city of Santiago selected: on the left is the list of all the cities, in the middle is the percentage change of the wood for each month of the year for the selected city, and on the bottom are small multiples of the main chart for each city. When the user hovers over other cities (image 7 and 8), the main chart animates to show data for both the selected city and the hovered city, allowing for a quick comparison between them. Because it was important to show the dimensional change of the wood both in relative and absolute values, and because each of those contained specific data, different visual representations were created and different animations and mechanisms were developed to compare the values in each one.

Chelsea Carlson

[Q] What do you think about data visualization/infographics?

[A] What I love is that the only real law of visualization is that you are faithful to the data—that leaves plenty of room for visual experimentation. I also like pushing the boundaries on what is considered an appropriate topic for data visualization by using seemingly mundane data sets—like how many times I check Facebook in a day—to tell interesting, relatable stories. I love being able to turn five years of convoluted airline mergers and acquisitions (The Rise and Fall of Airlines) into a beautiful and easily understandable image. That's the power of good data visualization, and that's why I love working in this medium.

[Q] What kind of design methods do you commonly use?

[A] For me, I start the design process with an interesting question. It doesn't matter how beautiful your data is, if the underlying question doesn't pique your interest, no one will bother putting the effort into interpreting your work.

From there, I start with spreadsheets and basic graphs, searching for a story in the numbers. Most data you look at won't surprise you, so I always try to look for the unexpected and the compelling hidden inside

Chelsea Carlson is a graphic designer and illustrator who loves creating things with data. After spending most of her childhood with a paintbrush in her hand, she began designing infographics and experimenting with data visualization while studying media studies and art at Scripps College in California. After graduating from Scripps, she began designing for Umbel, a data analytics start-up in Austin, Texas.

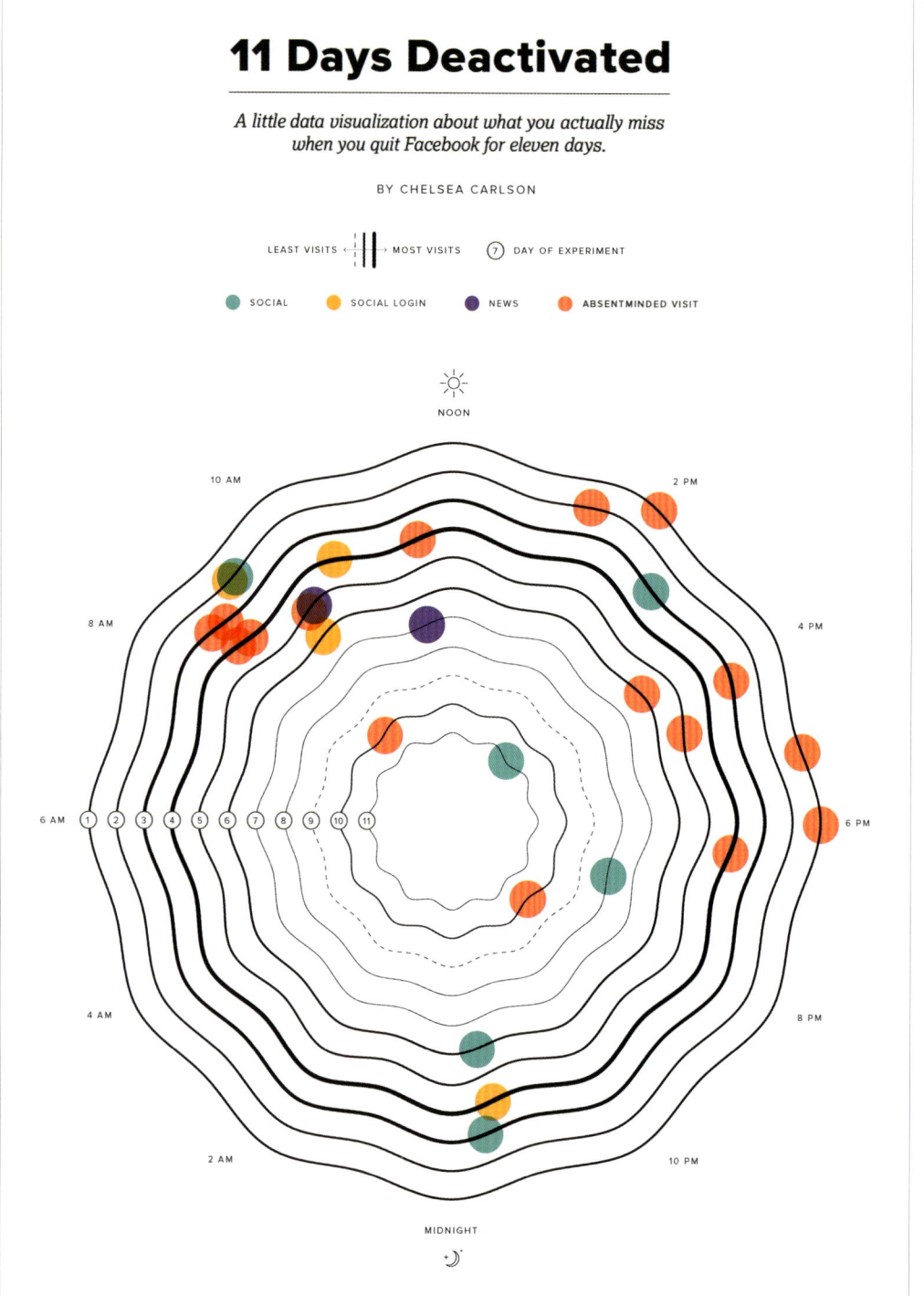

fields of boring data. Next I'll try looking at the data in a bunch of different formats, some conventional, some experimental. Finally, I'll start looking at how I can introduce color, shape, and a heavy dose of style to underline the most important information or draw interesting comparisons.

[Q] **What kinds of design elements do you commonly use?**

[A] My rule is to always let the data dictate the format. In the case of 11 Days Deactivated, I wanted to represent my perception of the passage of time—basically, that it became easier and easier for me not to check Facebook—in an unconventional manner. Arranging my days in concentric circles I sacrifice some precision of a line graph in exchange for a more emotionally accurate representation of the days.

I also played with the presentation of time in Slacking off at Work, where I used a spiral path to guide the passing day of work. In this case it was less important to know at exactly what time I ate lunch and more interesting to observe parts of the day where I quickly flitted from task to task, and begin to observe patterns of disruption and concentration in the colors and sizes of the shapes. Of course, sometimes conventional graphs, such as the line graphs in The Past, Present, and Future of Big Data Revenue, are still the best way to show change over time. It all depends on the data and the message.

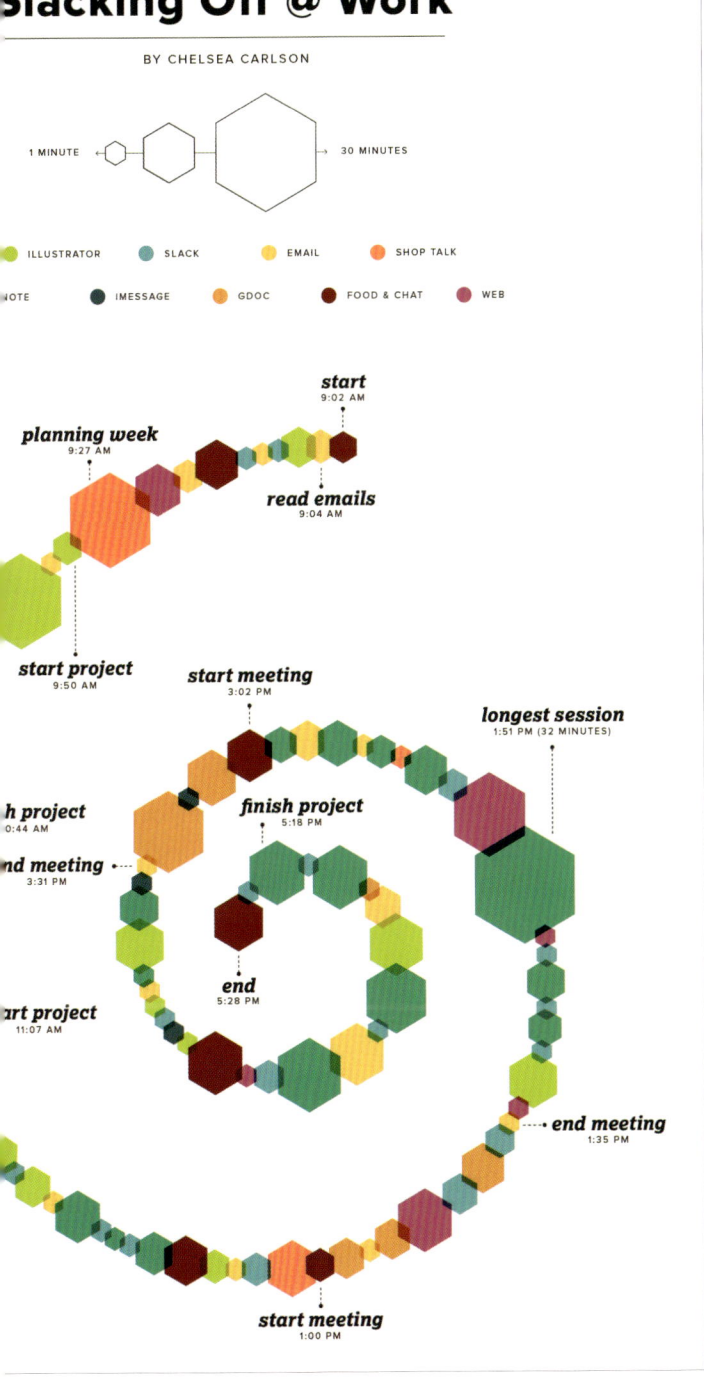

[1] 11 Days Deactivated

Credit: Chelsea Carlson
Completion: 2015

In this personal data visualization, the designer tracked what happened when she quit Facebook for 11 days. She had tracked each time she wanted to visit or accidentally visited Facebook, noting the reason and time, and finally chose to use an experimental tree-ring-inspired graph, which allowed her to keep time of day consistent while showing the density of visits with ring thickness.

[2] Slacking Off at Work

Credit: Chelsea Carlson
Completion: 2015

This data experiment shows one day of the designer's work, including every distraction, email break, and conversation. To emphasize the pattern of work, rather than the specific tasks, the designer included minimal detail. The focus is on the color and size of the shapes, making it easy to find patterns in the disruptive and productive parts of the day. The spiral path is a classic symbol of time, lending a sense of repetition and cycles to the daily work habits.

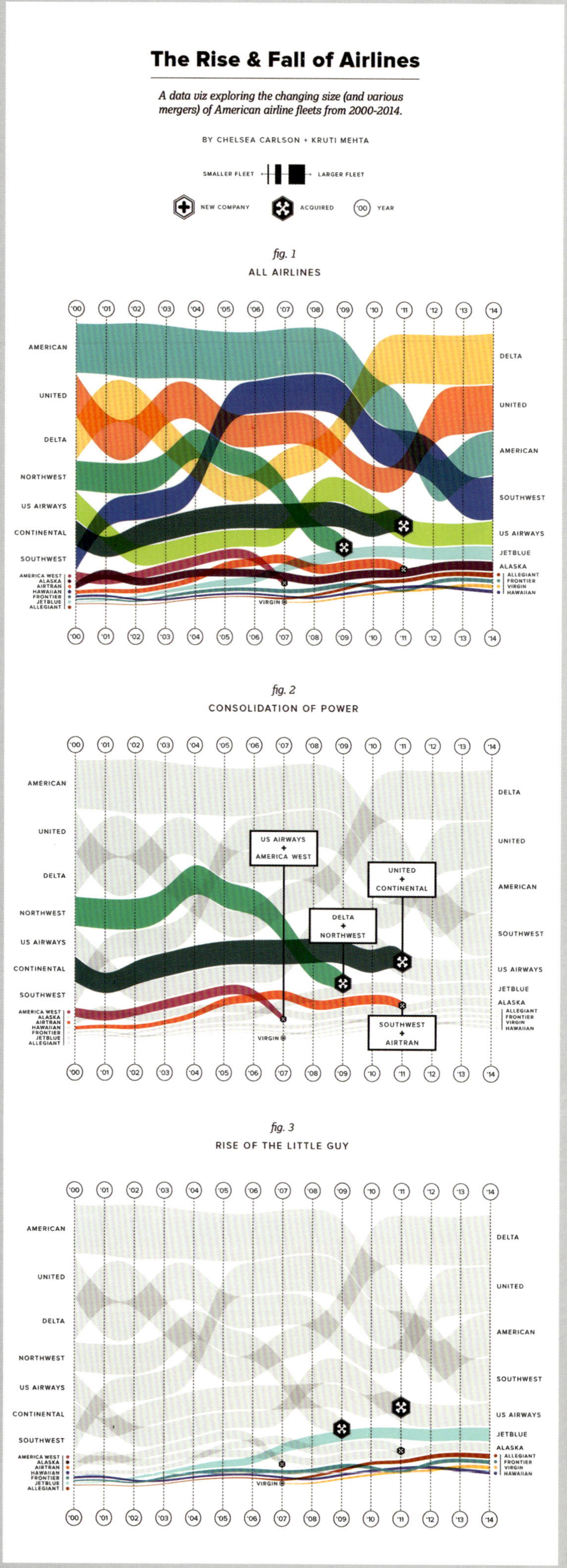

The Rise & Fall of Airlines

A data viz exploring the changing size (and various mergers) of American airline fleets from 2000-2014.

BY CHELSEA CARLSON + KRUTI MEHTA

SMALLER FLEET — ■ — LARGER FLEET

⬢ NEW COMPANY ⊗ ACQUIRED ⓪ YEAR

fig. 1
ALL AIRLINES

fig. 2
CONSOLIDATION OF POWER

- US AIRWAYS + AMERICA WEST
- DELTA + NORTHWEST
- UNITED + CONTINENTAL
- SOUTHWEST + AIRTRAN

fig. 3
RISE OF THE LITTLE GUY

[Q] Where are your works applied?

[A] All the works featured here were created for Umbel's data marketing blog, Truth in Data.

[Q] How do you turn boring and complex data into something interesting and understandable?

[A] There's an infinite amount of data out there, so the trick is wading through it until you find an interesting story. Anyone can make a graph out of anything. Visualization itself never makes data interesting. You have to strike a balance between presenting enough information to be meaningful, but not so much that you intimidate your viewers.

The power of data visualization is that it presents the facts, but also leaves room for interpretation. Two people looking at the same data visualization shouldn't necessarily come away with the same opinion. If there's a clear story, with room to disagree, I think I've done my job.

[Q] What is your suggestion for beginners?

[A] My biggest piece of advice for beginners is to focus on data that interests you. Dig for the story and you'll be compelled to find a way to tell it. Style is important, but the story is essential.

[3] The Rise and Fall of Airlines

Credits: Chelsea Carlson (design), Kruti Mehta (research)
Completion: 2015

The aim of this visualization is to explore the ebb and flow of the tightly regulated American airline industry through mergers and acquisitions since 2000. After playing with several different approaches, the designer settled on this colorful bump chart to illustrate the way in which the airlines seem to wrestle with each other for dominance in the market. She emphasized several concurrent narratives with color, including the rise of the small, specialty fleet.

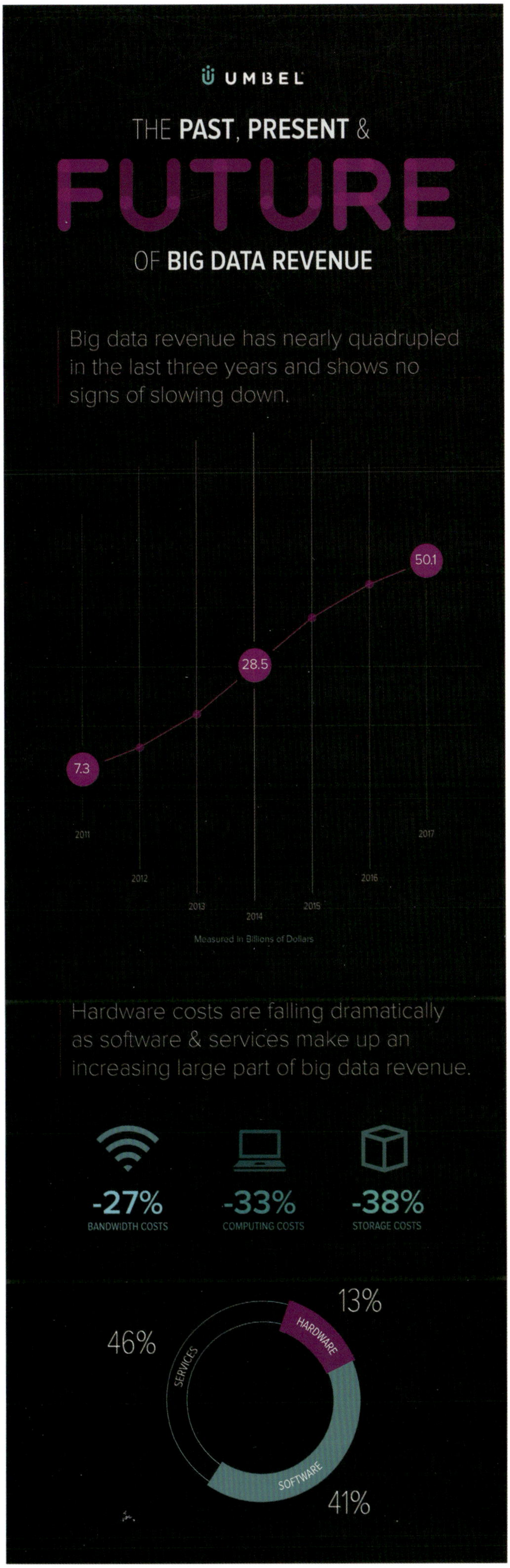

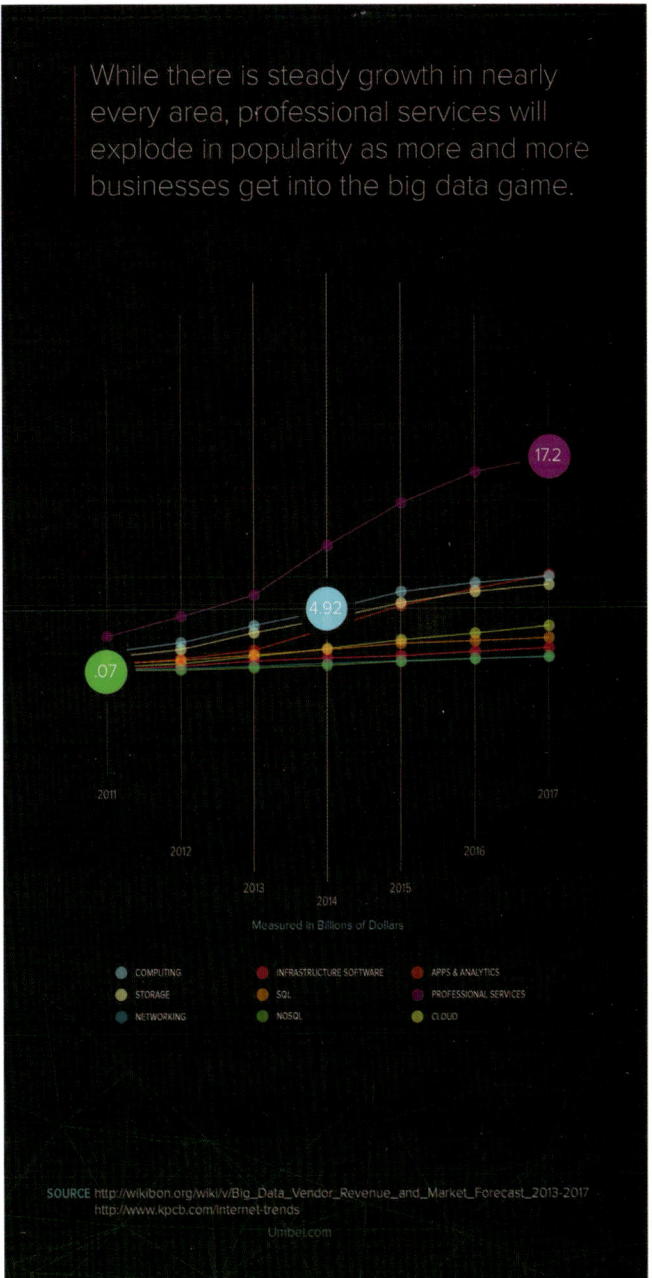

[4–5] The Past, Present, and Future of Big Data Revenue

Credit: Chelsea Carlson
Completion: 2014

This infographic of the recent history and predicted future of big data revenue uses very simple twists on pie charts and line graphs to show the changes underway in the industry. The designer took a minimal approach to the graphs, only providing the bare minimum in labels in order to streamline the story throughout the infographic. Each section builds on the one before, ending with the conclusion that professional services are the most lucrative sector of the big data industry in the near future.

Sabina Castagnaviz

[Q] **What do you think about data visualization/infographics?**

[A] I think it is a very interesting tool to better understand one or more topics and is wonderful work in which creativity is the center of everything. Each infographic is a new idea but it must never lose sight of the clear information.

[Q] **What kind of design methods do you commonly use?**

[A] Usually, we get a lot of messy data at the beginning, then we rearrange it according to importance. Then, once we have chosen the main topic, we sketch out an idea on paper, which will be realized with computer programming.

[Q] **What kind of design elements do you commonly use?**

[A] All kinds, from classical illustrations to pie charts, histograms, tables, trends, maps, flows, bubbles, etc. It is very important to understand the work and above all to find an original idea to show the news. For example, in the work The Scenery, I use the shape of a hand as a container of other forms (such as pie charts and histograms) that illustrate some numbers. Without these forms it would be impossible to explain a multitude of data, which would also be difficult to read and boring if placed individually in an article. In addition, it is important to be creative in the use of the forms, for example, the work Technology in the Classroom is visualized in concentric way.

[Q] **Where are your works applied?**

[A] We usually design for newspapers and websites.

[Q] **How do you turn boring and complex data into something interesting and understandable?**

[A] The data is often boring and incomprehensible, so the role of the infographic is making it understandable through a beautiful idea. Individual creativity is the heart of all works.

[Q] **What is your suggestion for beginners?**

[A] My suggestion is to be very curious about every possible topic and especially not to forget that the objective of the work is to explain something to the reader, and then the graphic must not only be beautiful, but clear. The reader must understand easily, otherwise they will turn the page immediately.

Sabina Castagnaviz is the infographic designer at RCS *Il Corriere della Sera*. She went to an arts high school in Milan and attended a series of professional courses in advertising graphics. In 1994, she started to work in a studio where exclusive infographic works were created for the two most important newspapers in Italy: *Il Corriere della Sera* and *Gazzetta dello Sport*. In 1998, she was hired by RCS *Il Corriere della Sera* in the infographic department, where, after 18 years, she still works.

[1] The Social Housing

Credits: Sabina Castagnaviz (author), Marcello Valoncini, Nicolas Vargas, Cristina Pirola, *Il Corriere della Sera*
Completion: 2015

This project is about the advance in Italy's social housing that proposes subsidized housing for those with an income between €15,000 and €55,000, giving them the chance to become owners in a shared building. The tenants require the commitment to create a network of solidarity in the building. The infographic explains what it is, when it was created, who is included, and how they are divided by region, analyzing the objectives in millions of euros, the investment decision, the number of houses, and the number of beds. A national fund of €2 billion, and a €1.5 billion investment were used to build 200 active projects.

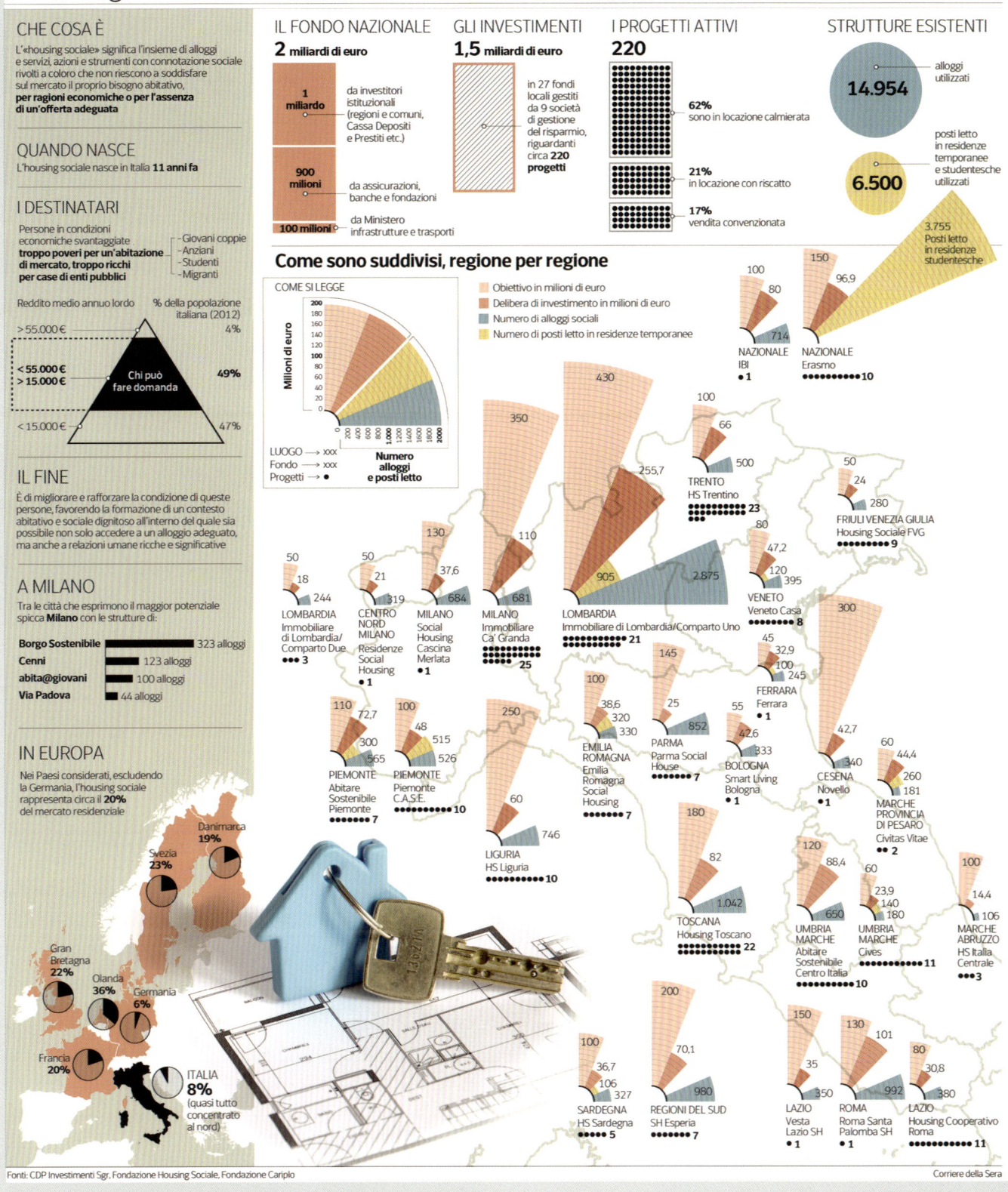

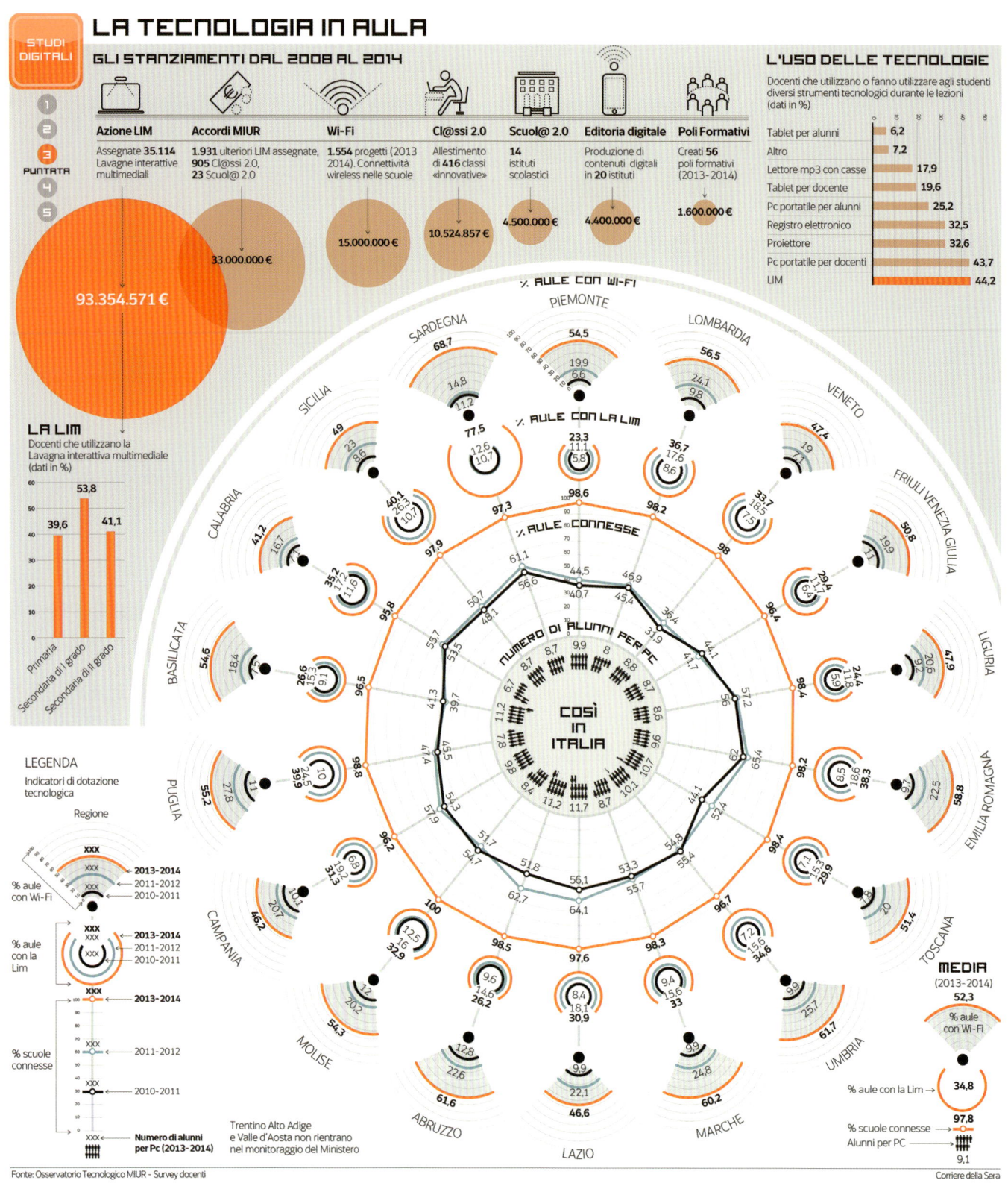

[2] Technology in the Classroom

Credits: Sabina Castagnaviz (author), Marcello Valoncini, Nicolas Vargas, Cristina Pirola, *Il Corriere della Sera*
Completion: 2015

From multimedia interactive whiteboards to smart classrooms, the infographic shows how the hi-tech study and the frontier of ultra-broadband changed our lives. In Italy, there are nine computers for every 100 students (the European average is 24). At the top of the infographic we can see how much money has been given to schools from 2008 to 2014, most of which was invested in interactive whiteboards. At the center is a comparison of the number of pupils for one computer from 2010 to 2014 by region, and then the data from the inside out is the percentage of the connected classrooms, the number of the classrooms with multimedia boards, and the percentage of the classrooms with Wi-Fi.

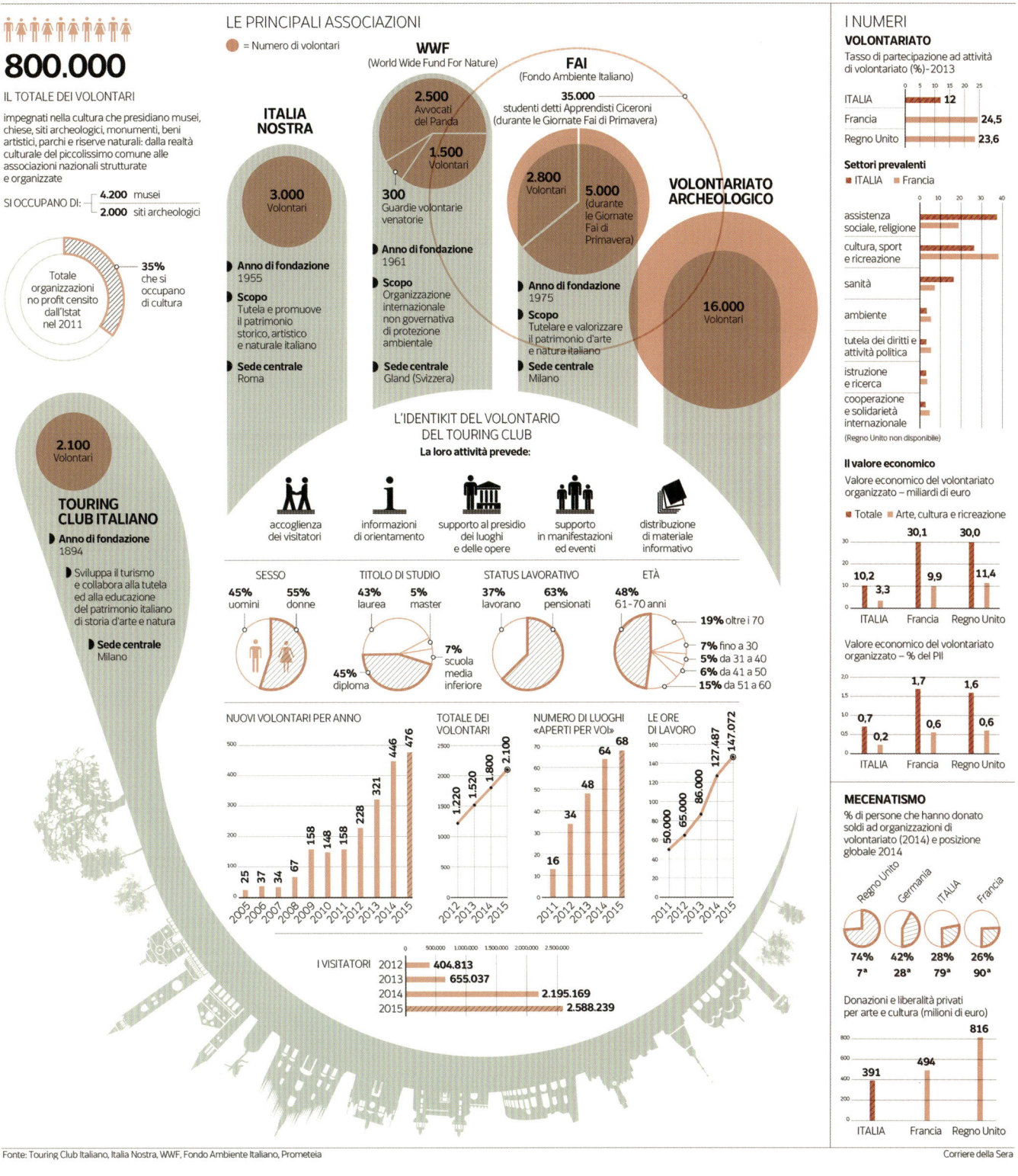

[3] The Scenery

Credits: Sabina Castagnaviz (author), Marcello Valoncini, Nicolas Vargas, Cristina Pirola, *Il Corriere della Sera*
Completion: 2015

There is a growing number of citizen volunteers, especially among young people, who take care of monuments, sites, and archaeological sites. In Italy there are almost 800,000. The infographic shows the main associations and their compositions: the number of volunteers, the year of establishment, the purpose, and the headquarters, and the center is the identikit of the types of volunteers. Over the years, there has been a very high increase in the number of volunteers and the number of hours they worked.

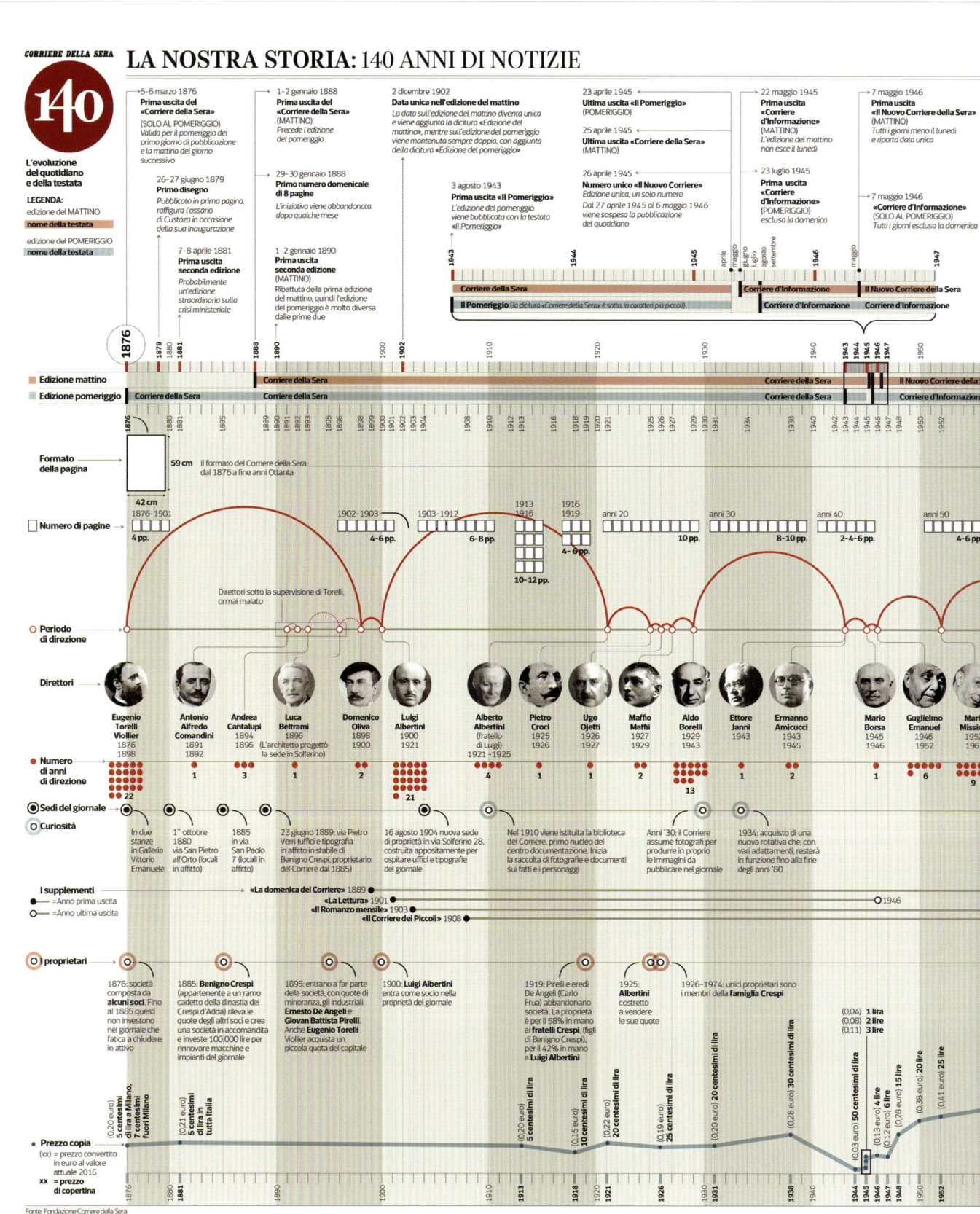

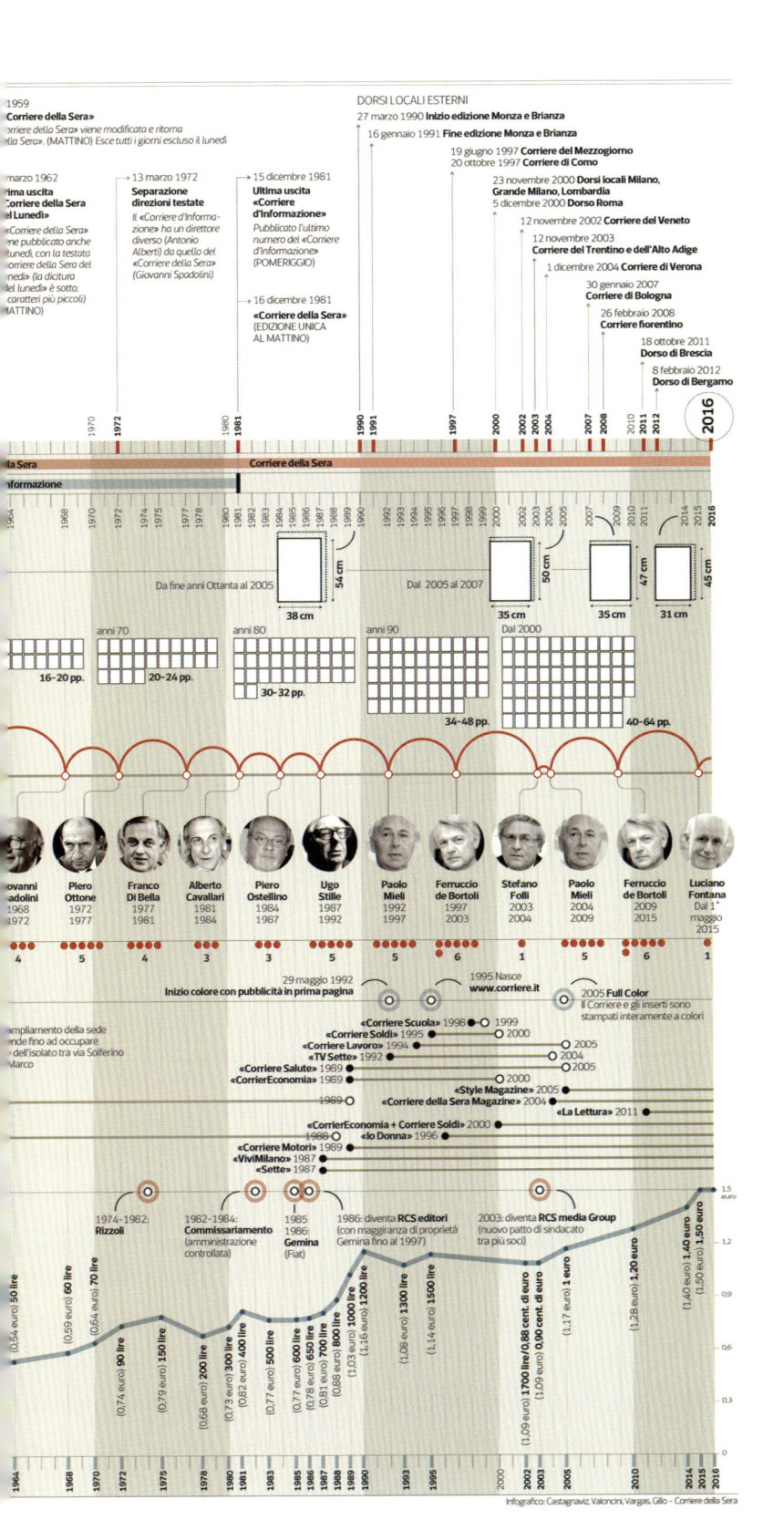

[4] Our History: 140 Years of News

Credits: Sabina Castagnaviz (author), Marcello Valoncini (author), Nicolas Vargas (author), Cristina Pirola, *Il Corriere della Sera*
Completion: 2015

On 6 March 2016, *Il Corriere della Sera* turned 140 years old. Its history is shown in this double-spread infographic: when it changed the name, the various editions, the different sizes, the number of pages, all directors and the years they worked, all the inserts, the different owners, and at the end, the price of newspaper converted to current value in euros.

Meng Chih Chiang

[Q] What do you think about data visualization/infographics?

[A] Data visualization is to unveil the story behind the world. It gives the data meaning and is always a good engaging way to help people understand the mystery behind the data.

[Q] What kind of design methods do you commonly use?

[A] Usually I combine several tools and software to accomplish one work. Different data and design formats can result in totally different methods. This way, I often study the data first and try to find sources online to help me solve the problem. There is a language, Javascript, which is always helpful to analyze data and produce amazing interactive visual style.

[Q] What kind of design elements do you commonly use?

[A] I don't have a common way to visualize something. Sometimes I use lines, circles, or maps, depending on what the data needs to convey. One thing I particularly like is dynamic pieces that can show people different perspectives inside one story or data set.

[Q] Where are your works applied?

[A] My pieces appear on the website at first, and then are applied to posters and books. I also make a video for each work to introduce behind-the-scenes and to elaborate on the design concept. The video is an intuitive way to make your data visualization understandable quickly.

[Q] How do you turn boring and complex data into something interesting and understandable?

[A] As a designer, making the visual appealing is very important. Using shapes, colors, and interactions is a great way to differentiate the data and to make something important. When you digest the data and output it in an interesting design, you are turning the boring into the interesting. There are no barriers with visual language. If your piece is well designed, then the viewer can understand the point very easily.

[Q] What is your suggestion for beginners?

[A] Be passionate and be hungry for big data. Always find the story behind the huge data sets, and don't let your discovery only appear in your mind, but in the eyes of the public.

As a Taiwanese artist and an award-winning designer, Meng Chih Chiang specializes in data visualization, UI/UX, and interactive media. She has worked as a digital designer for Medialand in Taiwan, and a creative designer and interactive designer for American Express and Hi-Res! respectively in New York. The highlights of her awards include: 2015 Red Dot Design Award: Communication Design, French Design Index Award Winner and Best CSS Award Winner, Adobe Design Achievement Awards, and the Lumen Prize.

1

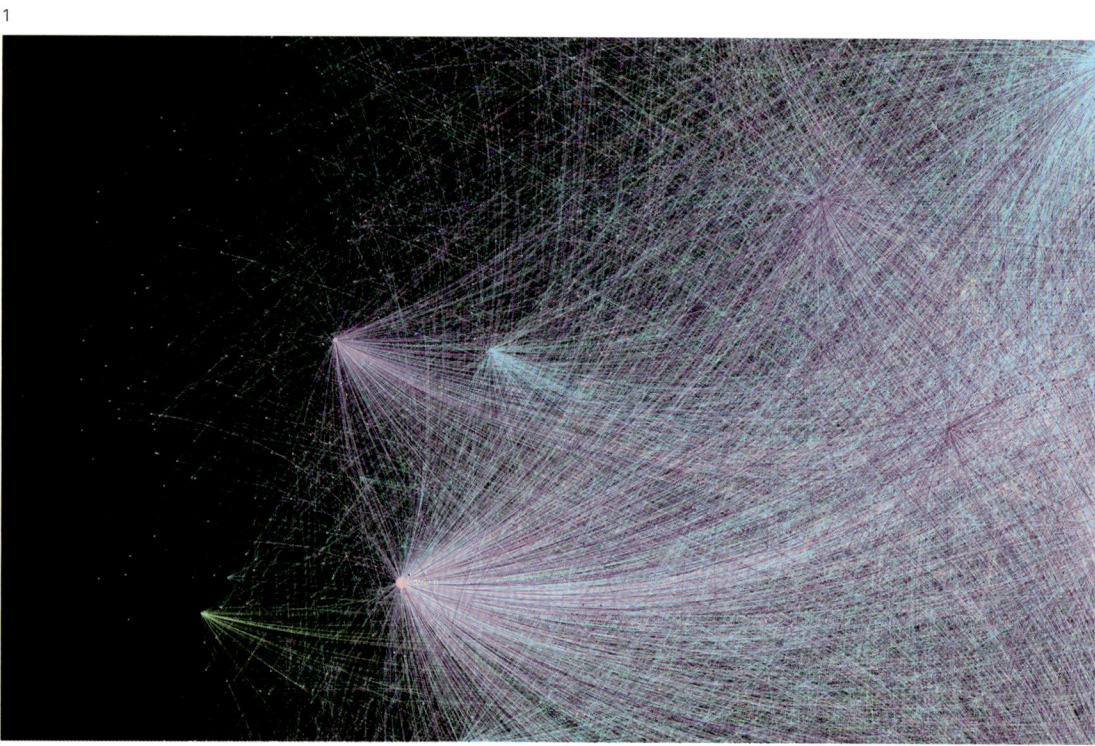

2

[1–6] A Stranger to Words

Credit: Meng Chih Chiang
Completion: 2013
Interactive link: www.mengchih.com/portfolio/a-stranger-to-words

This is an interactive network graph created by Meng Chih Chiang in 2013 to visualize her personal learning experience. Based on her daily reading report, the personal database of 23,358 words was created originally to express the curve of how she understood words. The complicated graph involves a great diversity of transformations, creating a mesmerizing interactive visual experience in which the language and the line of connection work in unison. Its goal is to introduce a new form of understanding language to reveal a connected system of underlying text algorithms in novel and insightful ways, and to unfold personal sentiments through the capabilities of information visualization.

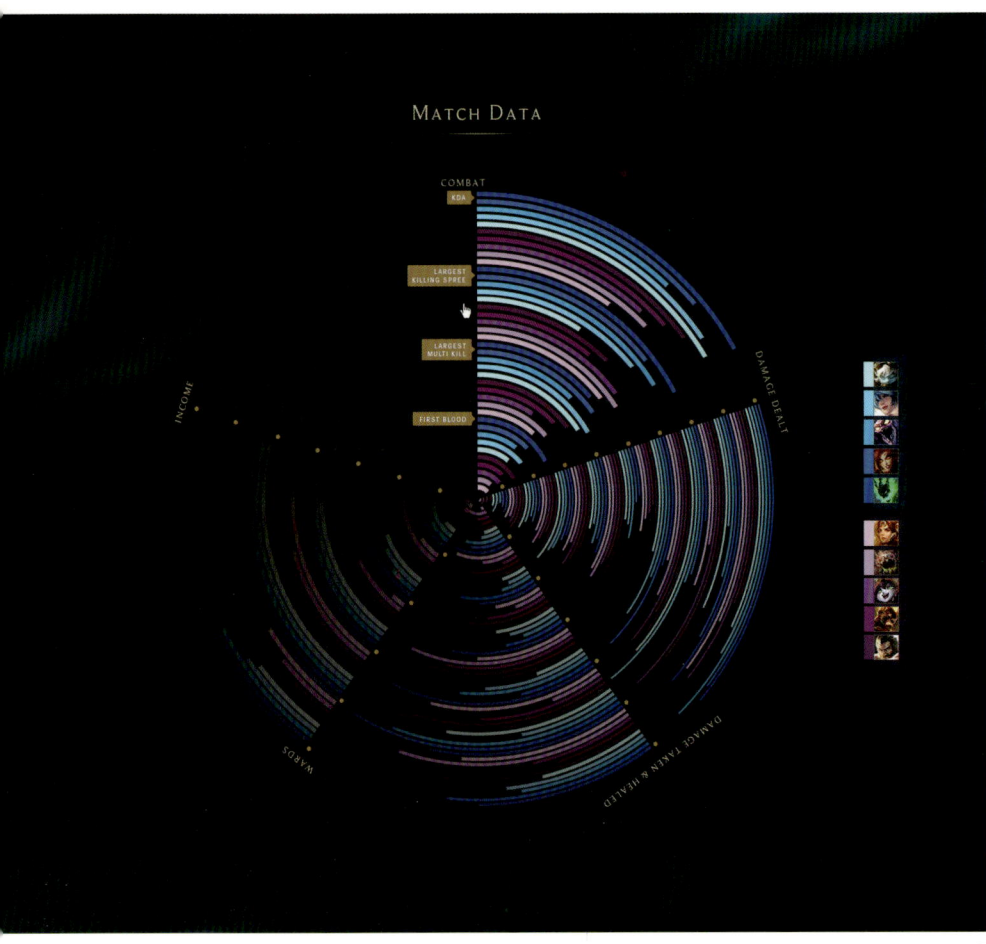
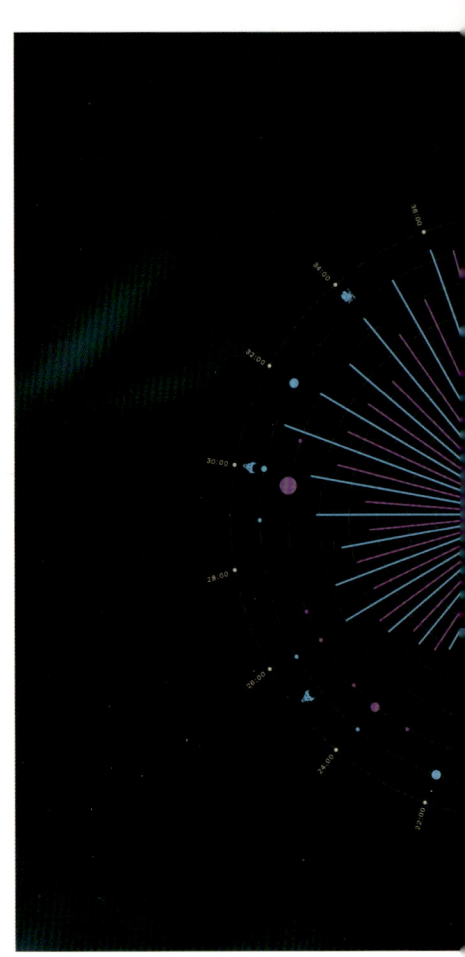
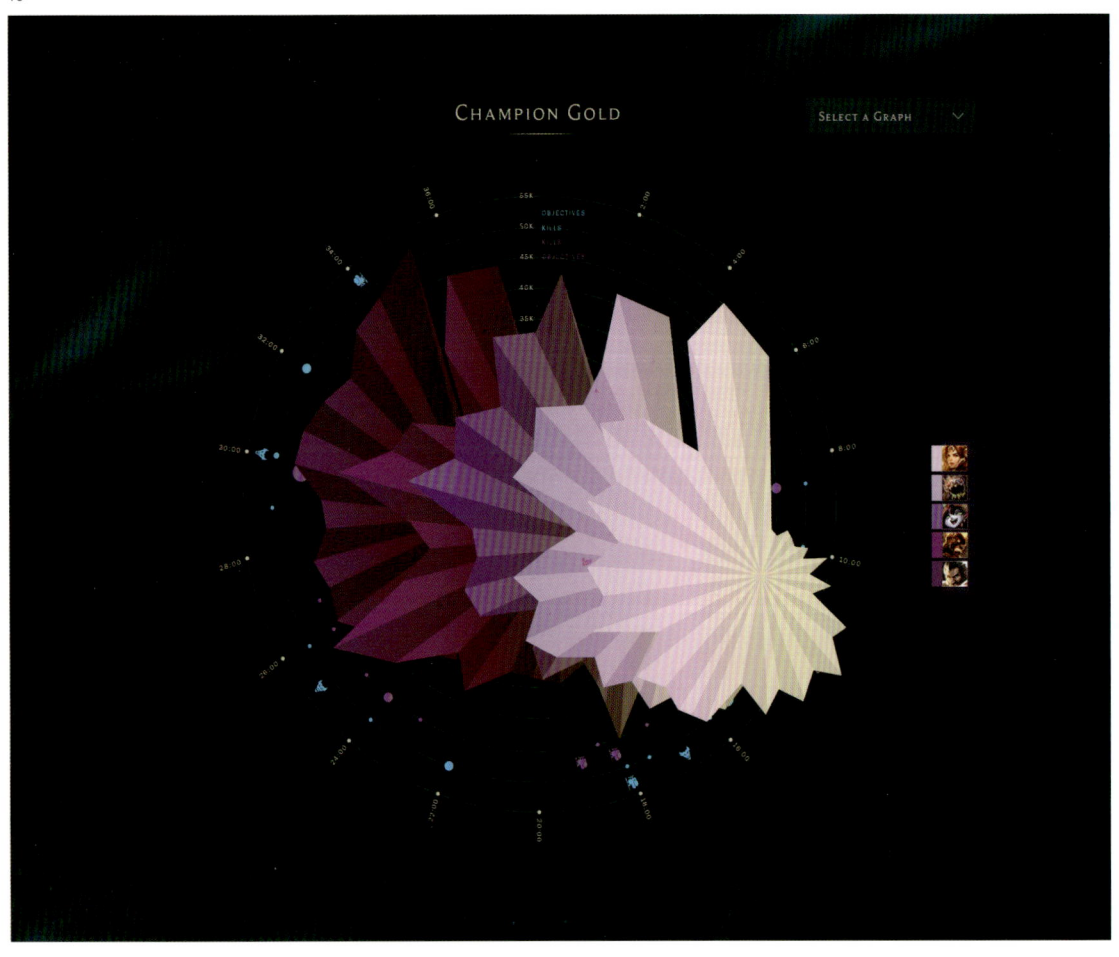

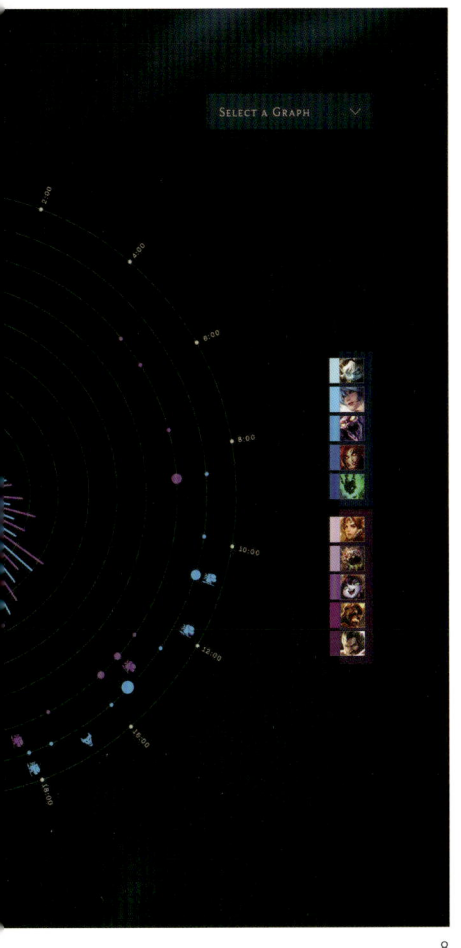

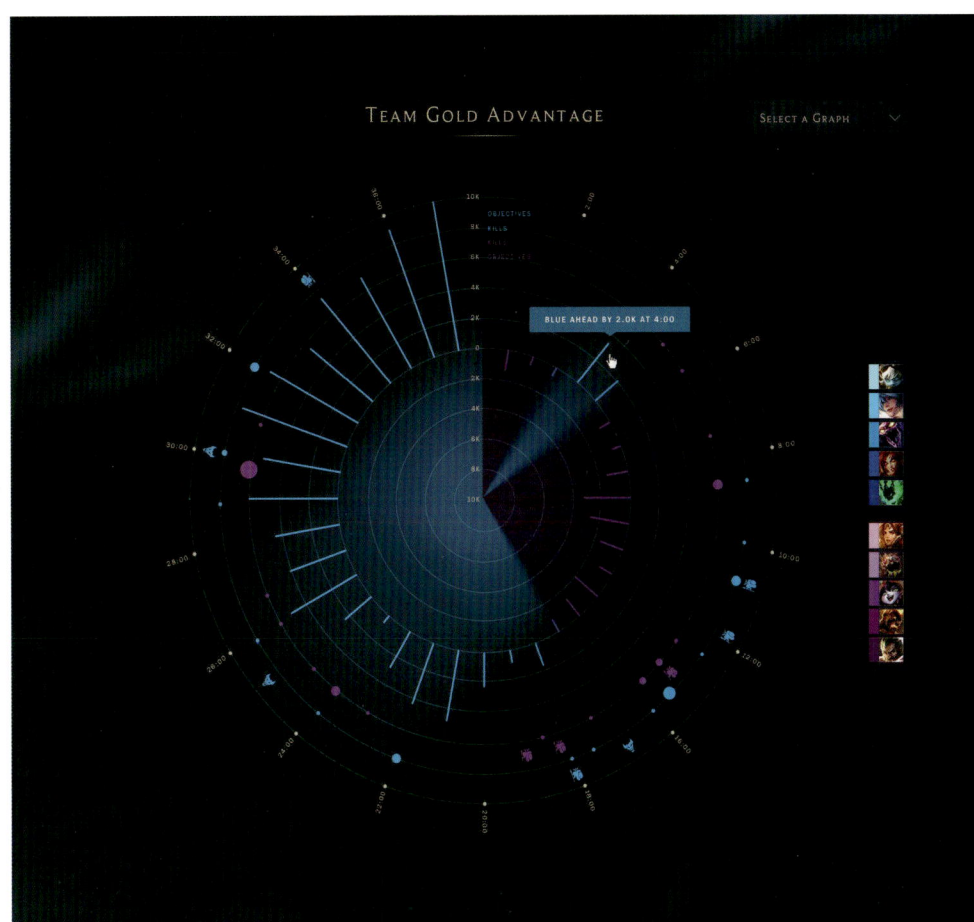

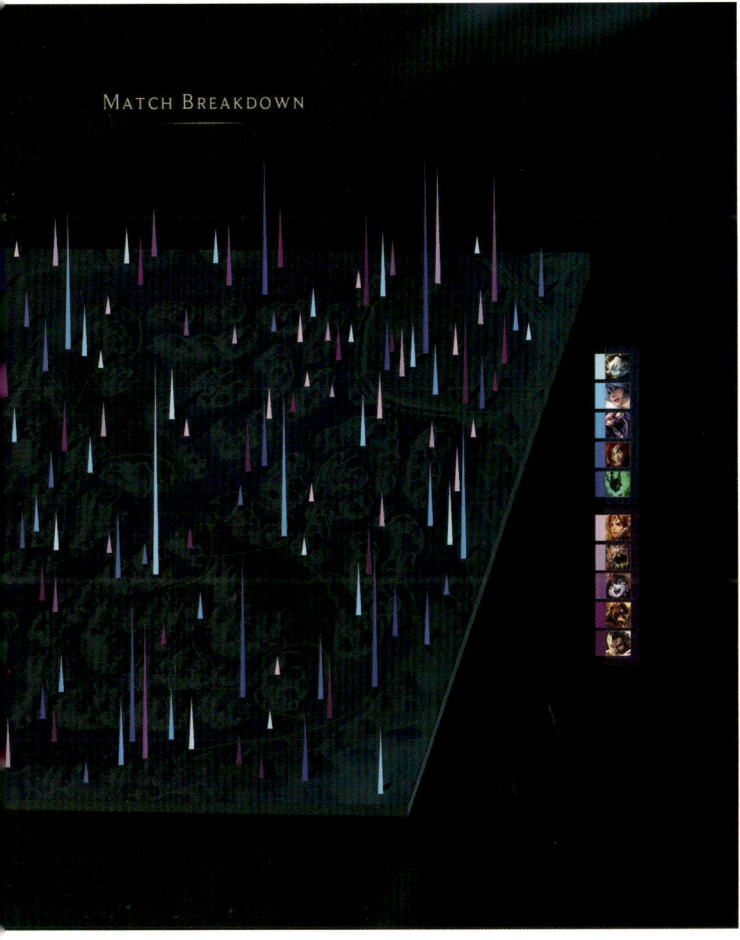

[7–11] Infographics for Match History

Credit: Meng Chih Chiang
Completion: 2015
Interactive link: www.mengchih.com/portfolio/infographics-for-match-history

This is an interface design for League of Legends, a multiplayer and real-time strategy video game. Match history is a record of past games the user has played, expanded and organized with graphs, charts, heat maps, and more to help tell the story of the most epic games. The goal is to deliver robust, intricate details about users' previous matches in an accessible, intuitive interface that expands the end-of-game information.

Cloudred

Cloudred is a digital design and online strategy studio located in New York City. It helps civic-minded organizations and businesses maximize their visibility online. Clients include the Mayor of London, the City of New York and UNICEF. Allen Yee, a co-founder and creative director for the data visualizations, grew up in San Francisco and practiced architecture and landscape architecture prior to his career in interactive design. Cyril Tsiboulski, the other co-founder, grew up in Moscow, Russia.

[Q] What do you think about data visualization/infographics?

[A] Data visualization is a way for designers and technologists to make sense of and give visual structure to complex data. Through using recognizable forms of visual representation, designers can reveal clear insights and patterns from data that would otherwise be overwhelming.

[Q] What kind of design methods do you commonly use?

[A] The data visualizations we have created to date are self-initiated, personal projects, so we can only speak to this particular process. Creating a data visualization is one way we distract ourselves from our client work and a way we can explore interesting facts and facets of our city.

We often imagine a client and the reasons why this person would want to use our visualization. It's important to us that there should be some sort of utility and functionality driving the direction of the visualization. We step into the shoes of this fictitious client many times in order to keep the work grounded and relevant.

We look at the data at a macro level before taking a sample to see if there are any interesting patterns. Allen typically doodles a lot in his sketchbook to explore different ways of representing the data or ways that one can interact with it. Though these sketches are often messy and unstructured, possible directions emerge from these artistic explorations.

When we're ready to give the visualization some visual structure, we'll design several iterations with a graphic program. We like to design quickly and assess the merits of each direction. Many directions will be discarded, and if we feel stuck we'll take a break, chat with each other, drink some coffee, and walk the dogs. We'll repeat this process several times until the visuals, data, and user interaction come together.

[Q] What kind of design elements do you commonly use?

[A] We don't have preconceived notions when it comes to design elements in our visualizations. Examining and reorganizing the data will sometimes lead to certain design elements. Above all, we aim for simplicity and clean, graceful visuals.

[Q] Where are your works applied?

[A] The data visualizations thus far have been web-based. We want as many people as possible to interact with our work.

1

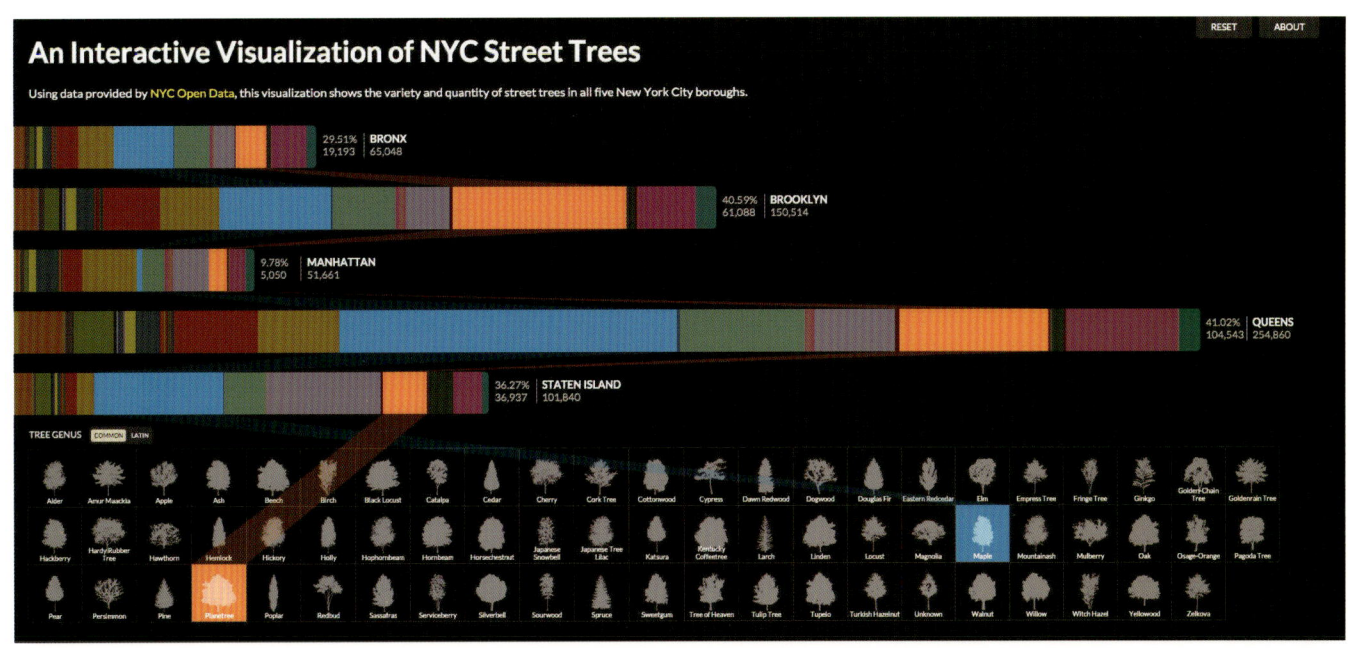

[1–3] An Interactive Visualization of NYC Street Trees

Credits: Allen Yee, Cyril Tsiboulski, Cristian Zapata
Completion: 2014
Interactive link: www.cloudred.com/labprojects/nyctrees

The designers were curious to visualize common and not-so-common trees planted in the five boroughs of New York City. Using data provided by NYC Open Data, this visualization shows the variety and quantity of street trees in all five boroughs. While this particular project visualizes trees that they love as an essential element of any urban place, they see this as an experiment or model to visualize other data sets in an additive and subtractive format.

[Q] **How do you turn boring and complex data into something interesting and understandable?**

[A] We allow ourselves to get overwhelmed by the data set so that we may find logical and intuitive ways to give it order. We fill our sketchbooks with freehand, messy sketches and rambling ideas. We design many iterations and discard a lot of ideas. We like to envision how a user would interact with the visualization and why they would even want to use it. We believe in beautifully designed interfaces that are accessible and informative.

[Q] **What is your suggestion for beginners?**

[A] Try. Create. Revise. Rest. Try again.

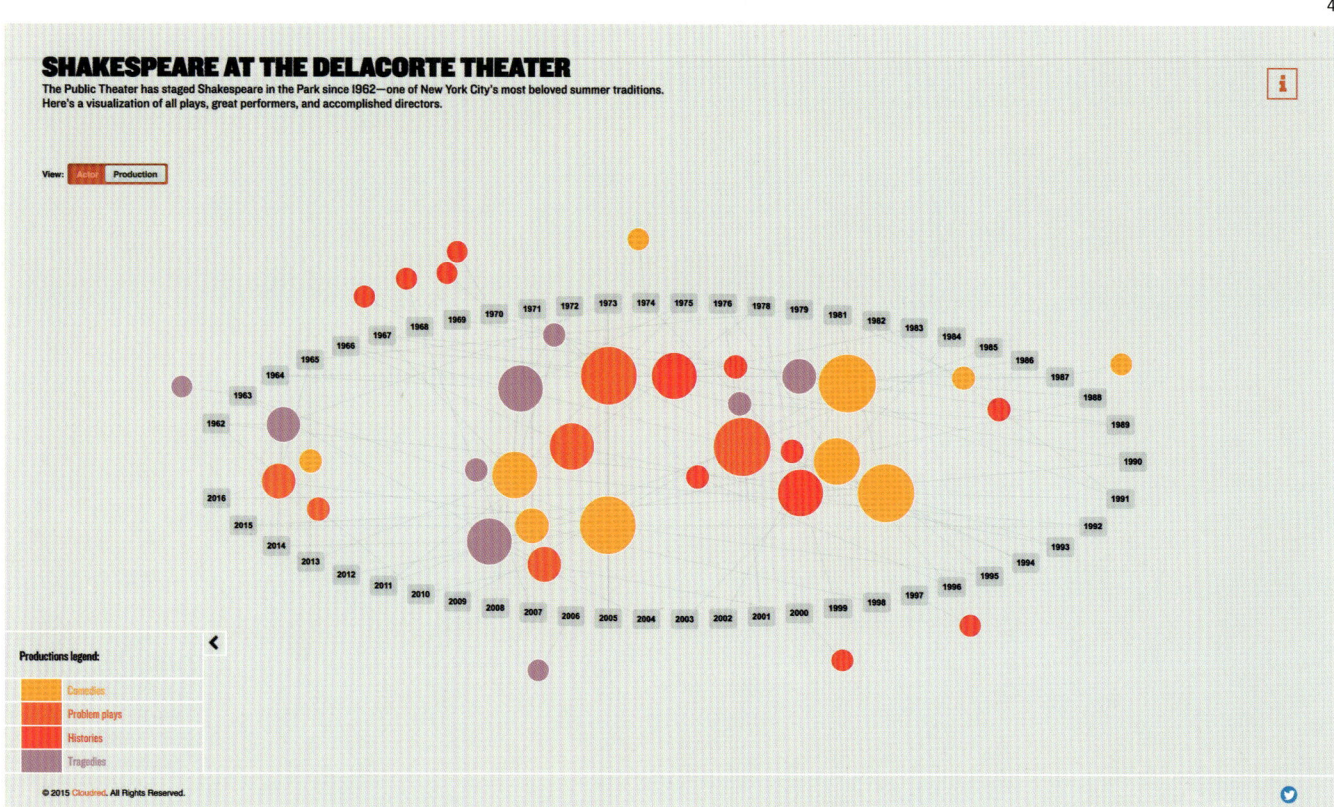

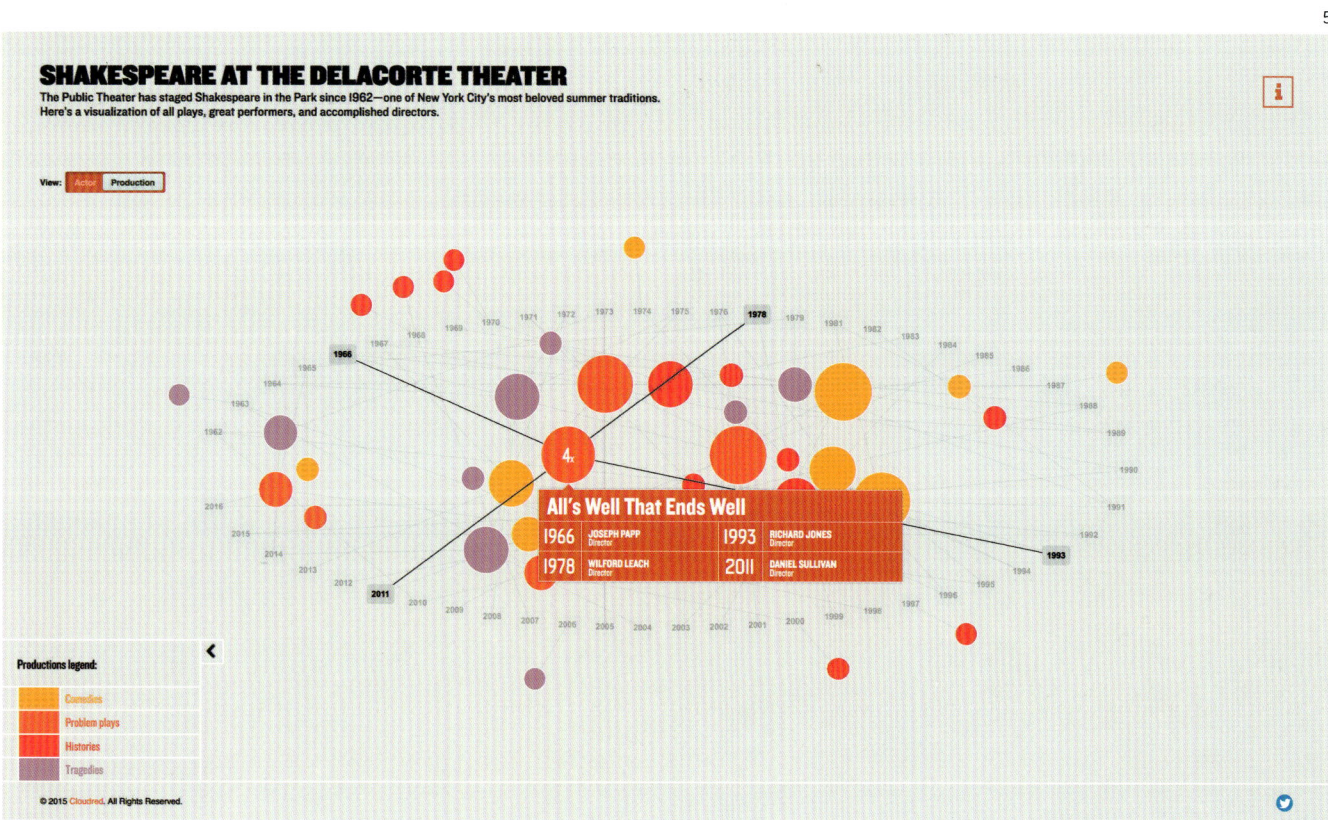

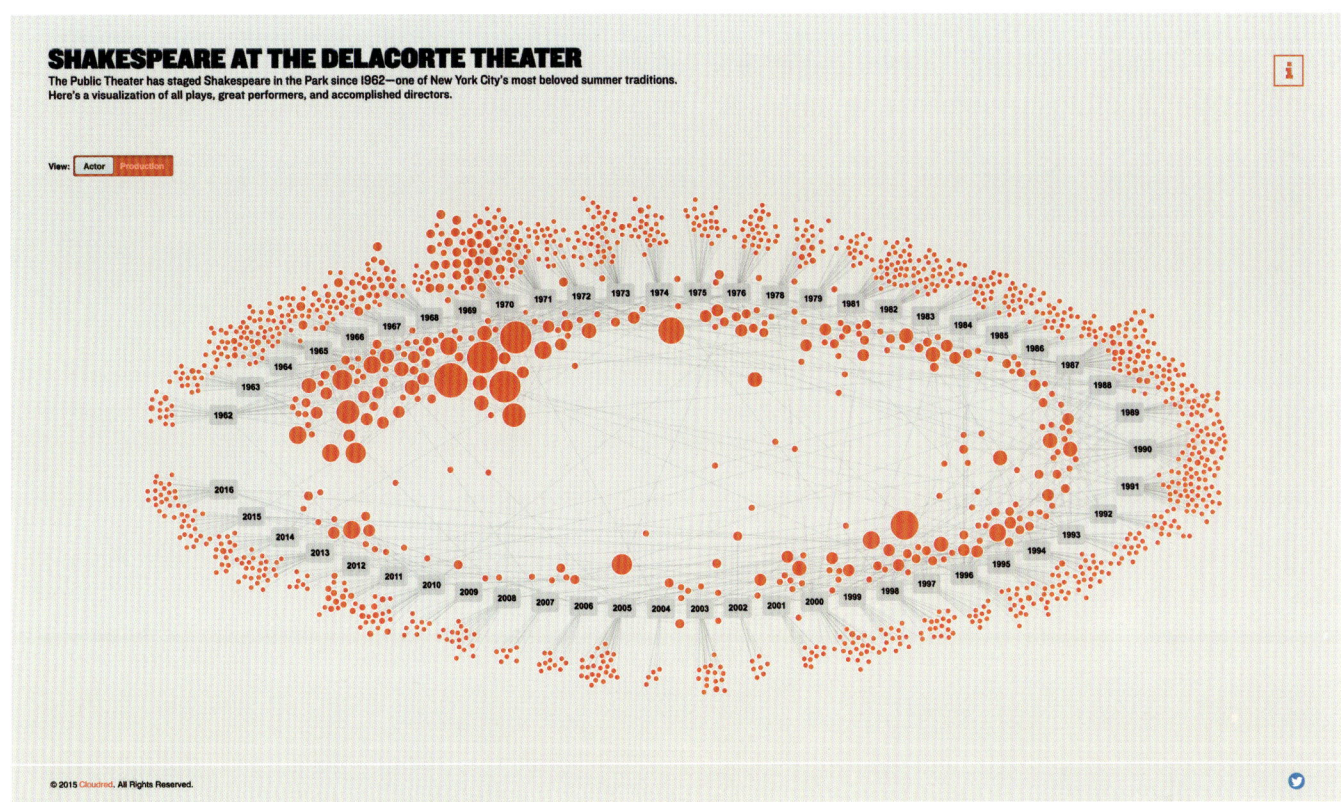

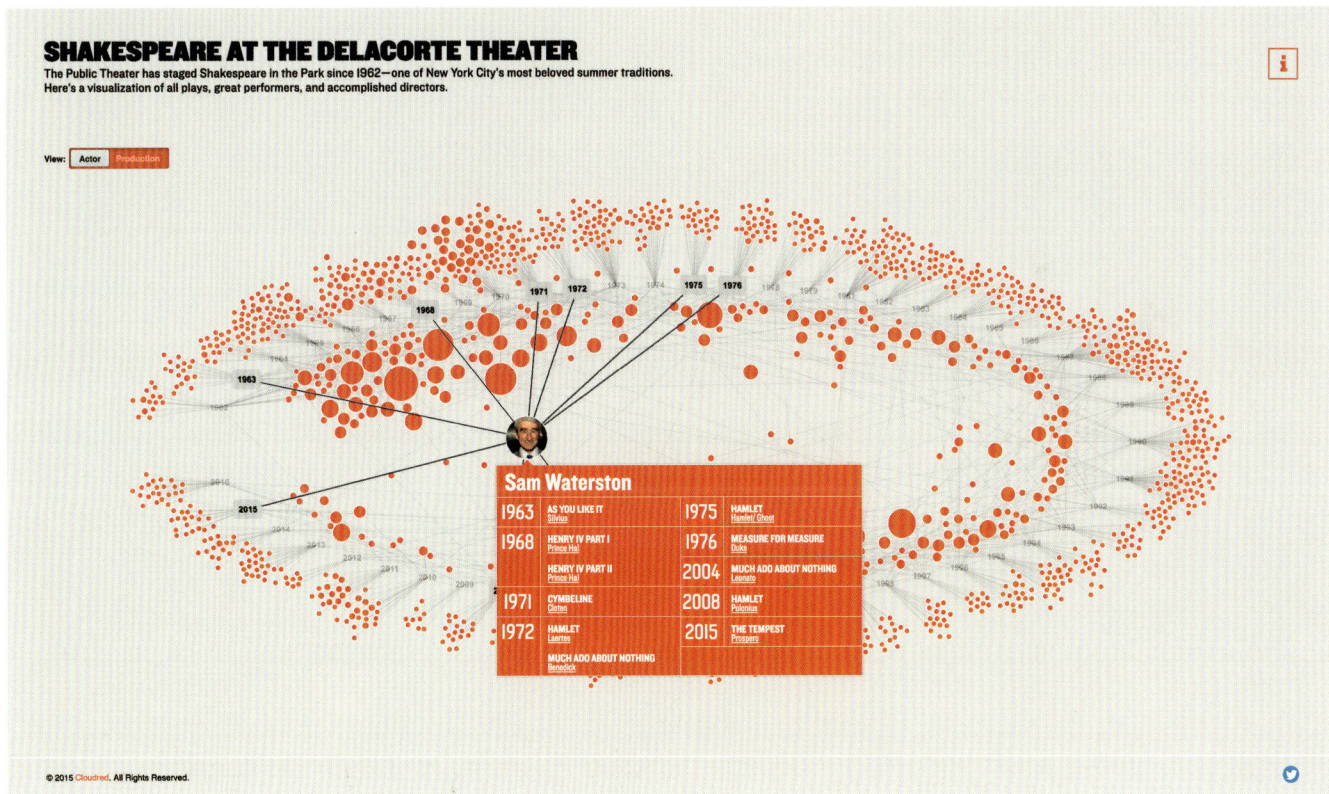

[4–7] Shakespeare at the Delacorte Theater

Credits: Allen Yee, Cyril Tsiboulski, Cristian Zapata
Completion: 2015
Interactive link: www.cloudred.com/labprojects/shakespeare

The designers were interested in visualizing a complex data set of productions, characters, and actors in a non-linear, time-based format. This visualization allows the user to discover who has played iconic Shakespearean characters such as Beatrice, Lear, or Hamlet at the Delacorte. They were also curious about the plays. Which are the most frequently presented? Do certain genres dominate? After many design layout variations, hours of data collection, and creative coding, they put together an interactive homage to this great summertime New York City institution.

Dataveyes

DATAVEYES

Dataveyes is a French data visualization studio founded in 2010. They help people understand, operate, and communicate their data. They translate data into experiences to share narratives, support new users, and make sense of a world increasingly shaped by algorithms. They design useful, relevant interfaces through their workflow, which revolves around both data and user needs.

[Q] What do you think about data visualization/infographics?

[A] We perceive there is a need to radically transform the way organizations, both public institutions and corporations, understand the value attached to data, and how they implement solutions to unleash their potential. Data has become a very valuable currency in the digital economy, thus making it vital to have interfaces that allow understanding, processing, and sharing of data.

The need for comprehension remains widely unsatisfied for two main reasons. First of all, data does not interpret itself, which results in everyone not being able to fully process what the message is. Besides, while this mass of data could reveal extremely useful information to better understand our environment, data too often remains in silos, scattered in different repositories that make it difficult to access and connect. This leads us to a strong conviction that unveiling the value and the information inside massive data sets is a great challenge to tackle.

[Q] What kind of design methods do you commonly use?

[A] We have developed a consistent working process revolving around three phases, in order to effectively translate unmet user needs into a relevant visual interface.

Phase 1—Immersion: This phase allows us to precisely define the expectations, technical constraints, as well as who the audiences are and what their behaviors are. During this phase, we also deeply analyze the data in order to fully understand the information it contains.

Phase 2—Conception: This phase allows us to translate scenarios of usage into interfaces, and into rules to manage information. We determine how all the elements should be assembled, visualized, and implemented within the application. We then specify the data processes as well as the technical choices.

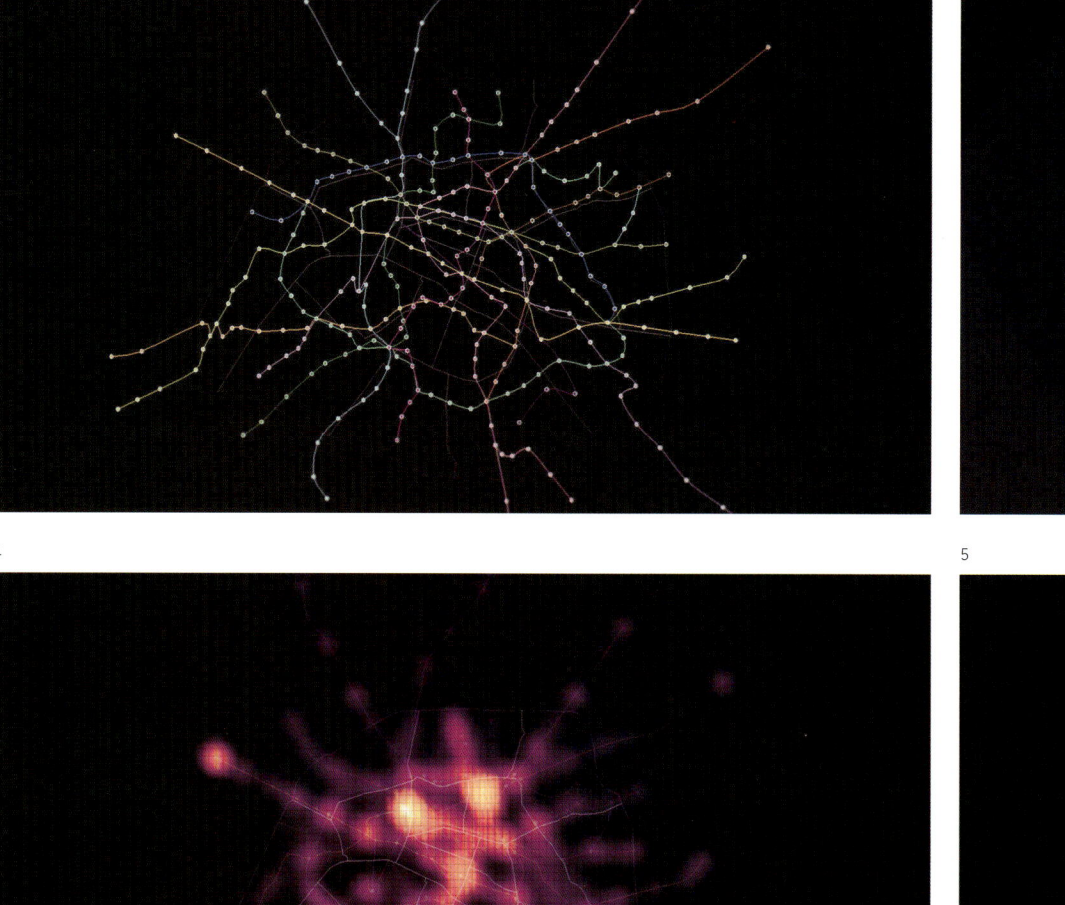

1

4

Phase 3—Development: During the production phase, designers and developers within our team work closely to develop the application.

[Q] **Where are your works applied?**

[A] We connect users to data through different kinds of digital interfaces: web and mobile applications, software, editorial contents, creative installations, etc.

[1–6] Metropolitain

Credit: Dataveyes
Completion: 2013
Interactive link: www.dataveyes.com/#!/en/case-studies/metropolitain

This is a new representation of a transport network shaped by metro data. The designers challenged the traditional way of representing the Parisian transport network by depicting a more realistic territory through data. They proposed a three-dimensional visualization in which the user can play with time and space variables. The interface materializes the data related to metro commuting, in a poetic way. This project led to research work on how users typically interact with three-dimensional interfaces, as well as the transition from visual design to service design.

3

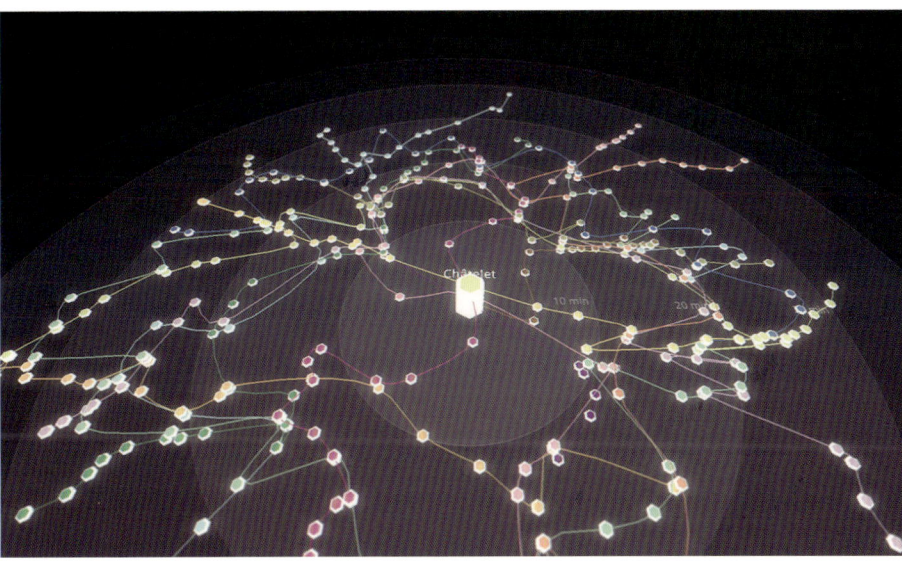

6

[Q] How do you turn boring and complex data into something interesting and understandable?

[A] We believe that the true potential lies at the fingertips of users, rather than within data centers. We perceive our mission to be at the very end of the data value chain, in close touch with users; this is where data-driven strategies are implemented, and where organization changes can be witnessed. We always keep the user in mind. Our ambition is to design bespoke interfaces, which will greatly help users grasp, process, and understand the data. We favor short, agile work cycles. They allow the creation of more mature tools on an ongoing basis, rather than a long tunnel of development that can divert us from the intricacies of the data.

We spend a great part of our time creating interfaces meeting non-standardized user needs. This is how we guarantee long-term relevance. We also develop our own proprietary technological components to capitalize on our research works.

We allow the whole organization to improve its data literacy. All along our creation and production process, we want to ensure that all stakeholders feel comfortable understanding the data, not only the people in charge of the tool's administration.

[Q] What is your suggestion for beginners?

[A] Read a lot about data and data visualization. Explore as many different visualizations as possible.

7

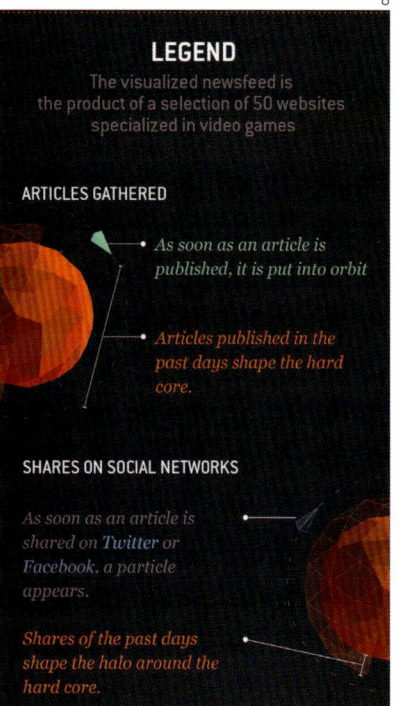

8

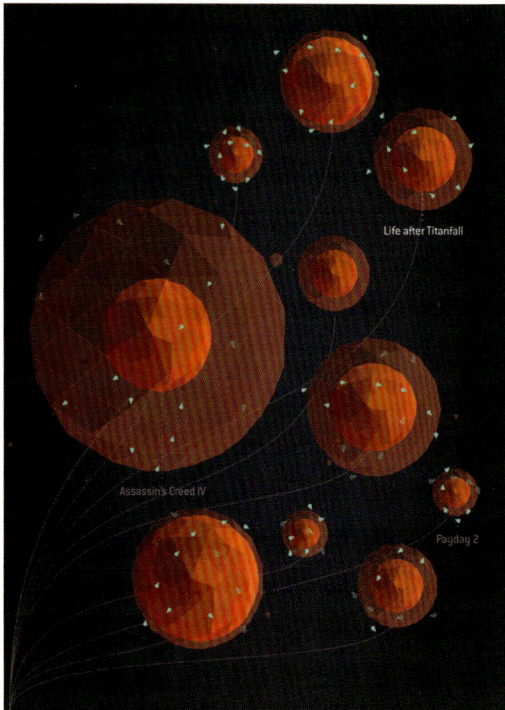

9

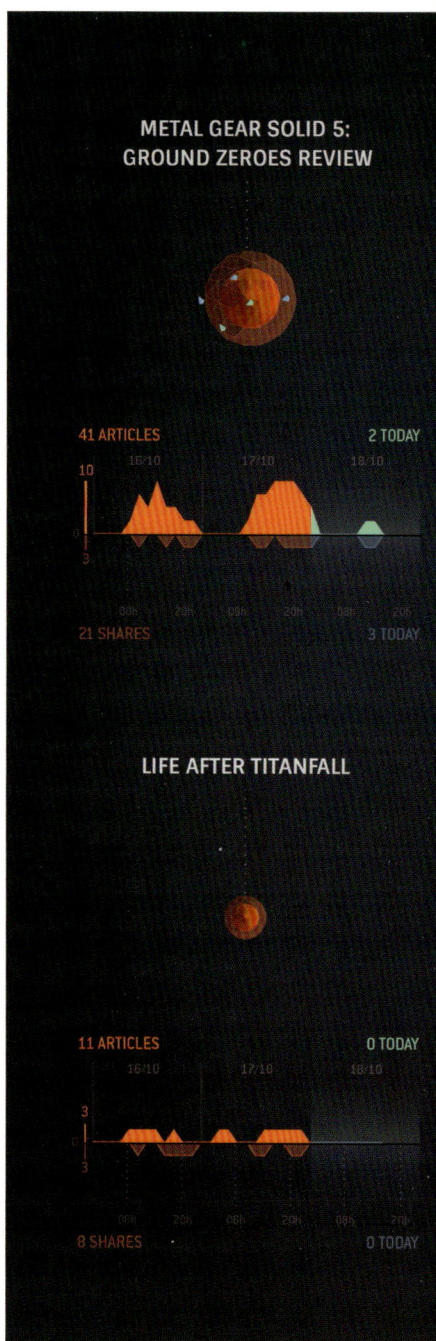

10

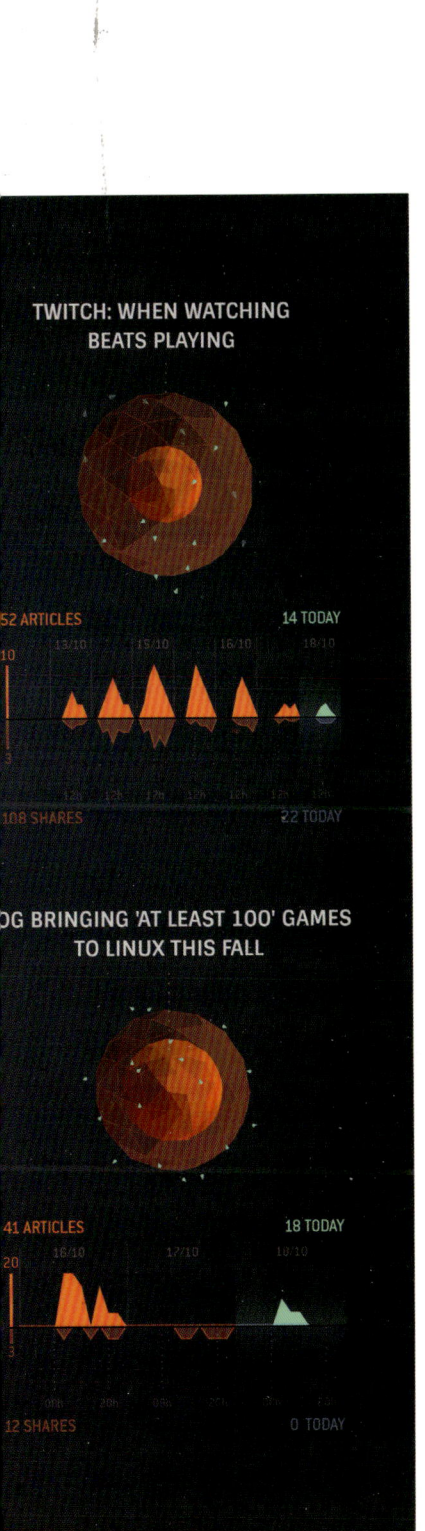

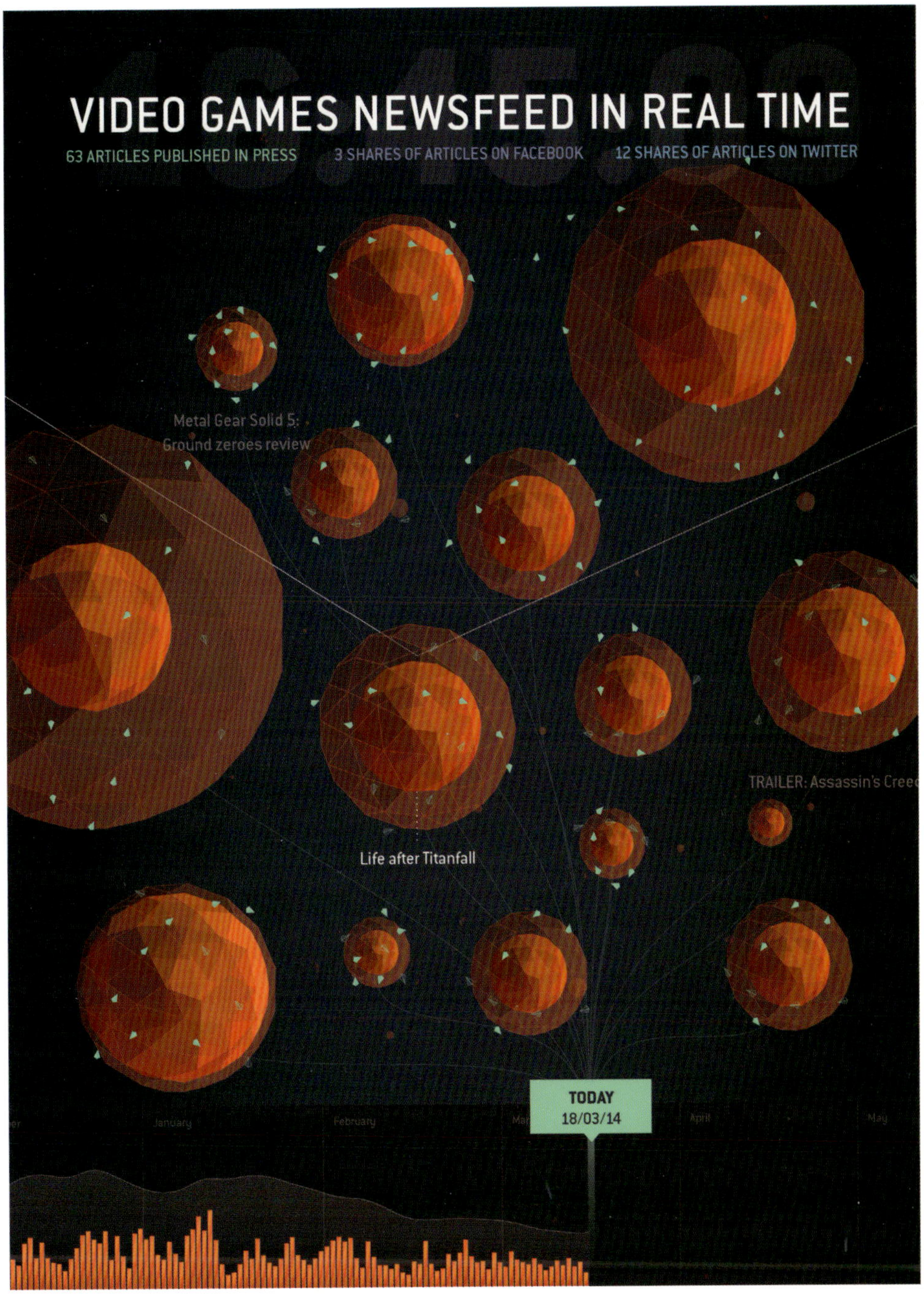

[7–11] News

Credit: Dataveyes
Completion: 2013
Interactive link: www.dataveyes.com/#!/en/case-studies/actualites

This is a visual, real-time setup for a video-game exhibition at the Paris Science Museum. The designers created a visual interface monitoring real-time newsfeeds on the topic of video games, for a special eight-month long exhibit at the Paris Science Museum. They translated the data coming from various media sources into a poetic, quiet landscape where each news topic was represented by a planet, and their echo on social networks by a halo, with recent articles orbiting them. The application gained a life of its own, as if it were animated by the mysterious energy of data. Projected onto a big screen, it provided analytical insight and updates during the eight months.

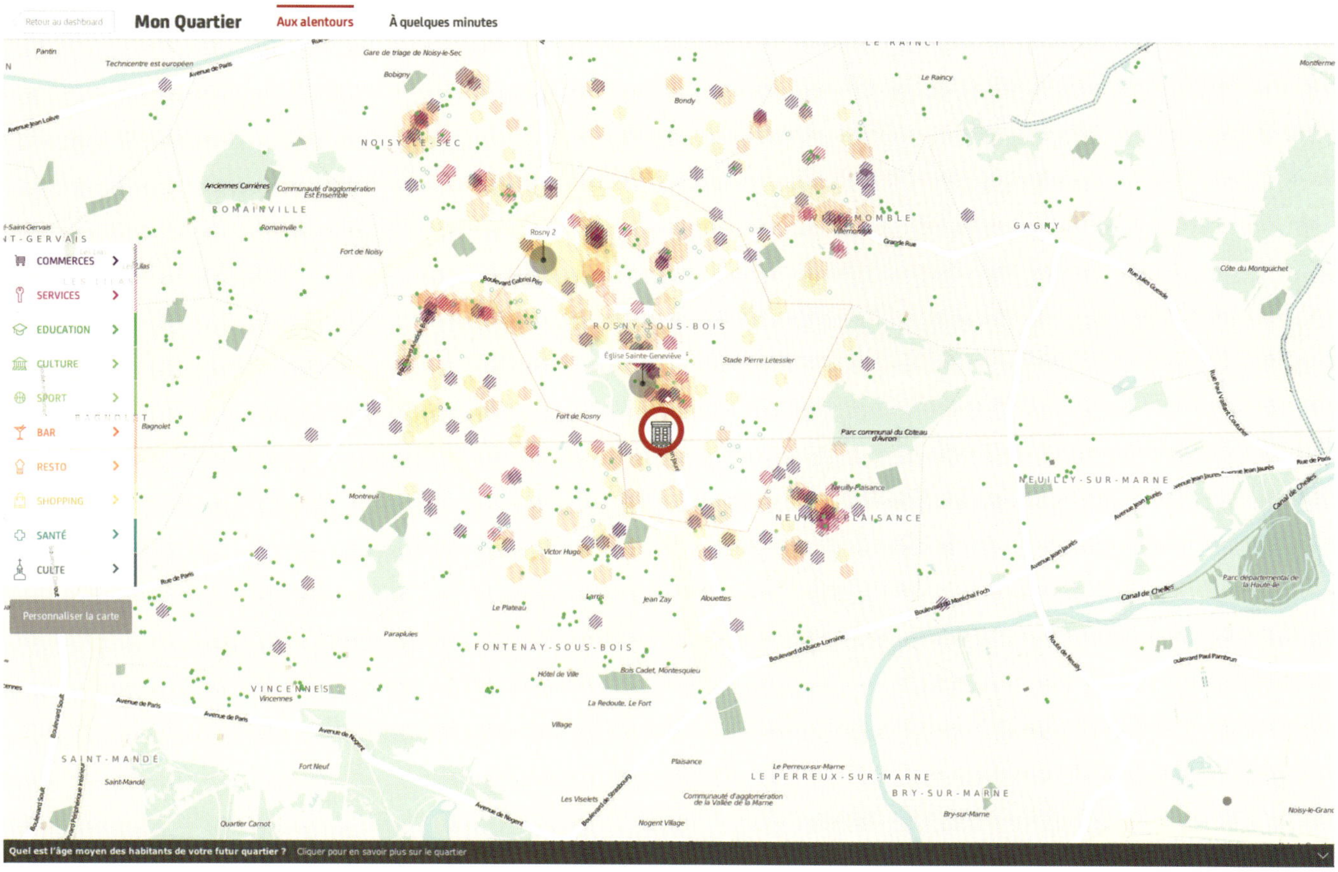

Mon Quartier	Aux alentours	À quelques minutes	

COMMERCES
SERVICES
EDUCATION
CULTURE
SPORT
BAR
RESTO
SHOPPING
SANTÉ
CULTE

Personnaliser la carte

Quel est l'âge moyen des habitants de votre futur quartier ? Cliquer pour en savoir plus sur le quartier

---

Mon Quartier	Aux alentours	À quelques minutes	

Voici la répartition des lieux par catégories pour la zone choisie.
Sélectionnez une catégorie pour en savoir plus

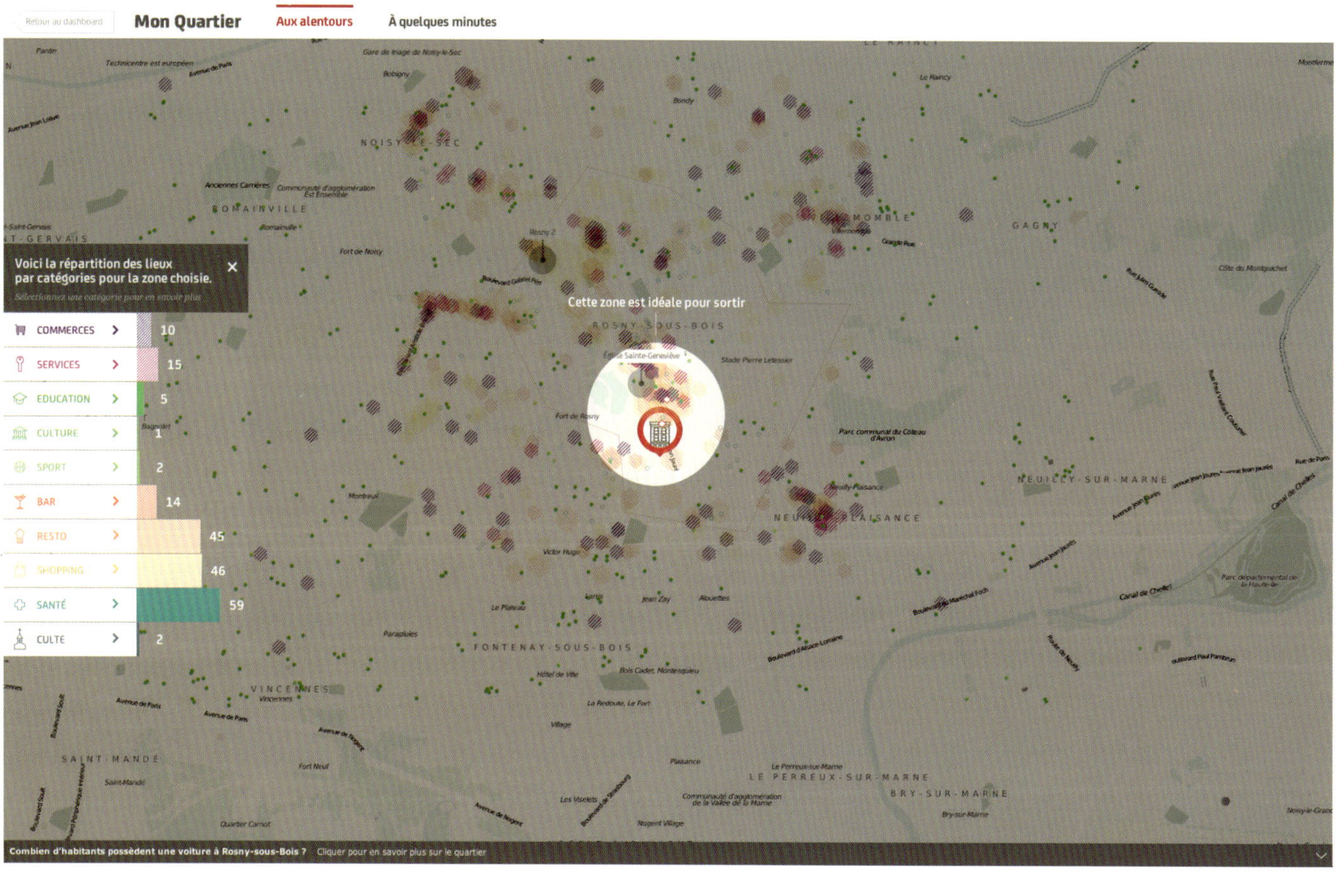

COMMERCES 10
SERVICES 15
EDUCATION 5
CULTURE 1
SPORT 2
BAR 14
RESTO 45
SHOPPING 46
SANTÉ 59
CULTE 2

Cette zone est idéale pour sortir

Combien d'habitants possèdent une voiture à Rosny-sous-Bois ? Cliquer pour en savoir plus sur le quartier

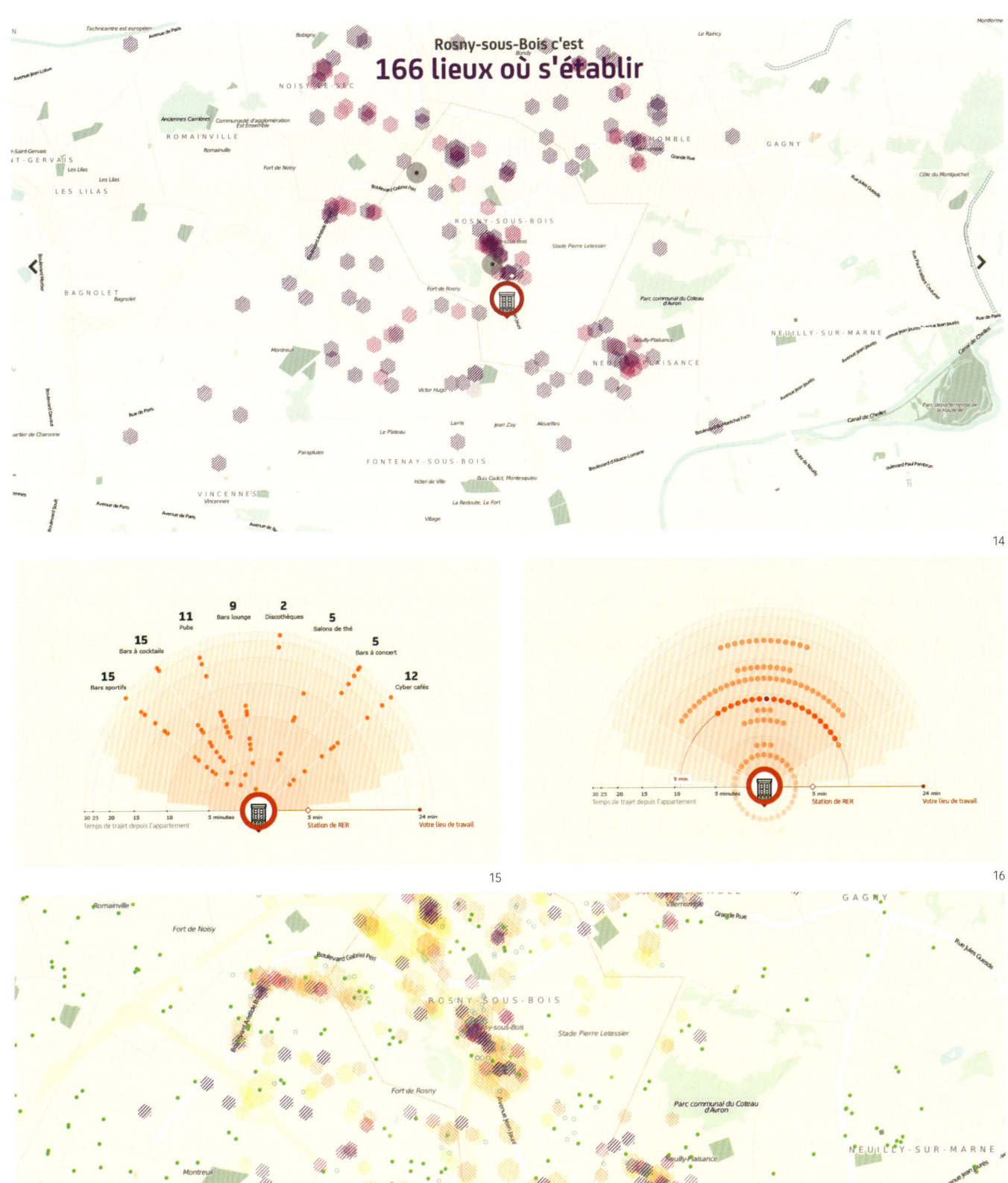

[12–17] My Neighborhood

Credit: Dataveyes
Completion: 2013
Interactive link: www.dataveyes.com/#!/en/projects/mon-quartier

This is an iPad web app to discover a new neighborhood. The designers assisted prospective property buyers with envisaging what their future neighborhood will look like, and explored the new opportunities available in their area. They created an app that leverages data about local amenities to paint the picture of a city through two dimensions: global atmosphere and accessibility. The map can be customized depending on what the user finds of interest. The app can be used on a computer, iPad, or smartphone.

Marcelo Duhalde

[Q] What do you think about data visualization/infographics?

[A] I think data visualization can be a very interesting tool to discover facts that are hidden in a bunch of data. Only it will depend on the visual journalist's skills to transform the data into something readable and attractive. The unreadable data visualization only helps to keep the information away from the most important actor, the audience.

[Q] What kind of design methods do you commonly use?

[A] After a long time researching and many hours of preparing the data, I always start with a series of sketches. My inspiration is more from the real world; some objects or patterns could help me to find a solution. I usually throw away the initial sketches, because at the beginning, ideas could be too literal, basic, or complex to work efficiently. It is necessary to spend more hours to discover which formula will be doable, visually fresh, and understandable.

[Q] What kind of design elements do you commonly use?

[A] My works are related to visual journalism and infographics, so I like to use geometric elements, transparencies, mostly vector, nothing really innovative, just the same elements that everyone uses.

[Q] Where are your works applied?

[A] We usually design mostly for newspapers and tabloid magazines.

[Q] How do you turn boring and complex data into something interesting and understandable?

[A] Data is not boring, actually, and the numbers can always be represented by different shapes. I think the key for a compelling result is to know the subject in depth and feel myself as a part of the audience. It is necessary to be very self-critical.

Marcelo Duhalde is an infographic designer, visual journalist, and illustrator. He works at SCMP as senior infographic designer, and previously worked as the deputy infographic editor at the Times of Oman. He has won more than 40 SND awards, 10 Malofiej medals, one Peter Sullivan's best of show (2015), and four gold medals at the WAN IFRA Asian media awards. His works have been published in several books, magazines, and infographic and data visualization websites in Europe, Asia, and the Americas.

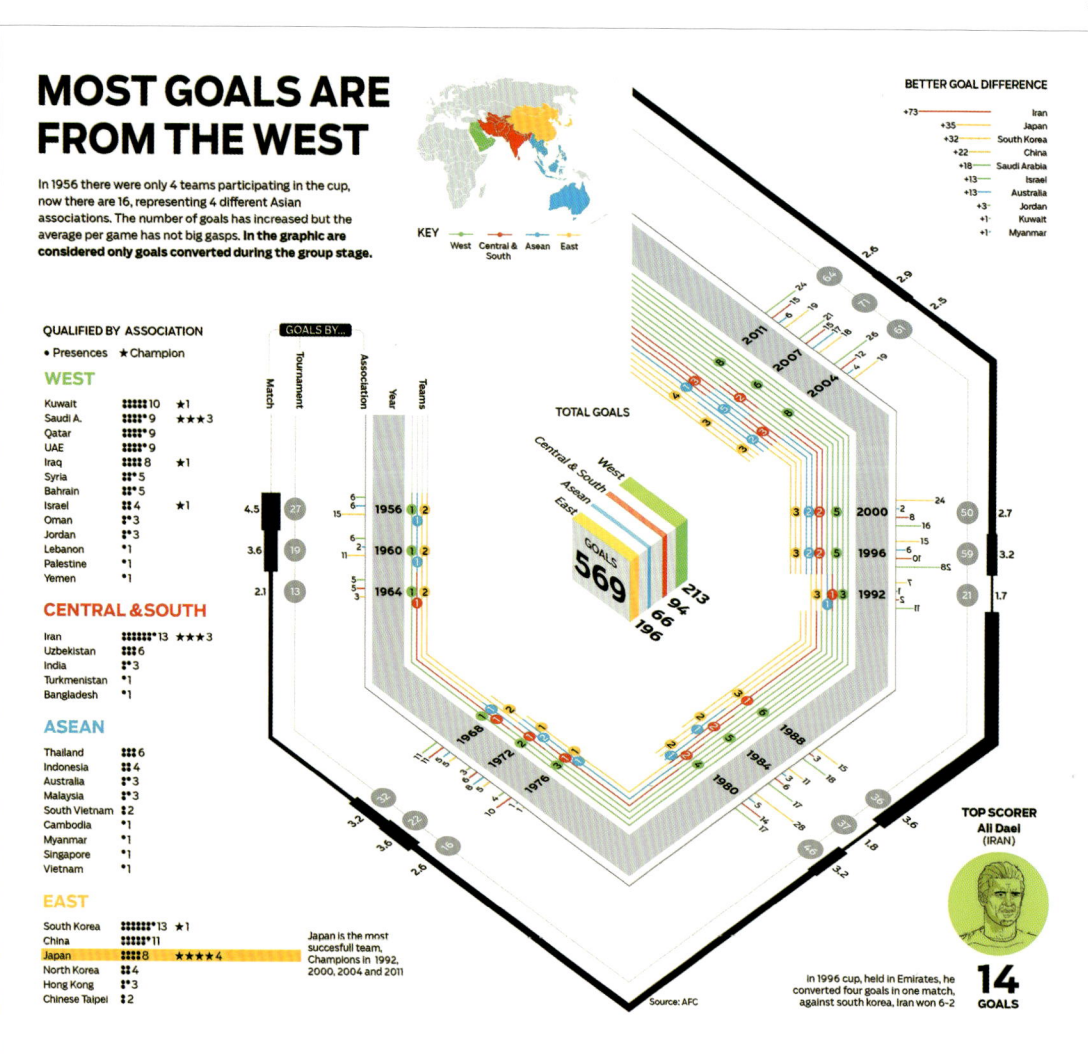

[Q] What is your suggestion for beginners?

[A] If you want to work as a visual journalist, you have to be passionate for the information, and be keen to spend many hours on research. Moreover, sketch sessions and several tests are also necessary to reach a goal. I have learnt that iteration is one of the core elements that every designer needs to consider seriously. The iteration helps you to reach a better understanding of the subject, and most importantly, it helps to find your specific skills for a project. It is essential to always show your sketches to your colleagues or people in general. Any opinion helps, and all critics leave certain knowledge and experience. You are working for the audience, so the audience can help to find the best formula.

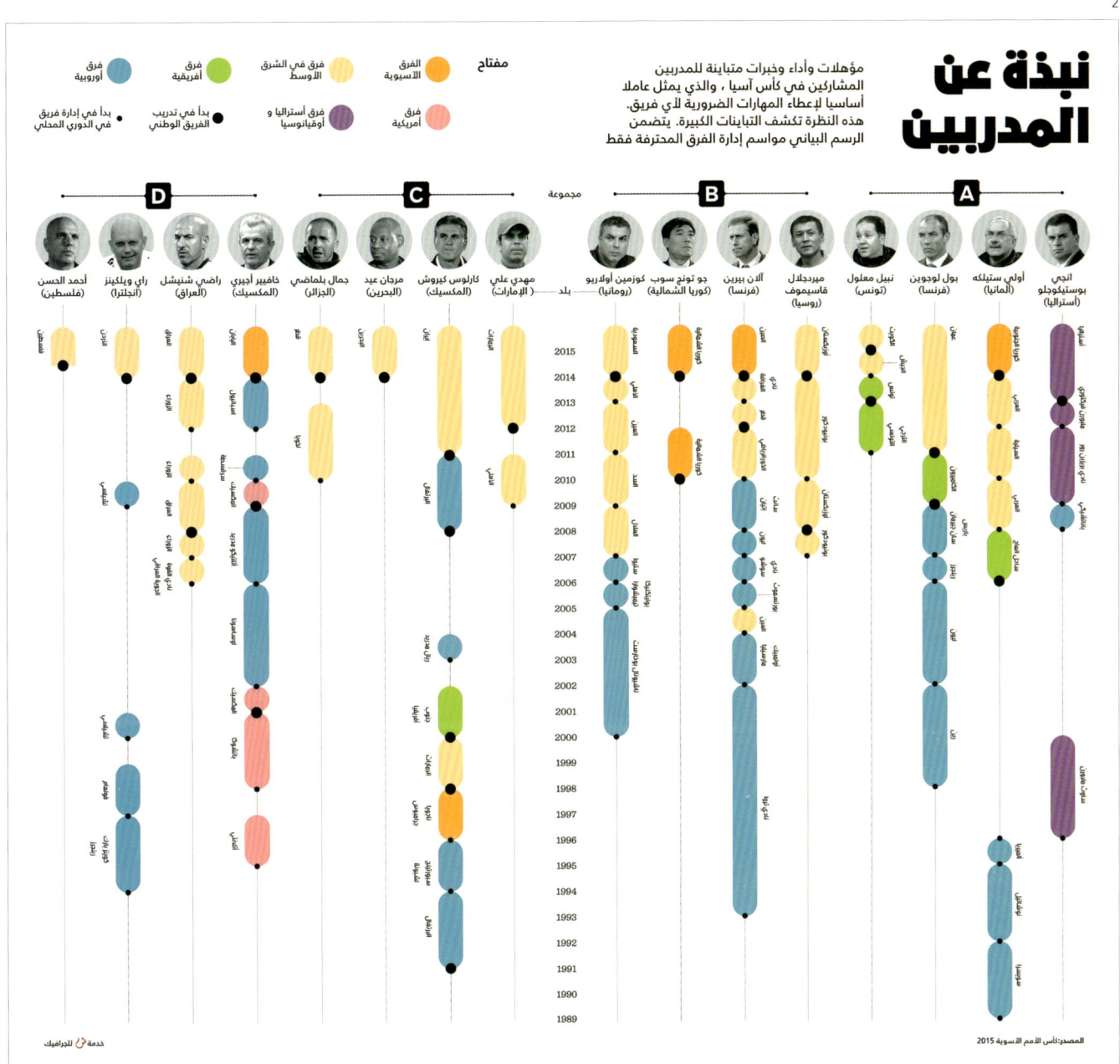

[1] Scores from the East

Credit: Marcelo Duhalde
Completion: 2015

This infographic is an overview of the history of the Asian Cup from 1956, and each side of the shape displays three versions of the tournament, ordered chronologically. The color key is to discover which of the football confederations has been most successful over the 55 years.

[2] Experienced Coaches

Credit: Marcelo Duhalde
Completion: 2015

To figure out if the men on the bench have good credentials and success history as a coach, the graphic shows all the teams and national teams in the professional lifetime of each coach. The big dots indicate the transfer from a team to a national squad.

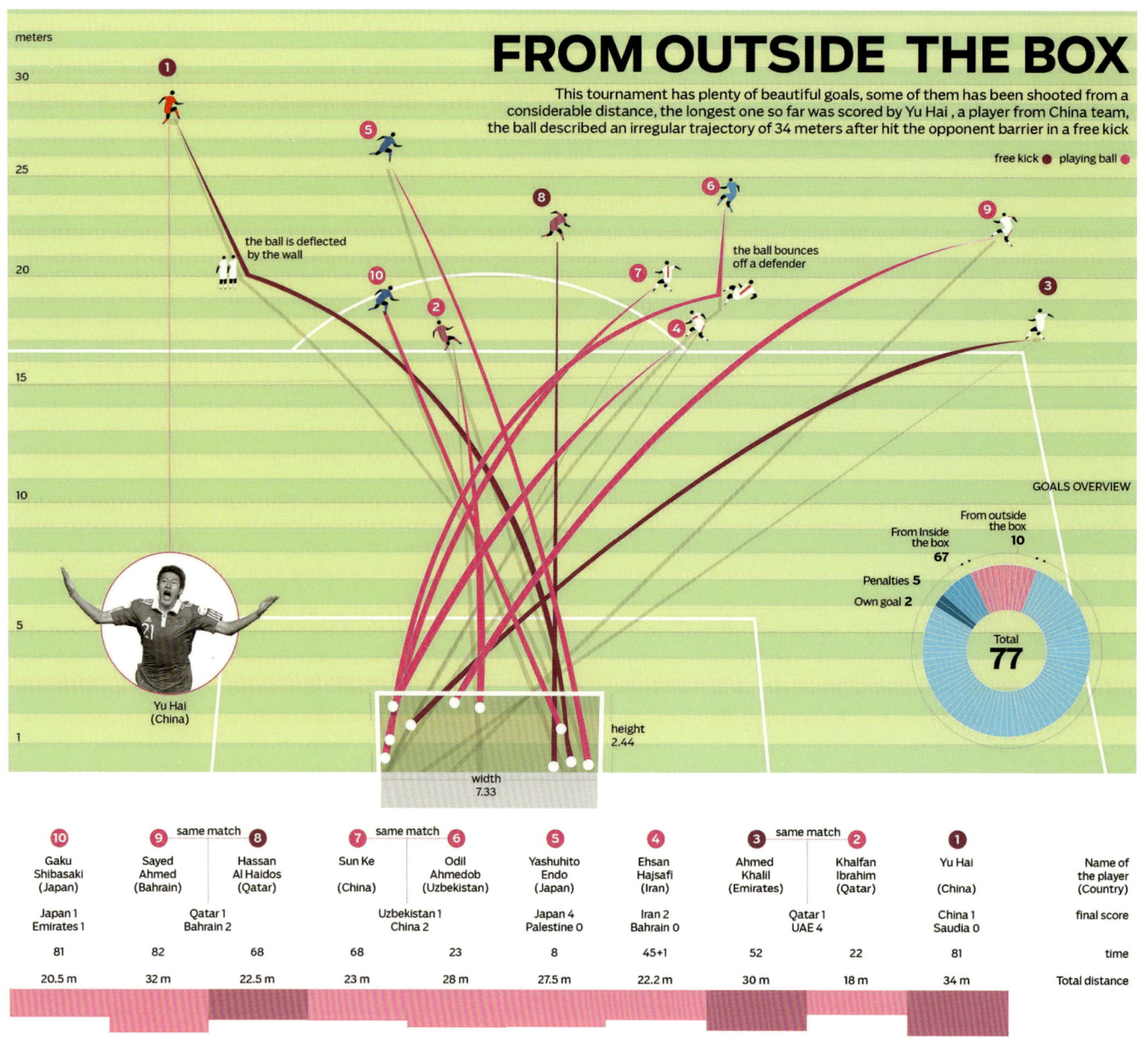

[3] From Outside the Box

Credit: Marcelo Duhalde
Completion: 2015

This tournament (Asian Cup Australia 2015) has plenty of beautiful goals, some of which have been shot from a considerable distance, and the longest one so far was scored by Yu Hai, a player from the China team. The stripes in the field help to count the distance from where the score was shot and if it was the product of a free kick or a playing ball.

[4] Waiting in the Row

Credit: Marcelo Duhalde
Completion: 2015

In the United States during 2015, 25 people were executed for crimes committed between 1984 and 2009. The graphic helps viewers to understand how long the stay the death row can be. Some of the convicted persons have spent more time waiting for the execution than as a free person.

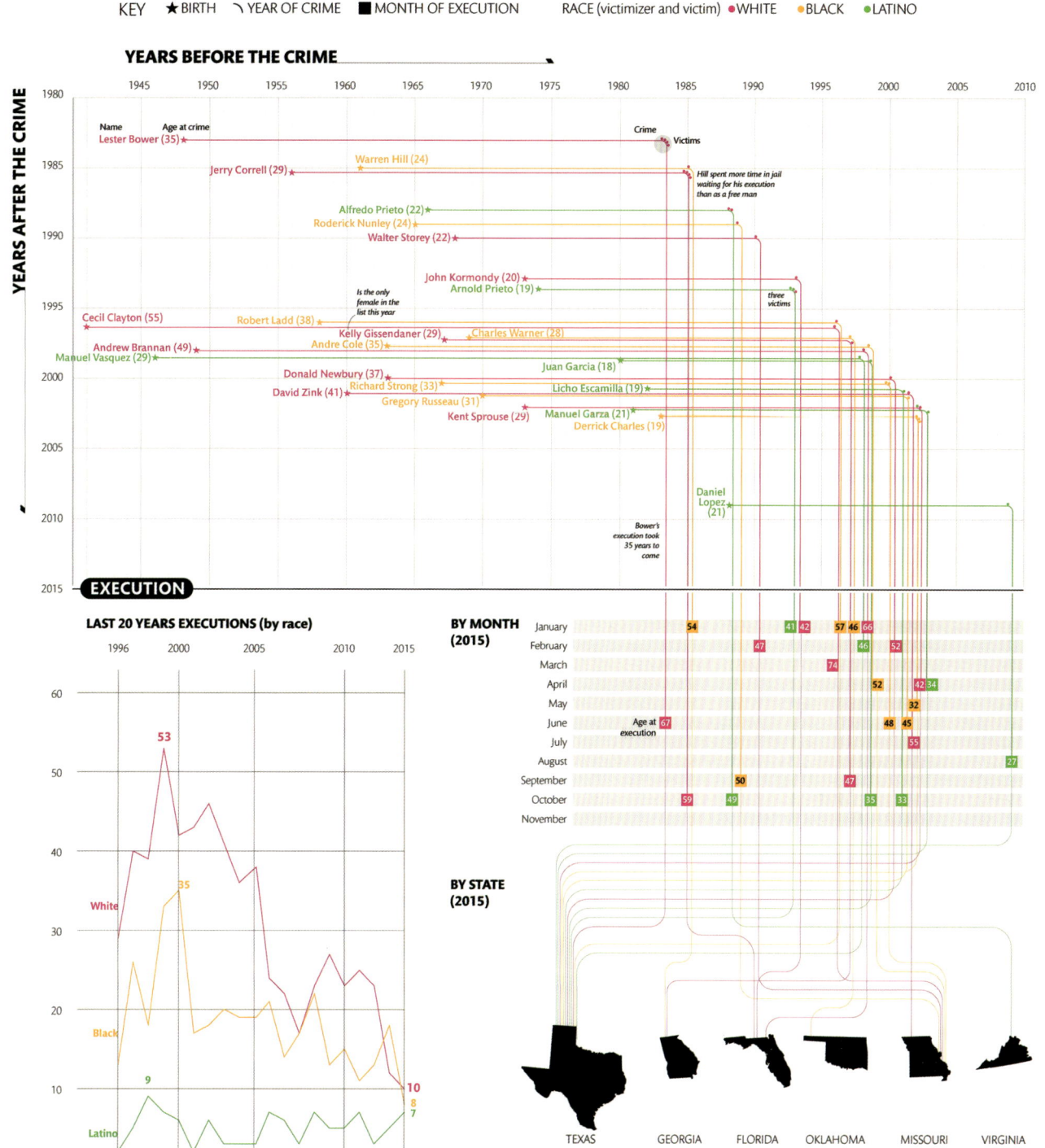

Antonio Farach

[Q] What do you think about data visualization/infographics?

[A] It's the future of storytelling. Data visualization is increasing its presence in all media at an accelerated rate. Data visualization represents the democratization of global information because it's massive and more accurate than simple infographics. Information can be transferred more easily through data visualization than through words. So I'm happy that I'm part of such revolution in communications.

[Q] What kind of design methods do you commonly use?

[A] I work my visualization manually (using design software for print) rather than automated software. That gives me freedom to create original forms.

[Q] What kind of design elements do you commonly use?

[A] I'm comfortable using just dots, lines, and a reduced color key.

[Q] Where are your works applied?

[A] Newspapers, magazines, posters, and websites.

[Q] How do you turn boring and complex data into something interesting and understandable?

[A] The first step is to research the topic and create the database. Once the data is complete, a double-check of it is mandatory. Once the data is correct, I do some sketching. It's good to explore many different layouts. Once the design is decided, I transfer the data into the design software.

Antonio Farach is a visual journalist with 18 years' experience of doing infographics and most recently doing data visualization, mostly for print media. Most of his experience is in newspapers. He likes to tell stories, and after a couple of years he had a good combination of skills (mathematics, drawing, and writing) that allowed him to call himself a visual journalist. His work has been published in Honduras (his homeland), the US, Canada, Switzerland, Luxembourg, Germany, France, Poland, Ireland, Spain, Emirates, Oman, Korea, and China. He has won more than 100 international awards in the fields of infographics and editorial design, including Malofiej's Peter Sullivan Award, the most highly regarded of all.

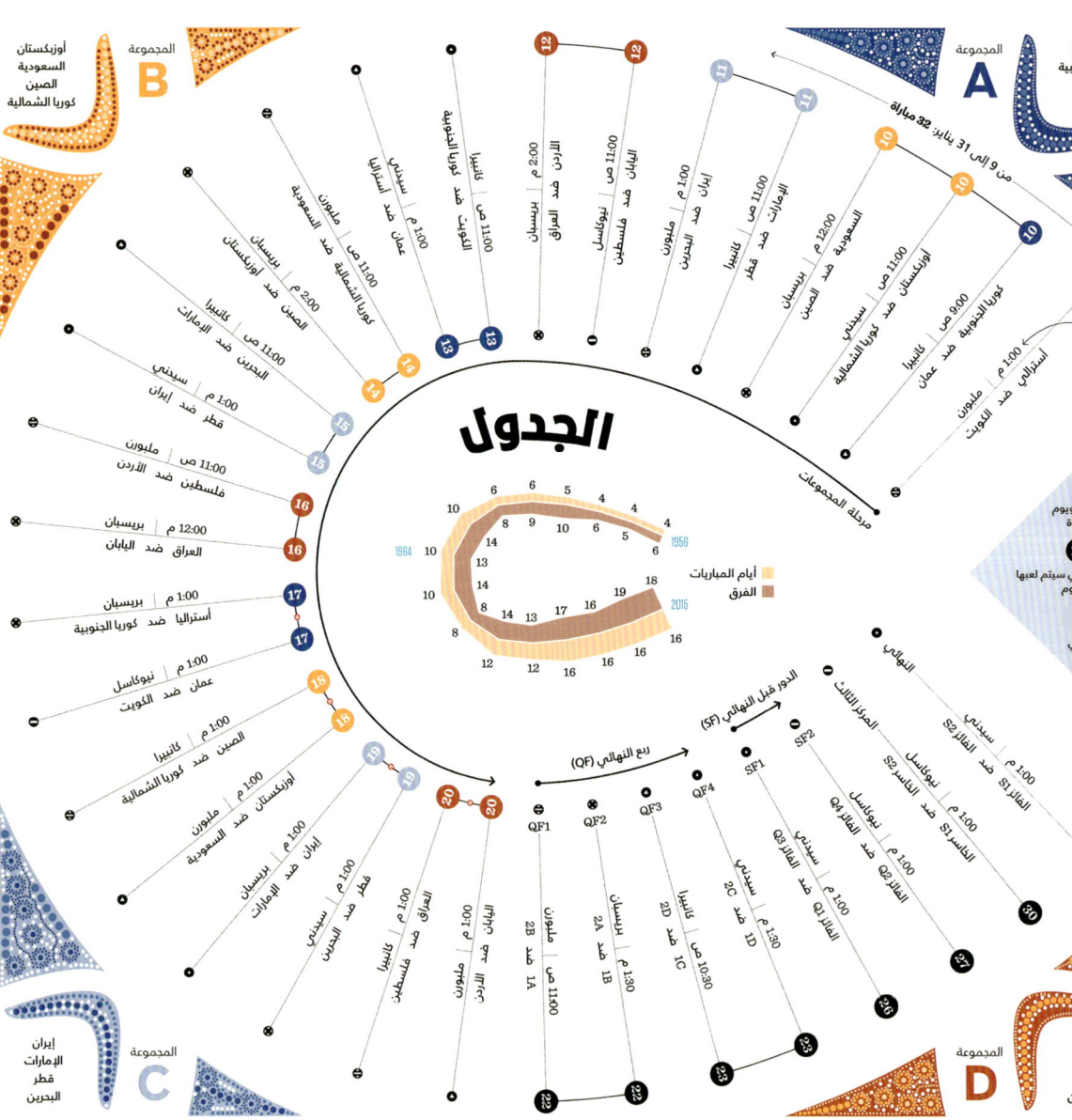

[Q] **What is your suggestion for beginners?**

[A] Include a good balance between beauty and understandability. Use color as information and use a reduced color palette. Explore new ways of presentation, or combine classic chart types to create new ones. Develop your own stories during your free time, don't do only the visualizations that editors or clients suggest or request. Look for the topics that you think are important.

[1] Venues and Schedule

Credits: Antonio Farach (art direction, research, graphics), Winie Ariany (illustration), Marcelo Duhalde (illustration)
Completion: 2015

This piece was published on the inauguration day of the Asian Cup 2015. Because the tournament was held in Australia, the look was inspired by the Australian aboriginal pointillism. It's a double-page infographic with the five stadiums of the competition shown on the right. Each stadium was assigned a small black icon that is shown on the left in order to know in which stadium a particular match was played. In the inner part, there is a timeline with data about the stadium attendance. This page also includes a location map with the five stadiums as well. The left page is the schedule of matches. Each match includes the information of the teams, time, stadiums, and groups (by color key). In the inner part, there is a timeline with the number of matches per tournament, and the list of all the teams by group is in the four corners.

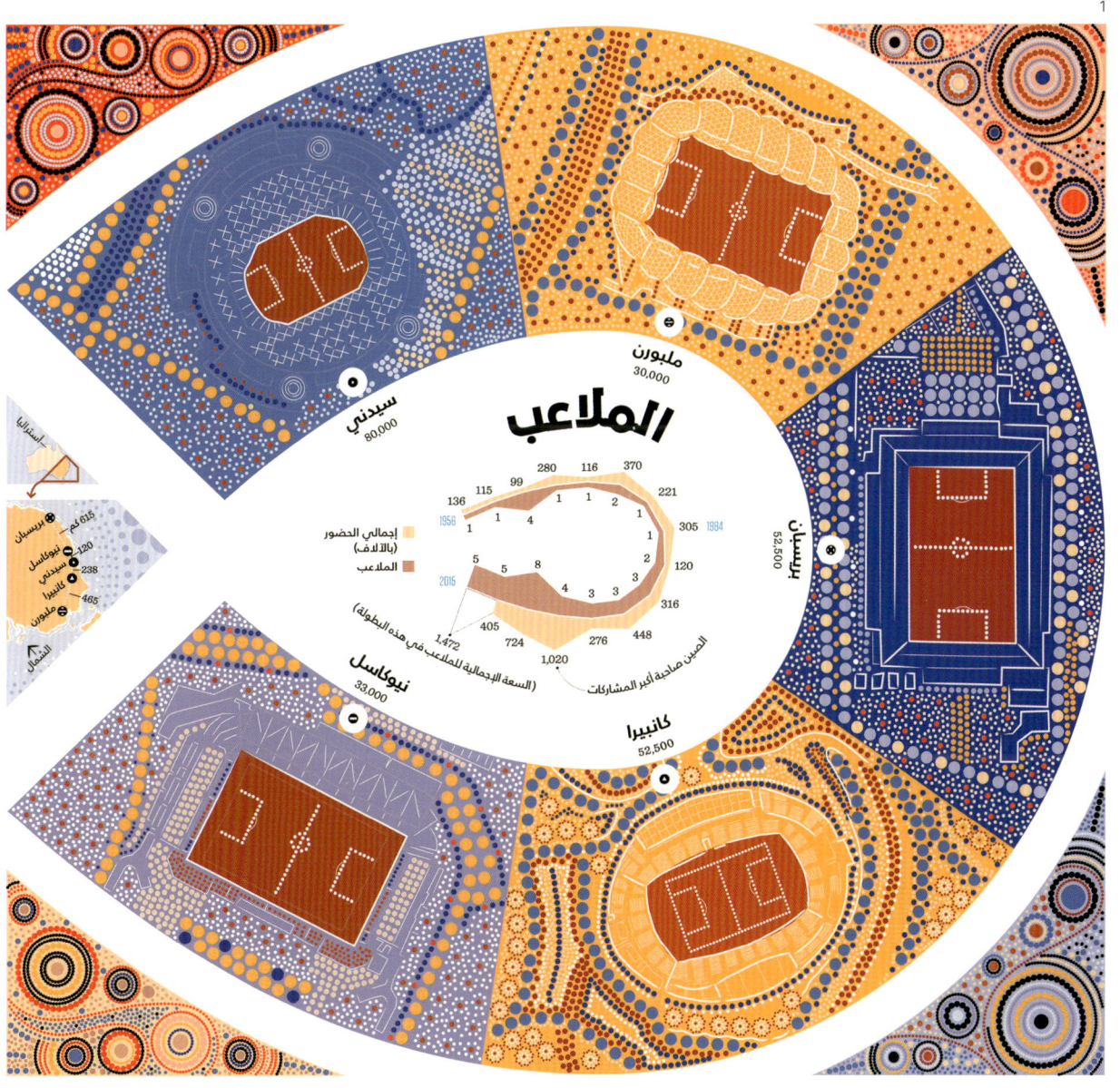

[2] Road to the Finals

Credit: Antonio Farach
Completion: 2015

This full-page infographic is showing all the matches played by the two teams that reached the grand final match of the Sultan Qaboos Cup 2014–15. The reader can follow the data backwards from the final (the top) or can start from the bottom. The flowing paths for both clubs are highlighted in blue and green. Such lines connect match scoreboards represented by black bubbles with the number of goals scored by each club. The graphic also includes instructions on how to read the graphic and secondary statistical charts related to the cup timelines for both teams (bottom right), most powerful clubs, tournament goal scorers, total goals, and scoreboards.

---

[3] Gulf Cup 21 Match Analysis

Credits: Antonio Farach (concept, graphics, art direction), Jay Cedro (graphics), Isidore Vic Carloman (graphics)
Completion: 2013

Nine hot-news infographics were published during the Gulf Cup 2013, in which there was a display of all passes executed in each match of the tournament. A typical tournament match day had two matches, so the designers published one full-page infographic with the passes analysis of the two matches. The layout is divided into two: the first match at the top and the second at the bottom. Each match has four diagrams, one for each 45-minute time period of each team's performance. Such diagrams are basically the fields in which the passes given were plotted in blue if they were successful and in red if they were not. The goals are represented in black. Each field is accompanied by lateral and longitudinal charts that summarize the total passes in order to know on which side of the field the team played most. The designers recorded the matches in video first, and after a 45-minute period finished, four designers plotted each given pass by watching the recorded video several times. One full page with the analysis of two matches was produced in about seven hours and delivered as hot news to appear in the newspaper the next day.

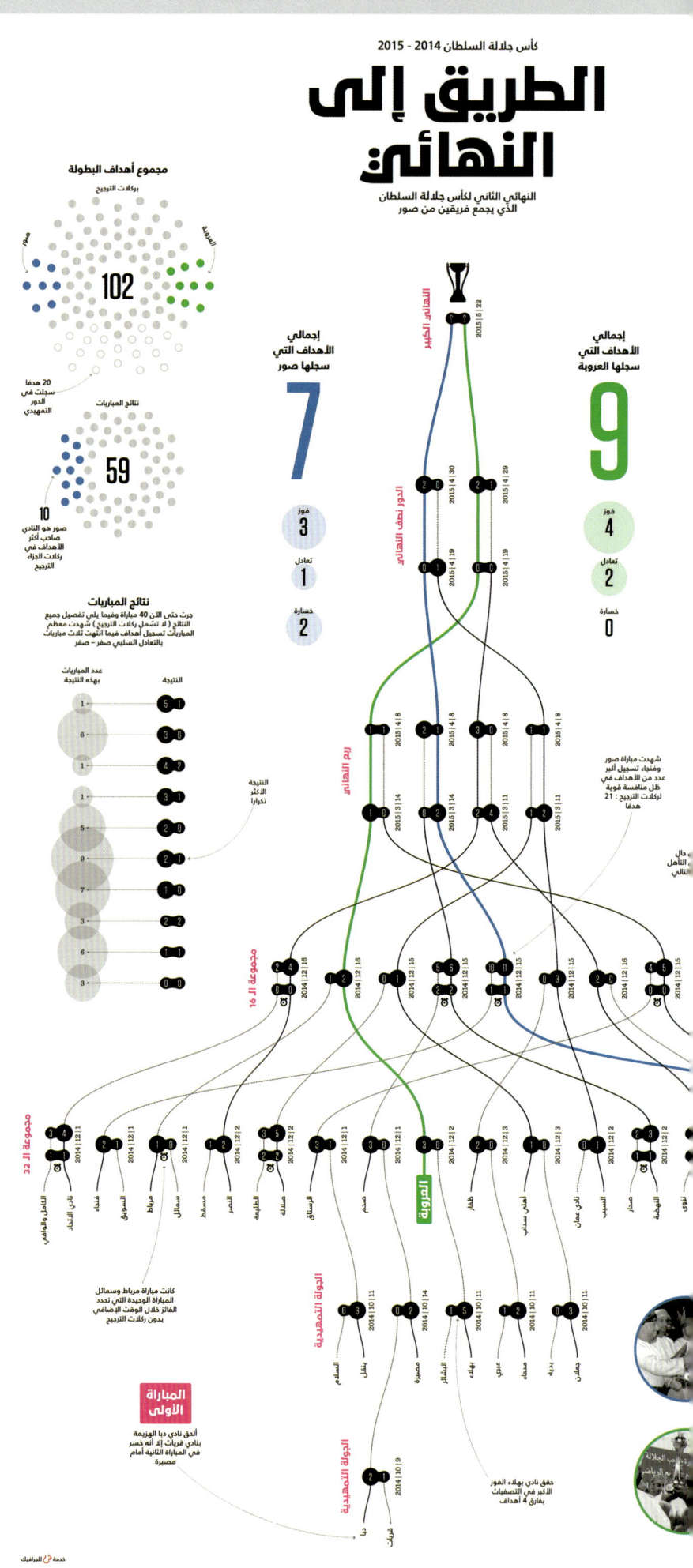

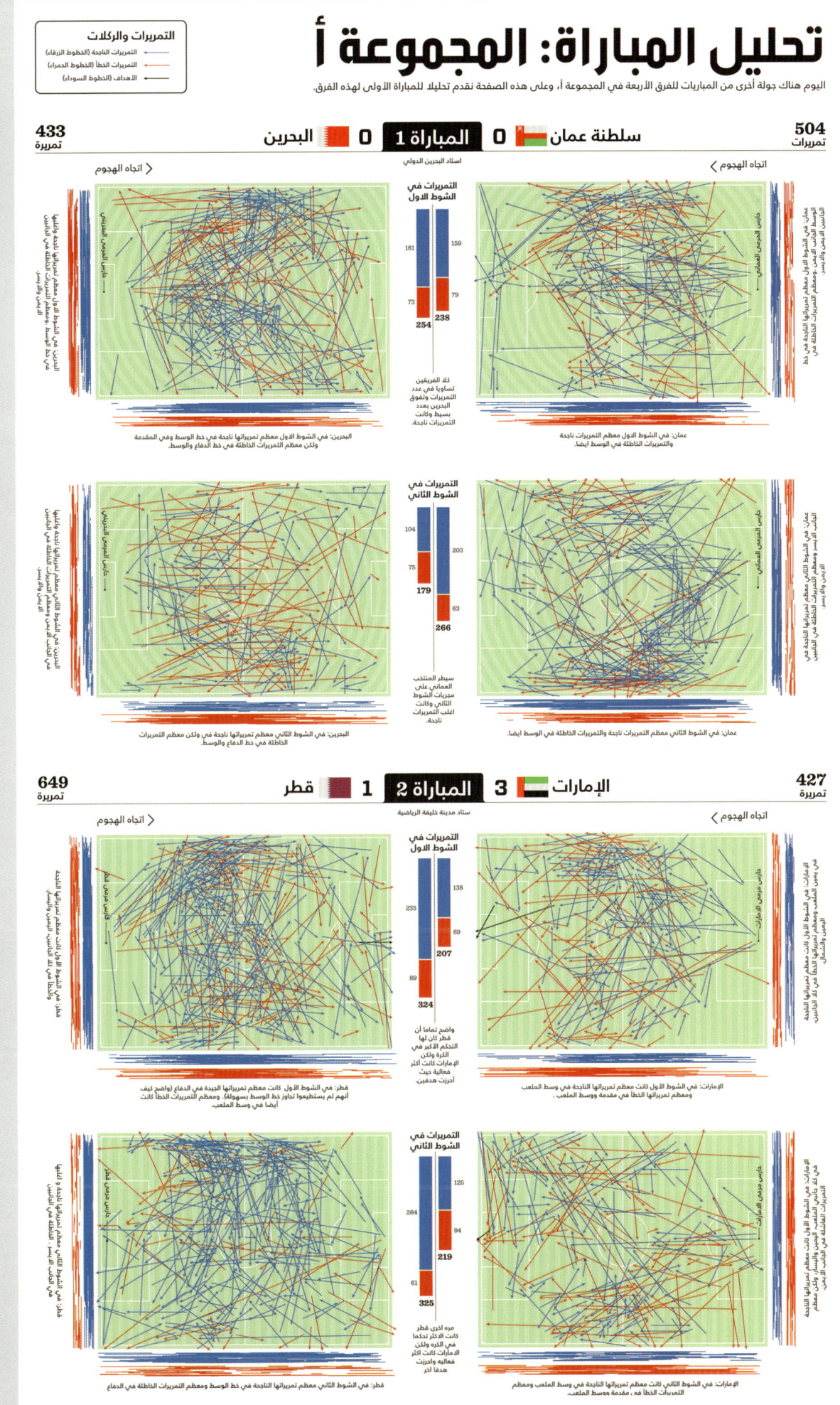

Artur Galocha

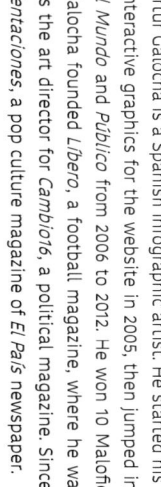

Artur Galocha is a Spanish infographic artist. He started his infographic artist career at *El Mundo* doing interactive graphics for the website in 2005, then jumped into paper and worked for *El Correo Gallego*, *El Mundo* and *Público* from 2006 to 2012. He won 10 Malofiej medals at Público. When Público closed, Galocha founded *Líbero*, a football magazine, where he was the art director. In 2014, he started work as the art director for *Cambio16*, a political magazine. Since April 2016, he has been the art director of *Tentaciones*, a pop culture magazine of *El País* newspaper.

[Q] **What do you think about data visualization/infographics?**

[A] I think it's a very useful tool to tell stories. It's the best way to explain things with large amounts of data or to explain processes.

[Q] **What kind of design methods do you commonly use?**

[A] The most important thing in infographics is the data. So it's vital to get sources and verify them. Once I have the data, I organize it and start to play with it to see how I can communicate with the reader, and then look for patterns that explain events.

[Q] **What kind of design elements do you commonly use?**

[A] I use graphics, icons, illustrations, photos, and so on, but the essential thing is the data that you want to deal with. I commonly use graphics (pie charts, flow charts, bars, etc.) to show the data, but one of the most important design methods is to organize the data in the best way. For that, I think it's better to have a very solid grid to organize it and guide the reader through the infographic.

[Q] **Where are your works applied?**

[A] I used to work for newspapers and magazines mostly, but sometimes I did little pieces for websites and some infographics like maps or simple graphics for books.

[Q] **How do you turn boring and complex data into something interesting and understandable?**

[A] I think the most important thing is to look for patterns, to guide the reader through the infographic. You've got to have a thesis. If you just put some data or some graphics in the page, the reader will think, 'Well, I see all the data but I don't know what it means', so you have to explain what you want to tell.

When you work with large amounts of data it's necessary to organize the data to make it understandable. Albert Einstein said, 'If you are able to explain it to your grandmother, then you understood it'. So that's the goal, to make it understandable for everyone.

[Q] **What is your suggestion for beginners?**

[A] To spend time thinking and playing with data, working with the computer to handle the tools. Watch a lot of infographics and try to understand how the designer put it onto the page and why. Keep trying even when you fail. At last, try to work with good infographic artists.

[1] The History of the World Cup

Credits: Diego Quijano, Artur Galocha
Completion: 2014

This infographic shows stats and differences between the first World Cup and the latest one. The ball, the trophy, the boots, and the shirts are being compared. There's also a graphic with all the finals and champions, all the goals, and the evolution of tactics during the history.

BRASILE 2014 SPECIALE

LA STORIA
Caccia al Brasile

Spagna leader nel ranking. Ma solo l'Italia può raggiungere i cinque volte campioni

di Ettore Intorcia

L'ultimo aggiornamento del ranking Fifa, sfornato proprio ieri, fotografa le gerarchie del calcio post-moderno: prima la Spagna, davanti alla Germania e al Brasile, con l'Italia solo nona. Ma la storia del mondiale racconta altro: c'è un tabellone che parla chiaro, nessuno come i padroni di casa verdeoro e una sola squadra, la nostra, che può agganciarli: *pentacampeon*, ecco l'obiettivo a cui solo l'Italia può puntare. E diventarlo lì, in casa loro...

FATTORE CAMPO. C'è qualcosa che ci accomuna, sebbene le nostre affinità, lì in Sudamerica, siano più concentrate al di là del confine, in Argentina. C'è qualcosa che ci accomuna, il sogno sfumato, che poi diventa incubo, di vincere il mondiale in casa. L'abbiamo provato, quel pugno allo stomaco, ventiquattro anni fa, cadendo al ritmo del tango di Maradona sotto il colpo di testa di Caniggia e sotto i colpi della solita sfiga che ai rigori, tendenzialmente, ha scelto (quasi) sempre di baciare noi.

Il Brasile era convinto di vincerlo in casa il suo primo mondiale nel 1950. D'altra parte, era andata quasi sempre così: l'Uruguay l'aveva conquistata per primo la Coppa Rimet, perché per primo aveva ospitato il mondiale. E poi era toccato a noi dare una dimostrazione di forza sul rettangolo verde: il trionfo azzurro nel '34 mentre tutto il Paese vestiva con la camicia nera. Fatta la regola, trovata l'eccezione: l'Italia vince in Francia (per rifarsi, dovrà organizzare il torneo del '98) e dopo la guerra anche il Brasile si arrende in casa, sul più bello, in finale con l'Uruguay: psicodramma di una nazione.

LE ALTRE. La storia del mondiale, che è evoluzione tecnica, tattica e tecnologica di uno sport, s'incrocia con la Storia, quella vera. La Germania che ci insegue a quota 3 è ancora quella Ovest: nel '90, ultima vittoria, il Muro era già crollato ma l'unità politica (e sportiva) doveva ancora realizzarsi. E l'Argentina, due successi, ha trionfato l'ultima volta nel 1986: più che la Germania sconfisse l'Inghilterra chiudendo vecchie ferite di una guerra freschissima.

RIPRODUZIONE RISERVATA

URUGUAY 1930

L'attrezzatura
La struttura della palla e il cattivo stato dei campi trasformano la divisa in qualcosa di più adatto per il lavoro che per lo sport.

- MAGLIA MOLTO LARGA
- CINTURA
- PANTALONI AL GINOCCHIO
- PUNTA RINFORZATA
- SEI TACCHETTI DI CUOIO
- PARASTINCHI

JOSÉ NASAZZI — Capitano dell'Uruguay

Il pallone
Nella finale del primo Mondiale, si giocò la prima parte con il pallone uruguaiano e la seconda con il pallone argentino.
- CAMERA D'ARIA DI GOMMA
- 10 STRISCE DI CUOIO (x2, x8)

Il trofeo
Coppa Jules Rimet
Raffigura la vittoria alata (Nike) che regge una coppa decagonale. Il Brasile la conquistò definitivamente nel 1970. Fu rubata il 19 dicembre 1983.
- ARGENTO "STERLING" PLACCATO ORO
- PIEDISTALLO DI MARMO
- 35 CM, 3,8 KG
- 1930 → 1970

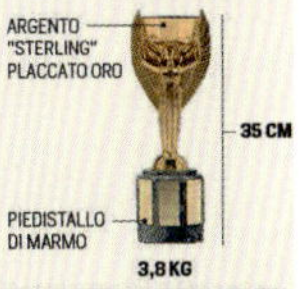

Il sistema di qualificazione
Hanno partecipato 13 delle 16 squadre invitate, così ottavi e quarti sono stati adattati per determinare una fase a gironi.
- GRUPPO A, B, C, D

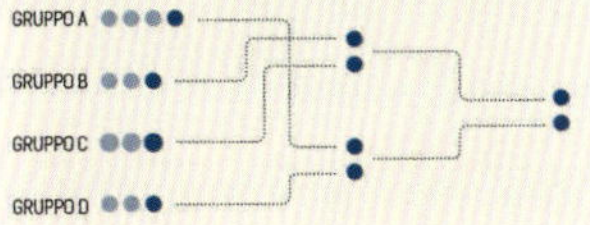

TUTTI I FINALISTI

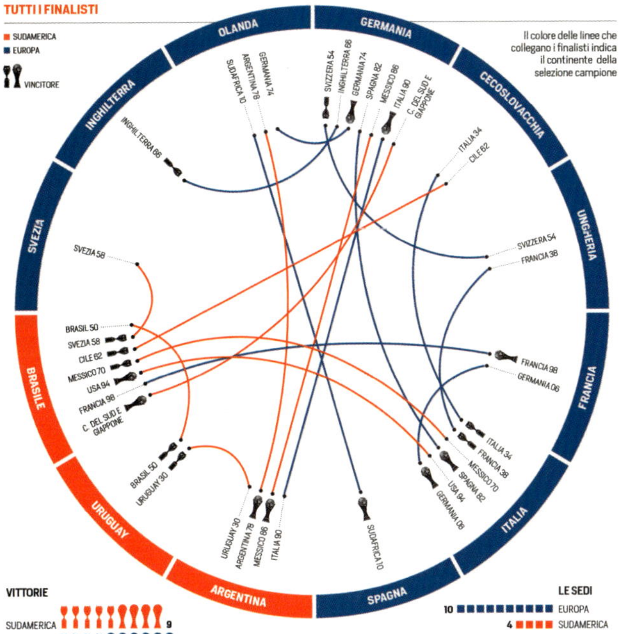

- SUDAMERICA
- EUROPA
- VINCITORE

Il colore delle linee che collegano i finalisti indica il continente della selezione campione.

VITTORIE
- SUDAMERICA: 9
- EUROPA: 10

LE SEDI
- 10 EUROPA
- 4 SUDAMERICA
- 3 NORDAMERICA
- 1 ASIA
- 1 AFRICA

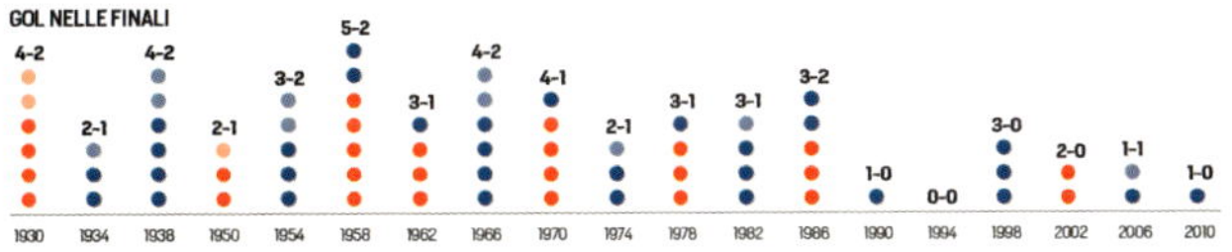

GOL NELLE FINALI
1930	1934	1938	1950	1954	1958	1962	1966	1970	1974	1978	1982	1986	1990	1994	1998	2002	2006	2010
4-2	4-2	4-2		3-2	5-2	3-1	4-2	4-1	2-1	3-1	3-1	3-2	1-0	0-0	3-0	2-0	1-1	1-0
2-1		2-1	2-1															

BRASILE 2014

L'attrezzatura
Realizzati con le più evolute tecnologie, i materiali in dotazione oggi si adattano perfettamente ai movimenti dei giocatori. Le scarpe Nike Magista sono la novità in questo Mondiale.

- TESSUTO SINTETICO
- POLIESTERE E LYCRA
- LA SCARPA HA UN CALZINO INCORPORATO
- PARASTINCHI IN CARBONIO

ANDREA PIRLO — Regista dell'Italia

Il pallone
A partire dal 1970 la FIFA sottomette il pallone a varie prove. Il Brazuca è il 12º pallone Adidas che si utilizza ai Mondiali.
- GOMMA SINTETICA
- RINFORZO
- GOMMAPIUMA
- 6 PARTI DI POLIURETANO (x6)

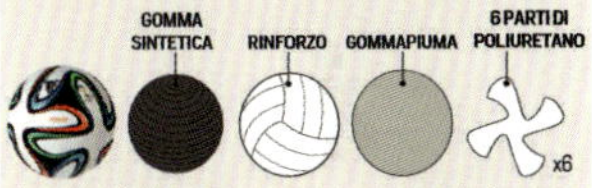

Il trofeo
Coppa del Mondo FIFA
Disegnata dall'orafo e scultore italiano Silvio Gazzaniga rappresenta due atleti che esultando sorreggono il mondo. I campioni in carica tengono il trofeo quattro anni, poi ricevono una replica.
- ORO
- MALACHITE
- 36,8 CM, 5,0 KG
- 1974 → 2014

Il sistema di qualificazione
Partecipano 32 squadre divise in otto gironi. Le prime due si qualificano per gli ottavi, quindi eliminazione diretta.
- GRUPPO A, B, C, D, E, F, G, H

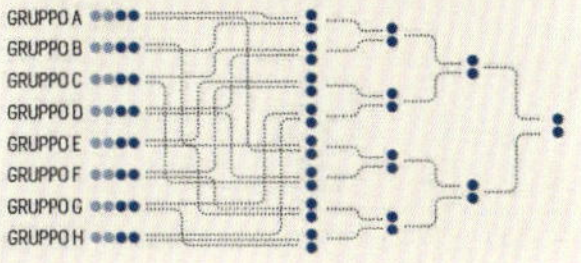

NUMERO DI SPETTATORI PER MONDIALE NEGLI STADI

Il calcio ha conquistato popolarità nel XX secolo: ci furono oltre mezzo milione di spettatori nel primo Mondiale, si è arrivati a superare i tre milioni nel 1994 e nelle ultime due edizioni.

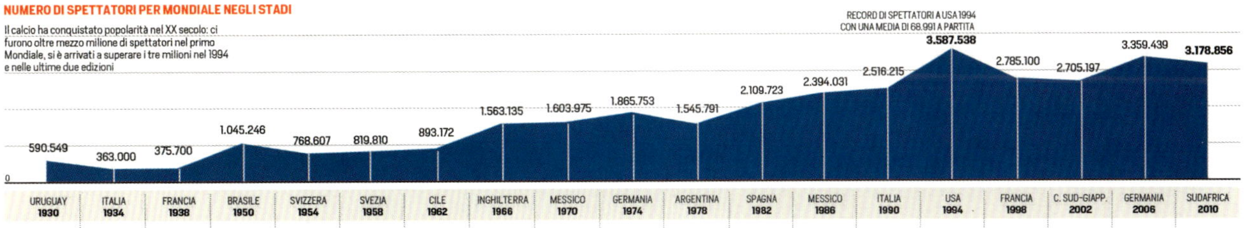

RECORD DI SPETTATORI A USA 1994 CON UNA MEDIA DI 68.991 A PARTITA

Mondiale	Spettatori
URUGUAY 1930	590.549
ITALIA 1934	363.000
FRANCIA 1938	375.700
BRASILE 1950	1.045.246
SVIZZERA 1954	768.607
SVEZIA 1958	819.810
CILE 1962	893.172
INGHILTERRA 1966	1.563.135
MESSICO 1970	1.603.975
GERMANIA 1974	1.865.753
ARGENTINA 1978	1.545.791
SPAGNA 1982	2.109.723
MESSICO 1986	2.394.031
ITALIA 1990	2.516.215
USA 1994	3.587.538
FRANCIA 1998	2.785.100
C. SUD-GIAPP. 2002	2.705.197
GERMANIA 2006	3.359.439
SUDAFRICA 2010	3.178.856

PARTITE E GOL

Mondiale	Partite	Gol
URUGUAY 1930	18	70
ITALIA 1934	17	70
FRANCIA 1938	18	84
BRASILE 1950	22	88
SVIZZERA 1954	26	140
SVEZIA 1958	35	126
CILE 1962	32	89
INGHILTERRA 1966	32	89
MESSICO 1970	32	95
GERMANIA 1974	38	97
ARGENTINA 1978	38	102
SPAGNA 1982	52	146
MESSICO 1986	52	132
ITALIA 1990	52	115
USA 1994	52	141
FRANCIA 1998	64	171
C. SUD-GIAPP. 2002	64	161
GERMANIA 2006	64	147
SUDAFRICA 2010	64	145

NEL 1954 SI SEGNARONO QUASI TANTI GOL COME NEL 2010 IN MENO DELLA METÀ DELLE PARTITE
VARIAZIONI CONTINUE NEL NUMERO DELLE PARTITE: 32 — 38 — 52 — 64

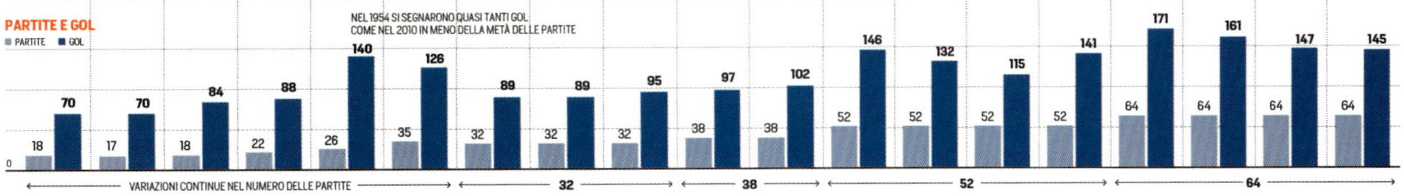

L'EVOLUZIONE DELLA TATTICA

1930. Un sistema offensivo
L'Uruguay conquistò la prima coppa con un sistema di gioco del tutto offensivo, molto simile a quelli in voga alla fine del XIX secolo.

1950. Un gioco più equilibrato
Con l'introduzione del fuorigioco, fu necessario rendere i reparti più equilibrati: si arrivò a un 3-2-2-3 che disegnava sul campo uno schema MW.

1954. Le modifiche ungheresi
Una tattica simile la adottata dall'Ungheria che nel 1954 raggiunse la finale. La modifica principale fu rafforzare il centrocampo a scapito di un attaccante.

1962. Il Catenaccio
Il sistema difensivo sviluppato soprattutto in Italia negli Anni Sessanta: quattro difensori marcano a uomo e un libero si muove dietro di loro.

1966. Appare il 4-4-2
I centrocampisti aiutano sia in attacco sia in difesa: in fase difensiva si crea una prima barriera, in fase di attacco il gioco si sviluppa maggiormente sulle fasce.

1974. L'arancia meccanica
Sviluppato dall'Ajax di Michels e adottato dalla Nazionale olandese, è il gioco totale: i giocatori si muovono per tutto il campo cambiando posizione di continuo.

1998. Il calcio moderno
La Francia vince il Mondiale del 1998 giocando senza esterni alti: i due terzini si muovono lungo tutta la fascia, il centrocampisti sono molto creativi e offensivi.

2010. Il tiki-taka
È il sistema sviluppato dal Barcellona e riproposto in Nazionale: un elevatissimo possesso di palla in un gioco che spesso prescinde da un attaccante puro.

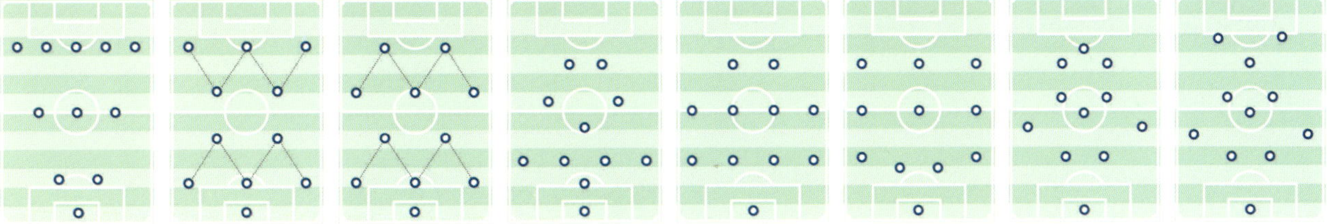

FONTE: FIFA, ADIDAS E 'INVERTING THE PYRAMID' DI JONATHAN WILSON
ARTUR GALOCHA

VENERDÌ 11 LUGLIO 2014 — **BRASILE 2014** — **VERSO LA FINALE** — *CORRIERE DELLO SPORT STADIO*

MÜLLER-MESSI
Come quelle sfide Matthäus-Diego

Lothar e "il pibe" gli ultimi a vincere la Coppa per Germania e Argentina; ora a chi tocca?

di Furio Zara
INVIATO A SAN PAOLO

Messi è un uomo che gioca da dio. Müller è una squadra che si è fatta uomo. La differenza è questa. E non è sottile. Del resto: è tutto nel solco della tradizione di Argentina e Germania. Riferimenti storici: Maradona, Matthäus. Gli ultimi due ad alzare la coppa del mondo per le rispettive nazionali. Diego nel 1986 all'Azteca di Città del Messico, Lothar nel 1990 all'Olimpico di Roma. Maradona & Messi: genio puro concentrato. Matthäus & Müller: il Bignami di una squadra riassunto in un solo giocatore.

L'ARGENTINO. Messi vive di luce propria, è baciato dal dio del pallone, gioca in un mondo suo. Quando fa il Messi sta due metri sopra il cielo, quando non lo sfuma e non incide: può trascinare l'Argentina (è successo nella fase a gironi), o può lasciarsela scivolare accanto, come è successo l'altra sera all'Itaquerao. Romero parava i rigori, l'Albiceleste faceva festa, e Messi conquistava la finale a sua insaputa. E' stato calcolato che corre di più. Ma ha smesso di segnare. Ultimo gol alla Nigeria, fase a gironi. Svizzera, Belgio, Olanda: a secco. Da tre partite. Sono 375' senza gol, un'eternità. La Pulce ha postato la propria felicità su Instagram dopo la conquista della finale. Stava al doping, niente zona mista. *«Sono orgoglioso di far parte di questa squadra. Tutta l'Argentina deve essere felice. Ora vogliamo la coppa del mondo».* Ha dedicato la vittoria ad un amico, giornalista, si chiamava Jorge «Topo» Lopez, 38 anni, è morto l'altra sera, prima della semifinale, in un incidente d'auto. Si conoscevano dal 2005.

IL TEDESCO. Di Müller non si può neppure dire che sia un uomo squadra. La squadra già c'è, eccome. Come detto: lui è un'intera squadra che si è fatta uomo. Sa fare tutto. Non ha un ruolo preciso. Ne ha molti. Diversifica. Löw gli chiede di fare il centravanti? Centravanti sia. Ma a modo suo. Löw decide che davanti è meglio piazzare Klose? Müller si sposta, un po' più in là, nel 3+1 offensivo dei tedeschi. Ma rimane sempre al centro del gioco. E' come se la Germania avesse bisogno di lui. I numeri che ha addosso sono impressionanti. L'età, innanzitutto: 24 anni. Con la Germania, 22 reti in 54 gare. Ai Mondiali ha segnato già 10 gol in 11 partite. Ronaldo, il Fenomeno, ha detto: *«Batterà ogni record, ha ancora un paio di Mondiali a disposizione».* E' stato capocannoniere quattro anni fa in Sudafrica con 6 gol. Qualche mese prima, a marzo, durante un'amichevole tra Germania e Argentina, Maradona - allora ct dell'Albiceleste - l'aveva scambiato per un raccattapalle. *«Toglietemi di torno il ragazzo»*, aveva intimato durante la conferenza stampa. I cinque gol brasiliani sono tutti pesantissimi: i tre che hanno schiantato il Portogallo, il gol anti-biscotto agli Usa (1-0, decisivo), il primo gol nella mattanza contro il Brasile. Nei momenti che contano, Müller c'è. Se Messi è speciale, Müller è normale. Se Messi è unico e brilla della sua unicità; Müller è molte cose insieme e brilla della luce di questa Germania.

©RIPRODUZIONE RISERVATA

FONTE: FIFA — DIEGO QUIANO E ARTUR GALOCHA

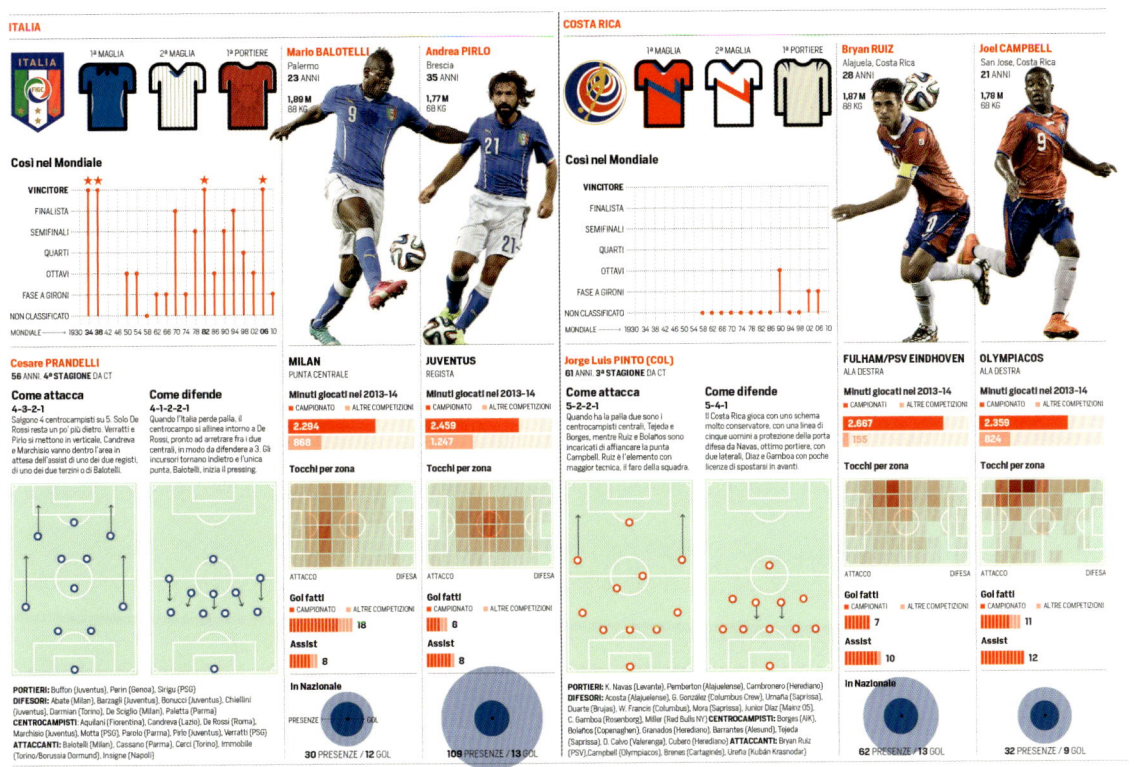

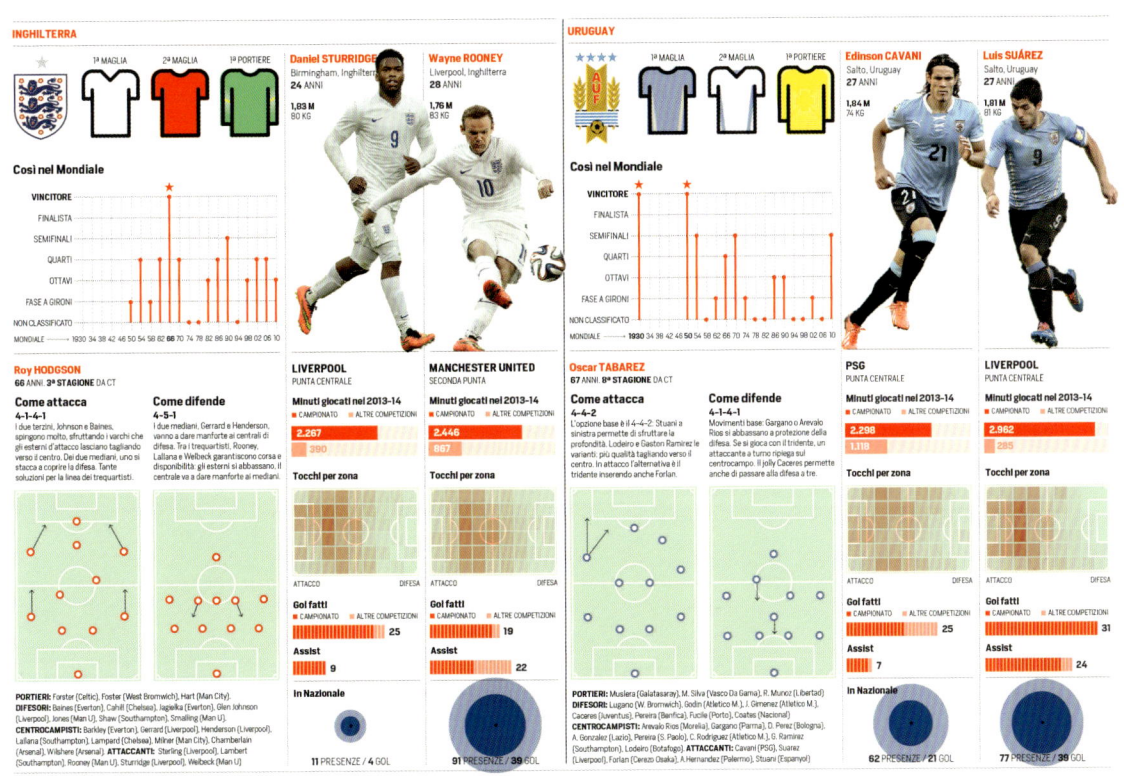

[2] Our Group

Credits: Diego Quijano, Artur Galocha
Completion: 2014

This is another infographic about the World Cup 2014 published in *Corriere dello Sport* (Italy). This one shows the teams that played against Italy in the first round of the World Cup (Costa Rica, England, and Uruguay), how they played, and how they moved in the field, as well as their star players.

[3–4] Germany and Argentina in the World Cups

Credit: Artur Galocha
Completion: 2014

This work analyzed all the matches between Germany and Argentina, the two teams that reached the World Cup final in Brazil in 2014. The first part of the infographic shows what round each national team reached in previous World Cups, then analyzes the top scorers of each team, the goals made, and the goals against in every World Cup, paying special attention to the matches the two teams played against each other in previous World Cups.

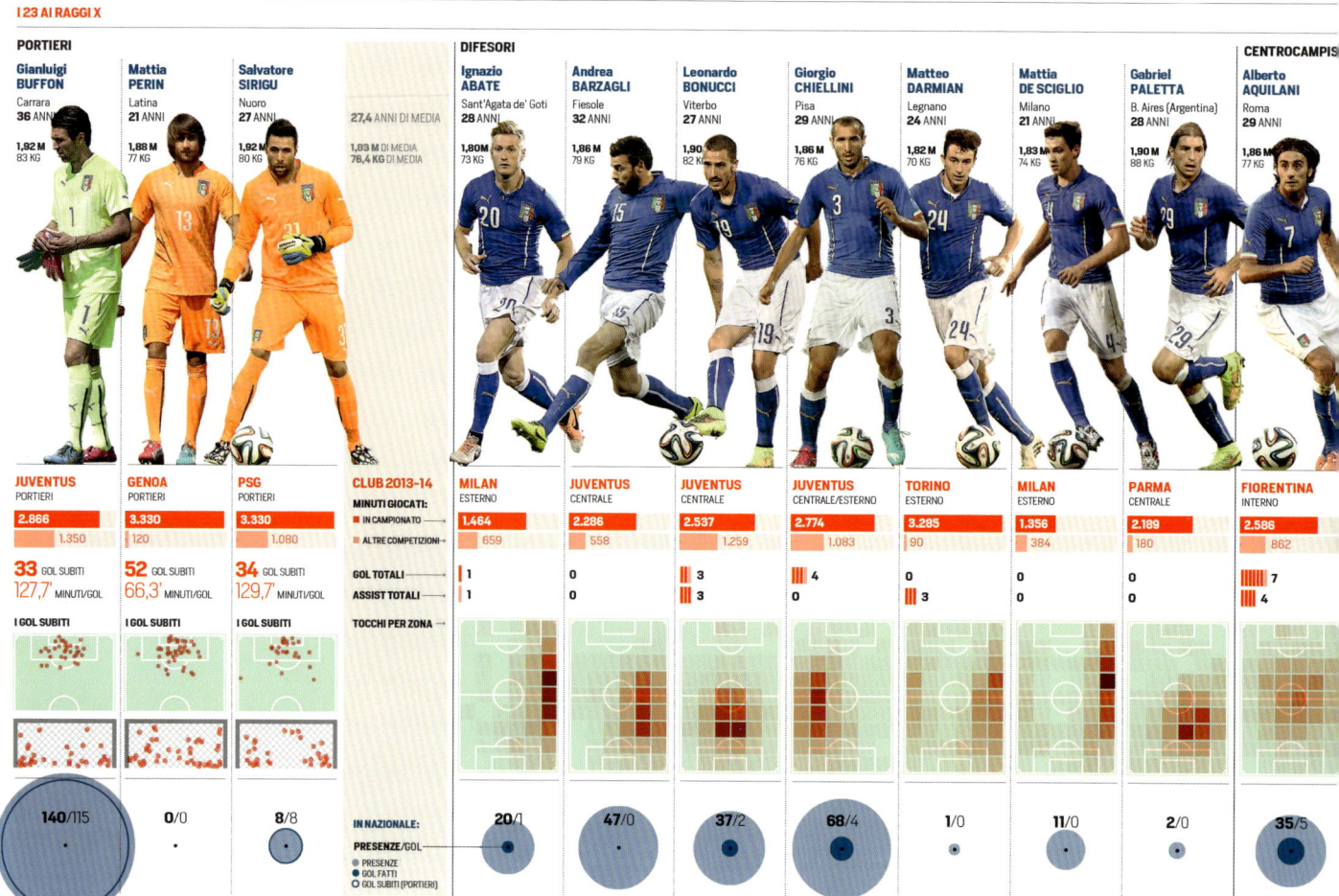

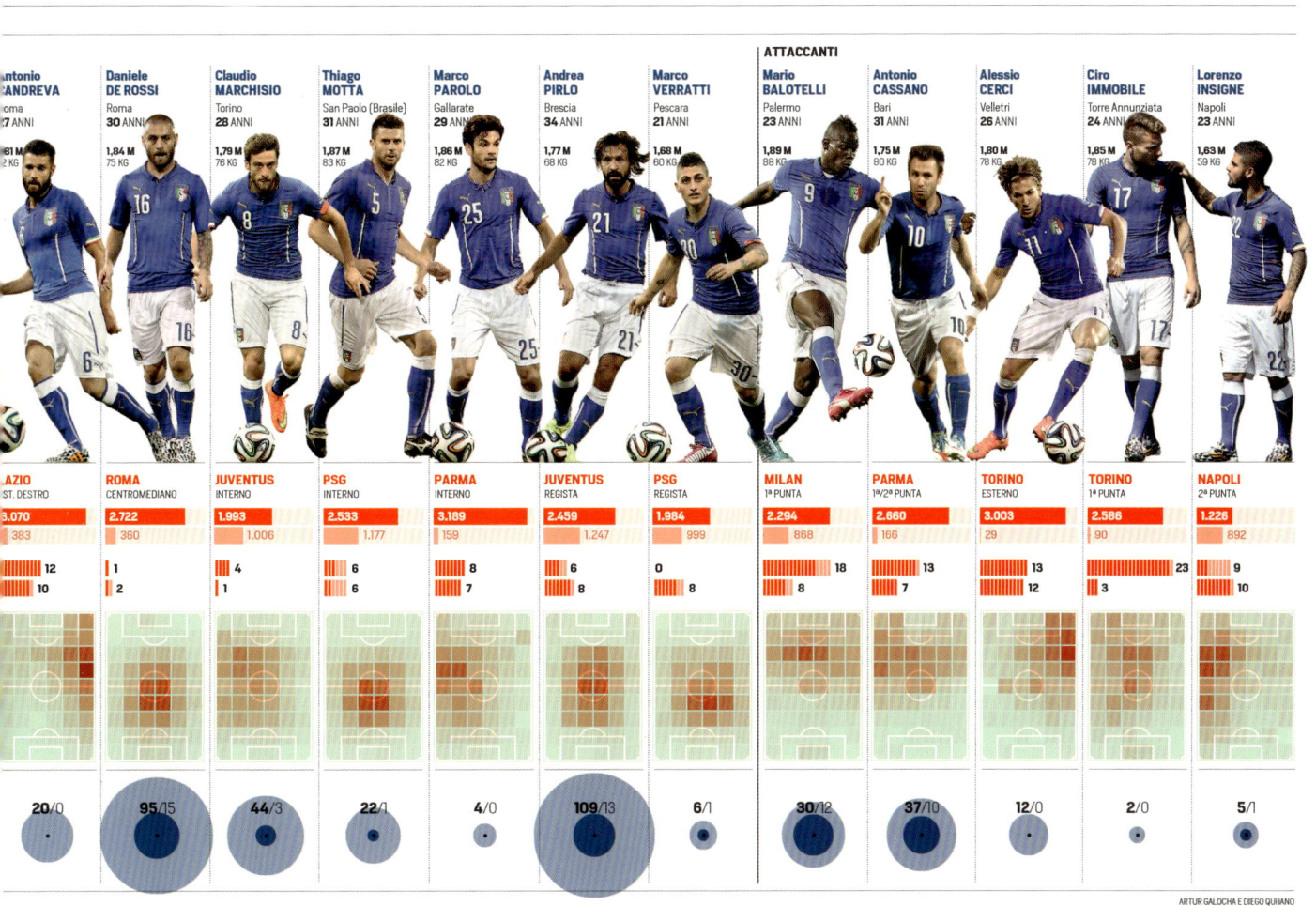

[5] The Blue Team

Credits: Diego Quijano, Artur Galocha
Completion: 2014

A week before the World Cup 2014, the designers started to publish an infographic everyday in *Corriere dello Sport* (Italy). This one shows the 23 players of the Italian national team with the statistics of the team and each player. The infographic shows the minutes played in that season, goals, assists, and the areas in the field where each player touched the ball.

Manuela Garreton

[Q] What do you think about data visualization/infographics?

[A] I understand data visualization as a visual interface that allows us to understand, and use information to acquire new knowledge. I think it is an area that has grown considerably in recent years due to the amount of data we are generating in the most diverse areas, partly because of the different technologies we have created that allow us to capture and store information. However, we know that the data itself does not have a meaning, since in a segregated and fragmented way it cannot complete a message, and therefore it is necessary to determine and evidence connections between data in order to get significant information. Such connections can be achieved by mapping discrete data into visual representations. Accordingly, I believe that visualizing data is a way to find meaning in the amount of information we generate about ourselves and the societies in which we live. In other words, it is a way of finding visual patterns that allow us to interpret the world around us.

On the other hand, in personal terms, my work in this area has allowed me to participate in interdisciplinary and collaborative projects in such diverse areas as plant biology, sociology, urbanism, and neuroscience, and this is the aspect that most excites and encourages me in what I do. Data visualization is an area that is currently being developed by different disciplines (journalism, science, programming, design, etc.) through different approaches and tools. The design approach is emphasizing the construction of visual information for the communication of a message to a user. And finally, from my own experience, I see design as a discipline capable of combining different areas of knowledge, which allows the development of innovative projects that hardly subscribe to a particular area.

[Q] What kind of design methods do you commonly use?

[A] Usually, when designing a data visualization, I spend a lot of time understanding the data, where it comes from, what its importance is, why a user would be interested in understanding and using it. At this point, I specify what the objectives are that the visualization must fulfill to finally be able to define the most suitable visual representations. For this, I always develop concepts that take shape through visual inspiration that could come from different areas such as science, music, art, and design. With these initial visual ideas, I begin to draw the first representations, and after a few iterations, I begin to develop them interactively.

Manuela Garreton is an information designer at the crossroads of data visualization, technology, and aesthetics. She develops interdisciplinary and collaborative projects as an assistant professor at Pontificia Universidad Católica de Chile, where she also teaches design and data visualization. She has a background in biology and design (Pontificia Universidad Católica de Chile) and a Master at the Interactive Telecommunication Program (ITP), New York University. She focuses her practice and research on visually representing relevant and meaningful data to make it available, understandable, and engaging.

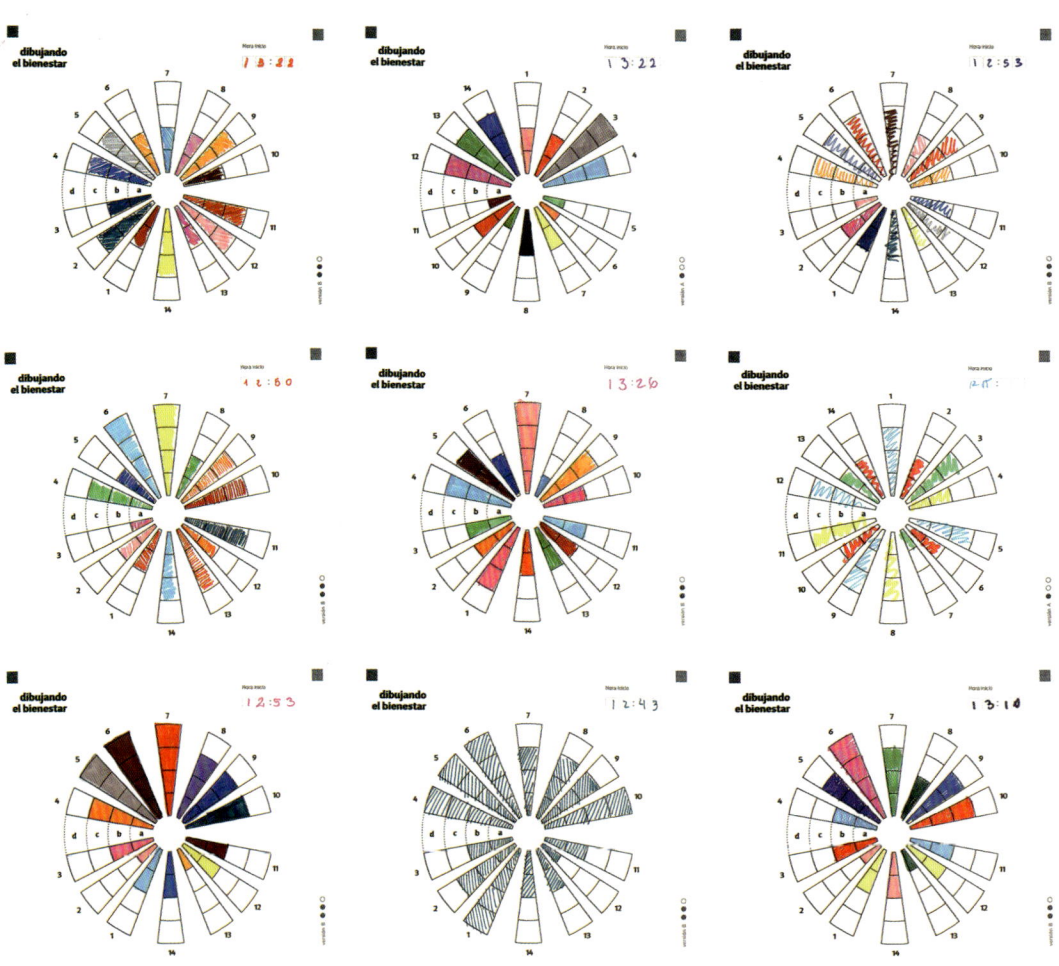

1

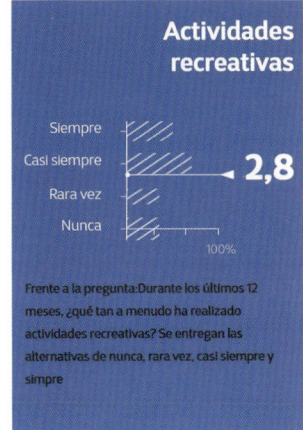
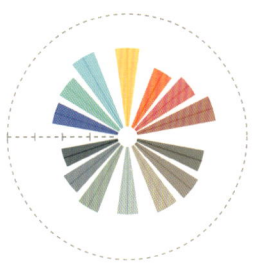

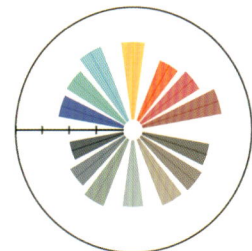

[1–3] Drawing Well-being

Credits: Manuela Garreton, Esteban Calvo
Completion: 2015
Interactive link: www.dibujandoelbienestar.cl/encuestas

This project aims to explore, through an interdisciplinary work, a new survey methodology that allows collecting, processing, and visualizing information about subjective well-being, transforming complex data into graphics that are easy to read and understand. The methodology consists of a survey built upon a set of questions and a radial graph used to color the answers, complemented with a technology that automates the processing and visualization of the information collected.

The project is based on a single radial graph that fulfills a double function: it is used to collect the data, and once it is completed it works as an easy way to interpret it. Each of the triangles comprising the graph corresponds to a question and is arranged in such a way that it is possible to interpret subjective well-being in terms of a context favorable or adverse and feelings of malaise or well-being.

[Q] **What kind of design elements do you commonly use?**

[A] I usually use basic geometric shapes, having in mind where the data set comes from and how I can represent it in a simple way. However, I take special care when choosing colors. In my experience, the color has been the key to transmitting information clearly, especially when I have multiple variables to represent.

[Q] **Where are your works applied?**

[A] I mainly develop interactive visualizations that have different purposes, some of which are designed for online media such as *The Revolving Door of Power*, that presents information on holders of high office in Chile, their connections with the private world, and their conflicts of interest. The purpose is to promote transparency, making the collected data widely accessible in visual format so that it can easily be consulted, read, and understood.

On the other hand, I have developed research projects where the way the data is gathered it is also an important part of the system. These projects approach data visualization as a tool to understand social phenomena, representing them in a way that can contribute to making decisions in complex realities. For instance, Drawing Well-being is a project designed to allow different organizations working with communities to actively participate in the process of gathering and managing data on their own subjective well-being.

[Q] **How do you turn boring and complex data into something interesting and understandable?**

[A] Understanding the data and enchanting myself with the stories that could be found in it. I think it does not have to do with the fact that data itself can be complex, but the problem is the lack of structure that allows us to interpret it. What I try to do is design the visual structure that will encourage us to find the meaning in data. In order to develop a visual representation of data, I try to find the story to be told and how to connect it visually and interactively in a non-linear narrative. I try to think a visualization in multiple layers of information that can draw the user's attention and then guide them to find and understand the information represented.

[Q] **What is your suggestion for beginners?**

[A] Enjoy what you do and dare yourself to experiment with the possibilities of the visual language while keeping in mind the contexts and needs of the people who will engage with the visualization.

4

[4] Map8

Credits: Manuela Garreton, Ciudad Emergente
Completion: 2014

Map8 visually represents the responses of almost 500 people who answered the question: 'Why did you go down to the river?' These responses were gathered during an event held in Santiago, Chile, in which citizens were invited to go across the river bed as a way of validating the feasibility of making it a public space for the city.

It is designed as a printed poster that allows at least two layers of reading. The first layer lets the viewer understand the number of answers that correspond to each type of response (represented by group and color), while in a second layer it is possible to read the original participants' responses.

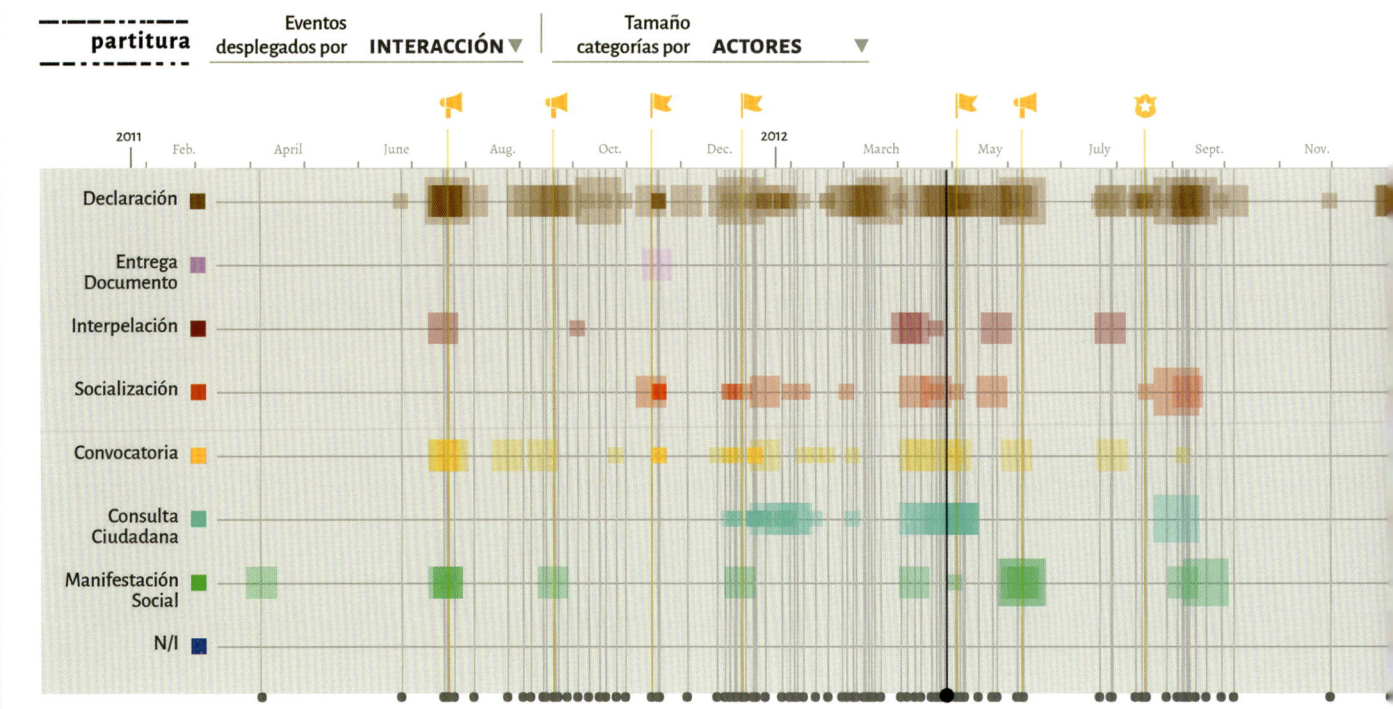

SoyCalama /
SoyChile.cl

CHARLA DE CALAMA PLUS: PLAN INTEGRAL PARA EL DESARROLLO DE LA CIUDAD

Sigue la campaña difusión Calama

Noticia sobre el Seminario "Ver para creer, Un Chile inclusivo es posible" donde participaron diversas mineras

+ Juan Pablo Schaeffer dio la charla "Asociatividad público - privado para el desarrollo de las ciudades"

7 Ago 2012

CONFLICTO N/I

ÁMBITO Infraestructura Urbana, Política

ACTORES Calama PLUS

ACTORES INVOLUCRADOS Gerente General de Asuntos Corporativos y Sustentabilidad Juan Pablo Schaeffer, Coordinador General Calama PLUS Gabriel Mendez, Gerente General de Medio Ambiente y Comunidad de Codelco Jorge Sanhueza

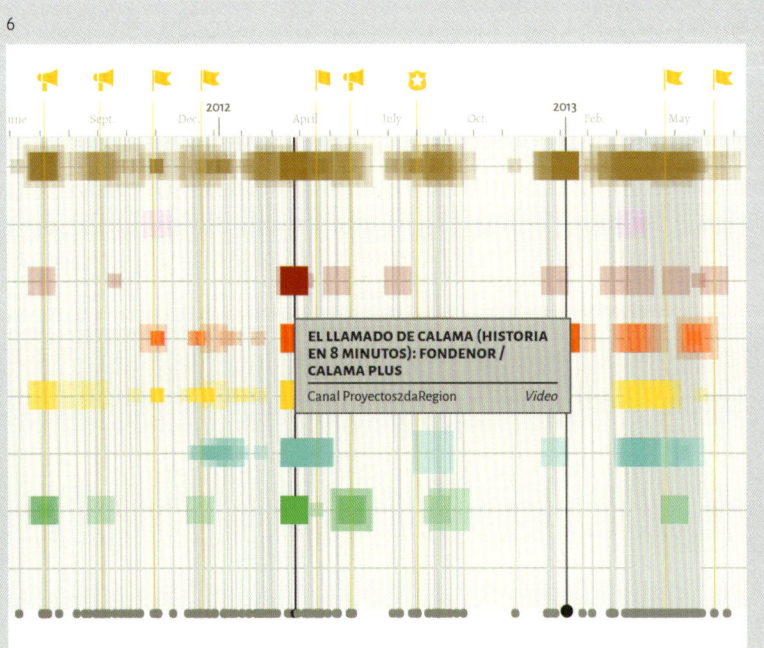

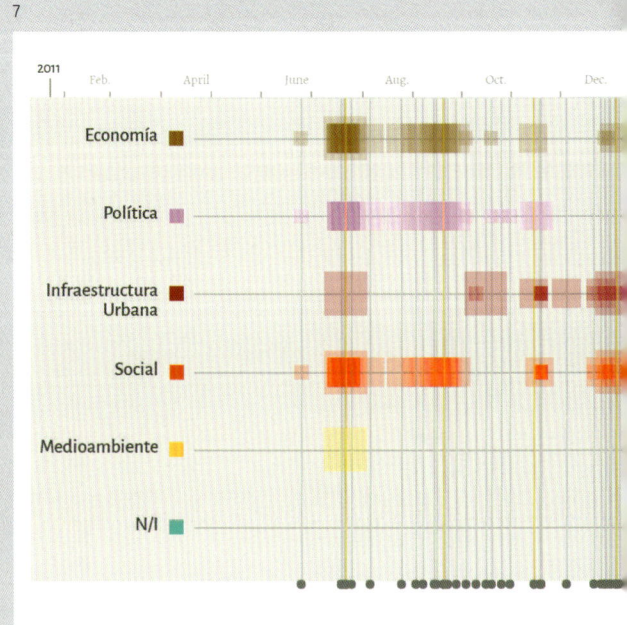

[5–7] Music Score

Credits: Manuela Garreton, Pablo Hermansen, Martin Tironi, Ricardo Vega
Completion: 2016
Interactive link: partitura.visualizacionycontroversias.cl/plus

This is an interactive platform that gathers, visualizes, and connects a series of printed and digital news about the impact of a participatory urban development plan for the city of Calama, Chile. This platform allows a temporary graphic navigation through the different actors, areas, conflicts, and interactions that come out of the urban project, managing to visualize their relationships, associations, concessions, and dissensions.

The graphic design of this project takes score as a visual and conceptual reference, since what is sought is to understand the dynamics and rhythms generated by facts that were collected in the news around the urban development of Calama.

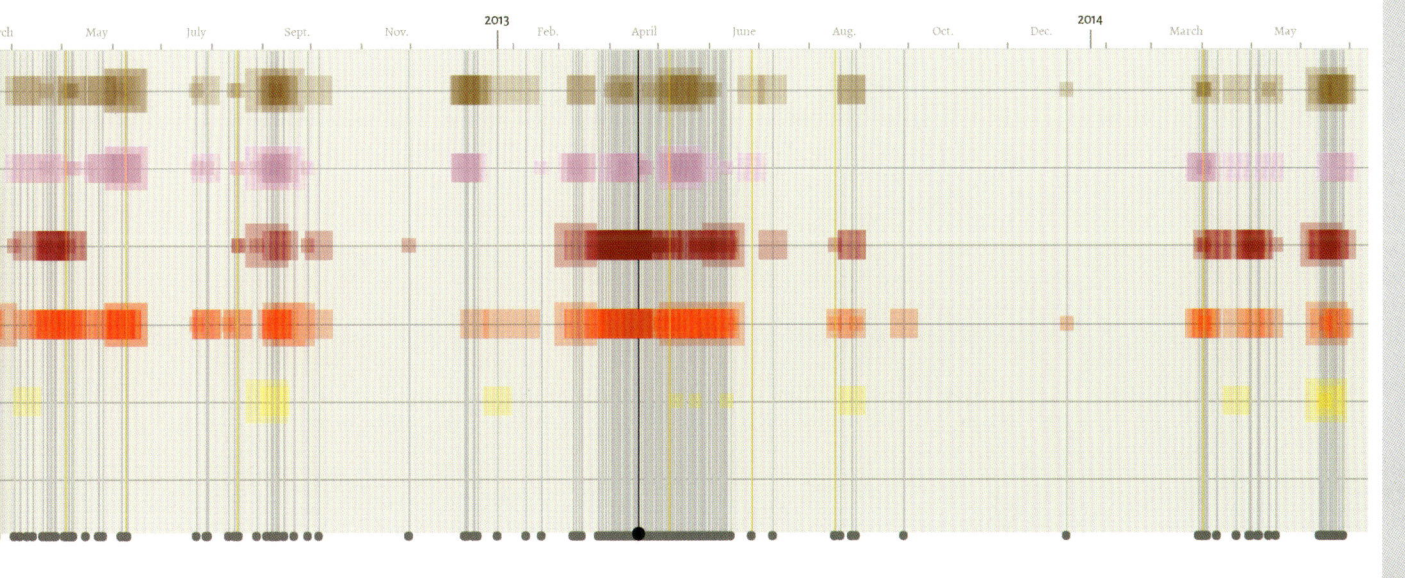

Stefania Guerra

Stefania Guerra is an information and graphic designer from Dissimo, a little village in the Italian Alps. She studied communication design at the polytechnic School of Design in Milan and she has been living and working there since graduation.

The author of the portrait is Glenn Harmon.

[Q] **What do you think about data visualization/infographics?**

[A] I think data visualization is a very powerful tool, because it allows people to understand very complex issues that otherwise are not so straightforward to understand only using words. That's one of the reasons why I choose to design data visualization with a social purpose.

[Q] **What kind of design methods do you commonly use?**

[A] The very first step I take is to understand the subject, and if necessary, reduce its complexity to a basic level of comprehension. This includes a first dive into the data, cleaning and analyzing it, and trying to catch the story it's hiding. Then it comes to the visual model, that's a matter of combining the right graph with the right style until I'm satisfied with the result.

[Q] **What kind of design elements do you commonly use?**

[A] I like basic shapes, flat design, quite minimalist, but every decision, from colors to shapes, has to make sense for the whole artifact, not just be pretty. I mostly use lines, circles, and squares combined with other types of graphs, like a basic histogram. In data visualization, the combination of forms is very useful when you have multiple sets of data to show.

[Q] **Where are your works applied?**

[A] My works are mainly used for editorial purposes, posters, books, and newspapers, but I'm following with interest the interactive scene and I can't wait to challenge myself in designing for websites or installations.

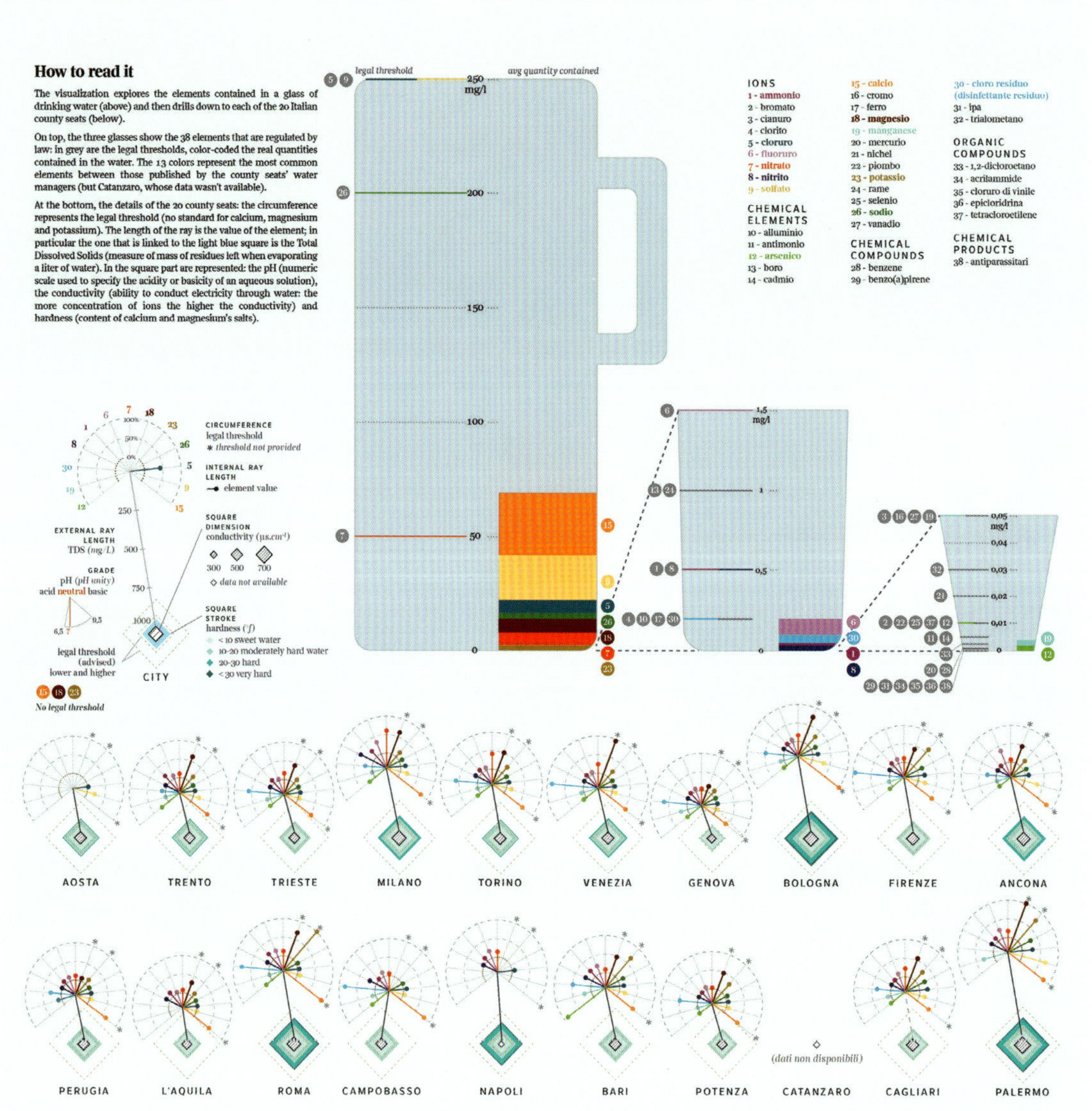

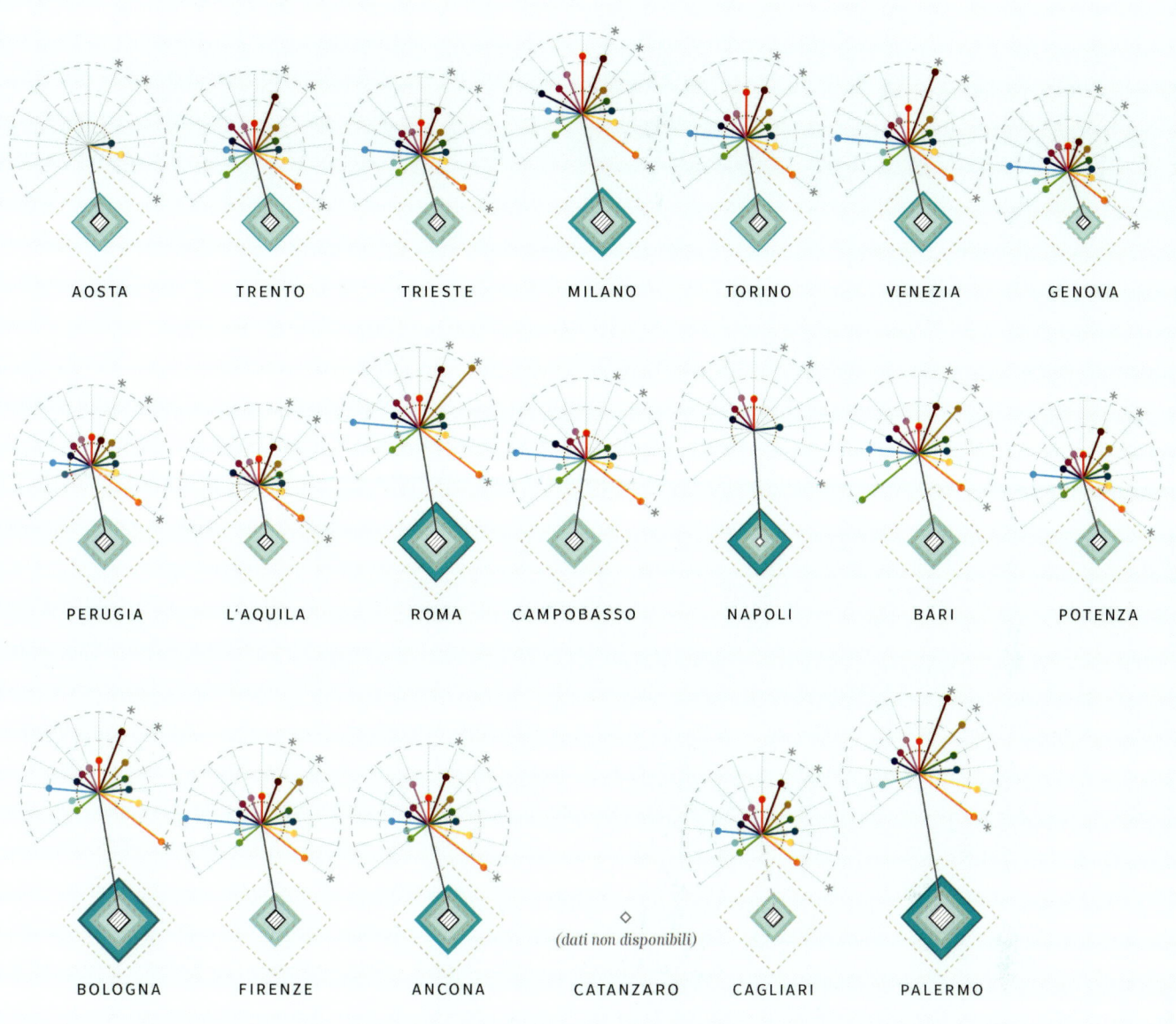

[1–2] What Is Drinking Water Made of, Besides Water

Credits: Stefania Guerra, Michela Lazzaroni
Completion: 2016

The main objective of the visualization was to promote the quality of drinking water, since Italians are one of the top consumers of bottled water. The visualization explores the elements contained in a glass of drinking water (above) and then drills down to each of the 20 Italian county seats (below).

On top, the three glasses show the 38 elements that are regulated by law: in grey are the legal thresholds, color coded are the real quantities contained in the water. The 13 colors represent the most common elements among those published by the county seats' water managers (excluding Catanzaro, whose data wasn't available).

At the bottom are the details of the 20 county seats. The circumference represents the legal threshold (no standard for calcium, magnesium, or potassium). The length of the ray is the value of the element, in particular, the one that is linked to the light blue square is the Total Dissolved Solids (measure of mass of residues left when evaporating a liter of water). The square parts represent the pH, the conductivity, and hardness.

[Q] **How do you turn boring and complex data into something interesting and understandable?**

[A] Passion is what drives my works: when I'm engaged with the topic and I think that my work could have an impact on someone, even if very little, I do my very best to make that happen. On the design side, I make my friends test the visualization, the visual model, and the data. It's very useful, because many of them do not work in my field, so they're like the majority of people I want to reach. If they understand, it's a good start.

[Q] **What is your suggestion for beginners?**

[A] I'm not really a suggestions person since I'm always looking for new and better ways to improve myself. I can tell you what works for me: be passionate, be open to everything, let other fields inspire you, and work until you feel comfortable showing what you've done.

3

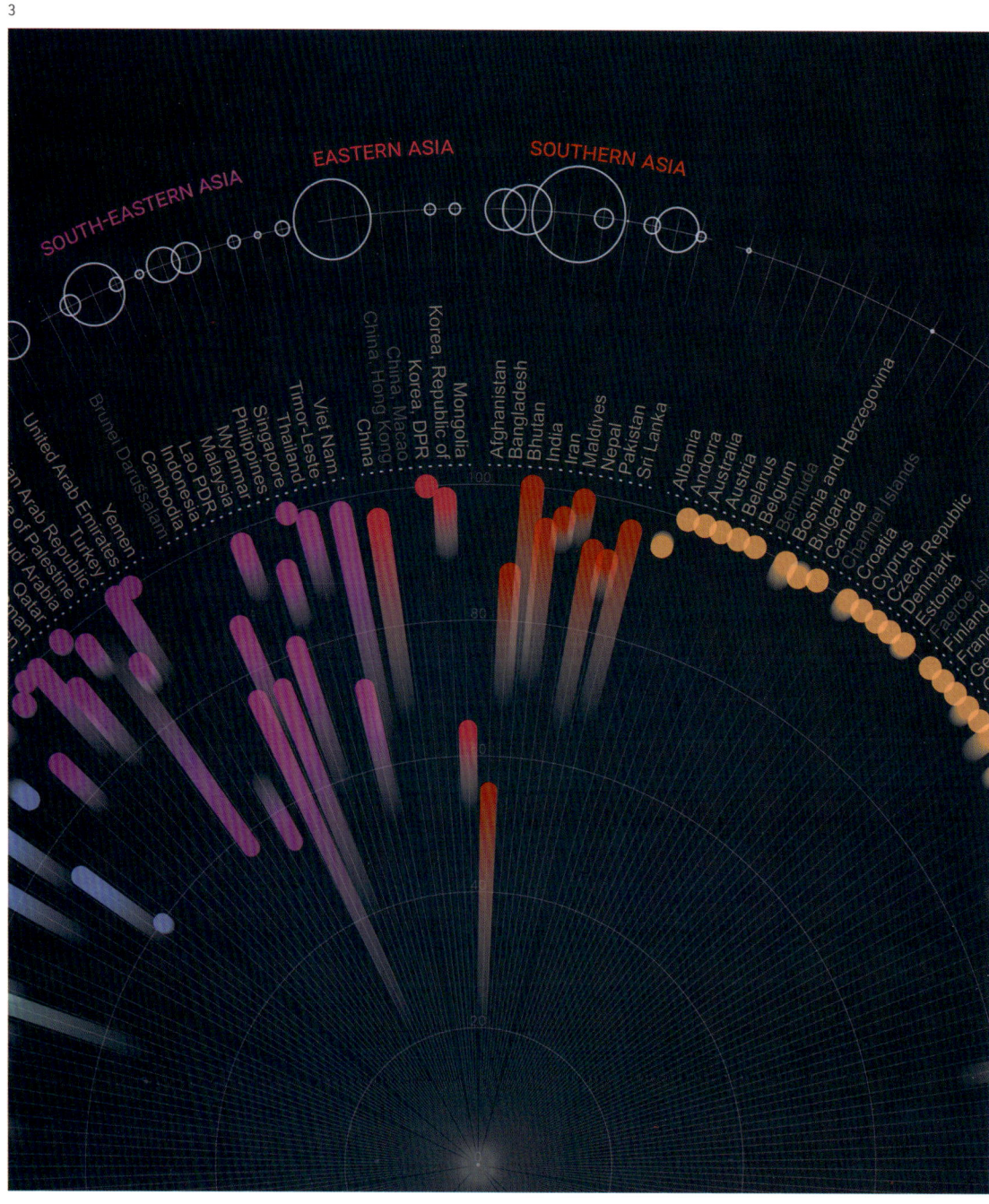

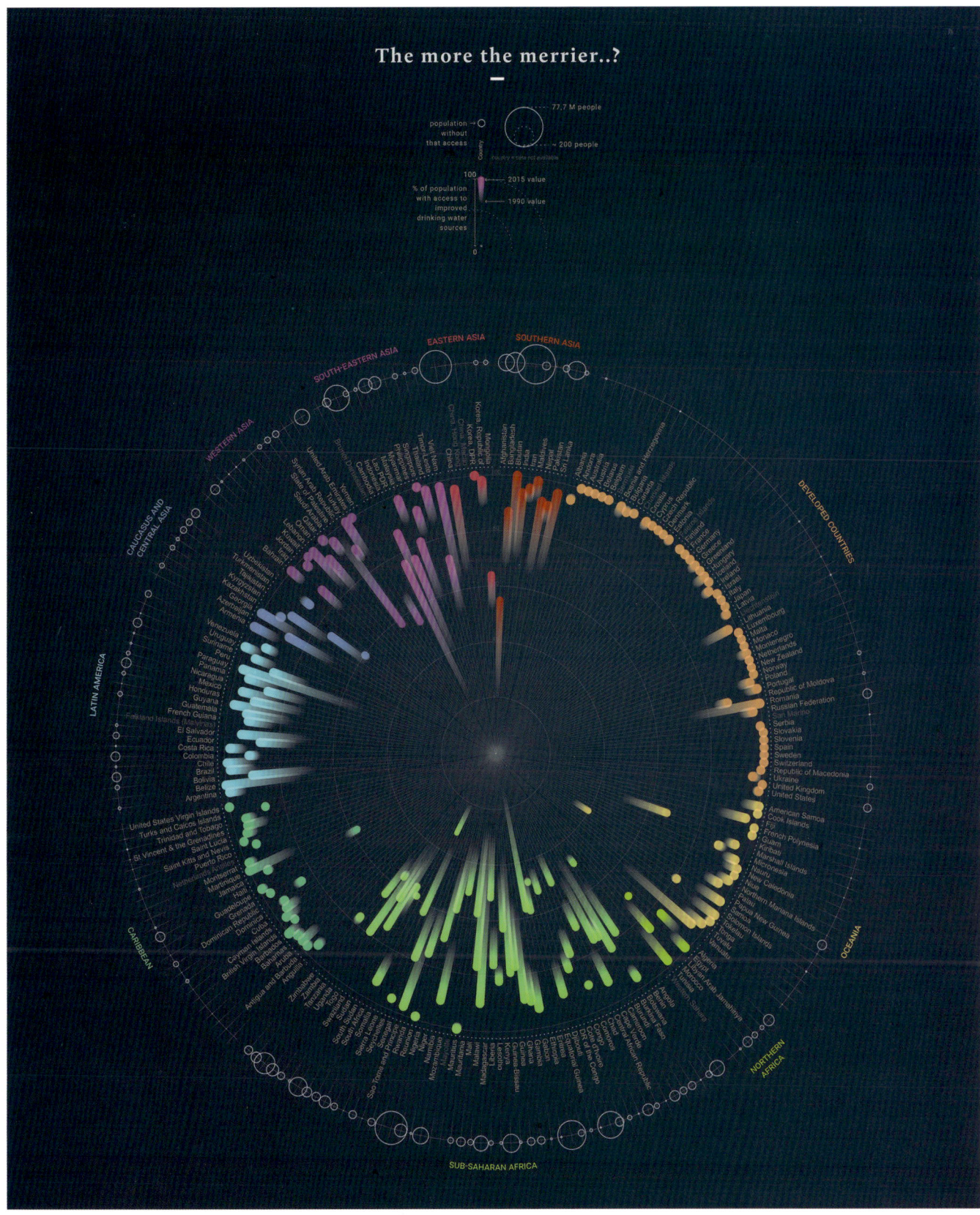

[3–4] The More the Merrier?

Credit: Stefania Guerra
Completion: 2015

Drinking water is the first basic right for every human being, but this seems to be not so simple to achieve. Even nowadays, with technology at its height, there are still people without proper access to drinking water while others are wasting it. This poster aims to raise awareness of this situation in a world where people have one or more smartphones while other are still struggling with an old drinking water system.

The visualization focuses on the change in the proportion of the population with access to an improved drinking water source from 1990 (or first year of submission of data) to 2015 (or latest year of submission of data) by country, comparing it to the size of the population (absolute number) that has no access to such an improved system.

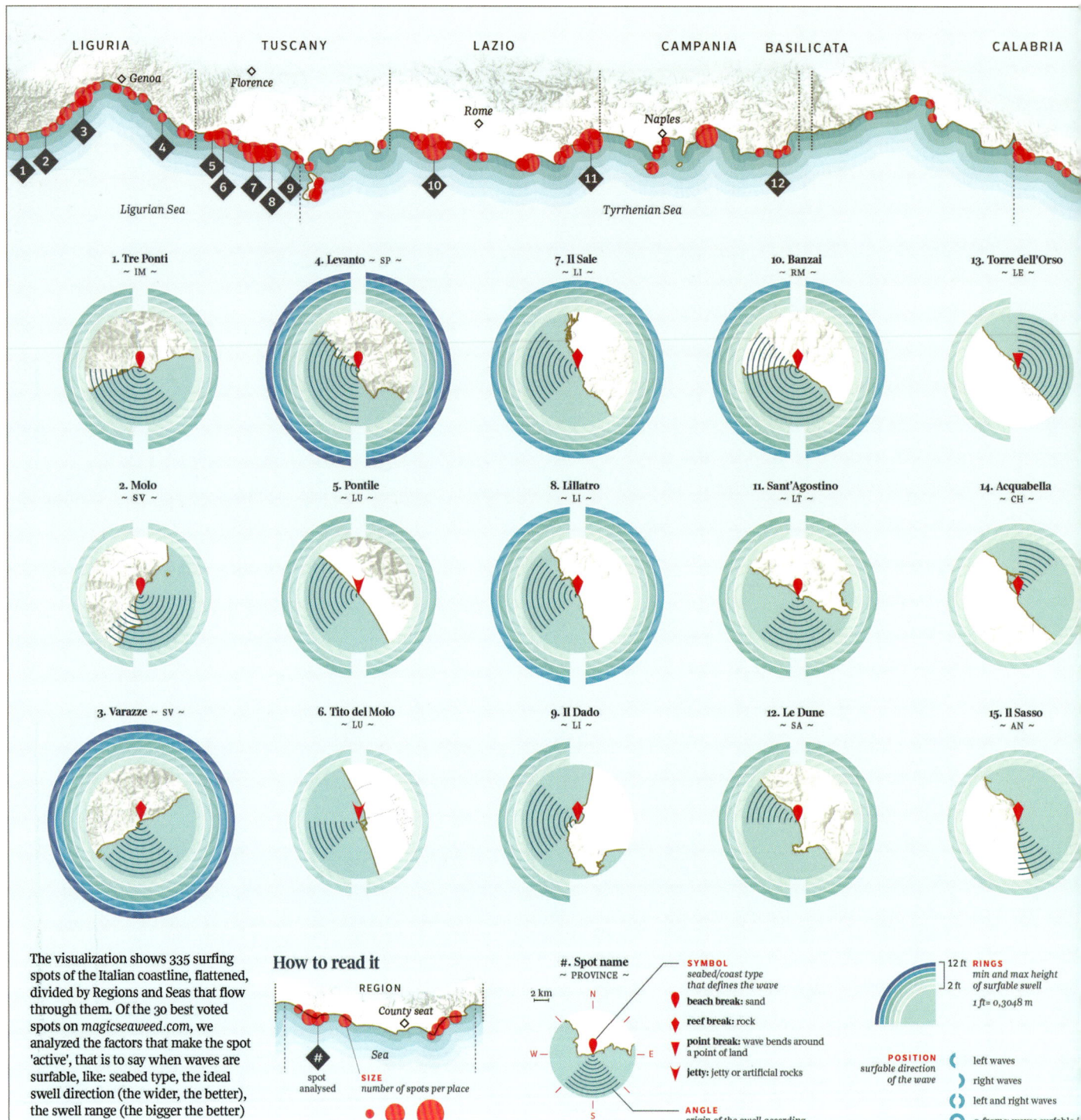

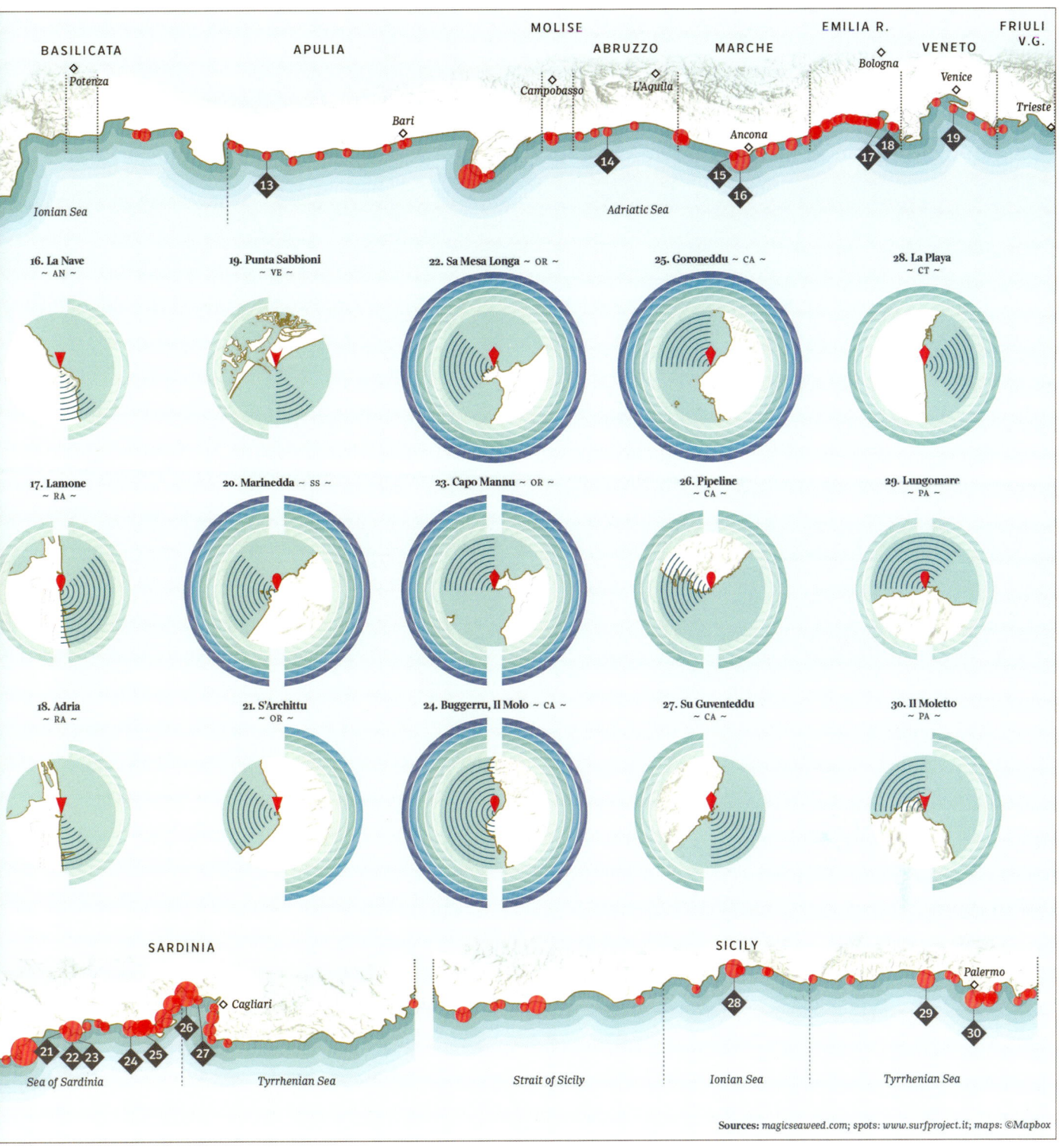

[5] Surfing in Italy

Credits: Stefania Guerra, Michela Lazzaroni, Giovanni Egeo
Completion: 2016

The visualization shows 335 surfing spots on the Italian coastline, flattened and divided by regions and seas that flow through them. According to the 30 best voted spots on magicseaweed.com, the designers analyzed the factors that make the spot 'active', that is to say when waves are surfable, such as seabed type, the ideal swell direction (the wider, the better), the swell range (the bigger the better), and the type of waves.

Hahn+Zimmermann

BC

The graphic design studio Hahn+Zimmermann was founded in Berne by Barbara Hahn and Christine Zimmermann in 2008. They work on projects in the fields of communication design, visualization, and design research for national and international clients as well as on self-initiated and non-commercial projects. Since 2007, they have been initiating and carrying out research projects for the Berne University of the Arts within the research area of knowledge visualization. Moreover, they are teaching undergraduate and postgraduate students from different universities in workshops on information visualization and visual analysis as well as giving lectures.

[Q] **What do you think about data visualization/infographics?**

[A] You can use information visualization to analyse a huge amount of data if you don't know yet what kind of knowledge is hidden in the data. In this case, infographics are a means to gaining knowledge. Or you can use visualizations to communicate data or a complex subject in a very comprehensible way. The illustrative and narrative aspects of infographics and the non-linear way of reading infographics enable the viewer to explore the content in a playful manner.

[Q] **What kind of design methods do you commonly use?**

[A] For us it is always important that we develop the graphic means used out of the content that has to be visualized. The graphic means should not be exchangeable and should help to communicate the content very precisely. The main challenge is to find the appropriate graphic element to represent a specific parameter of the data.

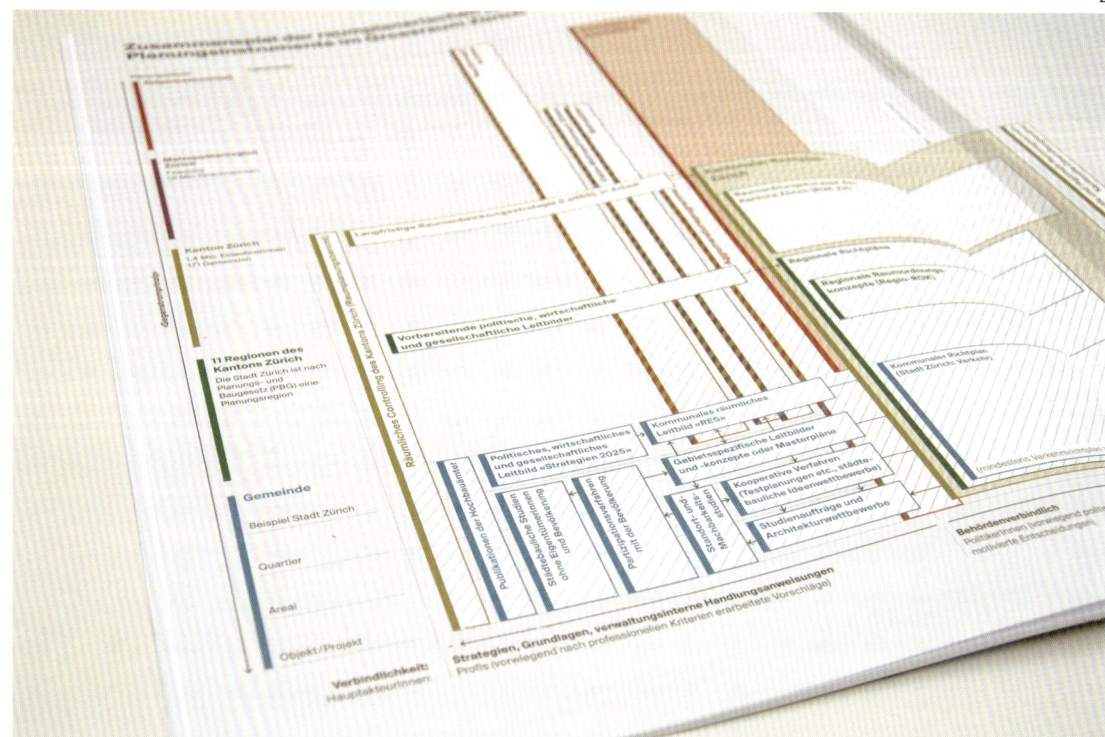

1

2

Our design method can be described as the systematic testing of content-relevant parameters and their adequate translation into visual variables. Thus the generated wide range of visual experiments and their constant evaluation characterize such a visually conducted design process. Three aspects play a significant role in this 'graphic transcription'. First, it is a matter of the type of information carrier, including typography, photography, cartography, or graphic elements. Second, it is a matter of graphic parameters, including size, color, opacity, brightness, angle, length/width/height, and structure/surface/material. Third, it is a matter of the graphic processing or visualization of, for example, abstraction, comparison/contrast, scaling, overlapping, and marking. Structured experimentation with these three levels of visual coding of content provides numerous options for developing a wide range of alternative presentation forms in information visualization.

The search for an appropriate graphic density is essentially a balancing act between complexity and reduction, whereby the objective is to assess and define the number of content-relevant parameters that can be displayed within one visualization. The goal is for the visualization to be sufficiently complex, but at the same time for the individual aspects to still be registered and comprehended by the observer.

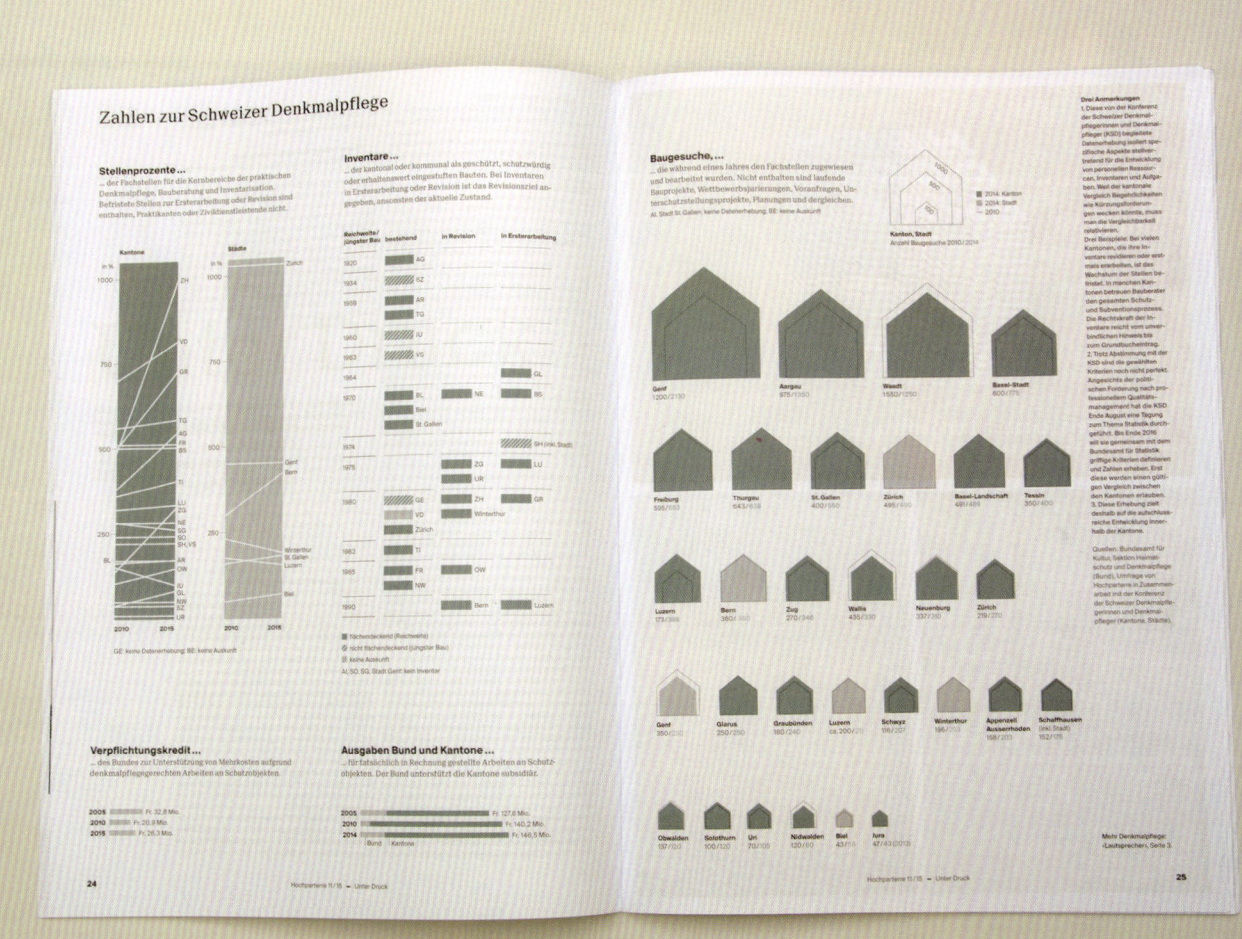

3

[1–3] Infographics for Hochparterre

Credit: Hahn+Zimmermann
Completion: 2014

The infographics were designed for the architecture and design magazine *Hochparterre*. In image 3, the facts and figures about the preservation of historical monuments in Switzerland are illustrated: the total employment percentage per specialist department (2010 and 2014) of each canton in Switzerland (on the left) and the comparison of the number of building application per year (2010 and 2014) of each canton department (on the right).

In the bilingual special issue *Stadtregionen Planen* (image 2), the double-spread infographic provides an overview over spatial and city planning tools of the urban regions in Zurich and Amsterdam and encourages the reader to compare the two cities.

[Q] What kind of design elements do you commonly use?

[A] We always try to use a wide range of different graphic elements such as typography, photography, cartography, and graphic elements (point, line, irregular form, etc.) as information carriers. As designers we have more elements at our disposal than only bars and pies.

[Q] Where are your works applied?

[A] We design infographics for many different clients and communication media. In the news sector we work for newspapers (e.g. *Die Zeit*) and magazines (e.g. *brand eins*, *Hochparterre*, *New York Times Magazine*) as well as for corporate publishing clients (SUVA, LGT Bank). We also design infographics for clients from the administration (e.g. federal administration or Department of Education of the Canton of Zurich) or science and university sector (University of Bern) as well as for clients from the private industry (e.g. Swisscom, Bank Julius Bär). The infographics are either applied to magazines, newspapers, books, brochures, or posters for exhibitions, or published on the web or on a screen.

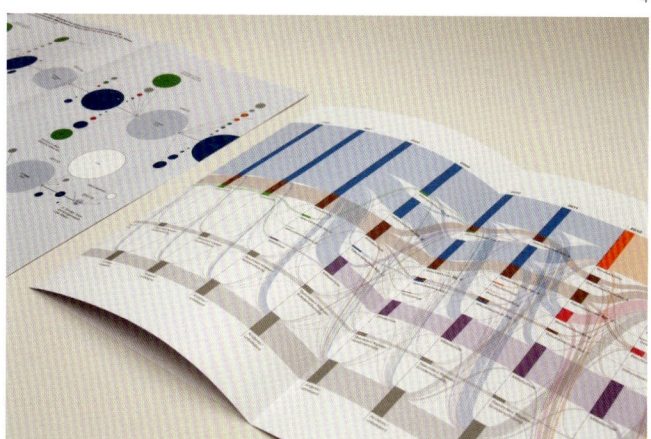

4

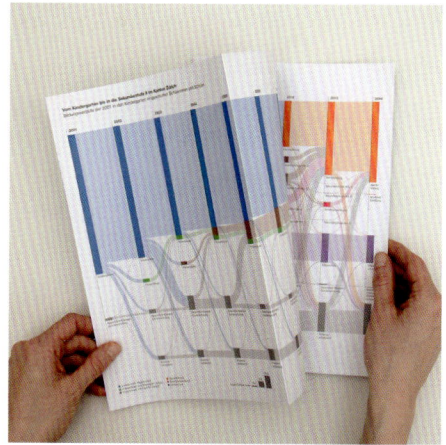

5

6

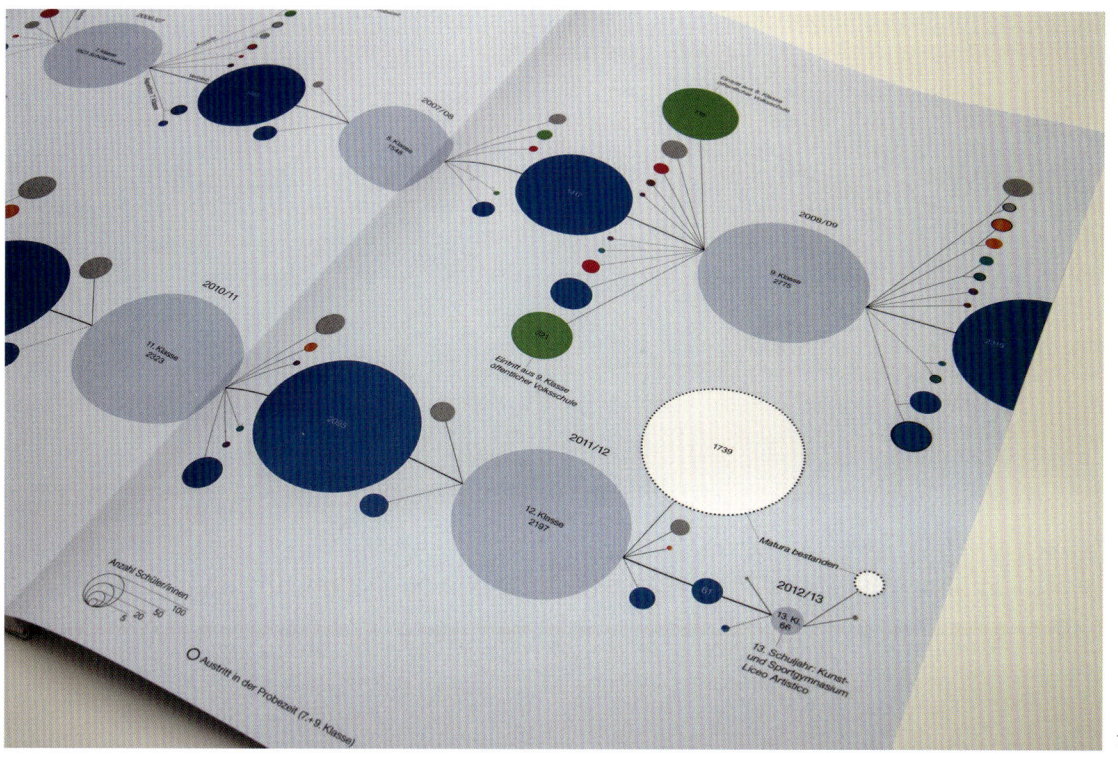

[4–8] Educational Pathways

Credit: Hahn+Zimmermann
Completion: 2016

The double-spread visualization (images 7 and 8) shows the educational trajectories of high school students within one year from 7th to 12th/13th grade between 2006 and 2013. It respectively shows how many pupils (size of the bubbles) entered and left the educational institutions (differentiated by colors), and if they finally passed the school-leaving examination or not.

The folded leaflet (images 4 to 6) shows the educational pathways of pupils between kindergarten and 11th grade between 2001 and 2014. The distinction is drawn between different progressions (regular, accelerated, delayed) and types of education (elementary school, vocational education and preparation, secondary school) differentiated by colors.

[Q] **How do you turn boring and complex data into something interesting and understandable?**

[A] The data itself is not boring for us. Most of the time we deal with very interesting and relevant content that has to be communicated. At the beginning the amount of data is often overwhelming. Then we start with trying to understand the data and analyzing the content. The next step is to sketch different ideas of a possible visual representation form. Our main goal is always to show a new aspect of the data or to make something visible that was not visible before. As John W. Tukey said, 'The greatest value of a picture is when it forces us to notice what we never expected to see'.

[Q] **What is your suggestion for beginners?**

[A] Data visualization is not making boring data look fancy and interesting. Data visualization is about communicating specific content and giving equal weight to information and aesthetics.

9

[9–13] Summa cum laude

Credit: Hahn+Zimmermann
Completion: 2014

The infographic poster exhibition for the night of research showed statistics about the PhD students who submitted their doctoral theses at the University of Bern in 2013, in a vivid, funny, and surprising manner. The infographics analyze and show which countries and cantons the PhD students are from, which gender they are, their names, which graduate school they belonged to, and the titles of their doctoral theses. During the event, many different people—students, professors, the doctoral students themselves, and their relatives—studied the posters in depth, showed each other the details of the infographics, found themselves or their PhD within the posters, and discussed the contents.

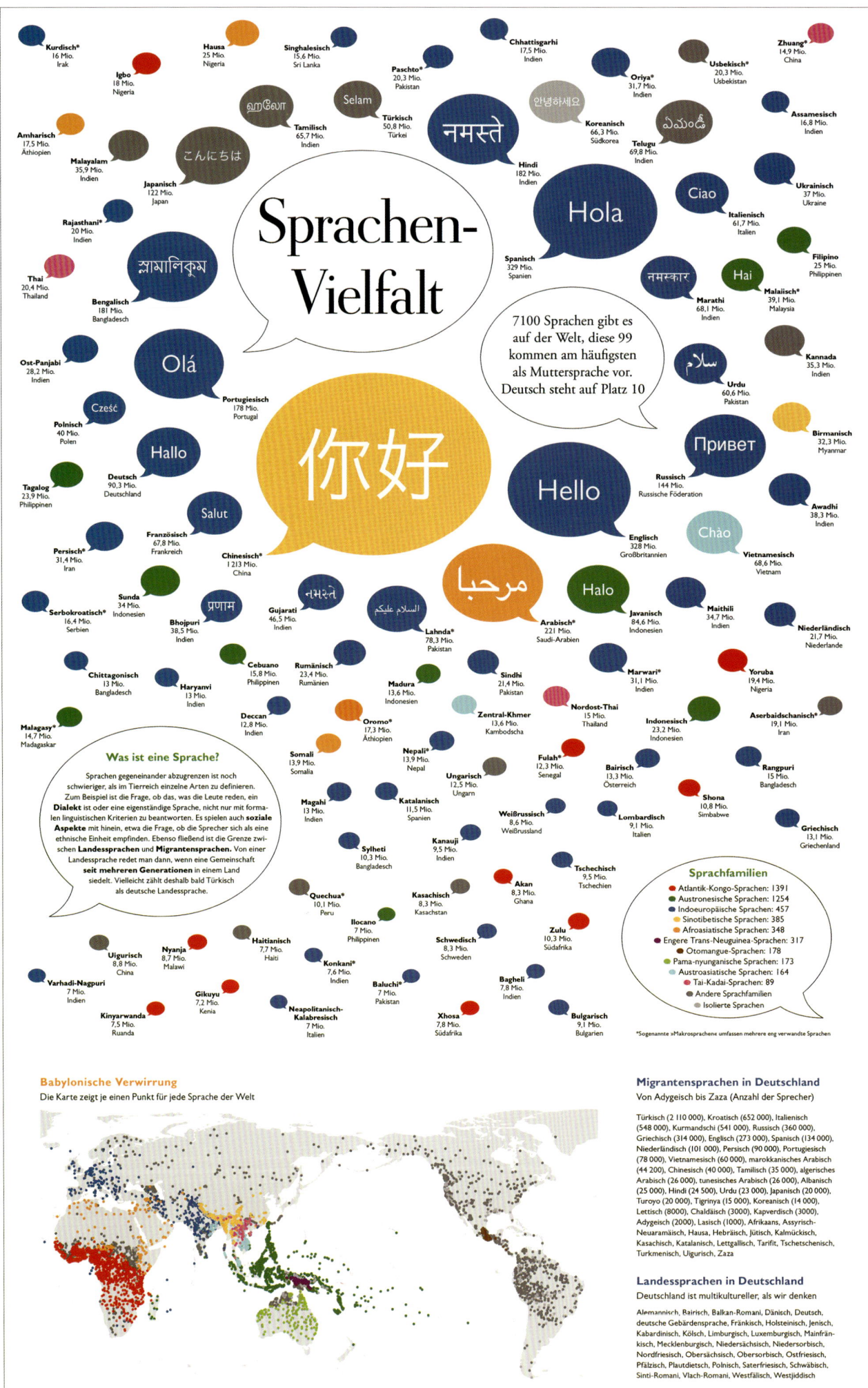

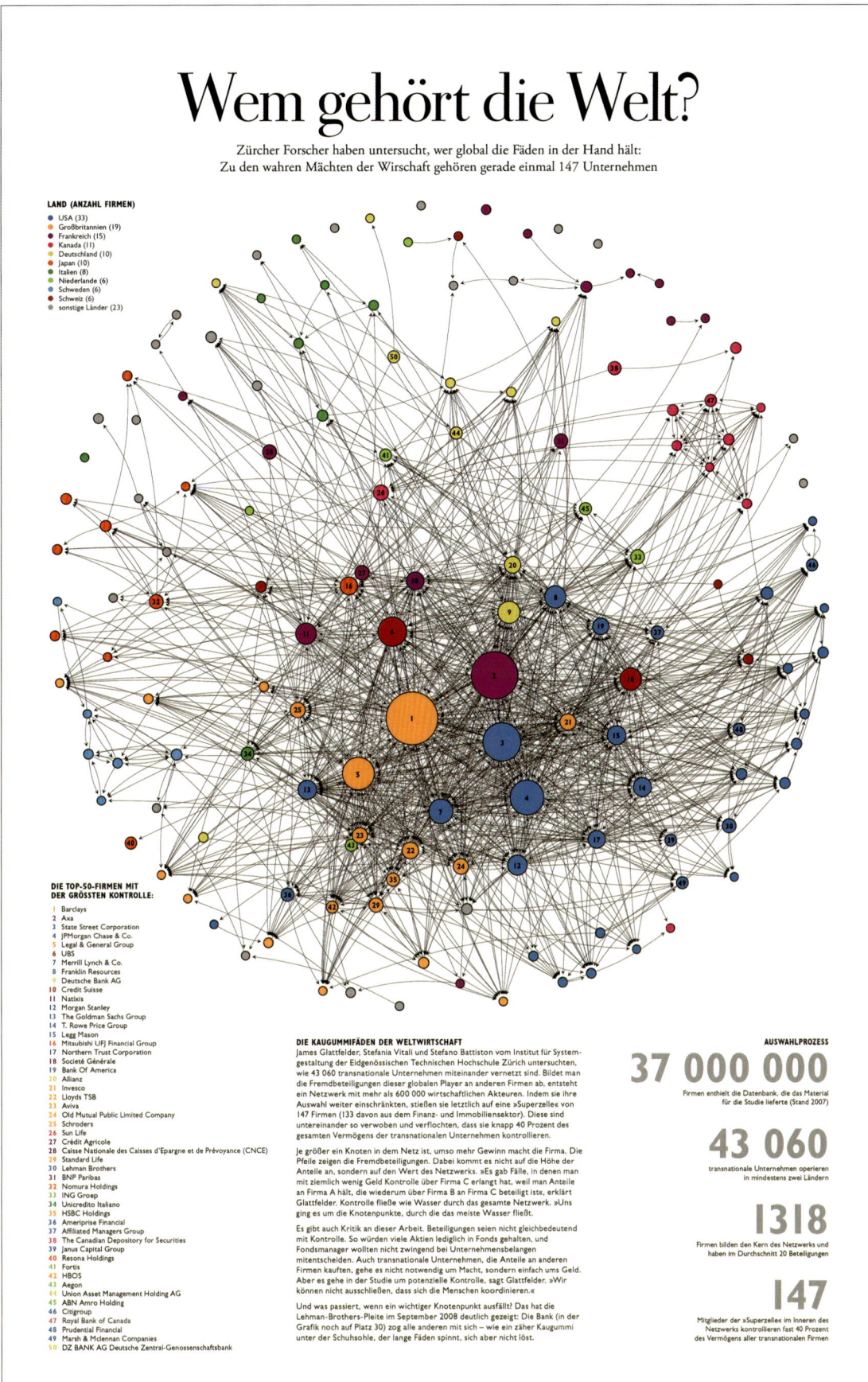

[14–15] *Die Zeit*
Infographics

Credit: Hahn+Zimmermann
Completion: 2013

The visualization in image 14 shows the 99 most common languages (mother tongue) in the form of speech bubbles with different sizes representing the number of speakers. The map further reveals the origin of the 7100 languages worldwide (points) and their belonging to different language families (colors). The visualization in image 15 shows an interdependent network of 147 firms dominating the world economy. The size of the bubble represents the revenue of a company, the arrows show minority interests, and the colors show the origin country of the firm.

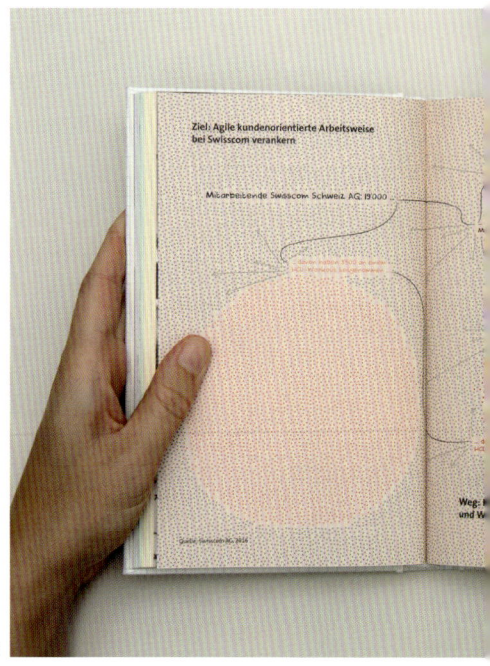
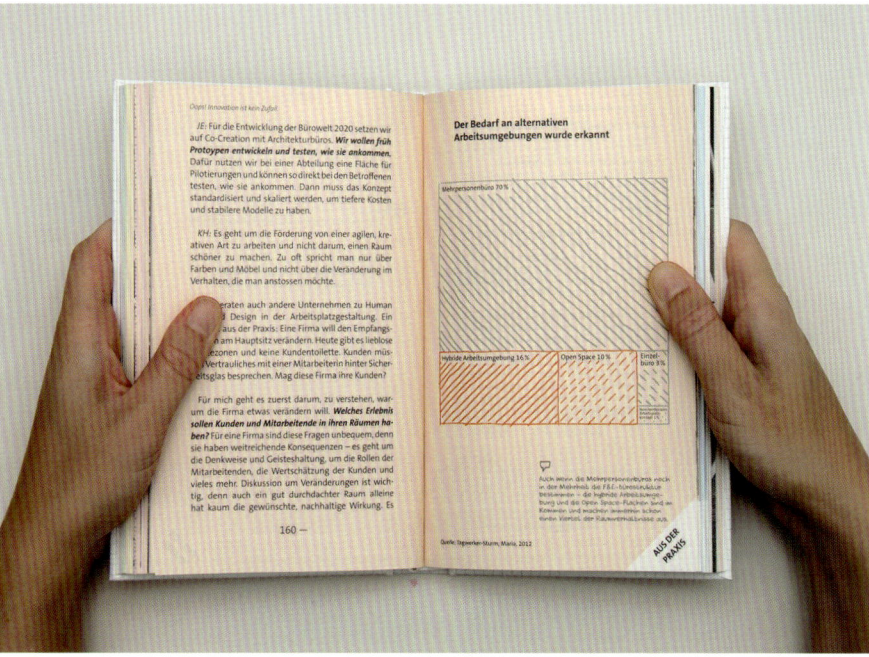
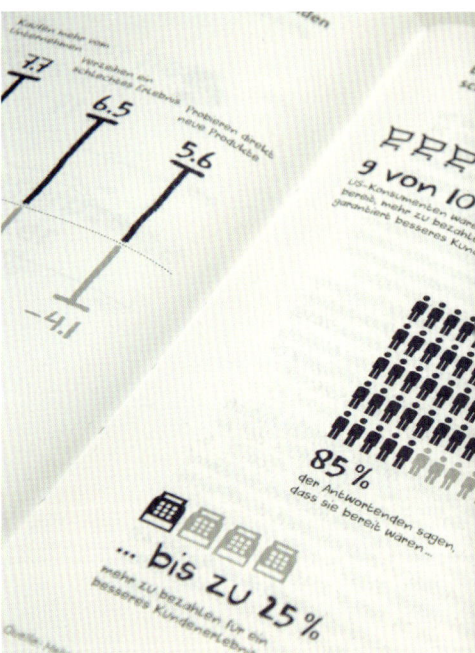
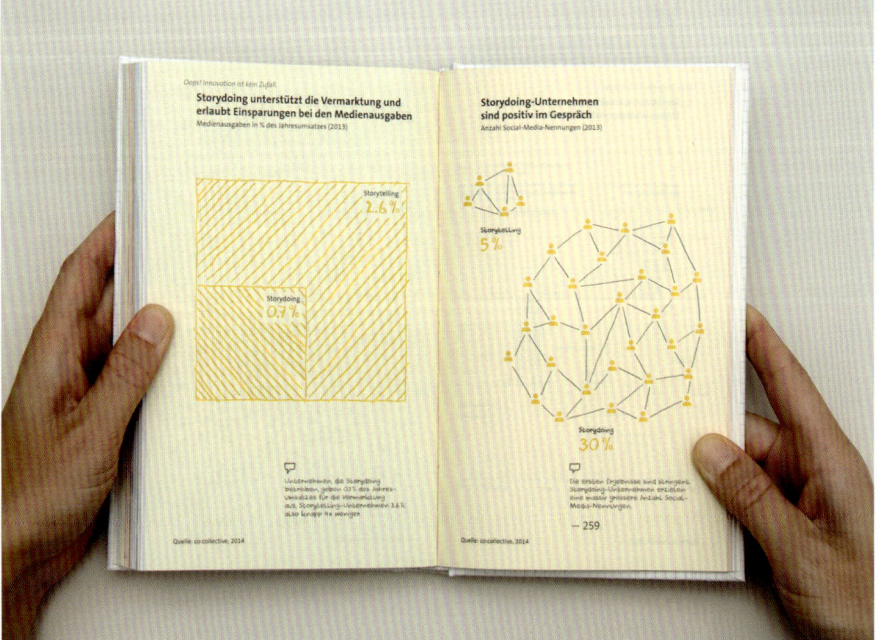

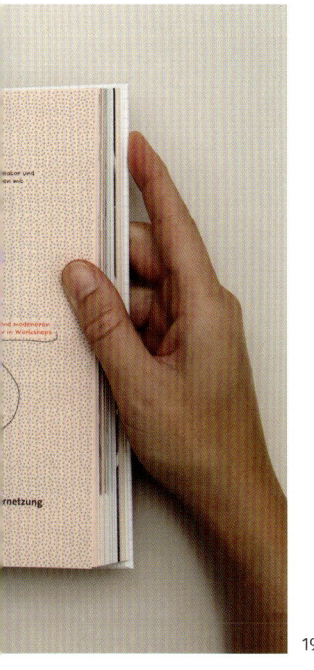

19

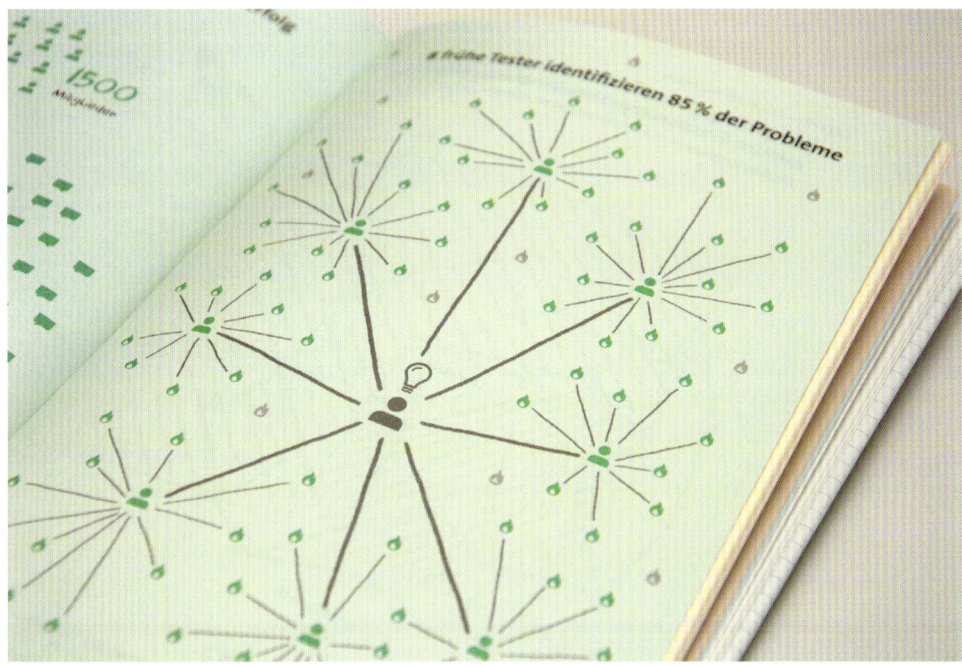

22

20

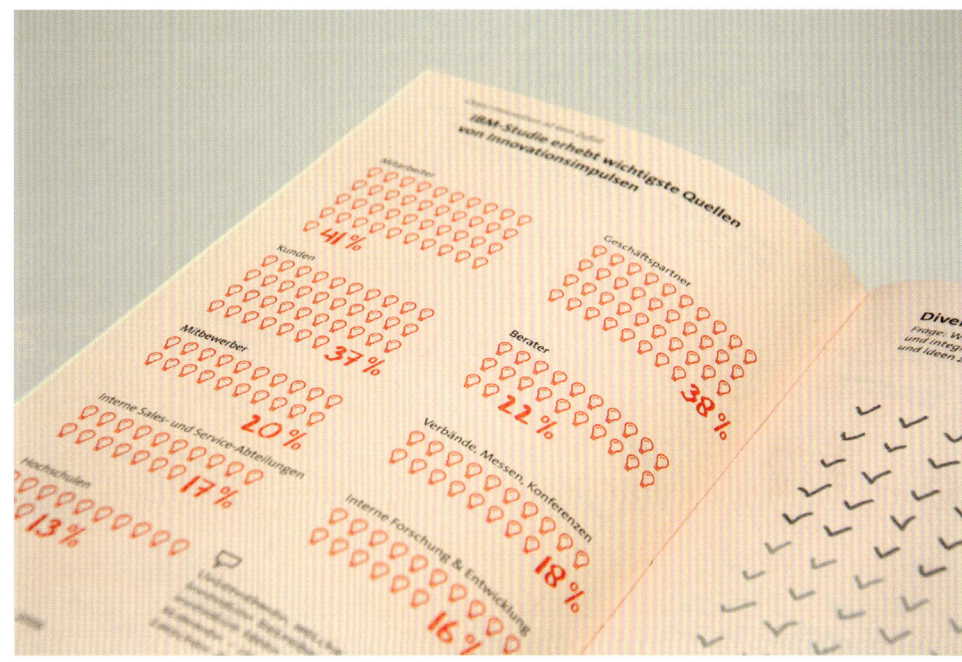

23

21

[16–23] Swisscom Publication

Credit: Hahn+Zimmermann
Completion: 2016

These 32 illustrative infographics are about design thinking and how innovation can be supported in a company. Facts and findings of various studies are shown in demonstrative illustrations and information graphics. The infographics supplement the editorial part of the Swisscom publication *Oops! Innovation ist kein Zufall*.

Heyday

[Q] What do you think about data visualization/infographics?

[A] Visual communication is an interesting and fast-growing field. Even though it has quite a long history, the development and possibilities to make something new or unique seem to be bigger than in other areas. And it's a good way to explain (sometimes difficult) content to a wide range of people. It gives us the chance to work with a large spectrum of clients from different fields.

[Q] What kind of design methods do you commonly use?

[A] The concept is the most important thing. No concept, no idea, no good result. So we try to sketch, scribble, and discuss (a lot) in teams before we begin to work on the computer.

Heyday is a design bureau focusing on visual communication and concepts, located in Bern, the capital of Switzerland. It consists of four members (Philipp Luethi, Ariane Forster, Andrea Noti and Sam Divers), all trained as graphic designers at several Swiss universities. They like the exact Swiss style as much as the playful style and try to be open-minded.

Total final energy consumption in Switzerland in 2014 with shares of renewable energy

Final energy consumtion 2014: 825'770 TJ

21.4 % Renewable energy Final consumption

13.97% Electricity
4.18% Wood
1.53% Ambient heat
0.76% District heating
0.32% Share of renewable energy from waste
0.30% Gas
0.27% Solar power
0.11% Liquid biogenic vehicle fuels

78.6 % Final consumption of non-renewable energy

[Q] **What kind of design elements do you commonly use?**

[A] We do not really prefer any design elements, because we think the infographic should always be orientated on the subject or content. We are open to every kind of visual realization, as long as it helps to communicate the content. So we've used so far almost every classic shape that exists. We mostly use circles and bars as a solid basis, and then experiment, transform, and reshape these forms until they conform to our visual idea and the aim of the infographic. The use of these basic forms depends on the message of the infographic, if we have to either transport information about the evolution (of the theme) or the actual status. The bar and circle forms appear in almost every product on the market, so the step of using real products or elements is quite small. We like to communicate with simple, meaningful objects and then implement our ideas, because most of our topics are quite complex.

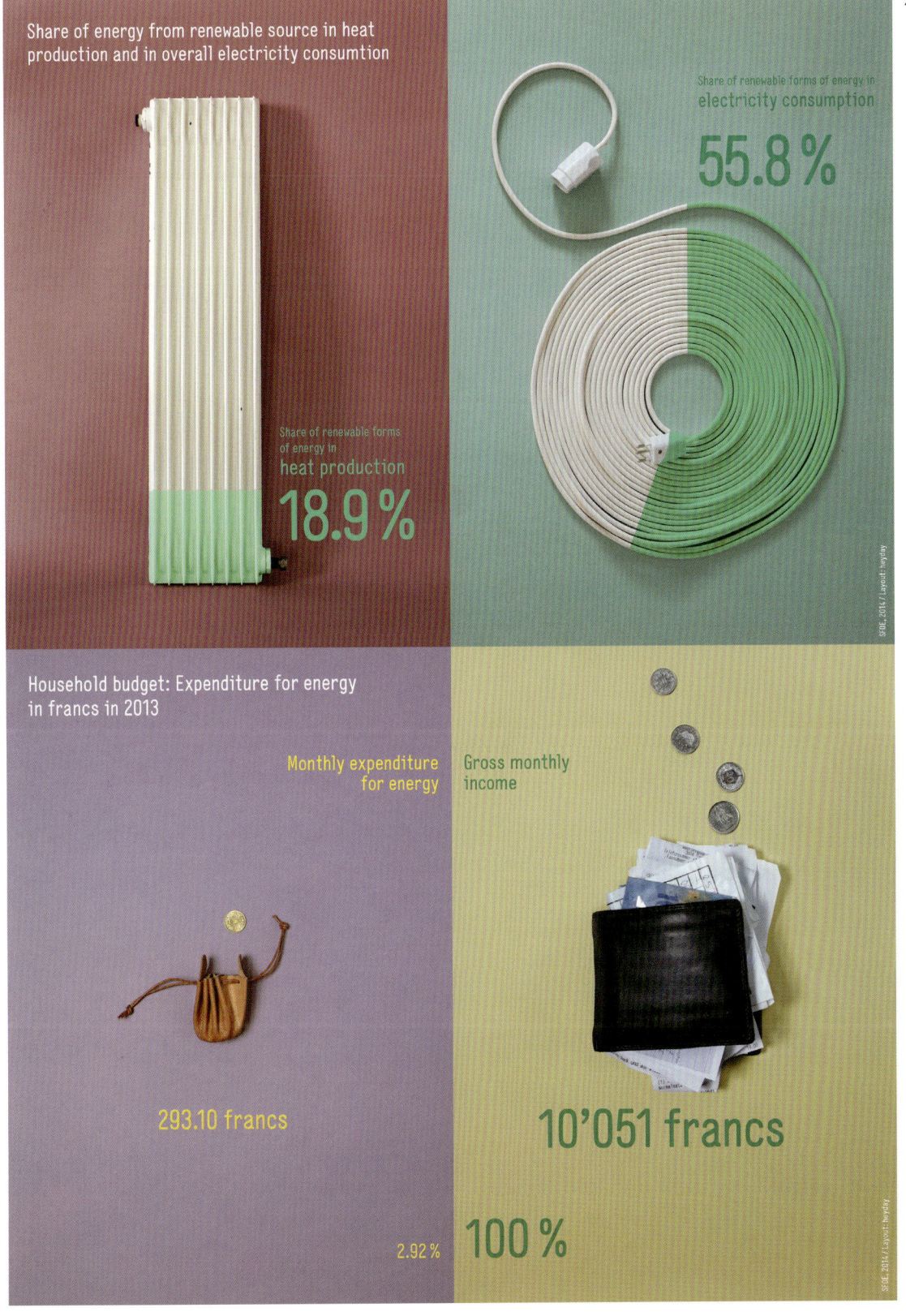

[Q] Where are your works applied?

[A] Mostly in brochures and on websites, sometimes also on posters and flyers.

[Q] How do you turn boring and complex data into something interesting and understandable?

[A] We try to get a sense of the content, going deeper into the subject matter and then peeling out the core, which can be interesting, useful or include astonishing details. And we try to have in mind that the viewer shouldn't fall asleep or yawn when they look at our infographics.

[Q] What is your suggestion for beginners?

[A] Be like a sponge. Stay innocent. And be always interested in social evolutions.

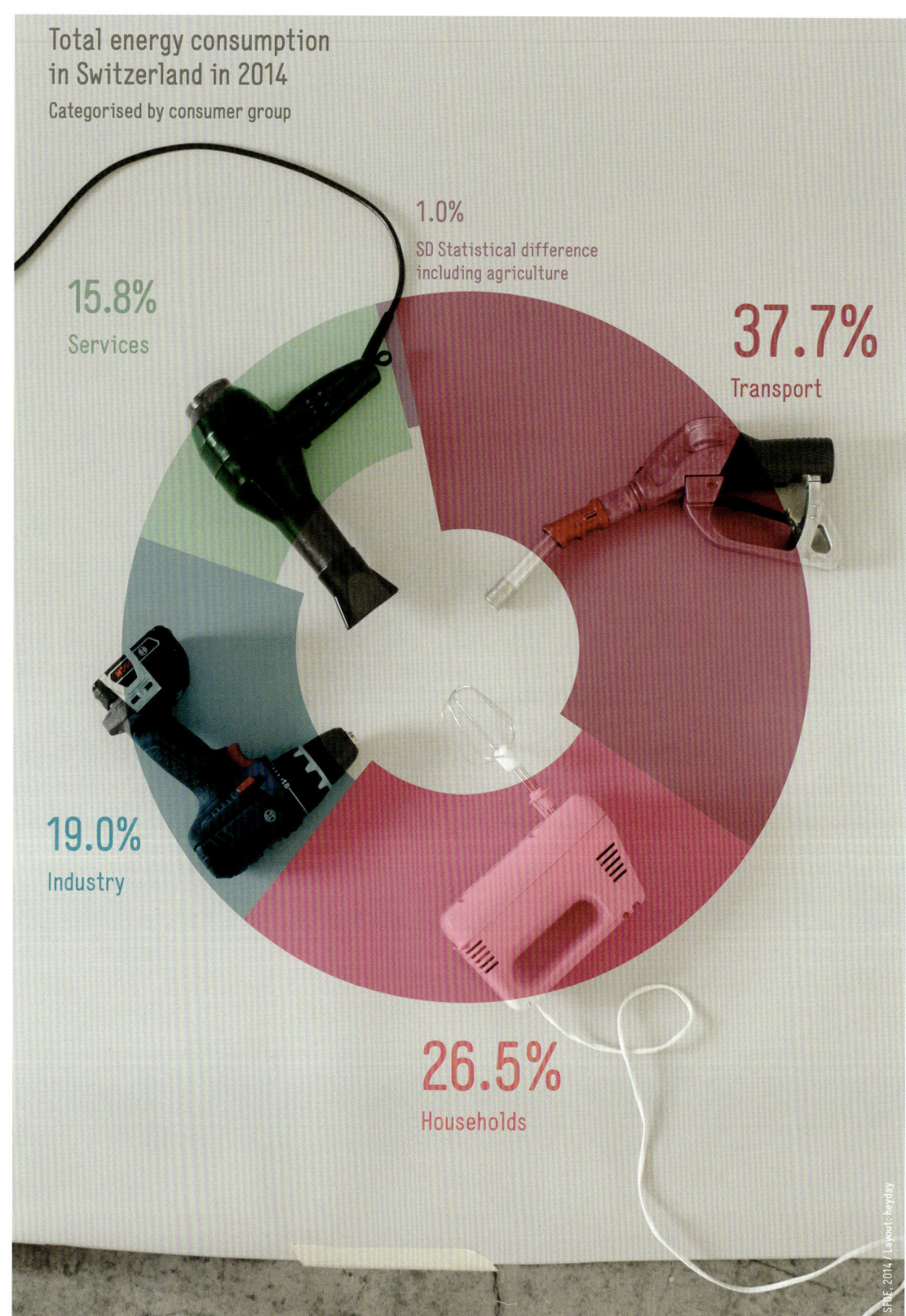

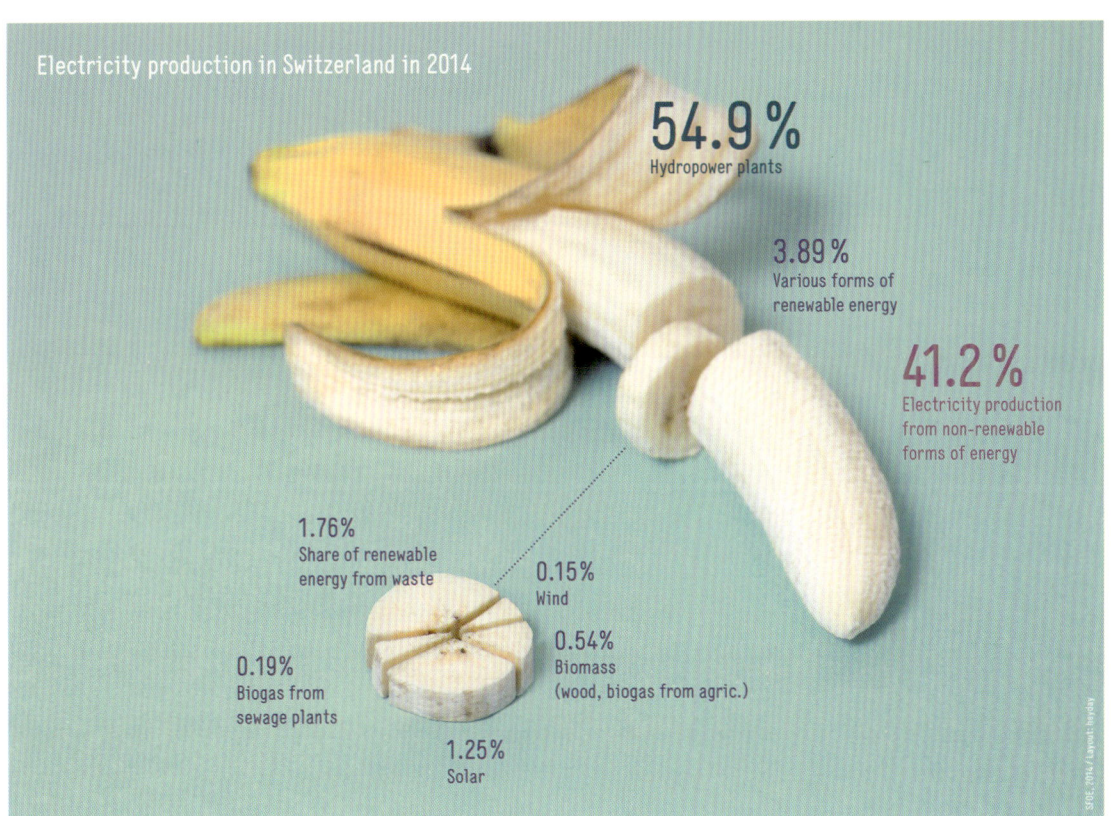

[1–5] Energy Consumption and Development in Switzerland

Credits: Heyday (concept, art direction, layout), Anja Schori (photography), Swiss Federal Office of Energy SFOE (client)

Completion: 2015

The infographics are used in several ways and for different activities, mostly to inform the public about the actual tendencies in energy consumption. So they must be presented in an appropriate, easy and quickly understandable way, being eye-catching and including enough detailed information. The main idea is to work with real, established, and known products, which act as symbols for a topic or content and simultaneously as screens, to demonstrate the proportionality. By setting them up on a plain, colorful background, their appearance becomes more striking and each topic gets an understandable icon.

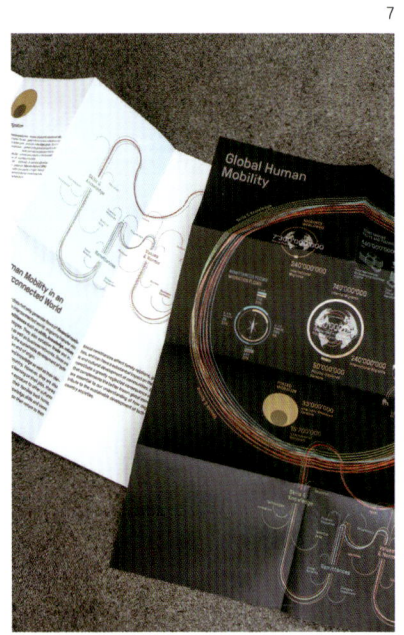

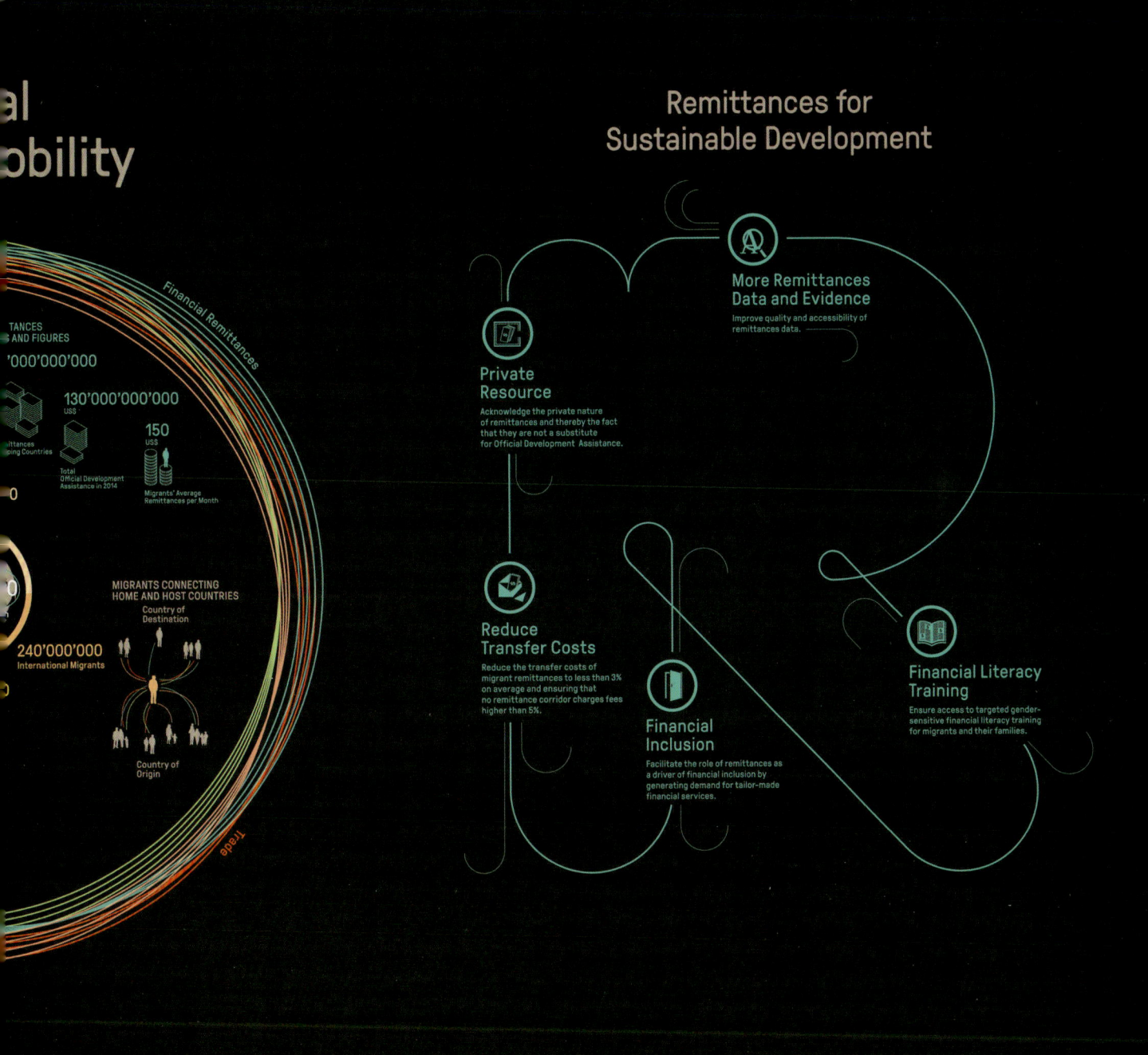

[6–8] Global Human Mobility

Credits: Heyday (concept, art direction, layout),
Albrecht Druck (printing), Lettra Design (booth panels),
Swiss Agency for Development and Cooperation (client)
Completion: 2015

The infographic has to show the complex context of the subject—migration—in an easily understandable and striking way that also has a distinct effect. The main idea is to show on one hand the migration flow and the emerging cultural and social exchange and the interaction, and on the other hand the dynamics of the different streams (knowledge, money, goods, etc.) that go with it. The colors and tonality reflect the positive social benefit of global migration.

Interactive Things

[Q] What do you think about data visualization/infographics?

[A] In our studio, we consider data visualizations as a tool that supports users to explore, analyze, and evaluate large data sets. These types of visual and interactive representations are often referred to as exploratory visualizations. A second important role that data visualizations play in a user's daily work with data is as a medium to communicate the insights that seem hidden within these data sets. These types of representation are best described as explanatory visualizations. The line between these two types is not strict and the exploratory and explanatory qualities are not mutually exclusive. In many powerful data visualizations, the user will be provided with means to enjoy both exploration and explanation. The best way to define the role of a data visualization is by considering its target audience, the context where it's being deployed, and the objectives the creator strives to achieve with it. When we evaluate visualizations, we typically do this with four dimensions grouped into data and design.

Data relevance examines the importance of the data for the specific context of the user. The data must hold substantial meaning for users and must motivate them to actively engage with the visualization. Data integrity evaluates the accuracy, consistency, and honesty of the data source and its provider. Design form analyzes whether the data is presented appropriately. The presentation needs to be clear, readable, and of a high aesthetic standard. Data function assesses the overall usefulness as a combination of usability, simplicity, and immersion.

[Q] What kind of design methods do you commonly use?

[A] The practice in our studio can be described as research-led design. That said, we do not stick to any dogma on how to work on our projects, nor do we force ourselves to replicate the same process for every project. Different organizations, domains, goals, and circumstances demand different means. On a big scale, our design process can be described as a set of four phases: discover, define, design, and develop. This description is not our own invention. It has been established and defined in design theory and gets applied in design studios all around the word. Divergent thinking and convergent thinking are applied in alternation. Each of the phases can be broken down into activities focusing on individual key objectives of the phase. For each activity, we have a set of methods that we can apply to conduct the activity. These can be well-established methods from the fields of ethnography, design research, cognitive science, information visualization, or computer science to more experimental or personal methods for acquiring knowledge, generating ideas, and developing concepts.

Discover: In the first phase we try to learn as much as possible about the project and discover its restrictions and opportunities. We explore the data and content, research the audience, analyze benchmarks, and gather requirements and stakeholder expectations. Our goal during this phase is to build a shared understanding of the project and its context to inform our future decisions.

Define: Combining the insights from our exploration, we work closely with our client to establish a strong product strategy. This includes the basic concepts for content, visualization, interaction, and technology. Collectively we specify what the product is going to be and what it won't. We define a project plan and specify the product scope.

Interactive Things is a design studio with a focus on data-driven digital products. They are a close-knit team of experts with backgrounds in interaction design, interface design, information design, data visualization, data science, and software engineering. They help organizations to innovate with their unique combination of skills in design and engineering. They create bespoke tools and experiences that assist, connect, and delight people, always putting the human at the center of attention.

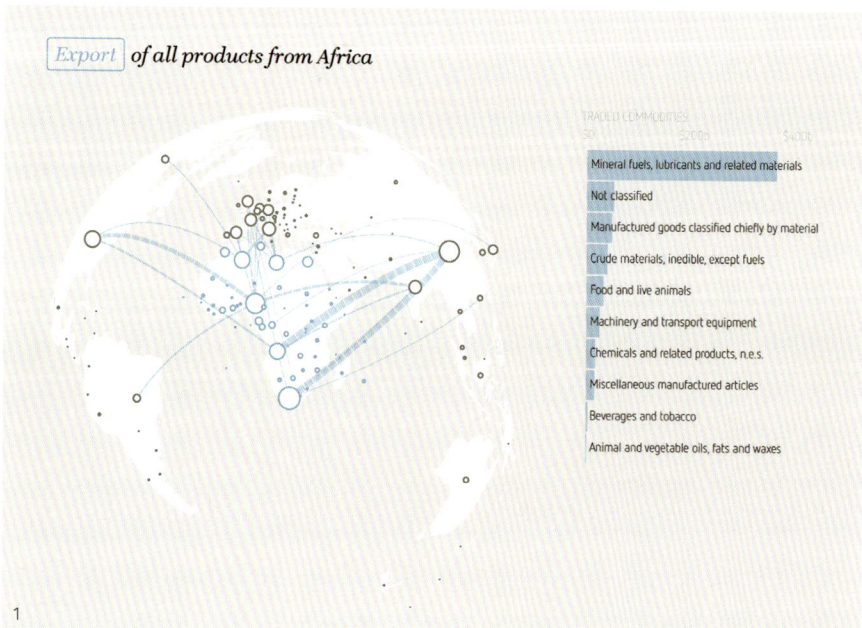

1

2

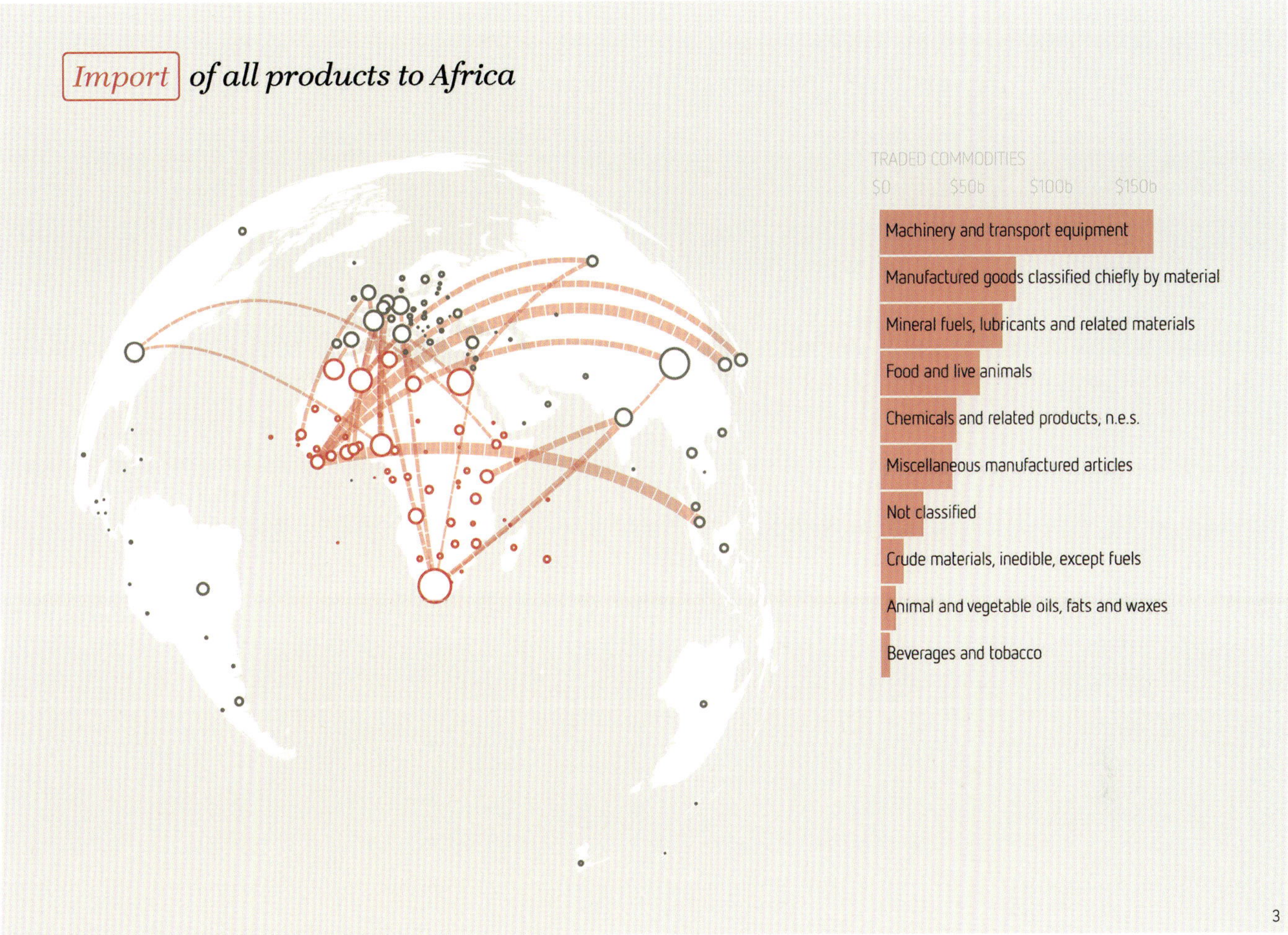

Import *of all products to Africa*

[1–4] Global Trade Africa

Credit: Interactive Things
Completion: 2014
Interactive link: lab.interactivethings.com/global-trade-africa

International trade, the exchange of capital, goods, and services across international borders, represents a significant share of the GDP of the countries of the African continent. This investigative report visualizes the world's imports from and exports to Africa to share insights about the most important partners and commodities.

At first sight, the visualization tells six stories that the designers found during the exploration and analysis of the data set. These stories highlight geographic trade trends, patterns, and distributions. The goal of these stories is to introduce you to the subject domain using bite-sized chunks of information. Once you're ready, you can explore the complete data set freely and discover your own insights. Trade relationships are visualized as connection lines between countries on a globe. The import and export quantities are represented by the thickness of the connection line, and the animated connection segments indicate the trade direction. A secondary chart beside the globe compares the commodity categories and allows us to drill down into the subcategories.

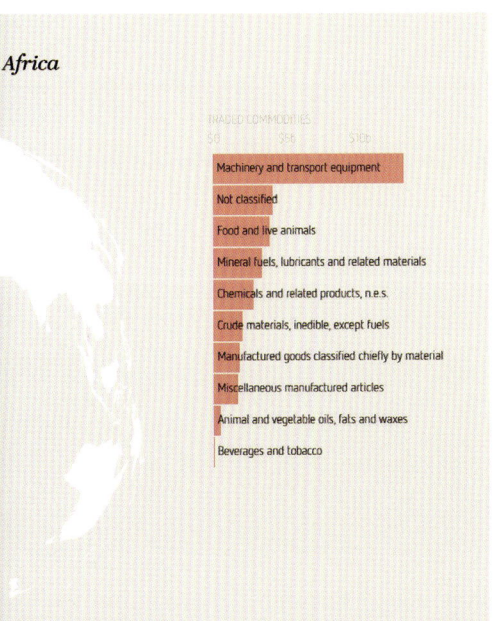

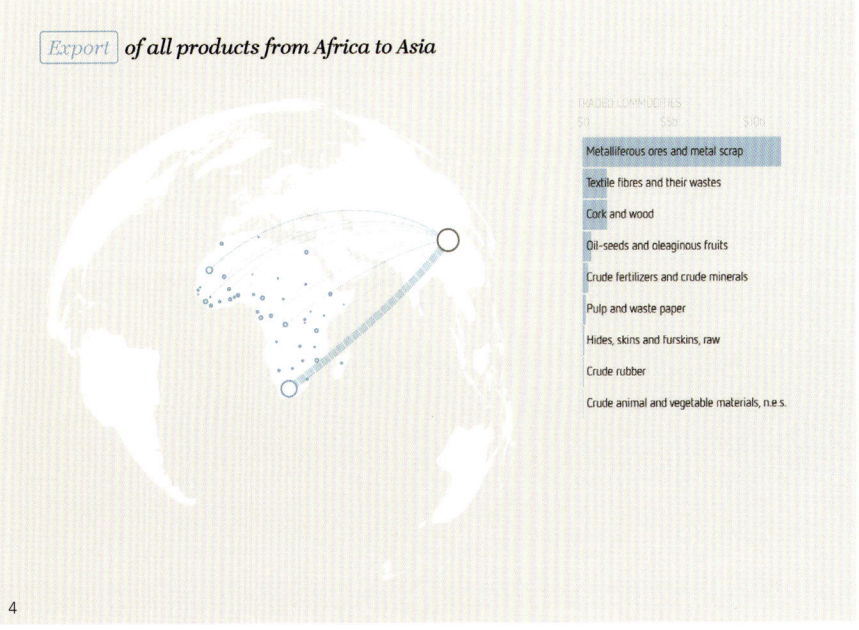

Design: We begin the design process by creating different approaches to each problem. Using prototypes and evaluation, we find the most effective way to present information and guide the user. Every design decision must prove its purpose and is executed with the highest attention to detail.

Develop: In the last phase, we implement the final application. This usually builds upon a series of prototypes that have previously been built as part of the design phase. Now is the time for the final rounds of evaluation with users, testing thoroughly in terms of usability, stability and security, and optimization for deployment. It's important to note that the phases can't be seen as closed steps. They rather represent a scaffolding for conducting a series of related and dependent activities. Therefore, the phases are interconnected and get repeated in iterations where necessary and appropriate.

[Q] **What kind of design elements do you commonly use?**

[A] When we look at commonly used design elements and visualization techniques, we see two different tendencies how people chose a direction that deserves attention. First, the visualization methods that have proven to be successful in making data understandable are plentiful. Therefore, it's easy to stick to what works and simply apply it to any problem space. Second, it's equally easy to disregard the proven techniques and instead strive for innovative ways to visualize the data at hand. We try to balance our design choices somewhere in the middle path of these two tendencies.

Our goal with our work is not necessarily to invent new techniques, although we certainly are not shy with experimentation. We put our efforts into finding the right, not the most innovative, solution to a problem. 'Right' can only be evaluated by considering closely the characteristics of the user and the data as well as the context in which the system is being used. Then again, we do not consciously look for predefined and ready-made visualization methods that can be applied to any problem. We analyze the data that we want to visualize and then encode the different dimensions using visual and behavioral attributes that can be processed pre-attentively by the human brain. This way, we make best use of the user's capabilities as a human and simplify and deepen comprehension of the information that we represent.

5

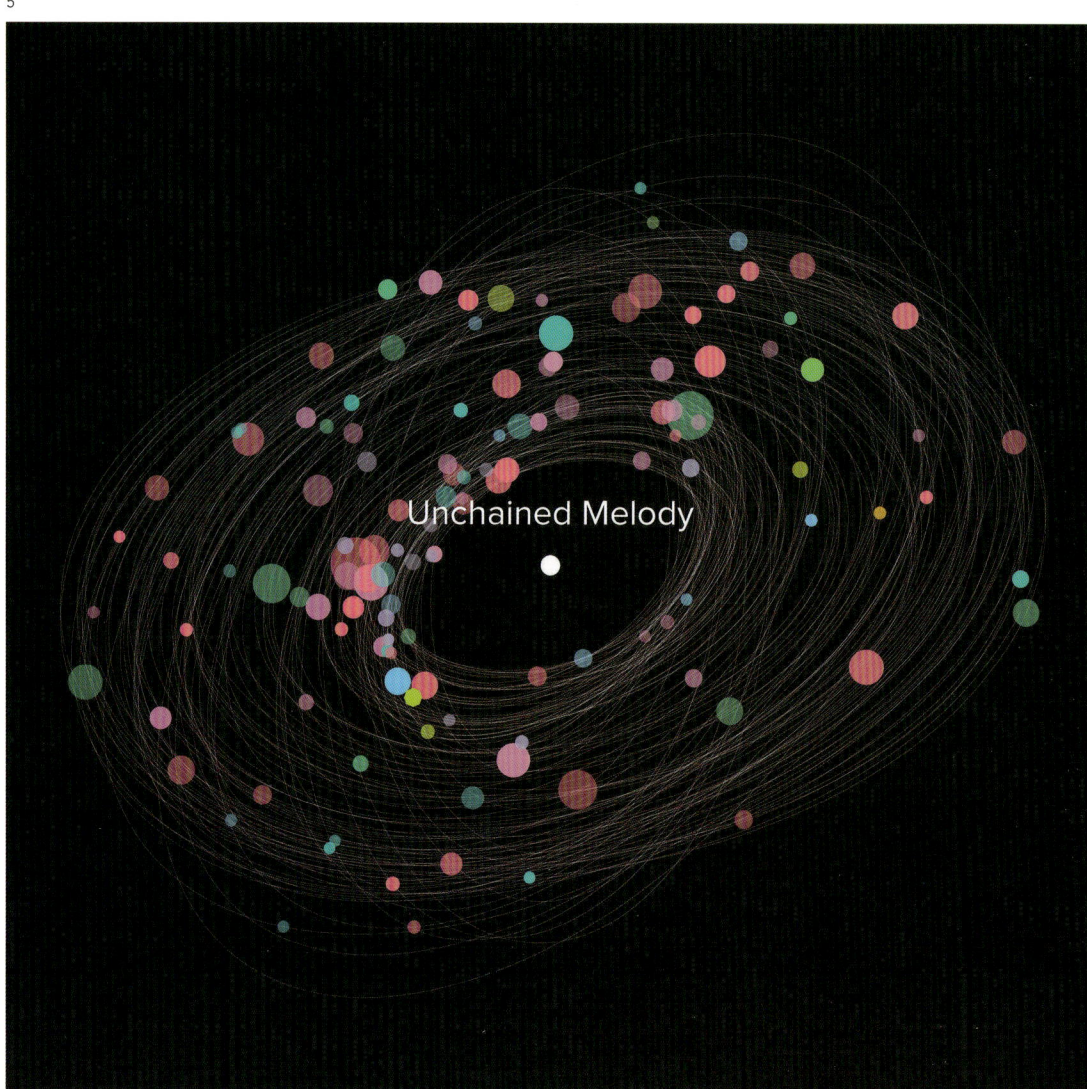

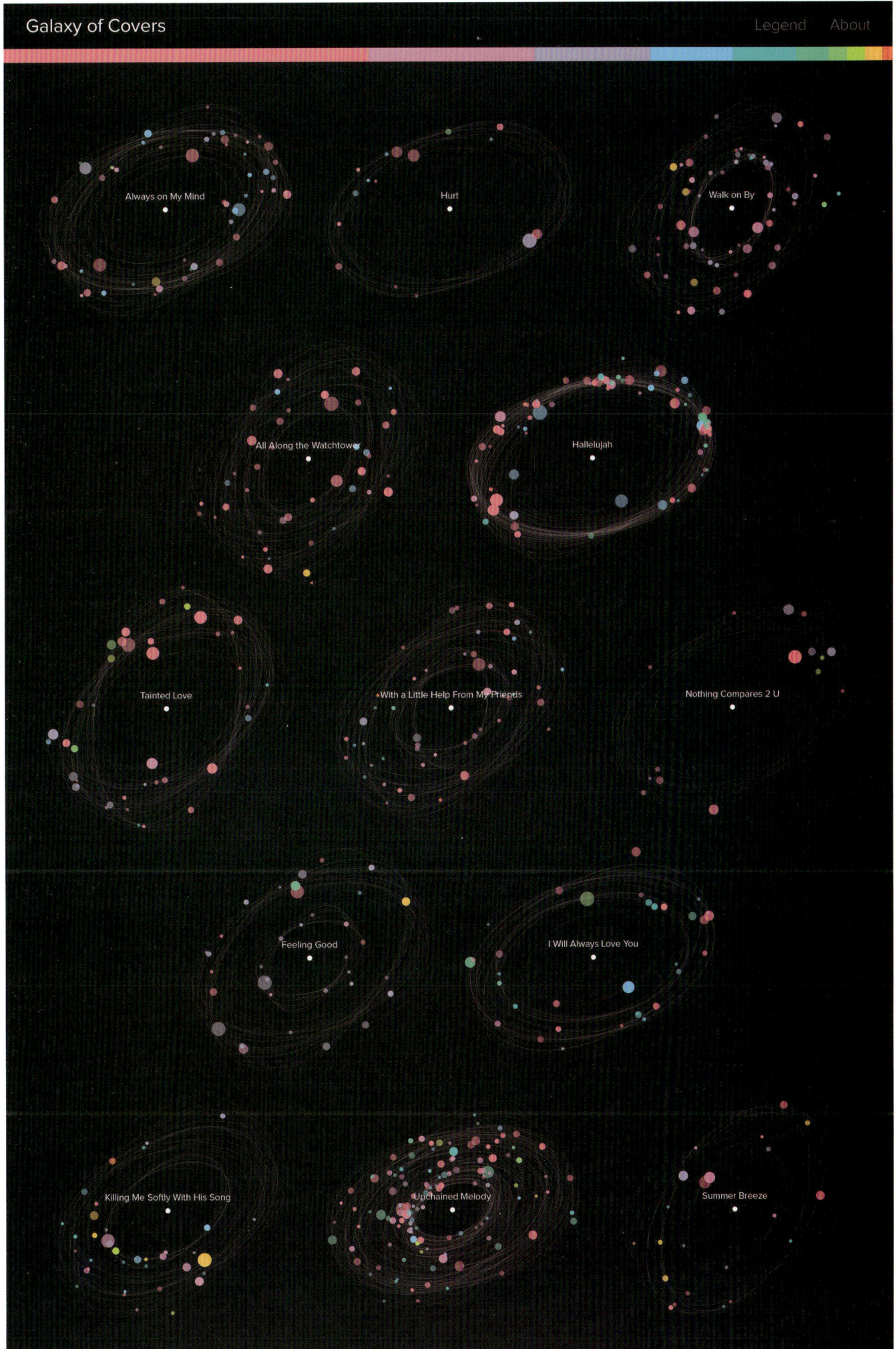

[Q] Where are your works applied?

[A] Looking at the works we are doing, you can easily distinguish two reccurring themes: user-centered design for interfaces between humans and machines, and data-driven design for interfaces between humans and information. If you would analyze our work in more detail, you would be able to place them on a range between these two themes with the majority of projects landing somewhere in the middle, where we have a strong overlap of requirements for solutions that are user-centered and data-driven at the same time. For us, this is the space where our capabilities can have the biggest impact. This is where we can contribute not only on a per-project basis, but hopefully to the design discipline as a whole. The intersection of user-experience design and data visualization is a space of increasing importance, considering the increasing amount of information available and the increasing ubiquity of computing capabilities. When we can create solutions that follow the best practices of these two fields, we are able to optimize interfaces for human capabilities while maintaining data integrity.

[Q] How do you turn boring and complex data into something interesting and understandable?

[A] As a design studio with the focus not only on data visualization, but also on user experience, it's evident that we follow fundamentally a user-centered design process. When I look closer at the individual phases that we typically go through when designing visualizations, I see 10 steps that are connected and get repeated as necessary:

1. Inform: We inform everyone on the team about the project in its entirety.
2. Prepare: We research, acquire, clean, and format the data.
3. Explore: We learn about the structure and texture of the data and what answers we will be able to draw from it.
4. Discover: We connect with the data and find stories, patterns, correlations, and challenges.
5. Sketch: We test out ideas visually based on the data to see if our ideas for the visual form are applicable and comprehensive.

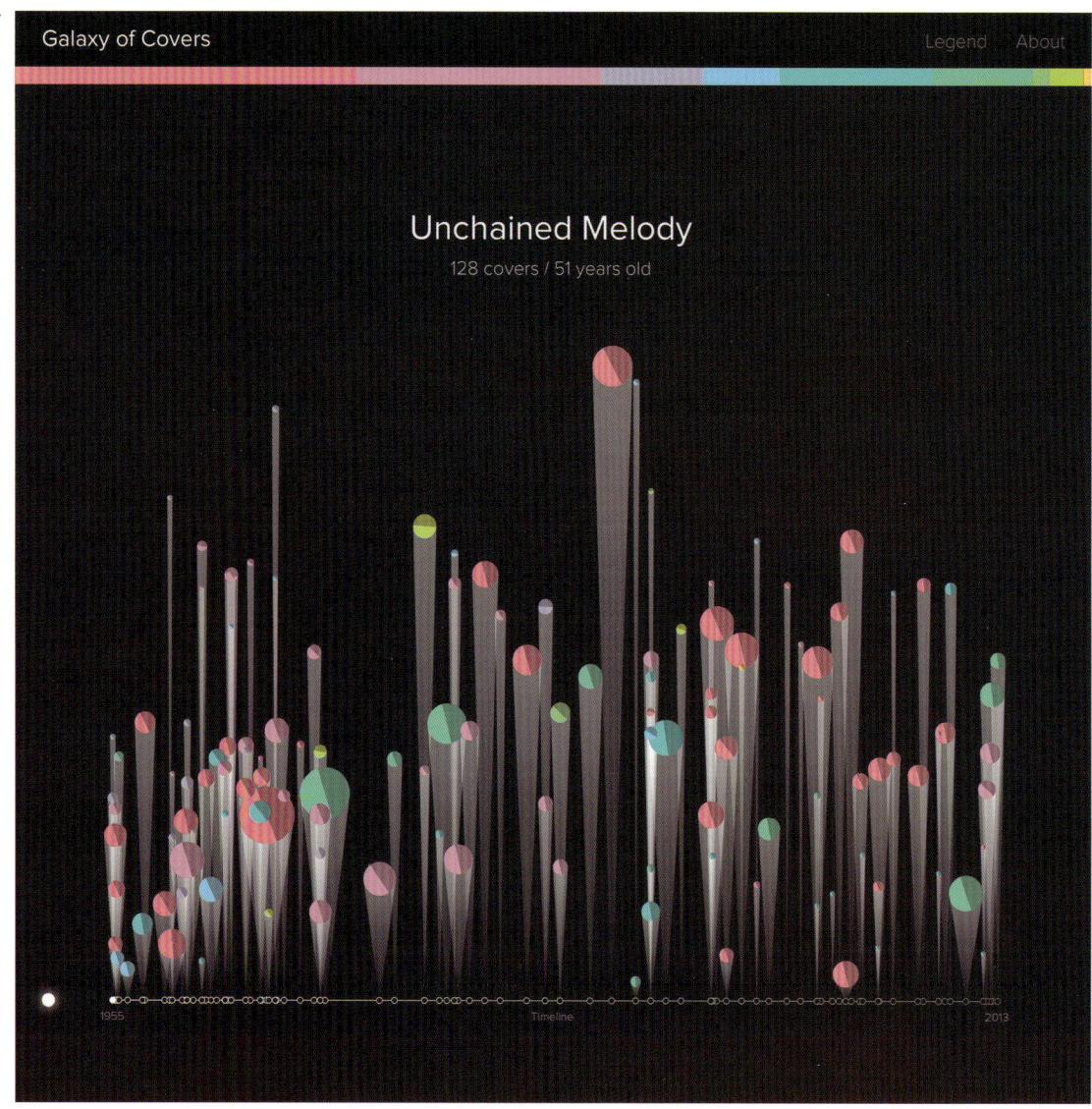

7

6   Question: We ask questions about our sketches to verify if the selected visualization methods truly provide valuable insights.
7   Design: We refine and finalize the visual and functional design of the visualizations and interfaces.
8   Develop: We implement a flawlessly working application.
9   Evaluate: We ensure that the solution is understandable, readable, usable, and useful, and make corrections and optimizations where necessary.
10 Deliver: We conclude the project by publishing and documenting it appropriately.

[Q] What is your suggestion for beginners?

[A] One general recommendation for anyone working in our field is to never lose your curiosity or your critical thinking. When we are curious, we keep searching for interesting, relevant, and exciting insights. When we are critical, we keep questioning our findings, assumptions, and interpretations. The dialectic process that we use by looking and questioning is what helps us make more meaningful discoveries.

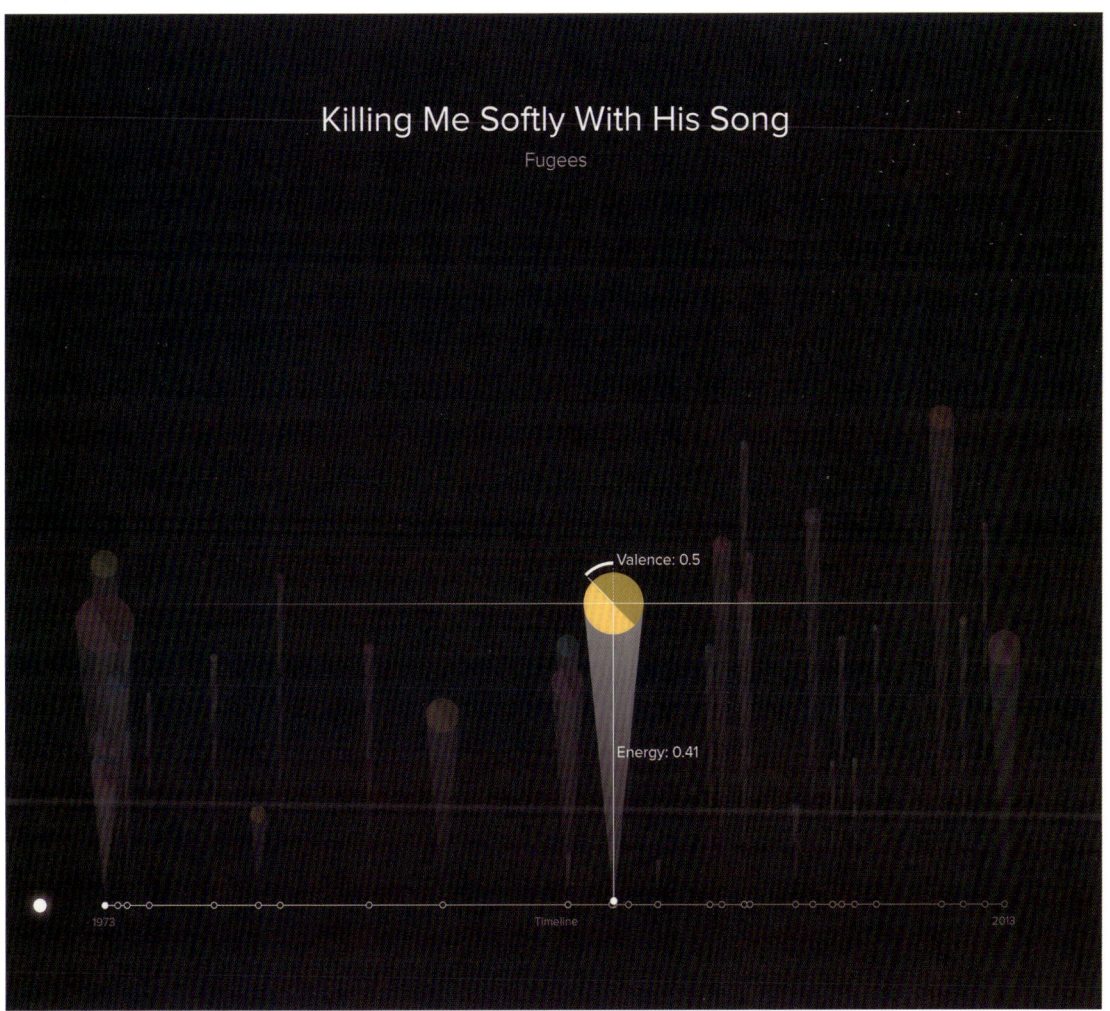

[5–8] Galaxy of Covers

Credit: Interactive Things
Completion: 2015
Interactive link: lab.interactivethings.com/galaxy-of-covers

Our most beloved songs might exist in hundreds of alternative versions created by other artists in distant decades. Those versions can differ in character and style and reach completely different audiences. The designers looked closely at the 50 most popular cover songs as well as the original works. The Galaxy of Covers visualization is the result of this analysis and allows the viewer to freely explore the evolution from idea to recording.

The panorama view shows the songs as individual planetary systems with the original song idea as the sun. Each planet represents a version of the song and its appearance indicates characteristics including genre, popularity, tempo, valence, energy, and speechiness. The radius of its orbit around the sun shows the years between the publication dates. This view allows us to compare the structure and density of the constellation of different songs from a high-level perspective. The detailed view of a planetary system lists the versions of one song in cross-section. The characteristics and positioning of the planets is consistent with the panorama. This view allows us to compare different versions of the same song individually.

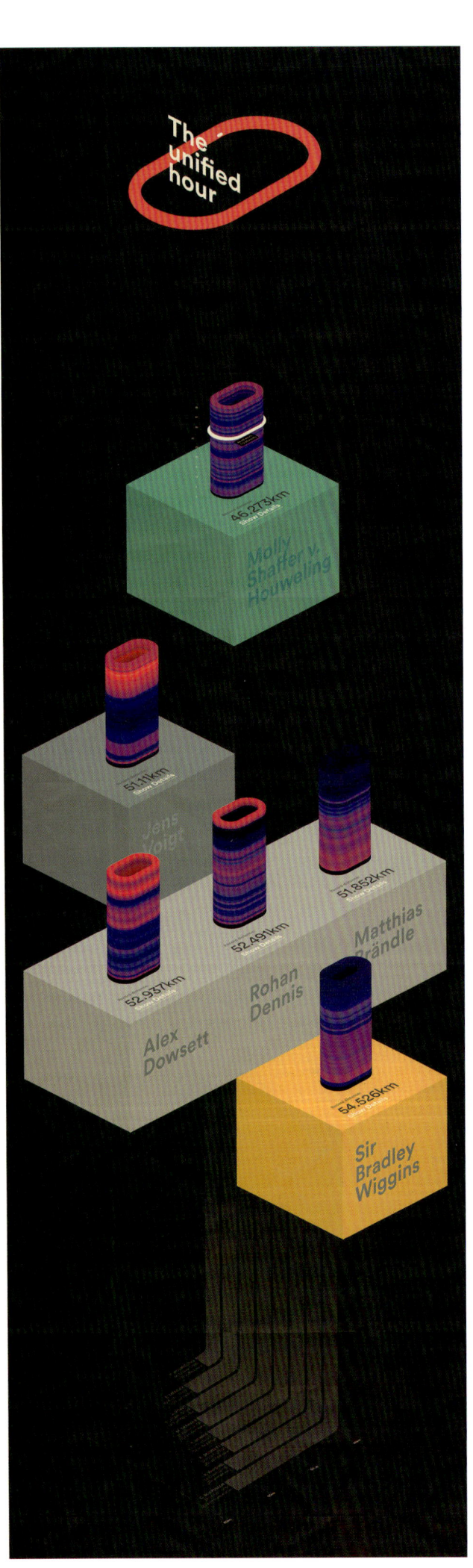

[9–15] The Unified Hour

Credit: Interactive Things
Completion: 2016
Interactive link: lab.interactivethings.com/the-unified-hour

The premise for the Hour Record cycling discipline is pretty simple: how far can a cyclist ride in one hour? There are no competitors, just the cyclist and their track bicycles in a velodrome. All that is left to do then is to start to pedal and keep turning left. While this does not sound too spectacular, the records made in this discipline have been held in high regard since the first official record in 1893 in Paris. The simple setup reduces external factors, such as road conditions in outdoor road racing disciplines, and allows for a nearly direct representation of an athlete's strength.

The designers wanted to understand how athletes in this discipline attempt to create new records. Using UCI (Union Cycliste Internationale) data for the attempts since the rule change in 2014, they visualized the different pacing strategies used to provide insight into how the various attempts differ and how they compare. From the visualizations, we can see that some athletes try to maintain a constant pace, while others have spikes of energy. Besides seeing each rider's pacing strategy, the visualization shows how environmental conditions such as atmospheric pressure and the altitude of the velodrome affect the record. As a user, we can even play with these parameters and see how they influence the record's distance.

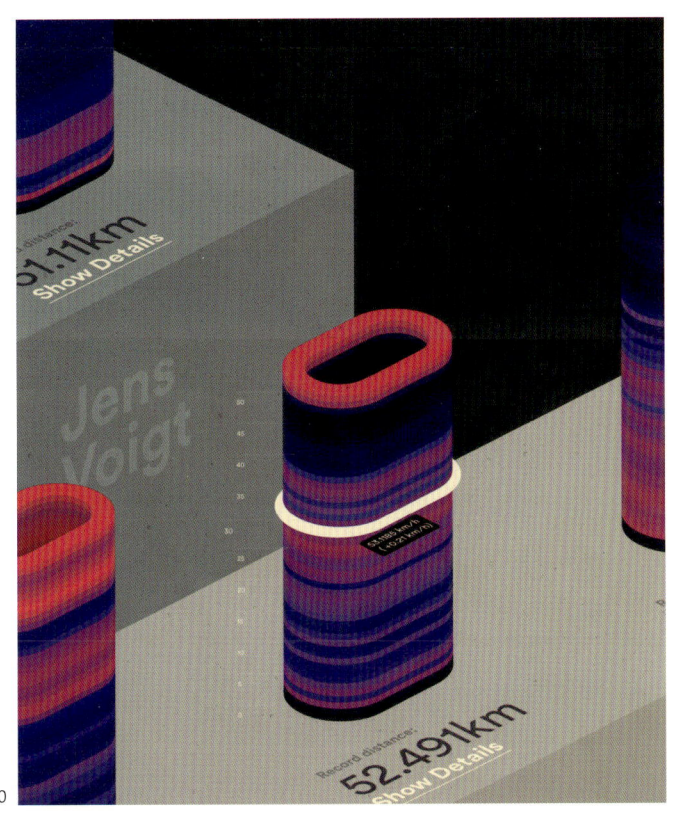
10

11

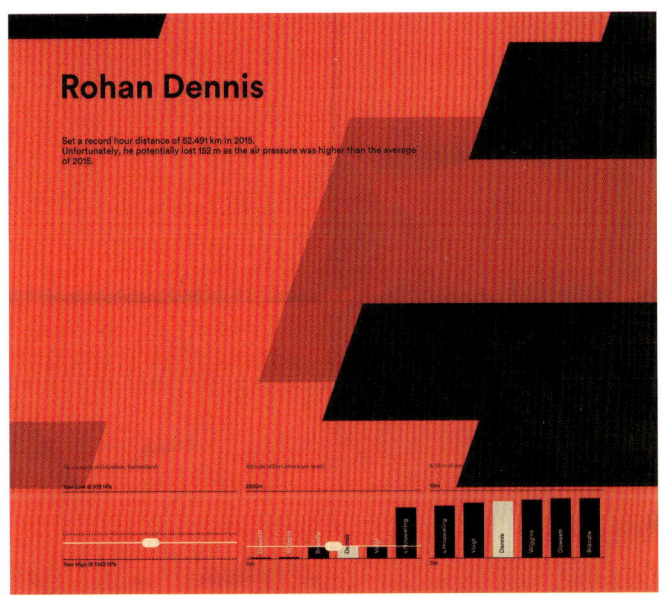
12

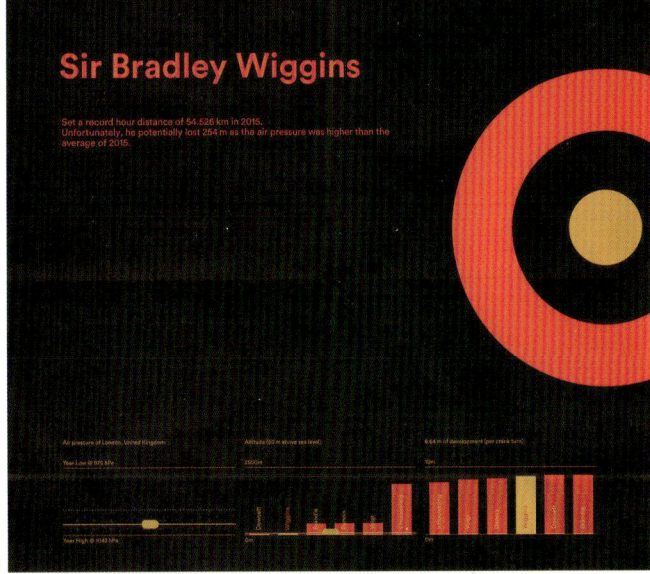
13

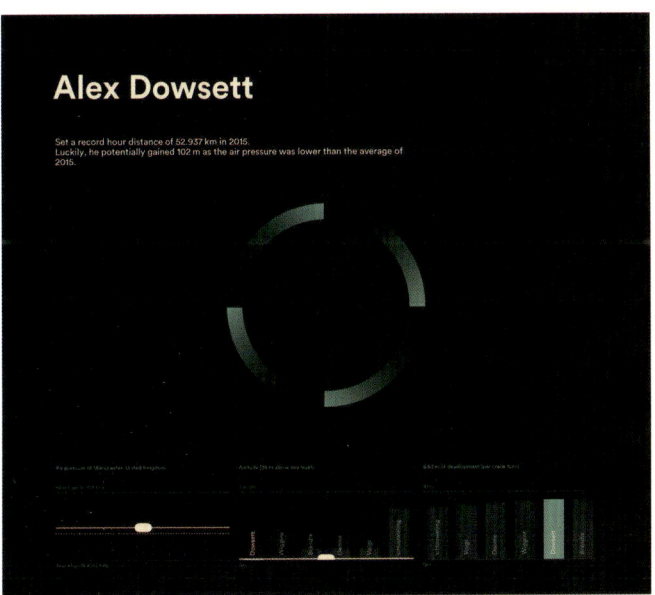
14

15

JESS3

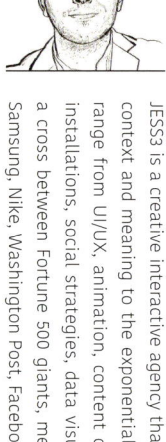

JESS3 is a creative interactive agency that specializes in the art of data visualization, adding context and meaning to the exponentially growing world of data around us. Their services range from UI/UX, animation, content creation, and digital PR to developing large-scale installations, social strategies, data visualizations, and infographics. Their client roster is a cross between Fortune 500 giants, media empires, and start-up powerhouses, including Samsung, Nike, Washington Post, Facebook, National Geographic, Microsoft, and Google.

[Q] What do you think about data visualization/infographics?

[A] Data visualization is what we do, so we naturally love it, as well as infographics, motion graphics, and interactive data graphics. Data visualization is, to us, a very broad term, as most of what we see is a form of 'data visualization'. Whether it is an advertisement for 90 percent fat-free yoghurt, a spreadsheet, the computer screen, or an amazing illustrated infographic, it is all data that's visualized with a purpose.

[Q] What kind of design methods do you commonly use?

[A] We have many methods and best practices that we employ for our data visualization projects and the top one would be matching a chart type to the data. On a basic level, most data types have a chart type that best suits it. For instance, a pie chart has very high stats when it comes to viewers understanding and absorbing the display of multiple percentages. The pie chart could end up being a pizza, a donut or even a ring of fire with a cat jumping through it, but in the end, your graphic will be easier to consume due to the underlying chart.

[Q] What kind of design elements do you commonly use?

[A] Grouping data in sections, or as we call it a 'narrative', is our most common design tactic. Users or viewers aren't digging into large meaty graphics like they used to, they now want it spoon-fed like a storybook of data. Without an immediately intuitive hierarchy for your data visual, many viewers will not bother.

Our types of graphs are selected mostly based on data comprehension. While we love data visuals, the purpose of our creations are not purely visual; their function is to be consumed and generate results for our clients. Based on this, we make sure our graphs or shapes work for the type of data. Making the data easier to comprehend gives our infographics the upper hand in fast consumption platforms such as social media and advertising.

An example would be percentages; while they can be plotted on most styles of chart, a pie chart is usually best for comprehension. Although this can change, you could have multiple percent categories with slight variations (making the differences hard or even impossible to distinguish). A more granular bar chart view focused on the variation range could be better in that situation.

[Q] Where are your works applied?

[A] As we mentioned, data visuals are everywhere, and so are our projects. We have worked on interactive television walls, created physical data visual jungles at SXSW, had felt puppets explaining charts for ESPN ratings, and plotted world social trends for US television presenters.

1

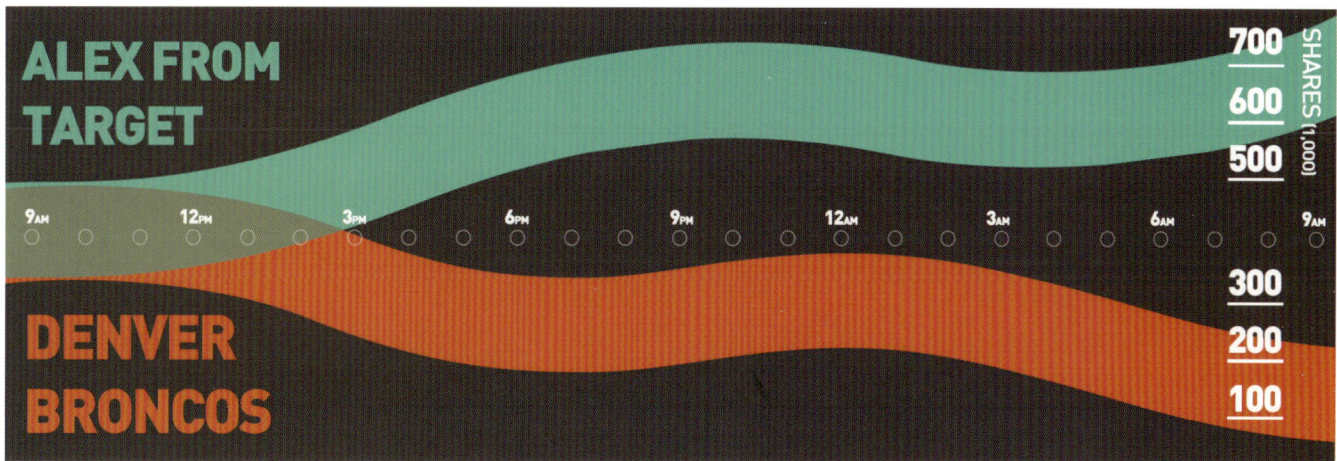

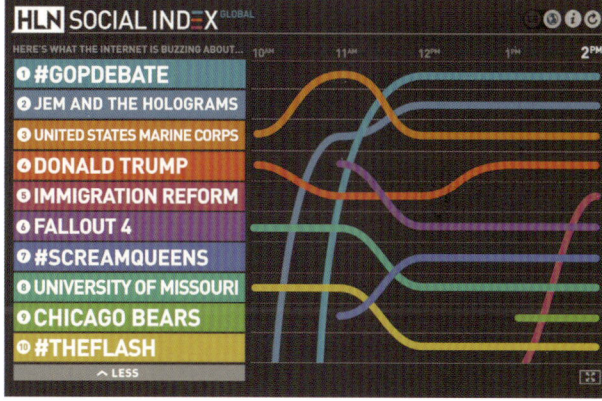

[1–5] HLN Social Index

Credit: JESS3
Completion: 2016

The HLN Social Index is a real-time, all-screens data visualization that ranks the top trends in conversation across social networks (currently accounting for Facebook, Twitter, and Google, with more sources coming soon). It is powered by HLN's proprietary trending algorithm, together with editorial context that explains what's behind the trend. With updates every hour, it's your guide to never missing out on what the internet is talking about, ever again. Their visual approach for this project was influenced by the company branding and on-air visuals. Interaction with the UI on television required large, easily digestible icons and text, in order to be functional.

[Q] How do you turn boring and complex data into something interesting and understandable?

[A] Push your visuals, go crazy with them and keep on pushing till it starts to affect how easy it is understand. We have a strong belief that data visuals should never be boring; just because you may be working with boring data doesn't mean your graphic should be boring too.

[Q] What is your suggestion for beginners?

[A] When doing your first data visual, don't jump straight to the visual. We recommend you look to the data for inspiration. Give the data some love, look it over, group it in sections, and experiment with ways those sections can interact or be linked. A good handle on the data you are using is incredibly valuable for the layouts and creative thinking.

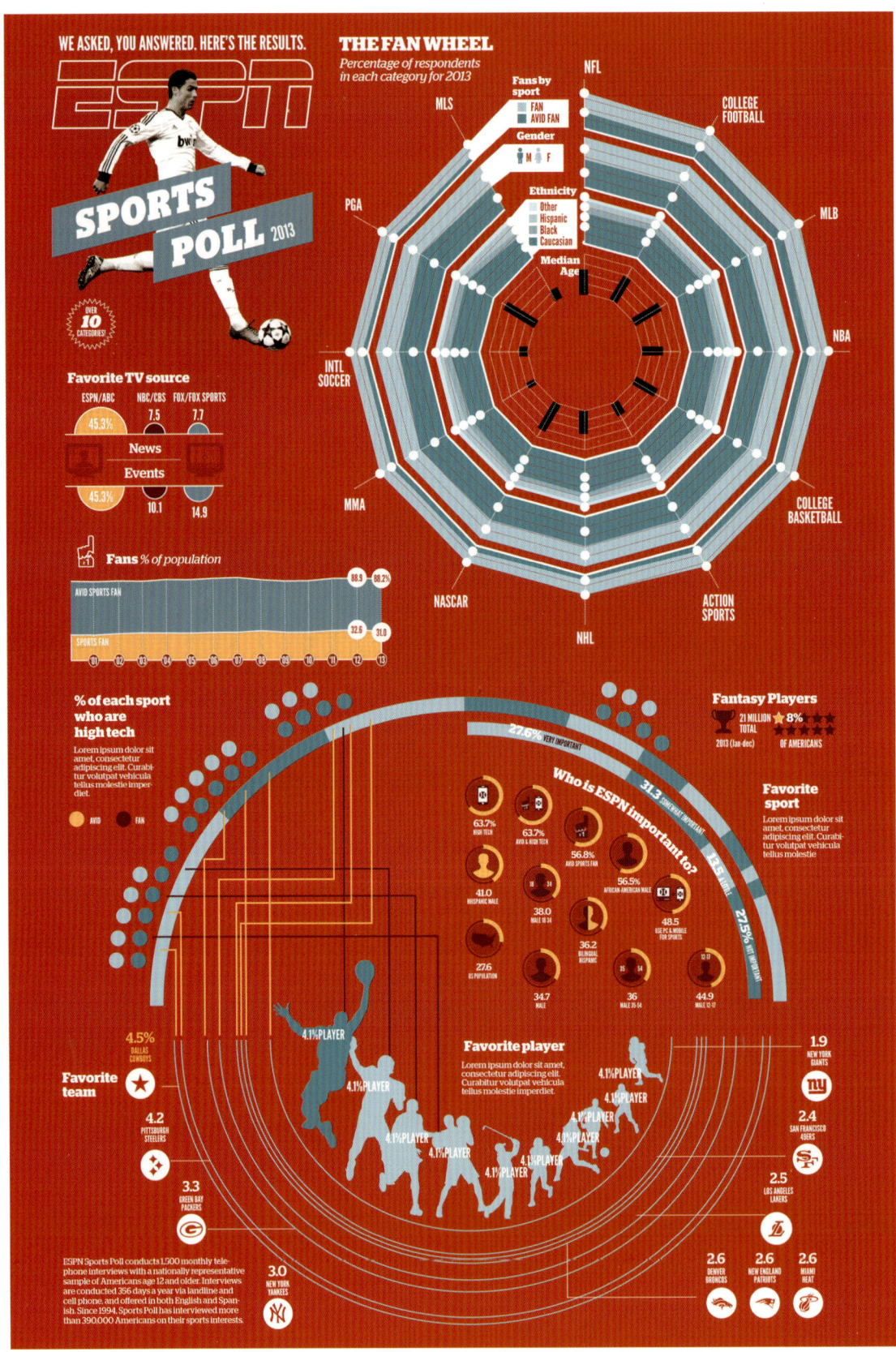

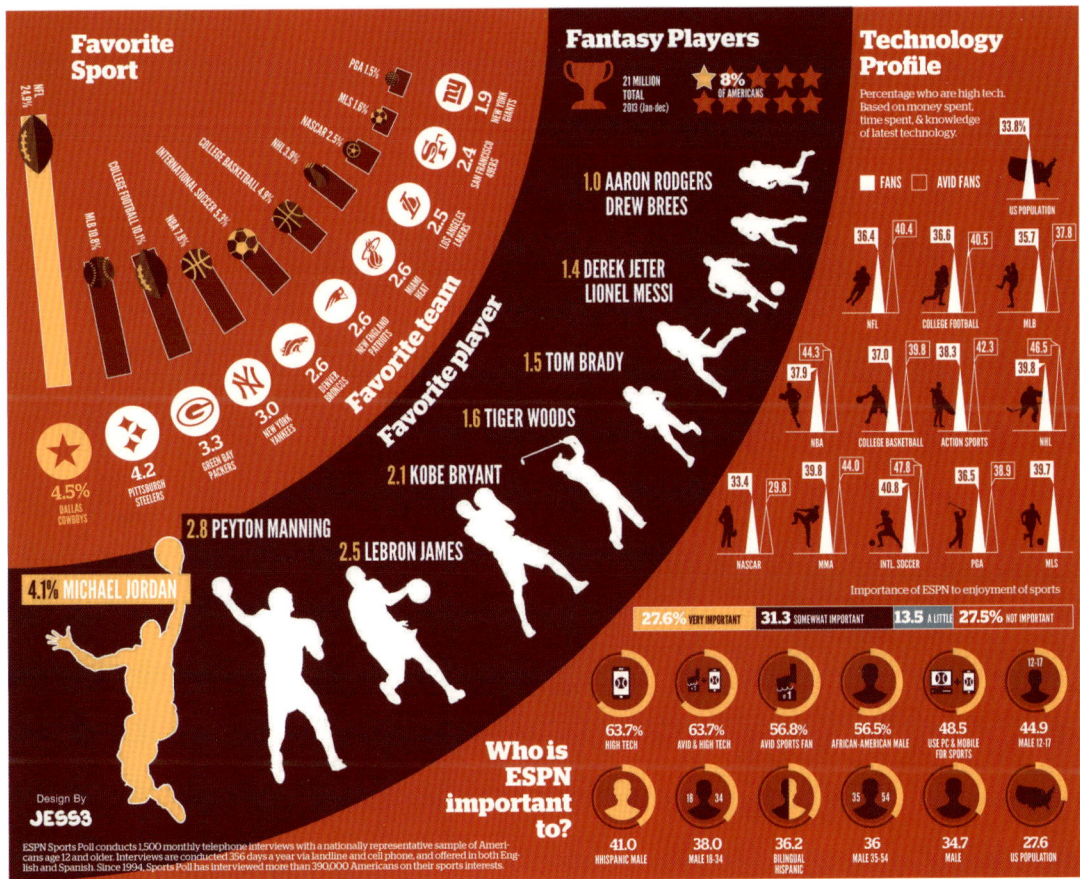

[6–8] Sports Poll Poster, Spring 2014 Update

Credit: JESS3
Completion: 2014

ESPN's annual Sports Poll attracts sports fans of all types. By using a ball, a puck, wheels, or fists, *ESPN* tracks and records the statistics for their fan base. The designers helped them compile these statistics into annually produced posters that are digestible, beautiful, and packed to the gills with sports data. They used a combination of smaller charts and text for these, considering that they are used for print.

LaTigre

LaTigre, directed by Luisa Milani and Walter Molteni, is a multi-disciplinary creative consultancy that specializes in refined visual design solutions and data visualization for various clients, including IBM, *The New York Times Magazine, Wired, The Guardian, New Yorker, Il sole 24 ore, Suddeutsche Zeitung, Die Zeit, Le Monde, ESPN* and so on. In 2012, LaTigre was awarded the Art Directors Club's Young Guns. In 2016, it was mentioned by New York Type Directors Club, Society of Publication Designers, and it was awarded gold by the Spanish Laus award.

[Q] What do you think about data visualization/infographics?

[A] Data visualization or infographics is an easier and faster way to read and understand concepts and information.

[Q] What kind of design methods do you commonly use?

[A] We always try to make the topic readable through aesthetic. This means that the visualization conveys the topic at first sight through the graphic elements used.

[Q] What kind of design elements do you commonly use?

[A] We use charts and bars, pattern and colors.

[Q] Where are your works applied?

[A] We usually design infographics for newspapers and magazines all over the world. Increasingly frequently, companies ask for data visualization in their company profiles, catalogues, website, etc. because it is an easy way to explain concepts and information about a lot of topics.

[Q] How do you turn boring and complex data into something interesting and understandable?

[A] We start thinking of an idea that leads all the charts. It's always important to consider who we are working for. That is to say the kind of magazine we are working for, who is the target, how it views the graphic project, etc.

[Q] What is your suggestion for beginners?

[A] We suggest thinking of data as a whole, to look at it as any other design project. The most important rule is clarity; never forget we are designers and our goal is functional.

1

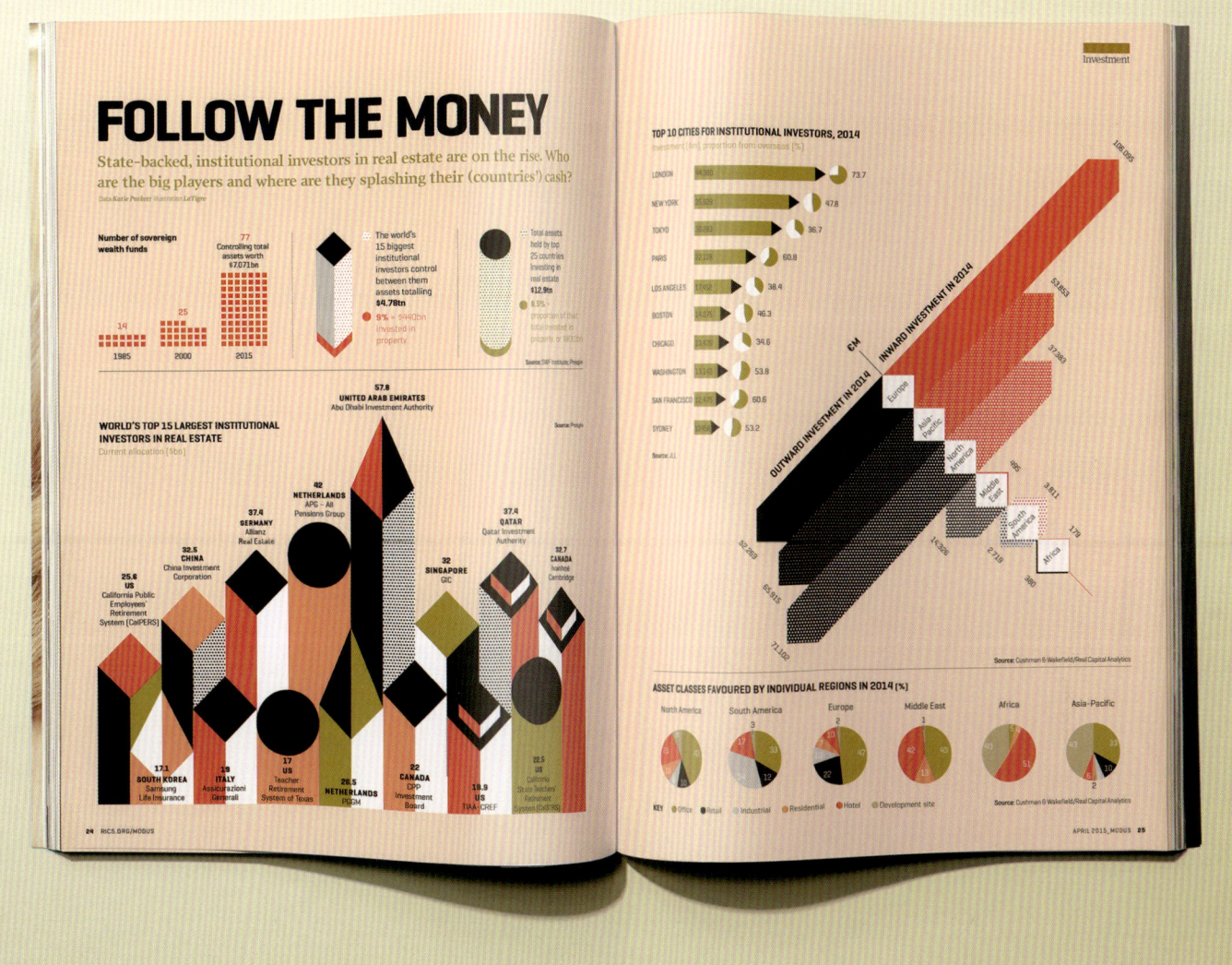

[1] Viv

Credit: Caleb Bennet (art direction)
Completion: 2014

It is the visualization of the Viv system, an intelligent personal assistant created by the makers of Apple's Siri. This technology enables people to interact by conversation with devices and services. This visualization shows how this technology works with simple daily life queries. The information is depicted in a very technical way like a workflow, and the forms are simple and the colors give them a vibrant thrill.

[2] Follow the Money

Credit: Christie Ferdinando (art direction)
Completion: 2015

This is a double-spread infographic about real estate. The form of the charts symbolizes the physicality of the city itself, focusing on the data report. In this way, the bar charts become three-dimensional and come out from the two-dimensional page. The vibrant color palette makes the data attractive and also the use of gold strengthens the concept of money involved in real estate.

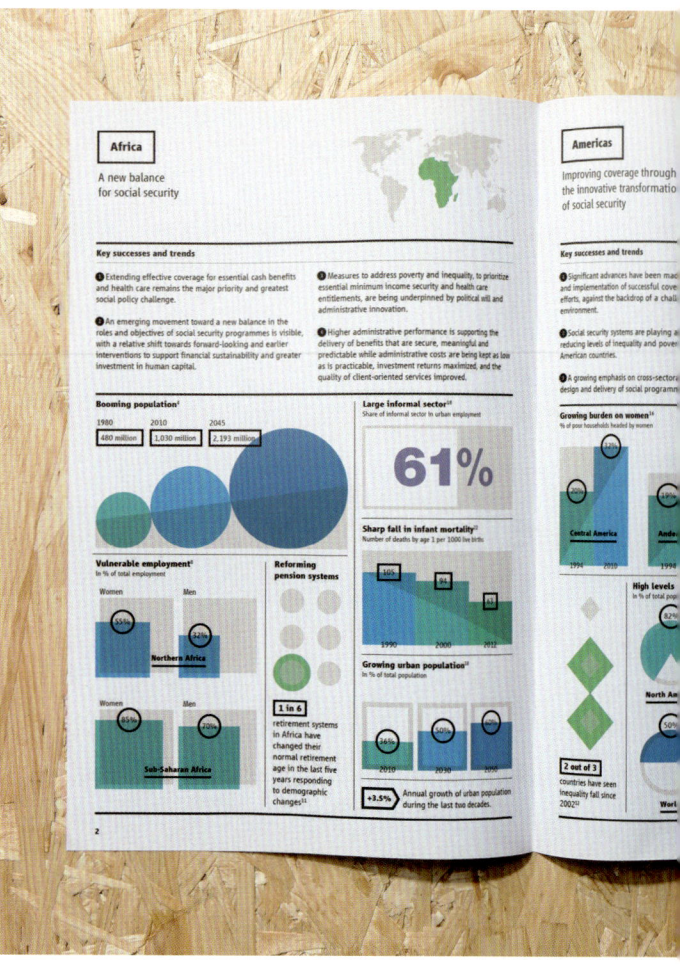
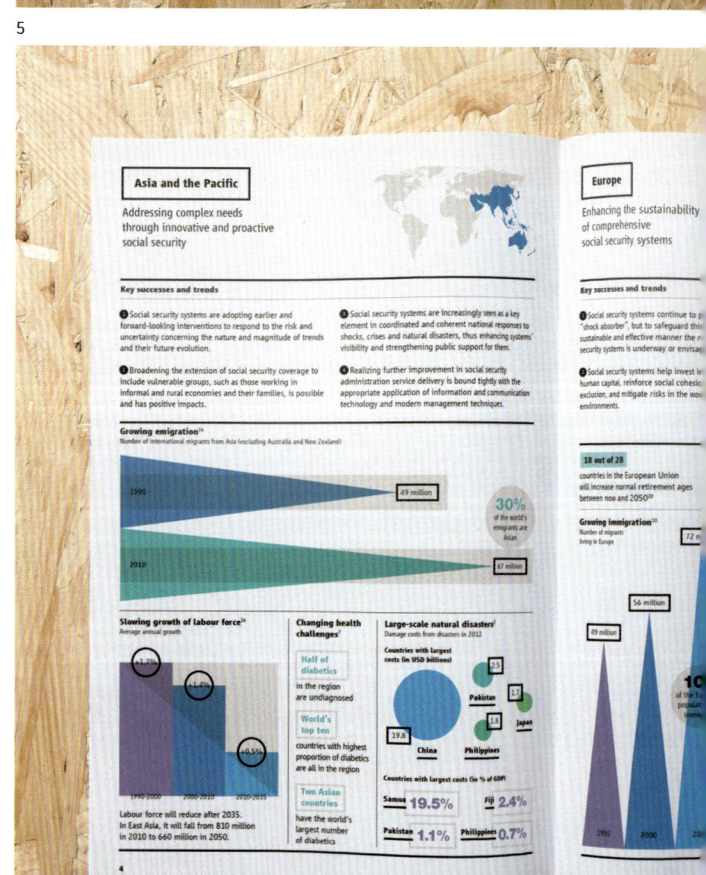

[3–7] Global Report 2013

Credits: Benjamin Bollmann (data and content),
Matteo Cremonini (photography)
Completion: 2013

The Global Report was on developments and trends for the International Social Security Association. The language used in the visualizations is direct in order to convey the scientific information as clearly as possible, with no frills. To achieve that, the forms used are simple circles, squares, rhombuses, and triangles. In this way, the focus of the pages is just the pure data itself.

6

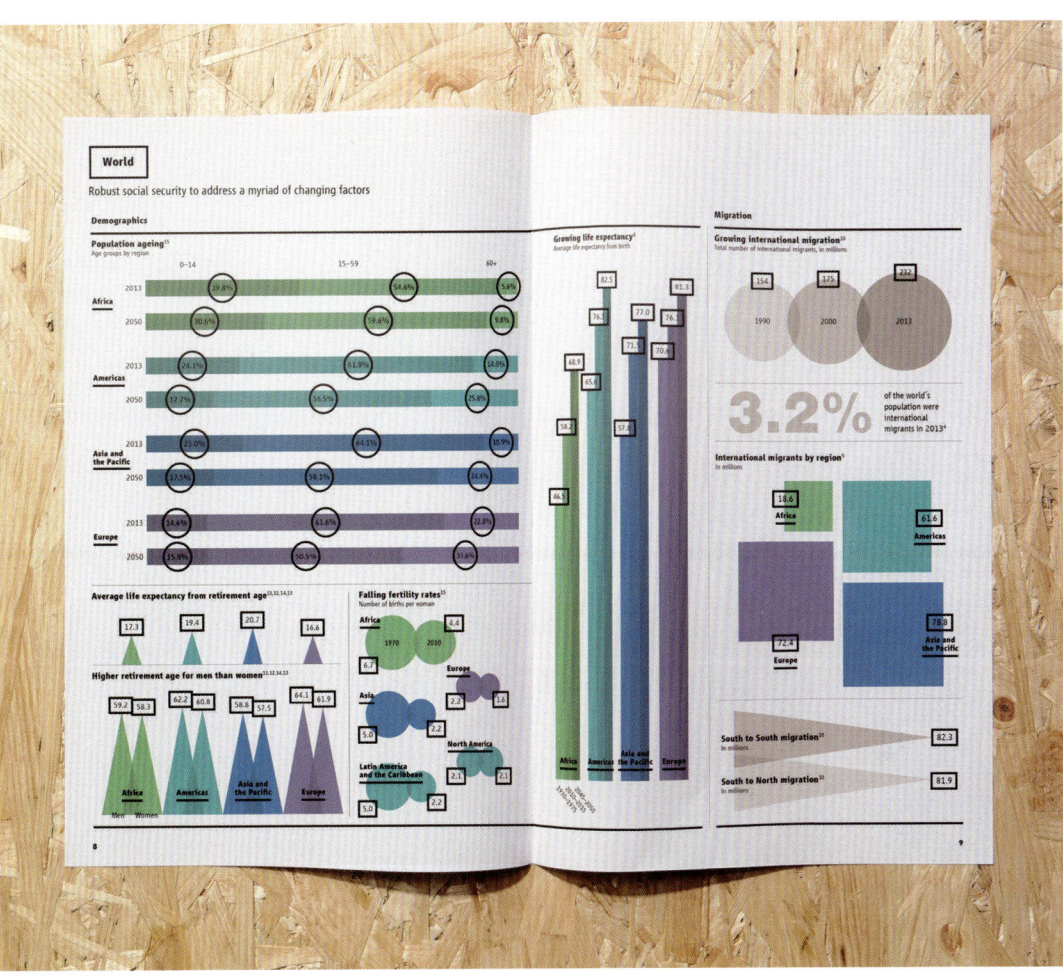

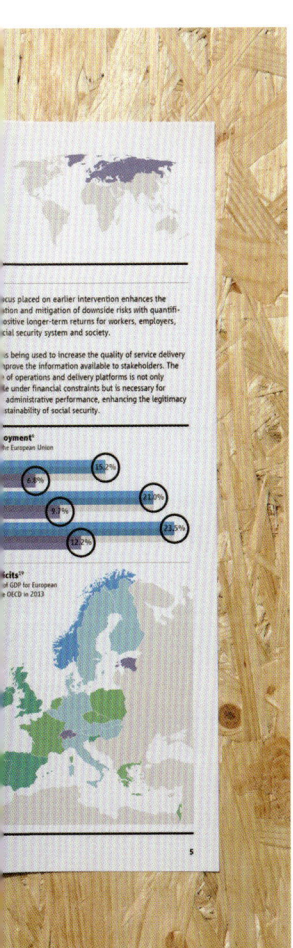

7

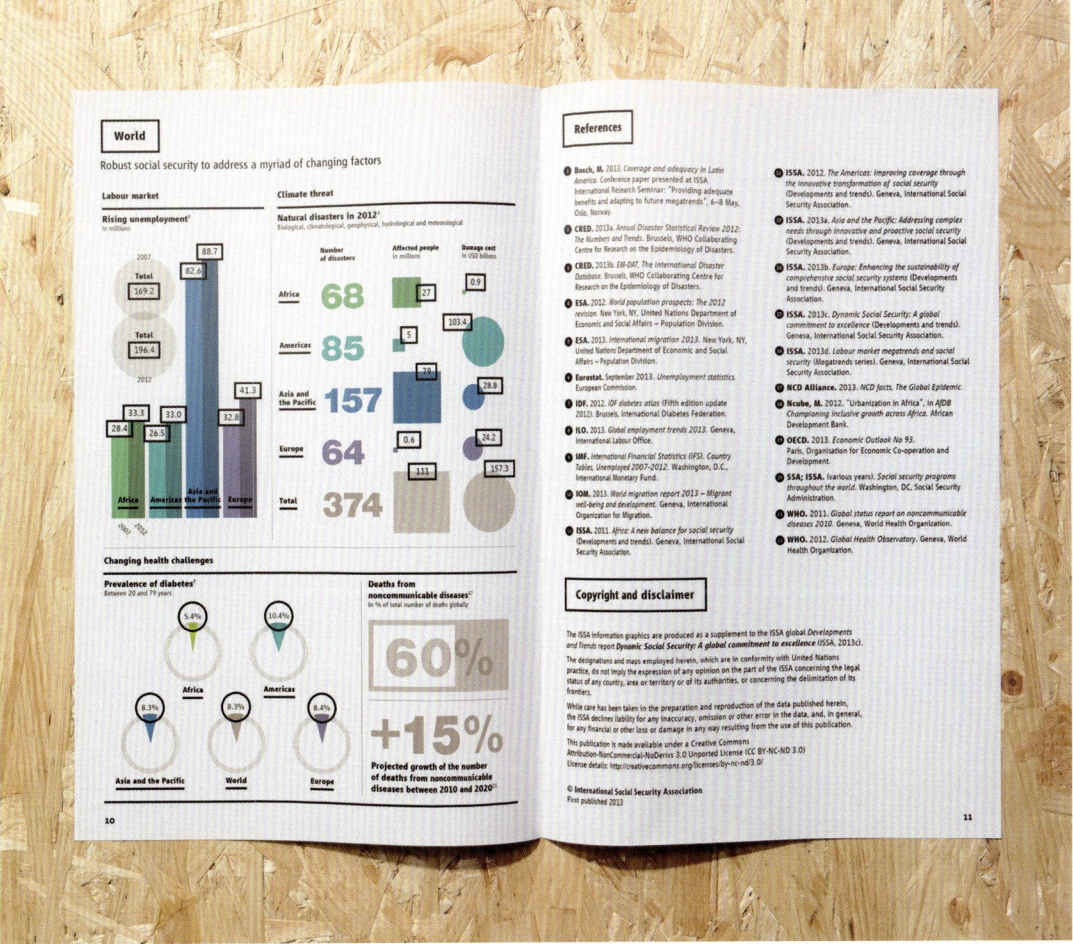

[8] Love vs Desire

Credit: LaTigre
Completion: 2014

This one-page infographic for *Die Zeit* magazine, shows the differences between love and desire. The idea stands behind the concept of these emotions and it is depicted with different gradient colors from pink to red and from red to yellow. The data changes below or above zero along with the emotions as related to love or desire.

[9–14] *Elephant Magazine* #25 & #26

Credits: Atlas (art direction), Matteo Cremonini (photography)
Completion: 2016

These infographics were realized for *Elephant Magazine* #25 and #26, a quarterly on contemporary art and visual culture. For issue #25, the infographic focuses on women in the art business and for issue #26, on Silicon Valley for and against creativity.

Both projects were used as special props strictly related to the artists' work or to a specific masterpiece. As an example, in *Elephant Magazine* #25 the bar charts represent the 'Top-selling living female artists'. Yayoi Kusama was depicted with the background of vivid yellow and black dots, as the artist's main characteristic is the obsession for polka dots. Cindy Sherman's bar chart was painted with red lipstick symbolizing her habit of role-playing with makeup and costumes in her photographic self-portraits. The idea has been applied also to the other artists' bar charts.

In *Elephant Magazine* #26, the infographics are related to the topic: as an example in the 'Silicon Valley tech timeline', the background is made of perforated laminate in order to make a grid, in which the cables, a symbol of tech and innovation, draw the timeline of the different companies' year of foundation.

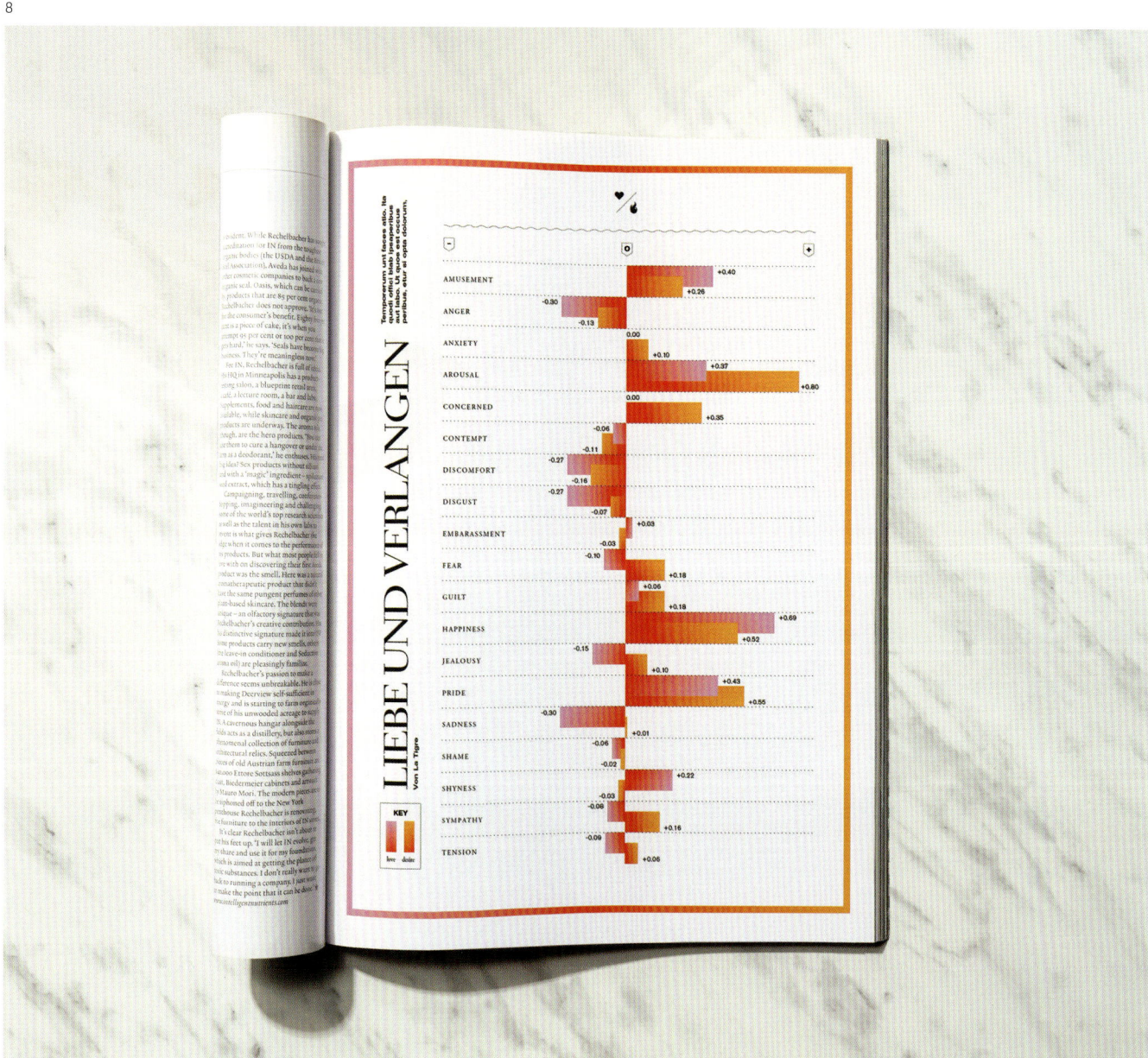

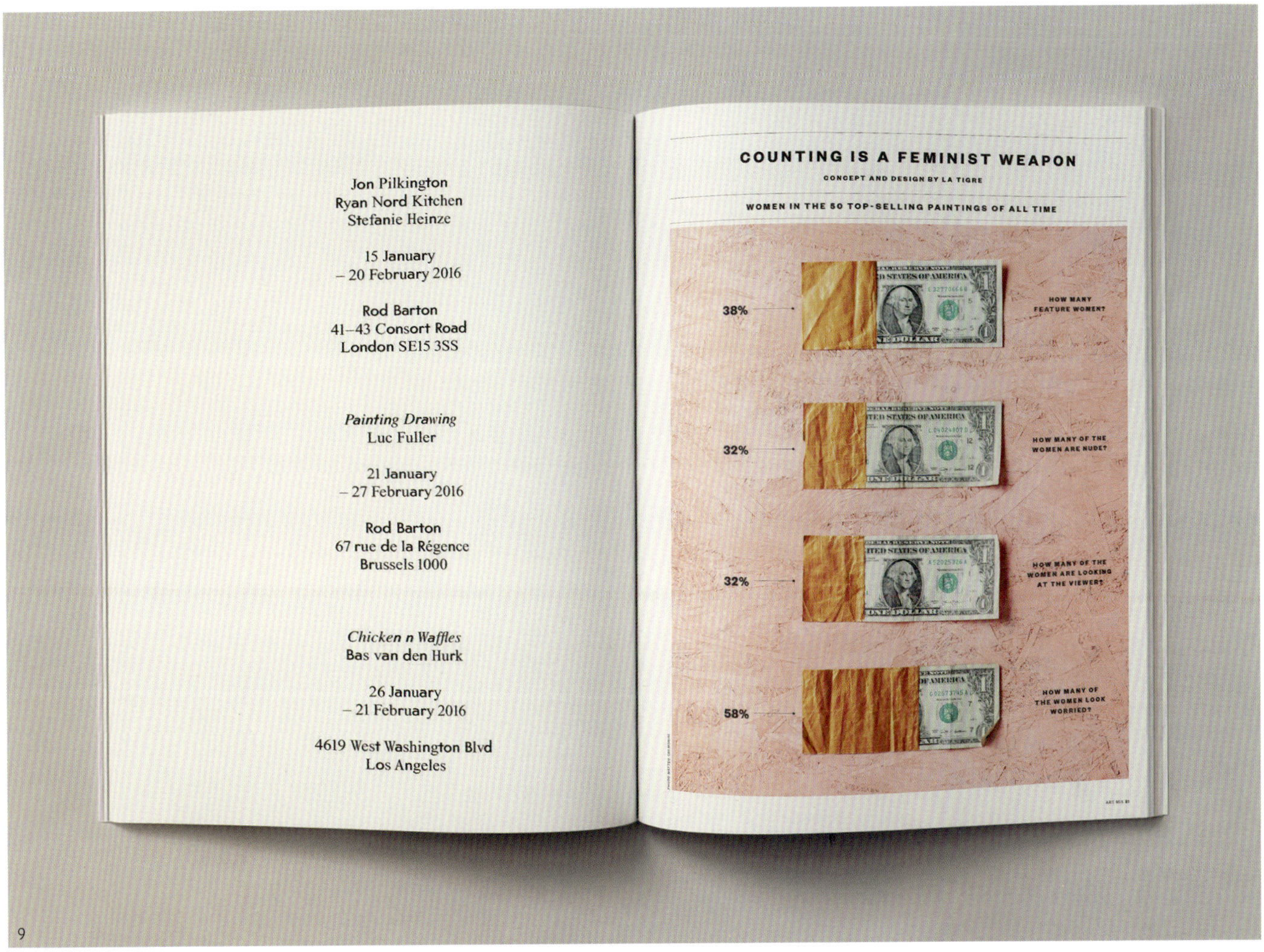

Jon Pilkington
Ryan Nord Kitchen
Stefanie Heinze

15 January
– 20 February 2016

Rod Barton
41–43 Consort Road
London SE15 3SS

Painting Drawing
Luc Fuller

21 January
– 27 February 2016

Rod Barton
67 rue de la Régence
Brussels 1000

Chicken n Waffles
Bas van den Hurk

26 January
– 21 February 2016

4619 West Washington Blvd
Los Angeles

COUNTING IS A FEMINIST WEAPON

CONCEPT AND DESIGN BY LA TIGRE

WOMEN IN THE 50 TOP-SELLING PAINTINGS OF ALL TIME

- 38% — HOW MANY FEATURE WOMEN?
- 32% — HOW MANY OF THE WOMEN ARE NUDE?
- 32% — HOW MANY OF THE WOMEN ARE LOOKING AT THE VIEWER?
- 58% — HOW MANY OF THE WOMEN LOOK WORRIED?

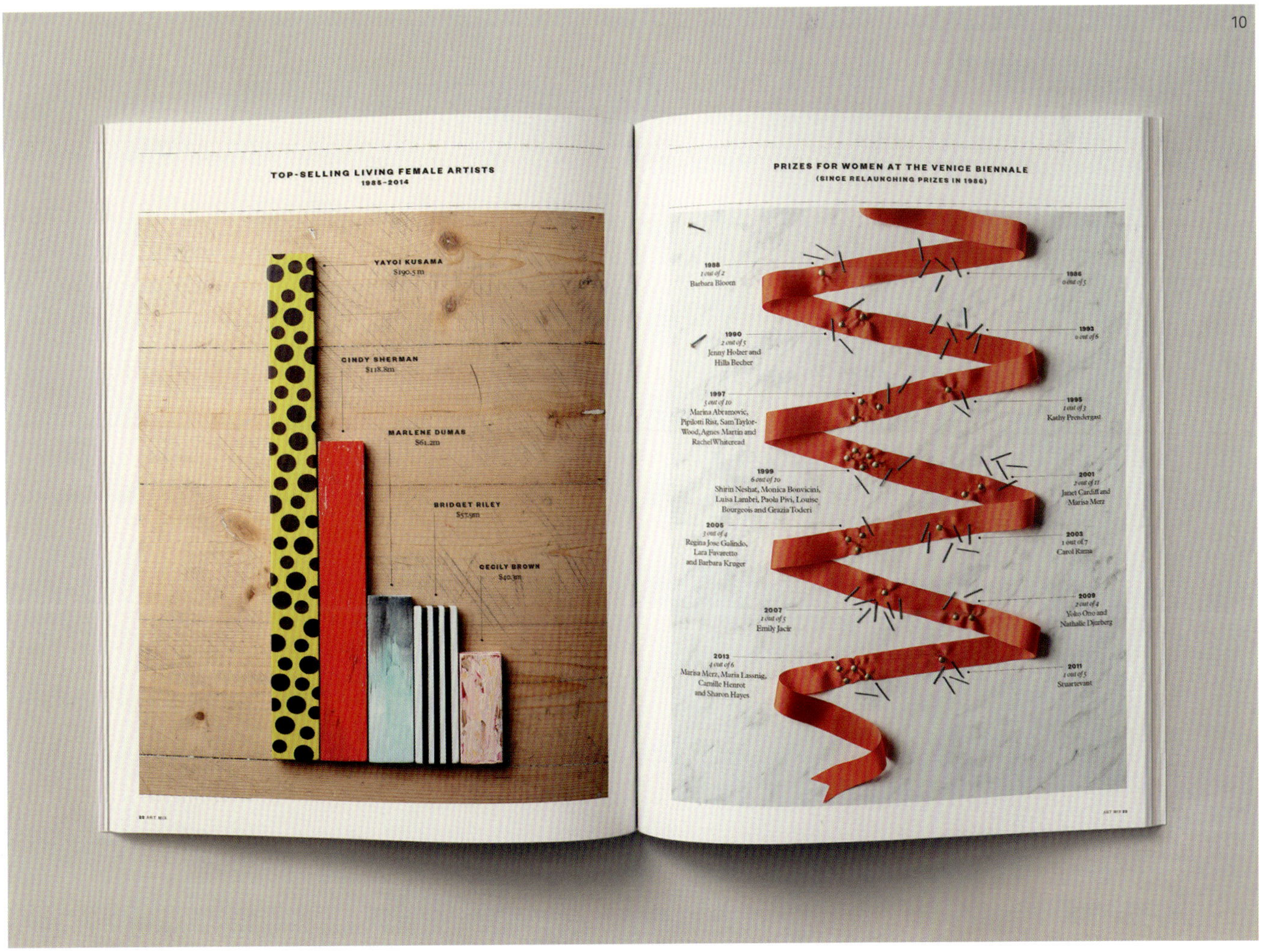

TOP-SELLING LIVING FEMALE ARTISTS
1985–2014

- YAYOI KUSAMA — $190.5m
- CINDY SHERMAN — $118.3m
- MARLENE DUMAS — $61.2m
- BRIDGET RILEY — $57.9m
- CECILY BROWN — $40.3m

PRIZES FOR WOMEN AT THE VENICE BIENNALE
(SINCE RELAUNCHING PRIZES IN 1986)

- 1986 — 1 out of 2 — Barbara Bloom
- 1986 — 0 out of 3
- 1990 — 2 out of 3 — Jenny Holzer and Hilla Becher
- 1993 — 0 out of 8
- 1997 — 1 out of 20 — Marina Abramović, Pipilotti Rist, Sam Taylor-Wood, Agnes Martin and Rachel Whiteread
- 1995 — 1 out of 3 — Kathy Prendergast
- 1999 — 6 out of 20 — Shirin Neshat, Monica Bonvicini, Luisa Lambri, Paola Pivi, Louise Bourgeois and Grazia Toderi
- 2001 — 2 out of 11 — Janet Cardiff and Marisa Merz
- 2003 — 2 out of 4 — Regina José Galindo, Lara Favaretto and Barbara Kruger
- 2005 — 1 out of 7 — Carol Rama
- 2007 — 1 out of 3 — Emily Jacir
- 2009 — 2 out of 4 — Yoko Ono and Nathalie Djurberg
- 2013 — 4 out of 6 — Marisa Merz, Maria Lassnig, Camille Henrot and Sharon Hayes
- 2011 — 1 out of 5 — Sturtevant

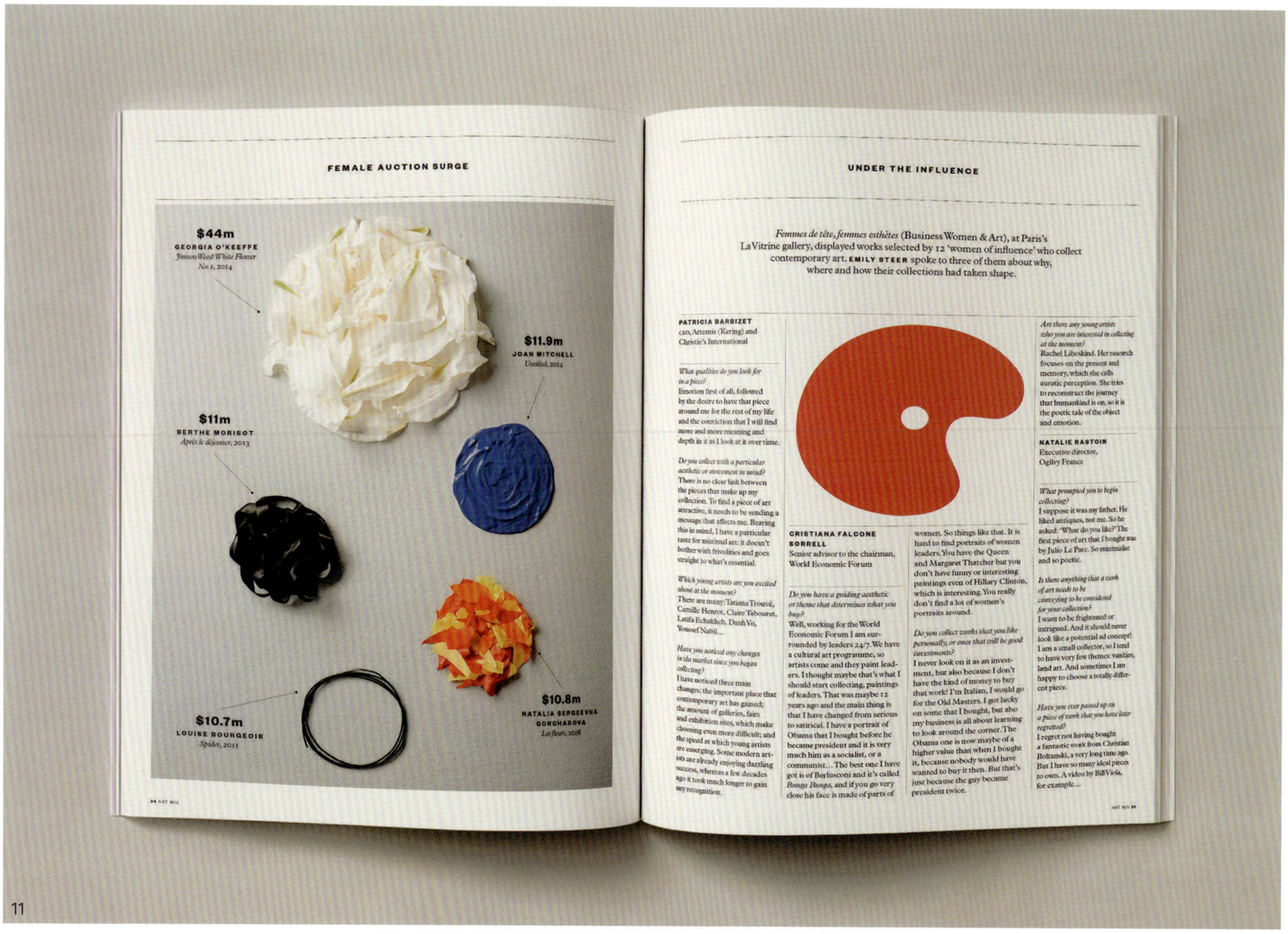

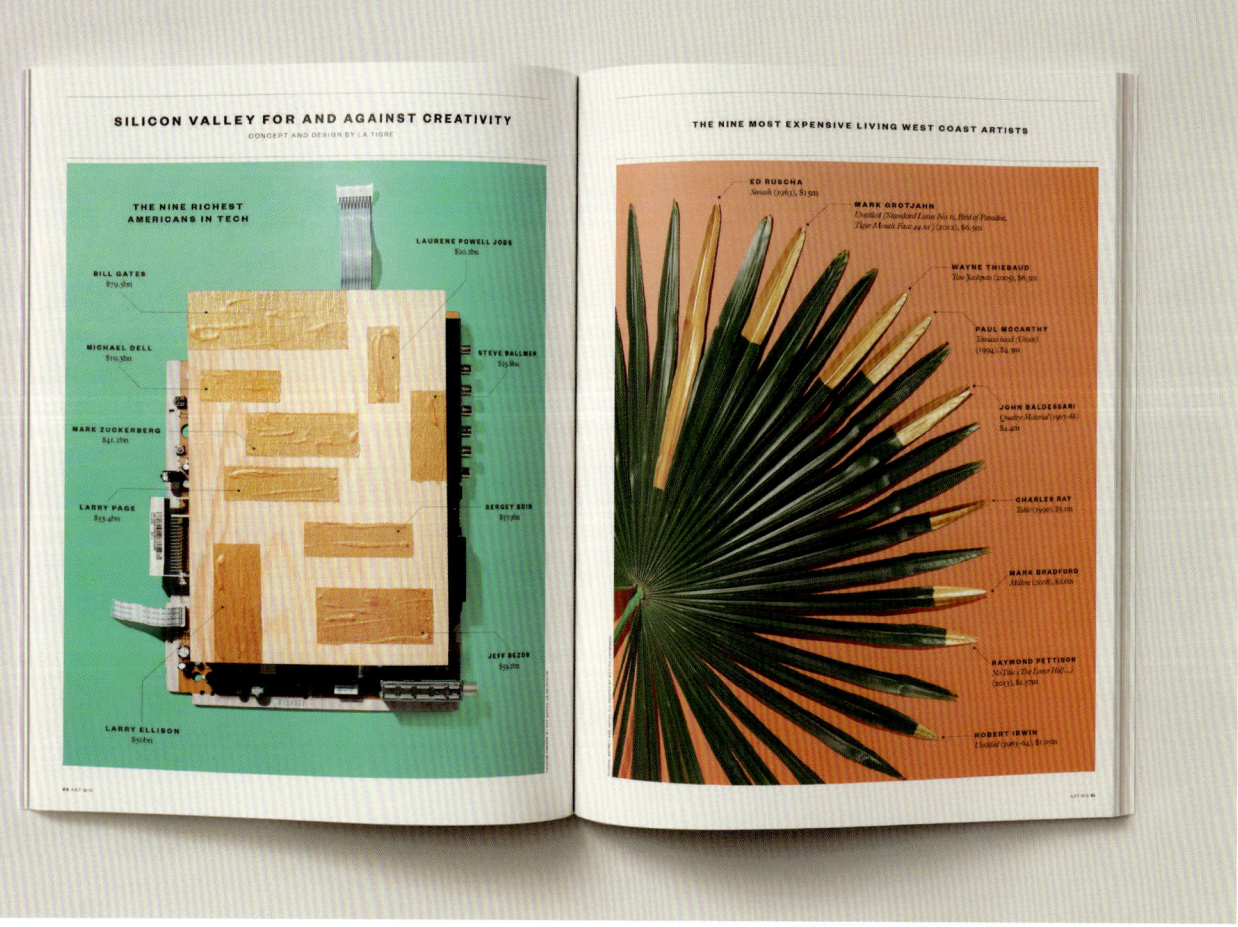

13

14

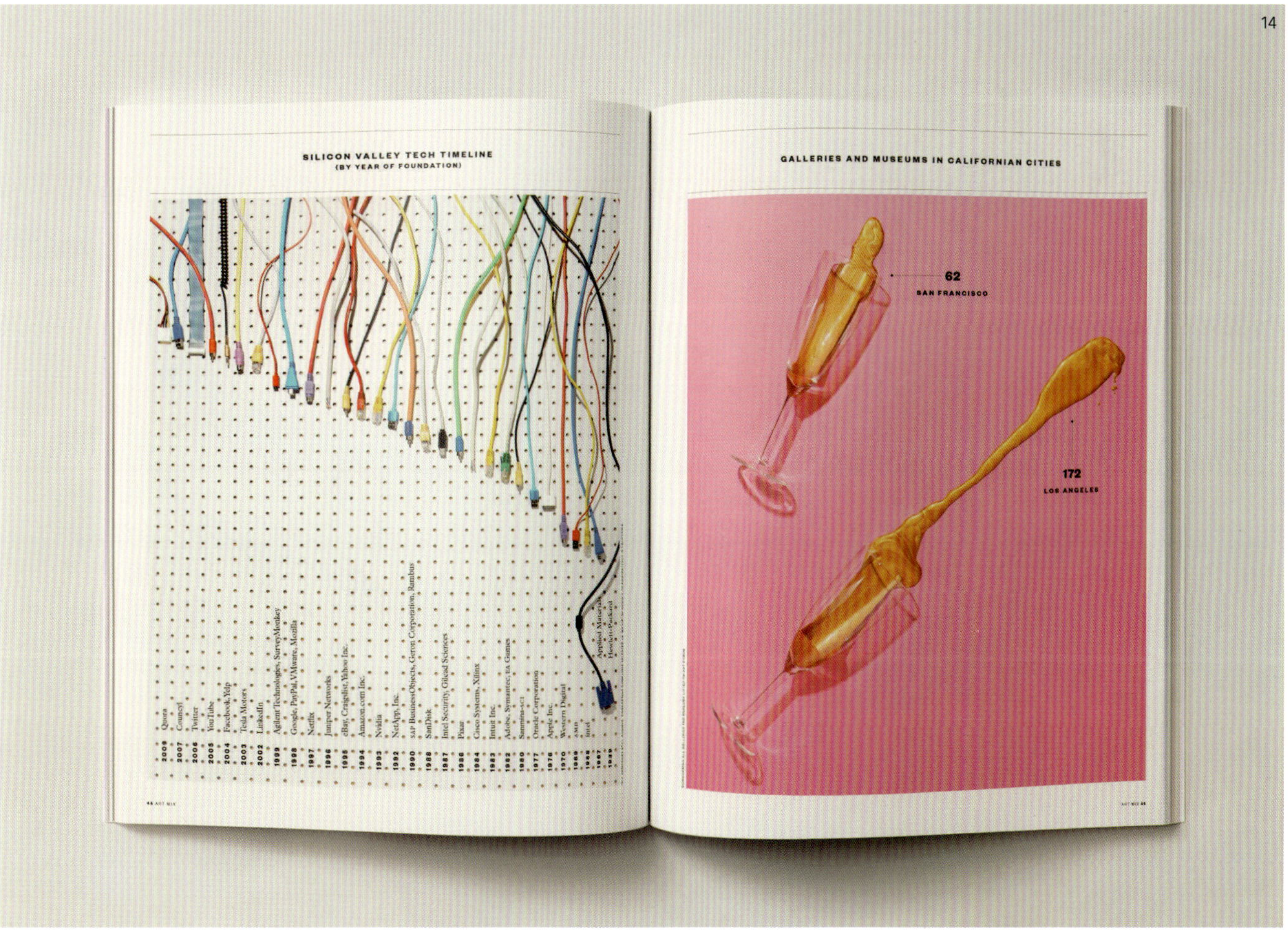

Susana Lopes

Susana Lopes has 14 years of work experience, and about 12 years of leadership. She has a master degree in design and visual culture, and she specializes in visual production design.

[Q] What do you think about data visualization/infographicss?

[A] Nowadays, information should be speedily retained, since we are constantly receiving new information. This information may capture our attention or not. Data visualization is possibly the most efficient and quickest way to pass on the information (data) in a simple and easily understandable manner, which would be difficult to communicate by any other methods.

[Q] What kind of design methods do you commonly use?

[A] My mind always searches for good information. The method, after some years of experience in the area, becomes intrinsic to everything we do and to all information we deal with. Information starts to be seen graphically and schematically and stops being seen as data, numbers, and letters.

[Q] What kind of design elements do you commonly use?

[A] Map, line, color, everything can be used to communicate the strength or the importance of the information. Usually, information is received as raw data, and then we start thinking graphically.

[Q] Where are your works applied?

[A] My works have already been applied to all types of media, however, it is most common to newspapers and websites.

[Q] How do you turn boring and complex data into something interesting and understandable?

[A] In the process of drawing the information, I love to find what it looks like. Sometimes if it is difficult, I will rethink the work with analysis: would it be understandable? Of course, this depends directly on the target of our work. Is a colleague going to see and read this type of information or is it a common reader who needs visual explanation?

[Q] What is your suggestion for beginners?

[A] Schematic and visual thinking/drawing is the best way to 'speak' if you don't have words to show. Keep it simple and keep thinking about what story you want to tell, at the beginning, middle, and end of the process.

[1] IRS: Tax with New Rules and Deadlines

Credit: Susana Lopes
Completion: 2016

Personal income tax (PIT) has suffered significant changes in 2016, mainly regarding the way incomes are taxed. These changes originated from the misunderstanding of the submission dates (constantly postponed) and related to the filling rules and invoice validation. This infographic indicates the timeframe in order to make it easier for taxpayers to comprehend the tax.

IRS 2016
IMPOSTO COM NOVAS REGRAS E PRAZOS DE ENTREGA

Uma das novidades do IRS a entregar este ano tem que ver com o padrão de tributação para contribuintes casados. Assim, em 2016, a regra é a tributação separada (que já era permitida aos casais unidos de facto), havendo, contudo, a opção pela tributação conjunta. Mas, para tal, ambos os cônjuges devem indicar essa intenção na declaração do IRS e entregá-la dentro do prazo. Este ano, existem também mais contribuintes dispensados de entregar a declaração do IRS, nomeadamente quem tenha auferido rendimentos iguais ou inferiores a 8.500 euros brutos em 2015.

Em 2016 não existe distinção de prazos consoante o modo de entrega da declaração do IRS (papel ou internet)

FEVEREIRO

MARÇO — até dia 15
- Estão disponíveis para consulta todas as despesas e encargos comunicados ao Fisco. Facturas referentes a despesas com saúde e educação (públicos), encargos com lares e imóveis comunicados pelas diferentes entidades até 19 de Fevereiro.

prazo inicial até 29 Fev

de 16 a 31
- Período de reclamação dos valores que constam do e-fatura.

prazo inicial 1 a 15 Mar

22 [até]
- Data limite para confirmar e comunicar faturas no sistema e-factura.

prazo inicial 15 Fev

ABRIL — de 1 a 30
- Primeira fase para entrega da declaração do modelo 3 do IRS (trabalhadores dependentes e pensionistas)

prazo inicial 15 Mar a 15 Abr

MAIO — de 1 a 31
- Segunda fase da entrega do IRS, destinada aos restantes contribuintes. Rendimentos do **trabalho independente** (vulgo, recibos verdes), de rendas, mais-valias, entre outros. Refira-se que as modelo 3 que incluam os anexos B, C, D, E, I e L terão de ser obrigatoriamente submetidas pela internet.

prazo inicial 16 Abr a 16 Mai

JUNHO / JULHO — até dia 31
- Data-limite para os contribuintes receberem a **nota de liquidação** do IRS.

Não se esqueça que, se não concordar com os valores constantes na nota de liquidação, poderá formalizar a reclamação através das vias tradicionais: declaração de substituição, reclamação graciosa, recurso hierárquico ou impugnação judicial.

AGOSTO — até dia 31
- Quem tiver de pagar **imposto além daquele que reteve** todos os meses em 2015, terá de fazê-lo até 31 de Agosto. Isto se cumpriu o prazo de entrega da declaração do IRS. Caso contrário, o prazo desliza até 30 de Dezembro.

438
REACTORES NUCLEARES NO MUNDO

EUA é o país com mais reactores nucleares activos (99), e também o que mais reactores encerrou (33) em 2015. Já a China está no topo da lista, como o país com mais reactores em construção (25), quase duplicando a sua capacidade actual (26). Caso todos os planos propostos ou planeados fossem concretizados a China atingiria um total de 230 reactores nucleares, ultrapassando os EUA que ficaria nos 126. O Japão que revive novamente a polémica das centrais nucleares com a reativação do segundo reactor pós Fukushima (2011) tem 3 reactores em construção e planos para mais 12.

Dados de outubro de 2015, em unidades.

Reactores nucleares em actividade

Encerramento permanente e 'Long Term Shutdown (LTS) ou operação suspensa

158 TOTAL

Em construção

Existentes	438
Em construção	68
Planeados	488
Encerrados	158

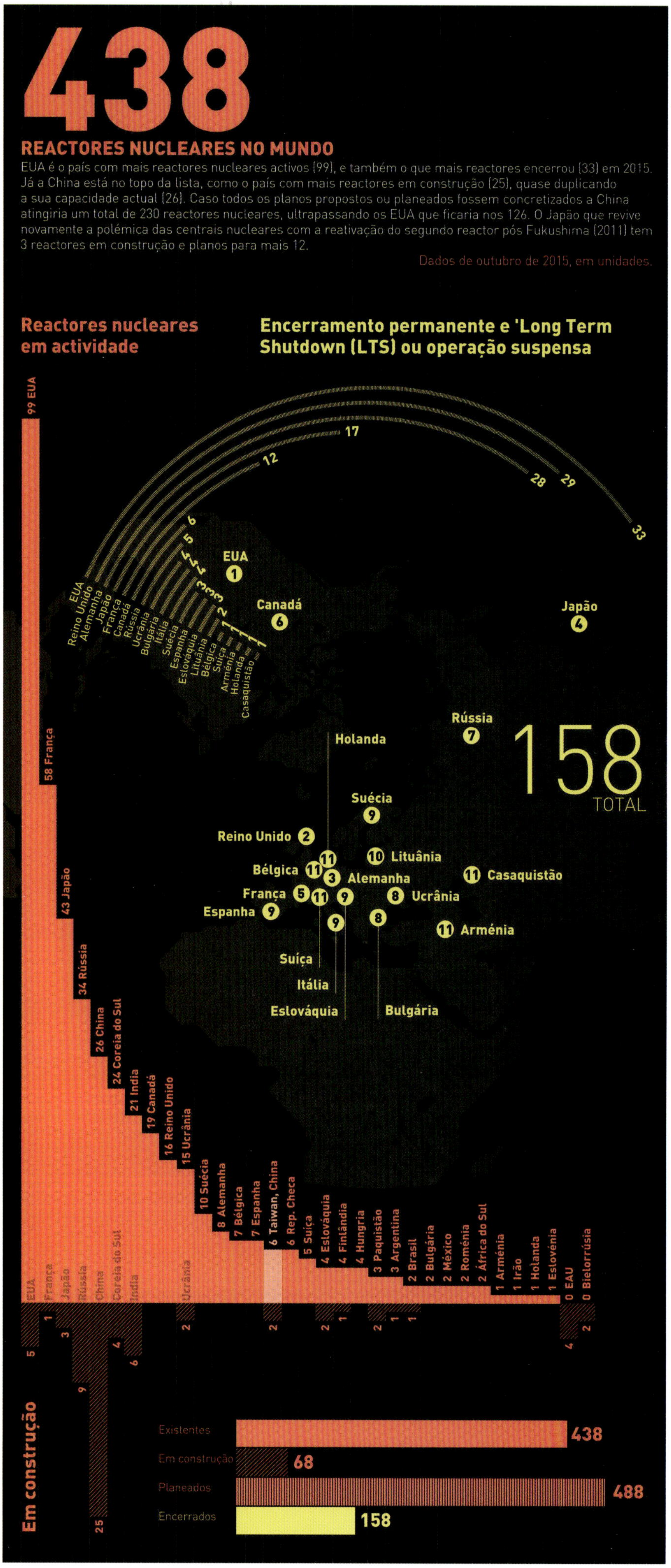

[2–3] World Nuclear Power

Credit: Susana Lopes
Completion: 2015

This work includes the investigation and analysis of the world nuclear reactors in actual reality, and intends to compare the trend of the nuclear reactors closed (in yellow) and active (in red).

Reactores nucleares planeados e propostos

488

São 16 os países que neste momento têm reactores nucleares em construção. Planeados ou propostos estão 488 novos reactores em 42 países. 14 destes países não têm actualmente nenhum reactor nuclear em funcionamento, incluindo o Casaquistão e a Lituânia, com um e dois reactores nucleares encerrados ou em LTS (respectivamente), planeam a construção de cinco (4 e 1).

País planeados e propostos (existentes - em construção)

China 179 (26-25)

Índia 57 (21-6)

Rússia 49 (34-9)

USA 22 (99-5)

Arábia Saúdita 16 (0-0)

Ucrânia 13 (15-2)

Japão 12 (43-3)

EAU 11 (0-4)   **Reino Unido 11** (16-0)

Vietname 10 (0-0)   **Irão 9** (1-0)

Coreia do Sul 8 (24-4)   **África do Sul 8** (2-0)   **Turquia 8** (0-0)

Polónia 6 (0-0)   **Canadá 5** (19-0)   **Indonésia 5** (0-0)

Tailândia 5 (0-0)   **Argentina 4** (3-1)   **Brasil 4** (2-1)   **Chile 4** (0-0)

Egipto 4 (0-0)   **Cazaquistão 4** (0-0)   **Rep. Checa 3** (6-0)   **Roménia 3** (2-0)

Suíça 3 (5-0)   **Bangladesh 2** (0-0)   **Bielorrússia 2** (0-2)   **Finlândia 2** (4-1)

Hungria 2 (4-0)   **Jordânia 2** (0-0)   **Malásia 2** (0-0)   **México 2** (2-0)

Paquistão 2 (3-2)   **Arménia 1** (1-0)   **Bulgária 1** (2-0)   **França 1** (58-1)   **Israel 1** (0-0)

Coreia do Norte 1 (0-0)   **Lituânia 1** (0-0)   **Holanda 1** (1-0)   **Eslováquia 1** (4-2)   **Eslovénia 1** (1-0)

FONTE: PRIS - Power Reactor Information System e World Nuclear Association. | INFOGRAFIA: Susana Lopes | susana.lopes@economico.pt

[4] Oil Prices Going Down

Credit: Susana Lopes
Completion: 2016

This chart presents the evolution of oil prices, with the purpose of showing that quotations decrease within one year in 2015, and also its monthly comparison.

---

[5] XXI Government: Which Universities Trained More Ministers

Credit: Susana Lopes
Completion: 2015

The infographic shows the level of education of the actual ministers (XXI Government) and the list of the universities that have trained many ministers. From the infographic we can see that the University of Lisbon is the one that trained more ministers than other universities. There are nine ministers in all, including two engineers trained at the Instituto Superior Tecnico and three economists trained at ISEG.

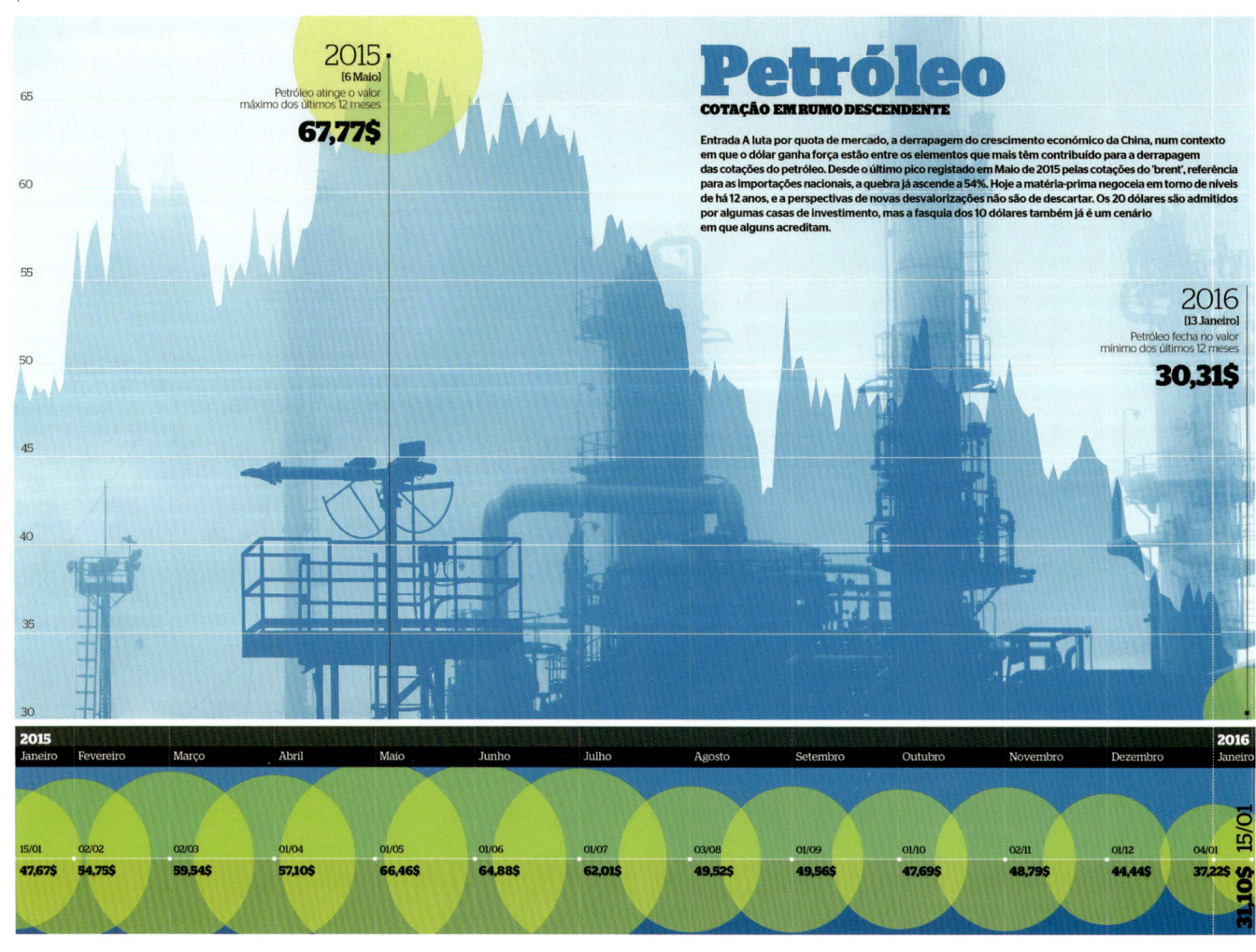

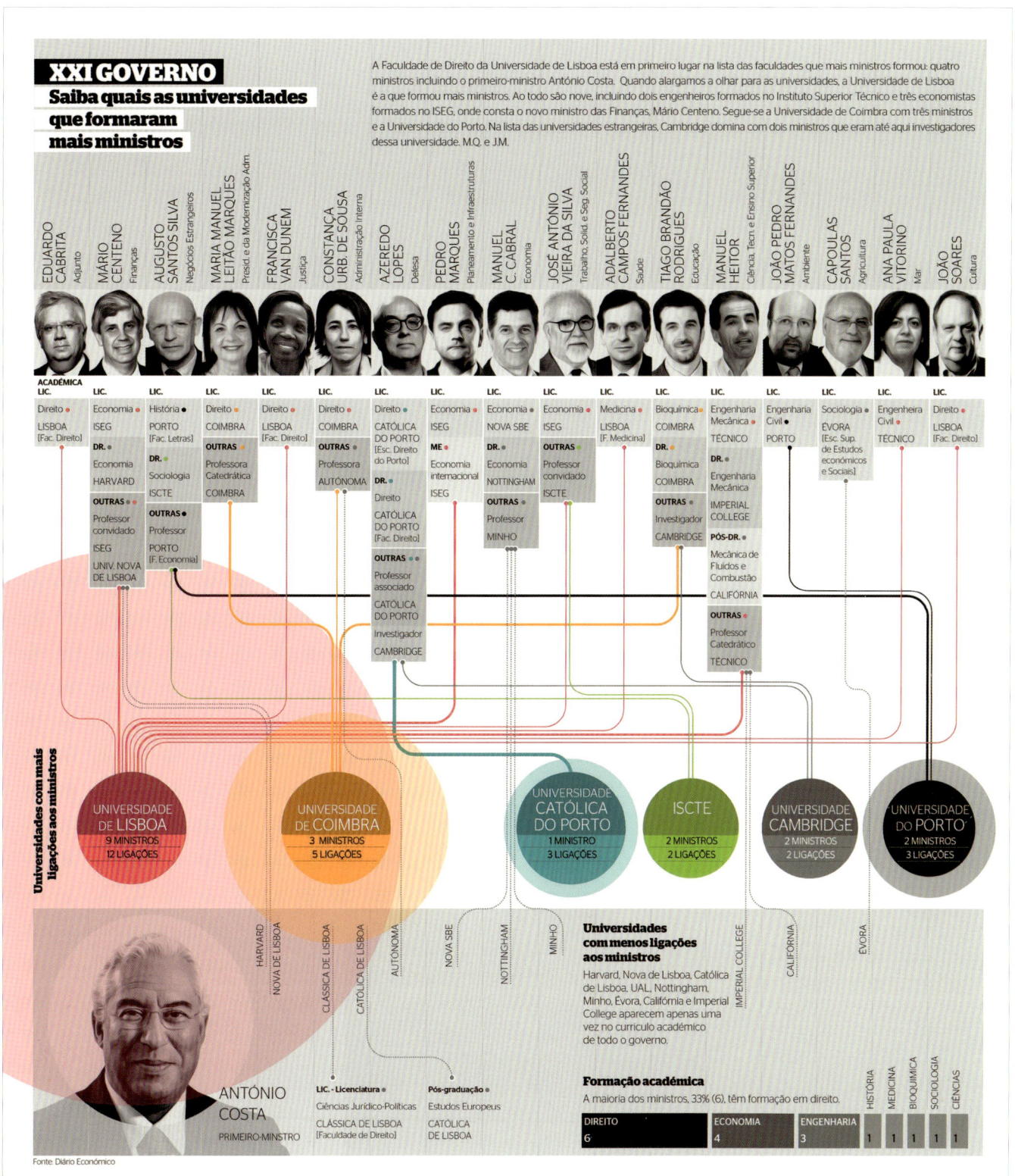

Massimiliano Mauro

Massimiliano Mauro is a multi-disciplinary designer. He joined *Wired* in 2012 where he learnt a lot in different fields, from digital publishing to data visualization and digital cartography. He believes in the power of visual exploration.

[Q] **What do you think about data visualization/infographics?**

[A] I believe that the first thing to do for an efficient visualization or infographic is to be the audience. 'To center the target you need to be the target.' It is not only about the aesthetics. Nowadays infographic is more a style than a project. Data visualization and infographics are like books that need a good story, and a good text is necessary.

[Q] **What kind of design methods do you commonly use?**

[A] Research analysis and a good brief are the basis. It is important to create sketches and ideas to share with people and colleagues, and select only the best, especially in editorial design, otherwise nobody will read anything or understand anything.

[Q] **What kind of design elements do you commonly use?**

[A] I really love a lot user interface. I think that data visualization and infographics should be like a control panel where the beholder can create their own story, link, and find something more. It is better to be a dash story, otherwise users will not read text.

Every infographic is a different project in which shapes can have different meanings. I really love to work with simple shapes and layouts to make the information more accessible for the readers. Shapes and icons are a universal language, for example, a triangle can stand for different directions according to the angles and its positions on the page.

One of my favorite projects is the one about gay rights in Europe, because it is not only a visual widget but also a metaphor in which the rainbow tiles that have fallen represent the missing elements in some countries. Also the rainbow shape is really similar to the floor layout of the Italian *camera da deputati* where the laws were proposed. Sometimes more layers of information and storytelling can be added to help the reader to understand the information displayed.

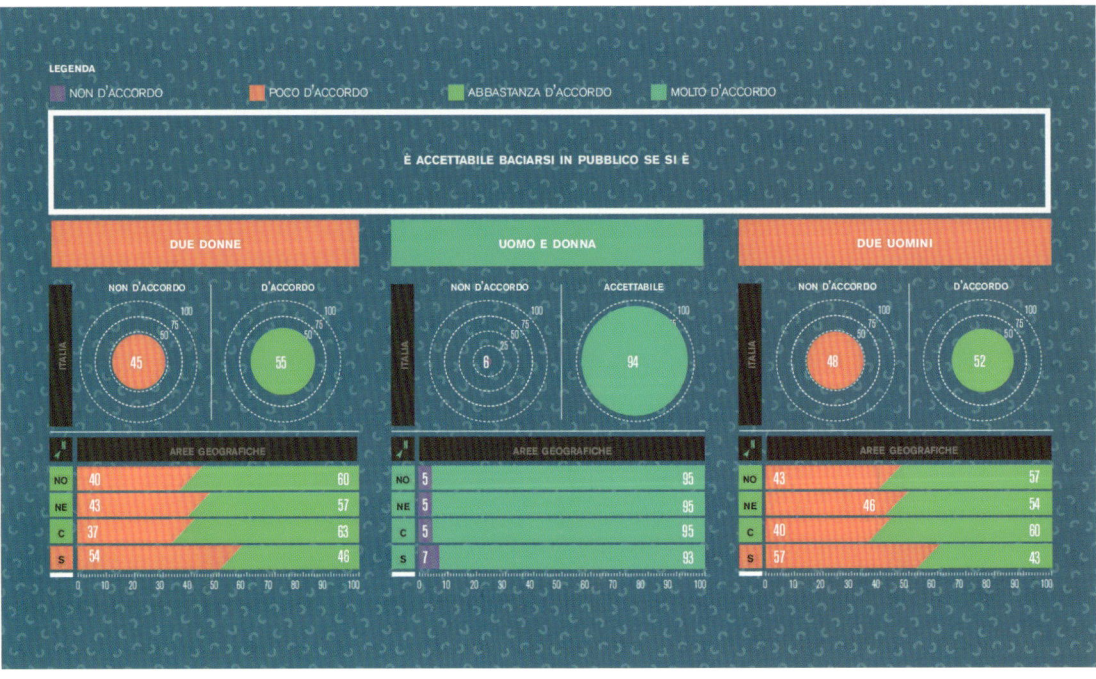

1

[1–3] Europe Is Gay-Friendly?

Credits: Corrado Garcia (art director), Marco Boscolo (journalist)
Completion: 2016

The infographic was made before the recognition of same-sex relationships by the Italian government on 20 May 2016. The data set has been visualized as a rainbow, where each country occupies a different sector from left to right according to their ranking in the gay-friendly index to give a quick overview of the number of countries that are 'gay-friendly' against those in which some rights are missing, partially recognized or forbidden. The designers used patterns and colors to generate a clear differentiation of the variables included in the data set. A flat color means that the right is recognized, the patterns are used when it is partially recognized or forbidden, and if the cell is empty it means that there are not laws about that subject.

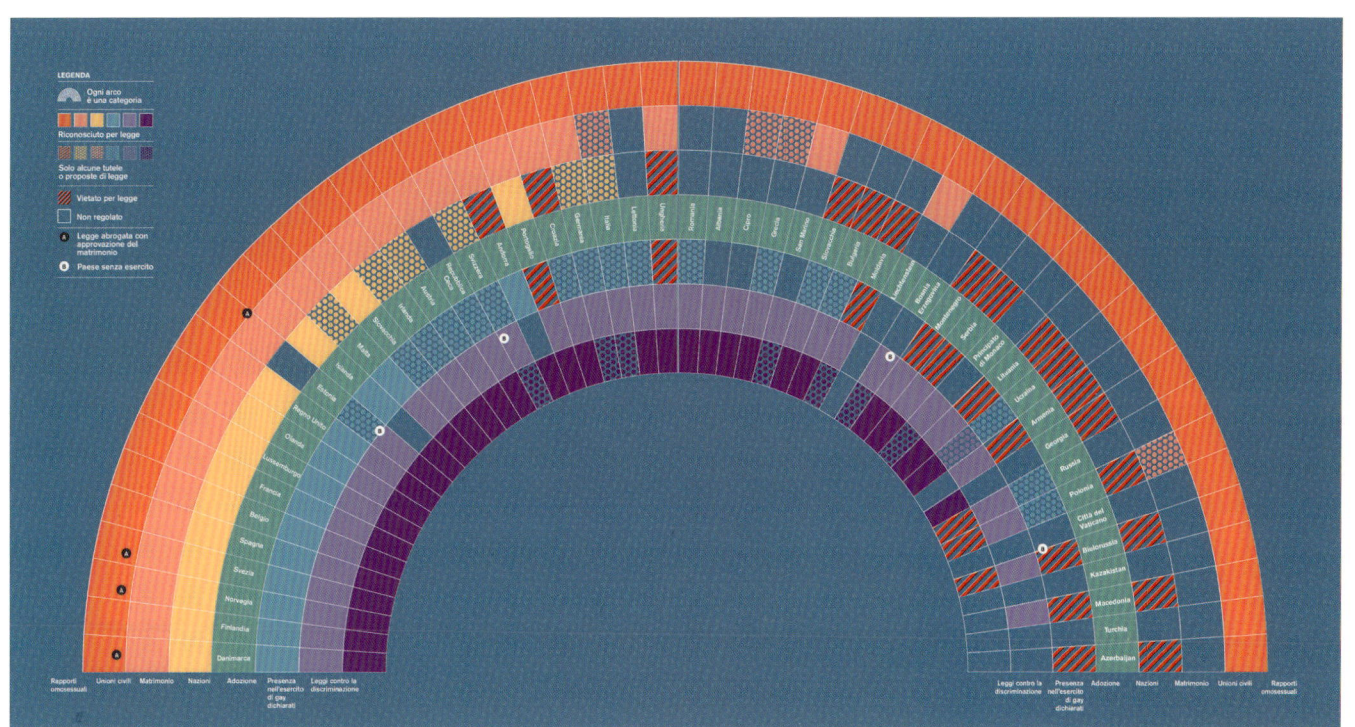

Quanto è gay friendly l'Europa?

Essere omosessuale o transessuale nel Vecchio Continente è meglio che in altre regioni del mondo. Ma all'interno dell'Unione le norme sono diverse: c'è chi ha legalizzato i rapporti omosessuali a fine '700 e chi solo nel 2000. Chi permette le nozze e chi ancora punisce la "propaganda gay". — MARCO BOSCOLO

COME SI LEGGE
Gli spicchi verdi, al centro, rappresentano gli Stati europei. Per ogni paese è visualizzata la sua posizione su sei temi, indicando se la richiesta della comunità omosessuale è stata riconosciuta per legge, proibita, regolata solo in parte o ignorata. Più un paese ha gli spicchi pieni di colore, più è gay friendly.

Fonti: Rainbow Europe Index Ilga - Europe, Fra

E se il tuo vicino di casa fosse gay?

L'adozione per le coppie omosessuali è ancora un tabù per quasi l'80% della popolazione italiana, ma sul matrimonio gay siamo molto più avanti dei nostri politici: una persona su due lo trova accettabile. È quello che emerge dall'indagine Istat dedicata alla percezione dell'omosessualità nel nostro paese. Dai baci in pubblico al coming out, ecco gli altri dati.

GLI ULTIMI SONO STATI IL Lussemburgo, dove persone dello stesso sesso si possono sposare dal primo gennaio, e la Slovenia, che il 3 marzo scorso ha approvato una nuova norma sul matrimonio. Lo scorso febbraio in Slovacchia un referendum contro il matrimonio tra persone dello stesso sesso non ha raggiunto il quorum nonostante l'appoggio di papa Francesco. La consultazione preoccupava l'Agenzia dell'Unione europea per i diritti fondamentali (Fra) che la considerava una minaccia ai progressi degli ultimi anni. «Sempre più paesi europei stanno approvando leggi che tutelano i diritti della comunità lgbt (lesbiche, gay, bisessuali, transgender)», sottolinea Blanca Tapia, la portavoce dell'Agenzia. Ciò nonostante i dati mostrano che la situazione rimane variegata, con il blocco meno tollerante dei paesi dell'Est che si contrappone a un Ovest più aperto. «La strada per vedere garantiti più diritti è quella di promulgare leggi di tutela», aggiunge la portavoce. Questione che in Italia è nel limbo da tempo. Di matrimonio non si parla e ogni volta che si è toccato il tema delle unioni civili, Pacs o Dico che fossero, le proposte sono state affossate prima ancora che si arrivasse al voto parlamentare. Ora il Partito democratico ha in canna un documento che promette di portare in aula a breve, almeno a sentire le intenzioni della relatrice del testo, la senatrice Monica Cirinnà. In Italia manca anche una legge specifica per combattere le discriminazioni di genere. Ma è tutto il paese che, guardando i dati Istat, ha ancora un blocco culturale nei confronti del mondo lgbt. Soprattutto al Sud, dove il vedere due uomini prendersi per mano è considerato inaccettabile da un italiano su due. Stessa proporzione anche sull'accettazione delle relazioni omosessuali. Rimangono anche gli stereotipi sulle "lesbiche donne mascoline" e sui "gay uomini effeminati". A guardare il bicchiere mezzo pieno, queste posizioni medie non sembrano rispecchiare quelle dei giovani italiani, che si professano più aperti. Ma, sottolineano alla Fra, proprio le persone lgbt più giovani sono le più esposte alle discriminazioni, a scuola e in altri contesti pubblici.
— MARCO BOSCOLO

[Q] **Where are your works applied?**

[A] I work for digital and editorial design.

[Q] **How do you turn boring and complex data into something interesting and understandable?**

[A] For boring data, making an illustration might be a good way. Complex data doesn't mean complex visualization. It can be really impressive, but it also needs to be explained with simple visualization. It is really important to see different points of view and slice through the mass of information.

[Q] **What is your suggestion for beginners?**

[A] Study a lot of theories of information design and cartographies. Also neuroscience is helping designers to understand how the brain sees.

4

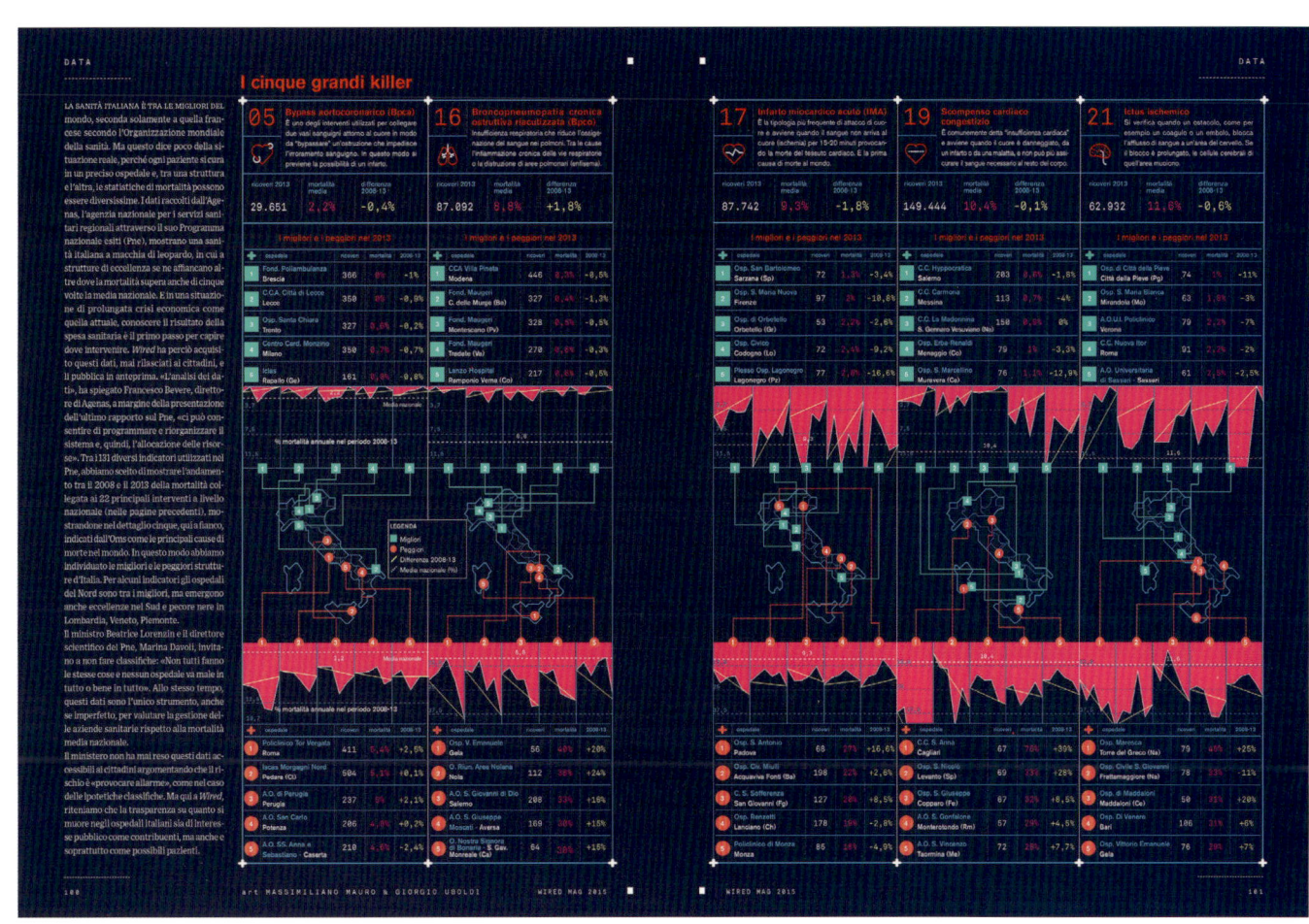

[4–5] The Russian Roulette of Public Health

Credits: Corrado Garcia (art director), Marco Boscolo (journalist), Giorgio Uboldi (first spread of data visualization)
Completion: 2015

The designers analyzed data about public health in Italy. In the first spread, the reader can find the five main causes of death in Italian hospitals, marked in red. To show the tendency of these markers, a yellow line represents the number of deaths between 2008 and 2013. The second spread is an overview of the hospitals and their death rate showing the five best hospitals where patients are more likely to survive and the five worst where patients are more likely to die, as well as the worst hospitals in the second appointment.

Santiago Ortiz

Santiago Ortiz is the chief data officer at Drumwave, where he also leads a research team called Moebio Labs. He is a mathematician, data scientist, interactive visualization developer, and inventor. He creates and develops innovative and interactive-rich projects for the web, based on data.

[Q] What do you think about data visualization/infographics?

[A] Data visualization is a new language we're just starting to explore. It can express complexity, structure, dynamic processes, objective and subjective ideas, and even emotions. I'm fascinated with patterns that emerge in very diverse phenomena and in extremely different scales, especially when new complexities are formed: in the creation of galaxies, proteins, multicellular organisms, cities, or innovative ideas. All these dynamic processes also generate data, and information visualization offers a window to them. All these processes are also interactive—complexity emerges from the interaction of simplest parts, so I explore how to mimic these interactions in the cognitive experience of the people faced with the visualization interfaces.

[Q] What kind of design methods do you commonly use?

[A] The methodology I and my team use is called inductive iterative, and more informally, naive methodology. It starts by exploring data without strong domain knowledge, trying to find all possible relations among variables and using multiple analytical, visual, and interactive approaches. The result of the first iteration is a landscape that we use to start creating a dialogue with the data holder, a dialogue that will lead to new iterations of development, driven by detected opportunities and value. This is a process that goes beyond just the visualization results, it aims to extract value from the data, and interactive visualization is one very important part of it, but we use all the tools data science provides.

We develop dynamic data visualizations that are a very rich type of visualizations based on 16 main characteristics, which are multi-dimensional approaches to data, multiple-scale navigation, exploration in multiple levels of sampling and aggregation of huge databases, temporal simulation (the 'play button'), multiple views on same data set, allowing the user to combine variables, and so on.

[Q] What kind of design elements do you commonly use?

[A] Our naive approach rejects the imposition of shapes or patterns into the visualization. Instead shapes, forms or patterns, geometries and visual structures tend to emerge from the data itself. That said, certain geometries and spatial archetypes often appear, such as spheres or fractals (due to the inner spherical, cyclical, or fractal nature of the data).

[Q] Where are your works applied?

[A] Our works are applied to companies from all industries, built for the web or internal networks, and operated on modern browsers.

1
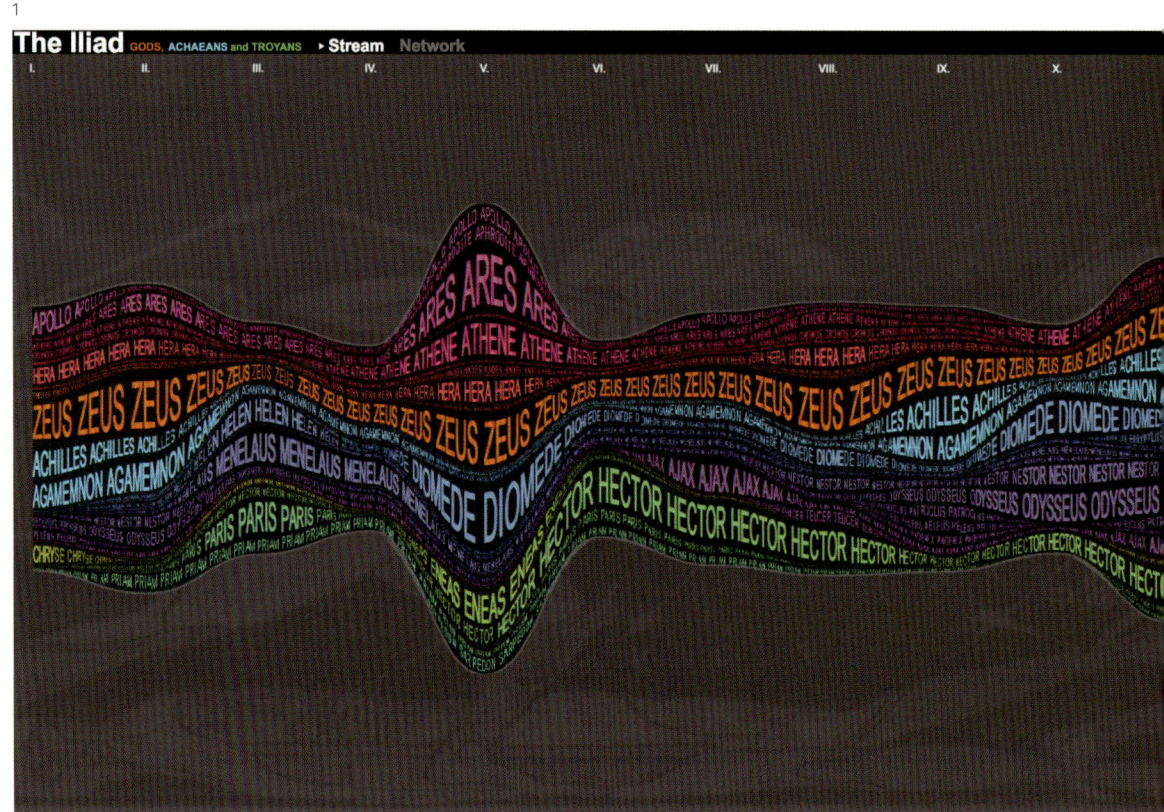

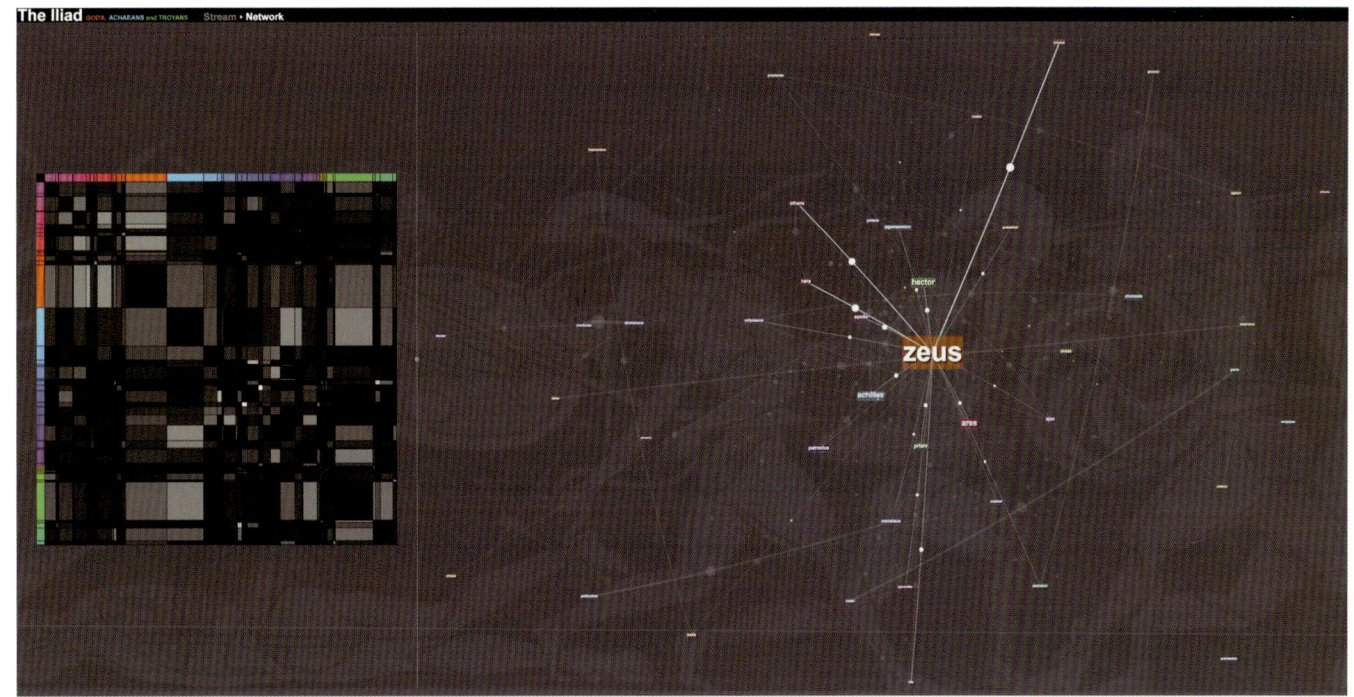

2

[1–2] The Iliad: Gods, Achaeans and Troyans

Credit: Santiago Ortiz
Completion: 2012
Interactive link: www.moebio.com/iliad

When the designer thought about what things deeply interest him besides data, and if he could use data visualization to touch that, one of the main answers was literature, which in fact is also data. The Iliad was then one of the first projects he built at that time. He chose Homer's *Iliad* for its universal importance and resonance, and also because it has a very interesting flow of characters that literally enter and leave the arena. There are also three categories of characters—Achaeans, Trojans, and gods—all appearing in different moments with different motivations, which are shown exactly in the word flow. The designer also wanted to give access to the text, so the visualization works not only as a 'pattern depiction'—an analysis—but more as a guide that accompanies lectures.

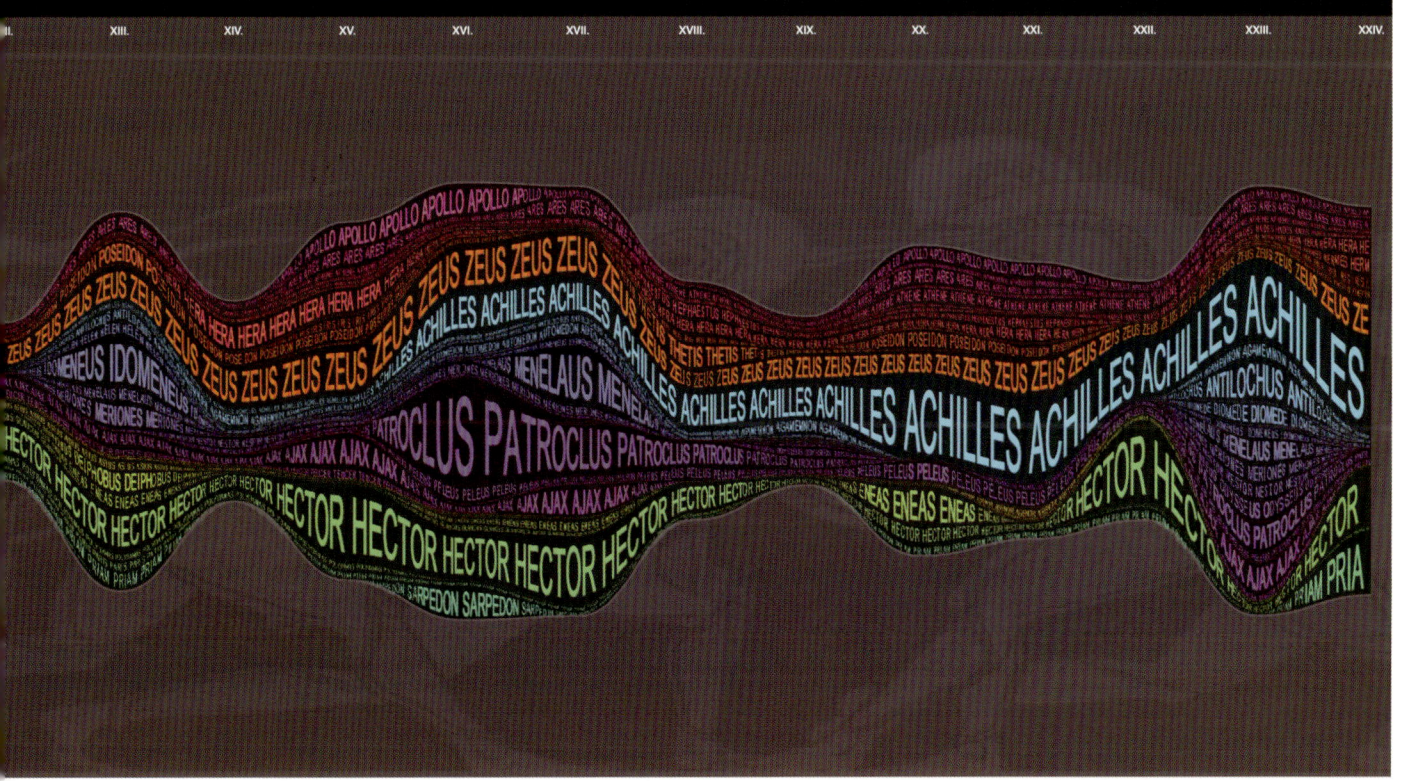

3

[Q] How do you turn boring and complex data into something interesting and understandable?

[A] I deeply disagree that data is boring. Data, the information it contains and the reality it represents, is always extremely interesting. It is often just cryptic in the way it appears. And if a visualization is good, that is because it allows the reader to perceive that rich reality. It may seem that the visualization is interesting, but the visualization is just the window.

[Q] What is your suggestion for beginners?

[A] A photographer should be interested by the reality she wants to capture, and then by the photography discipline, the camera, and the techniques. A photographer who is not insanely curious about the world can't be a great photographer. A photographer explores the world. If they do portraiture, they explore human emotions; and if they do landscapes, they are necessarily an adventurer. Then, of course, a photographer also studies photography, but that's secondary. Translate all this to visualization and it also holds. Beginners tend to think that visualization is about doing visualization, when in reality is about understanding the world through data.

4

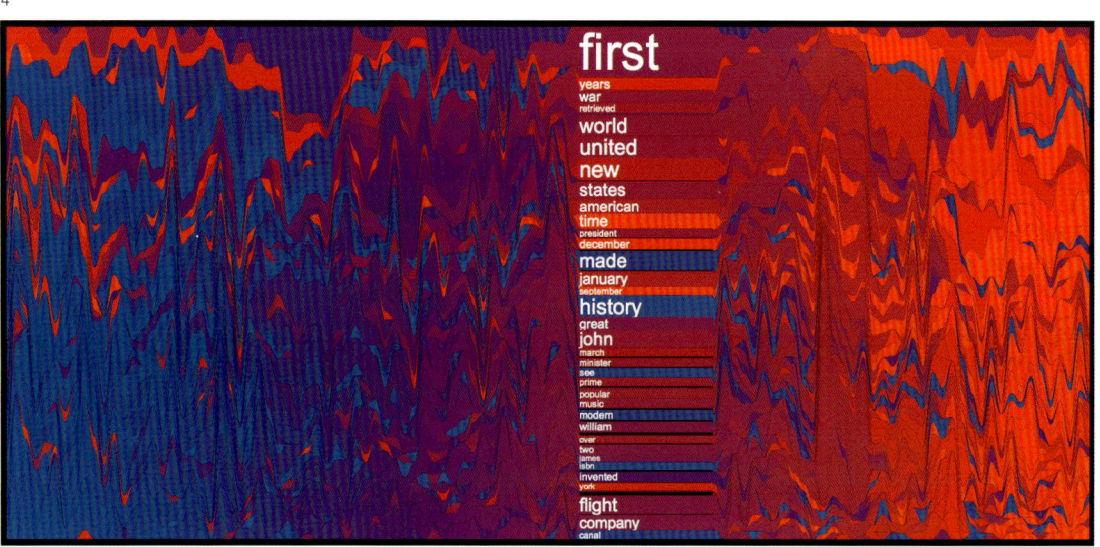

[3–5] History Words Flow

Credit: Santiago Ortiz
Completion: 2012
Interactive link: www.moebio.com/research/historywordsflow

Wikipedia is of course an amazing source of information, not only for its content but also for the multiple structures it contains. Whereas people access the articles mainly by search means, there are many other interesting ways to navigate and read contents, for instance, day, month, year, decade, or century. Articles tell a story and provide a perspective. The designer scrapped most of those articles and analyzed the words being used. He expected more continuity, which would be expressed as words' relevance being more stable though time, but there are a lot of words spiking and disappearing. This project could also be seen as an attempt to build automatically, via available data, a sort of histomap, the famous 1930s word history flow diagram.

5

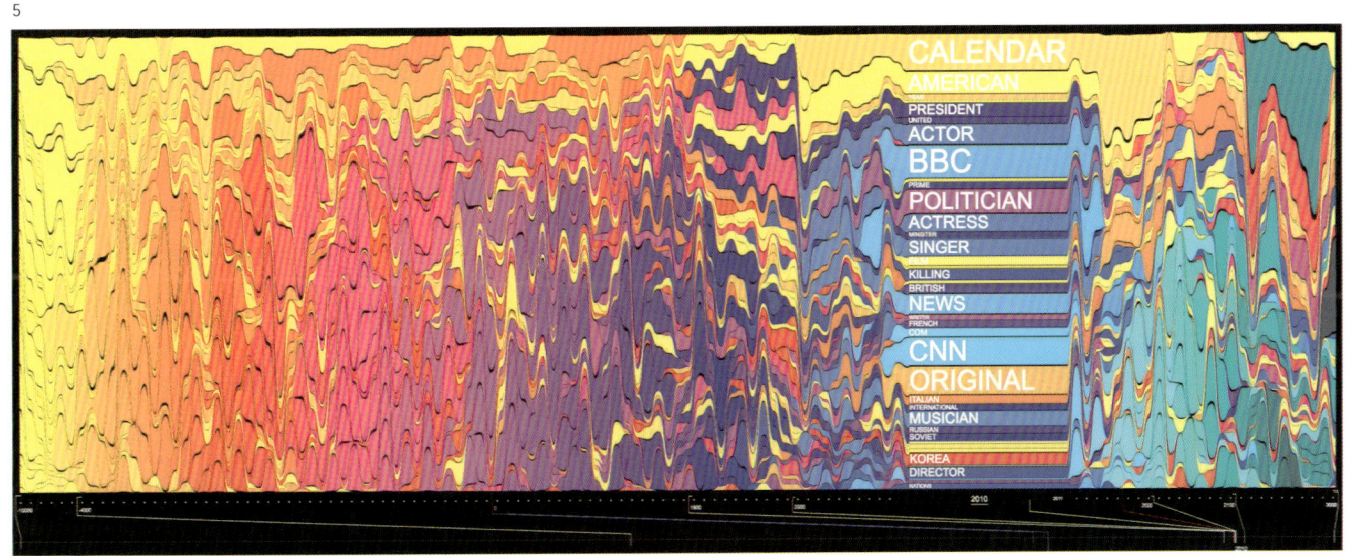

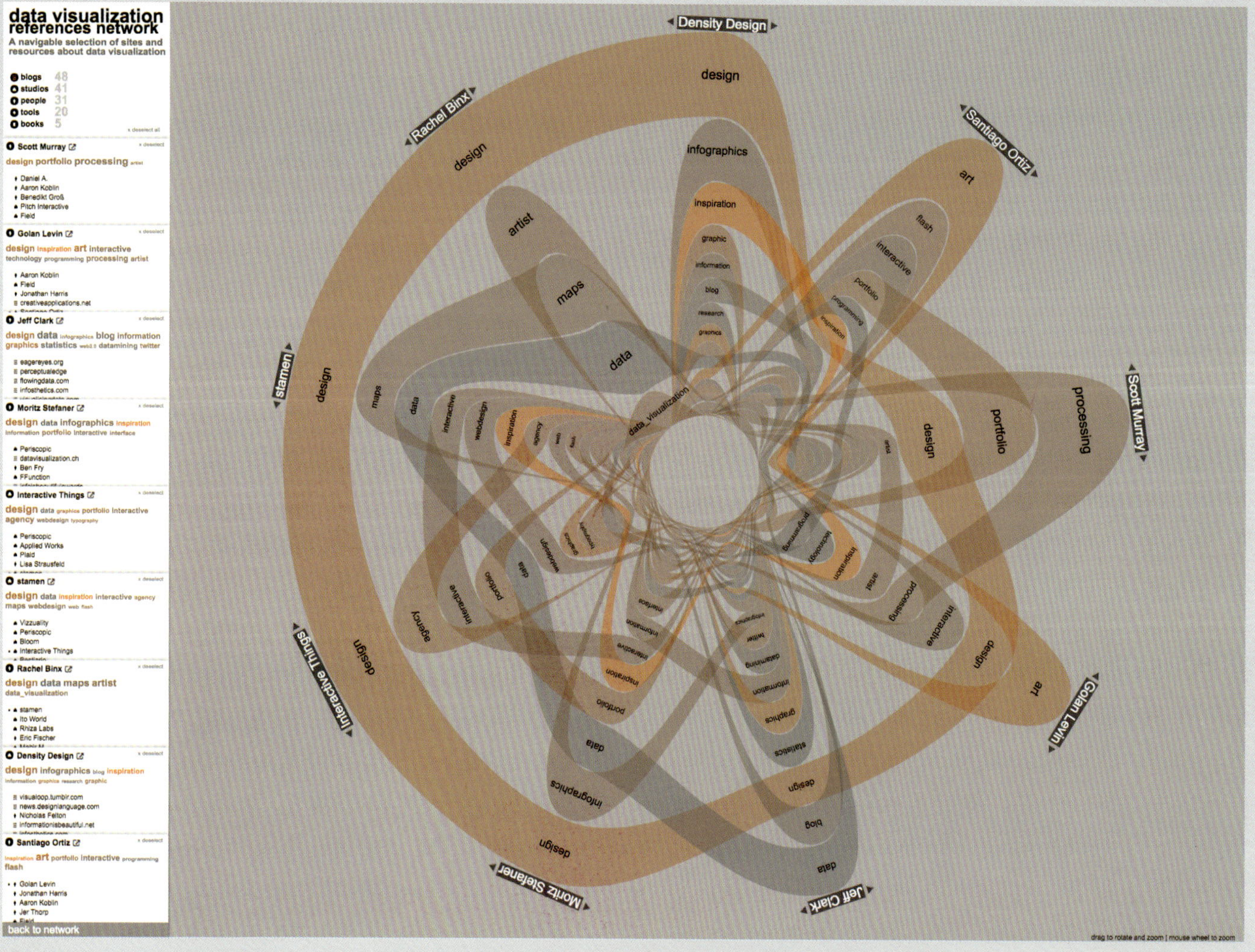

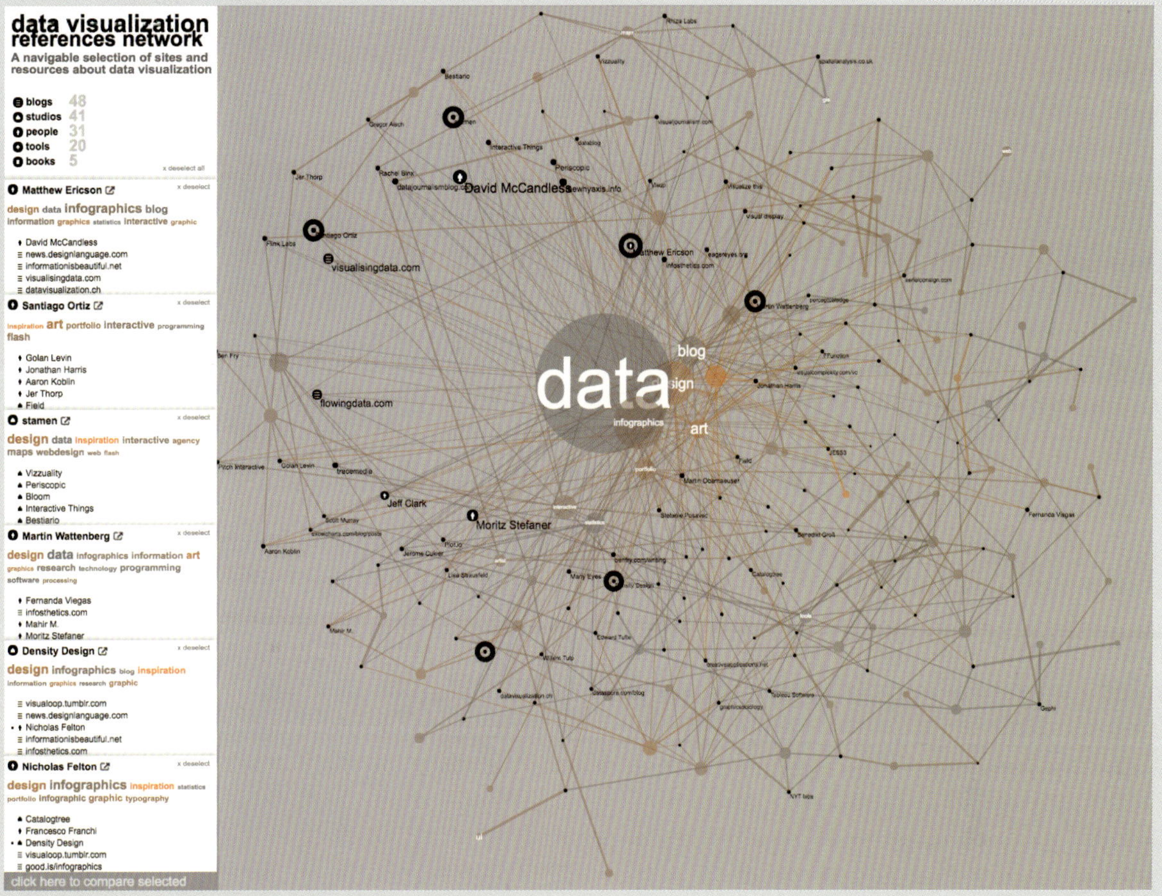

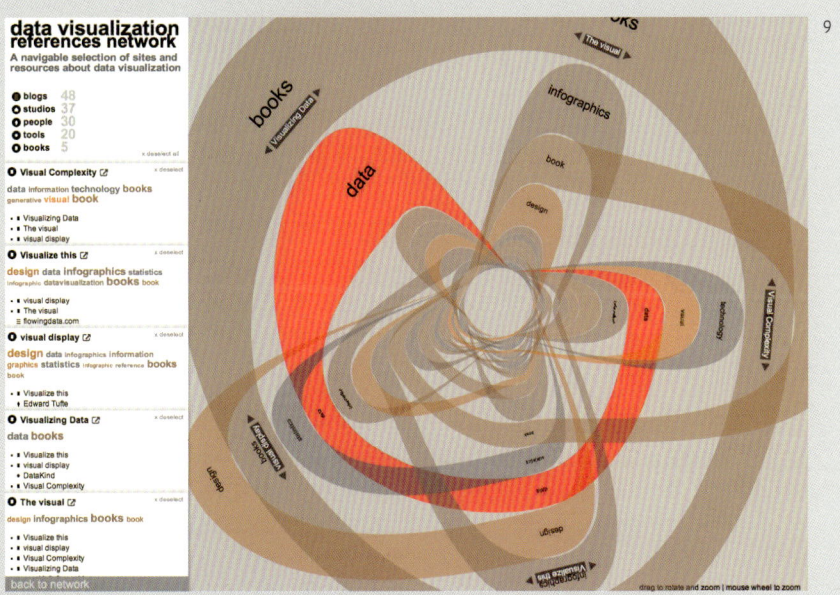

[6–9] Visualization Resources Network

Credit: Santiago Ortiz
Completion: 2012
Interactive link: www.moebio.com/datavisnetwork

When the online bookmarking service Delicious was still used a lot, it provided information on how different people perceived a website. People would bookmark a site and then attach a series of tags. The designer was thus always paying attention to what tags people used when bookmarking his website and projects, which told him a lot about impact and perception. Was his work being classified as experimental or artistic? Were the technical aspects such as the programming language more relevant than the content and concepts included in his work? He soon realized these questions were better addressed in comparison with other interactive data visualization creators and studios. And this is how he ended up building his project. The project then allows for selecting a series of entities (people, studios, books, etc.) and comparing them based on the tags people used to classify them.

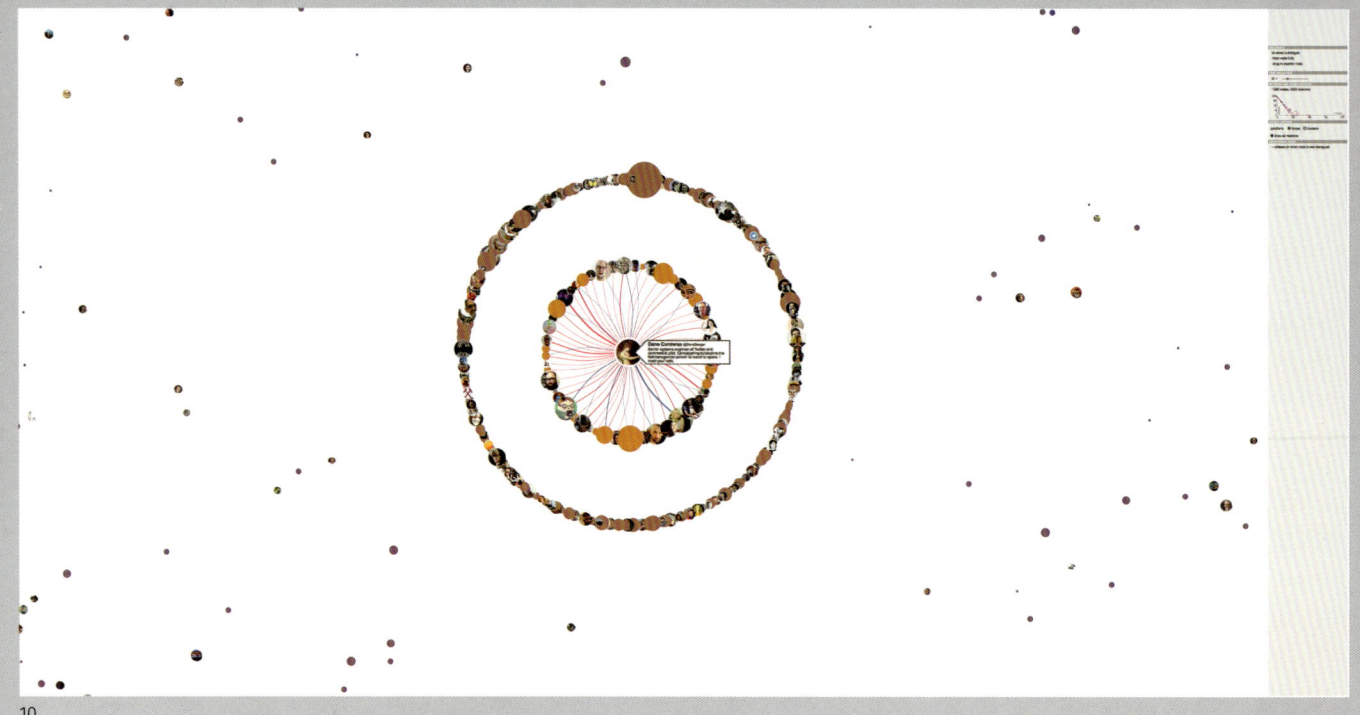

10

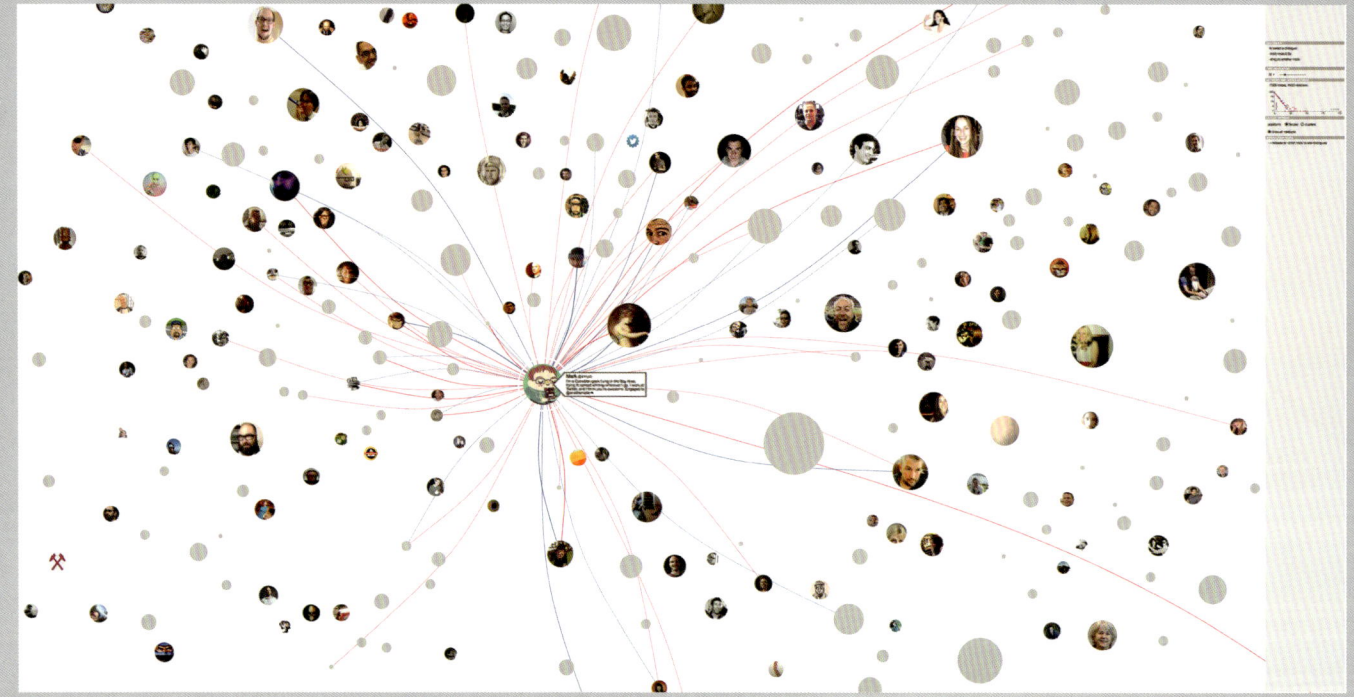

11

[10–14] Twitter Network

Credit: Santiago Ortiz
Completion: 2013
Interactive link: www.moebio.com/newk/twitter

In this network visualization, the nodes are all Twitter employees (at the time of project development), and the relations are the flows of conversations through Twitter and all the tweets the employees sent to each other in one week. The resultant visualization clearly depicts the clusters that match departments at Twitter and other groups. The interactive visualization allows for multiple actions, such as selecting nodes, exploring all the conversations or short paths between any two accounts.

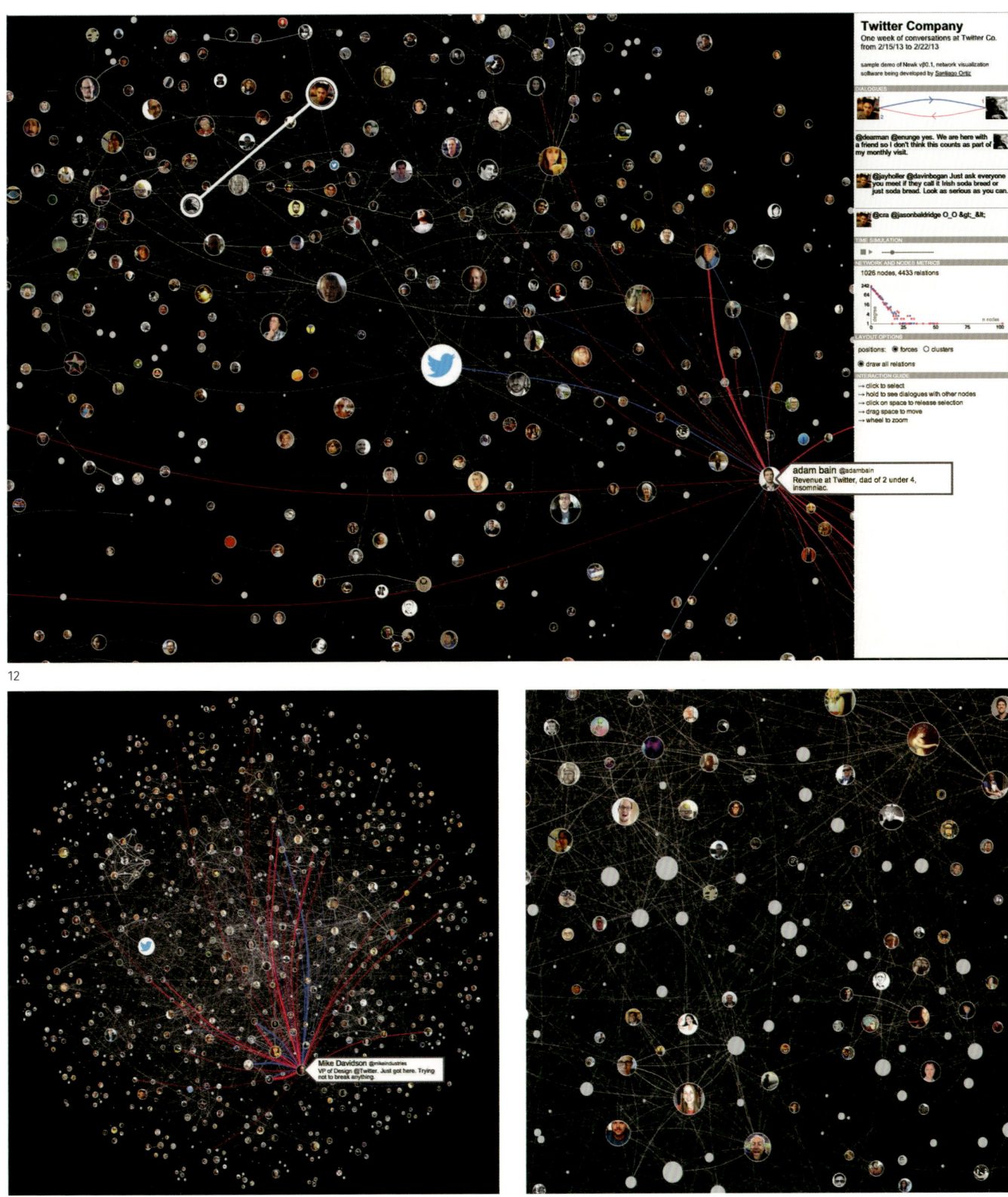

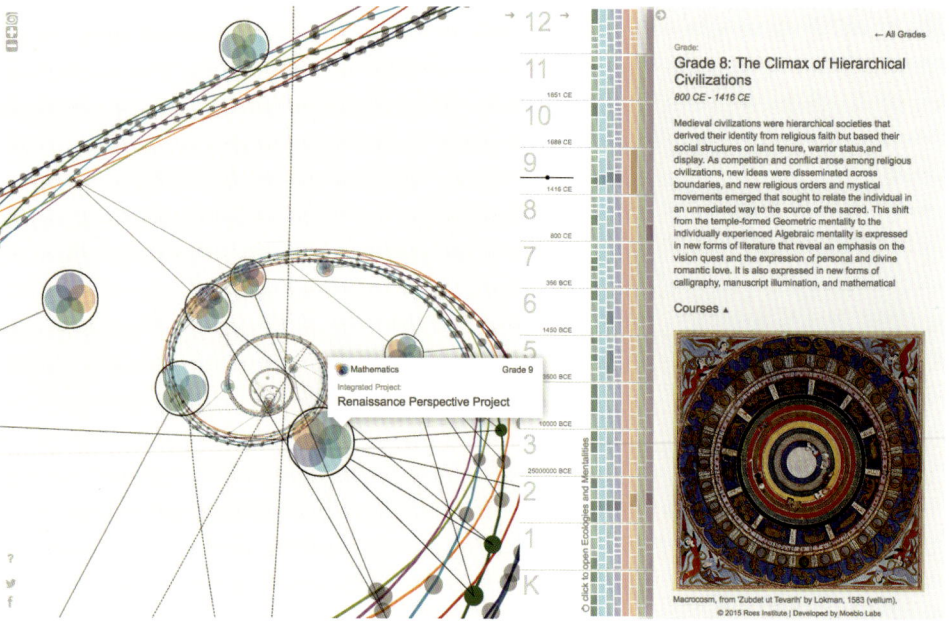

[15–17] Ross Spiral

Credits: Santiago Ortiz, Daniel Aguilar, Ross Institute
Completion: 2015
Interactive link: spiral.rosslearningsystem.org/spiral/#

The Ross Spiral Curriculum is a literary narrative of the evolution of human consciousness. It is taught chronologically through the grades as a dynamic system expanding in complexity. Cultural history is at the core of the Ross Curriculum, interwoven with all of the other domains. While each discipline offers its own rigorous curriculum, integration between domains creates a dynamic choreography of learning. Using this interdisciplinary approach, each grade focuses on a particular historical period and theme. The Spiral provides a cohesive architecture for analysis of the past as a dynamical system and enables students to more fully understand the present while envisioning the future.

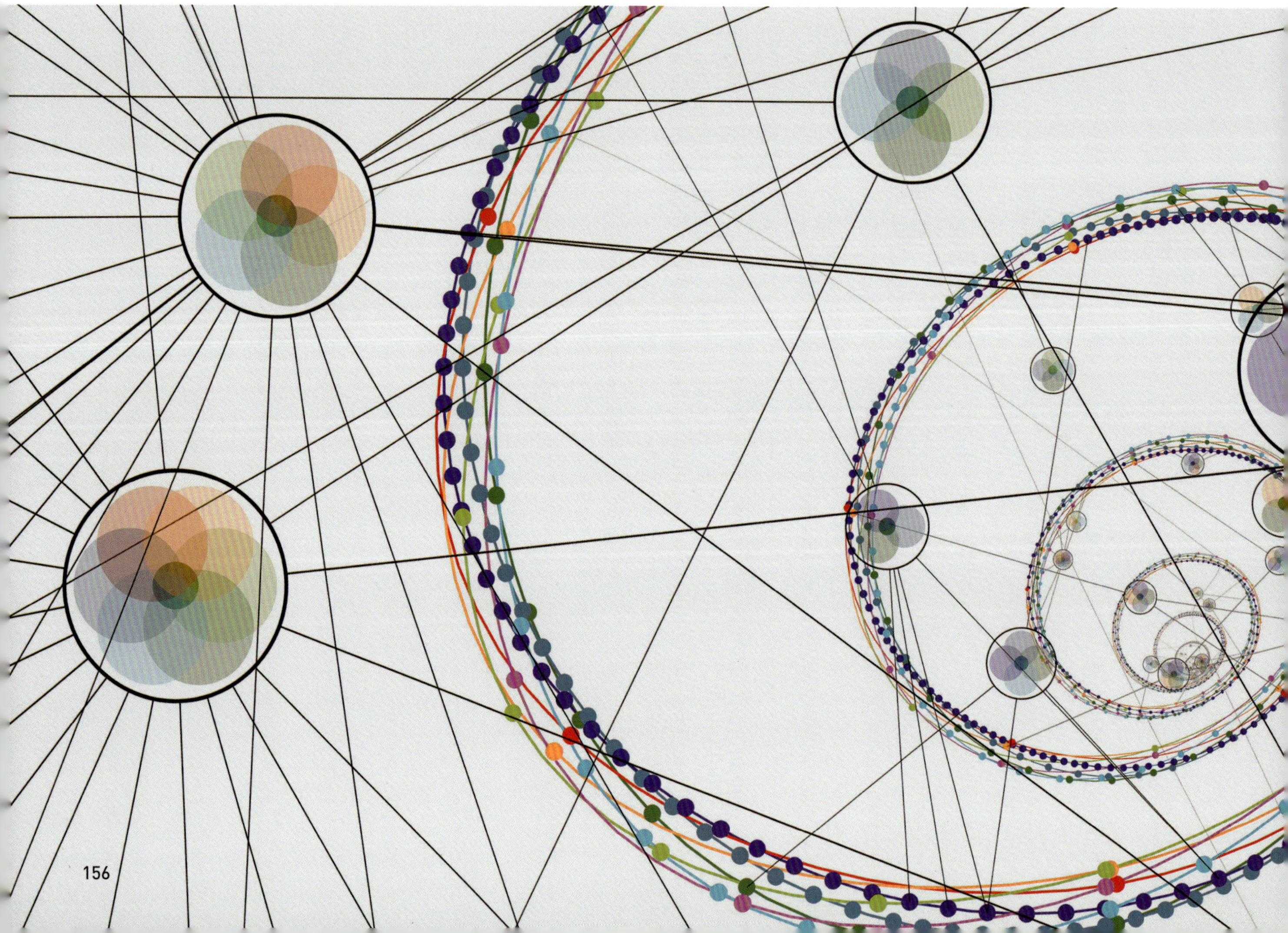

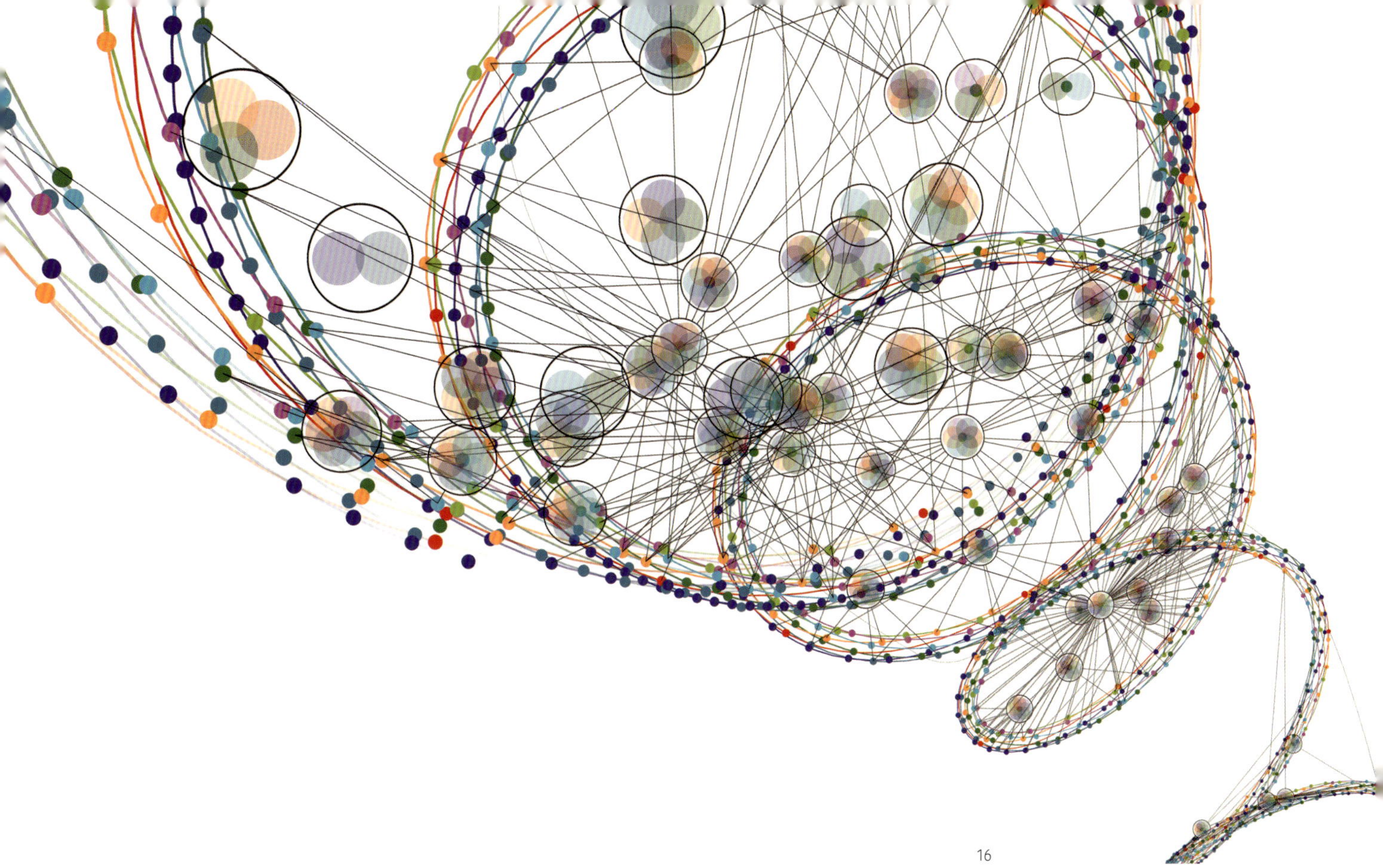

16

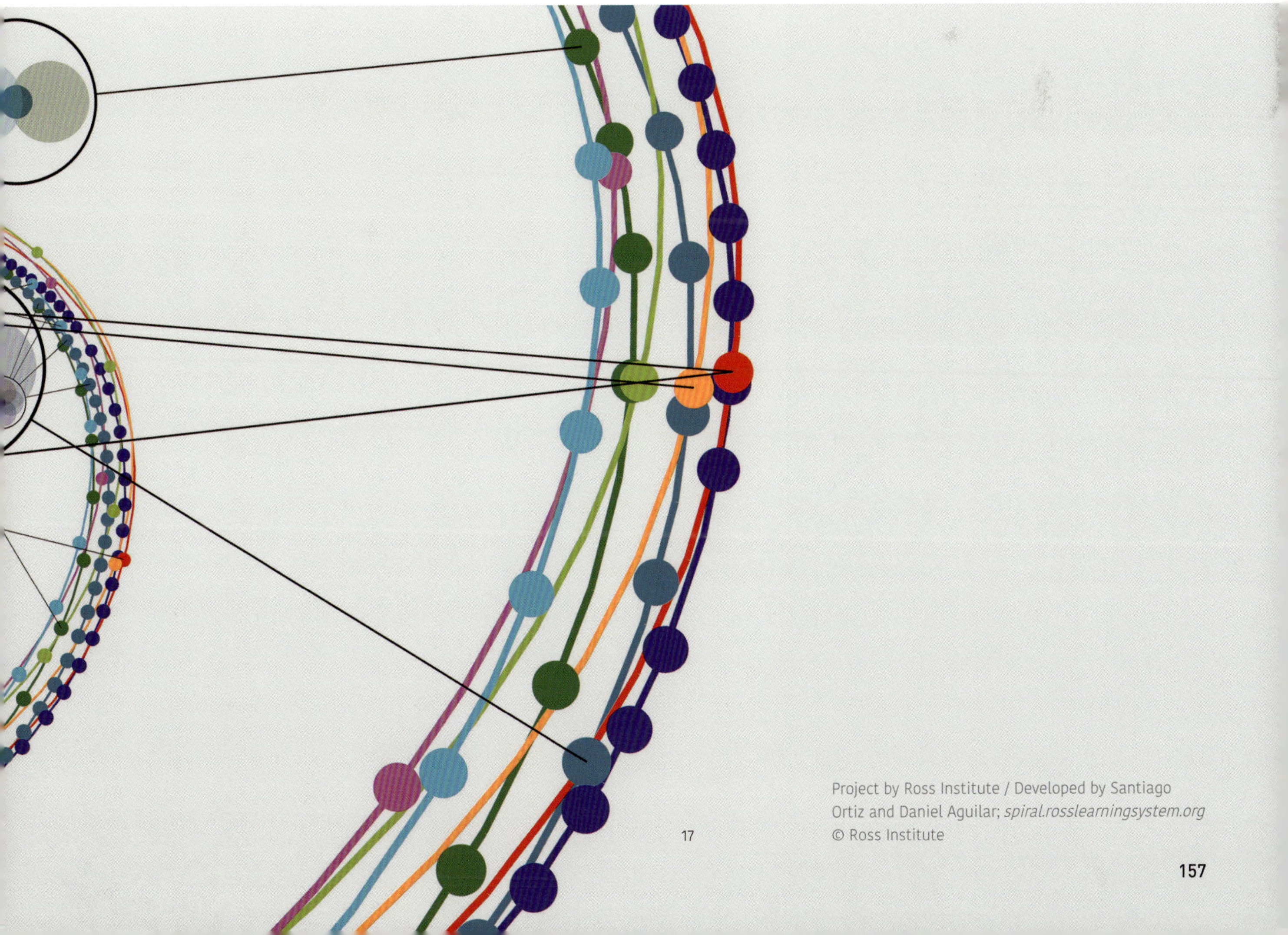

17

Project by Ross Institute / Developed by Santiago
Ortiz and Daniel Aguilar; *spiral.rosslearningsystem.org*
© Ross Institute

Valerio Pellegrini

Valerio Pellegrini is an information designer based in Milan. After graduating in communication design at Politecnico University in Milan, he obtained a master degree with a thesis titled 'Minerva–Data Visualization & Kant's Work' that won the Kantar Information Is Beautiful award in 2013 and in 2016.

[Q] What do you think about data visualization/infographics?

[A] Data visualization is a very powerful tool, capable of making information accessible, clear, and effective. It helps us understand reality.

[Q] What kind of design methods do you commonly use?

[A] My method is basically made of two moments: at first I study and analyze data and the phenomenon, which also implies actual work on data; and then I choose the best way to make it graphically visible and available, trying to pander and give strength to the theme, but also designing and, after rounds of drafts, realizing a structure that can work and show all the aspects and relations among the information.

[Q] What kind of design elements do you commonly use?

[A] I tend to use structures that can assume the most appropriate and concrete functional perspective. I usually prefer not to rely on pre-existing matrices, but try to analyze, interpret, and visualize the phenomenon in a

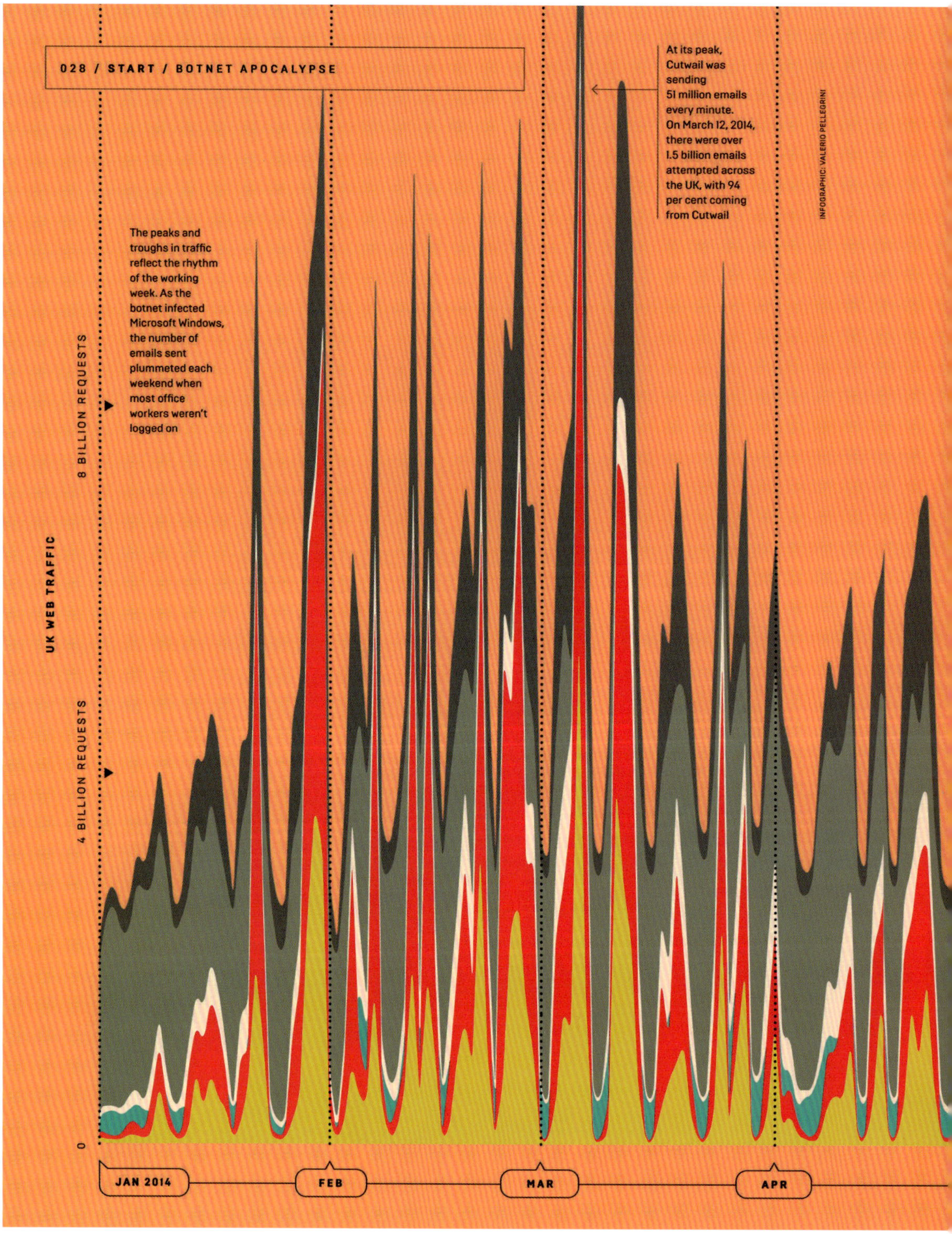

028 / START / BOTNET APOCALYPSE

The peaks and troughs in traffic reflect the rhythm of the working week. As the botnet infected Microsoft Windows, the number of emails sent plummeted each weekend when most office workers weren't logged on

At its peak, Cutwail was sending 51 million emails every minute. On March 12, 2014, there were over 1.5 billion emails attempted across the UK, with 94 per cent coming from Cutwail

UK WEB TRAFFIC

8 BILLION REQUESTS

4 BILLION REQUESTS

JAN 2014 — FEB — MAR — APR

INFOGRAPHIC: VALERIO PELLEGRINI

new, transversal, and efficient way. The structures in my works usually take into account the type and amount of data available. In this process there are no pre-defined and functional structures by definition applicable to particular types of data, except at a very basic level.

As an example, in my artwork Pantheon, you can see two main structures, a timeline and a time alluvial diagram together. The first part covers an introductory role, both at a subject level and at the historical framing of characters. Then it follows a group of these characters according to different categories. On some occasions, I use geometric structures to outline and make information more accessible, but the creative process, by definition, never follows predetermined structures.

[Q] **Where are your works applied?**

[A] My works appear in daily and weekly newspapers, magazines, books, websites, and other devices and platforms according to the client.

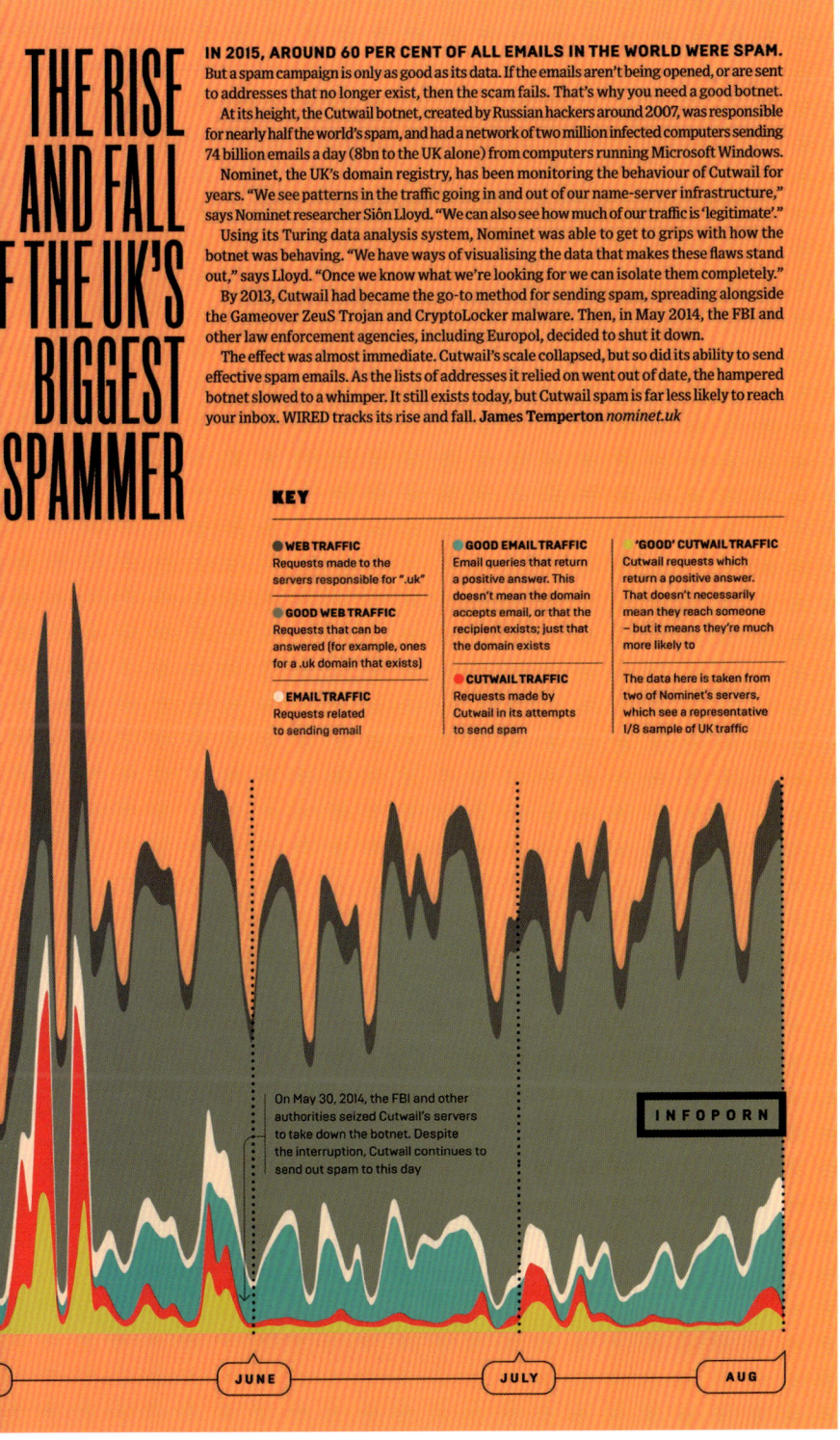

[1] The Rise and Fall of the UK's Biggest Spammer

Credit: Valerio Pellegrini
Completion: 2016

It is an artwork for *Wired UK* on UK's biggest spam service from January to August 2014 referring to total email traffic. In the graph, you can see the moments of major and minor activities of botnet. The peaks and troughs of the visualization reflect the rhythm of the working weeks. As the botnet infected Microsoft Windows, so the number of emails sent plummeted each weekend when most office workers weren't logged on.

[Q] How do you turn boring and complex data into something interesting and understandable?

[A] To me, the best compromise is keeping data visible, readable, and comparable, while providing a visually clear and interesting, yet never deceptive or too noisy, structure. In order to achieve this, I use tools I've learnt during my career, but also with personal aesthetic and functional choices.

[Q] What is your suggestion for beginners?

[A] My advice for young designers approaching this profession is to understand what the elements are simplifying, and make the communication of phenomena more effective, such as the use of symbols, the study of maps, and color palette choices. They can make communication fluent even if wordless, and let a phenomenon be explained visually.

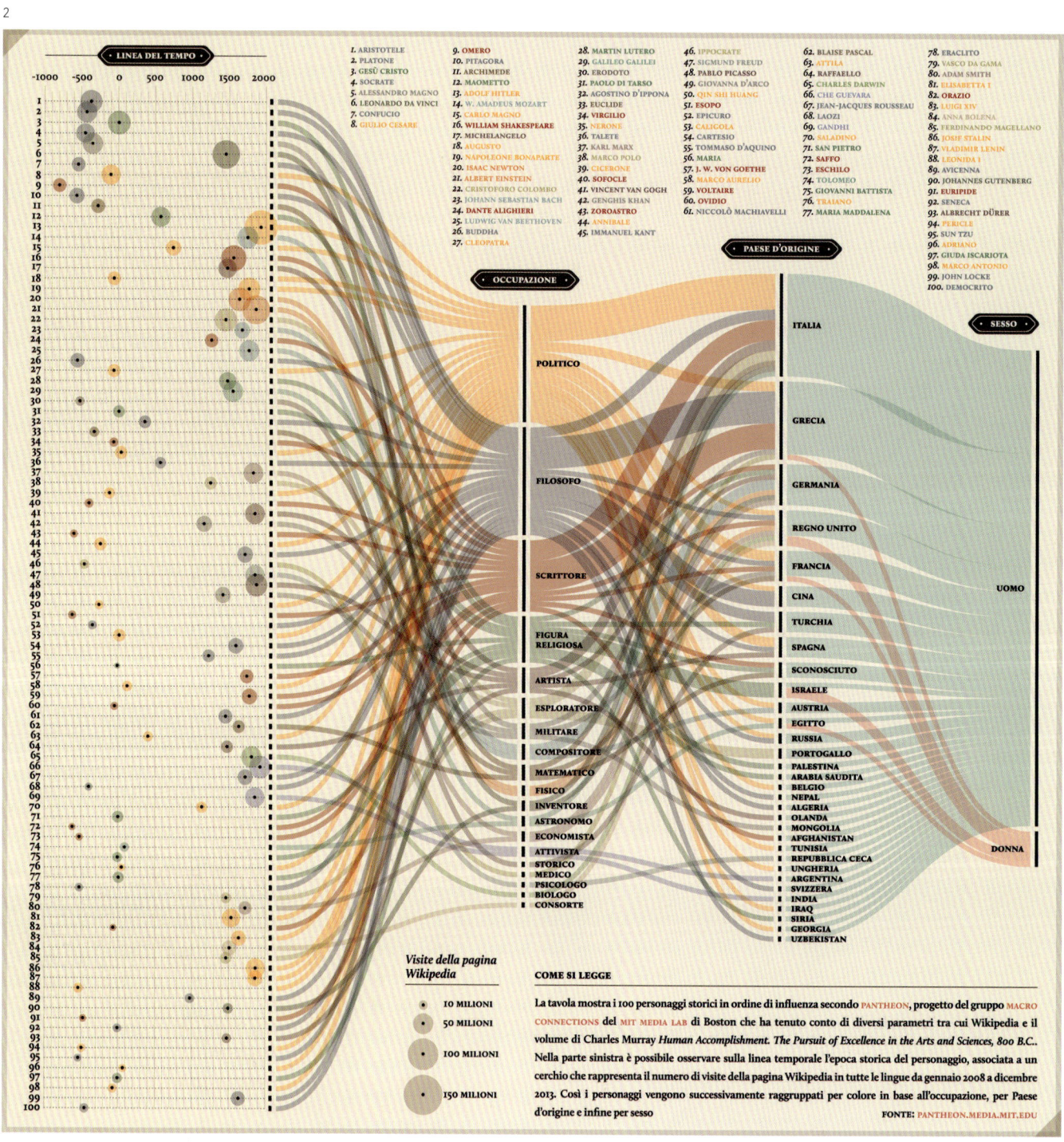

[2] Pantheon

Credit: Valerio Pellegrini
Completion: 2015

The artwork shows the first 100 historical figures in order of influence according to Pantheon, a Macro Connections group of the MIT Media Lab of Boston project that took into account various parameters, such as Wikipedia and *Human Accomplishment: The Pursuit of Excellence in the Arts and Sciences, 800 B.C. to 1950* by Charles Murray.

The timeline on the left shows the historical epoch of the character associated with a circle that represents the number of visits to its Wikipedia page in all languages from January 2008 to December 2013. The characters are then grouped by color according to employment, country of origin, and then gender.

[3] FBI's Most Wanted

Credit: Valerio Pellegrini
Completion: 2016

The artwork shows all those wanted by the FBI, grouped by type of crime committed. Each line is defined, starting from the center, by total rewards allocated for each type of crime, by the first three nations of belonging, by the average age, by category, and by the number of criminals arranged in radius around their hexagons. The size of each flag is related to the number of criminals belonging to each category. In case of equal position in ranking, all the flags are shown.

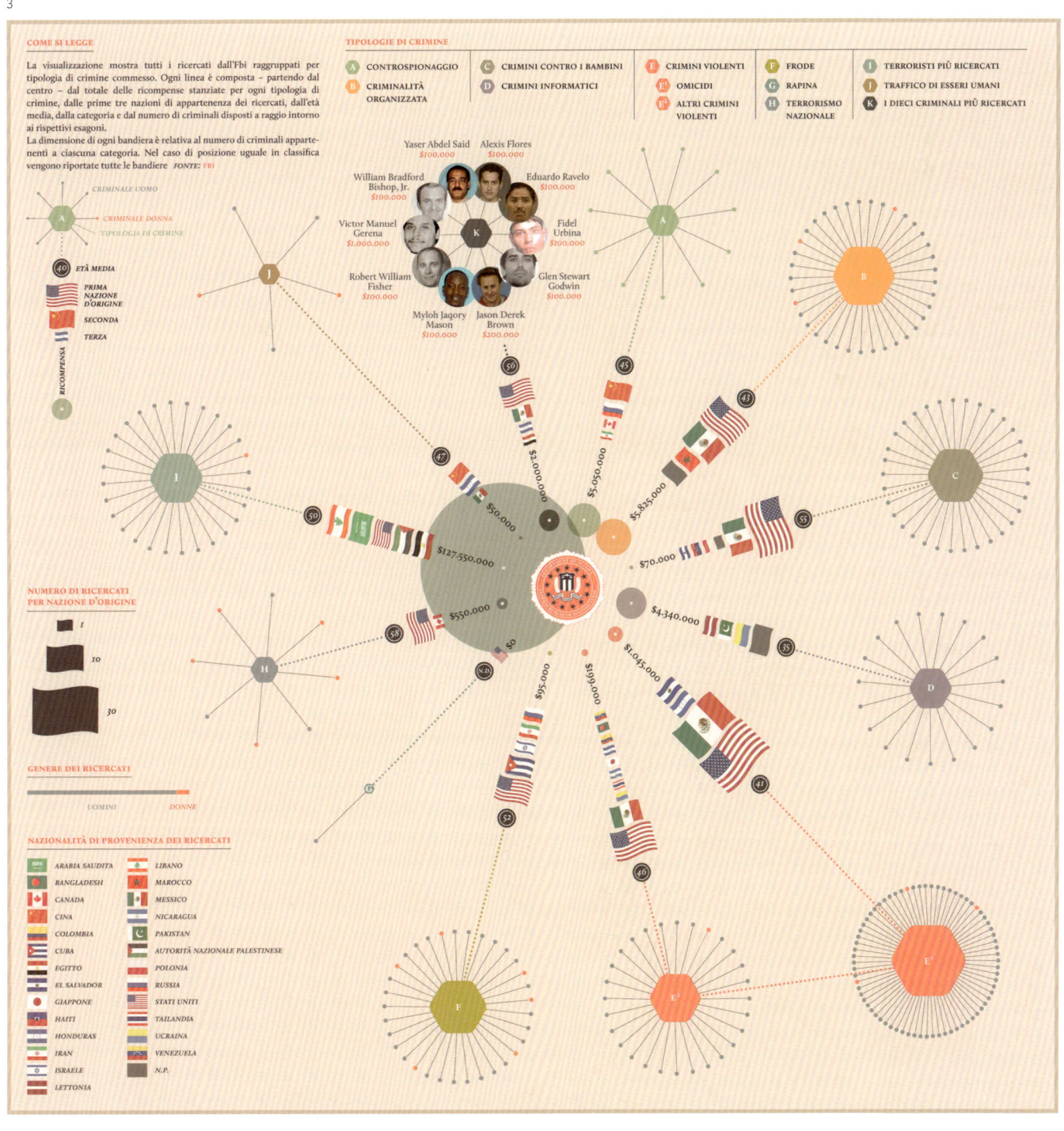

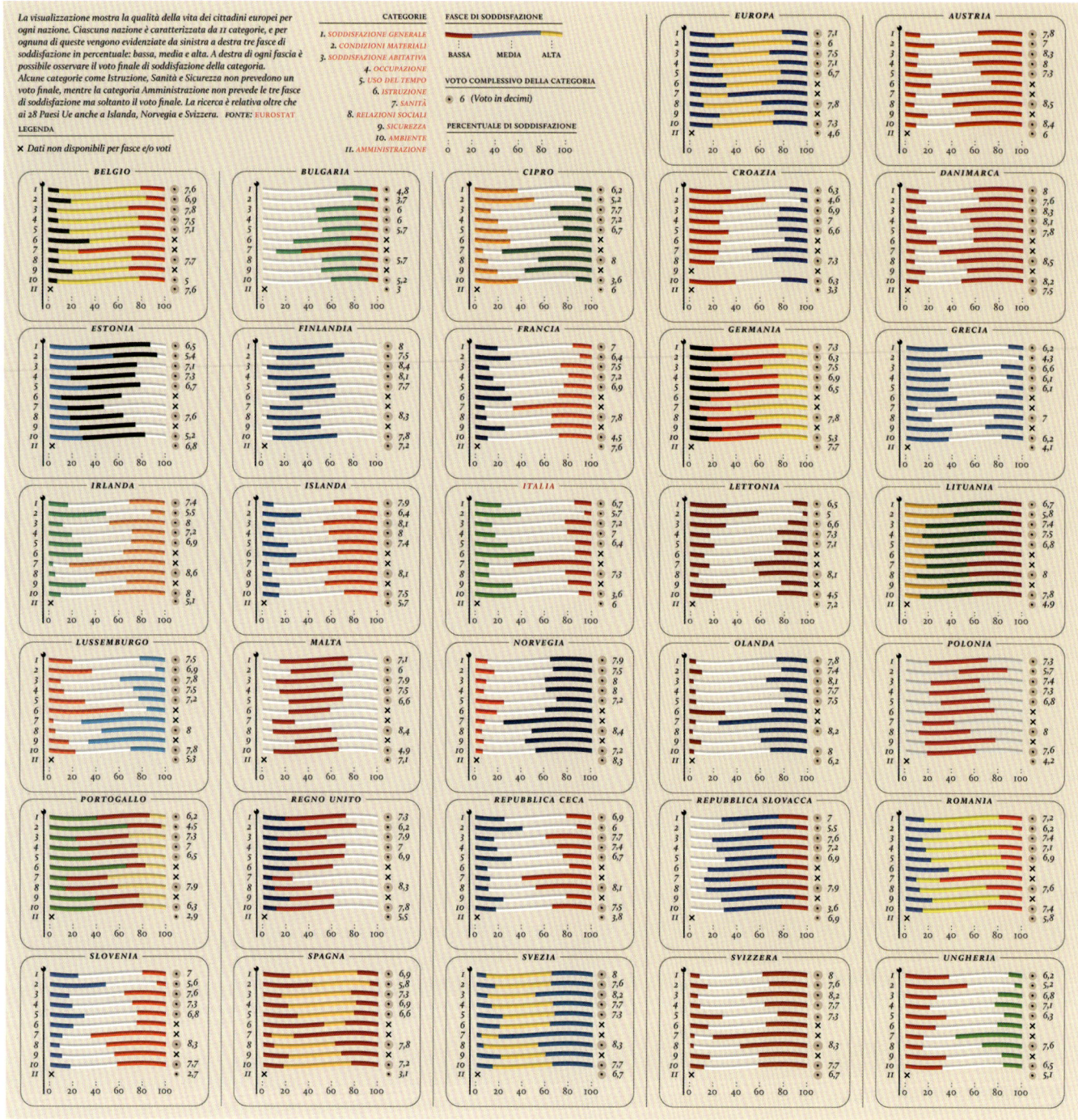

[4] The Quality of Life in Europe

Credit: Valerio Pellegrini
Completion: 2015

The artwork shows the quality of life of citizens for every European nation. Each nation is characterized by 11 categories, each of which highlights three satisfaction bands in percentages from left to right: low, medium, and high. On the right of each band is the final satisfaction vote for each category. Some categories such as Education, Health and Safety do not provide a final grade, while the Administration category does not include the three levels of satisfaction but only the final grade. The research is related not only to the 28 European countries, but also to Iceland, Norway, and Switzerland.

[5] Auditel

Credit: Valerio Pellegrini
Completion: 2015

This is the artwork for *Il Corriere della Sera—La Lettura* #189 about Auditel (the company involved in data collection of TV viewing in Italy). The visualization shows Auditel data over the last three years on the national broadcasters, grouped by publisher, according to daily time slots. The stream graph in the middle shows the total, while the outer graph represents daily average contacts for each time slot.

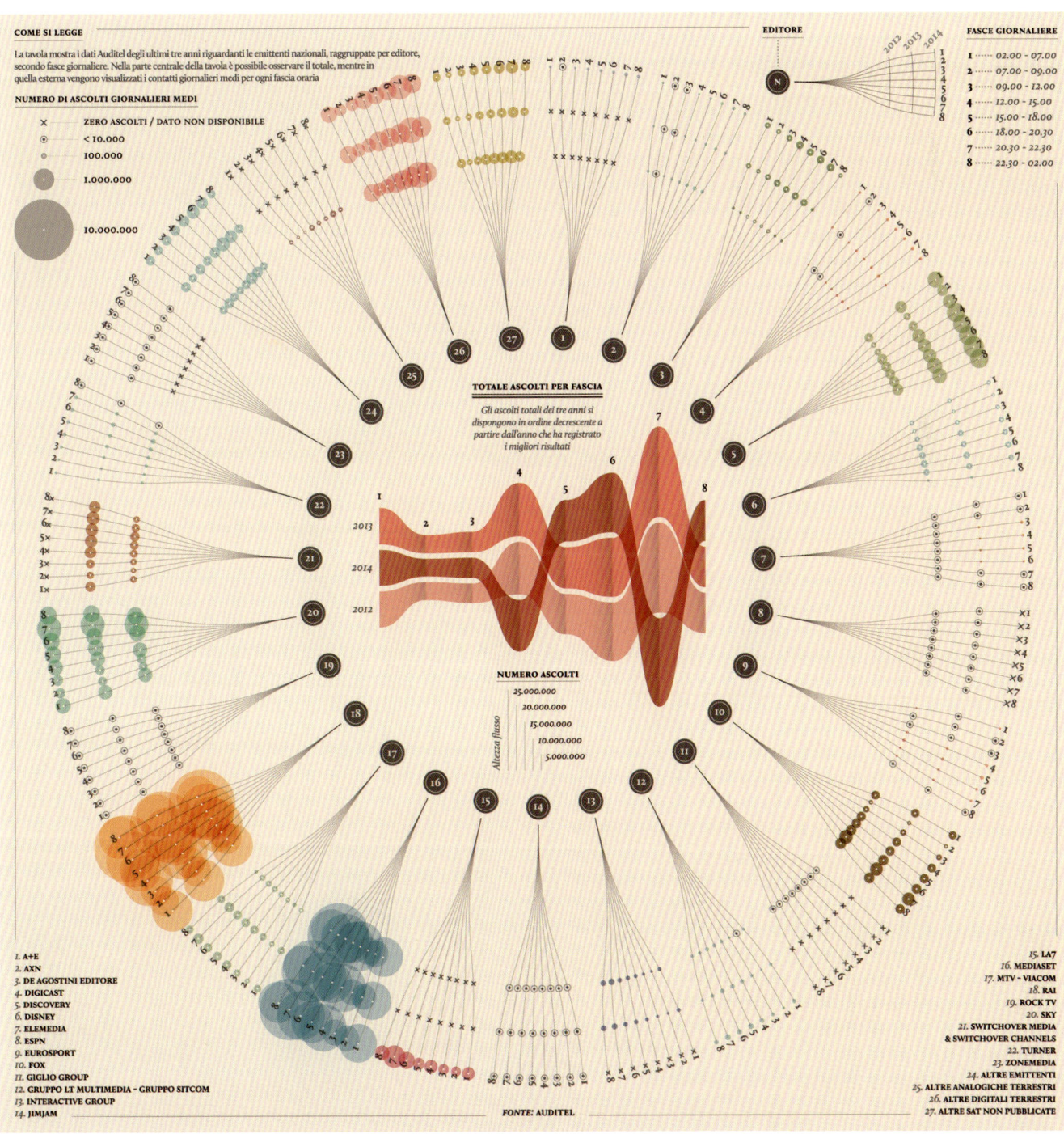

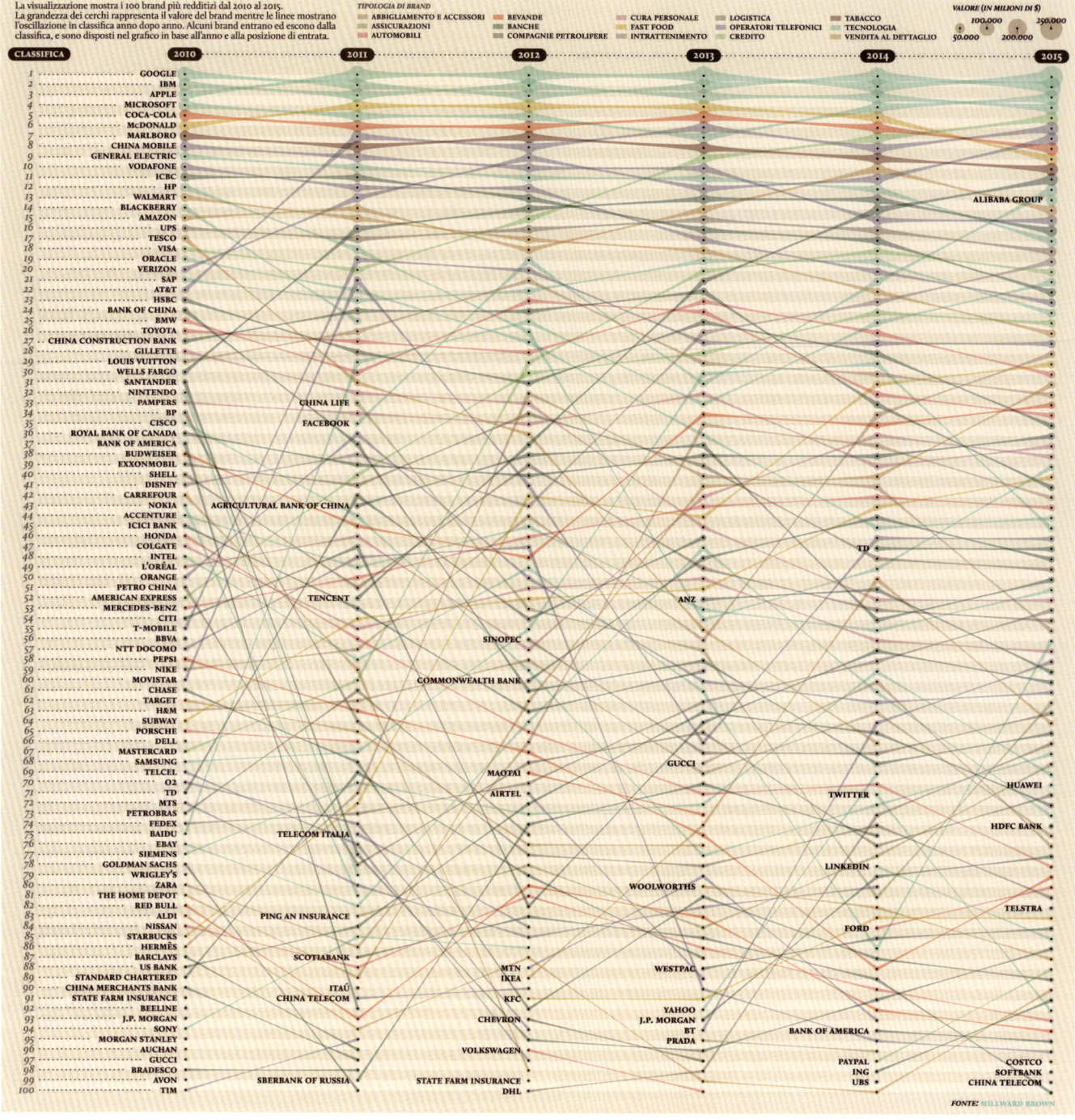

[6] 100 Most Valuable Brands

Credit: Valerio Pellegrini
Completion: 2015

The artwork for *Il Corriere della Sera—La Lettura* shows the 100 most valuable brands from 2010 to 2015. The size of the circles represents the value of the brand, while the lines show the fluctuation in ranking year after year. Some brands come in and out of the rankings, and are arranged in the chart according to the year and the position of entry.

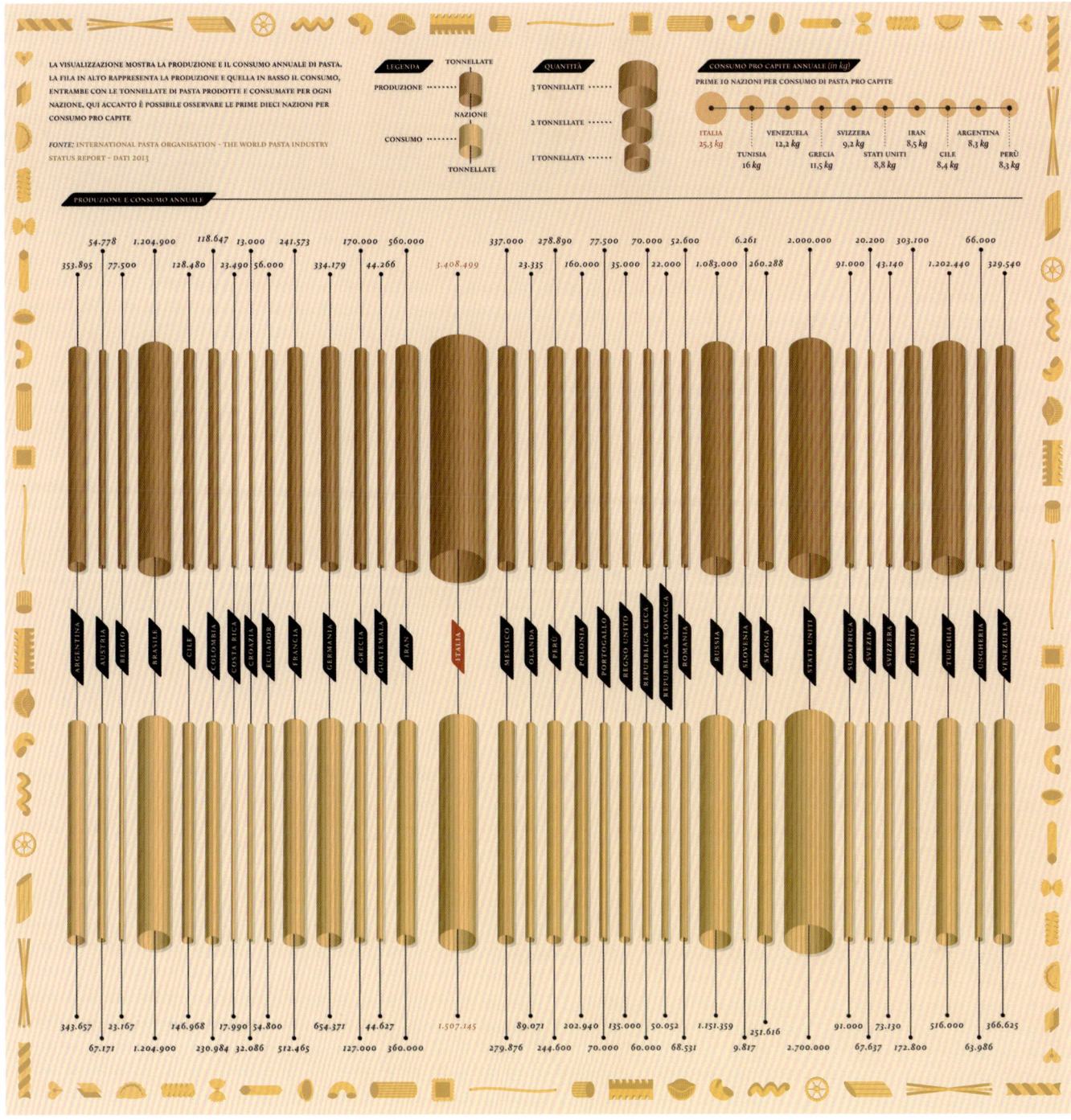

[7] PASTA

Credit: Valerio Pellegrini
Completion: 2016

This is an artwork for *Il Corriere della Sera—La Lettura* about the production and consumption of pasta in the world. In the central part there is a comparison between production and consumption of pasta in tonnes per country, while at the top there are the top 10 countries for per capita consumption of pasta in the world.

Periscopic

PERISCOPIC
DO GOOD WITH DATA

Periscopic is an award-winning data visualization firm. They convert raw data into visual and interactive experiences that allow people to empathize and understand. They help companies and organizations promote data transparency and public awareness. From endangered species to sustainability, politics, and social justice, it is their goal to use technology to visualize solutions that engage the public and deliver messages of action. The tagline 'Do good with data' describes their philosophy, as well as their approach.

[Q] What do you think about data visualization/infographics?

[A] We like them and believe they are helpful in making sense of data.

[Q] What kind of design methods do you commonly use?

[A] We have a diverse skill set that involves data wrangling, analysis, strategy, design, development, and management. Our design-specific methods involve research, conceptualising, brainstorming, information architecture, visual design, interaction design, and motion design.

[Q] What kind of design elements do you commonly use?

[A] It depends on the project. Often it includes data presentation methods that are sometimes accented by illustrations, photographs, dots, lines, circles, squares, triangles, polygons, and other shapes, as well as colors. We use whatever visual shapes best convey the insights we've identified in the data. Sometimes that takes the form of lines, polygons, or circles, and other times it takes the form of specialized presentation methods that we've invented or customized to suit our needs. Usually this will be informed by the type of data we are presenting (qualitative or quantitative, and within that, ordinal or nominal, or discrete or continuous). Color is often used to help emphasize an aspect of the data, or distinguish between variables.

[Q] Where are your works applied?

[A] Our work is most often found online, in books, and occasionally in brochures.

[Q] How do you turn boring and complex data into something interesting and understandable?

[A] We ask a lot of questions, do a thorough strategy phase, explore the data from many angles, and keep iterating our ideas until a design makes sense.

[Q] What is your suggestion for beginners?

[A] Be fierce and fearless. Educate yourself about data presentation methods, and if your focus is design, either educate yourself about design best practices, or go to design school. Consider learning a tool like Tableau. Find a data visualization firm and do an internship. Sketch, and try to think of your data visually.

1

[1–3] Growing Hope

Credits: Periscopic, MSNBC
Completion: 2013
Interactive link: www.periscopic.com/our-work/growing-hope

As a part of MSNBC's Growing Hope campaign, Periscopic developed this online, multilevel visualization of the hopes and concerns submitted by individuals across the nation. With a strong emphasis on helping to enable change in local communities, MSNBC traveled to various cities and college campuses to learn about the factors that motivate people to make a difference. Many of the events had a physical tree onto which visitors could hang a written 'hope' for the future. Periscopic extended this concept to MSNBC's website, where visitors could browse through dozens of topics, and thousands of hopes were submitted in real time.

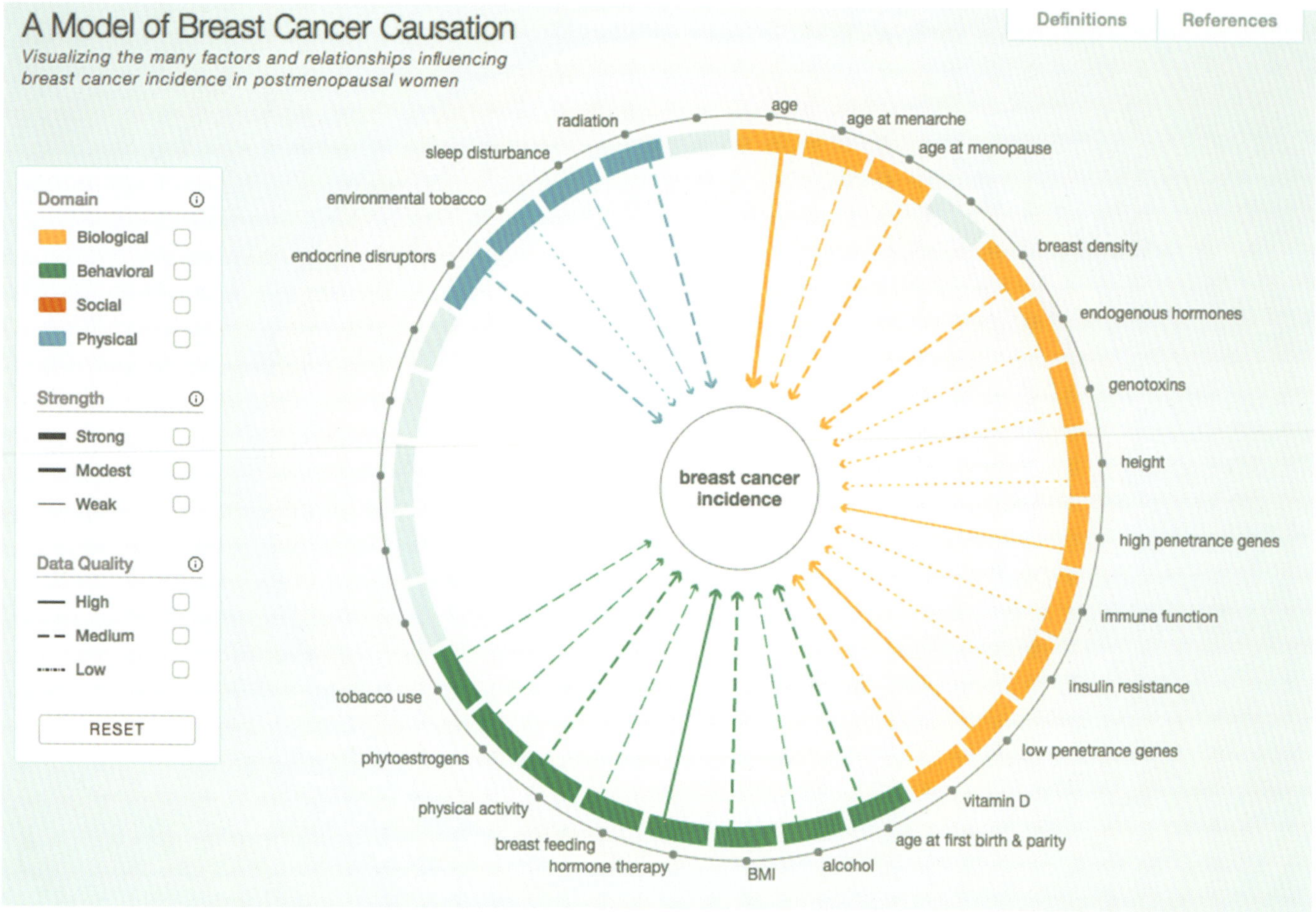

A Model of Breast Cancer Causation
Visualizing the many factors and relationships influencing breast cancer incidence in postmenopausal women

Definitions | References

Domain
- Biological
- Behavioral
- Social
- Physical

Strength
- Strong
- Modest
- Weak

Data Quality
- High
- Medium
- Low

RESET

Factors around the wheel: radiation, sleep disturbance, environmental tobacco, endocrine disruptors, age, age at menarche, age at menopause, breast density, endogenous hormones, genotoxins, height, high penetrance genes, immune function, insulin resistance, low penetrance genes, vitamin D, age at first birth & parity, alcohol, BMI, hormone therapy, breast feeding, physical activity, phytoestrogens, tobacco use → **breast cancer incidence**

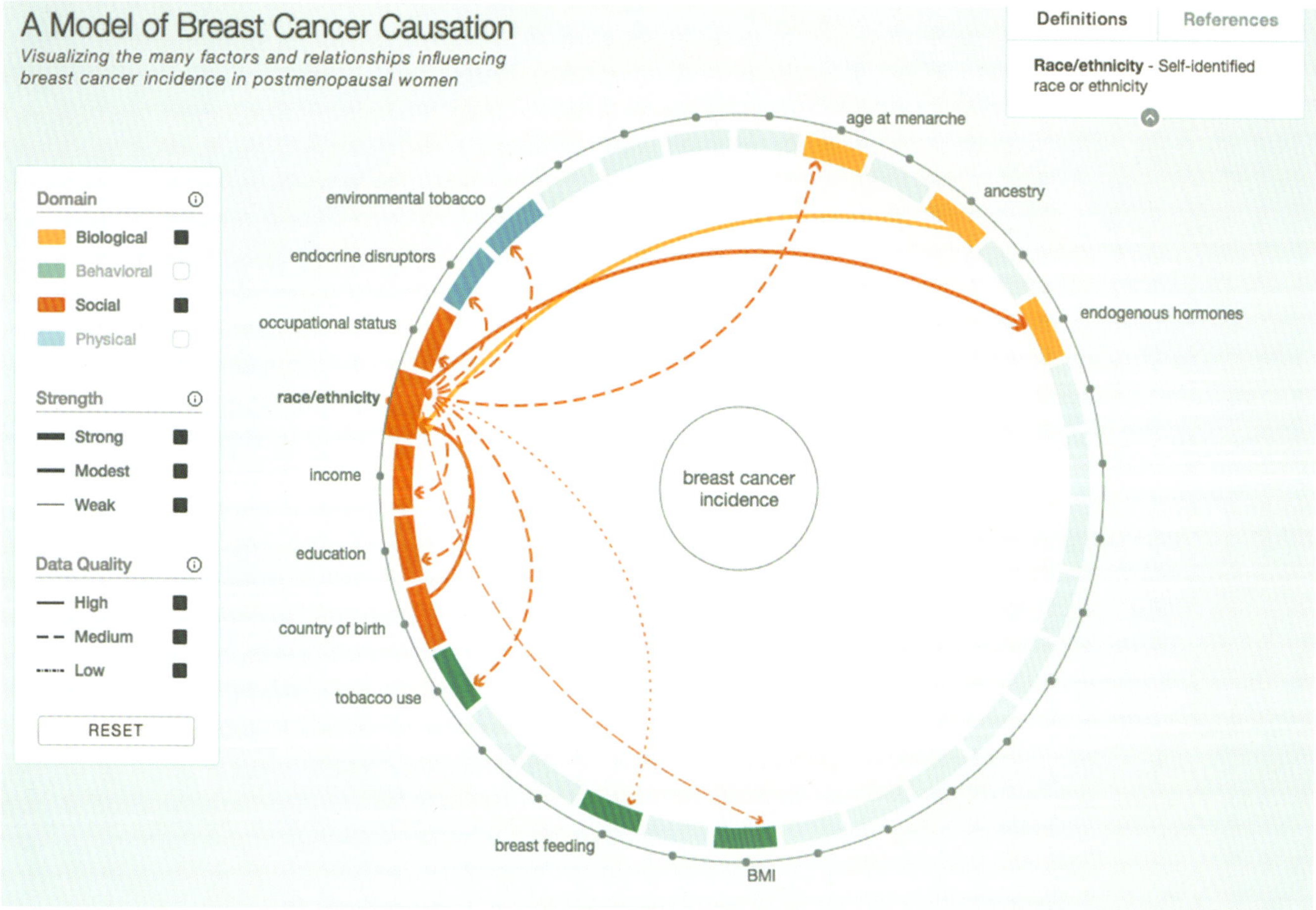

A Model of Breast Cancer Causation
Visualizing the many factors and relationships influencing breast cancer incidence in postmenopausal women

Definitions | References

Race/ethnicity - Self-identified race or ethnicity

Domain
- Biological
- Behavioral
- Social
- Physical

Strength
- Strong
- Modest
- Weak

Data Quality
- High
- Medium
- Low

RESET

Factors shown: age at menarche, ancestry, endogenous hormones, environmental tobacco, endocrine disruptors, occupational status, **race/ethnicity**, income, education, country of birth, tobacco use, breast feeding, BMI → breast cancer incidence

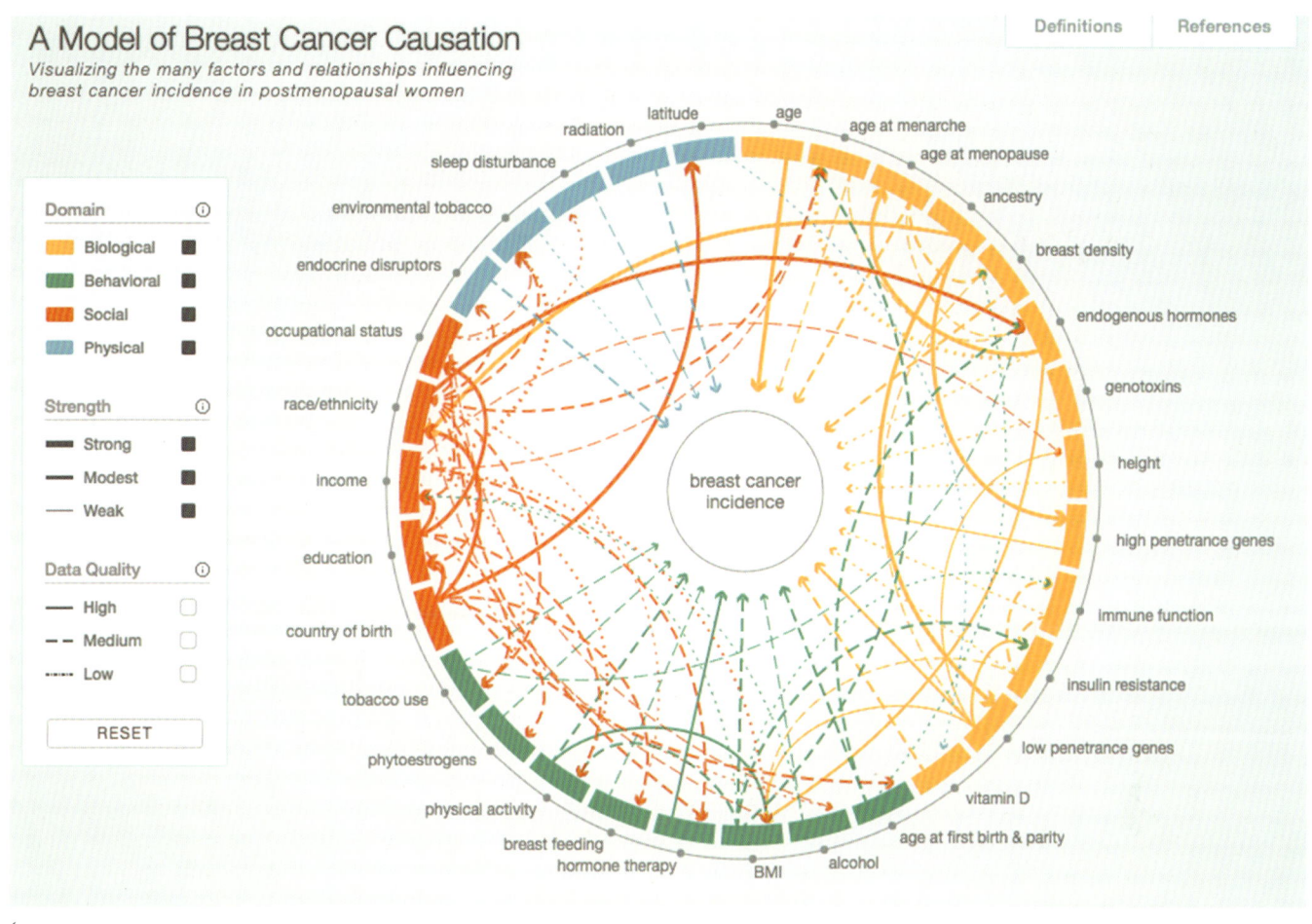

[4–6] A Model of Breast Cancer Causation

Credits: Periscopic, University of California San Francisco
Completion: 2014
Interactive link: www.periscopic.com/our-work/visualizing-breast-cancer-causation-in-postmenopausal-women

Working closely with scientists at University of California San Francisco, Periscopic designed and built an exploration tool that visualizes the direct and indirect factors that influence breast cancer in post-menopausal women. The researchers at UCSF had been collaborating with experts in the breast cancer field for over a year to create a paradigm that synthesized insights from various sources, and this tool allows visitors to explore the relationships between biological, social, behavioral, and physical factors, as well as quality of data and strength of influence. It also easily demonstrates which factors influence the occurrence of breast cancer, as well as demonstrating how many of the factors influence each other.

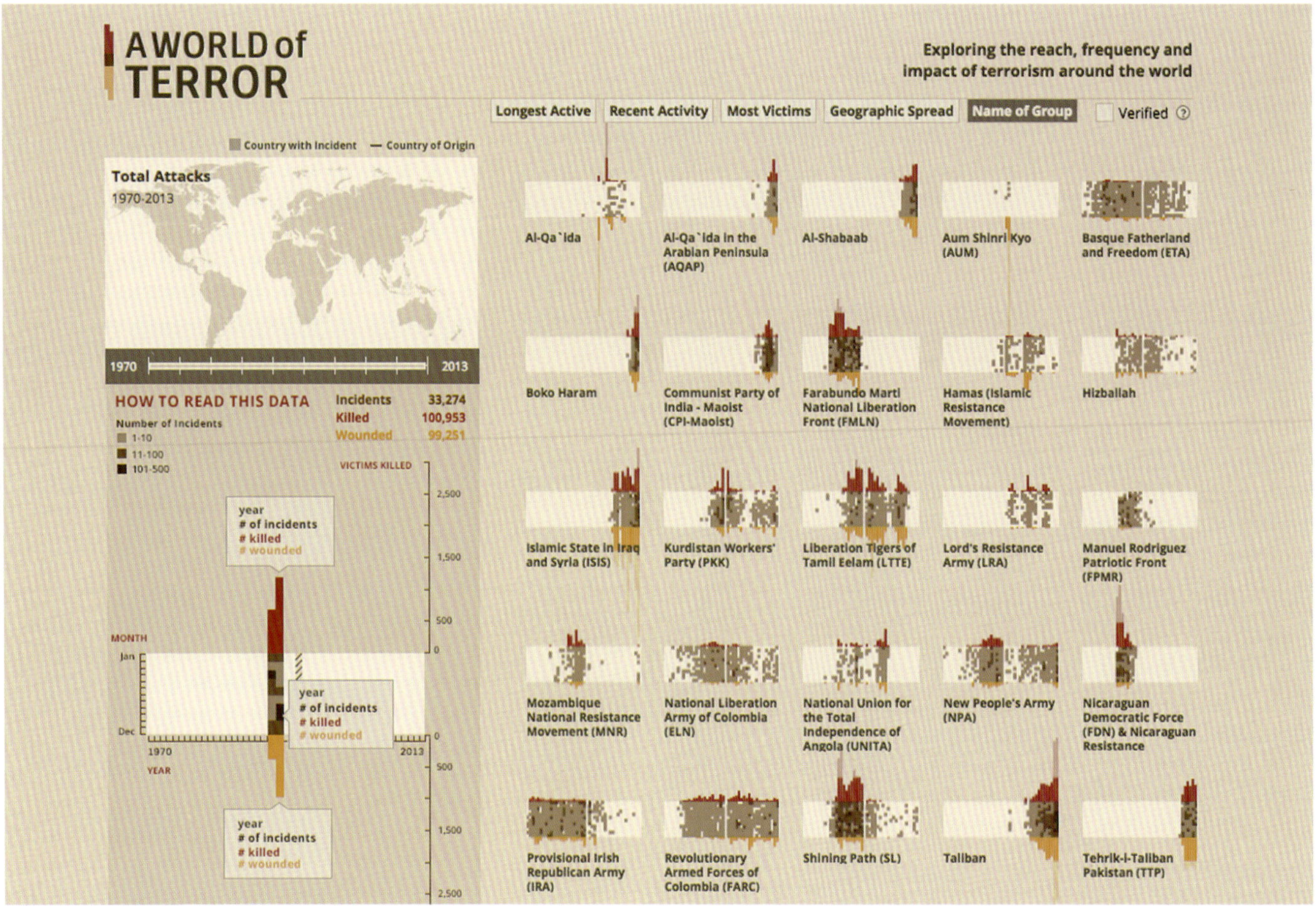

A WORLD of TERROR
Exploring the reach, frequency and impact of terrorism around the world
Longest Active
Recent Activity
Most Victims
Geographic Spread
Name of Group
Verified
Country with Incident
Country of Origin
Total Attacks
1970-2013
1970
2013
HOW TO READ THIS DATA
Number of Incidents
1-10
11-100
101-500
Incidents 33,274
Killed 100,953
Wounded 99,251
VICTIMS KILLED
2,500
1,500
500
0
year
# of incidents
killed
wounded
MONTH
Jan
Dec
1970
2013
YEAR
Al-Qa`ida
Al-Qa`ida in the Arabian Peninsula (AQAP)
Al-Shabaab
Aum Shinri Kyo (AUM)
Basque Fatherland and Freedom (ETA)
Boko Haram
Communist Party of India - Maoist (CPI-Maoist)
Farabundo Marti National Liberation Front (FMLN)
Hamas (Islamic Resistance Movement)
Hizballah
Islamic State in Iraq and Syria (ISIS)
Kurdistan Workers' Party (PKK)
Liberation Tigers of Tamil Eelam (LTTE)
Lord's Resistance Army (LRA)
Manuel Rodriguez Patriotic Front (FPMR)
Mozambique National Resistance Movement (MNR)
National Liberation Army of Colombia (ELN)
National Union for the Total Independence of Angola (UNITA)
New People's Army (NPA)
Nicaraguan Democratic Force (FDN) & Nicaraguan Resistance
Provisional Irish Republican Army (IRA)
Revolutionary Armed Forces of Colombia (FARC)
Shining Path (SL)
Taliban
Tehrik-i-Taliban Pakistan (TTP)

7

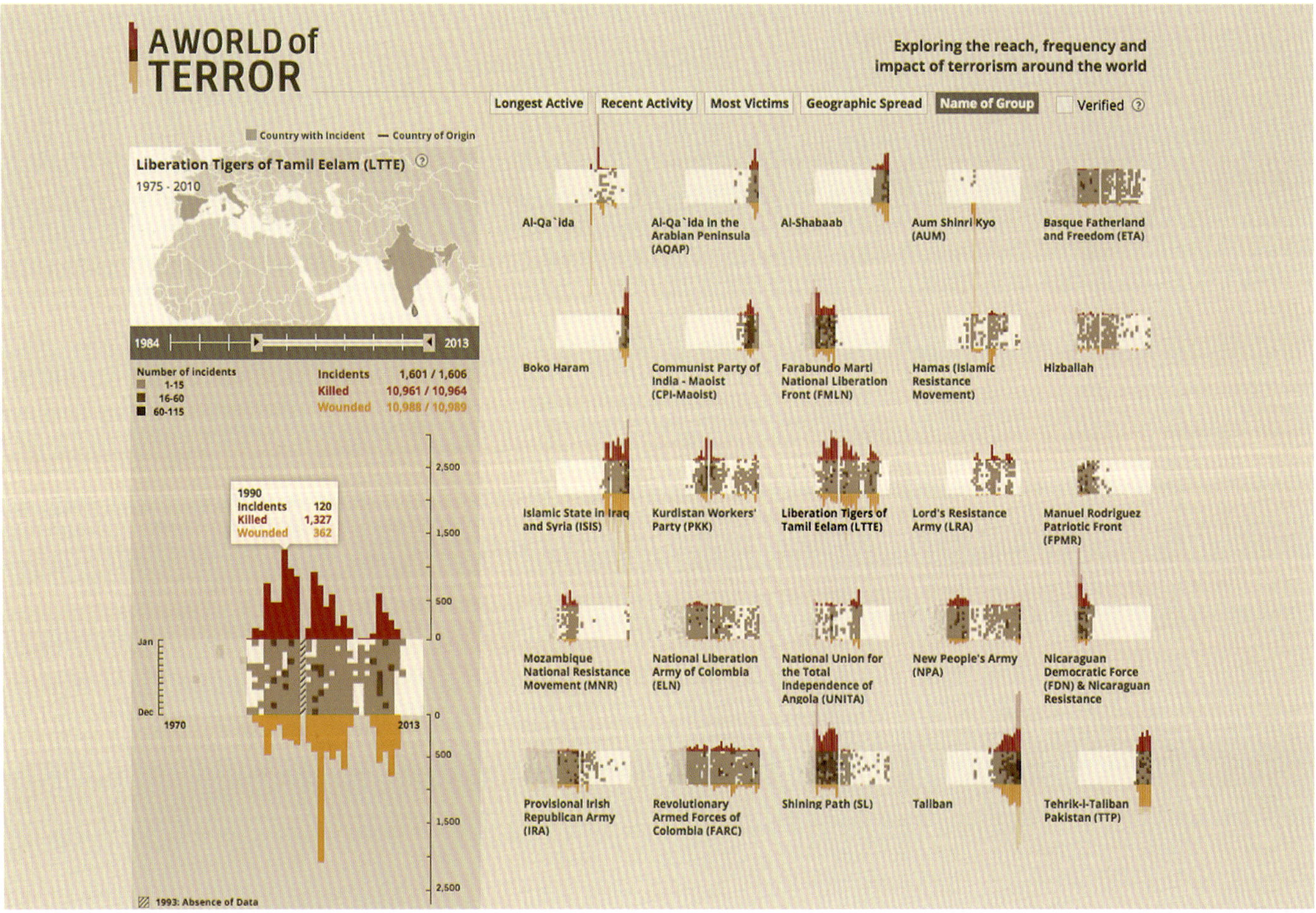

A WORLD of TERROR
Exploring the reach, frequency and impact of terrorism around the world
Longest Active
Recent Activity
Most Victims
Geographic Spread
Name of Group
Verified
Country with Incident
Country of Origin
Liberation Tigers of Tamil Eelam (LTTE)
1975 - 2010
1984
2013
Number of incidents
1-15
16-60
60-115
Incidents 1,601 / 1,606
Killed 10,961 / 10,964
Wounded 10,988 / 10,989
2,500
1,500
500
0
1990
Incidents 120
Killed 1,327
Wounded 362
Jan
Dec
1970
2013
1993: Absence of Data
Al-Qa`ida
Al-Qa`ida in the Arabian Peninsula (AQAP)
Al-Shabaab
Aum Shinri Kyo (AUM)
Basque Fatherland and Freedom (ETA)
Boko Haram
Communist Party of India - Maoist (CPI-Maoist)
Farabundo Marti National Liberation Front (FMLN)
Hamas (Islamic Resistance Movement)
Hizballah
Islamic State in Iraq and Syria (ISIS)
Kurdistan Workers' Party (PKK)
Liberation Tigers of Tamil Eelam (LTTE)
Lord's Resistance Army (LRA)
Manuel Rodriguez Patriotic Front (FPMR)
Mozambique National Resistance Movement (MNR)
National Liberation Army of Colombia (ELN)
National Union for the Total Independence of Angola (UNITA)
New People's Army (NPA)
Nicaraguan Democratic Force (FDN) & Nicaraguan Resistance
Provisional Irish Republican Army (IRA)
Revolutionary Armed Forces of Colombia (FARC)
Shining Path (SL)
Taliban
Tehrik-i-Taliban Pakistan (TTP)

8

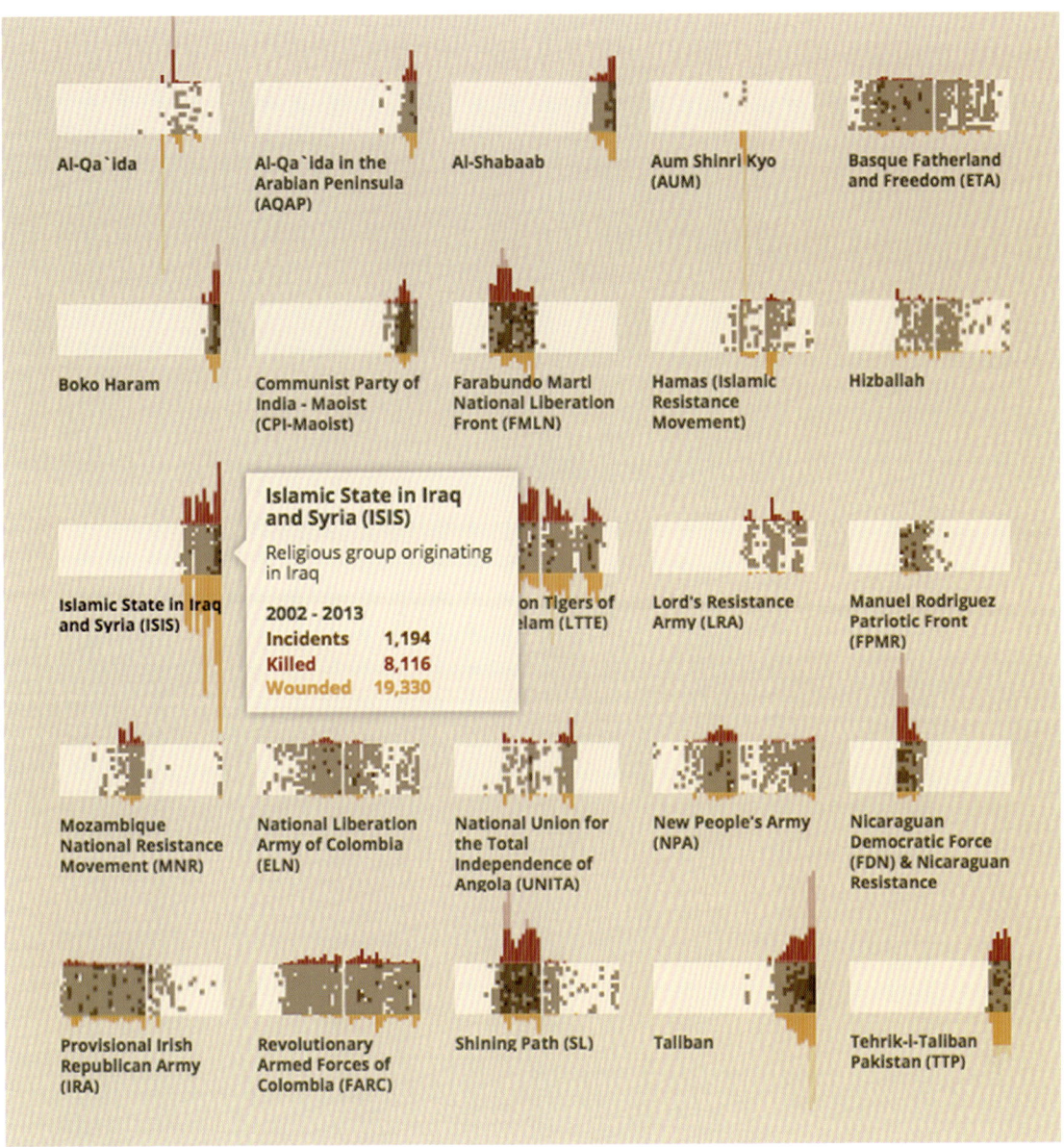

[7–9] A World of Terror

Credit: Periscopic
Completion: 2013
Interactive link: www.periscopic.com/our-work/exploring-the-reach-frequency-and-impact-of-terrorism-around-the-world

Through this project, Periscopic mapped the reach, frequency, and impact of the most active terrorist entities around the world. The data comes from the National Consortium for the Study of Terrorism and Responses to Terrorism's (START) Global Terrorism Database (GTD), which includes incident-level data from open data sources around the world from 1970 to 2013.

There are more than 3065 organizations and groups listed in the GTD, and to identify the top 25 organizations who use terrorist tactics, Periscopic determined the groups with the most killings, the most wounded, and the most incidents. They wanted to make sure they were inclusive of all actions, not just the most physically harmful. They aggregated these three lists and took the top 25 organizations (most were in the top 30 for all three categories). This top 0.8 percent of groups account for more than 26 percent of the 125,087 incidents.

Sara Piccolomini

[Q] What do you think about data visualization/infographics?

[A] Data visualization always opens me up to new perspectives, and it lets me deal with various issues in different ways and every project I work on is a unique challenge. I love to bring order and a sense of beauty to what otherwise would not be understood, and I am fascinated by turning complexity into something meaningful and memorable thanks to visual representation.

[Q] What kind of design methods do you commonly use?

[A] I think that my approach to visualization can be defined as 'instinctive'. When I look at a data set, I immediately try to understand which shapes and colors fit best. I think that is important to find a fine balance between an ordered, accurate, and scientific display of information and an aesthetically beautiful composition of colors and form.

[Q] What kind of design elements do you commonly use?

[A] I often get inspired from old renaissance books of astronomy or geography. I love the elegance and the details of this first kind of visualization. I also love using geometrical shapes and pastel colors.

[Q] Where are your works applied?

[A] I usually work for newspapers or online magazines that deal with visual representation of information.

[Q] How do you turn boring and complex data into something interesting and understandable?

[A] Before using any software, I create sketches in big white paper with a pencil and markers. It helps me to understand the connections and the interrelations of the information without feeling bound by the limits of technology. A deep comprehension of the data set is the first step for a good and understandable visualization.

[Q] What is your suggestion for beginners?

[A] I think data visualization is a really exciting field of visual communication. The complexity of a data set might scare the beginner at first, but I think it hides a great beauty. Data sets are not just numbers, they are events, time, places, in some sense they are stories. The designer is a visual writer; telling stories and making them memorable is the potential of data visualization.

Sara Piccolomini is an information designer based in Milan. She studied at Politecnico di Milano where she obtained a Masters in Communication Design. Her very first approach to information visualization was at university with Density Design. Here, she worked on the first data visualization project called Galileo Follower, a data visualization website that highlights Galileo Galilei's network of relationships through the analysis of the exchange of letters with his contemporaries. In 2014, she also worked for the Visual Agency that specializes in infographics and data visualization.

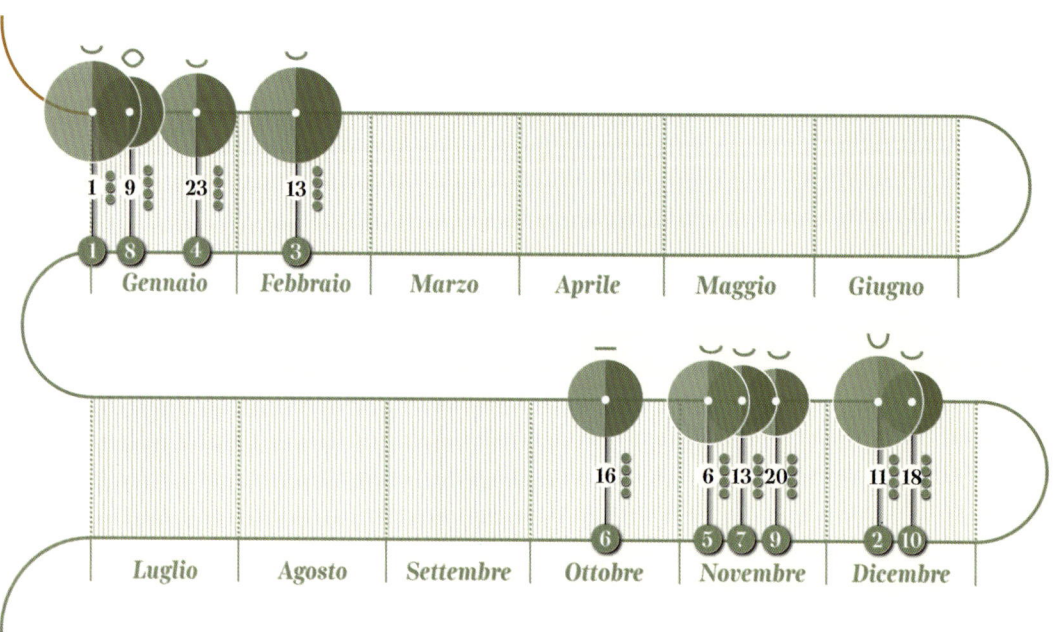

1

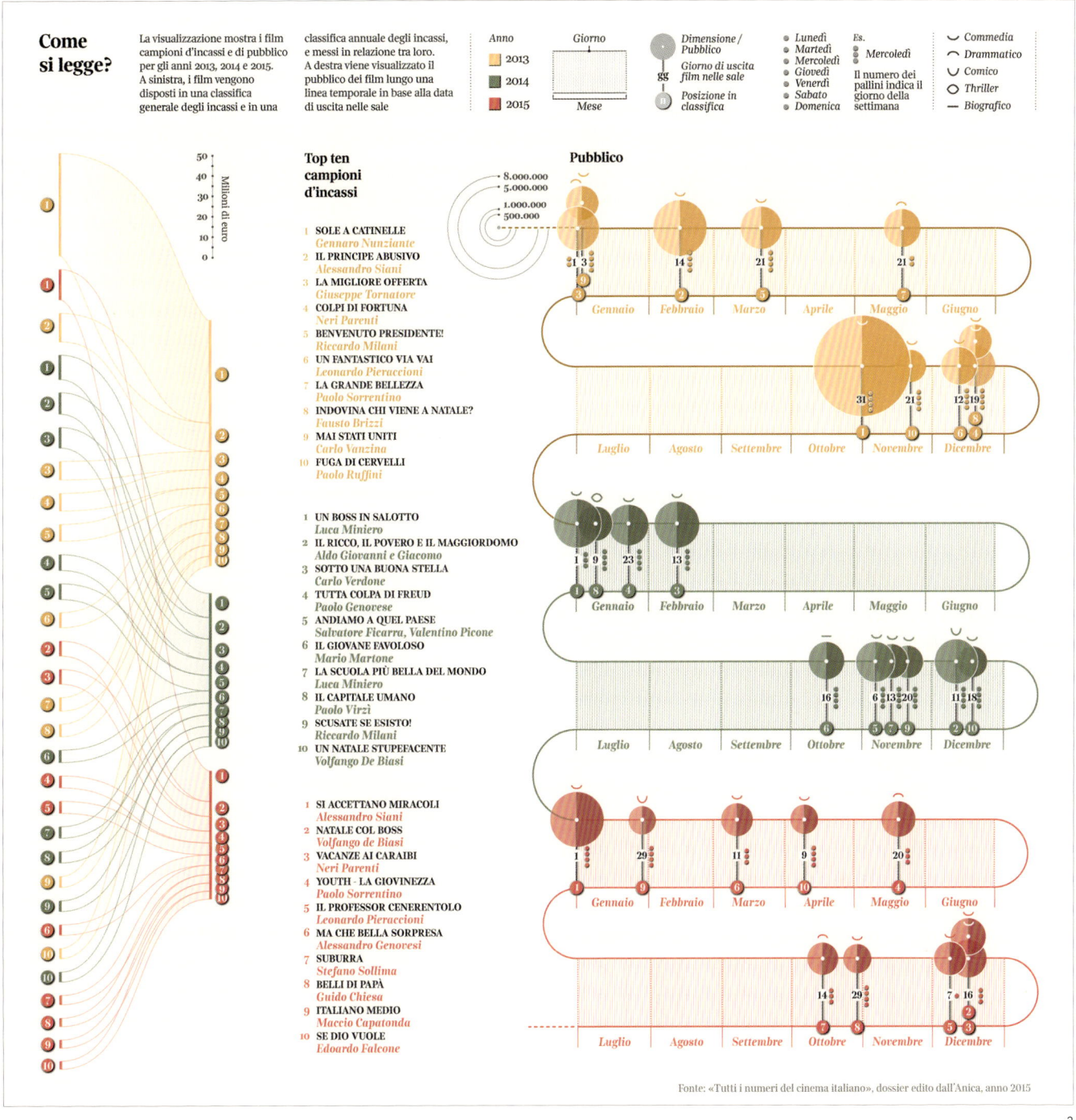

[1–2] Box Office Cinema of Italia

Credit: Sara Piccolomini
Completion: 2016

The visualization for *Il Corriere della Sera—La Lettura* shows the box-office ranking for Italian movies of 2013, 2014, and 2015. On the left there is a global ranking for these three years in relation with the top 10 of each year, on the right is the size of the audience who saw each movie in a timeline according to the date of debut in theaters.

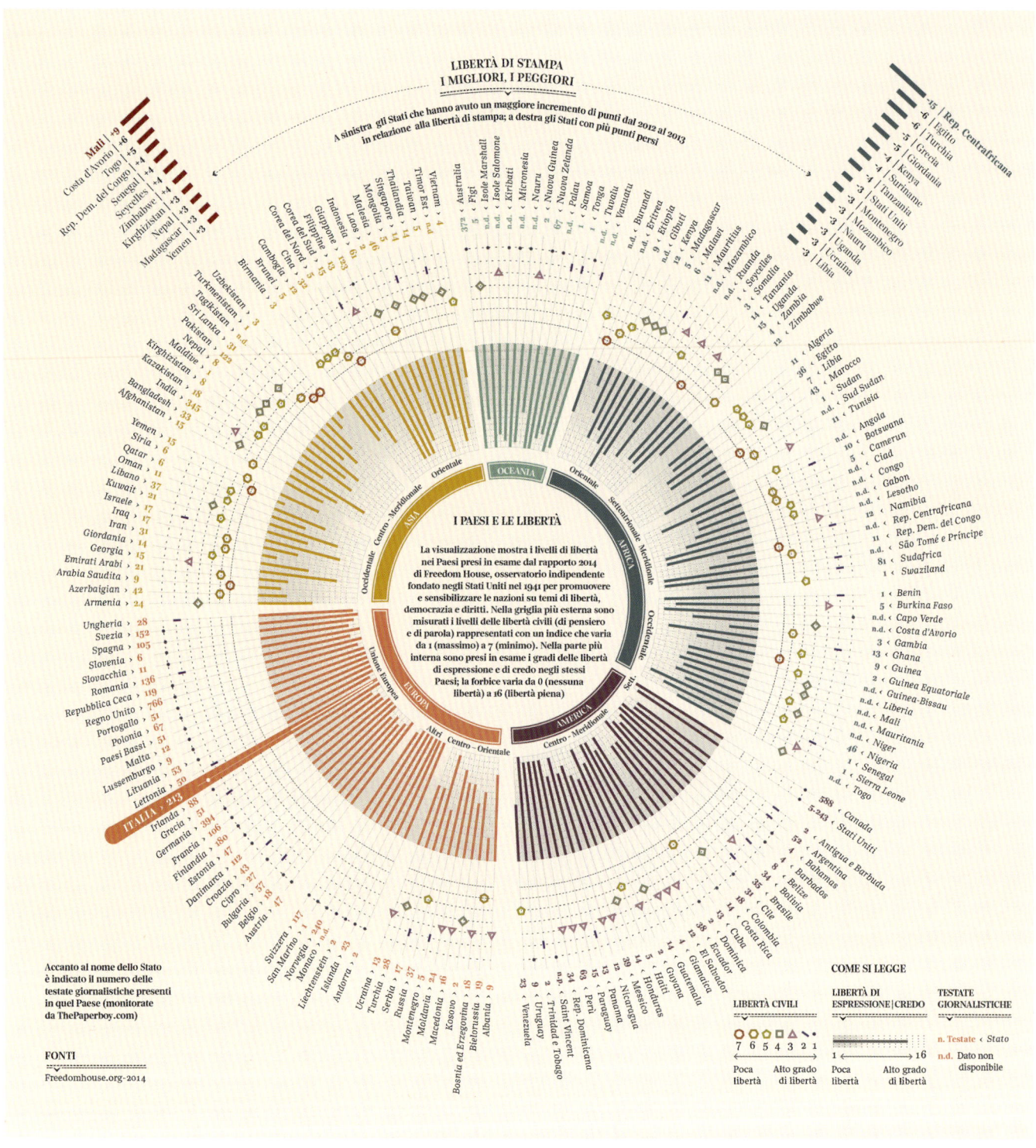

[3–7] Freedom in Countries

Credit: Sara Piccolomini
Completion: 2015

The visualization for *Il Corriere della Sera—La Lettura* explores the levels of freedom in countries according to *Freedom in the World*, Freedom House's flagship publication, which is the standard-setting comparative assessment of global political rights and civil liberties. Each country is assigned a numerical rating—from 1 to 7—for civil liberties, with '1' representing the most free and '7' the least free. The degrees of freedom in expression and belief (the gap varies from 0—no freedom, to 16—complete freedom) are visualized with a circular histogram, and the number of newspapers for each country is reported near the name of the country.

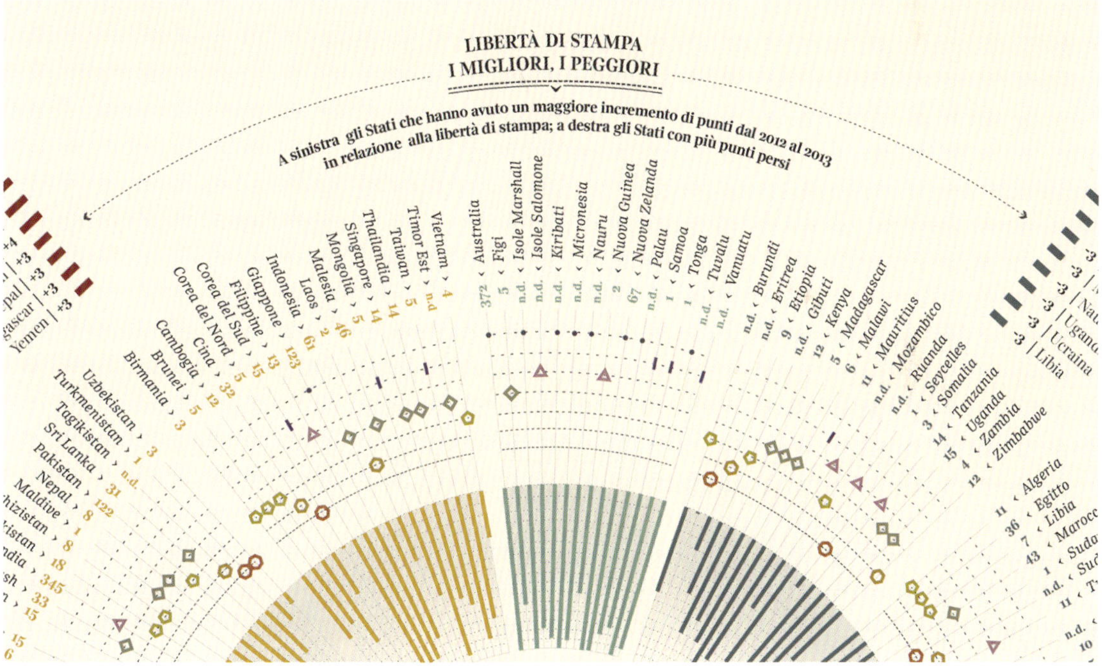

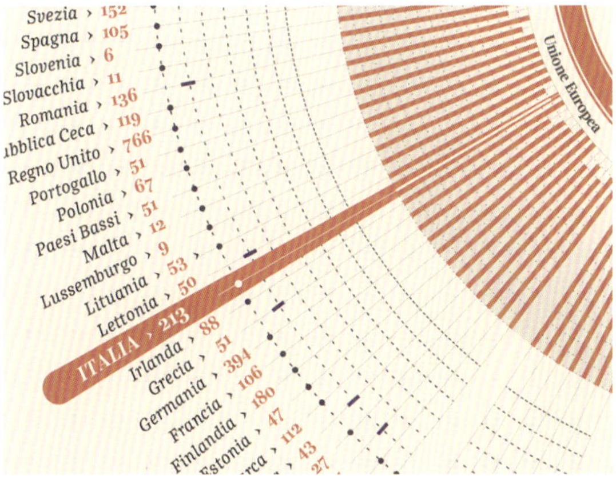

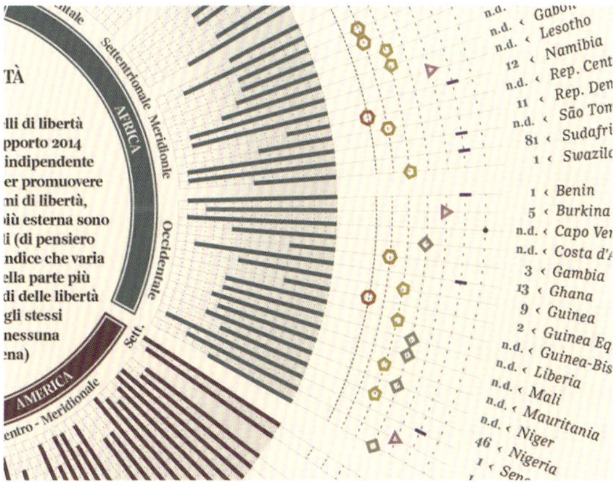

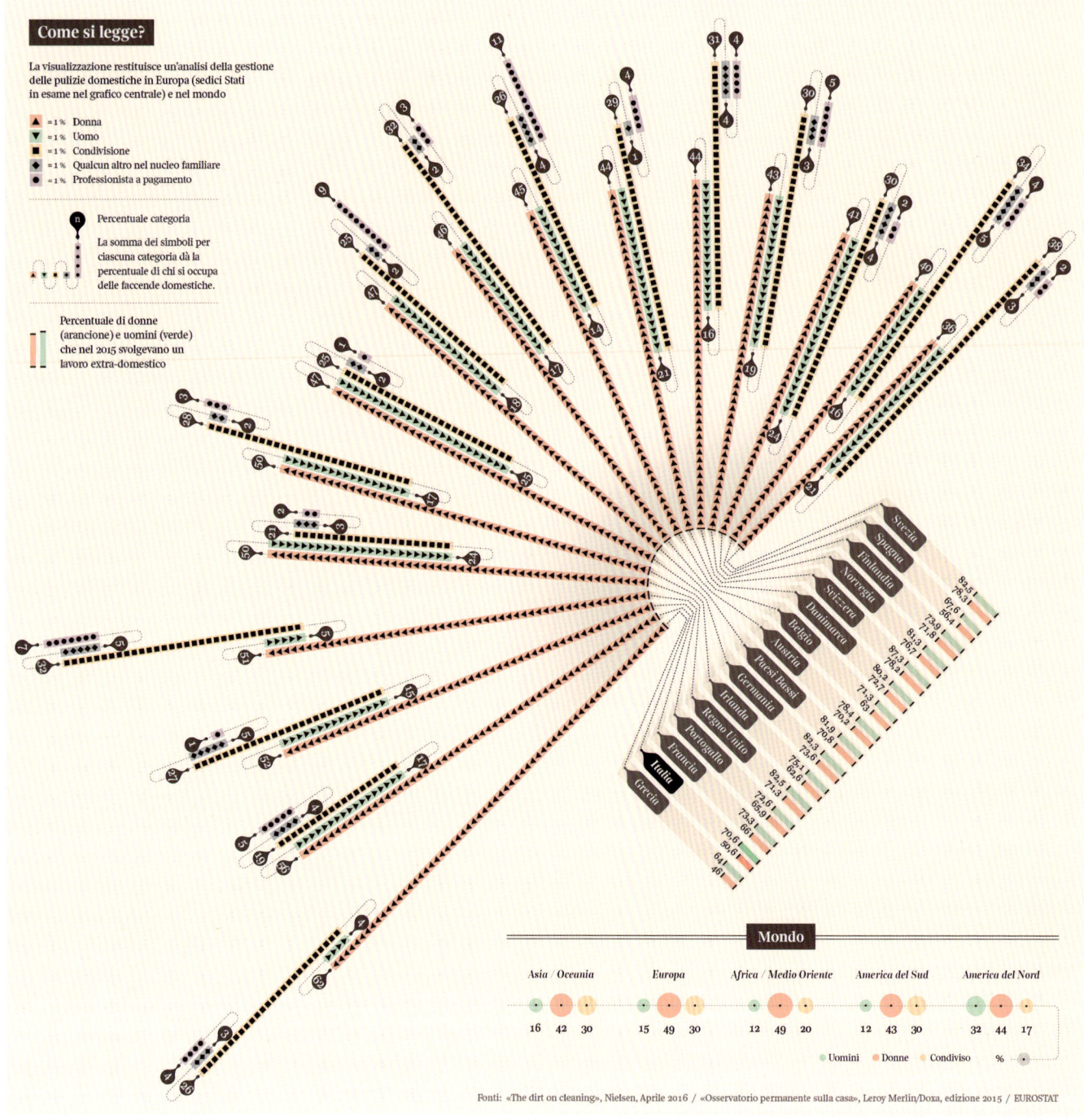

[8] Who Does the Housework?

Credit: Sara Piccolomini
Completion: 2016

The visualization for *Il Corriere della Sera—La Lettura* provides an analysis about house cleaning in Europe (16 states in the middle graph). Each colored symbol represents 1 percent of the people who do the house cleaning for each state (woman, man, sharing, someone else in the household, a professional). The sum of the symbols gives the percentage of those who look after the house cleaning. The bar graph shows the percentage of women (orange) and men (green) who have a job outside the home in 2015. The small graph in the lower part of the visualization shows the percentage of the people who do the housework by region (Asia or Oceania, Europe, Africa or Middle East, South America, North America).

[9] The Numbers of Culture in Italy

Credits: Sara Piccolomini, Politecnico di Milano
Completion: 2014

The data used in the visualization was extracted from the report 'I numeri della cultura in Lombradia' (The number of culture) drawn up from the Lombradia region in 2009. The visualization shows the distribution of the museums in Italy and the inflow of visitors in various regions. The area of each central white polygon shows the number of museums in a region, while the number of vertices shows the number of museum typologies. The polygons radially arranged represent the museum typologies, such as history and natural science, ethnography and anthropology, history, archaeology, science and technology, territorial, art, and specialized. In the lower part of the visualization, there is an insight into the distribution of visitors: the area of circumferences show the number of visitors for each region in Italy.

THE NUMBERS OF CULTURE IN ITALY

Visualizing data concerning the distribution of museums in Italy (2006)

The data used in the visualisation below are extracted from the report "I numeri della cultura in Lombradia" drawn up from Lombradia region in 2009.
The visualisations show the distribution of museums in Italy and the inflow of visitors in the various regions.

DISTRIBUTION OF NON-STATE MUSEUM IN ITALY

NON-STATE MUSEUMS

- AREA OF POLYGONS — *Number of museums*
- NUMBER OF VERTICES — *Number of museum typologies*

MUSEUM TYPOLOGIES

- AREA OF POLYGONS — *Number of museums*

1-50 musuems / 51-100 musuems / 101-150 musuems / 151-200 musuems

- History and natural science
- Ethnography and anthropology
- History
- Archeology
- Science and technology
- Territorial
- Art
- Specialized

377 TOSCANA | 324 EMILIA ROMAGNA | 318 PIEMONTE | 316 LOMBARDIA

274 MARCHE | 266 VENETO | 253 LAZIO | 207 SICILIA

  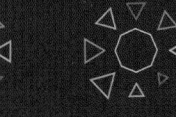

148 LIGURIA | 145 SARDEGNA | 138 CAMPANIA | 138 FRIULI V. G

131 TRENTINO A. A | 115 PUGLIA | 111 ABRUZZO | 104 CALABRIA

96 UMBRIA | 48 BASILICATA | 33 MOLISE | 24 VALLE D'AOSTA

DISTRIBUTION OF VISITORS

Piemonte, Valle D'Aosta, Lombardia, Trentino A.A, Veneto, Friuli V.G., Liguria, Emilia Romagna, Toscana, Umbria, Marche, Lazio, Abruzzo, Molise, Campania, Puglia, Basilicata, Calabria, Sicilia, Sardegna

VISITORS

AREA OF CIRCUMFERENCE — *Number of visitors*

61.707 visitors | 14.248.166 visitors

PROJECT BY
Sara Piccolomini

FACULTY
Ciuccarelli Paolo
Fattore Marco
Mandato Stefano
Ricci Donato

TEACHING ASSISTANTS
Matteo Azzi
Michele Mauri
Azzurra Pini
Giorgio Uboldi

Project developed during the integrated course final synthesis studio

THE BLACK DATA OF PIEMONTE

Visualization of the distribution and evolution of fatal car accidents from 1997 to 2011 in Piemonte (Italy)

The visualization shows how many fatal car accidents occur in each province and district of Piemonte region. One of the most unexpected thing is that, statistically speaking, women are better drivers than men: women have much more chances not to have a fatal accident than men. Another thing that can be infer from data is an overall decreasing trend in the number of fatal accidents. It's probably due to safer vehicles on the road and increased awareness of drivers.

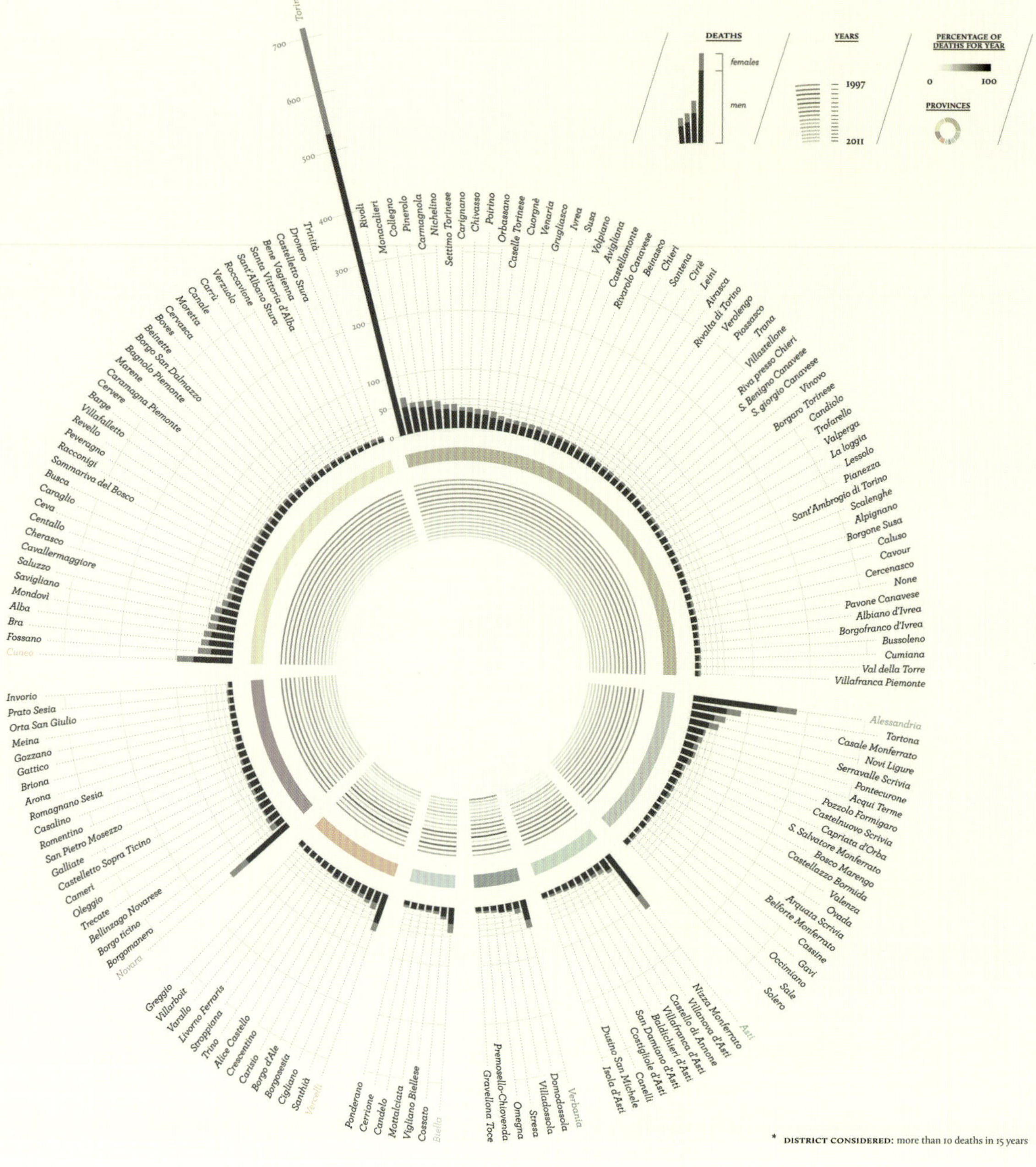

* **DISTRICT CONSIDERED:** more than 10 deaths in 15 years

PROVINCES AND NUMBERS OF DEATHS

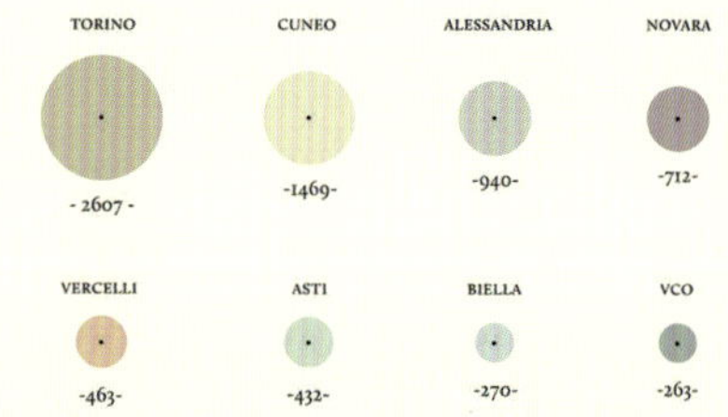

TORINO — 2607 —
CUNEO — 1469 —
ALESSANDRIA — 940 —
NOVARA — 712 —
VERCELLI — 463 —
ASTI — 432 —
BIELLA — 270 —
VCO — 263 —

EVOLUTION OF FATAL CAR ACCIDENTS (1997-2011)

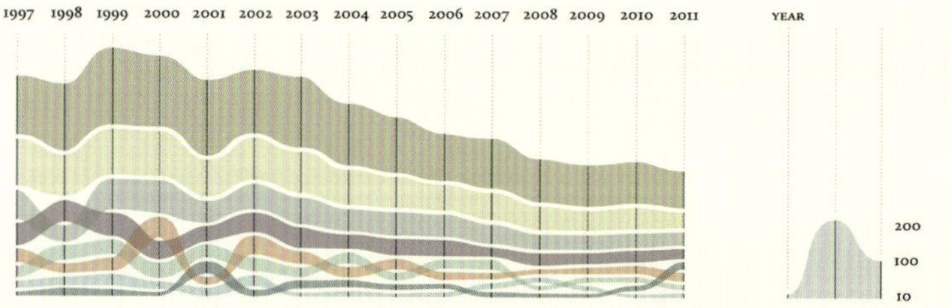

PROJECT BY
Sara Piccolomini

FACULTY
Ciuccarelli Paolo
Fattore Marco
Mandato Stefano
Ricci Donato

TEACHING ASSISTANTS
Matteo Azzi
Michele Mauri
Azzurra Pini
Giorgio Uboldi

Project developed during the integrated course final synthesis studio

DEN-SITY GN+

[10–11] The Black Data of Piemonte

Credits: Sara Piccolomini, Politecnico di Milano
Completion: 2014

The visualization shows how many fatal car accidents occurred in each province and district of the Piemonte region. Statistically speaking, women are better drivers than men: men are much more likely to have a fatal accident than women. Another thing that can be inferred from the data is an overall decreasing trend in the number of fatal accidents. It's probably due to safer vehicles on the road and increased awareness of drivers.

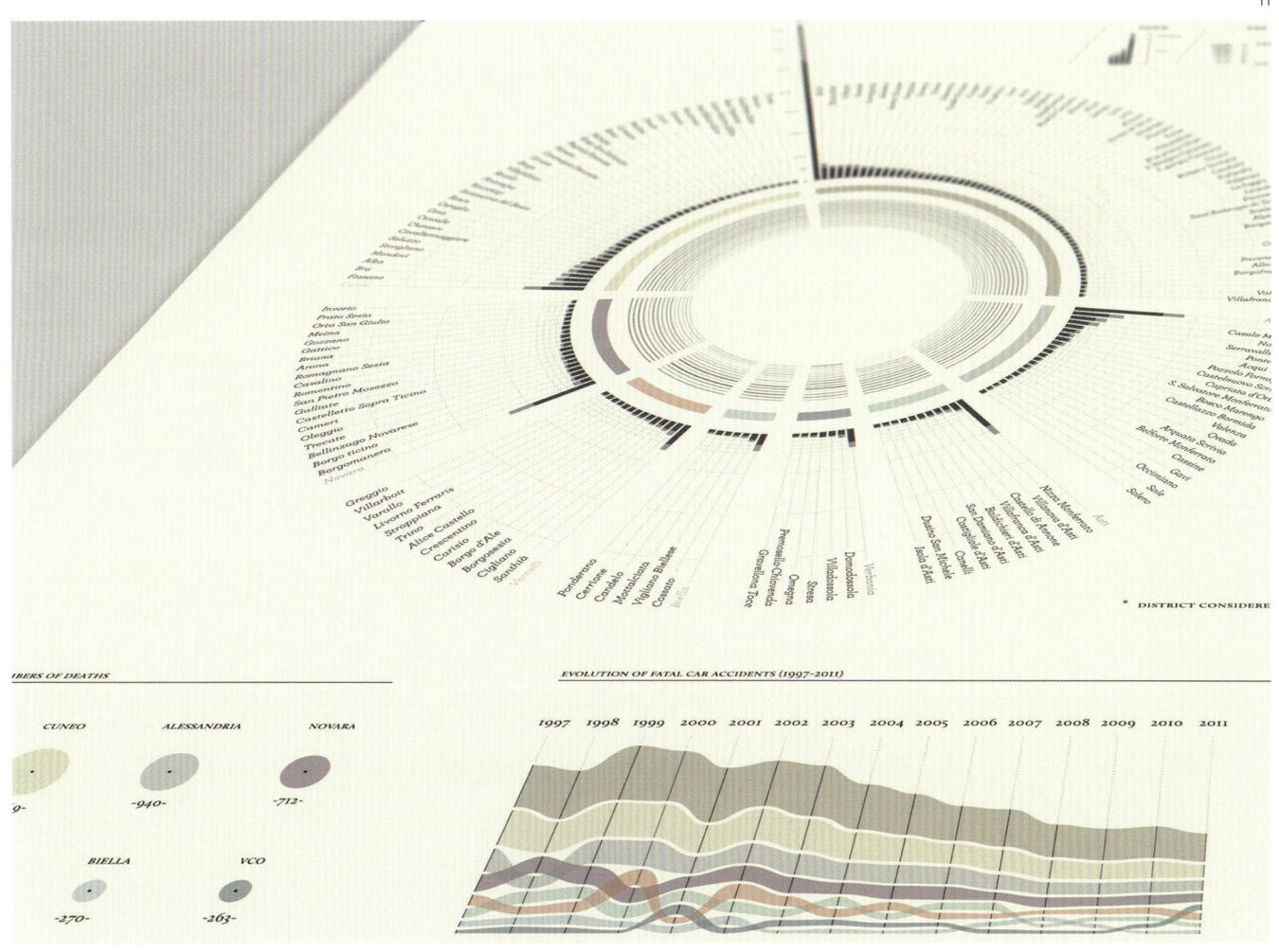

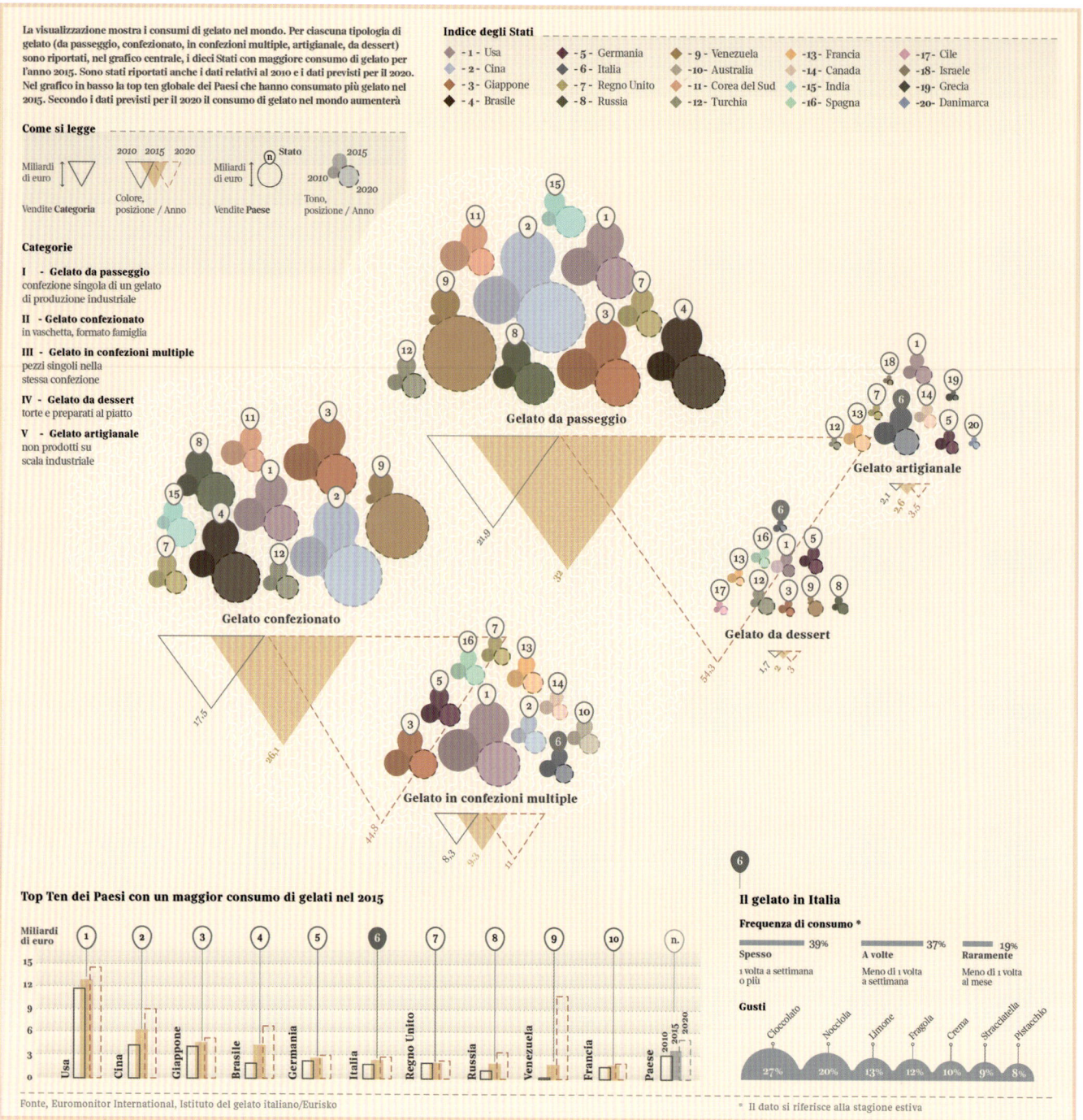

[12–15] World Ice-Creams Consumption

Credit: Sara Piccolomini
Completion: 2015

The visualization for *Il Corriere della Sera—La Lettura* shows the market value in euros for ice creams in the world. For each category of ice creams (single portion dairy ice cream, impulse ice cream, retail artisanal ice cream, ice-cream desserts, multi-pack dairy ice cream) the 10 countries with the higher consumption of ice creams in 2015 have been reported. Data related to 2010 and data expected for 2020 have also been reported. The graphs at the bottom show the top 10 countries that consume more ice creams in 2015 and the data related to Italian consumption. Overall, according to data provided by Euromonitor International, the consumption of ice creams in the world will increase until 2020.

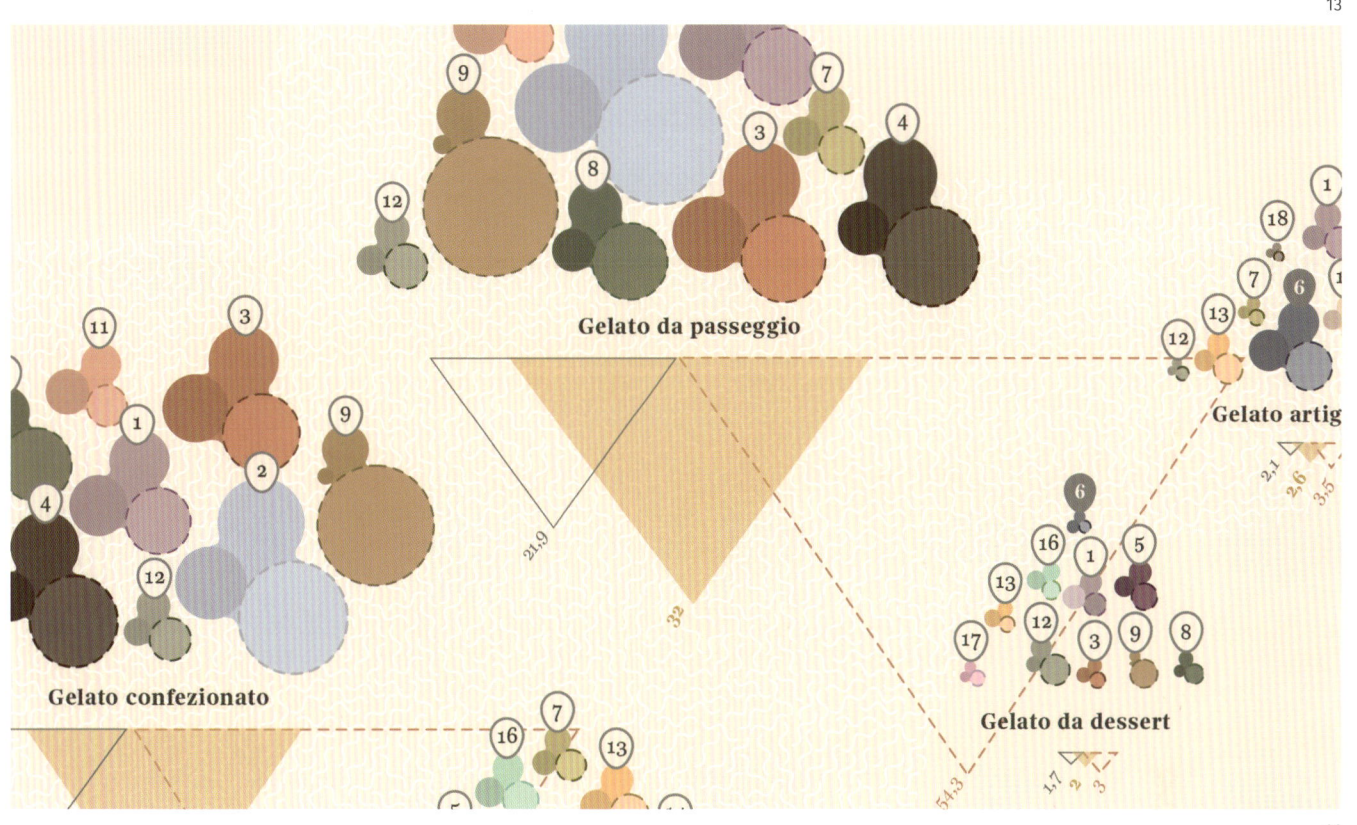

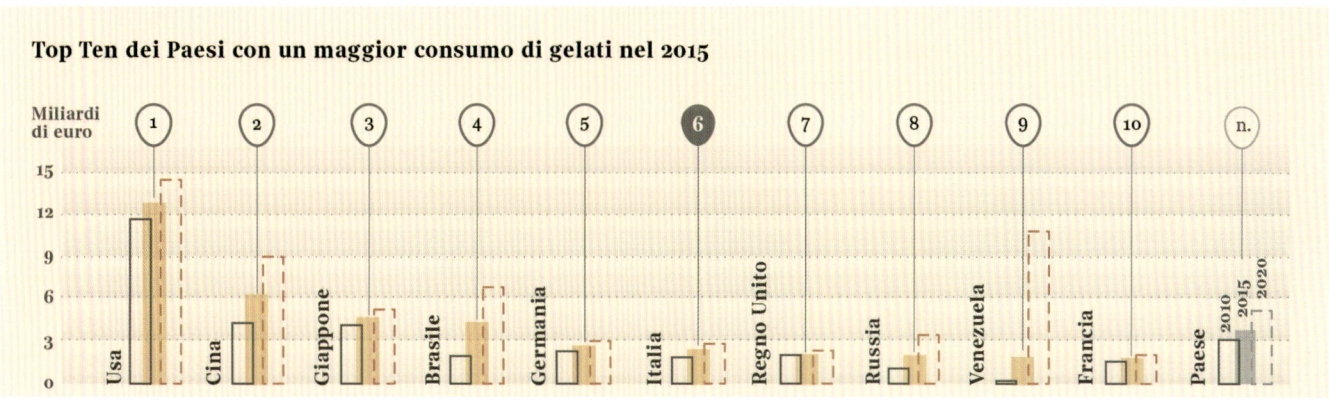

Top Ten dei Paesi con un maggior consumo di gelati nel 2015

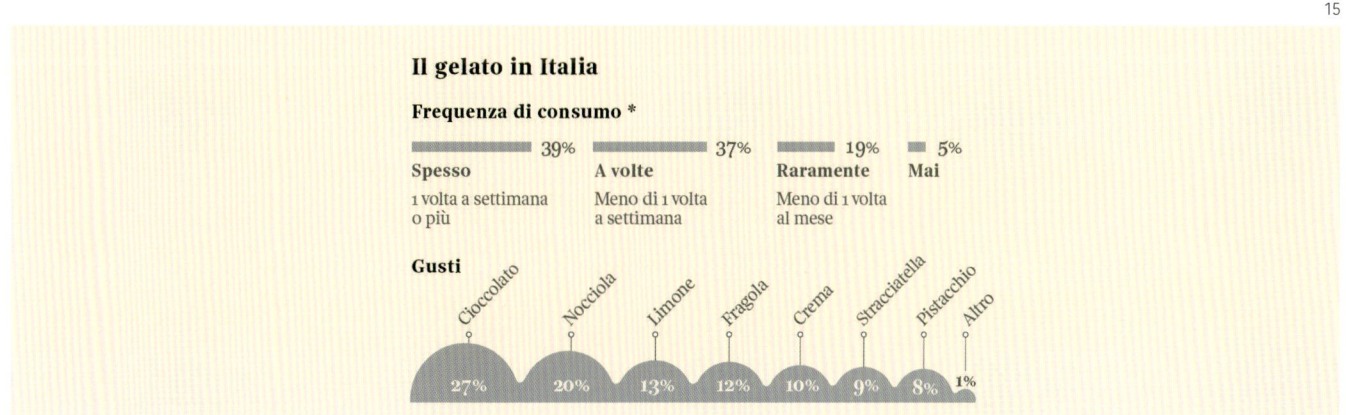

Il gelato in Italia

Frequenza di consumo *

- 39% **Spesso** 1 volta a settimana o più
- 37% **A volte** Meno di 1 volta a settimana
- 19% **Raramente** Meno di 1 volta al mese
- 5% **Mai**

Gusti

Cioccolato 27% · Nocciola 20% · Limone 13% · Fragola 12% · Crema 10% · Stracciatella 9% · Pistacchio 8% · Altro 1%

Pitch Interactive

PITCH INTERACTIVE, INC.

Pitch Interactive is a data visualization studio, founded by Wesley Grubbs, that focuses on using new technologies to address complex data. Their works span illustrations, physical installations, projections, console interfaces, software applications, websites, and textiles, and have been showcased in many internationally acclaimed publications.

[Q] What do you think about data visualization/infographics?

[A] I think data visualization is like a bridge that helps us understand complex information, especially in today's world, where data is collected en masse and tools are needed to help explore and discover relationships within the data.

[Q] What kind of design methods do you commonly use?

[A] Specifically for design, all we really do is apply simple things, such as shapes, colors, positions, and text size etc., to data points and allow the data to drive the visual output. For example, applying the size of a shape to the population of major cities and the color of the shape to the air quality can give us a very quick and clear picture of whether or not there is a correlation between population and air quality.

[Q] What kind of design elements do you commonly use?

[A] For aesthetics, we try to work with design elements that match the intended audience. For data art pieces, we will play with more abstract patterns and colors. For journalism organizations, we apply more conservative and well-established methodologies and palettes. It's great to be able to play and create work along this spectrum.

[Q] Where are your works applied?

[A] So many different media. Interactive digital walls, projections, websites, magazines, textiles, broadcast, books, museums, exhibits, and even video games.

[Q] How do you turn boring and complex data into something interesting and understandable?

[A] I have a hard time thinking any data is boring. It's all a matter of perspective. I believe that when you give a narrative and context to data, you help people understand it better. For our drones piece, we dramatized the data by using darker colors and building an animated sequence to highlight key events in the history of drone strikes. It's about how you tell the story through visual attributes that may blend with animations and interactivity.

1

[Q] **What is your suggestion for beginners?**

[A] Educate yourself. Find out what draws you to data visualization and research. When I started more than 10 years ago, I would go through *National Geographic* magazines and cut out all of the diagrams and charts that I thought were interesting, and collect them in a book and study them. What made them work so well? I did the same with other popular magazines, like *Wired*, and would find out how to recreate these with illustration tools and then with code.

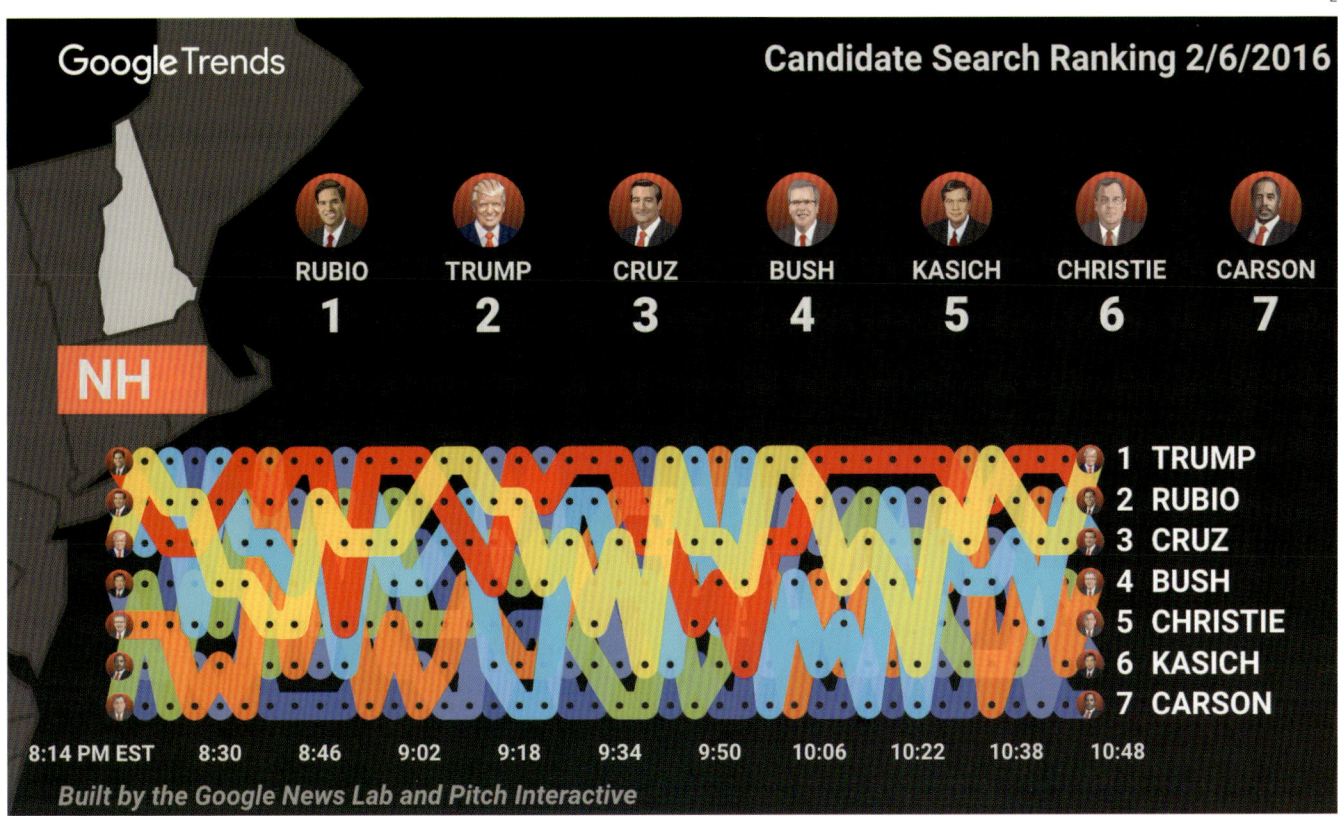

[1–3] Presidential Debates Search Interest Tool

Credits: Wesley Grubbs (creative director), Nick Yahnke (technologist), Adam Florin (technologist), Jessica Hamel (technologist), Mladen Balog (designer), Katarina Madrid (project coordinator)
Completion: 2016
Interactive link: www.pitchinteractive.com/work/GoogleDebates.html

This presidential debate search data platform toured the nation with the Google News Lab team to accompany their presidential debate media filing centers and spin rooms. The work circulated the spin rooms, media centers and was broadcast in national news on a 21-by-12-inch multiscreen wall. Pitch Interactive built the entire tool from the CMS to the front-end visuals, including a remote-control system for Google News Lab to manage the different views.

This tool's front-end visuals depict real-time Google search data in three alternating views: national-level ranked search interest of candidates; state-by-state ranked candidate search interest; and minute-by-minute candidate/debate topics search interest horse races. The CMS enabled the horse races to be exported as animated gifs allowing shareability. The work went viral on multiple social media and newscast platforms during each debate. These visuals were designed with the journalists and reporters in mind, giving them insight into what people were googling in real time during debates.

[4] Montpellier

Credits: Wesley Grubbs (creative director), Nick Yahnke (technologist), Mladen Balog (designer), Shujian Bu (software support), Ri Lui (image production)
Completion: 2013

This is a large-format data art piece depicting complaint data from the city of Montpellier in France as a vibrant, layered diagram. Pitch Interactive, commissioned by the Contemporary Cultural Center La Panacée in Montpellier, chose to represent each complaint by a color, and form a shape from layers created by locations in which a complaint was reported. The radius of the circles is defined by how many complaints were reported of that type in the area.

[5] Disease Squeeze

Credits: Wesley Grubbs (creative director), Jessica Hamel (technologist), Mladen Balog (designer)
Completion: 2016

This is a print piece that shows how life expectancy has risen for decades all around the world, but according to the Institute for Health Metrics and Evaluation, the increased numbers really just show people living for more years with debilitating ailments and diseases. This data visualization depicts the causes of premature deaths and disabilities, showing the differences between DALYs (disability-adjusted life years) in developed countries and those of developing countries.

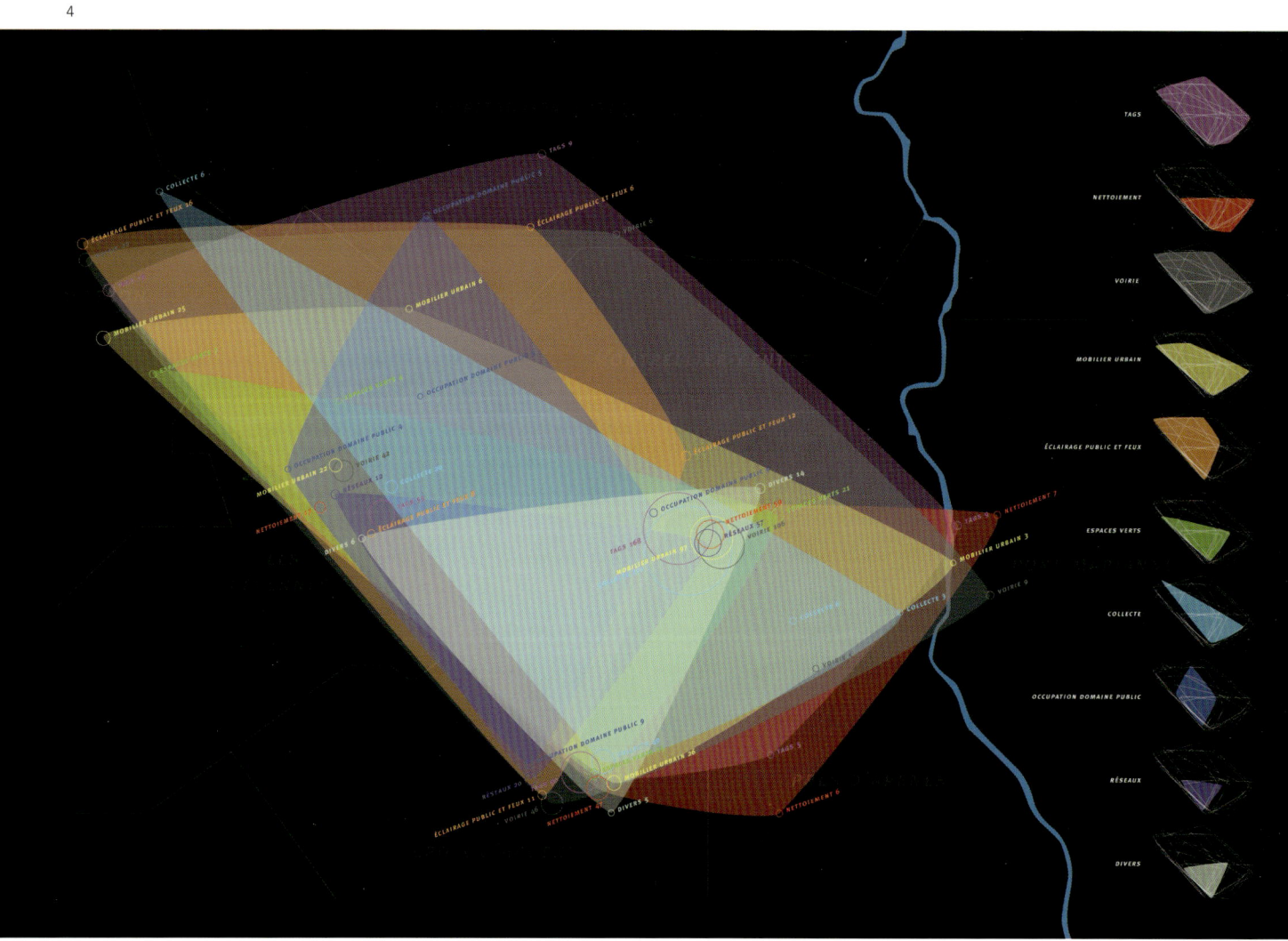

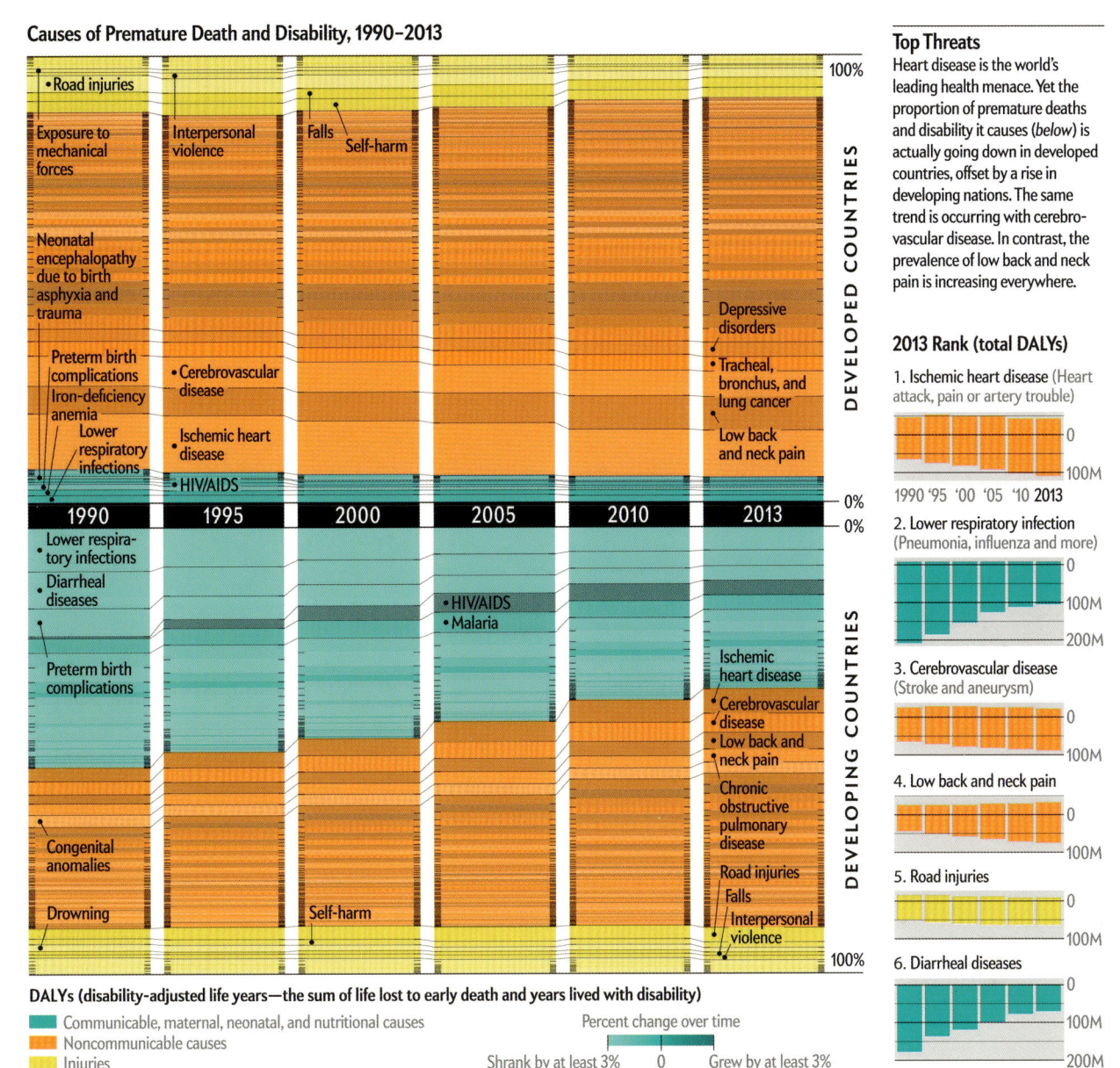

Disease Squeeze

Developing countries are battling illnesses of rich and poor

Life expectancy worldwide has risen for decades. But more people are living more years with debilitating ailments, according to a new study by the Institute for Health Metrics and Evaluation in Seattle. In developed countries (*top of graphic*), the trouble comes almost entirely from noncommunicable conditions such as heart and lung disease and back pain (*red*)—ills typically associated with lifestyle choices such as diet and exercise. In developing nations, however (*bottom*), the prevalence of these ailments are increasing rapidly, even as those countries continue to try to stamp out communicable diseases such as diarrhea and malaria that have plagued them for decades (*gray*). If developing nations are clever, though, they can create health policies that impede the new threats and continue to reduce the old ones. "Knowing what's coming," says Amy VanderZanden at the institute, "they can prioritize what they should do."
—*Mark Fischetti*

[6] Tech Executive Compensation

Credits: Wesley Grubbs (creative director), Adam Florin (technologist), Anna Hodgson (designer)
Completion: 2015

This is an infographic showing the tech industry compensation trends for executive positions by region, sector, and funding round. Using a salary survey produced by CompStudy, Pitch Interactive studied the trends of CEO, COO, CFO, CTO, Head of Engineering, and Head of Sales wages over the last five years. They found the most interesting trends of compensation in funding rounds, specific sectors, and by region, though the survey data covered other parameters such as company head count, revenue, target/actual bonus, and equity.

[7] An Unprecedented Drought

Credits: Wesley Grubbs (creative director), Mladen Balog (designer)
Completion: 2015

This is an infographic on California's dry spell that plots data from the Palmer Hydrological Drought Index, a soil-moisture algorithm designed to measure the long-term impact of drought. The graph focuses on index values that fall outside the normal moisture range. It also includes trend lines to trace overall fluctuations in each region's drought conditions.

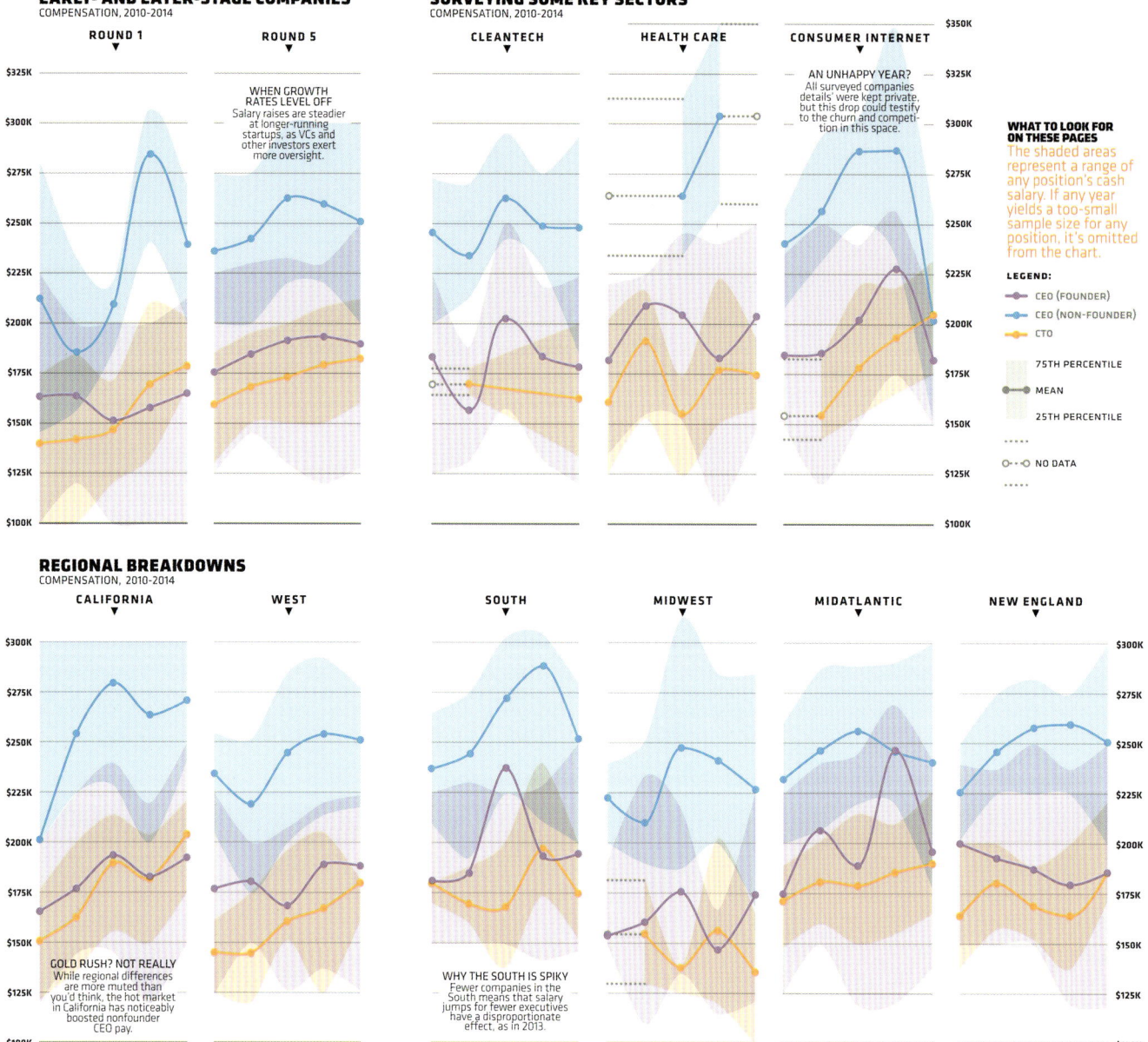

An Unprecedented Drought

By any measure, the current drought in California is historic. The chart below is based on the Palmer Hydrological Drought Index, a soil-moisture algorithm designed to measure the long-term impact of drought by taking into account reservoir levels, groundwater data and other slow-moving indicators. The data make clear that although extreme conditions—both wet and dry—have become more frequent since the 1970s, all regions of California have experienced an overall drying trend in recent decades.

Wet Spell
Recent dry years have been punctuated by unusually rainy years, but that moisture has not offset the overall drying trend. Similar patterns occurred centuries ago; the decades-long medieval megadroughts that appear in California tree-ring records also included occasional rainy years.

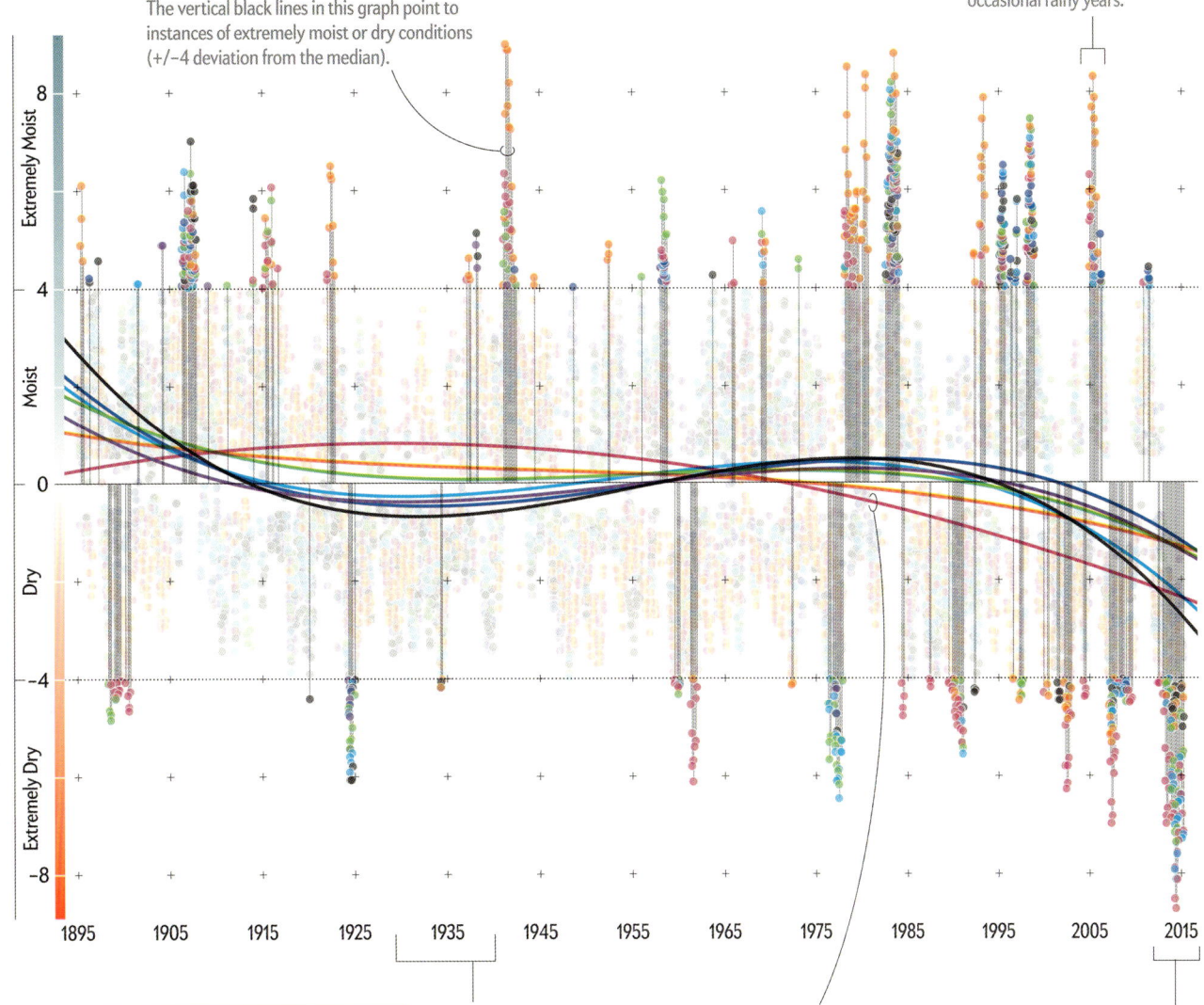

The vertical black lines in this graph point to instances of extremely moist or dry conditions (+/−4 deviation from the median).

Palmer Hydrological Drought Index
Each dot on the graph above represents one month's Palmer Hydrological Drought Index value for each of seven regional divisions. Dots within the "normal" range (+4 to −4) are faded into the background.

- North Coast Drainage
- Sacramento Drainage
- Northeast Interior Basins
- Central Coast Drainage
- San Joaquin Drainage
- South Coast Drainage
- Southeast Desert Basins

The Dust Bowl Years
California was largely spared the ill effects of the Dust Bowl, which is why displaced farmers from the Great Plains fled there in search of work.

Trending Dry
The solid curves are polynomial trend lines tracing overall fluctuations in the conditions in California's seven regional divisions. The increasing density of vertical gray lines after 1975 indicate an increase in the frequency of both extreme conditions—both wet and dry. Overall, however, every trend line bends downward during this period, indicating that every region in the state is trending dry.

Widespread and Long-Lived Drought
One unusual and unpleasant feature of the current drought is that so many different regions in this large and geographically varied state are experiencing it at an extreme level.

Raconteur Media

[Q] **What do you think about data visualization/infographics?**

[A] Data visualisation is an artistic way to turn complex information into an engaging story, designed in a powerful way.

[Q] **What kind of design methods do you commonly use?**

[A] Our infographic dashboards are created with one goal in mind: to present information effectively and clearly. Each piece is developed through a well-thought-out process of data analysis and interpretation, prototyping of the space, and illustration.

[Q] **What kind of design elements do you commonly use?**

[A] In every dashboard we develop, we interpret sets of data and create a theme that is unique and aims to evolve our design style each time. Our design strategy is to ensure the information presented is clear, but also

Raconteur Media is a publishing house and content marketing agency. They produce regular special reports for *The Times* and *The Sunday Times*, as well as content marketing solutions and bespoke market research for brands. They combine premium editorial, analysis, and graphic design with a commitment to high-quality executions in print and online across all of their services to ensure their content informs, inspires, and influences thought leaders worldwide.

IDENTIFYING DISRUPTION IN THE SUPPLY CHAIN

TOP 10 CAUSES AND IMPACTS OF SUPPLY CHAIN DISRUPTION
Relative proportion of survey respondents

N/A · Low impact · Medium impact · High impact

- Unplanned IT or telecommunications outage
- Adverse weather
- New laws or regulations
- Loss of talent/skills
- Outsourcer failure
- Transport network or disruption
- Cyber attack and data breach
- Energy supply issue
- Product quality incident
- Business ethics incident

Source: Business Continuity Institute 2015

TOP 10 CONSEQUENCES OF SUPPLY CHAIN DISRUPTION

- Loss of productivity — 58%
- Customer complaints — 40%
- Increased cost of working — 39%
- Loss of revenue — 38%
- Impaired service outcome — 36%
- Stakeholder/shareholder concern — 29%
- Damage to brand image — 27%
- Product release delay — 23%
- Delayed cash flows — 2%
- Expected increase in regulatory scrutiny — 14%

PREFERRED RISK MITIGATION STRATEGIES
Preference on a scale of one to ten (ten being most preferred)

- Strong suppliers
- Time compression
- Visibility
- Global logistics competency
- Predictive modelling
- Air freight
- Additional inventory
- In-source or near-source
- Reserve funds
- Purchase insurance

Source: UPS 2014

TOP 10 CHALLENGES FOR THE SUPPLY CHAIN
Global survey of senior executives in manufacturing

- Lack of information across the extended supply chain — 42%
- Inadequate IT systems — 38%
- Excess inventory — 35%
- Aligning operations to real-time fluctuations in customer demand — 35%
- Lack of skilled talent — 30%
- Lack of competitive cost structure — 27%
- Effectively supporting new product launches — 25%
- Ensuring sufficient supplier capacity to meet demand — 19%
- Supplier performance in terms of risk, reliability and quality — 14%
- Responsiveness to changes in demand or product mix — 14%

MOST FEARED RISKS
1. Natural catastrophes
2. Political change, embargoes and war
3. Globalisation affecting specialised suppliers

Source: Allianz 2015

ORIGINS OF SUPPLY CHAIN DISRUPTION
Percentage of survey respondents

- Immediate supplier — 50%
- Supplier's supplier — 21%
- Much lower down the supply chain — 8%

to push boundaries of style and interpretation. It would be difficult to categorize all the shapes and styles of graphs we usually use, as we have a very editorial approach to our data visualization. We analyze the story of each infographic before thinking of each graph, so that it has a theme and a consistent idea. Once we know this, we look for the right design. Overall, we try and make each infographic as different from the next as possible. On each one, we aim to have a variety of graphical and illustrative elements to ensure a very dynamic design.

[1] Supply Chain Strategies

Credit: Raconteur Media
Completion: 2016

This infographic needed to efficiently convey the specific information the designers wanted to present: outlining the top 10 causes and impacts of supply-chain disruption, preferred risk mitigation strategies, and most feared risks. They deliberately avoided too much design intricacy, opting for a very linear and divided layout, while always keeping the organic feel of the design and theme. The subtle illustrative element used throughout ensures that the strong creative element, which is directly related to the brand style, is presented and noticeable, but without taking anything away from the more serious tone of the design.

[2] The Insight Economy

Credit: Raconteur Media
Completion: 2016

Big data can be a minefield of information for companies to digest. In this infographic, the designers took a look at the similarities and differences between the customers and fans of various consumer brands to see patterns and trends in supposedly unrelated audiences. The production editor came across the data for this piece through online research and managed to prototype the visual interpretation for the graph straight away. There are many stories to tell with this graph, but with a very straightforward way of reading it. It is one set of data that takes up a lot of space, so it had to be intriguing and eye-catching. The colors used are also quite bold to immediately make the reader stop and pay attention.

2

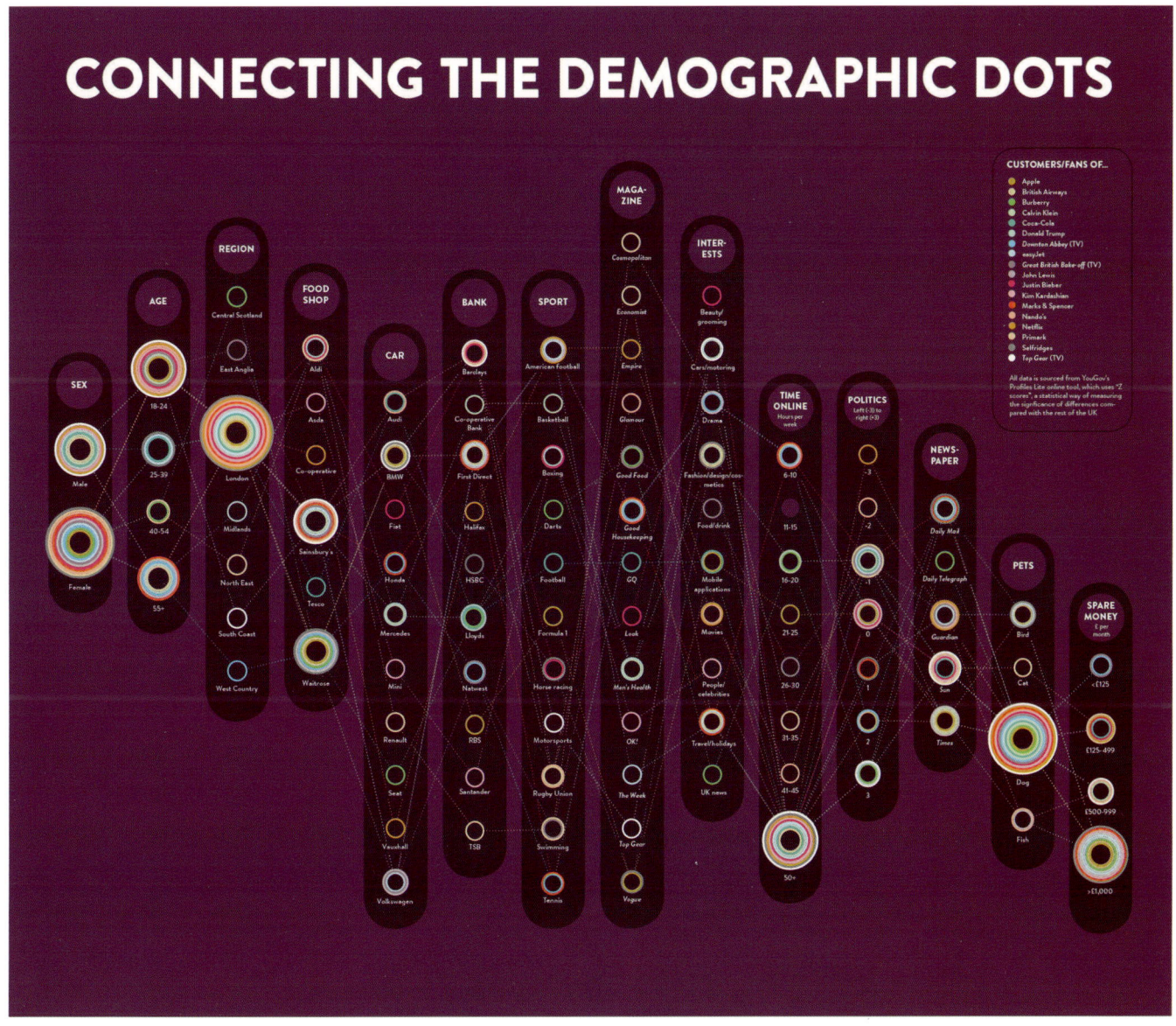

[Q] Where are your works applied?

[A] Our special reports are published in *The Times* and *The Sunday Times* newspapers in both print and digital, and others are applied to video, website, and printed content solutions for clients.

[Q] How do you turn boring and complex data into something interesting and understandable?

[A] There is a fine line between ensuring a graph is innovatively designed and also easily comprehensible. That is the art of infographic design. We achieve this effectively through striking the right balance between having a key part for the editorial team to play in prototyping the piece (as they are responsible for sourcing the data) and giving the creative designers enough freedom to compose creative elements.

[Q] What is your suggestion for beginners?

[A] Push the boundaries. Review your work. Always innovate.

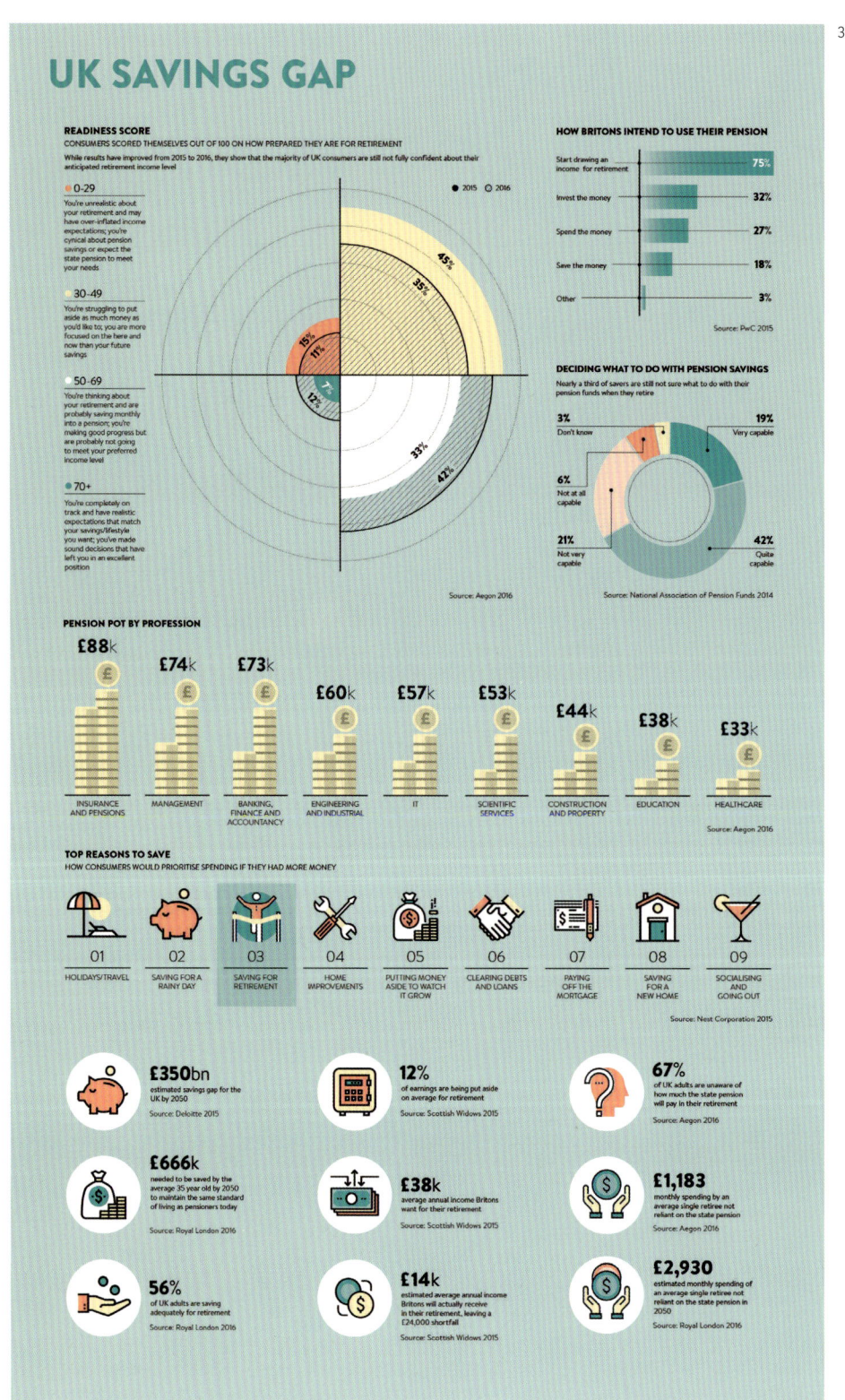

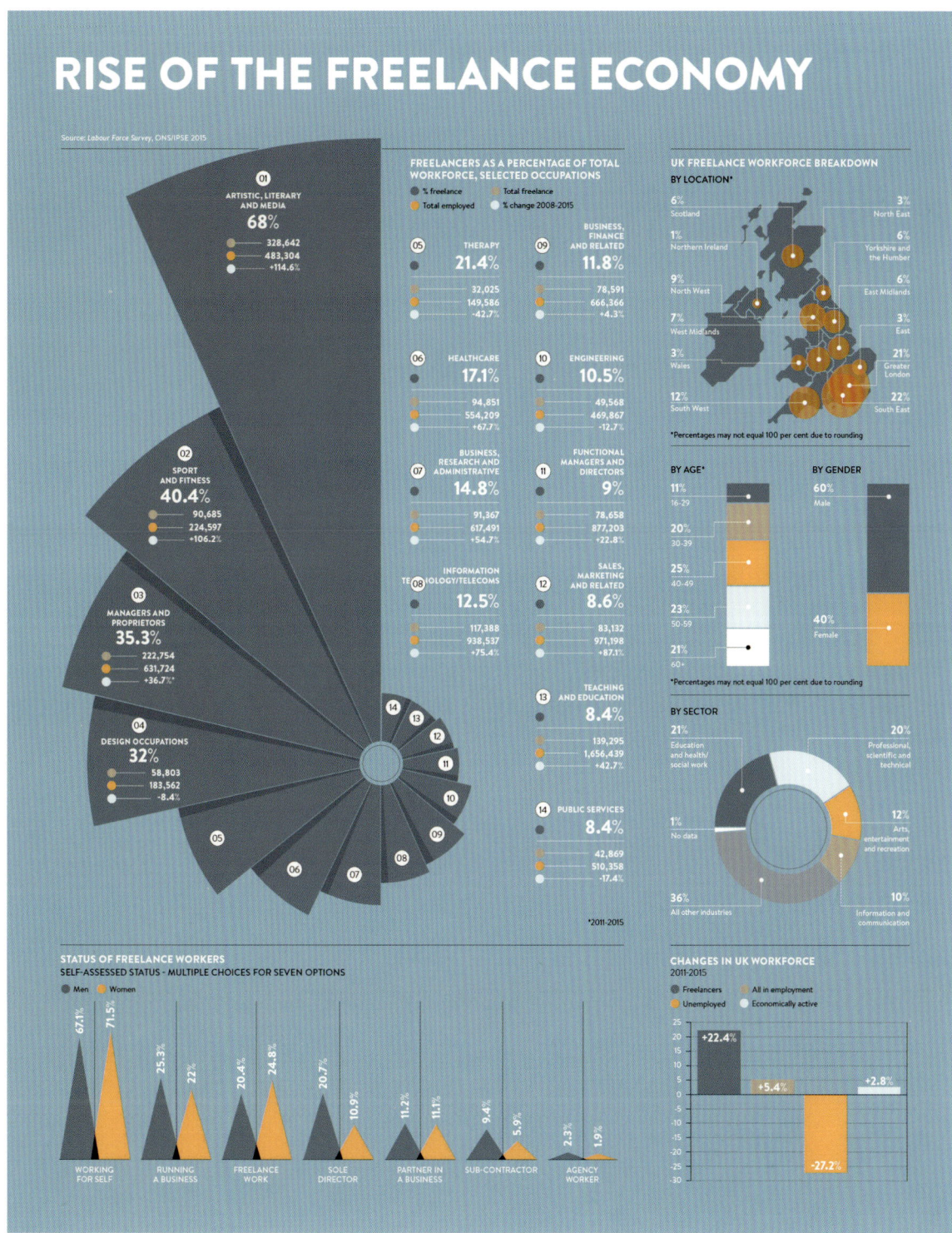

[3] Workplace Pensions

Credit: Raconteur Media
Completion: 2016

Pensions can be quite a 'dry' topic to express creatively, so it was indeed a challenge for the creative team to design this information. The infographic is charting consumer readiness for retirement, showing how Britons intend to use their pensions and pension pots, categorised by profession. The idea was to keep this dashboard quite clean and linear, ensuring a distinctive separation of styles, with a more 'mathematic' look to the top section, whereas the bottom half is more illustrative. The separated ideas work well in creating a balanced and harmonious design throughout, ensuring the seriousness of the topic, while engaging the reader through high quality design.

[4] Future of Outsourcing

Credit: Raconteur Media
Completion: 2016

The data sets for this piece were sourced through significant research. Once the final graphs were confirmed, the editorial and design teams prototyped the spread to ensure consistency with the rest of the publication, and the general creative idea made sense with the story being told. This infographic shows how freelancing is growing and offering benefits for both the freelance worker who gains autonomy, and the company that needs specialist skills on a project-by-project basis. The creative thought behind it was to have one hero graph, consisting of the element with the largest amount of information, surrounded by other illustrative elements.

Matthew Rowett

Matthew Rowett is an information designer based in London. Currently he is more than halfway into his first year at Signal Noise, and before this he worked for four years at The Design Surgery. One of his personal infographics was shortlisted for the Information Is Beautiful Awards.

[Q] What do you think about data visualization/infographicss?

[A] Both disciplines are incredibly important to help people make sense of complex information. Humans are naturally very visual beings and so we can process and understand concepts far quicker once they're visualized. Data visualization enables us to quickly notice trends and compare values. Infographics are generally more about creating an interesting story or narrative that connects pieces of information.

[Q] What kind of design methods do you commonly use?

[A] Here is an example of the steps I will go through when producing a piece of data visualization. First, examine the data and the brief to understand what is being compared and what needs to be highlighted. Second, decide which visualization method can best communicate the story of the data within the format and space given. Third, process the data and make any necessary adjustments such as reordering axis or values. Fourth, produce the visualization. Sometimes I'll work with a developer to make a more complicated visualization. Fifth, I can begin reformatting the graphics, apply styling, create labels, etc.

For an infographic, as I mentioned previously, a story sits at its heart. The process is more likely to vary compared to data visualization because infographics can take many different forms and are not required to follow many conventions. One method that I apply to all my infographics is connecting and grouping information in an interesting or logical format. I use these groupings to build the chapters in the story. The group might sit together as a module in the user interface, or be connected together by a piece of illustration that connects to a larger illustration. Once I've prepared the format of the story, then I can start making it pretty.

[Q] What kind of design elements do you commonly use?

[A] I try to use geometric shapes, layouts, and patterns as much as I can because this always looks pleasing to the eye. You can still create very diverse shapes, and the geometric principles will help you maintain consistency in the look and feel in everything you do.

[Q] Where are your works applied?

[A] The work I did for Fishything was a social media project where I produced infographics on hard-hitting subjects that could still be highly detailed and sharable. I hosted the infographics on my website, but the main audience reach came through social media.

1

2

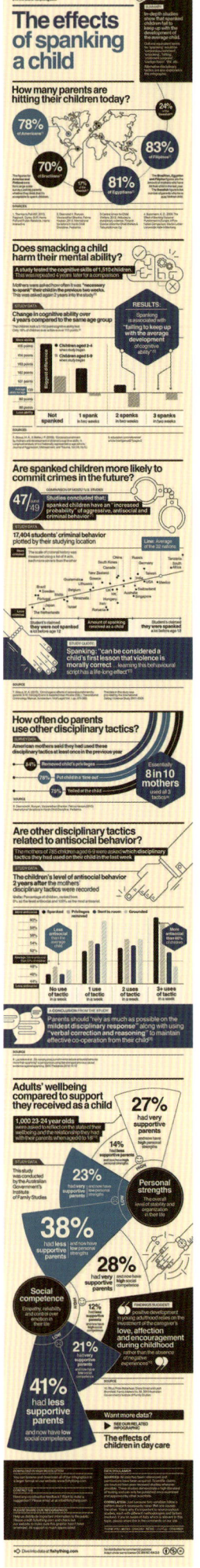

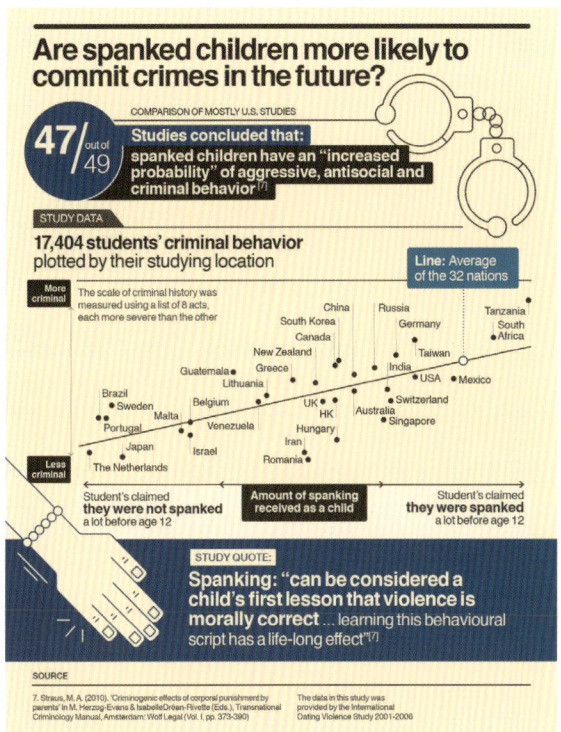
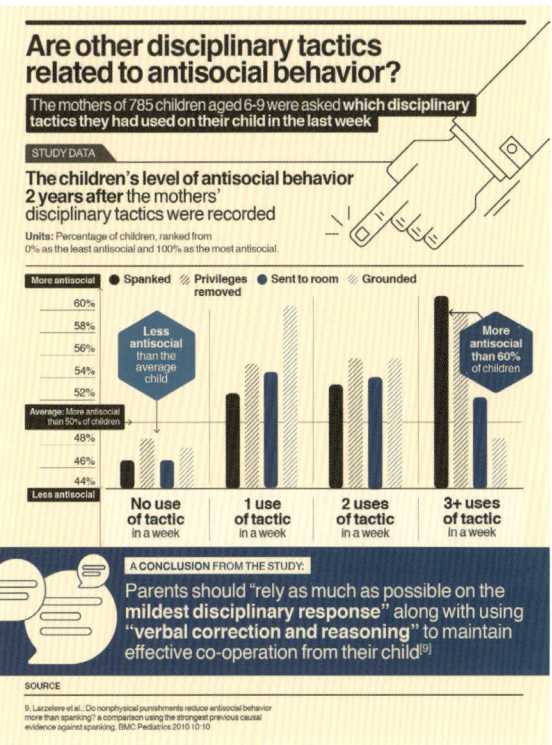
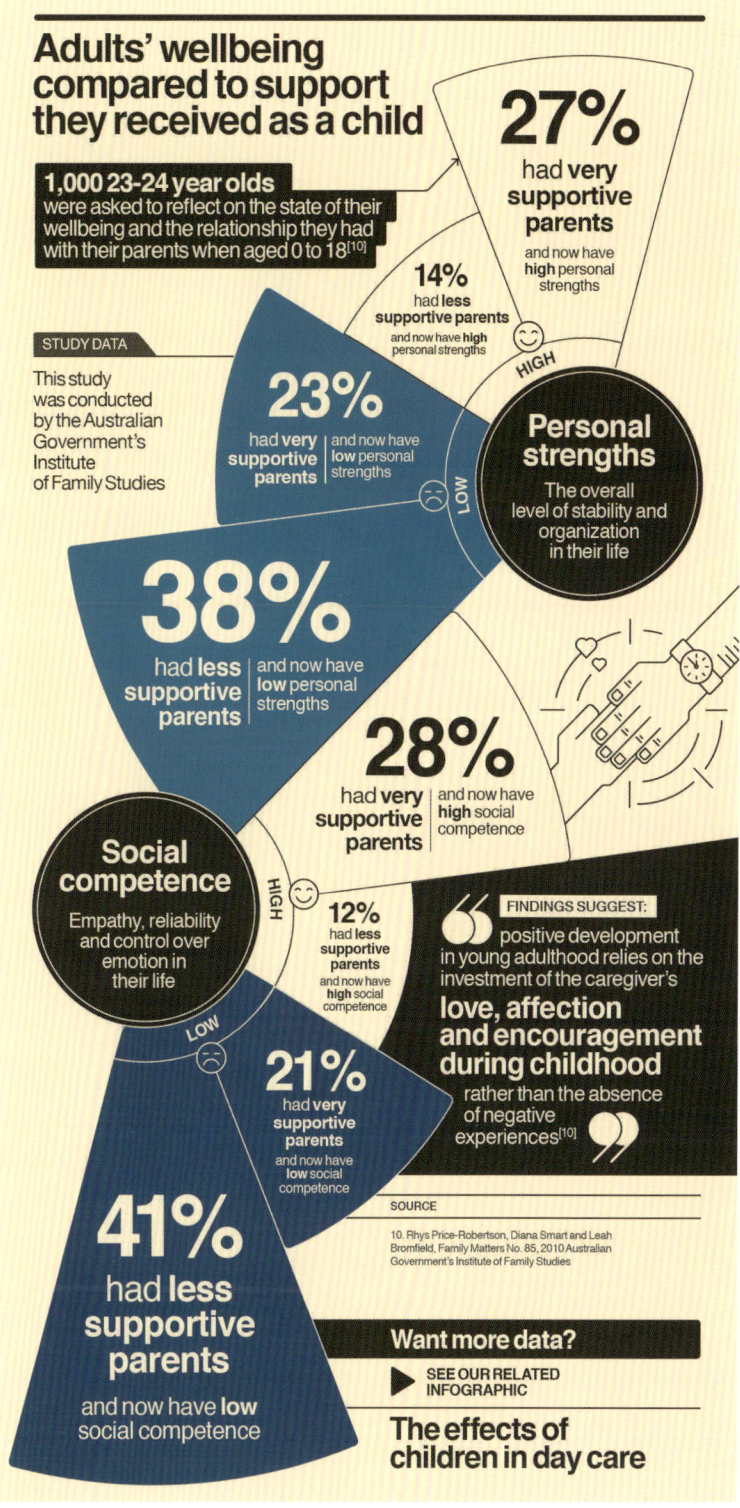

[1–5] The Effects of Spanking Children

Credit: Matthew Rowett
Completion: 2014

In recent years, the designer came across research about the effects of physically harming children as a form of discipline. He was shocked to learn how prevalent spanking children is. The term 'spank' to Americans is the equivalent to what the British would call 'smacking' as a way of telling a child off. There isn't anyone who provides scientific evidence that hitting a child affects them positively, so why do so many parents claim it's the right thing to do? This infographic collects scientific data that is available about the long-term effects of spanking and explores other ways parents can positively influence their children.

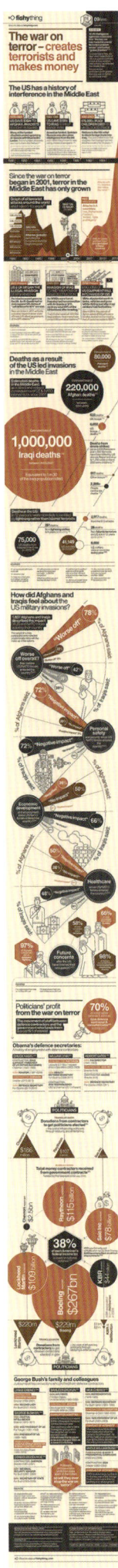

[Q] How do you turn boring and complex data into something interesting and understandable?

[A] These are some of the many methods that I think help you do this. Find what is important, interesting and/or beautiful in your data and focus in on that. Even if the data really is boring, you can still make it look good through good design styling and accompany it with a thought-out narrative. Always think about the user's perspective. How will the information relate to them? You will get more engagement when you focus on how the data is relevant to aspects of the audience's life. User-experience design methods are essential to creating something that is understandable to the audience. This means consistent use of color, line weights, and shapes. This also involves using hierarchy and layout to create a logical narrative that guides the user through the design.

[Q] What is your suggestion for beginners?

[A] I think different approaches work for different people. For me, I began by trying to create similar work to what other people had made. This gives you something to aim for while you focus on learning the design techniques. Then using online tutorials and asking for tips from your fellow students/colleagues should help you understand how to use the design tools you need. Like with any skill, the more you do it, the easier it becomes. Eventually you'll be able to foresee how a piece of data can look in visual form simply because you've seen a similar format before.

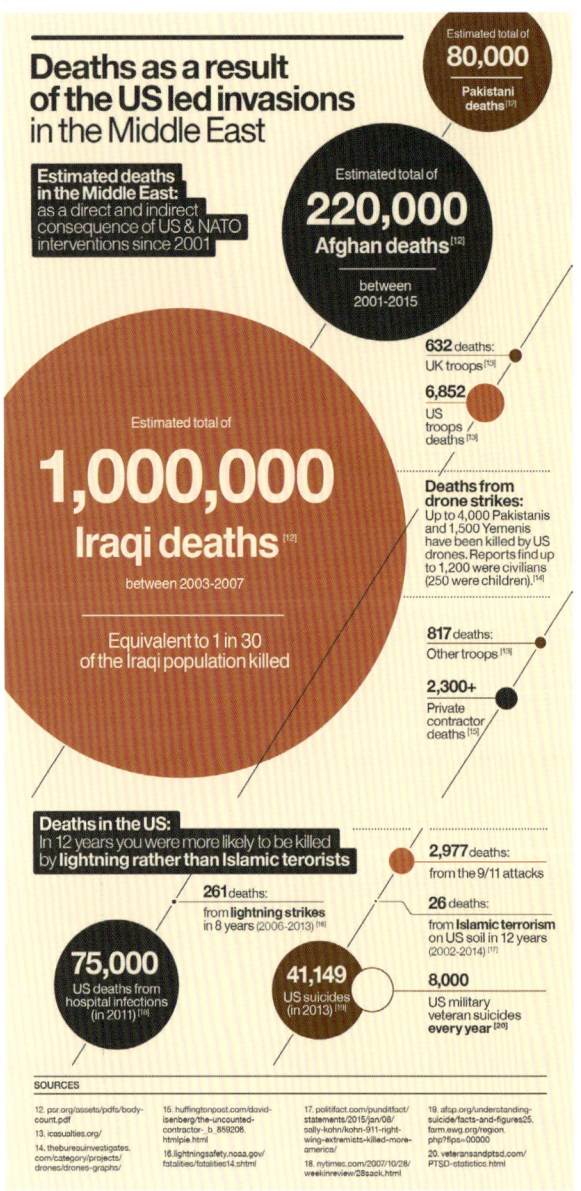

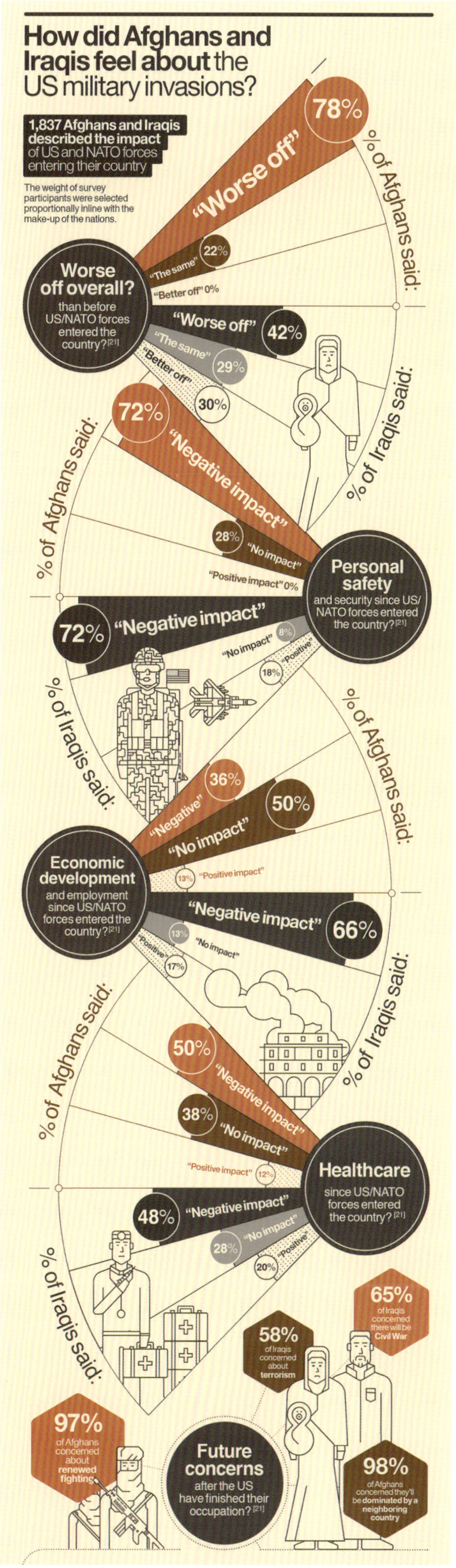

[6–10] War on Terror

Credit: Matthew Rowett
Completion: 2014

Sixteen US intelligence agencies concluded, 'The Iraq war has made the overall terrorism problem worse' and fueled 'global jihadism'. This infographic was made to help people see the bigger picture about Western-backed wars in the Middle East. The data reveals three important points: the actions of the West have only increased instability in the Middle East; the Iraqis and Afghans who are being 'helped' by the US actually think that the US is making matters worse; by following the money and politics, there is a clear incentive for politicians to be at war and use large amounts of taxpayers' money to fund it.

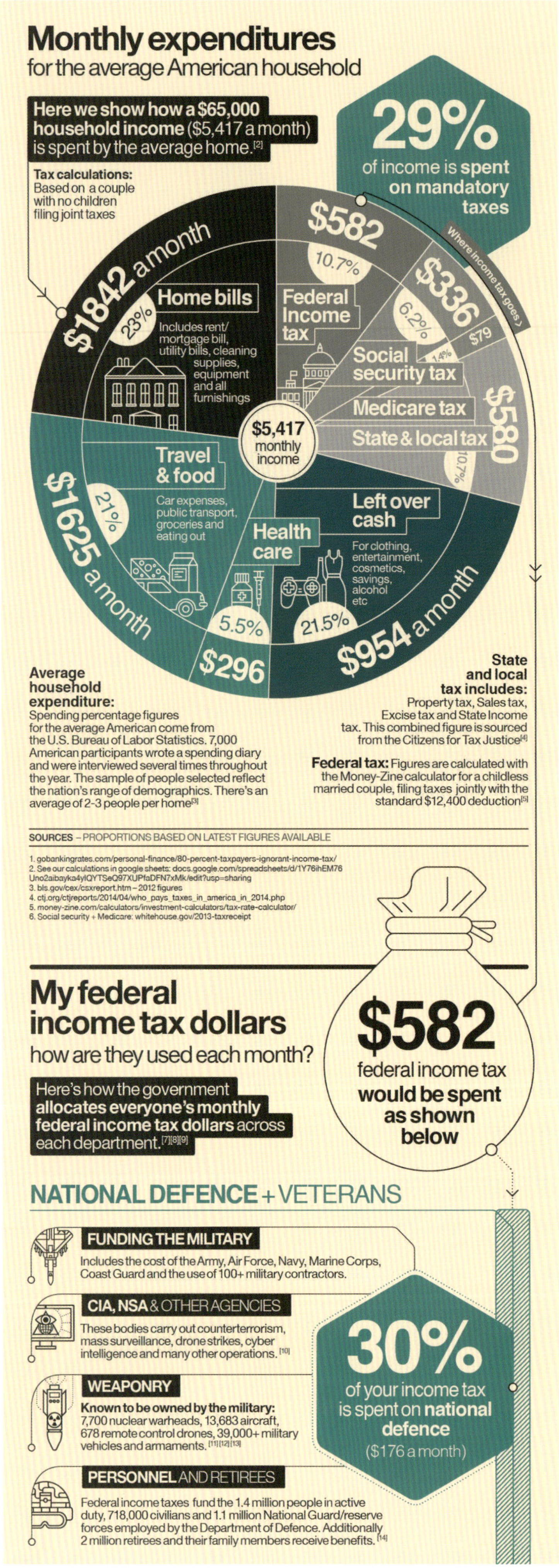

Monthly expenditures
for the average American household

Here we show how a $65,000 household income ($5,417 a month) is spent by the average home.[2]

Tax calculations: Based on a couple with no children filing joint taxes

29% of income is **spent on mandatory taxes**

(where income tax goes)

- $1842 a month — 23% — **Home bills**: Includes rent/mortgage bill, utility bills, cleaning supplies, equipment and all furnishings
- $582 — 10.7% — **Federal Income tax**
- $336 — 6.2% — **Social security tax**
- $79 — 1.4% — **Medicare tax**
- $580 — 10.7% — **State & local tax**
- $954 a month — 21.5% — **Left over cash**: For clothing, entertainment, cosmetics, savings, alcohol etc
- $296 — 5.5% — **Health care**
- $1625 a month — 21% — **Travel & food**: Car expenses, public transport, groceries and eating out

$5,417 monthly income

Average household expenditure:
Spending percentage figures for the average American come from the U.S. Bureau of Labor Statistics. 7,000 American participants wrote a spending diary and were interviewed several times throughout the year. The sample of people selected reflect the nation's range of demographics. There's an average of 2-3 people per home[3]

State and local tax includes: Property tax, Sales tax, Excise tax and State Income tax. This combined figure is sourced from the Citizens for Tax Justice[4]

Federal tax: Figures are calculated with the Money-Zine calculator for a childless married couple, filing taxes jointly with the standard $12,400 deduction[5]

SOURCES – PROPORTIONS BASED ON LATEST FIGURES AVAILABLE

1. gobankingrates.com/personal-finance/80-percent-taxpayers-ignorant-income-tax/
2. See our calculations in google sheets: docs.google.com/spreadsheets/d/1Y76ihEM76 Uno2aibayka4yIQYTSeQ97XUPfaDFN7xMk/edit?usp=sharing
3. bls.gov/cex/csxreport.htm – 2012 figures
4. ctj.org/ctjreports/2014/04/who_pays_taxes_in_america_in_2014.php
5. money-zine.com/calculators/investment-calculators/tax-rate-calculator/
6. Social security + Medicare: whitehouse.gov/2013-taxreceipt

My federal income tax dollars
how are they used each month?

Here's how the government **allocates everyone's monthly federal income tax dollars** across each department.[7][8][9]

$582 federal income tax **would be spent as shown below**

NATIONAL DEFENCE + VETERANS

FUNDING THE MILITARY
Includes the cost of the Army, Air Force, Navy, Marine Corps, Coast Guard and the use of 100+ military contractors.

CIA, NSA & OTHER AGENCIES
These bodies carry out counterterrorism, mass surveillance, drone strikes, cyber intelligence and many other operations.[10]

WEAPONRY
Known to be owned by the military: 7,700 nuclear warheads, 13,683 aircraft, 678 remote control drones, 39,000+ military vehicles and armaments.[11][12][13]

30% of your income tax is spent on **national defence** ($176 a month)

PERSONNEL AND RETIREES
Federal income taxes fund the 1.4 million people in active duty, 718,000 civilians and 1.1 million National Guard/reserve forces employed by the Department of Defence. Additionally 2 million retirees and their family members receive benefits.[14]

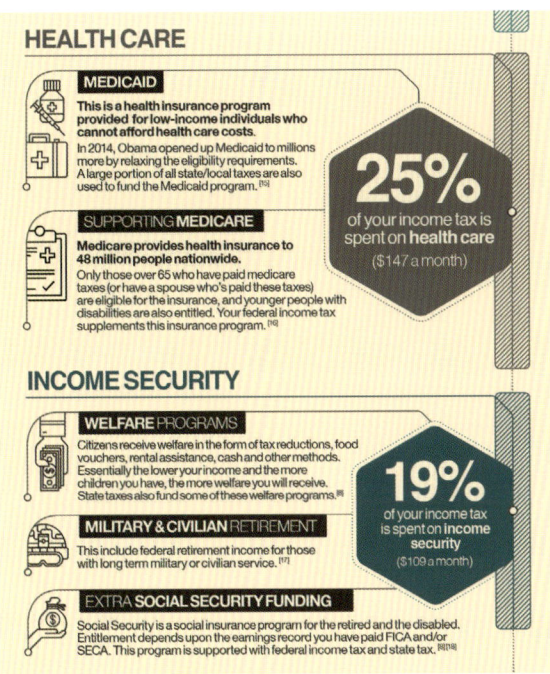

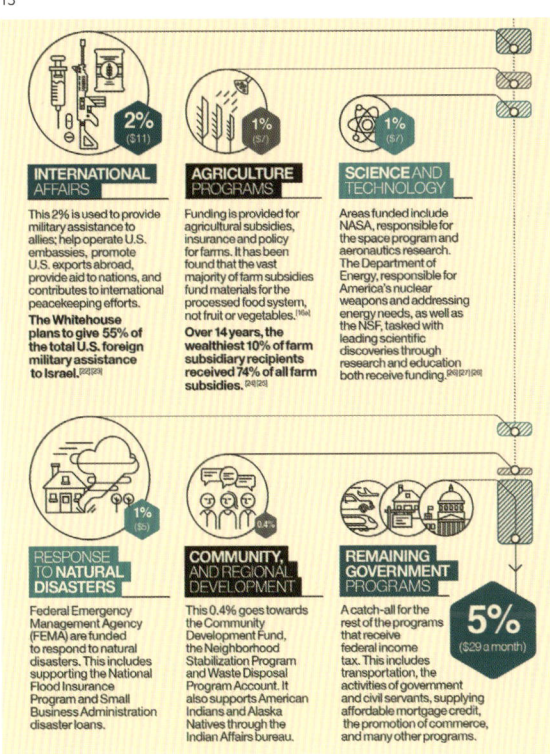

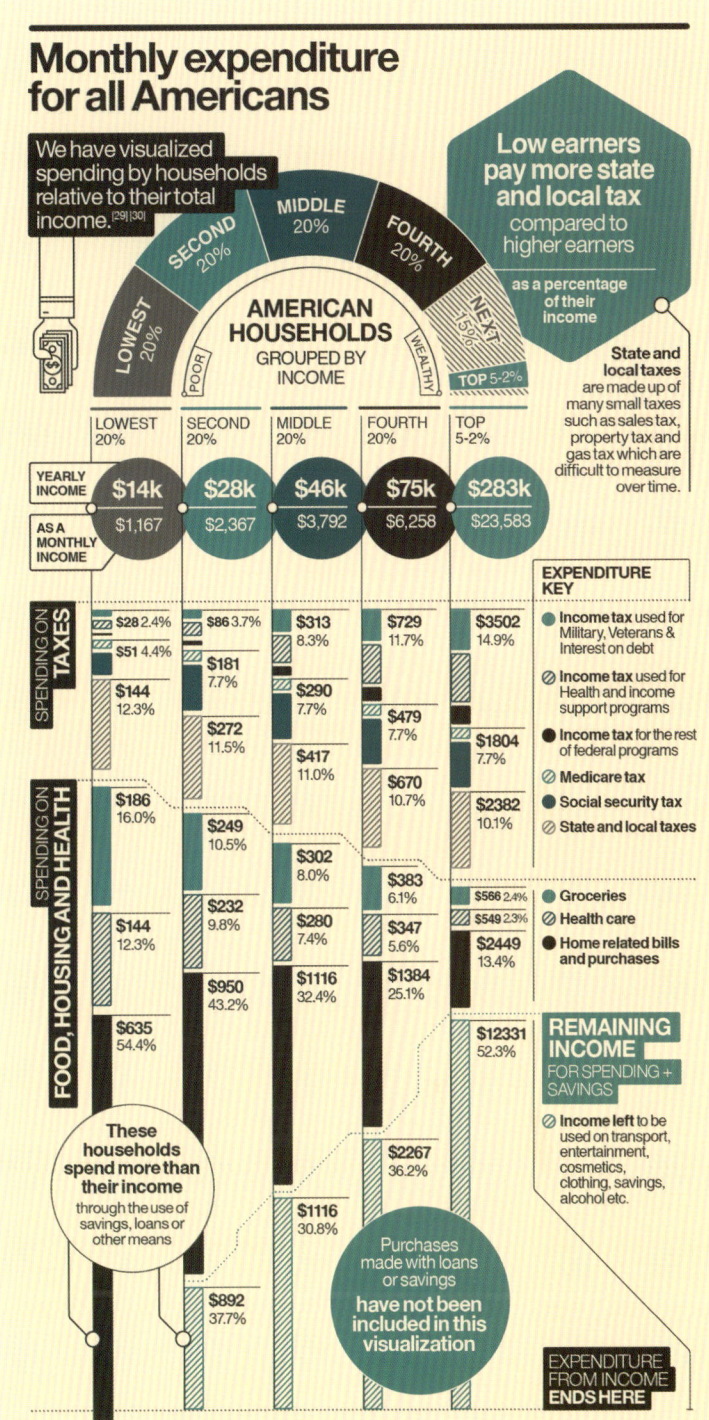

[11–15] Where do Your Earnings and Taxes Really Go?

Credit: Matthew Rowett
Completion: 2015

There's a big knowledge gap when it comes to taxes. In a recent poll, 4 in 5 Americans admitted they didn't know how their income tax dollars are used. This infographic answers that question in detail. To give people more perspective, the designer has visualized the proportions of expenditure for the average household, and shown how the government distributes the spending of federal income tax dollars. There is even a breakdown for different wage levels so you can see how much of your tax dollars fund each aspect of the government spending each month.

Signal Noise

Signal Noise is a London-based data design agency. It aims to make sense of its clients' complex worlds. Originally founded in 2010 by Matthew Falla, Christian Thümer, and Hem Patel, Signal Noise has a strong user-centric approach and combines the disciplines of information design, UI/UX design, and technical development to help clients understand and communicate their data by creating data-driven content and business intelligence tools.

[Q] What do you think about data visualization/infographics?

[A] Data visualization is a visual lens in today's increasingly complex world. Our world is made up of information and most of it is invisible. Data is our means of recording this information so that we can look at it and analyze it. We live in an era of ever increasing amounts of information to the point of overload. This makes it ever harder to pay attention and gain some understanding about the world we live in and what surrounds us.

Data visualization is a visual lens that allows us to see what is otherwise invisible or abstract. We, at Signal Noise, believe that the power of visualization is worth 10,000 words. We use our skills of simplifying complex concepts and communicating them in a way that is engaging as well as informative and useful.

[Q] What kind of design methods do you commonly use?

[A] By combining traditional information and communication design skills with the dynamic world of interaction design, we are able to create highly engaging and data-driven content and tools. Using interactive models allows us to layer the data in a way that is easier to understand and is also able to cater for multiple audiences, which we refer to as skimmers, waders, and divers. Depending on the requirements, often form does follow function—making sure that the understanding and legibility of the data is paramount and avoiding overly artistic interpretations of the data. In terms of process, we have an established process of Simplify, Beautify, Usify™.

[Q] What kind of design elements do you commonly use?

[A] Keep the data display as clean as possible and choose colors carefully with intuition in mind. Help to guide the user by placing emphasis on the most important or interesting facts.

[Q] Where are your works applied?

[A] Most of our works are implemented digitally in the form of a website, microsite or web-based tool. Other projects are produced in printed magazines, as digital PDFs or as animations. We are now doing more non-digital installations, whereby the data is user-generated, using materials such as balloons, string, stickers, and big pieces of paper.

[Q] How do you turn boring and complex data into something interesting and understandable?

[A] Find the story. All data has one, so it's a matter of finding enough data to tell the story. Find a narrative that the audience can relate to. That way it will become much more understandable. Sometimes contextual information can be of great help to aid understanding.

[Q] What is your suggestion for beginners?

[A] Keep it simple and question everything, and understand your audience.

[1] Data Breaches

Credits: Robert Wilson, Signal Noise
Completion: 2015

This visualization explores the digital and physical data breaches between August 2014 and August 2015, mapping every publicly disclosed incident involving more than 1000 records by company, sector source of breach, and potential threat level.

I got 448 problems but — no actually, they're all breaches.

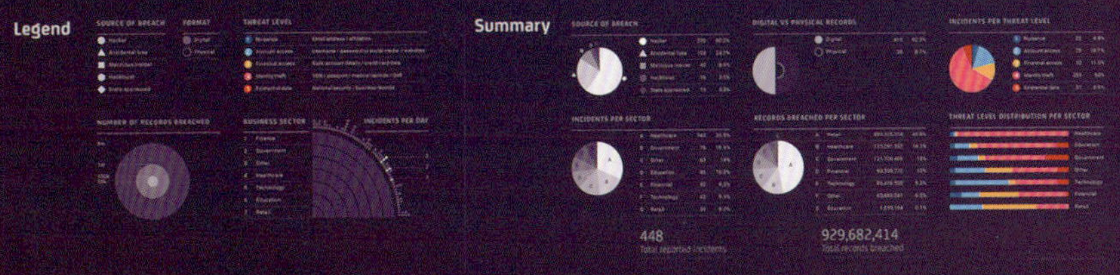

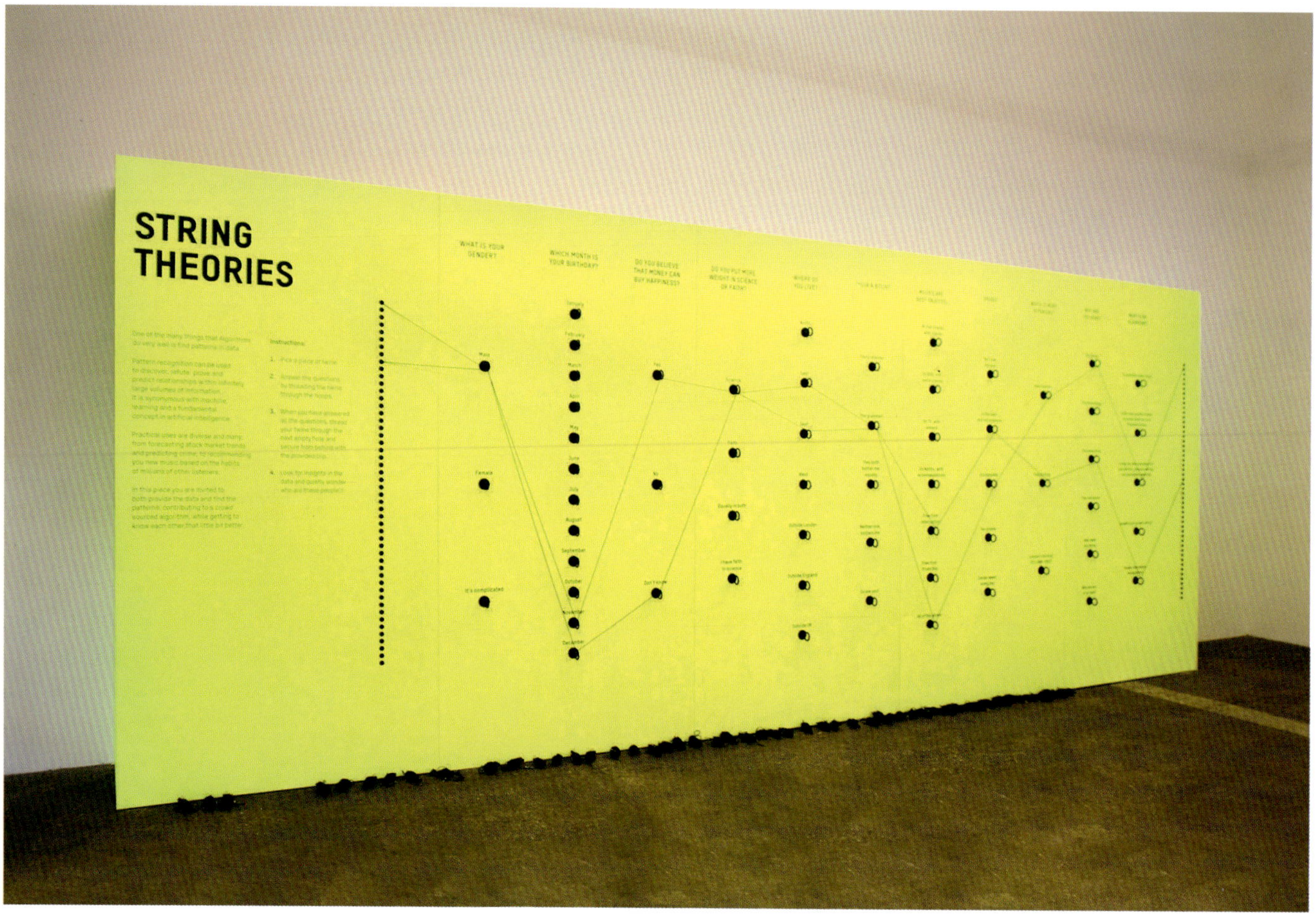

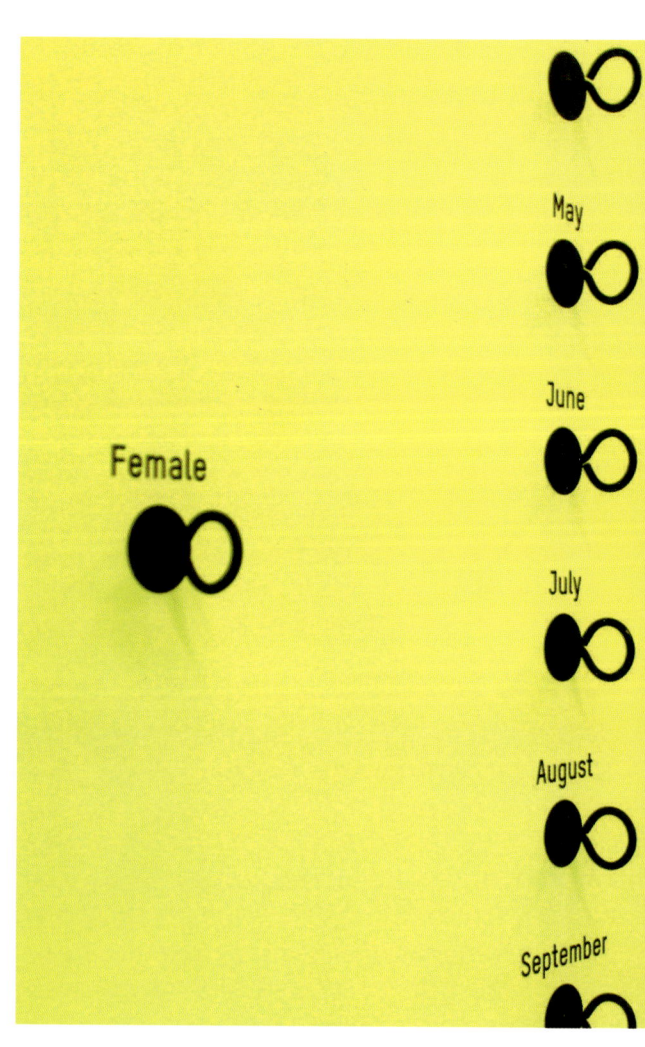

[2–6] String Theories 1

Credits: Robert Wilson, Matthew Falla, Signal Noise
Completion: 2014

This is an interactive component of the Art of the Algorithm exhibition. One of the many things that algorithms do very well is to find patterns in data. Pattern recognition can be used to discover, refute, prove, and predict relationships within infinitely large volumes of information. Practical uses are diverse and many, from forecasting stock-market trends and predicting crime, to recommending new music for you based on the habits of millions of other listeners.

String Theories invites the audience to create a unique algorithmic visualization. By answering a series of personal and opinion-based questions, the participants leave a trail of answers that become the visualization. By the end of the exhibition, the pattern of this data provides an insight into the minds and behaviors of the participants.

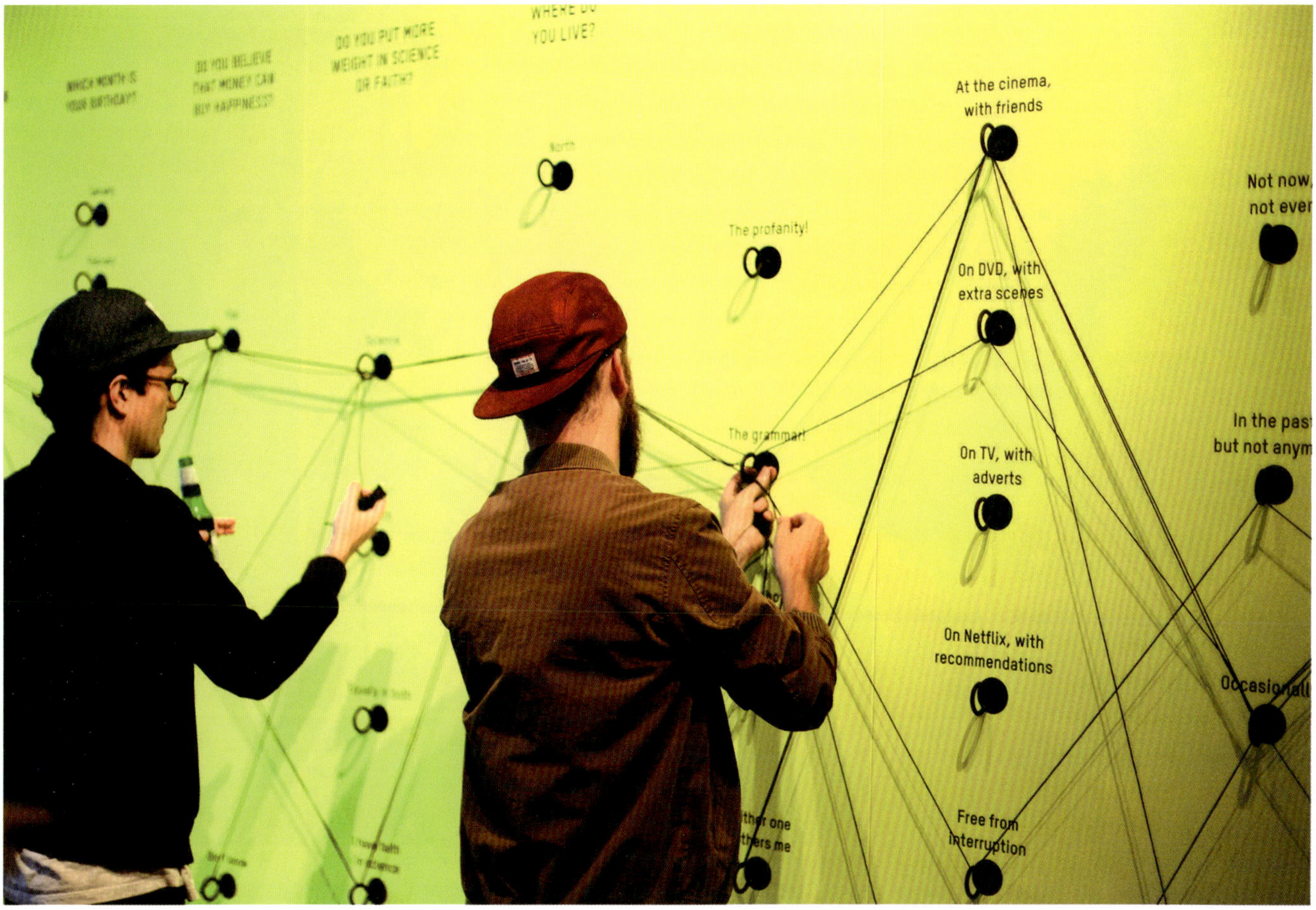

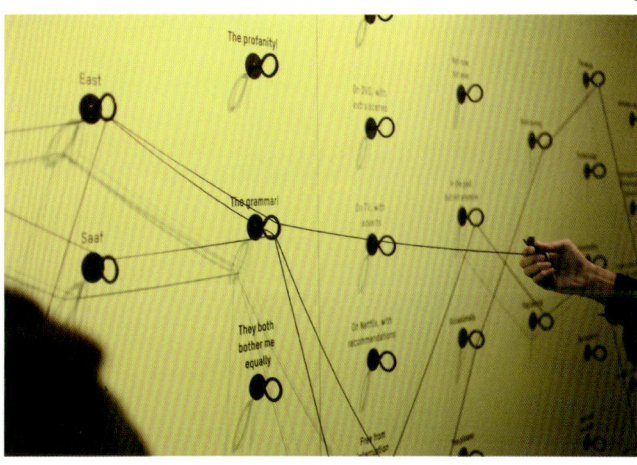
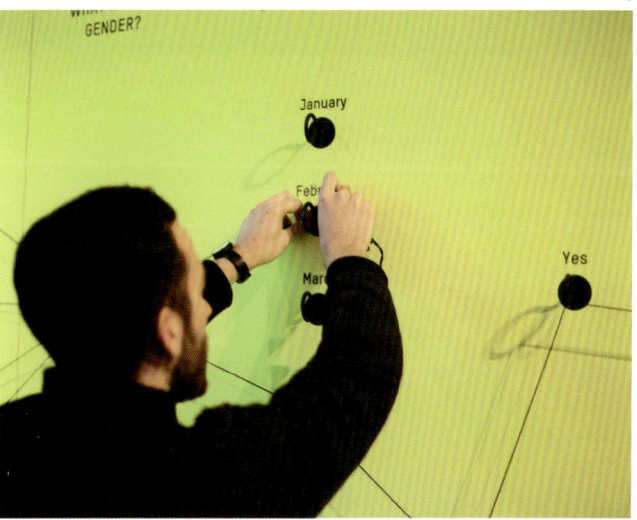

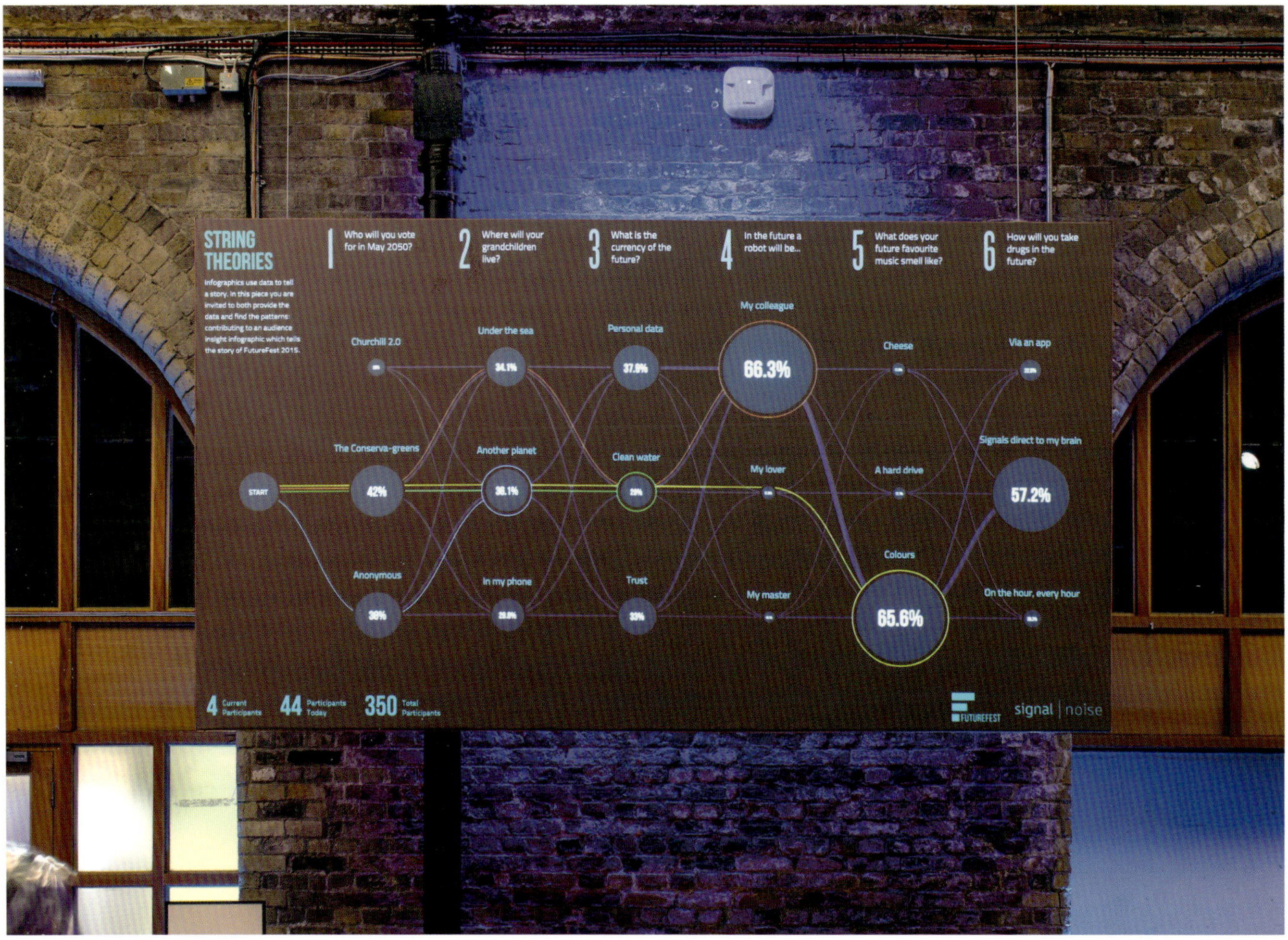

[7–8] String Theories 2

Credits: Robert Wilson, Signal Noise
Completion: 2015

This is an interactive data visualization for the Future Fest 2015 exhibition. String Theories is an interactive data installation that aims to capture and map the sentiments and opinions of visitors to the Future Fest festival. Users will be able to answer the questions and leave their own data trail, which will take its place among the network of past visitors' trails to create an instant and ever-growing data visualization.

[9] Rings of Fire

Credits: Robert Wilson, Signal Noise
Completion: 2016

The visualization is looking at 100 of the world's hottest chilis, sorted by heat ranking, species, and lineage. Alongside indexing the heat of the chilis, the designers had fun exploring family trees and wanted to show the individual species. The hybridization information tells you which chilis have been created through cross or selective breeding and the original plants they come from. That said, the world of the 'super-hots' is notoriously one of rumor and hearsay, so the exact parentage of some will always remain a heated debate.

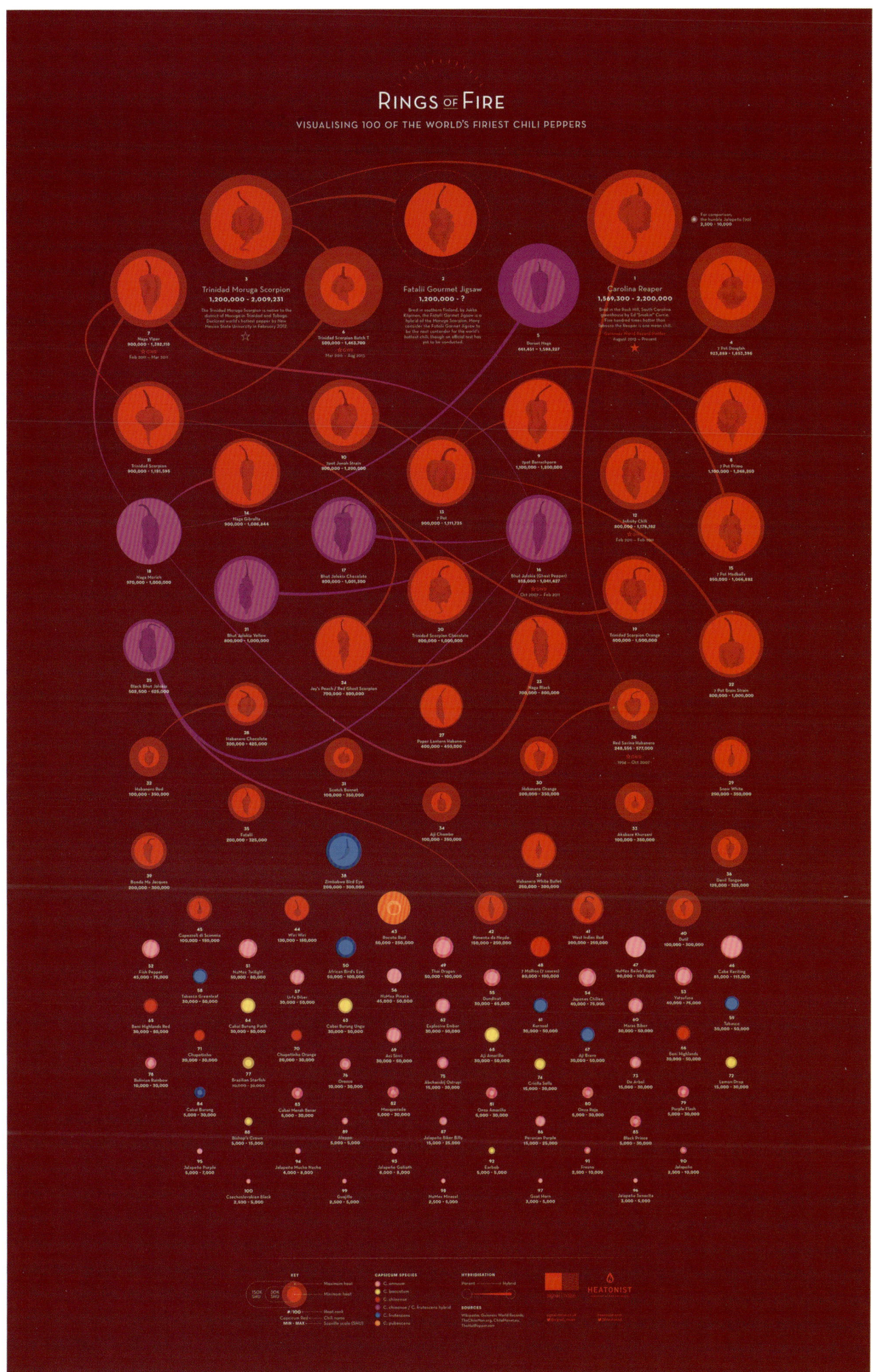

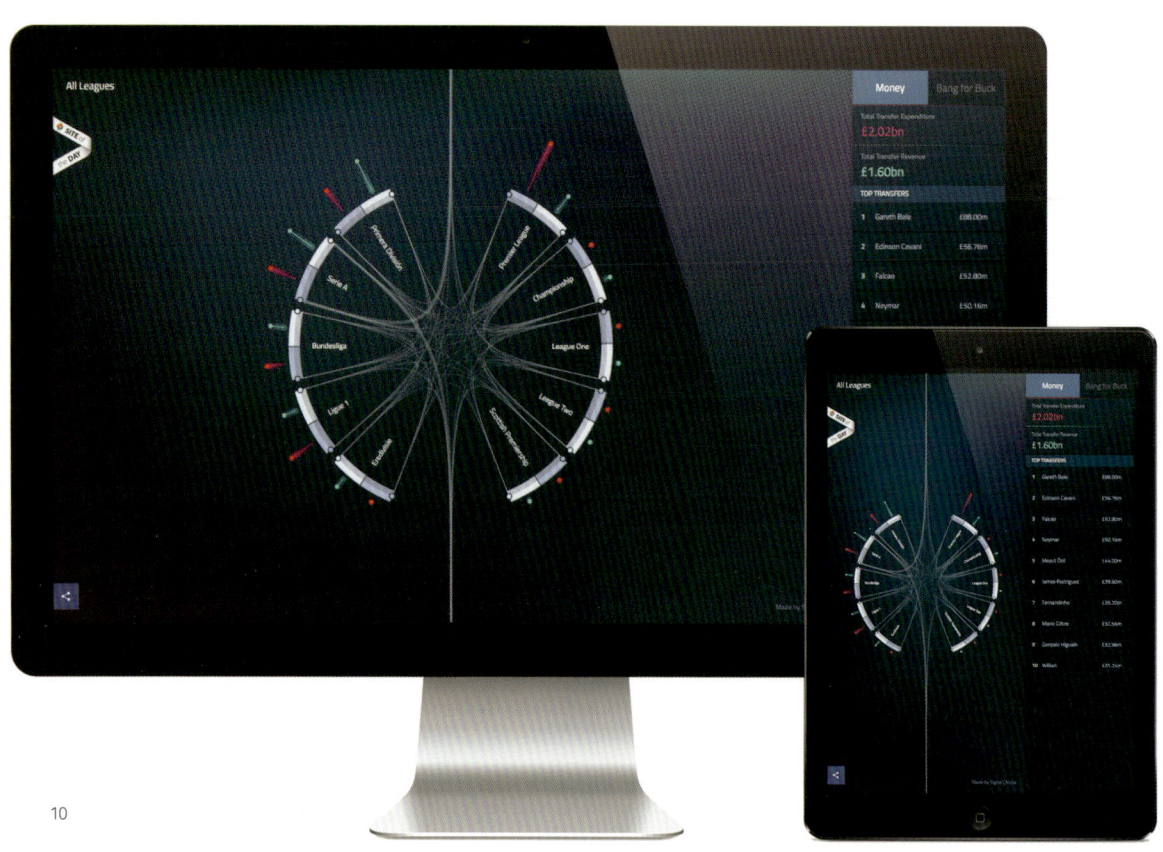

10

11

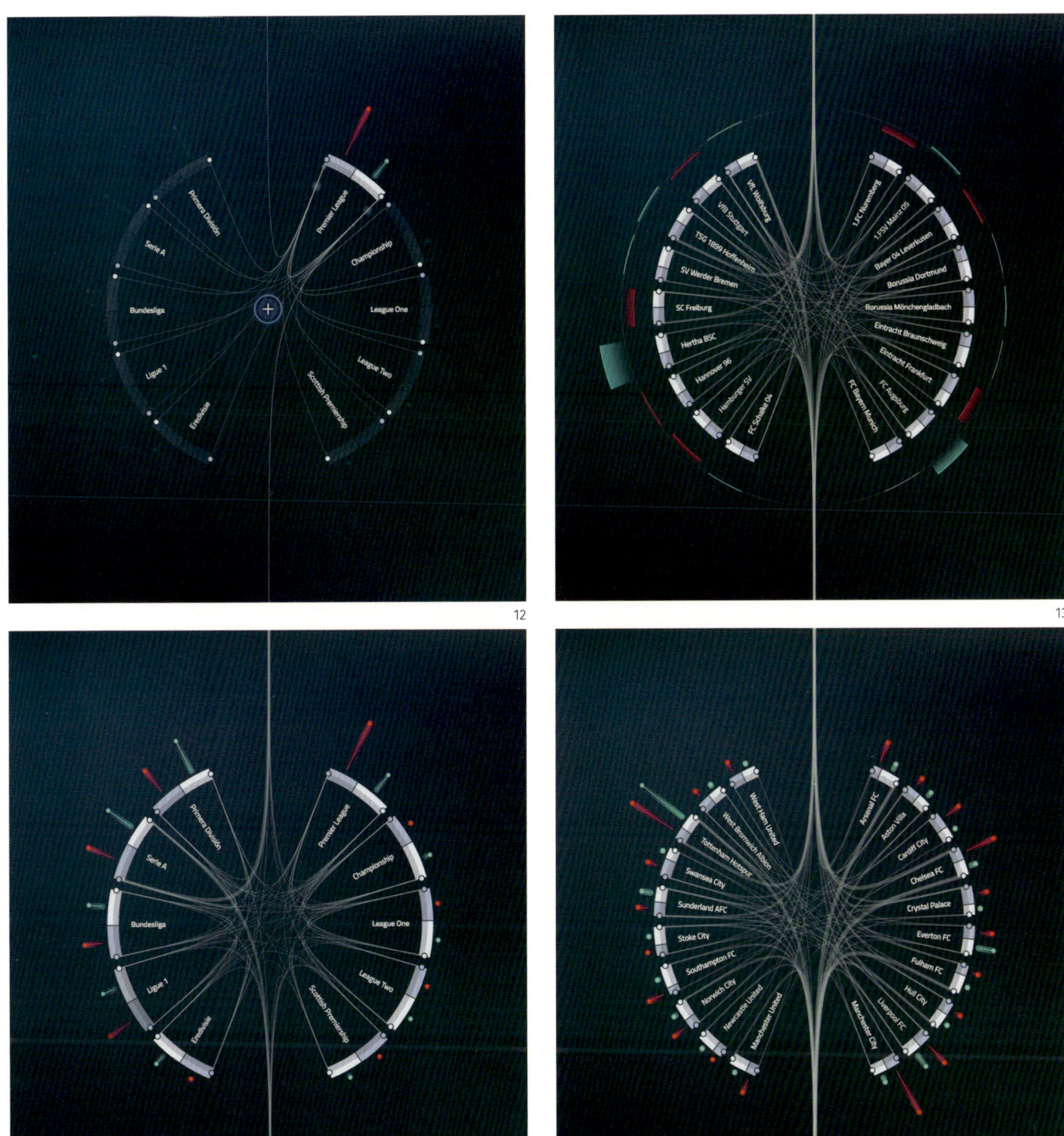

[10–15] Transfer Window

Credit: Signal Noise
Completion: 2014

This is an interactive visualization using live data from European football transfers and the impact it has on each club's league position. Every day, the site pulls in data about the 10 main European leagues and clubs within them, and visualizes all player transfers and lifts the lid on which teams are actually getting value for money.

The huge sums of money that accompany modern transfers are always an area of hot debate. With a dynamic interface for tracking a club's league position over the season and the amount they spend on new players, the site reveals which teams are getting the most 'bang for their buck' and which ones have wasted their money.

South China Morning Post

South China Morning Post's (SCMP) multiple-award-winning graphics and magazine design department is lead by Darren Long, a British art director based in Hong Kong. Over the past three decades, he has launched and rejuvenated dozens of magazines and newspapers in London, Kuala Lumpur, and Hong Kong.

[Q] What do you think about data visualization/infographics?

[A] The challenge is to present information directly, clearly and in a visually compelling manner. Visual presentation has always been an integral part of the storytelling process when reporting news. In our current, fast-paced environment, infographics are no longer merely supplementary to the editorial process but are increasingly the actual medium used to tell the story. Today's graphics engage the full news cycle, requiring research, reporting, data analysis, conceptualizing story ideas, and sketching alternative plans, culminating in the graphic's realization.

[Q] What kind of design methods do you commonly use?

[A] At *SCMP* we adapt our design approach to the story we want to tell. We are keen to humanize the story, so drawing and composition are key elements to our approach. Once we have established the central theme, we will introduce a hero image to act as the cornerstone for the composition. Additional elements will orbit the central visual. Editing is a crucial process as we continue to distill everything to the absolute essence.

[Q] What kind of design elements do you commonly use?

[A] Timelines, maps and charts, scales and relationship diagrams. We look for elements that our local audience can easily relate to. For instance, when a politician was discovered with 200 million yuan stashed in his basement, we showed how a single stack of bank notes would be 200 meters tall, approximately the same height as a landmark building our readers would be familiar with in the Causeway Bay shopping district.

[Q] Where are your works applied?

[A] The *South China Morning Post* is a newspaper, so we produce infographics for print and digital. Each platform has unique formats that impose certain conventions and restrictions. With print, what you see is what you get, so the story needs to unfold immediately to be accessible to the reader. Digital has the advantage that a reader can interact directly with the graphic and drill deeper into the story by clicking on buttons.

[Q] How do you turn boring and complex data into something interesting and understandable?

[A] We look for the human element in a story. This can be as direct as drawing the story's chief protagonist, or if a more abstract approach is appropriate, we might use flowing, tapering lines to describe a business deal. By using drawings and a subtle palette, we are able to keep the design unified and coherent. Hand-rendered drawings in pencil, or pen and ink provide a warm and sympathetic visual counterpoint to the data, which can often appear cold or dry.

[Q] What is your suggestion for beginners?

[A] Two things. First, learn the history of your craft. Infographics have been around a long time. Neolithic cave paintings, ancient Egyptian hieroglyphs and medieval illuminated manuscripts all contain extensive information in their images. Looking to historical solutions can provide great inspiration. French civil engineer Charles Minard's 1869 cartographical depiction of Napoleon's invasion and retreat from Russia is one such milestone. Another is Harry Beck's influential London Underground map from 1933, which forgoes geographic accuracy in order to better describe junction points. Second: edit. If a fact is not essential to understanding your key argument, drop it. Less is always more.

[1] Measuring the Rule of Law

Credits: Marcelo Duhalde, *South China Morning Post*
Completion: 2016

The World Justice Project collects data on 113 governing systems every year. The designers took a representative look at some of the factors that constitute good governance. The graphic shows how Hong Kong and mainland China compare to the worst and best performers. The rating is from 0 to 1. '1' indicates the most rigorous application of rule of law, through an open court system. The gap between Hong Kong and mainland China in each year is shown by different colors.

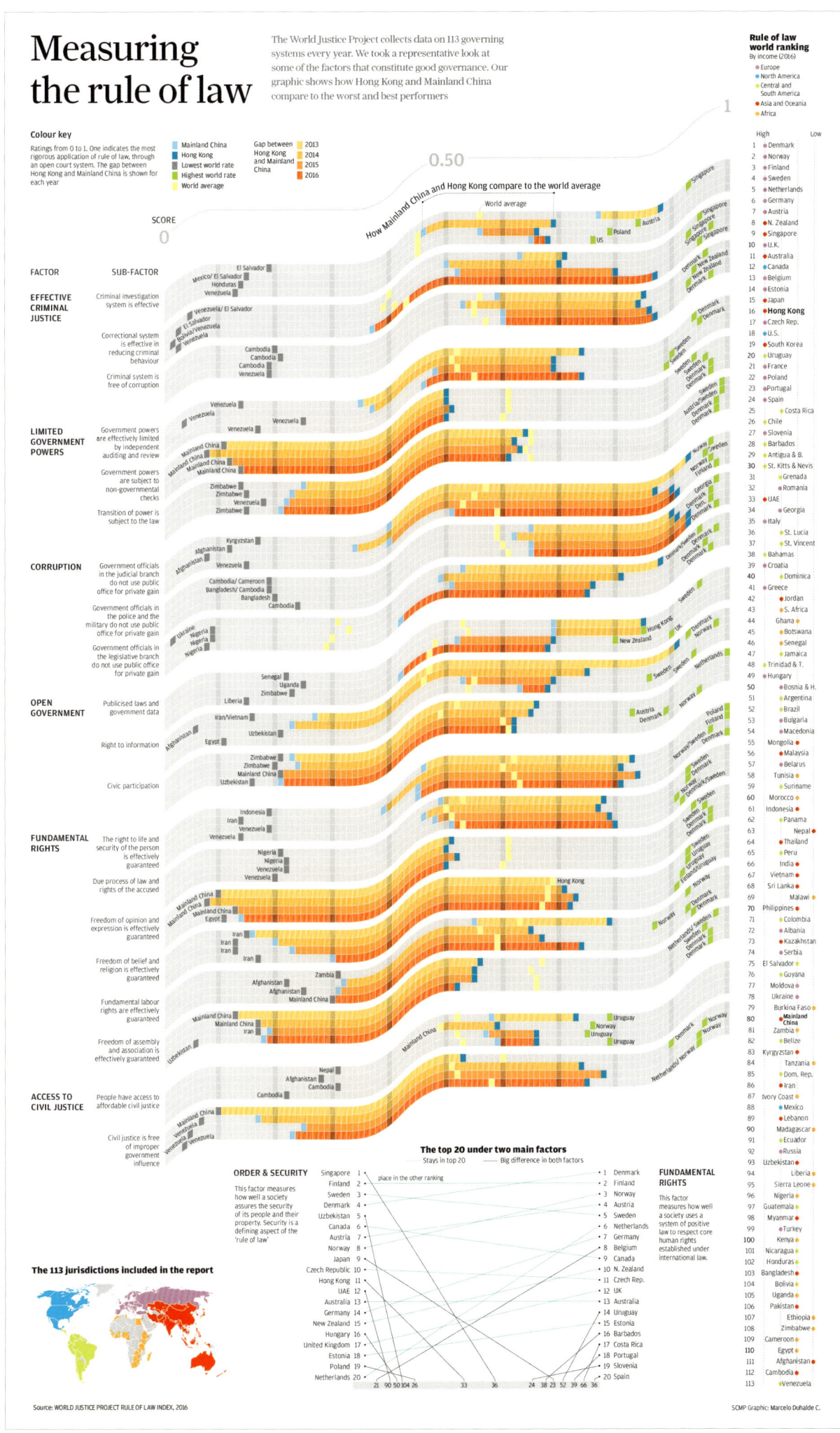

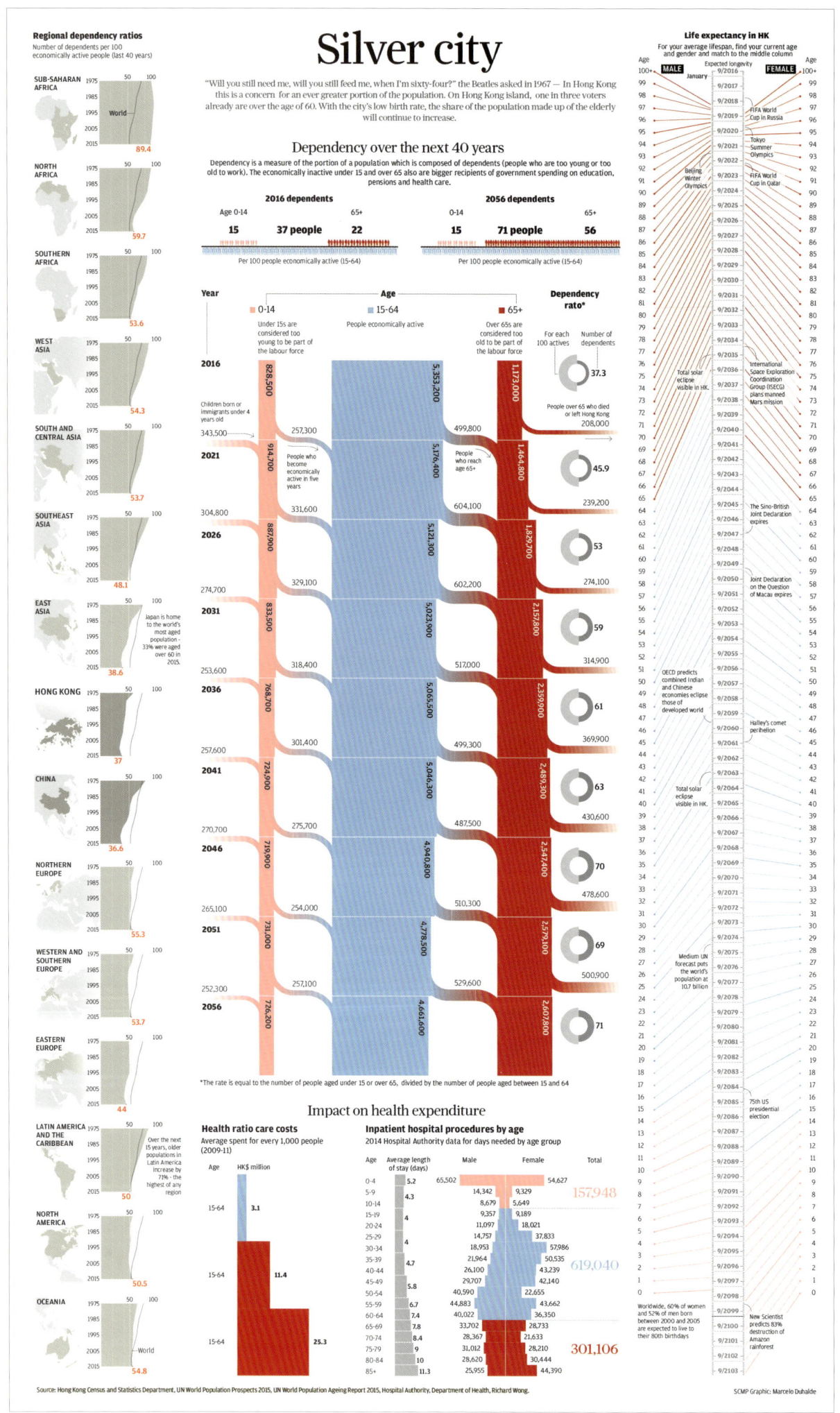

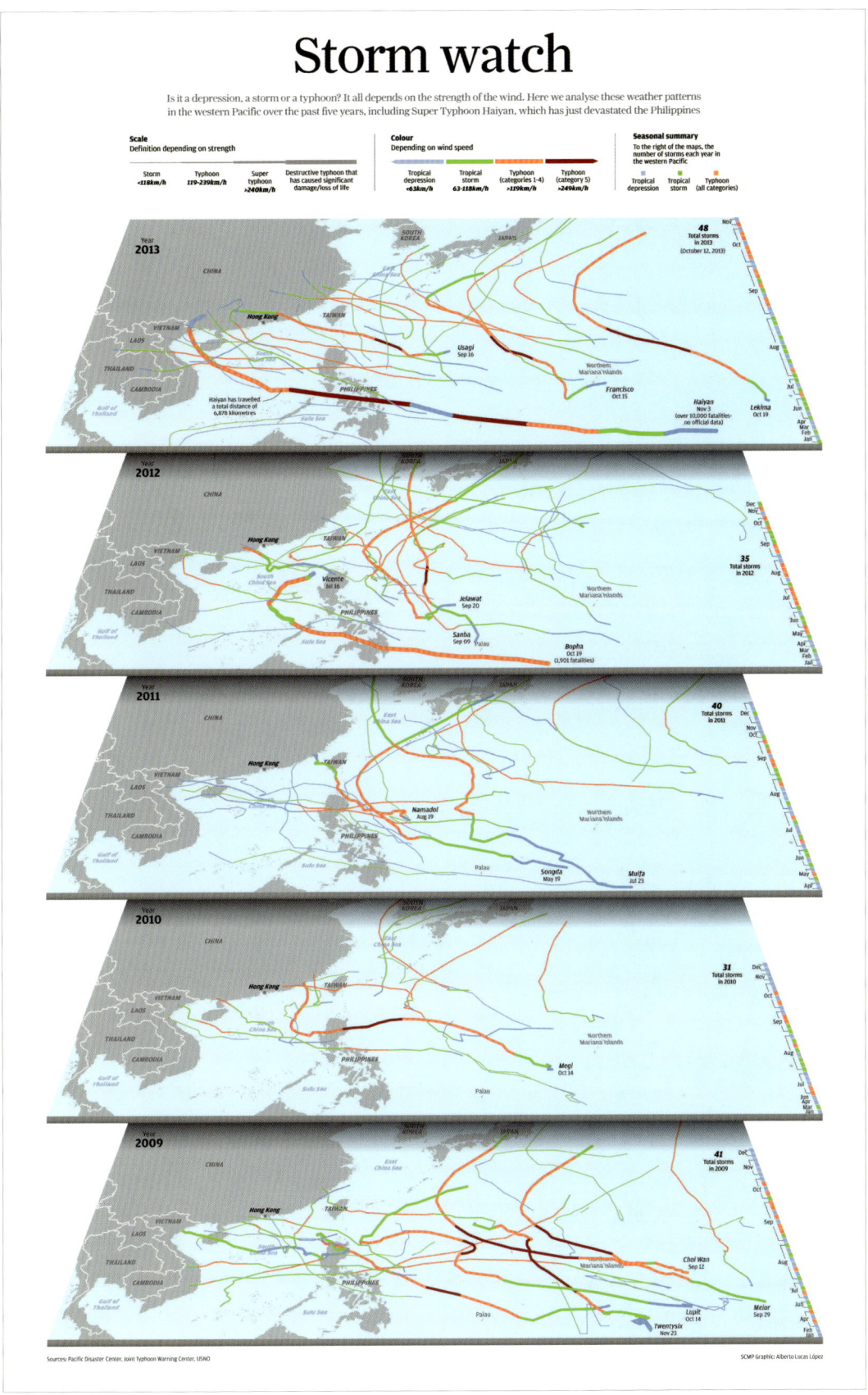

[2] Silver City

Credits: Marcelo Duhalde, *South China Morning Post*
Completion: 2016

'Will you still need me, will you still feed me, when I'm sixty-four?' the Beatles asked in 1967. In Hong Kong this is a concern for an ever greater portion of the population. In Hong Kong, one in three voters is over the age of 60. This infographic shows that with the city's low birth rate, the share of the population made up of the elderly will continue to increase.

[3] Storm Watch

Credits: Alberto Lucas López, *South China Morning Post*
Completion: 2013

Is it a depression, a storm, or a typhoon? It all depends on the strength of the wind. This infographic analyzes these weather patterns in the western Pacific over the past five years, including Super Typhoon Haiyan, which devastated the Philippines.

[4] The Cost of a Family in Hong Kong

Credits: Lau Ka-kuen, Dan Bland, *South China Morning Post*
Completion: 2016

Hong Kong has one of the world's lowest fertility rates. Anecdotal evidence suggests young people reel at the cost of raising a child, so the infographic studies how much bringing up a child actually costs by looking at three hypothetical families from different income brackets. The graphic assumes that both parents are in full- or part-time employment and want to maintain similar lifestyles to their pre-child years.

---

[5] The Sum of the Parts

Credits: Alberto Lucas López, *South China Morning Post*
Completion: 2016

China's rapid economic growth has had a great influence in the world for two decades. This graphic visualizes the nation's year-on-year growth by region over the past two decades. With an original chart format, the graphic provides a new method for understanding China's change in GDP.

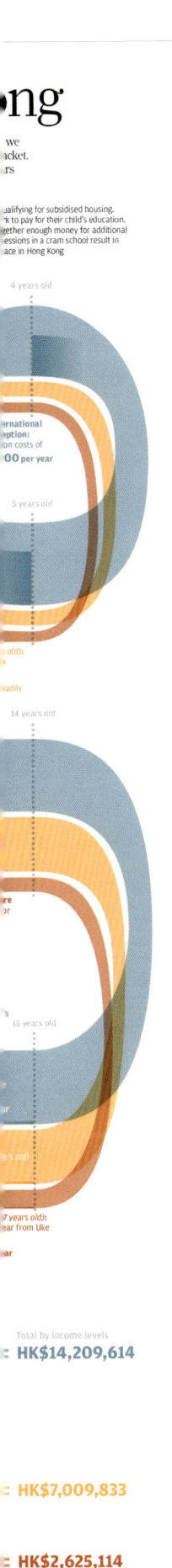

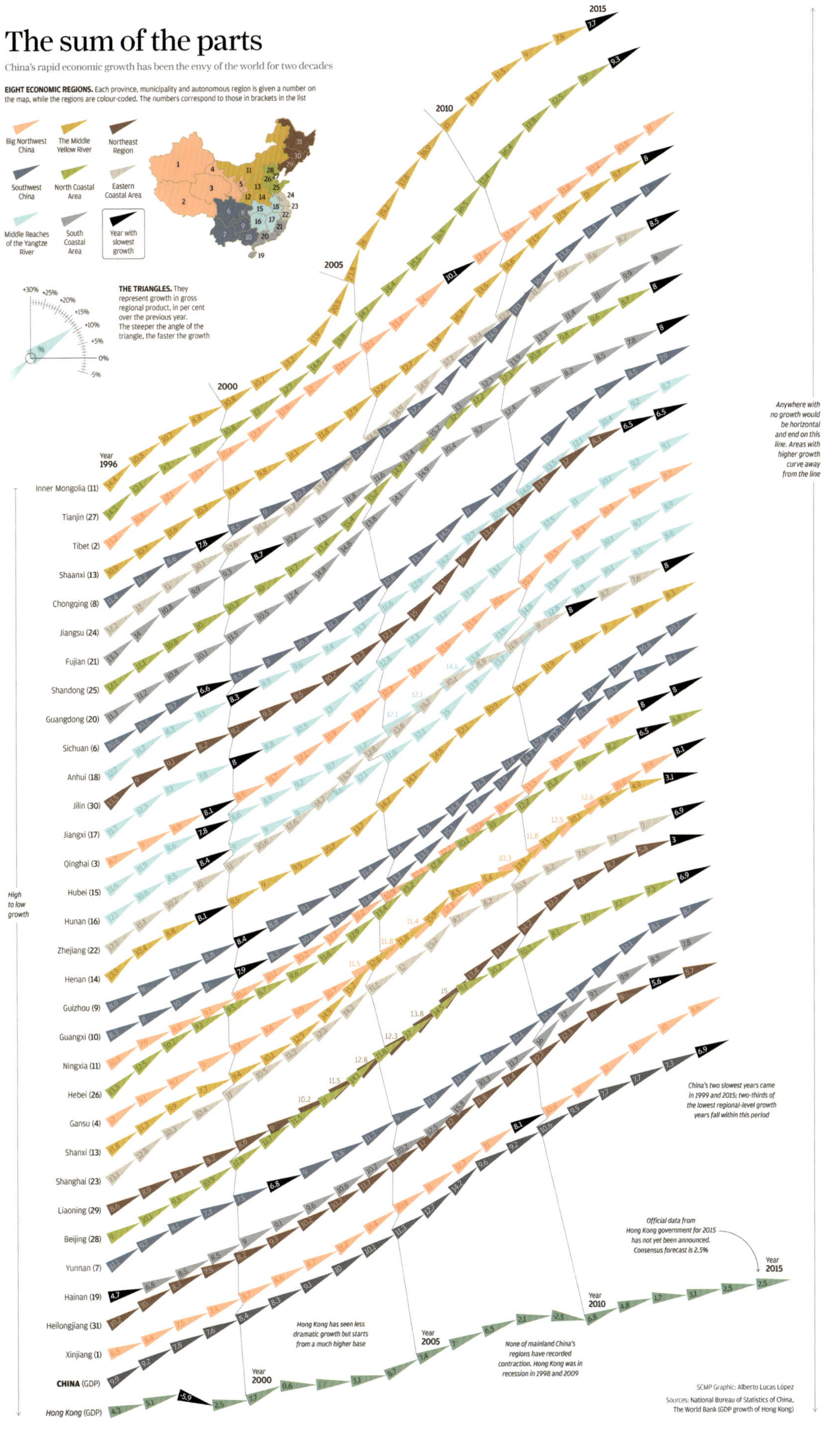

Moritz Stefaner

TRUTH & BEAUTY

Moritz Stefaner works as an independent designer, consultant, and researcher. He helps organizations, researchers, and businesses to find truth and beauty in relevant and meaningful data. He has worked with clients including Google, FIFA, Skype, and DPA, and has long-term consulting relationships with the OECD, the World Economic Forum, and the Max Planck Research Society.

[Q] What do you think about data visualization/infographics?

[A] Data visualization is one of our most important tools to make sense of a messy world, together. Only by bringing abstract phenomena into the realm of the tangible and experiential can we make complexity graspable and manageable.

[Q] What kind of design methods do you commonly use?

[A] It depends a bit if I work on a client commission or a self-initiated work. In the latter case, I might just be inspired by a certain phenomenon, data set, or technique that I want to try out. When working for a client, there is usually a bit more context, goals, and constraints to consider. Usually, at the beginning, I ask the client for two things: a data sample and some answers to a few questions clarifying the context and basic motivation of the work.

The basic set of questions I usually ask are:

- Why are we doing this?
- What are you hoping to achieve?
- Who are we targeting?
- How is the end product going to be used?
- How are we publishing?
- What data do we have available?
- Which other existing materials should we take into account?
- Which constraints do we have?
- Who is responsible for what?
- Who else is doing something similar?

To me, answers to these questions are really important to understand why the client thinks a data visualization is important, and also to understand when the project is done and successful. Often, both the client and I realize that half of these questions cannot be answered yet, but that's fine, as long as we make sure to answer them along the way.

As mentioned, the other important component in this first conceptual phase is to have a data sample. On the one hand, we want to know very early if the data is interesting enough to create a great visualization. Rather than trying to 'blow up' dull data with spectacular visuals, I try to achieve a position where we have much more data than we want to use in order to be able to edit down, put into perspective, and distill. The other important information to gather is if the data seems sufficient to reach the project goal at all. Very often, my clients overestimate the depth, and completeness of the data they have available, and it is good to determine that right away.

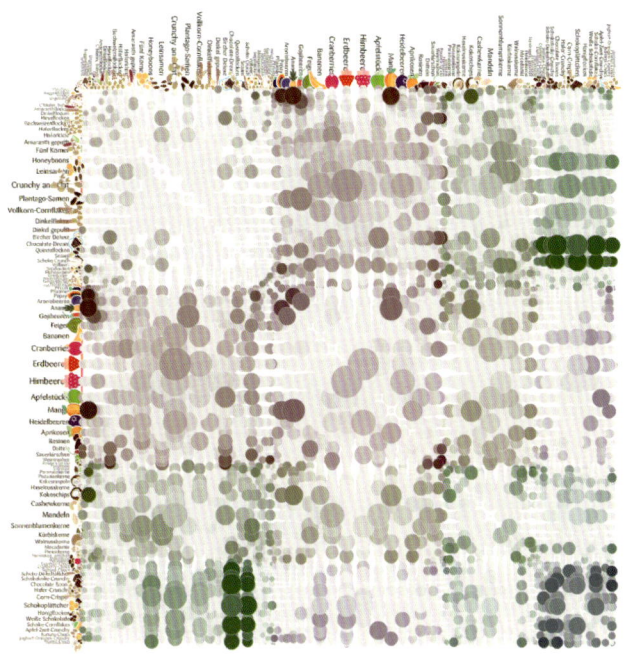

1

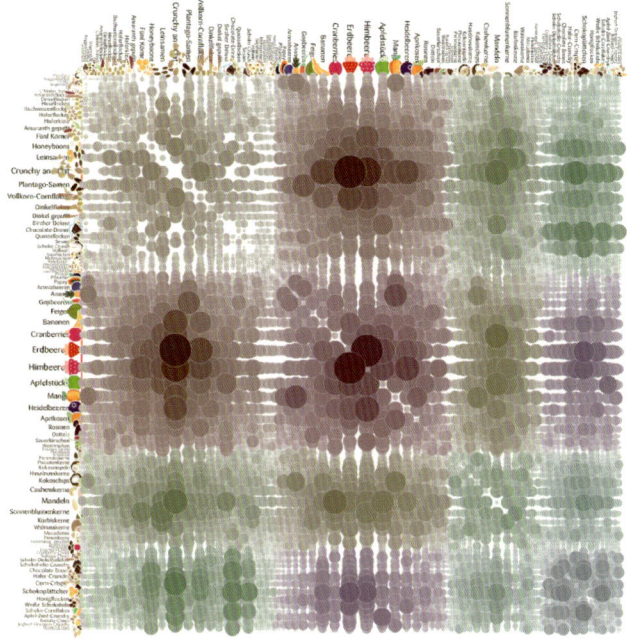

2

The third reason why I need data early in the process is that my design approach requires that I immerse myself deeply in the problem domain and available data very early in the project to get a feel for the unique characteristics of the data, its 'texture', and the affordances it brings. It is very important that the results from these explorations, which I also discuss in detail with my clients, can influence the basic concept and main direction of the project. To put it in Hans Rosling's word, 'Let the data set change your mind set'. Why? Some ideas sound great on paper, but are dull when we look at them using real data. Other times, totally new ideas can come into play from the close dialogue with the data, based on things we discover and learn along the way. So, it is really a process of continuous exploration, creating a view on the data answering a few questions, but raising new ones, so I create new views on the data to answer these questions and find new ones again. In this phase, it is really important to move fast and not get too married to specific solutions yet, so usually, I make really simple, generic charts.

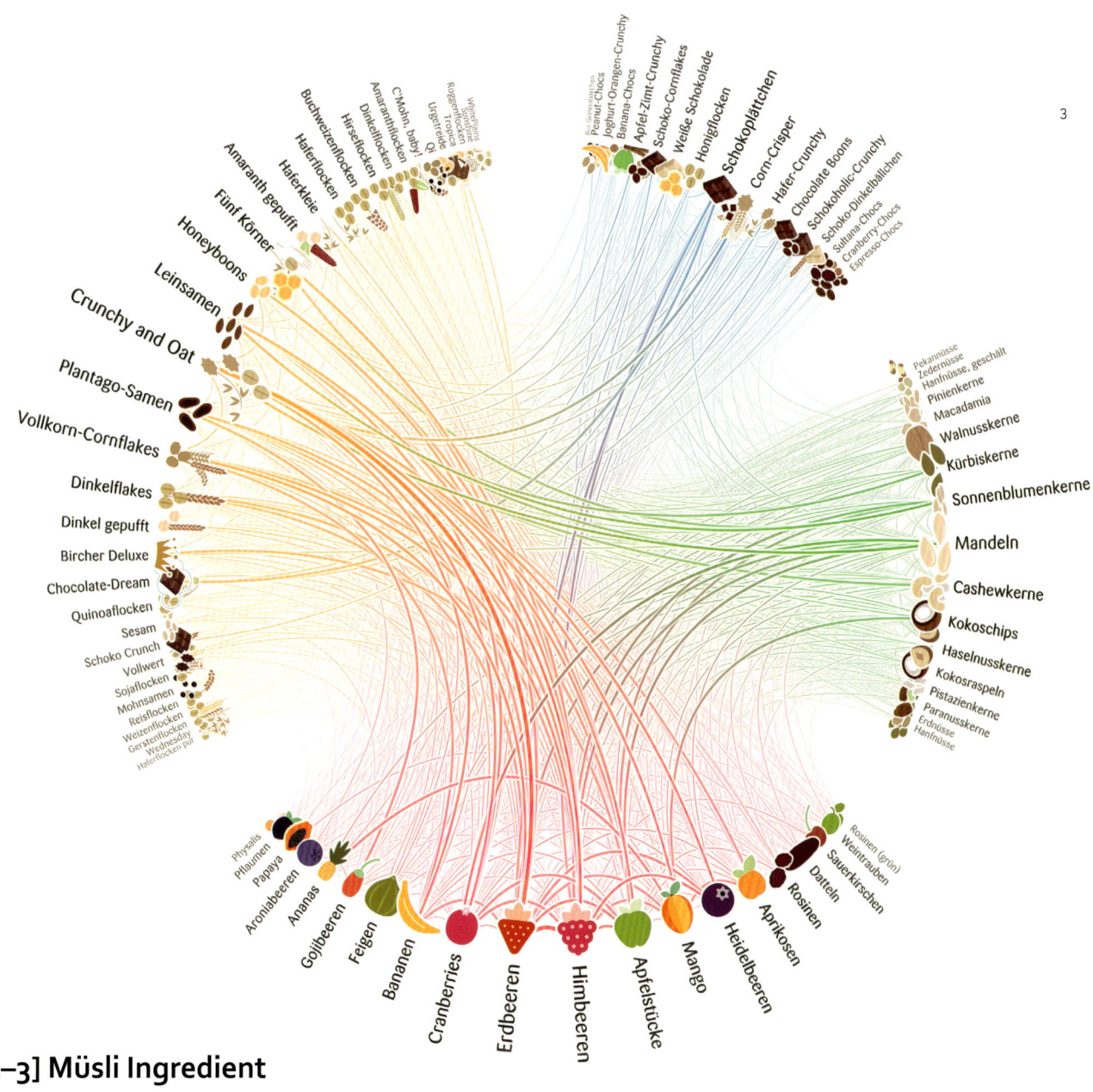

[1–3] Müsli Ingredient Network

Credit: Moritz Stefaner
Completion: 2012

The German start-up Mymuesli offers individual, custom-mixed mueslis by mail order. For their fifth anniversary, Moritz Stefaner was commissioned to analyze and visualize how their clients combined the ingredients they offer. The result was a straightforward radial network visualization, with the ingredients grouped by category (base mueslis, fruit, nuts, sweets, etc.). Some niceties have gone into the line rendering, with gradient strokes (depending on the categories of the connected nodes) and white stroke outlines to facilitate visual perception of the depth stacking. Some interesting insights can be gained from this visualization: fruits are the most popular ingredient, and are often combined with each other. Sweets and nuts, however, are rarely combined.

[Q] **What kind of design elements do you commonly use?**

[A] I usually try to use the visual encoding that works best for the data and tasks at hand. Which visual variable is the most expressive and most fitting for my most important data dimensions? Which shapes are recognizable, readable and fit the topic? In short, form follows data, function, and content. If I would limit myself to some favorite shapes or elements, I won't be able to find the best visual language in each project.

[Q] **Where are your works applied?**

[A] The spectrum of works I do ranges from static print graphics (journals, reports) to websites, high-end custom visualizations (such as large-screen displays, interactive installations) to data sculptures, and even food!

[Q] **How do you turn boring and complex data into something interesting and understandable?**

[A] When the data has been explored sufficiently, it is time to sit down and reflect. What were the most interesting insights? What surprised me? What were recurring themes and facts throughout all views on the data? In the end, what do we find most important and most interesting? These are the things that will govern which angles and perspectives we want to emphasize in the subsequent project phases. Often, I will also estimate and price the concept and data exploration phase separately from the second, more clear-cut design and production phase. Sometimes, we will also let the project end after the data exploration phase, because the data is less interesting than we thought or does not match the client's expectations. But, in fact, I consider these projects 'successful failures' and a real service to the client, as I prevented them from spending money on something they don't want or need.

When it comes to coding and producing data visualizations, it is important to keep in mind that not all design decisions can be made in advance. So, also during the production phases, a vital ongoing discussion between code, design, and data analysis is really important. The other important thing to note is that in the end, the details can make a great difference to whether people enjoy and use your data visualization, or are confused by it. As they say, the last 20 percent are the second 80 percent, and a lot of work can and should be put into getting a help section, legends, annotations, an introduction and so on into proper shape, and testing the whole product with a few users. And, once the product is out, a lot can be learnt from observing people interacting with it. How much time do users spend with your visualization? Which options do they discover and which are they missing? When do they comment on or link to it? Which parts of the project do they find most interesting to mention and refer to? Quite often, I would love to do a second iteration after the first launch, because only once the product is out 'in the wild' can we see more clearly its strengths and weaknesses.

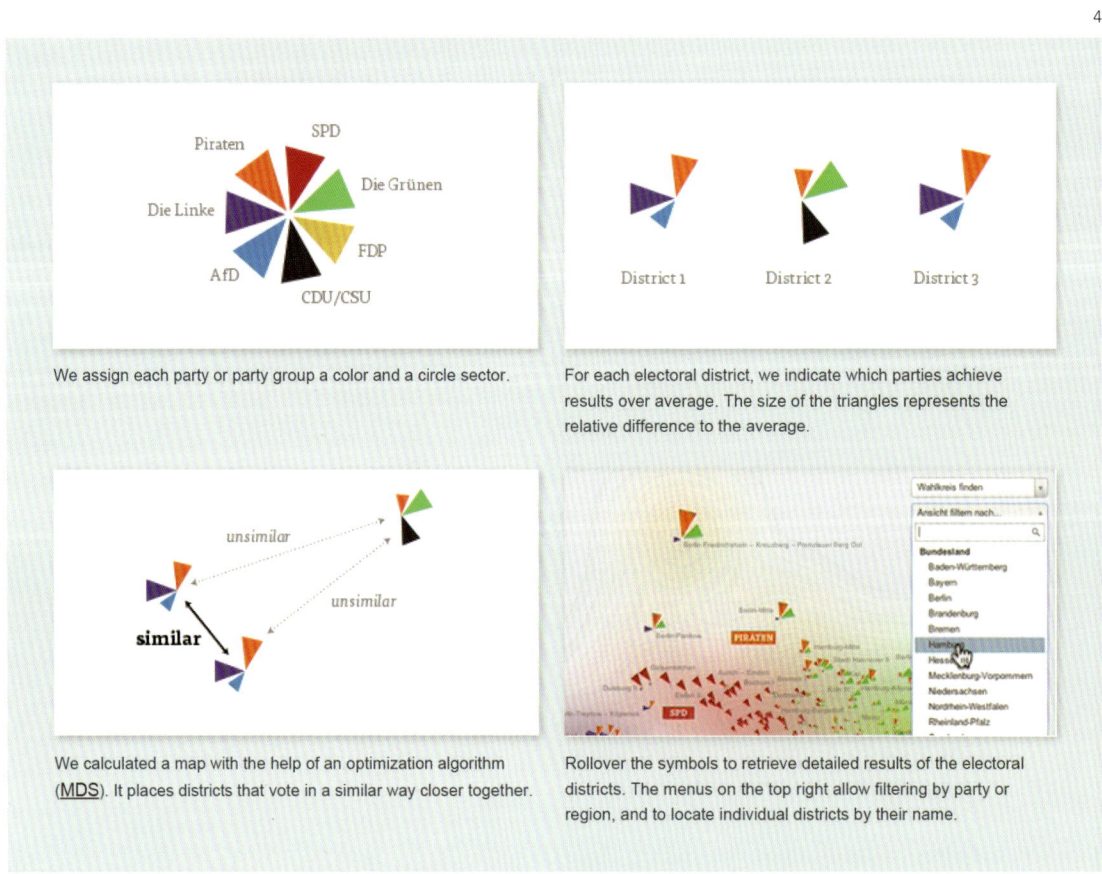

We assign each party or party group a color and a circle sector.

For each electoral district, we indicate which parties achieve results over average. The size of the triangles represents the relative difference to the average.

We calculated a map with the help of an optimization algorithm (MDS). It places districts that vote in a similar way closer together.

Rollover the symbols to retrieve detailed results of the electoral districts. The menus on the top right allow filtering by party or region, and to locate individual districts by their name.

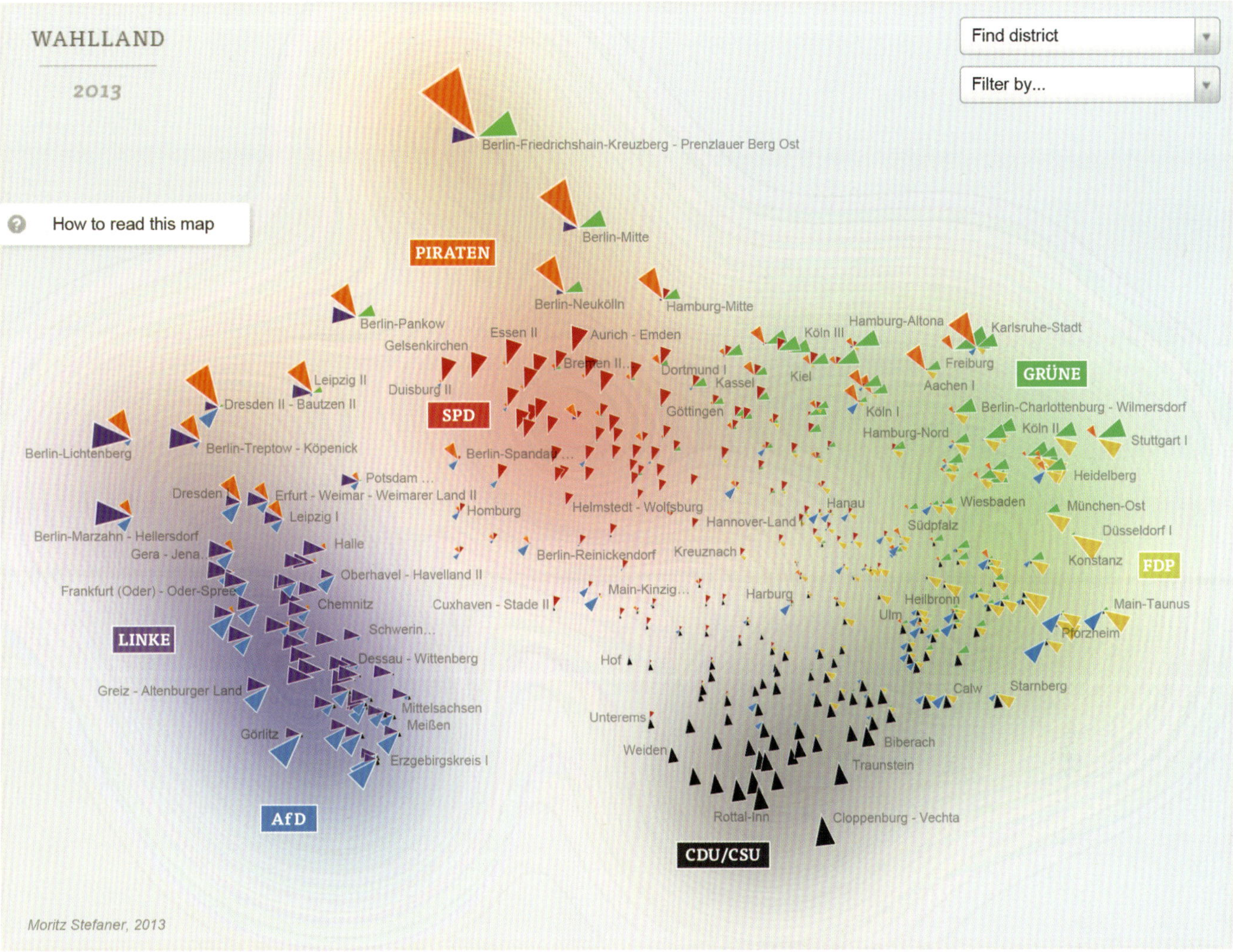

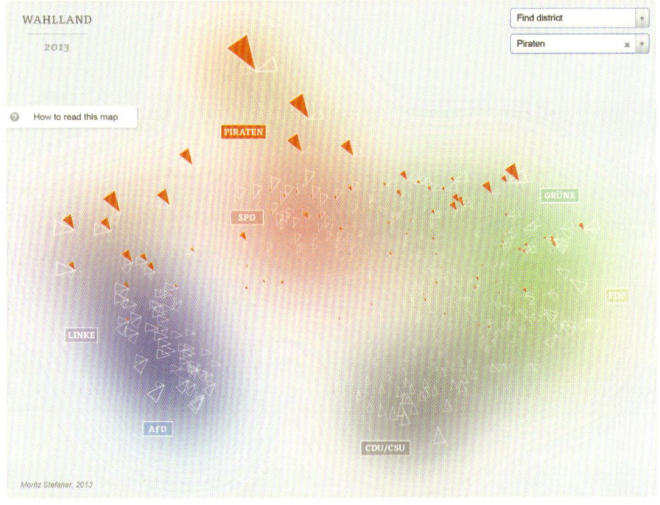
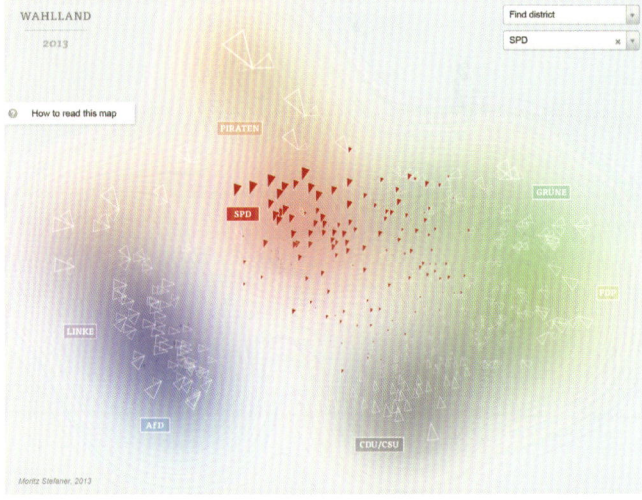

[4–7] Wahlland

Credit: Moritz Stefaner
Completion: 2013

Wahlland (Electionland) presents a whole new kind of election map for the German Bundestag elections 2013. Instead of showing the electoral districts' results on a geographic map, or in a table, we are charting a new land—Electionland—where all the districts that vote in a similar way are also located nearby. This new kind of map allows us to see Germany grouped by lifestyles, preferences, and attitudes. The triangles indicate results above the average for a specific party in a district. The colors represent the parties, whereas the size represents the relative difference to the average result of that party overall. A few smaller parties were combined into groups.

To sum up, my main advice is to use data as early as possible in the process, take it seriously and not just treat it as a vehicle for your ideas. Accordingly, it is a good idea to plan with a long data and concept exploration phase, and to accept that data visualization projects are just a bit non-linear, unlike the production of a brochure or a simple website.

[Q] **What is your suggestion for beginners?**

[A] If you want to produce information visualizations, you need to be able to work with the data directly. So you should learn about statistics and programming. Of course, you should also look into the arts, graphic design history, and visual language. If you master all those, then nothing can go wrong. I would recommend to get used to producing 10 to 20 different solutions to each challenge, and to draw many sketches for any project. You need to be honest about which ones work and which ones don't. Don't be afraid to fail. Sometimes you'll have a good hunch in the beginning, but more often you will need to look at many different variations of how to present the data using the right graphic form. That's the other crucial component to being successful in this business: you need to design a lot to become a good designer.

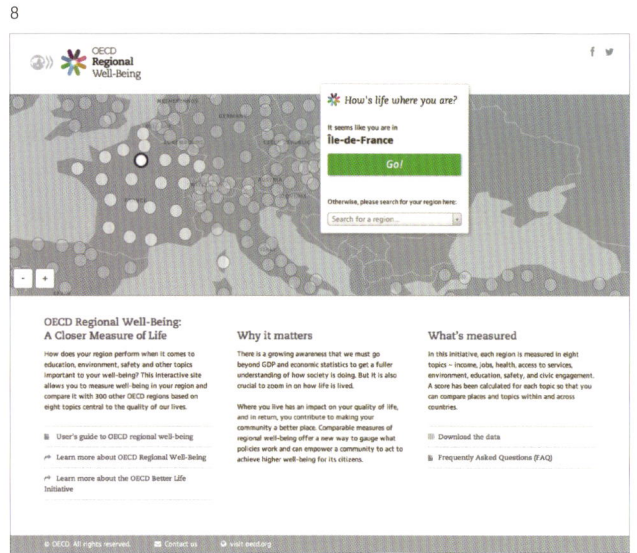

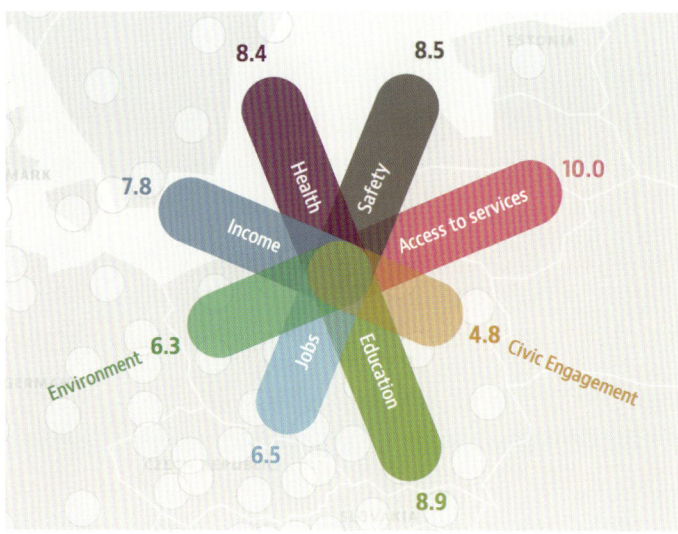

[8–11] OECD Regional Well-being

Credits: Moritz Stefaner, Dominikus Baur
Completion: 2014
Interactive link:
www.oecdregionalwellbeing.org/DE4.html

The site presents an exciting new perspective on more than 300 regions worldwide. As we all know, conditions inside a country can differ quite drastically, so going beyond the country averages presents an important step in the Better Life Initiative.

The user experience of the site is very consciously centered on the comparison of single regions in their context. Instead of presenting complex overviews, we start the experience with what people know best—their own home region. How does it compare to other regions in their country? And across all OECD regions? How have things developed over time?

The key visual elements, the multicolored star charts, represent the diversity of aspects we need to consider when talking about regional differences. Each region receives a unique symbol, representing its particular well-being profile. This design principle was pioneered in the famous flower design of the OECD Better Life Index, which was part of the same initiative.

Reflecting your own region in context provides a natural starting point for further explorations. One particular option we offer is the 'Regions with similar well-being' section, which suggests regions with similar indicator values all over the world. Who knew that Texas and Scotland are actually not that far apart when it comes to well-being (well, except for the Safety aspect)? Or that Berlin has a similar profile to Alsace?

From a design point of view, the main challenge has been to deal with the complexity and scale of the data set. With 10 indicators per region, most of which also have trend values, and 362 regions in the data set, the site provides access to more than 7000 data points. In designing the site, we made sure to introduce a hierarchy of information that presents the most important values at a glance, but at the same always provides the context to a single data point that makes it meaningful, and reveals deeper information.

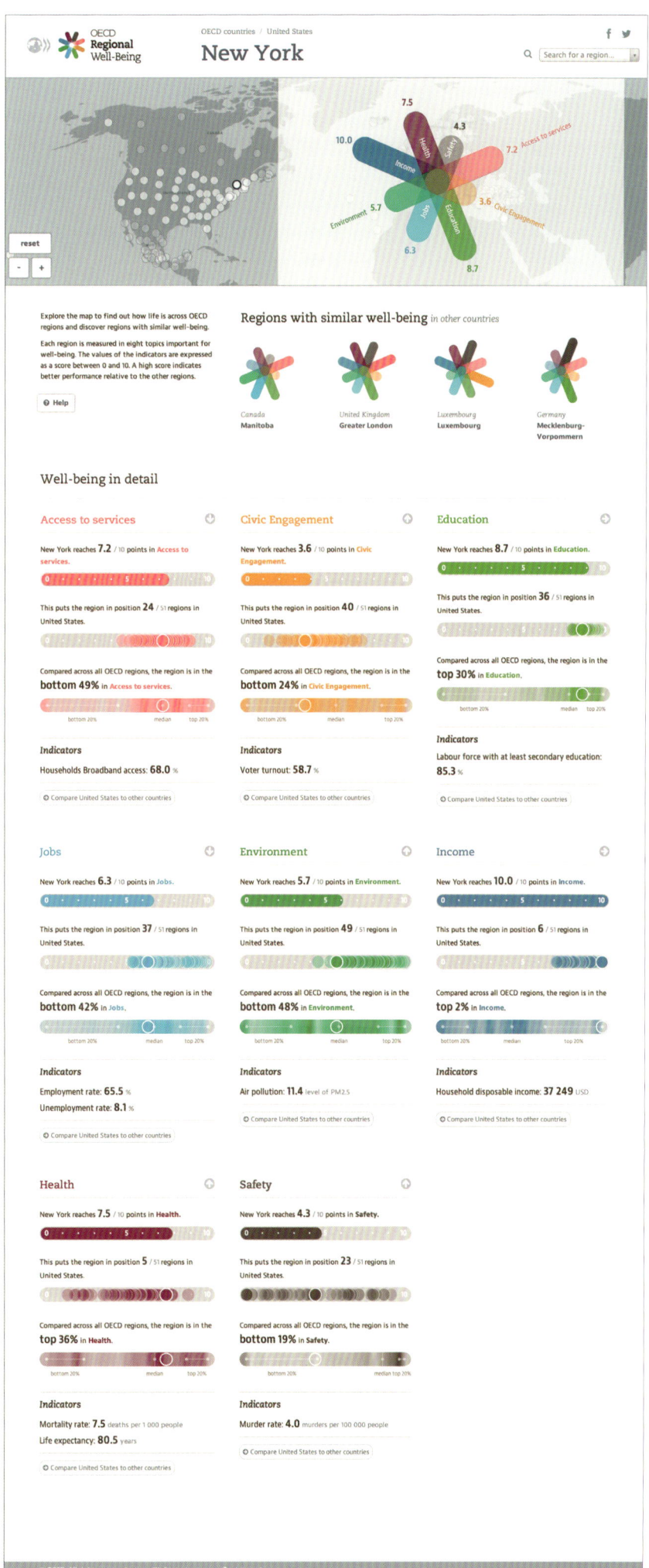

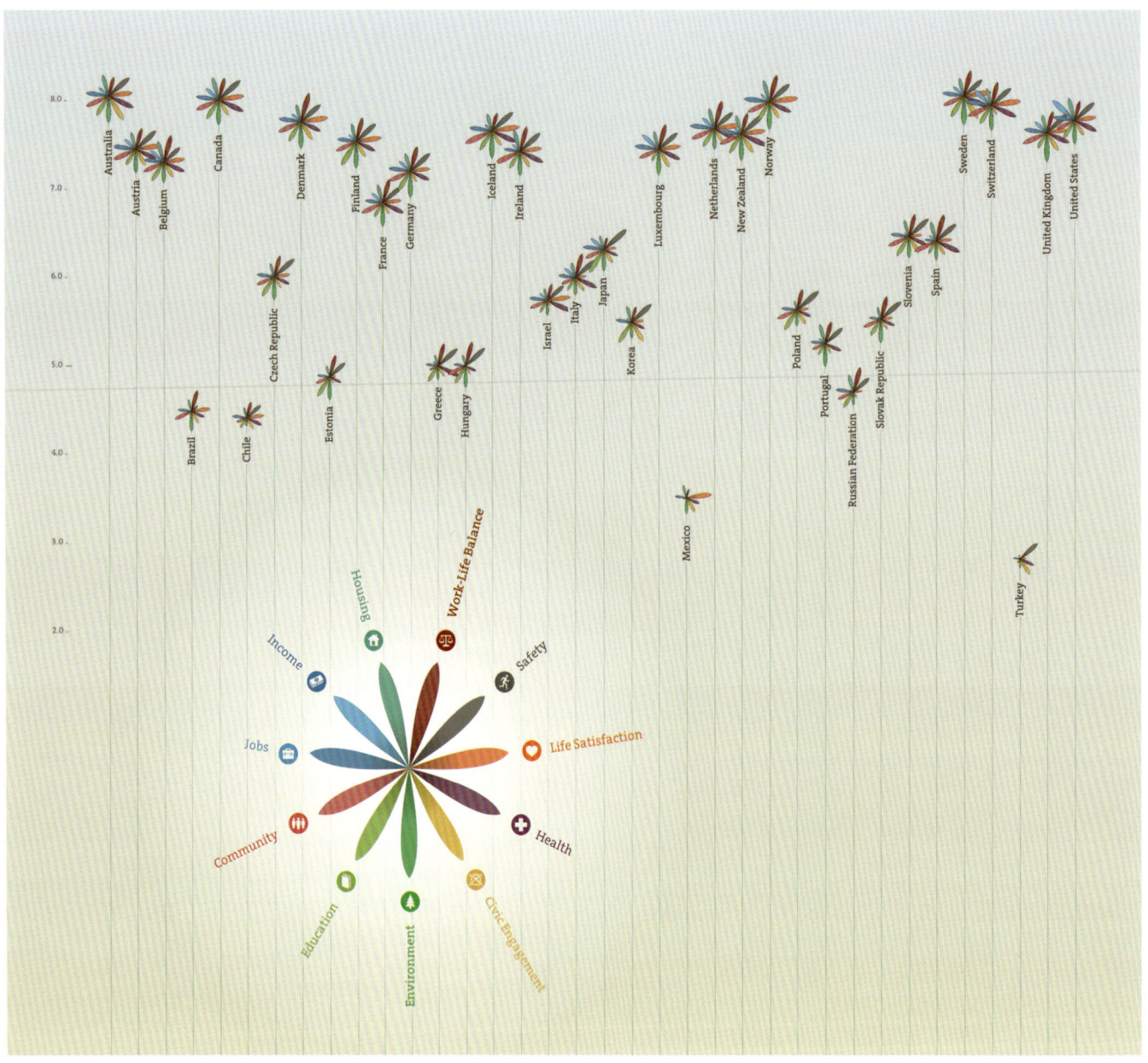

[12–16] OECD Better Life Index

Credits: Moritz Stefaner, Raureif GmbH
Completion: 2016
Interactive link: www.oecdbetterlifeindex.org/#/31211111111

The OECD provides a forum in which governments can work together to share experiences and seek solutions to improve the economic and social well-being of people around the world. Together with the agency Raureif, Moritz Stefaner worked on an interactive application called 'Your Better Life Index'. It is designed to let the user visualize and compare some of the key factors, such as education, housing, and environment, that contribute to well-being in OECD countries. But instead of presenting one authoritative country ranking, users can set their own priorities in a playful environment.

'We chose a natural metaphor to represent the different countries: each nation is represented by one flower, and each of its petals stands for one of the available topics. When the user makes, for instance, education more important, the education petals will become wider, and thus more visible. At the same time, countries with a good education score will rise more to the top, and "grow stronger". Our goal was to make these quite dry statistics immediately experienceable and encourage a playful experience of quite abstract numbers.'

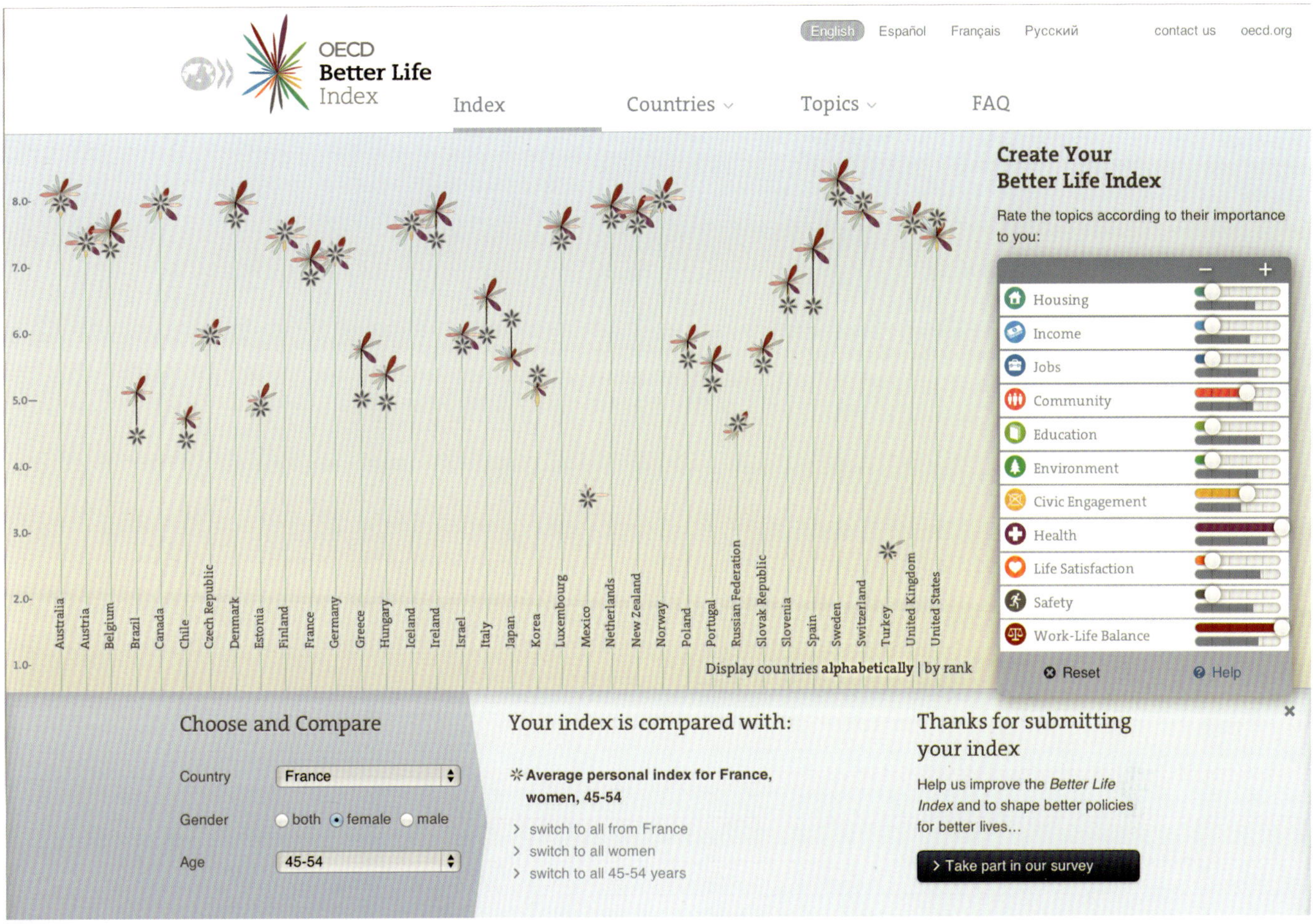

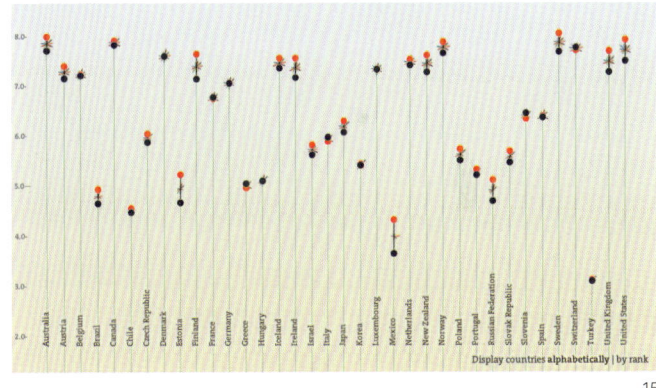

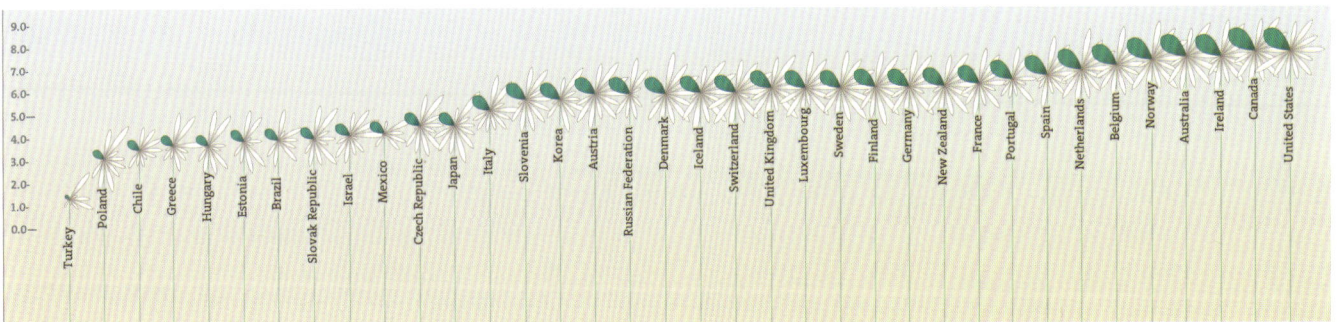

[17–21] Selfiecity

Credits: Lev Manovich, Moritz Stefaner, Dominikus Baur, Daniel Goddemeyer et al
Completion: 2014
Interactive link: www.selfiecity.net

Selfiecity investigates how people photograph themselves with mobile phones in five cities around the world. The project analyzes 3200 Instagram selfies shared in New York, Moscow, Berlin, Bangkok, and Sao Paulo (640 from each city).

Selfies were already the subject of many discussions in popular media. However, if we simply scan images tagged as selfies on Instagram, or observe people around us taking self-portraits, it's hard to quantify patterns, or systematically compare selfies from multiple cities taken by people who differ in age and gender. Are all selfies taken by young people? Do men take many selfies? Are we all trying to copy celebrities in choosing how we represent ourselves? Are there any significant differences between selfies shared in New York and Moscow, or Berlin and Bangkok? Selfiecity is the first project that investigates such questions systematically, using a carefully assembled large sample of selfies and tools of statistics, data, and data visualization.

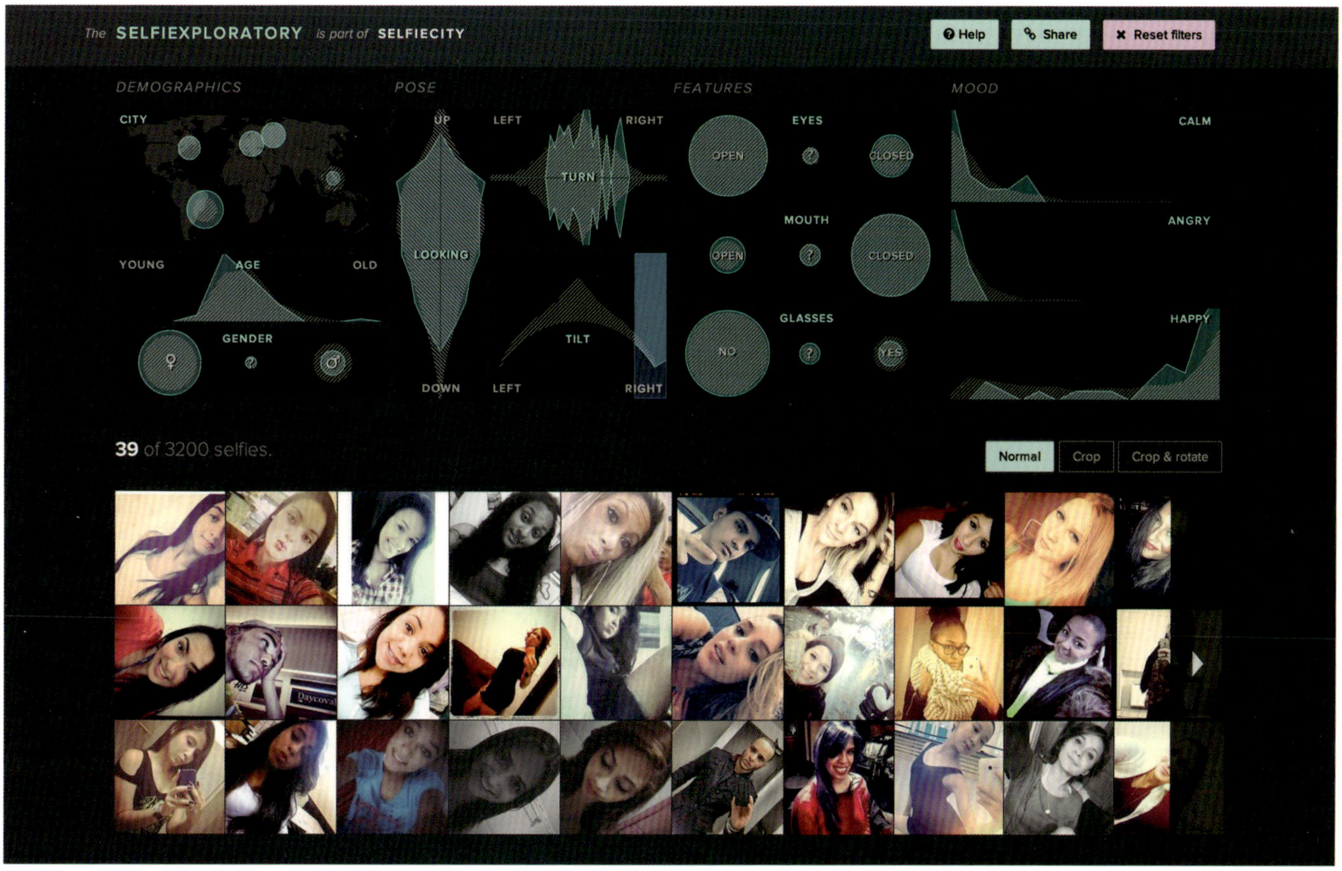

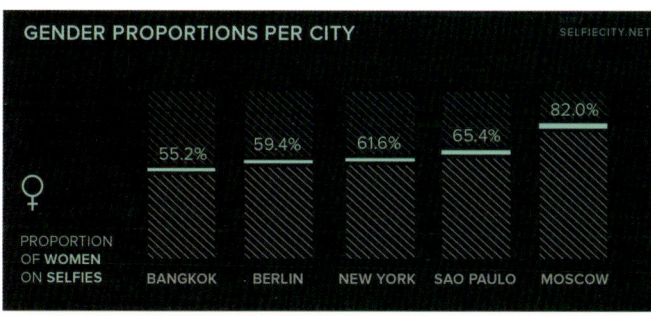

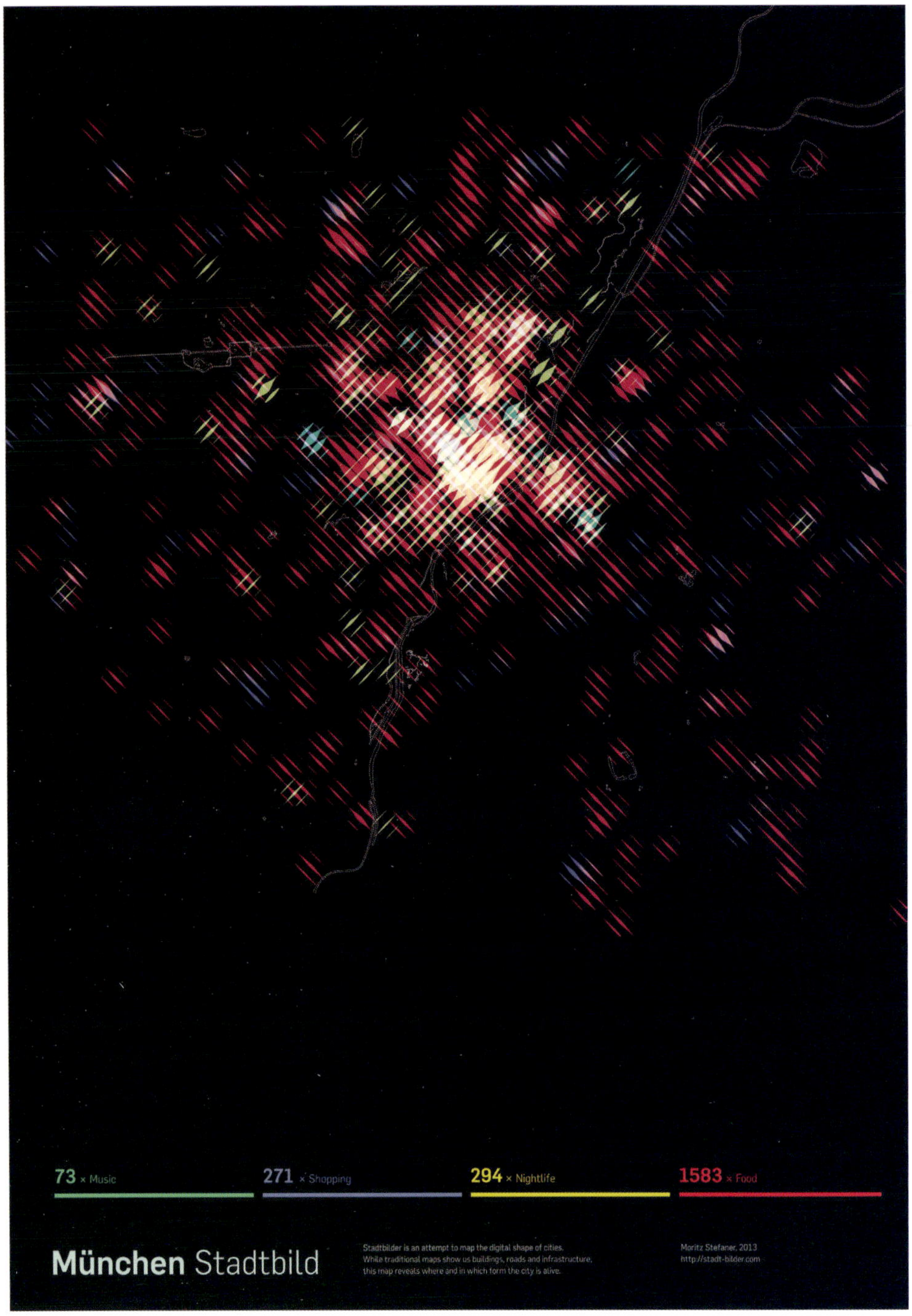

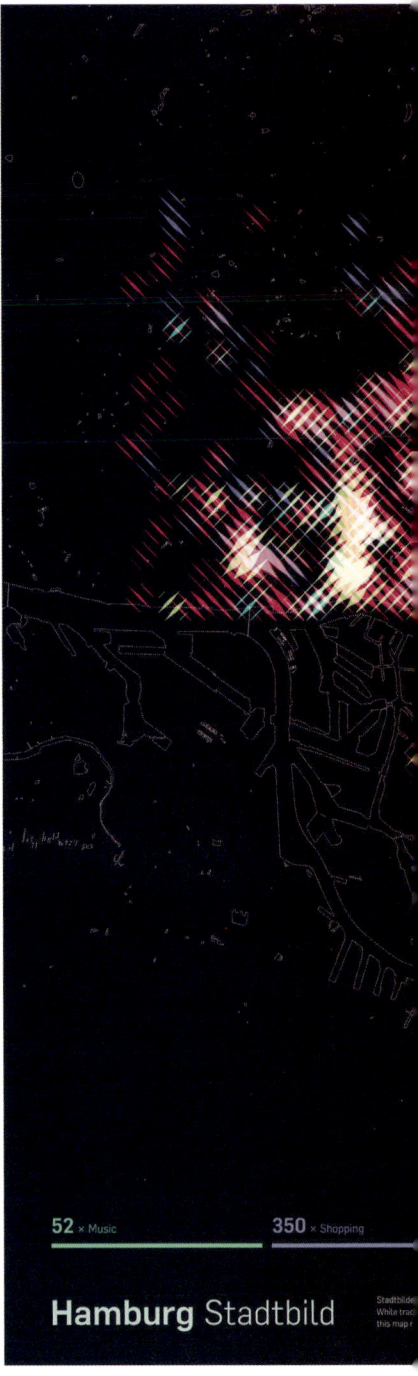

[22–24] Stadtbilder

Credit: Moritz Stefaner
Completion: 2013
Interactive link: www.stadt-bilder.com/#Hamburg

Stadtbilder is an attempt to map the digital shape of cities. While traditional maps show us buildings, roads, and physical infrastructure, these maps reveal where and in which form the city is alive. The maps show an overlay of all the digitally marked 'hot spots' in a city, such as restaurants, hotels, and clubs, collected from different online services. What they don't show are the streets, the railroads, and the buildings. The only exception is the rivers and lakes, for they help to frame the information for the viewer and also influence the shaping of the cities.

Berlin Stadtbild

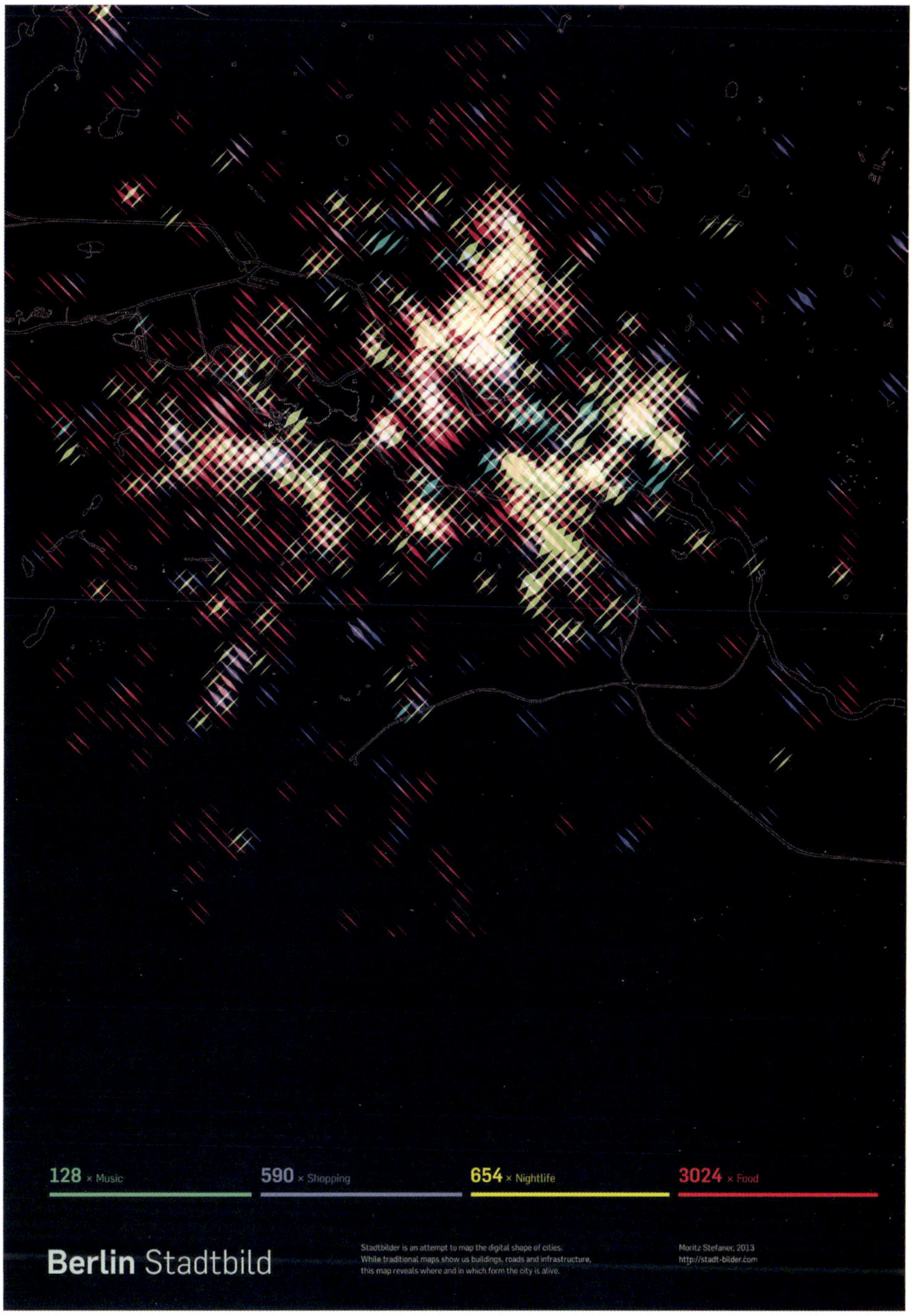

| 128 × Music | 590 × Shopping | 654 × Nightlife | 3024 × Food |

Stadtbilder is an attempt to map the digital shape of cities. While traditional maps show us buildings, roads and infrastructure, this map reveals where and in which form the city is alive.

Moritz Stefaner, 2013
http://stadt-bilder.com

Duncan Swain

Duncan Swain is co-founder and creative director of Beyond Words Studio, which is a studio that produces data visualization across any platform, including digital, physical, print, film, and motion graphics. He also co-founded Information is Beautiful Studio before starting Beyond Words and, prior to that, was creative and editorial director at the BBC.

[Q] **What do you think about data visualization/infographics?**

[A] I think visualization is entering a new era and it's our job to explore data and how it's manifested in different, more engaging, and ambitious ways. There are untold stories buried in myriad data sources still waiting to be discovered, unraveled, and put into a form people can understand, and we want to be a key part of how that's achieved.

[Q] **What kind of design methods do you commonly use?**

[A] We have a specific process to follow at Beyond Words and our starting point is to always ask, 'What's the story?' This more editorial phase of our process is super-important. This also kicks off the research phase where we're either using the data we have or, more often, on the hunt for supplementary data sets to shine a different light on our story and provide more context. From there, we move into sketching, then designing and finally coding or building if it's a non-print piece.

[Q] **What kind of design elements do you commonly use?**

[A] Selecting the right elements to display the data is initially one of the most difficult things to grasp. There are lots of rules and methodologies behind what is the right chart for the type of data you're trying to display. For us, it all comes down to whether or not we can understand the data via the device we've chosen. Our mantra is: 'You can't design what you don't understand', so that's the crucial first step—understand your data.

1

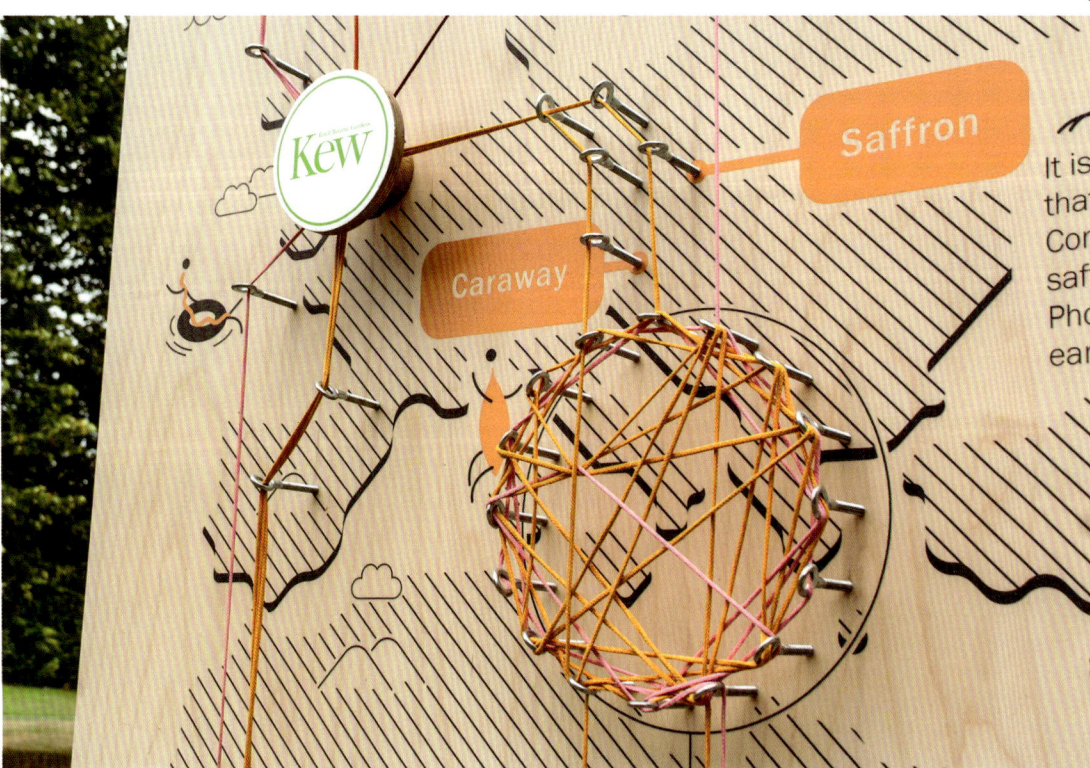

2

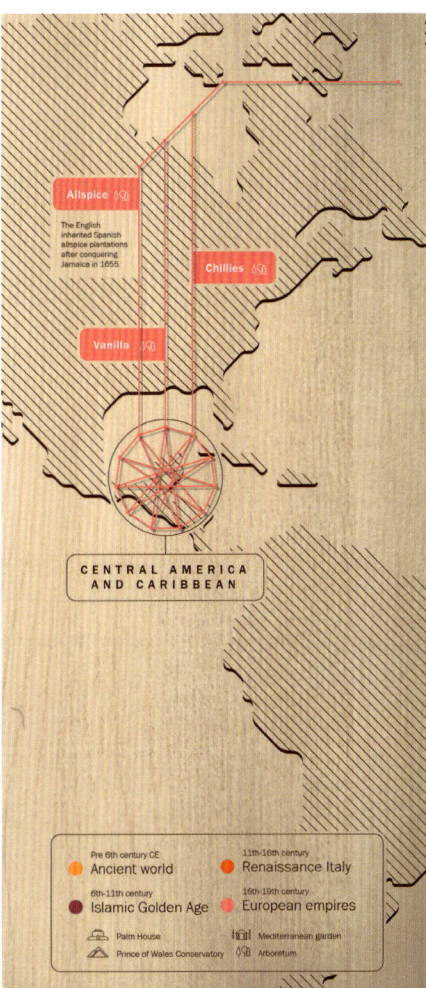
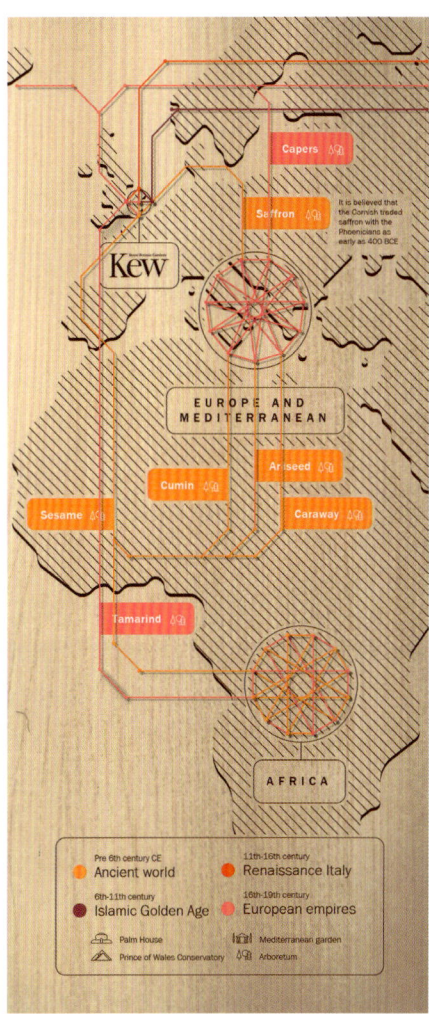

[1–3] Kew Gardens— Full of Spice

Credit: Beyond Words Studio
Completion: 2015

The Royal Botanic Gardens at Kew has the world's largest, most diverse collection of living plants. For summer 2015, the design agency created three physical data installations on the history, health benefits, and geography of spices for Kew's Full of Spice festival. They took a microscope to these mystical commodities to visualize the stories behind something that we all pretty much take for granted.

[Q] Where are your works applied?

[A] We work across every platform available. Most of our work lives in digital, and we work across all the usual platforms—web, tablet, mobile—with a lot of interactive pieces. Motion graphics and moving image-based visualizations are also a big part of our repertoire and we've done some static pieces for print, too. We also make physical data visualization installations and love crafting pieces that occupy space in the 'real' world and use more organic, tactile materials.

[Q] How do you turn boring and complex data into something interesting and understandable?

[A] By looking for the hook—what's in the data that will entice people into the piece we're creating. Our backgrounds in journalism help hugely with that because it's often the same challenge there: looking for a story and selling it in with a headline. And sometimes we're just trying to do something cool or beautiful, which can be enough to engage people, too.

[Q] What is your suggestion for beginners?

[A] To self-educate. Read and read and read. There's a lot of history of data visualization and a lot of theory and methodology too, but it's also an evolving and changing area. So you need to be part of what's going on now while also acknowledging what's gone before.

4

[4–5] Sweet Tweets

Credit: Beyond Words Studio
Completion: 2014

With Sweet Tweets, the designers wanted to literally show spikes in Twitter traffic over time so people could easily spot where the highs and lows occurred. Using a radial column chart was a really good way of doing that. Peaks are easy to spot and using a circular motif brings to mind a clock, which suits data about events happening over a certain time period.

Some tweets made during the broadcast of the *Great British Bake Off*, a massively popular show in the UK, were disregarded. They scrapped tweets that mentioned particular hashtags such as contestants' names, and just monitored Twitter activity to see where the general public got excited about particular things that happened during the broadcast.

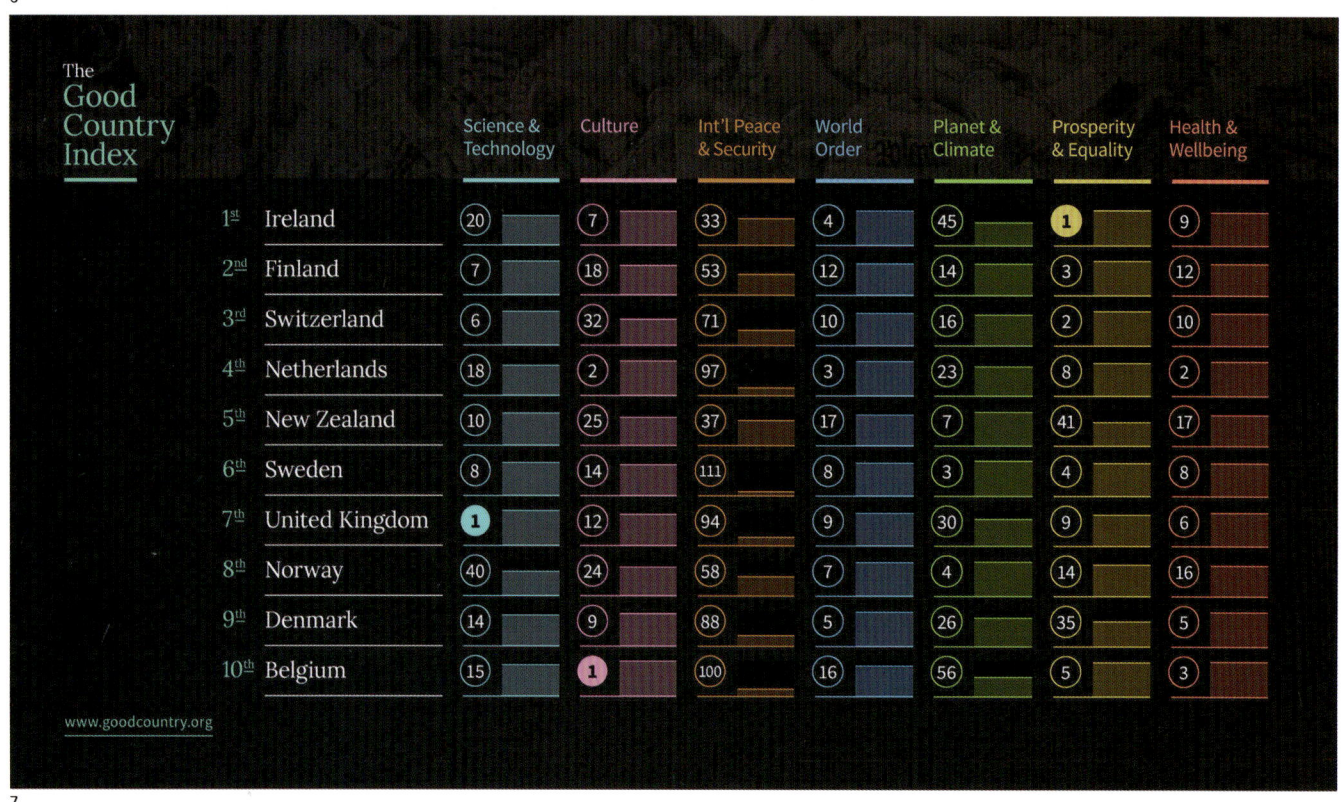

[6–10] Good Country Index

Credit: Beyond Words Studio
Completion: 2014

The idea of the project is simple to describe but complex to visualize. It measures each country's contribution to the common good and what it takes away, relative to its size. The designers had to portray a range of data, giving each country a balance sheet showing at a glance whether it's a net creditor to humankind, a burden, or something in between. It was a gratifying and heart-warming labor of love to build something that achieved these rather lofty goals.

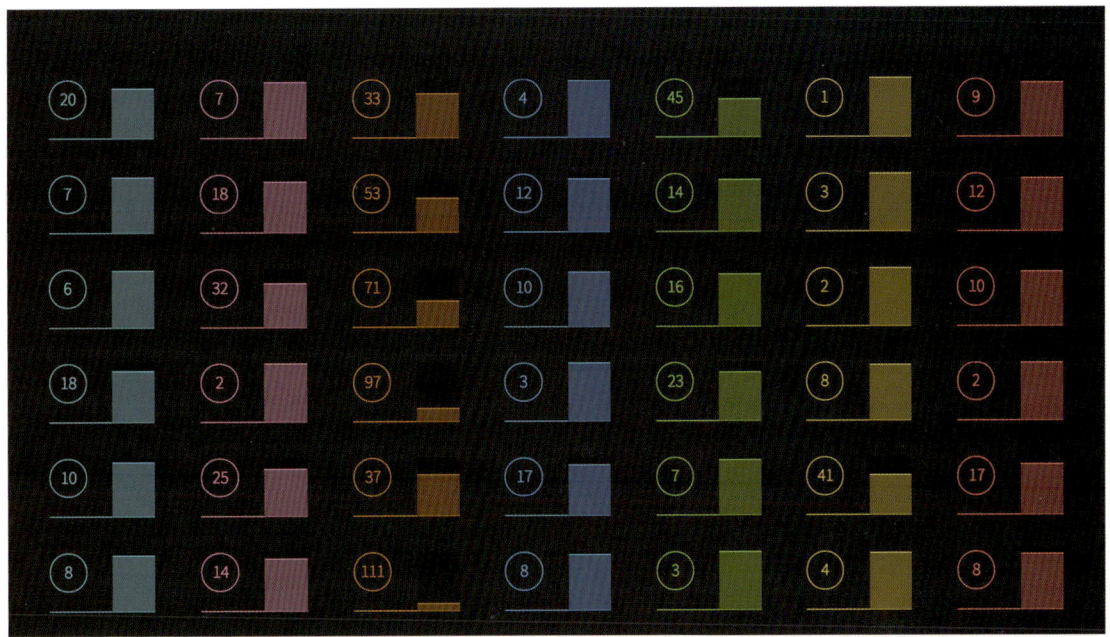

The Design Surgery

The Surgery

The Design Surgery is a creative agency based in London. They have had a hand in many areas of the creative industry from interior design through to large-scale event management. More recently, the focus has been in three key areas: editorial design, brand management, and data visualization.

[Q] What do you think about data visualization/infographicss?

[A] We work to ensure that our infographics and data visualizations are cutting edge and designed to connect with the audience. We look at how raw data can be turned into striking, easy-to-understand visual stories.

[Q] What kind of design methods do you commonly use?

[A] Before we start creating an infographic, we first of all establish the message or the story that needs to be told through the data. We research markets, products, and customer journeys to ensure that the infographic will connect with the intended audience. Then we analyze the data and look for patterns that will lead to a better understanding of the product and put it into a context that the reader can clearly understand.

It is important to simplify complex information, helping to reveal the hidden connections, patterns, and stories underneath. We visualize the data with a minimal words to create maximum impact. When all this is done, we then make recommendations on the creative look including design, color, style, and the implementation of any brand guidelines.

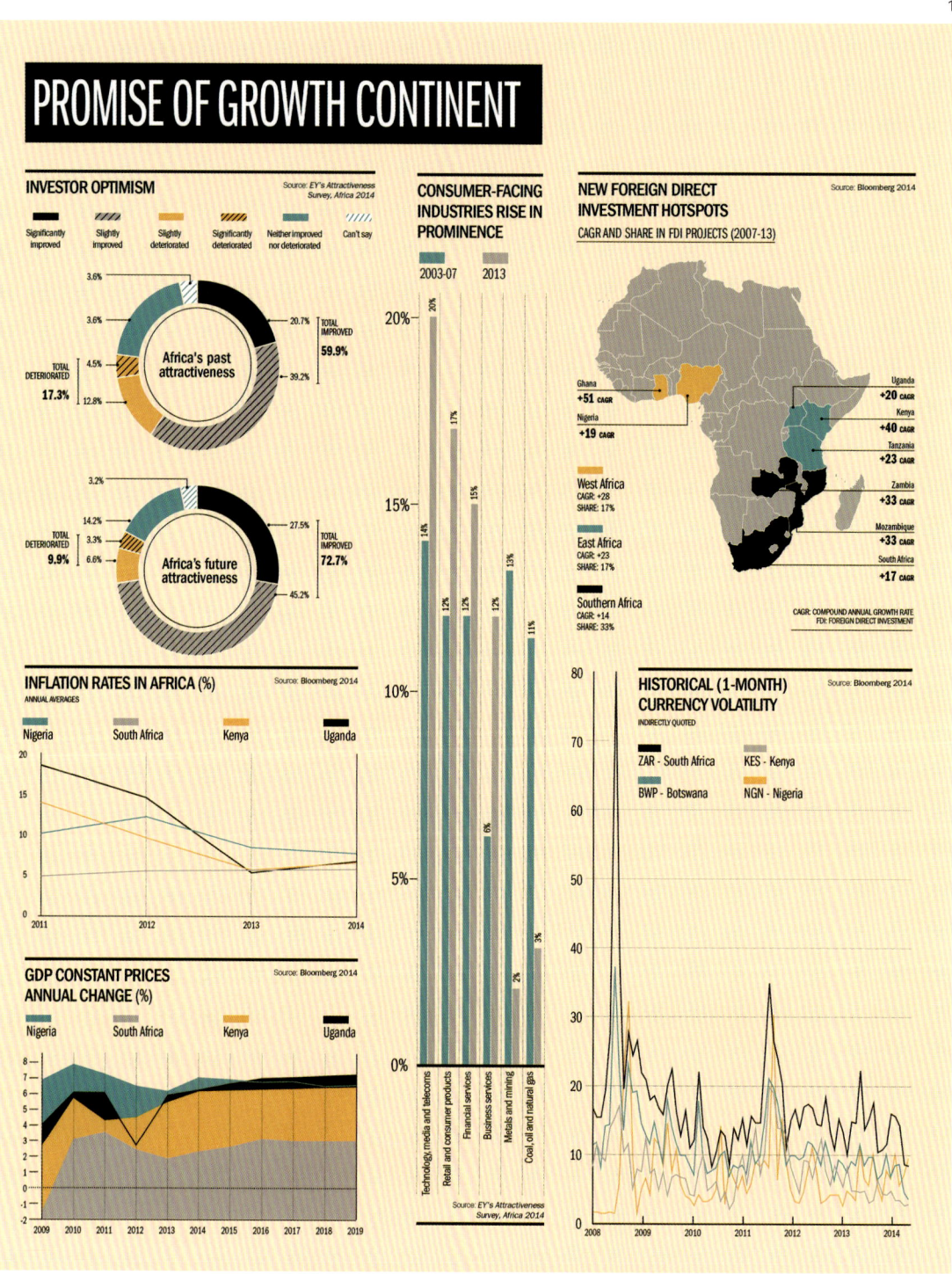

[Q] What kind of design elements do you commonly use?

[A] Graphs and charts are a key component of data visualization, however, we also like to use icons and illustrations to add visual interest in cases where the data is not necessarily comparable.

[Q] Where are your works applied?

[A] We develop creative works for print and online interactive and animated infographics. These infographics appear across numerous platforms, including newspapers, magazines, reports, apps, and across the web on countless devices.

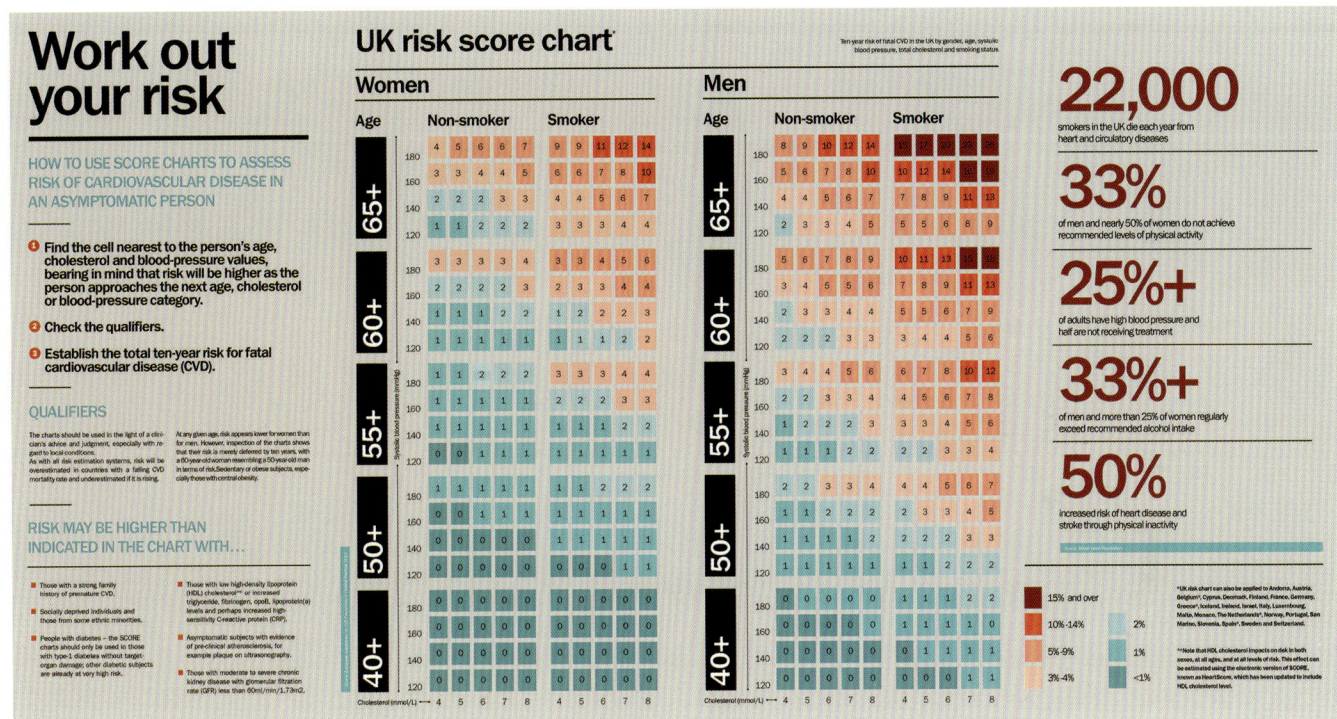

2

[1] Trading Strategies

Credit: The Design Surgery
Completion: 2014

This broadsheet infographic describes recent trends in Africa's investment growth. The Design Surgery used a variety of visualization methods to break down complex trading data and to highlight emerging trends. It was vital that trends and spikes in trade and currency were able to be accessed quickly and interpreted easily by the reader.

[2] Cardiovascular Health

Credit: The Design Surgery
Completion: 2014

This infographic dashboard was designed to assist readers to assess their risk of cardiovascular disease. Through the use of colors and an easily digestible chart, users are able to measure up their risk of the disease against a variety of factors including age and smoking status. Key statistics are used alongside the main feature for added context and interest.

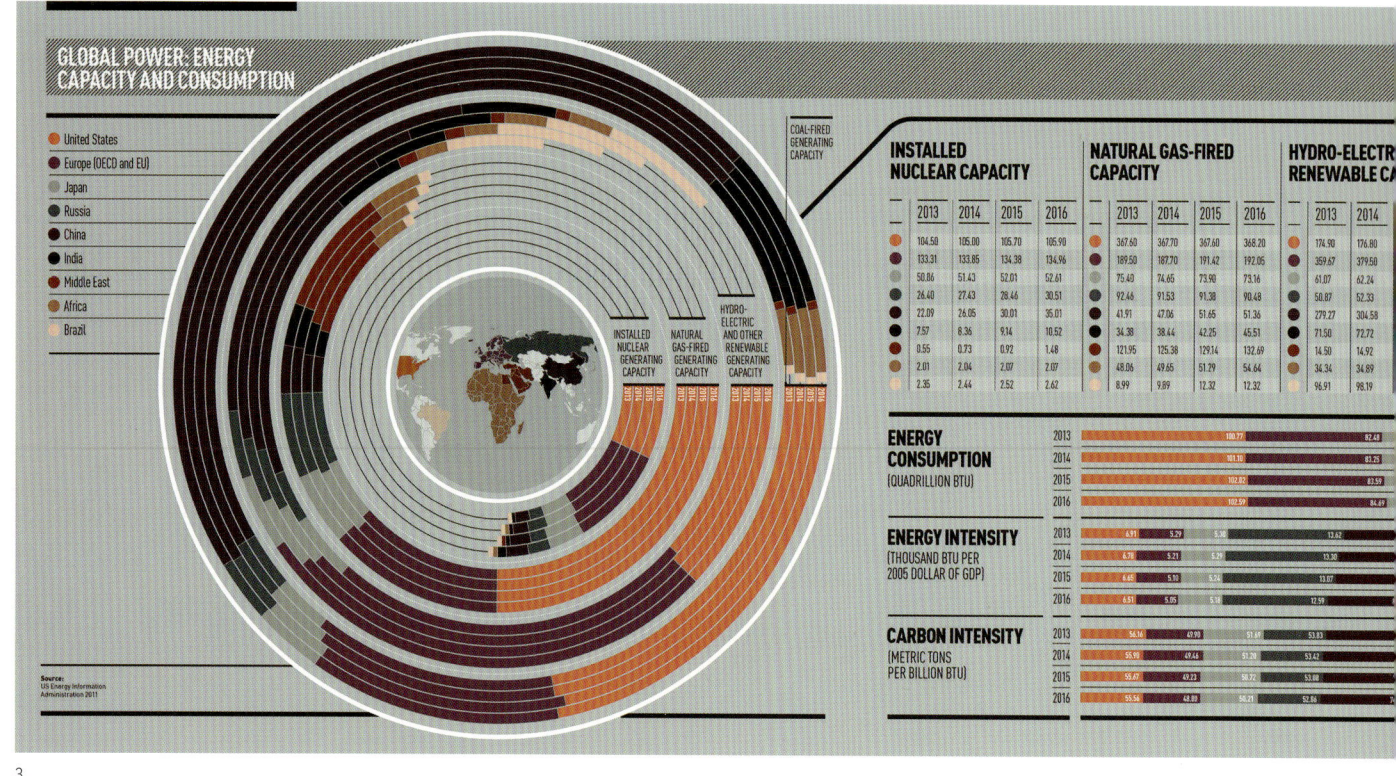

[3] Powering the Future

Credit: The Design Surgery
Completion: 2014

The data visualization piece analyzes the growth paths of developing countries and their energy consumption. To make the complex information more accessible to a reader, The Design Surgery condensed and visualized the data set into a striking infographic centerpiece. Data was divided across various categories and used in conjunction with a map to create an easily analyzed reference.

[4] Business Outsourcing

Credit: The Design Surgery
Completion: 2014

This infographic dashboard illustrates the trends in the European outsourcing market. By using a bold and complementary color palette, The Design Surgery brought simple data sets to life, making them easily comparable by size and proportion. The dashboard provides a concise, yet visually compelling, snapshot into business and outsourcing trends.

[Q] How do you turn boring and complex data into something interesting and understandable?

[A] By understanding the key trends and stories within complex data sets, we ensure that the information is used to its full potential. By applying a narrative, any data set can be transformed into a piece that is engaging and visually stunning.

[Q] What is your suggestion for beginners?

[A] A key piece of advice is to always make sure that you understand the intended audience for the infographic and be clear on what story needs to be told through the visualization.

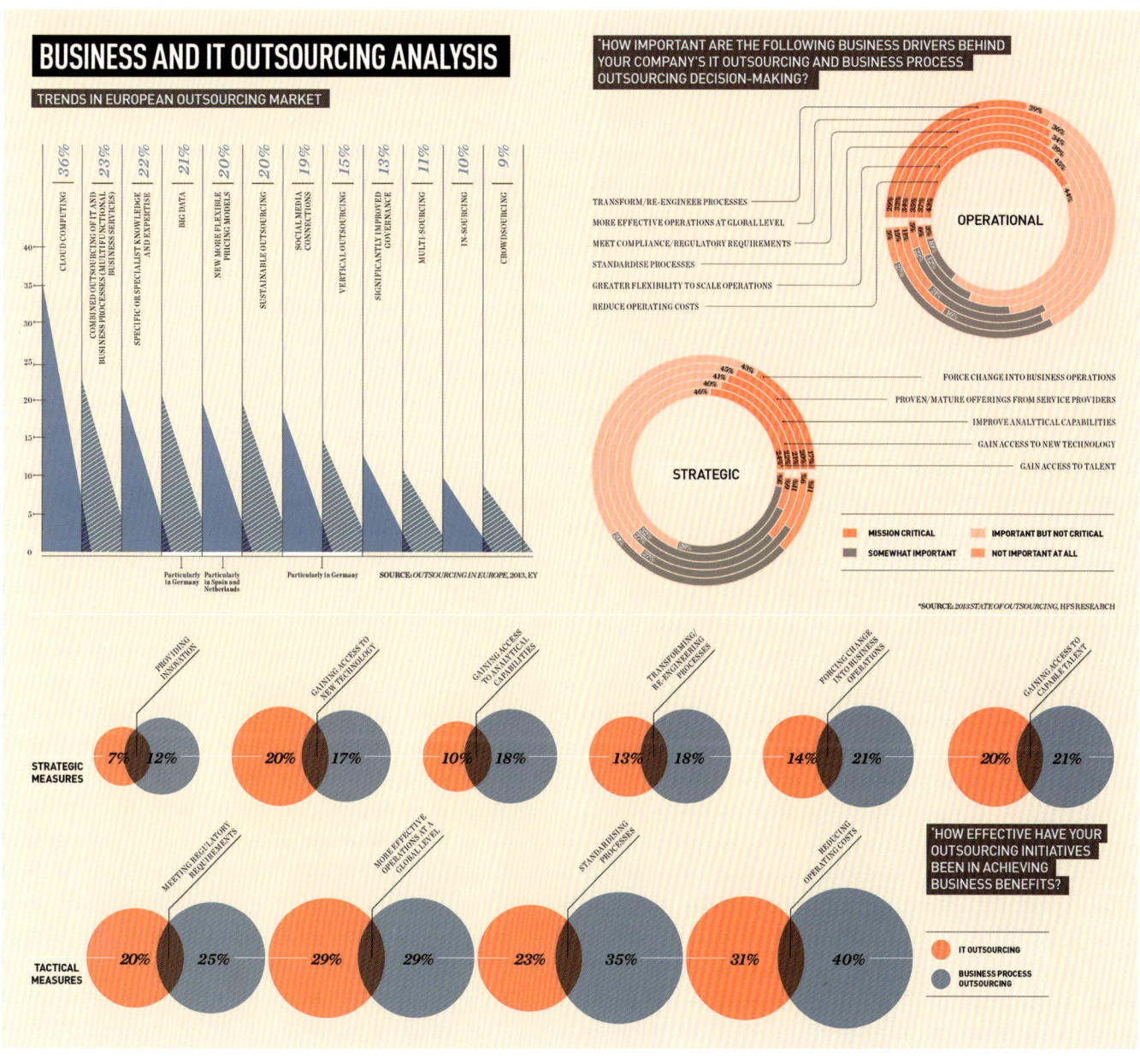

Roxana Torre

Roxana Torre is an independent media designer specializing in interactive data visualization. Her work consists of transforming data into a visual representation that can be easily understood and explored by users. The result varies from simple, interactive maps or charts to more complex web applications showing different aspects of the data. Clients include governmental, non-governmental, and educational organizations as well as commercial companies in Europe and the US.

[Q] What do you think about data visualization/infographics?

[A] I see data visualization as a way of 'giving life' to data, transforming it into information—something that people are able to understand.

[Q] What kind of design methods do you commonly use?

[A] The starting point of a project is always data and a bunch of ideas related to how to turn the data into something visual and interactive. I always start my projects by experimenting with the data, so it's essential to have a real (or very close to real) data set before starting instead of dummy data. I explore the data in different ways using basic tools and programming simple charts, and based on this I make sketches on paper until I find something that is worth being used for further development.

When working for clients, there's mostly a concrete need to show specific aspects of the data depending on the purpose of the visualization and who the target audience is. Other projects are more open, so during the exploration phase I try to find out which insights of the data are interesting to be shown. The process in both cases is always iterative because while exploring different ways of showing the data, new characteristics or peculiarities are found, which might mostly result in reconsidering the approach and the way the data is represented. During these iterations various people will take a look and review the intermediate results, this works as a quality control during the process.

[Q] What kind of design elements do you commonly use?

[A] I use a lot of geometrical shapes like circles or squares and when possible I create icons to reflect different aspects of the data. I also use standard charts when that's the best solution (possibly with a little twist).

[Q] Where are your works applied?

[A] All my projects are interactive, so they will be shown on a screen, mostly on websites.

[Q] How do you turn boring and complex data into something interesting and understandable?

[A] To make data understandable, I present different aspects of the data graphically in different views. The idea is mostly that at first view the user will get a global overview of the data, and while exploring the interface (for instance, by filtering or sorting), the user will get further insights into the data. Adding playful features always helps to make the exploration experience more engaging, and it's essential to provide all visualizations with enough textual explanation and a legend.

1

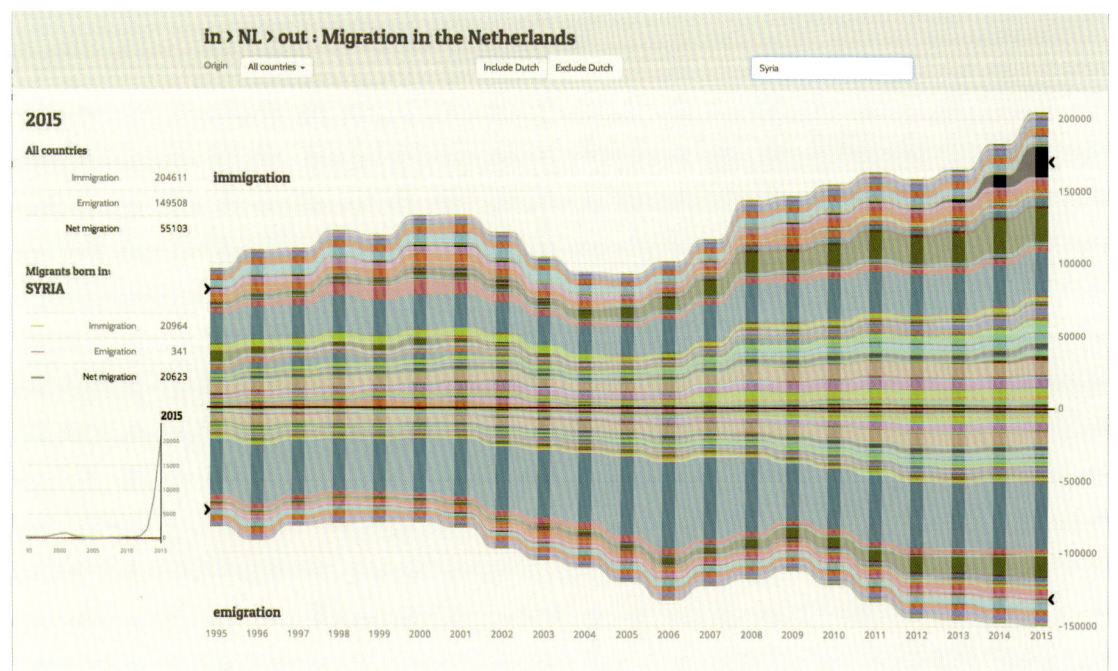

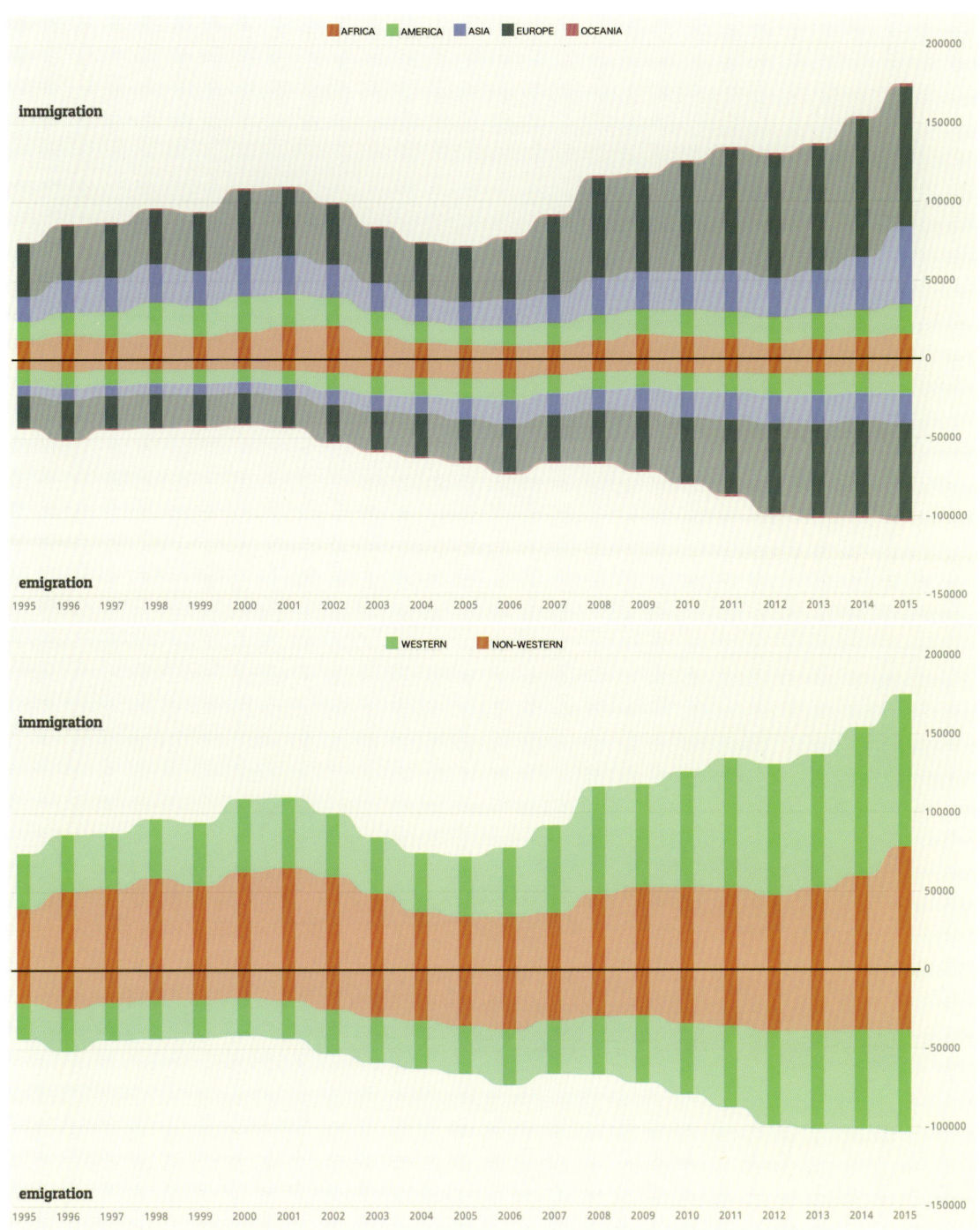

[1–2] Migration in the Netherlands

Credit: Roxana Torre
Completion: 2016
Interactive link: www.torre.nl/nlmigration

This interactive chart shows migration in the Netherlands between 1995 and 2015 based on migrants' country of birth. It's divided into two parts: the positive vertical axis shows immigration while the negative axis shows emigration. Each colored layer represents a different country of birth, ordered alphabetically. When hovering over these layers, more information about the migration from the chosen country becomes visible.

It's easy to see that each year, apart from immigration, there's a substantial number of emigrants. Some of these emigrants are probably people that are going back to their own countries, but there's also a large number of Dutch people settling abroad. Between 2003 and 2007, net migration has been negative, which means there were more emigrants than immigrants.

It's always a great challenge to find a good balance between complexity and understandability. When you have been working for a while on a project, sometimes you need to take a bit of distance and check with other users to see if what you are doing still makes sense to them. Furthermore, when talking about complexity, it's necessary to concentrate on a target audience while designing the interface and the visualizations. Some projects are meant to be seen by a broader audience, so you will need to keep the visualization simple enough. Other times when you are working on a complex subject for a more specialized audience, you might expect the user to make an effort to understand the visualization (and the subject). You cannot always reduce all data to one or more simple charts.

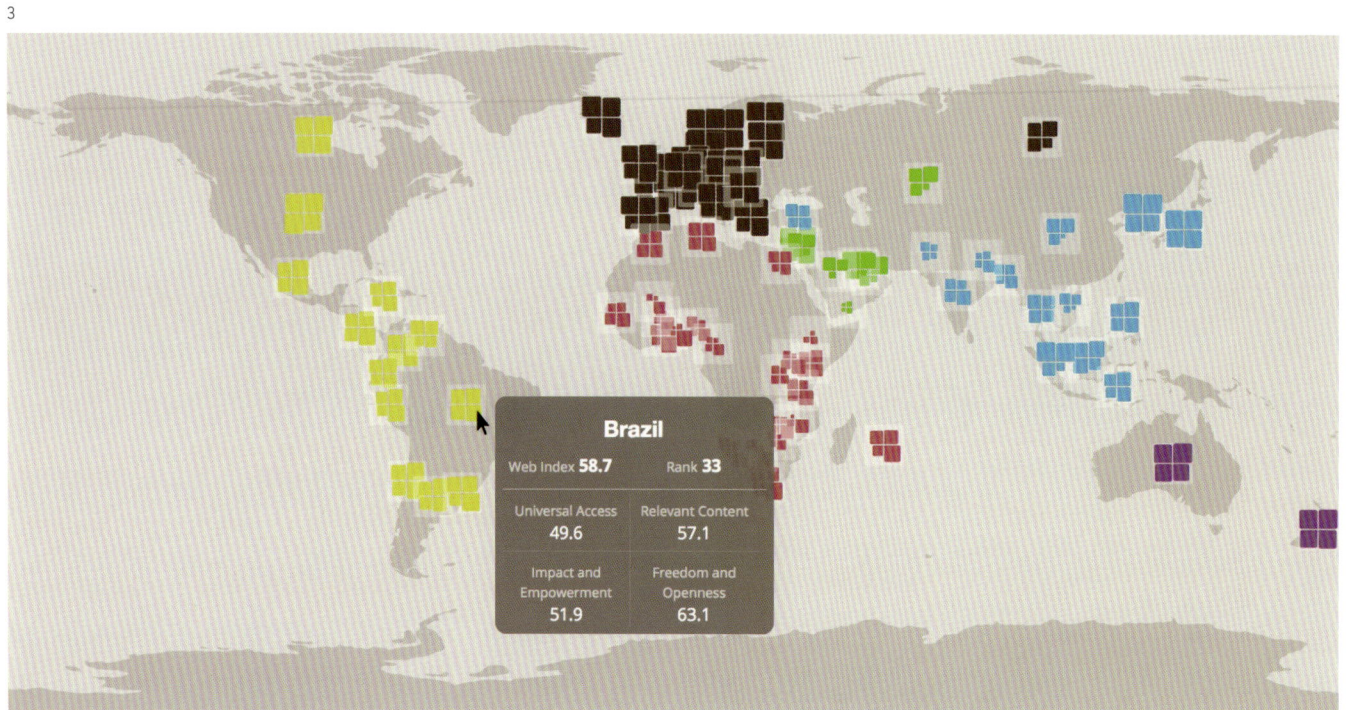

[Q] **What is your suggestion for beginners?**

[A] Like most of us did, I would suggest starting your own projects: think of an interesting subject, find the data, and create something. One important piece of advice is that sooner or later you will have to learn a programming language because while you will be able to make some progress using existing tools, at some point you will hit the limitations. There's enough learning material online to get into the subject depending on what your interests are.

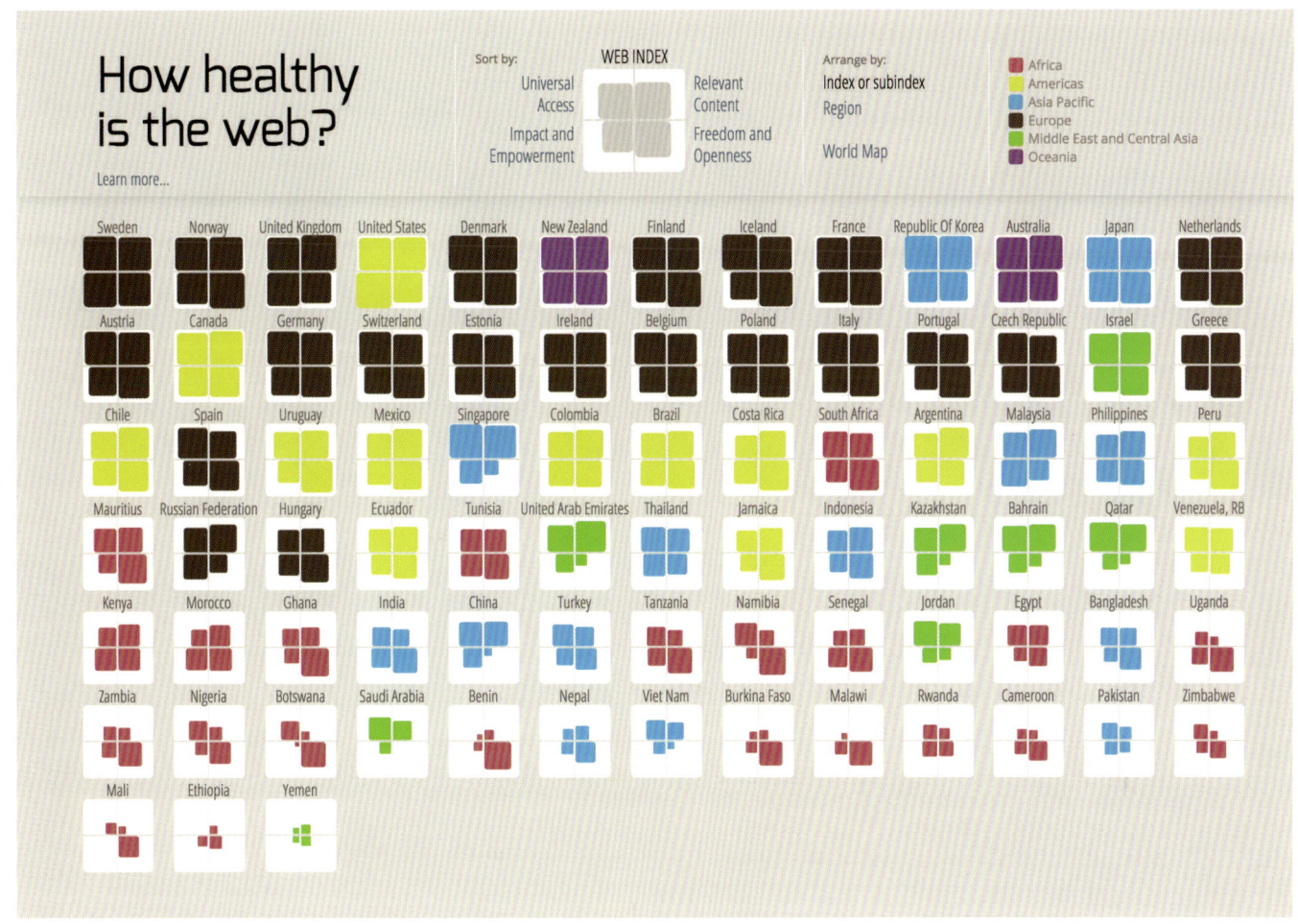

[3–5] How Healthy Is the Web

Credit: Roxana Torre
Completion: 2014
Interactive link: www.torre.nl/webindex

The web index is a measure of the web's growth, utility, and impact around the world. It has been designed and produced by the World Wide Web Foundation. This is an interactive visualization that allows exploration of the different components of the web index in different countries. Each country is represented by an icon divided into four squares, each of which gives a measure of the following subindexes: universal access, relevant content, freedom and openness, and impact and empowerment. It's possible to sort the countries according to each of these components and the interface allows for displaying the icons on a geographical layout.

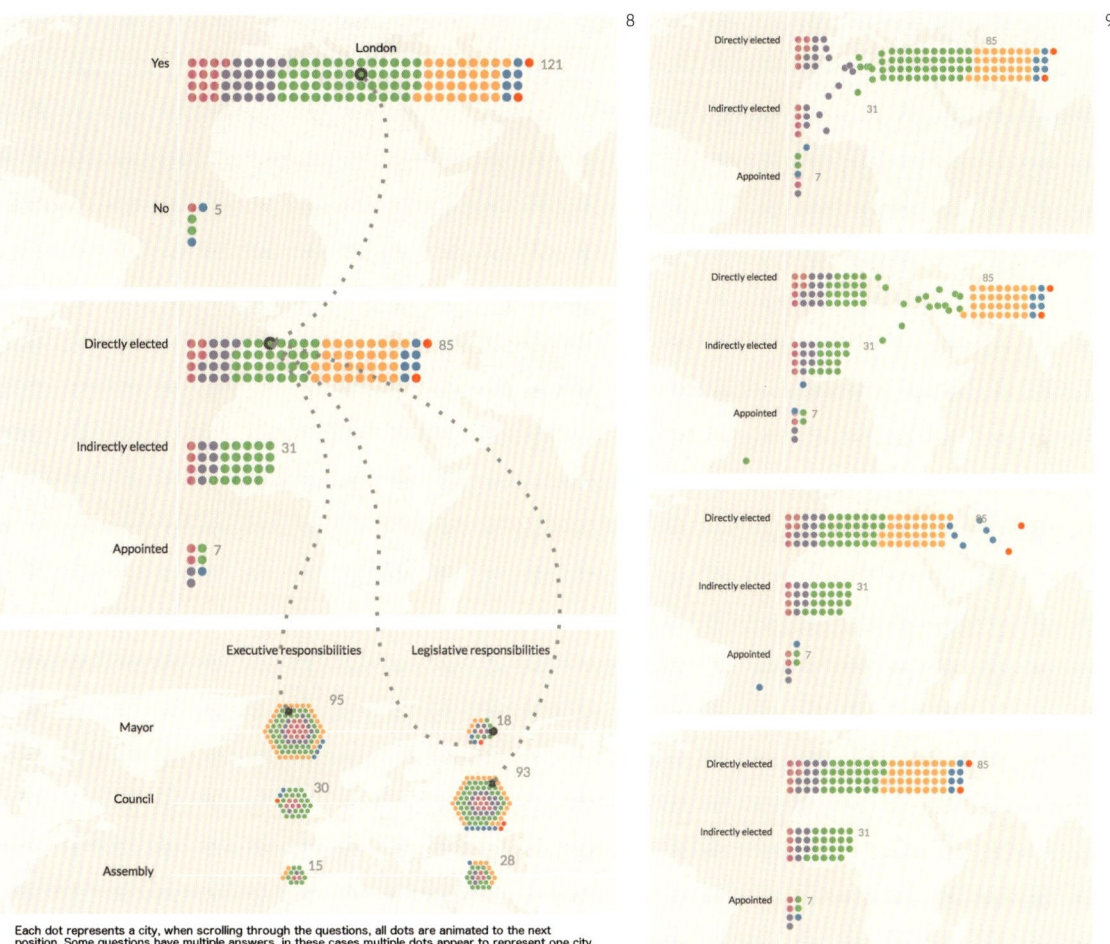

[6–9] How Cities Are Governed

Credits: Roxana Torre (data visualization design and development), Alex Starr (website design), Nuno Ferreira da Cruz (project coordinator), Enora Robin (researcher), Andrea Rota (development)
Completion: 2016
Interactive link: www.urbangovernance.net/en

This is an online platform for the first global Urban Governance Survey initiated by LSE Cities in partnership with UN-Habitat and UCLG.

The survey results are displayed in an interactive visualization where each colored dot represents a city. It's possible to scroll through the survey questions while the dots group together according to the given answers. This allows the user to see the total survey answers while at the same time it's possible to identify individual results of a city.

The dots can be colored according to world region, population, or city wealth. When selecting a city, additional information is displayed, and it's possible to highlight multiple cities while viewing the results.

Jan Willem Tulp

Jan Willem Tulp is a data experience designer. With his company TULP interactive, he creates data visualizations that balance clear communication and aesthetics. He has created visualizations for organizations such as the European Space Agency, Nature, *Scientific American*, Nielsen, the World Economic Forum, and Unicef. His works have been published in several books and magazines, and he speaks regularly at international conferences.

[Q] What do you think about data visualization/infographics?

[A] Data visualization and infographics allow you to get an understanding of a data set that is otherwise hard to understand. As humans we are very good at understanding visual patterns and structures, so communicating insights in data visually is only natural to us. There are, however, many choices involved on the data, technical, conceptual and design levels. So, it does require some knowledge and skills to make the right decisions. In general, it is a very effective way of communicating insights from data, which can also be very engaging and a joyful experience.

[Q] What kind of design methods do you commonly use?

[A] I do have a process that is common for most projects—usually getting a sense of the data is a first requirement, just to understand the potential for a visualization. This is followed by design prototyping and exploration to find out what visual representation of the data works for that particular situation, context, goal, and audience. Finally, once the raw concept is established, it is turned into a production-ready visualization, where attention to detail is very important.

[Q] What kind of design elements do you commonly use?

[A] Basically, visualization is mapping from data to visual elements. This means that the visualization contains elements that are always data-driven. In that sense, you only have a few basic visual elements available, such as points, lines, and areas. The data then drives the various properties, such as position, size, length, or color. This already yields so many possible design choices and it requires some skills to make the choices to produce good results.

All of my work is always custom data visualization. This means that I write custom software that reads in a data set, and my software turns this into a visual representation. I do make use of technical libraries that contain functionalities to help me write my code more efficiently and effectively. But these are just small building blocks, and I am always very flexible in what I eventually make. My visualizations are always designed for a specific situation, a specific audience, and within a specific context. This means that I don't have a fixed set of graphs or shapes that I often use (though it may look like that in hindsight, perhaps), but instead I design a visualization for a specific situation.

For instance, for the Goldilocks project, my project brief was very open: create an interesting visualization for the space-themed opening night of the Visualized 2015 conference in New York. I then looked for an interesting data set, which was about exoplanets (planets outside our solar system). The data set I found was particularly interesting, because it had several parameters about habitability of planets, which was not available in other data sets about exoplanets. This then became my focus point of the visualization: habitable exoplanets. Then I tried to come up with interesting ways to visualize this data, so that on the one hand the various aspects of habitable exoplanets are explained, and on the other hand it also would become a visually interesting graphic to look at. That, in general, is what I always try to do: find a balance between being informative and creating beauty. Sometimes you lean more to the informative side, sometimes more to the aesthetics side.

[1] Edible or Medical

Credits: Jan Willem Tulp, TULP interactive
Completion: 2014

This project was commissioned by Natural Recall (Italy) who asked image makers from all over the world to create an image that shows the interconnection between humans and plants, which was going to be shown at an exhibition in Venice, Italy, and published in a book. This visualization is based on the data set from Plants for a Future and shows the medical and edible uses of several plants as a network visualization. The more to the left a plant (a circle) links to, the more edible uses it has, and the more to the right, the more medical uses it has. Lines connect a plant with all its uses.

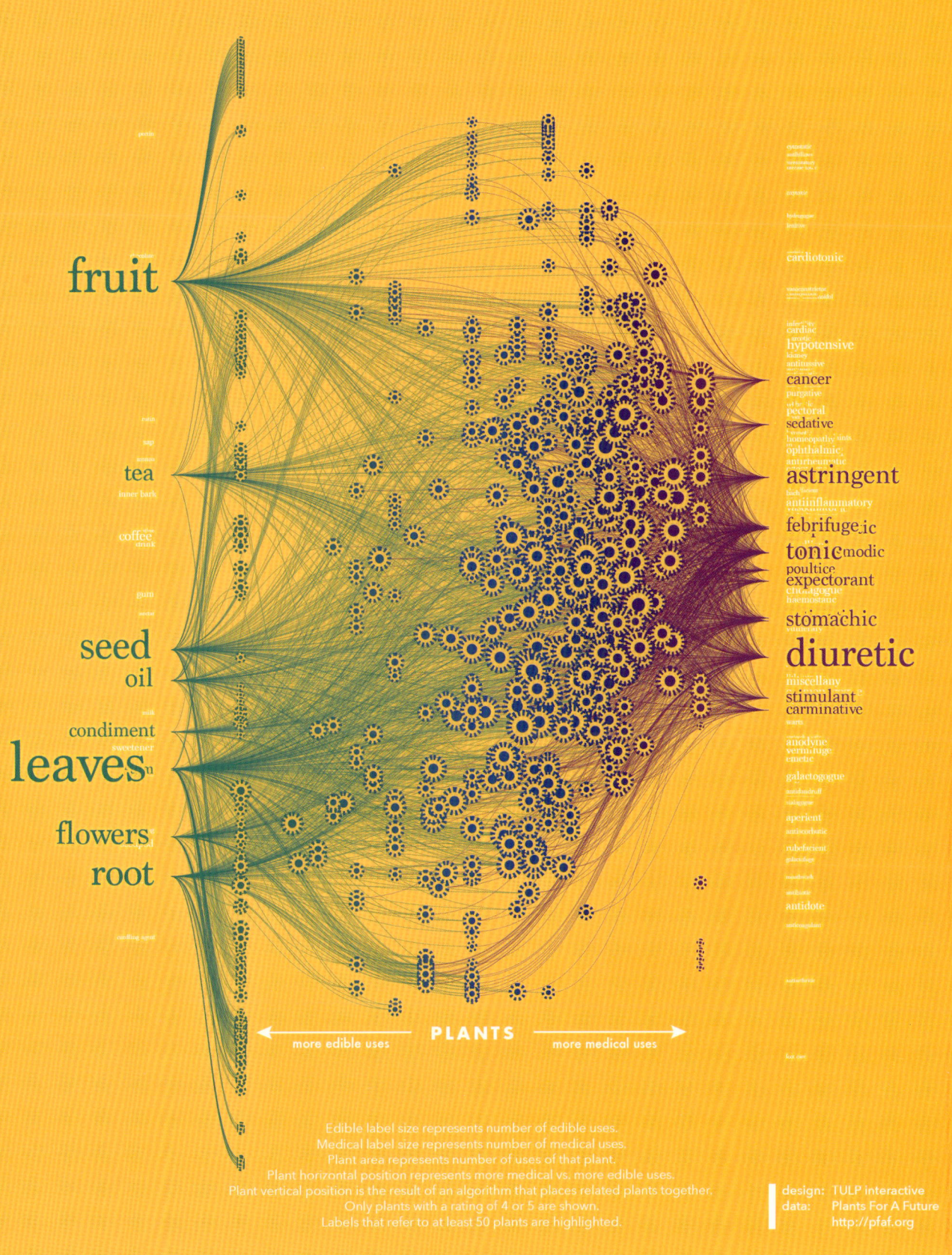

[Q] **Where are your works applied?**

[A] Most of my visualizations are used to communicate insights to an audience. Sometimes they're interactive and available online, and sometimes they're used in print. Occasionally they're created as an animation without interactivity. Sometimes I create visualizations that are tools to be used by an organization internally to explore a data set, and recently I started a new initiative called Office Data Art, which is a visualization based on a company's data, to be framed and hung on the wall.

[Q] **How do you turn boring and complex data into something interesting and understandable?**

[A] This is a difficult question to answer in general, but some of the elements that may help are guiding a user through a set of insights, instead of assuming a user will understand. I also believe that details, whether in the data, the concept or the design, will make your visualization more sophisticated. Making a visualization relevant for a user is something that could make a visualization more engaging. Using metaphors, such as using the colors of the concept in your visualization, if possible, is something that can help make the users understand better what it's about (a visualization about trees with green colors could make more sense than making the data look pink, for instance).

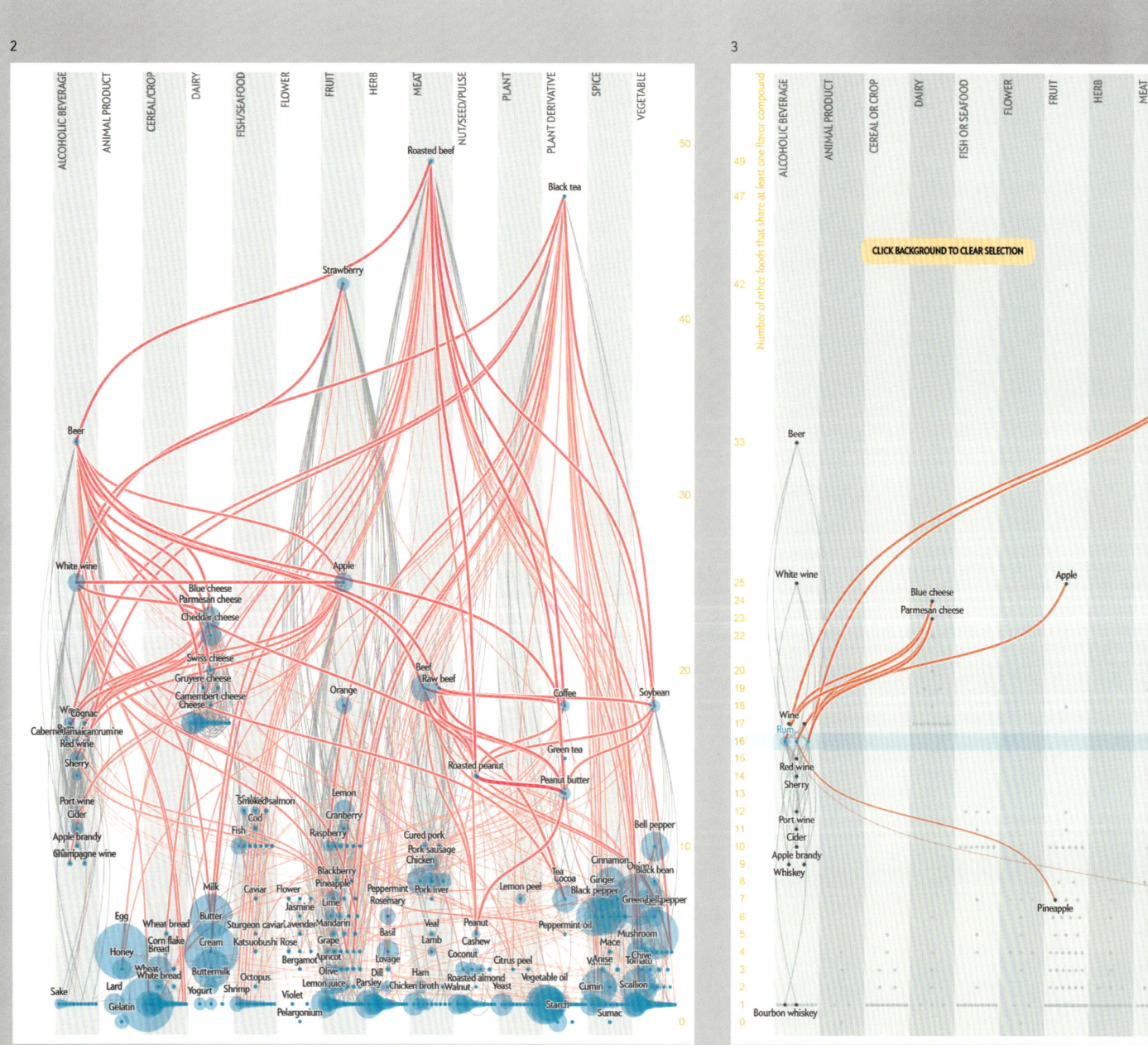

[2–4] Flavor Connection

Credits: Jan Willem Tulp, TULP interactive
Completion: 2013
Interactive link: www.scientificamerican.com/article/flavor-connection-taste-map-interactive

This project, created for *Scientific American*, is both a print graphic and an online interactive visualization, which shows the connections of foods that go well together. It is a redesign of the original network diagram in a research paper. Foods are connected if they share compounds. The thicker the line is, the more compounds they share. The columns are food categories, the circle size is the prevalence value of the food in a large recipe database, and the vertical position is based on the number of connections a kind of food has to other kinds.

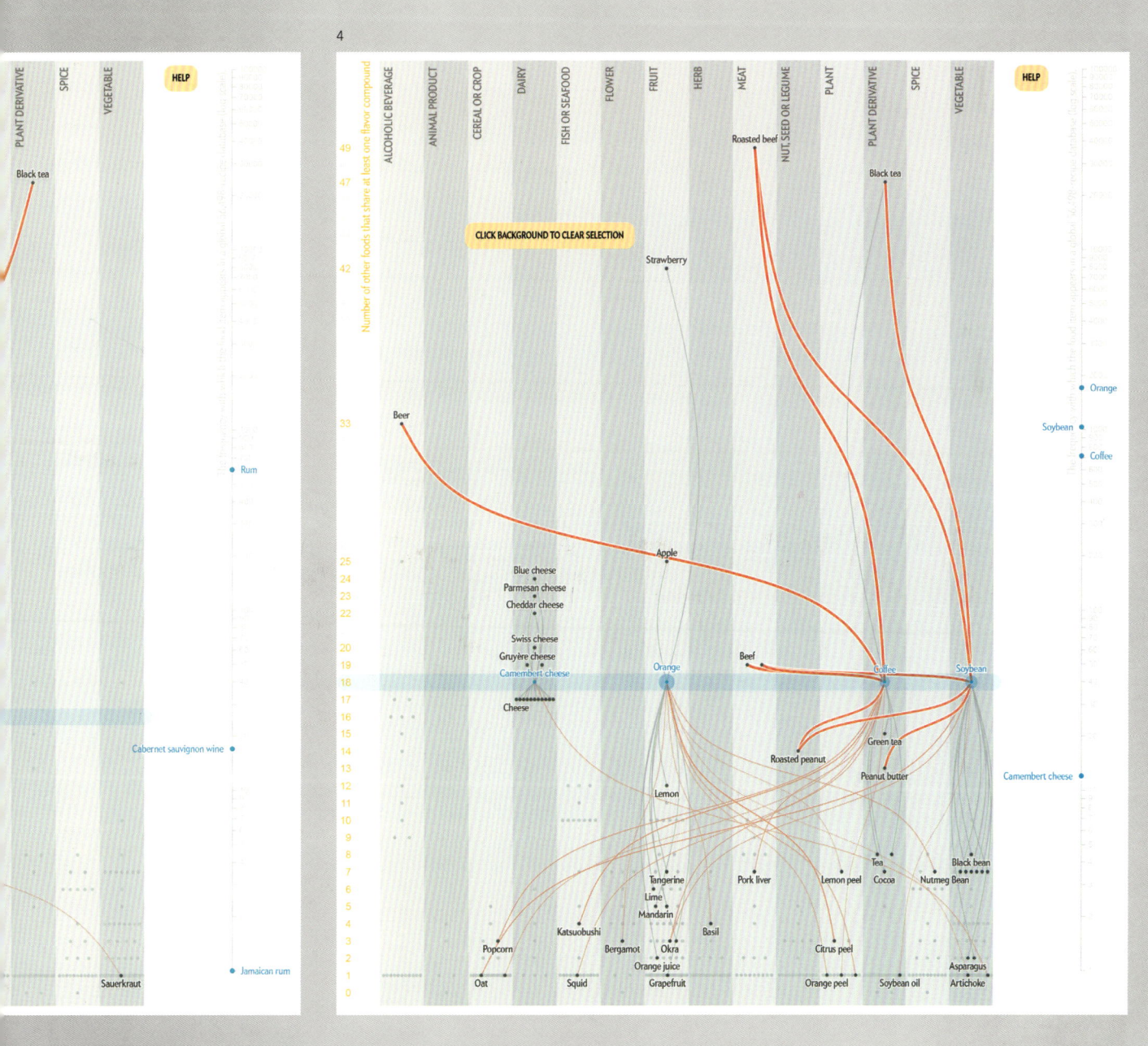

[Q] **What is your suggestion for beginners?**

[A] Data visualization is an art and a science. There is theory behind visual representation of data, so it is useful to learn about that and read books. I also recommend getting inspiration from works that are already out there. Finally, the most important recommendation would be to just do it. You learn most by doing. Be critical of your own work, ask others to give feedback, and learn from it, then your next visualization will be better than the previous one. I believe that I'm still improving, primarily just by doing it often.

5

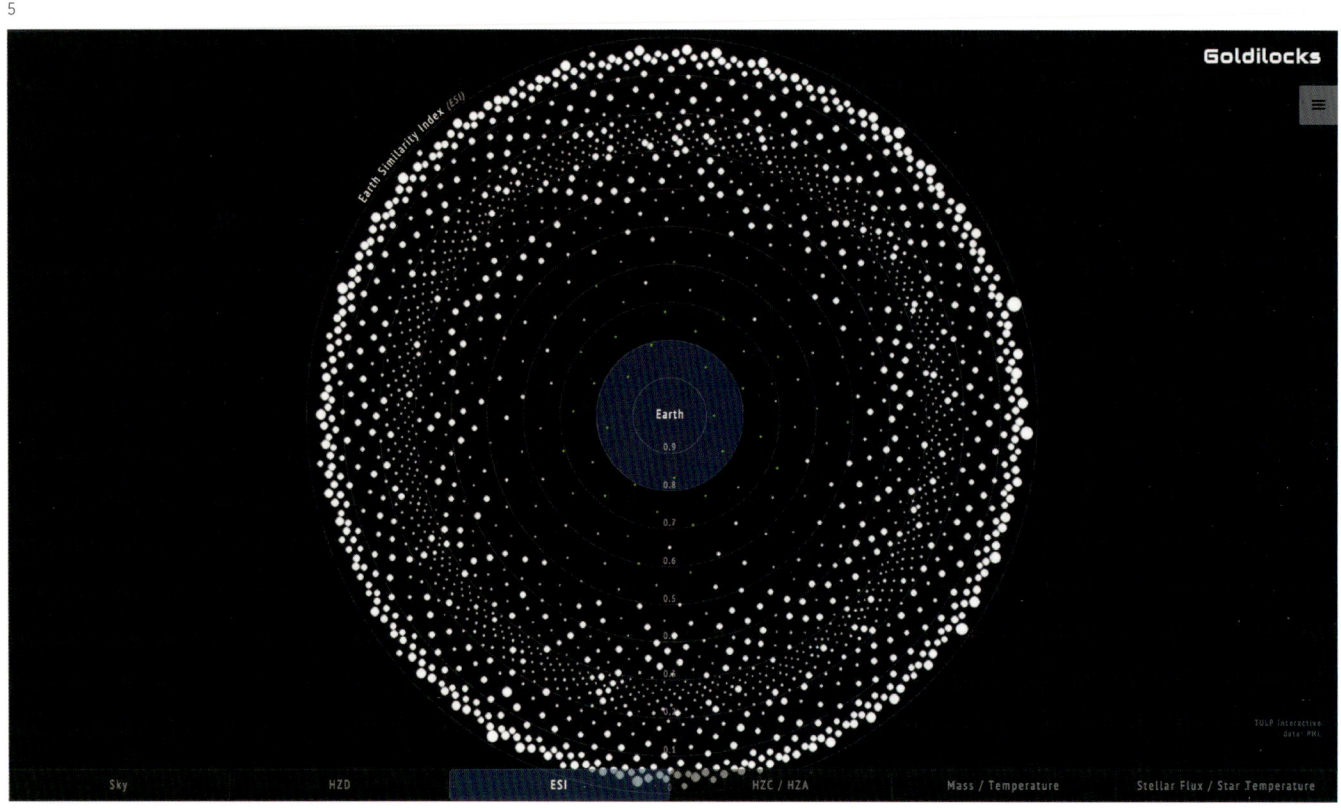

6

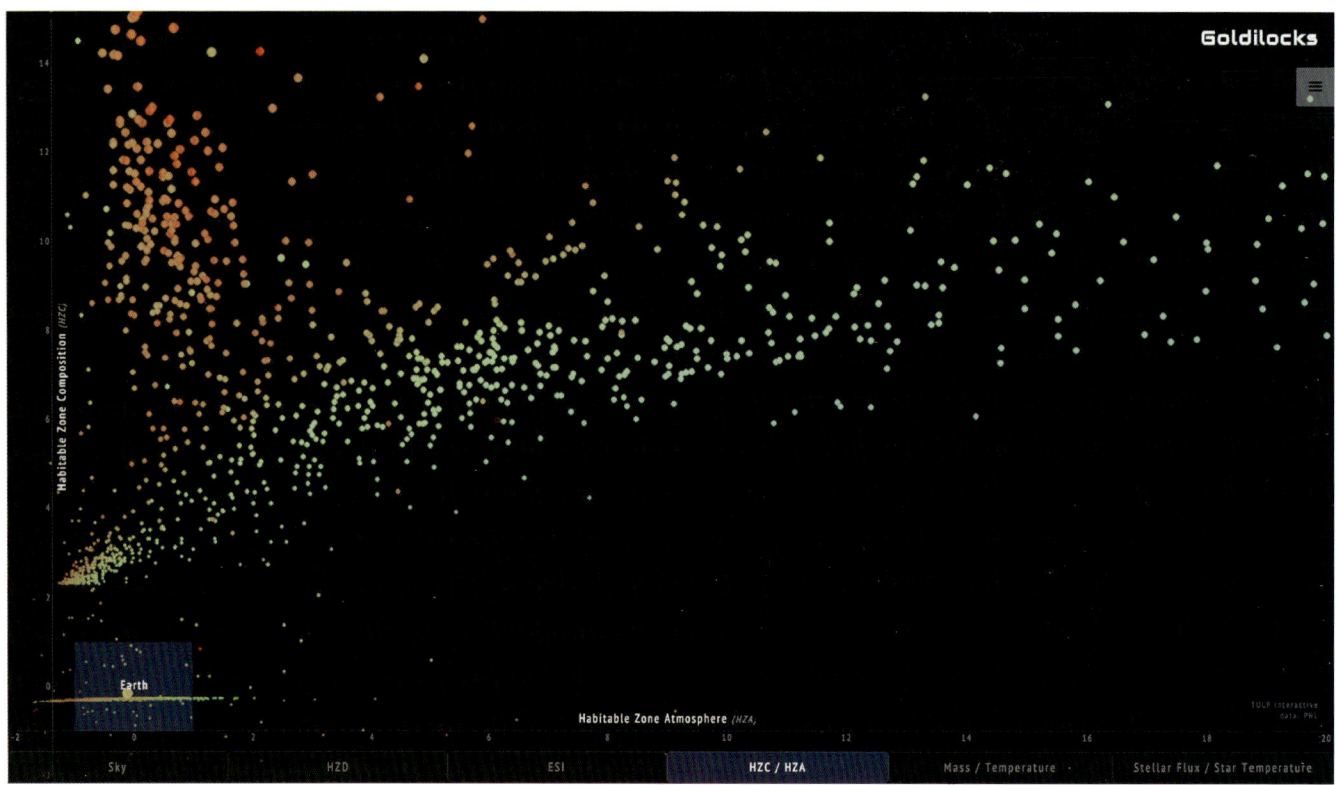

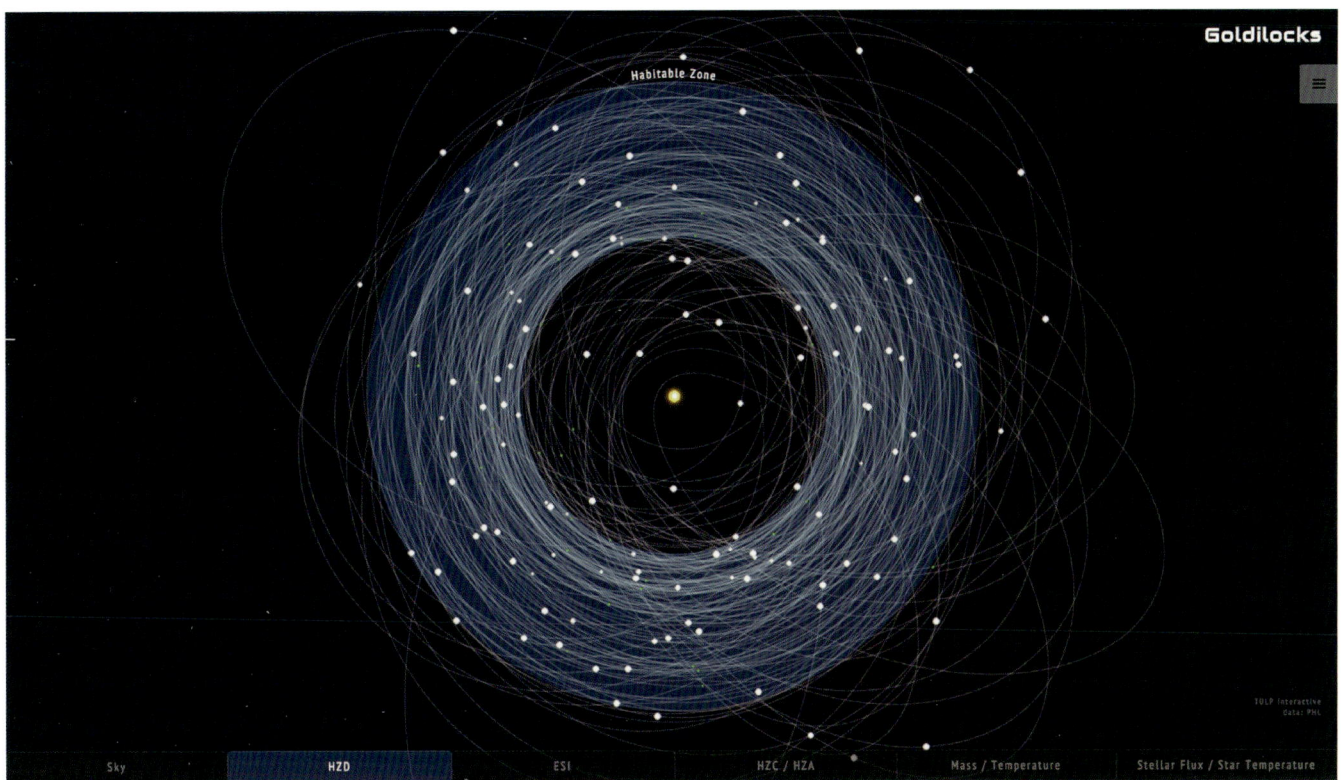

[5–8] Goldilocks

Credits: Jan Willem Tulp, TULP interactive
Completion: 2015
Interactive link: goldilocks.info

Goldilocks is a project commissioned by the Visualized conference in New York for their space-themed opening night of the 2015 conference. It is an interactive visualization that shows various aspects of exoplanets that have properties that scientists mark as potentially habitable. The visualization shows several views of the data, highlighting different characteristics in each view. This particular view is the sky view that shows where all the exoplanets are positioned in the sky.

Gemma Warriner

[Q] What do you think about data visualization/infographics?

[A] Information visualization is a practice focused on the generation of meaningful visual displays of qualitative and/or quantitative data types.

[Q] What kind of design methods do you commonly use?

[A] The information visualization processes and methodologies I practice largely depend on the project output and type of data being visualized. Typically, once a set of data has been established, I spend time decoding and 'playing' with the information. This process allows me to engage with and discover interesting patterns and trends within the data that are often difficult to distinguish initially. 'Playing' with the information in this way often involves a process of defamiliarization where the same data set is transformed, rearranged, or put into a different context to allow these insights to present themselves.

[Q] What kind of design elements do you commonly use?

[A] Scale, color, and text-based design elements are common and effective, however, the formal qualities are highly dependent on the project intent and material output (screen, digital, print, etc.).

[Q] Where are your works applied?

[A] Typically, the application of information visualization works considers the project's intent and the type of stakeholder the project speaks to. My project Twenty-Fifty is a series of large-scale posters found in an exhibition context.

[Q] How do you turn boring and complex data into something interesting and understandable?

[A] Effective information visualizations communicate information simply. Information visualizations are often aesthetically pleasing but tend to compromise legibility for visual appeal, making them ineffective in their communication. To turn 'boring and complex' data into something interesting and understandable asks that the designer undergoes a process of decoding such data sets through exploring and re-presenting interesting patterns and unexpected moments that may have otherwise gone unnoticed.

[Q] What is your suggestion for beginners?

[A] I think it's a dangerous design decision to begin with data visualization as an anticipated output. My advice to designers would be to begin with the brief and consider data visualization if and only when appropriate to the solution.

Gemma Warriner is a visual communication designer and educator at the University of Technology, Sydney. Her work reflects her interests in information visualization, food design, and brand experience, with projects spanning across both print and digital platforms. Gemma's designs have been recognized by the Australian Graphic Design Association (AGDA), Graphis, Kantar Information is Beautiful awards, Adobe, and the Dieline.

1

[1–5] Twenty–Fifty

Credits: Gemma Warriner, Kate Sweetapple
Completion: 2013

Twenty–Fifty is a visual exploration of the global food crisis predicted for the year 2050, a result of the inability of the Earth's natural resources to meet future demand. The project presents a series of eight data visualization posters, each exposing one primary issue responsible for this future crisis. It looks closely at population growth, urbanization, food production, food waste, genetic modification, climate change, consumption trends, and agrobiodiversity as the main influential factors.

Through sourcing and photographing food that is representational of the designer's own data visualizations, the project intends to both challenge and educate consumers about how the future may unfold. Twenty–Fifty explores the use of shape as an effective way in which information can be visualized. Distinctly different from more traditional shape-based data representations, this series of posters interprets shape through the images of food objects, each communicating a different factor of the predicted 2050 food crisis. The supporting graphic overlay highlights the specific data each shape makes reference to.

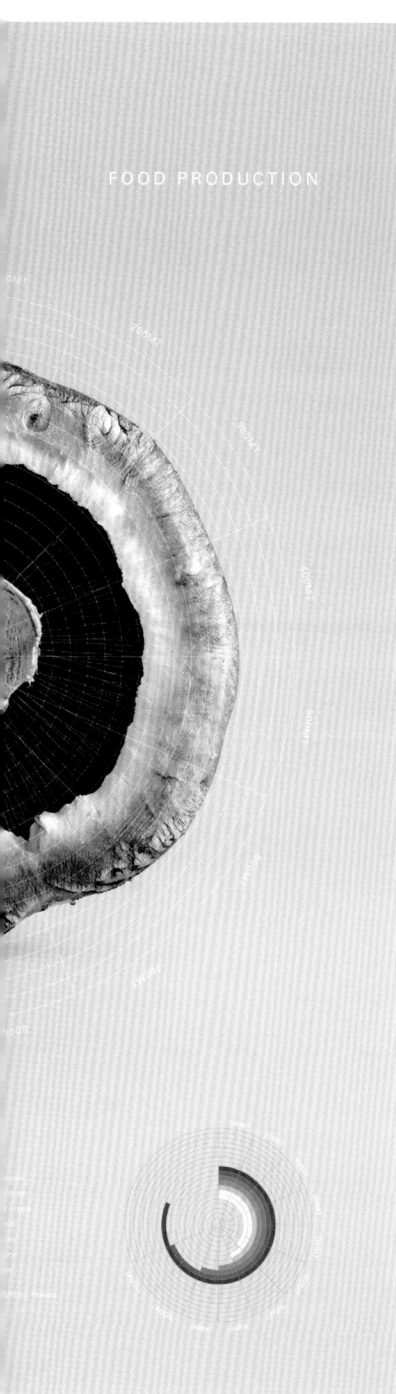

Krist Wongsuphasawat

Krist Wongsuphasawat holds a PhD in Computer Science, focusing on information visualization, from University of Maryland, College Park. During the day, he is a staff data scientist at Twitter, where he applies data visualization to improve how data scientists, engineers, and product managers interact with and understand rich and massive data sets. In addition to that, he helps Twitter's PR team tell stories from Twitter data via interactive visualizations. At night, he explores open data sets and personal visualization projects.

[Q] What do you think about data visualization/infographics?

[A] I am passionate about data. For me, data is snapshots of the world. Each data set has its own stories. Some are obvious. Some are hidden. Some are expected. Some are surprising. Visualization is my key to unlocking these hidden stories and revealing them to other people.

Data visualization can make complex things easy to understand, taking advantage of our amazing visual perception to process large amount of information rapidly. I get excited when I discover new information from data and enjoy challenging myself to design how to communicate them visually to others.

[Q] What kind of design methods do you commonly use?

[A] I usually ask three big questions, based on Tamara Munzner's why-what-how framework.

Why am I doing this?

Is it to present known information or story? If so, what is the story? If the idea is too broad, I will prepare additional time to analyze data. Is it to help users explore complex data sets looking for insights? If so, what kind of insights are we hoping to surface? Or is it to create something for pleasure? If so, the possibilities are limitless.

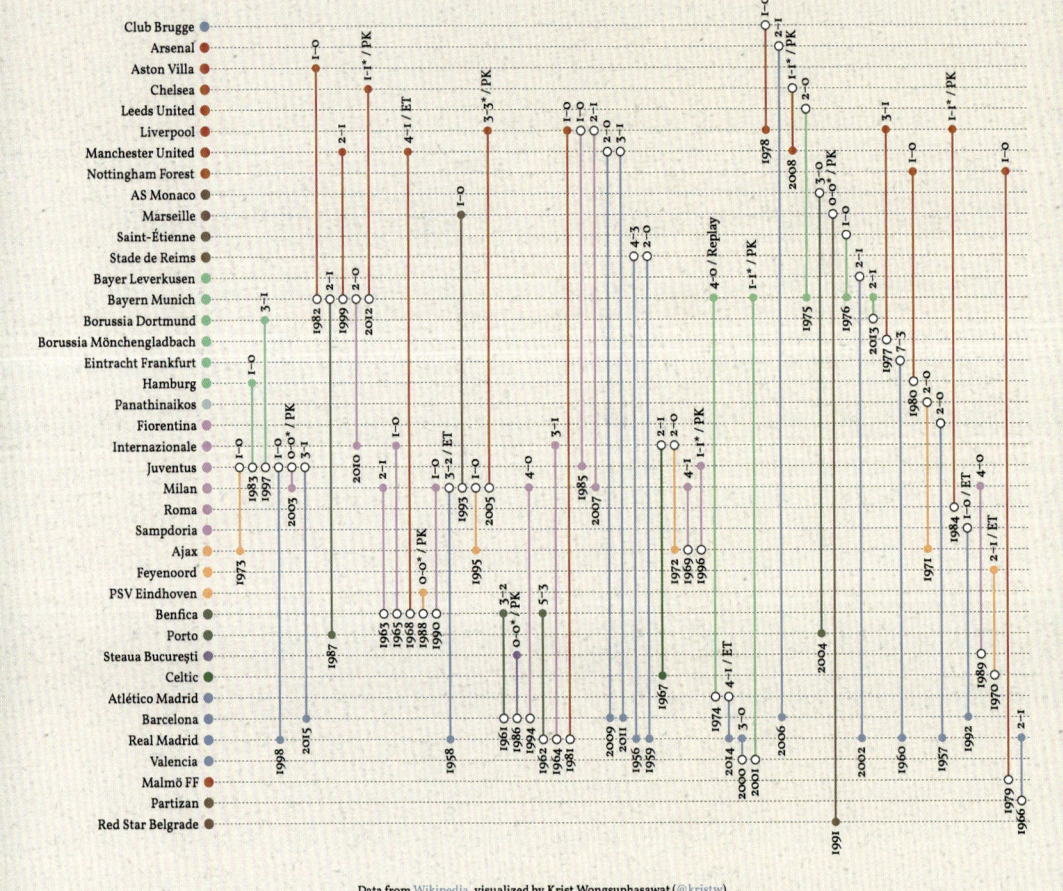

What is the data?

This will help me plan further how to collect, clean, and process them. I will try to obtain sample data as soon as possible as it is very important for shaping the project directions. There were many projects that start with unrealistically ambitious expectations. Prototyping on real data sets will bring the expectations closer to reality.

How should I visualize the data?

Once the goals are set and data is ready, it is time to start prototyping. I select the most appropriate visual encoding that I think will address the design goals. Then I add interactions to provide additional information on demand. I usually follow the information visualization mantra: overview first, zoom and filter, then details on demand. I always get feedback from colleagues or stakeholders. One simple way to check the design yourself before asking others is to prepare a demonstration in which you use your visualization as if you are a user to find insights. Then I revise according to feedback and refine the details. Often I have to go back and clean the data. Once I have received further feedback and refined, it is ready to publish.

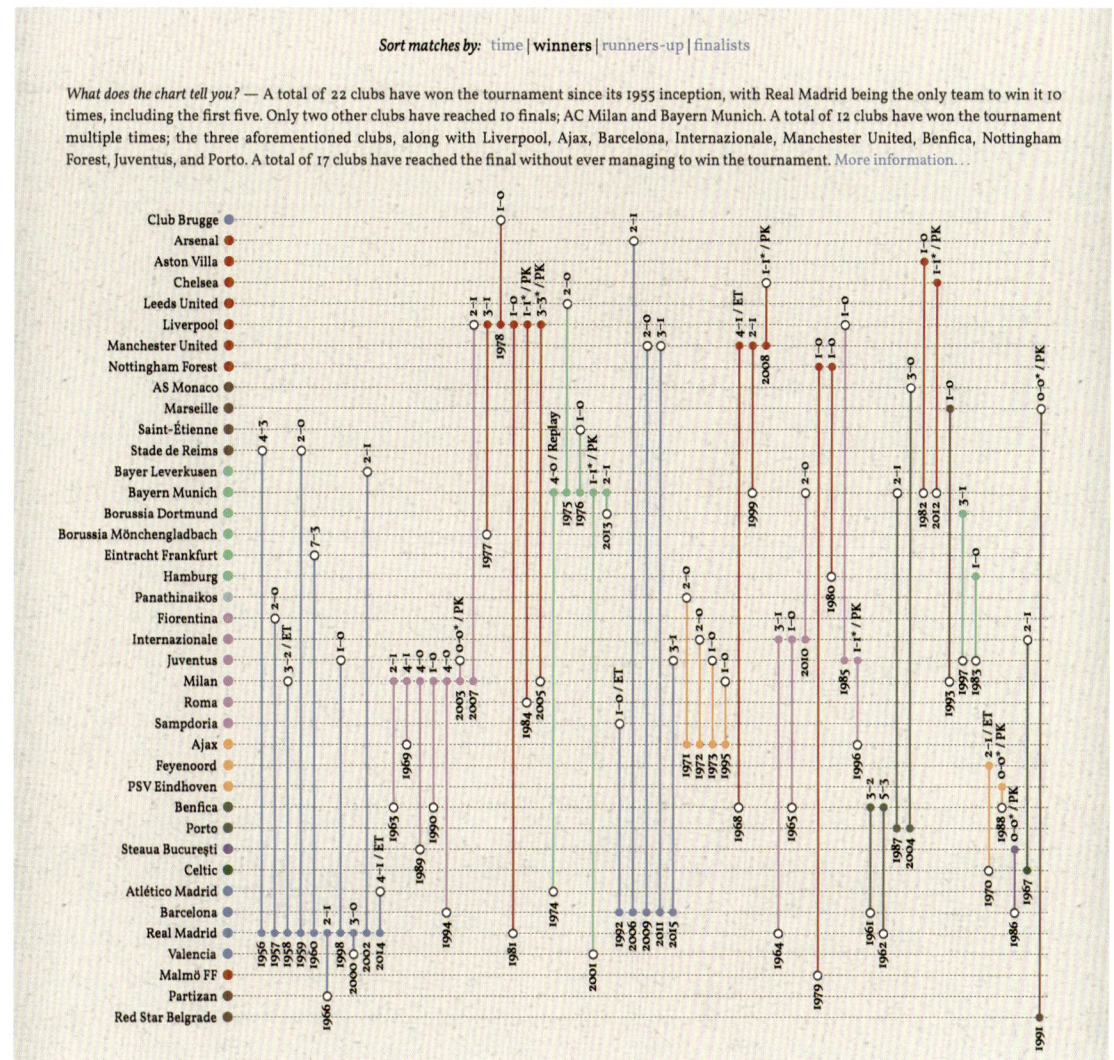

[1–2] The History of European Cup and UEFA Champions League Finals

Credit: Krist Wongsuphasawat
Completion: 2015
Interactive link: kristw.github.io/uclfinals

Before the final between Barcelona and Juventus in 2015, the designer was curious about the previous winners and quickly put together this work. Since it was about history, the visualization was designed to look like a page from a book. All teams that participated in the finals are listed, then colored and grouped by their nations. Each vertical line represents one year of the competition with its two ends marking the finalists. Solid and hollow circles indicate winners and runners-up, respectively. The designer gained several insights by changing how the lines are sorted while exploring the data. This led him to integrate the findings and ability to interactively sort the lines into the final piece.

[Q] What kind of design elements do you commonly use?

[A] Lines, shapes, and colors.

[Q] Where are your works applied?

[A] I like to empower the audience by allowing them to interact with the visualization, so most of my works are interactive pieces on websites. These works can be adapted to other printed formats as well. The UEFA Champions League Final work was printed as a poster and people loved it.

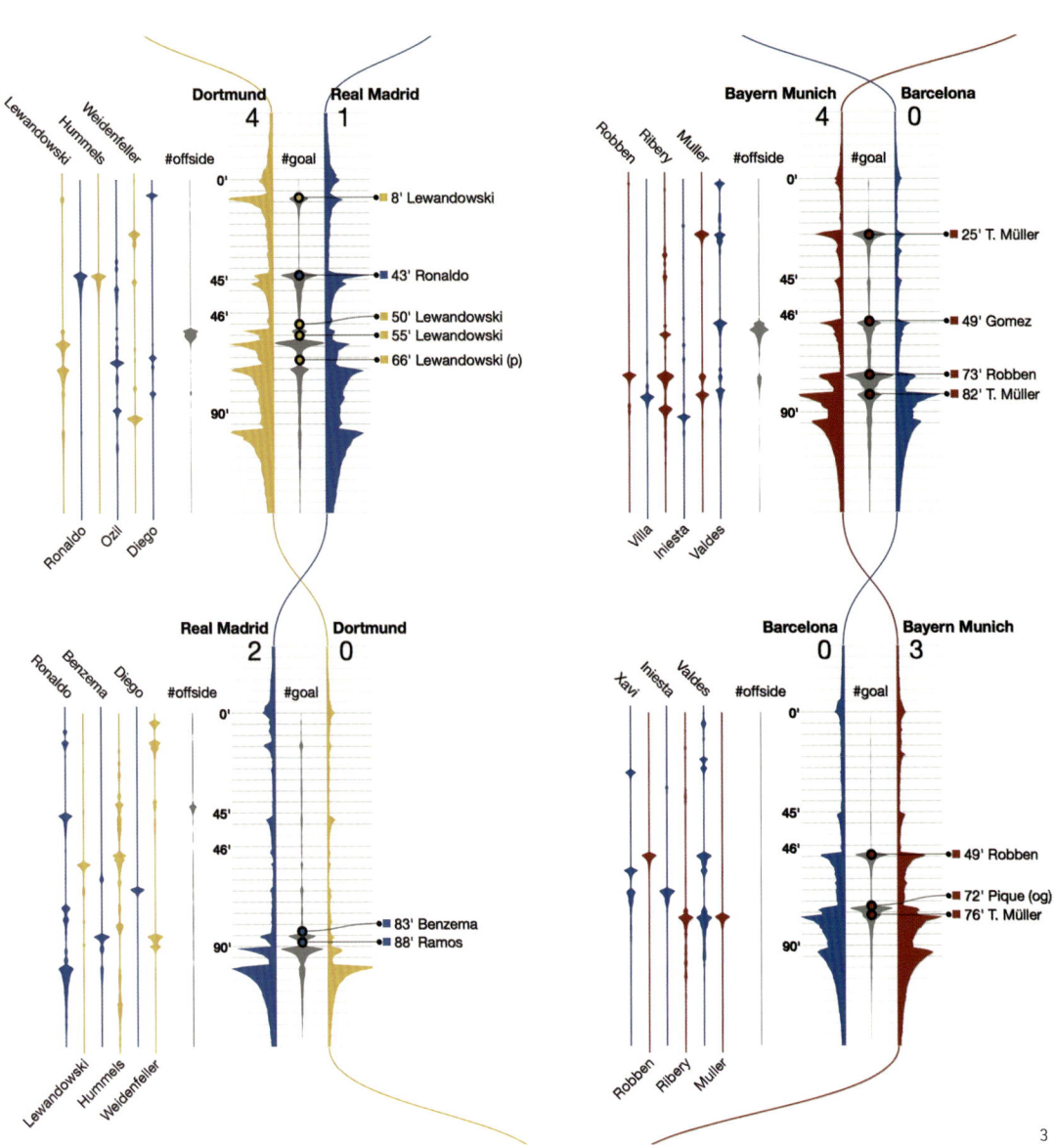

[3–5] UEFA Champions League

Credit: Krist Wongsuphasawat
Completion: 2013
Interactive link: uclfinal.twitter.com

This project was published before the final to tell stories about the tournament based on fans' activities on Twitter. It aims to capture the entire competition in a single view, providing both overview of the tournament and individual matches. To achieve this, the designer first visualized tweets about each match to highlight interesting moments. Time flows from top to bottom and the width of the graphs are proportional to the number of tweets. Spikes usually appear when something interesting happened. These per-match visualizations are arranged into a layout commonly used in sports for knockout tournaments. Graphs of the same team are connected. The final design shows an overview of each team's path in the competition: how far it went through, when it was eliminated. A closer look reveals the details about each match: moments that excited the fans, reactions after each goal, players' influence, etc.

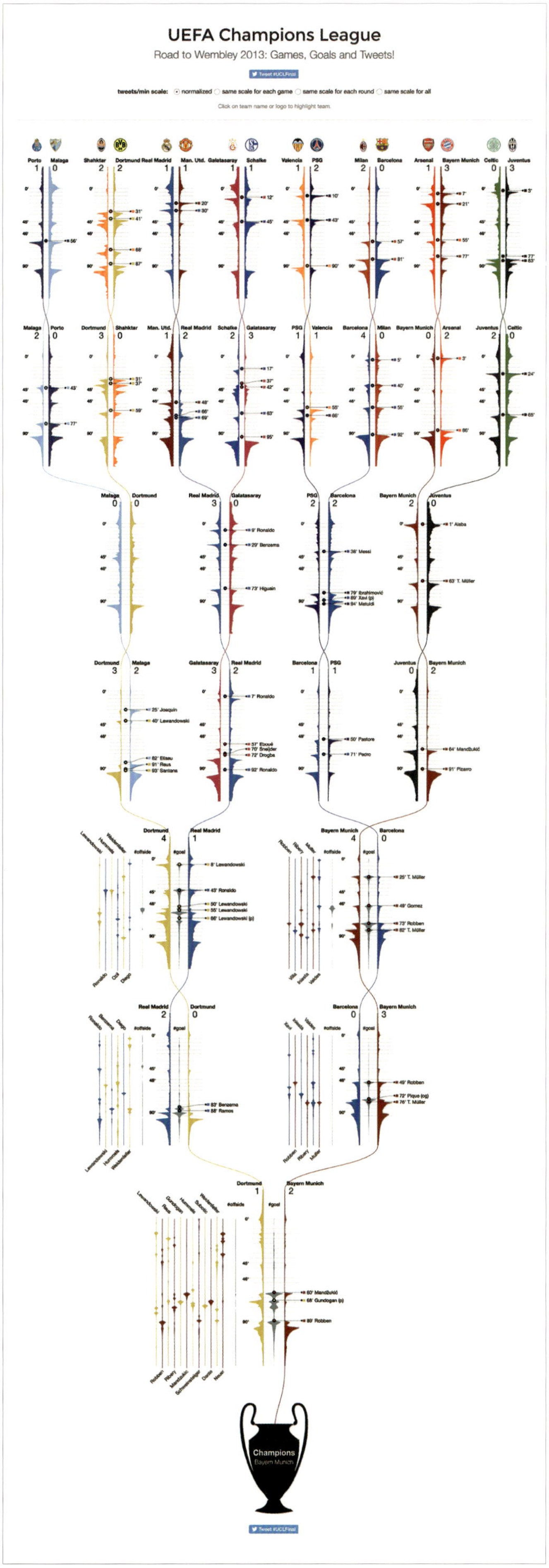

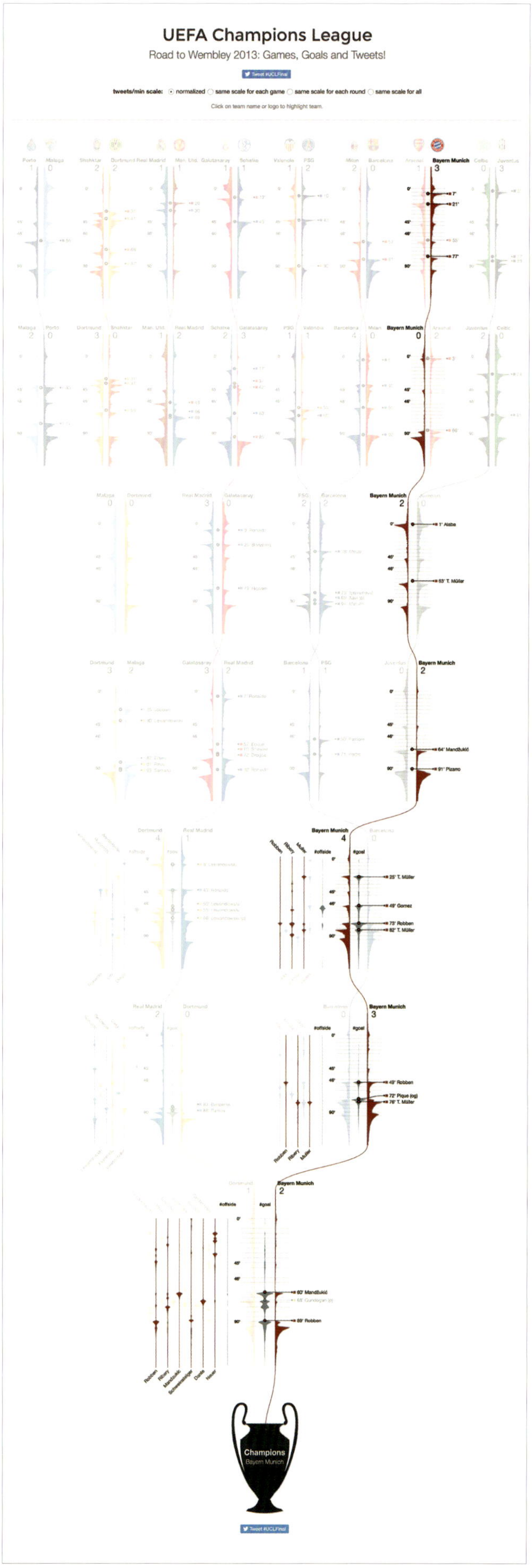

[Q] **How do you turn boring and complex data into something interesting and understandable?**

[A] In my opinion, the reasons many people consider data boring and complex is because they are overwhelmed by the amount of data and cannot interpret or make sense of the data in a way that is useful or related to them. Therefore, my role is to learn what the target audiences are interested in, analyze data, find interesting insights, get rid of the noises to reveal the interesting parts, choose visual representations that are effective in highlighting them, and then add interaction to provide additional information on demand.

[Q] **What is your suggestion for the beginner?**

[A] Start developing visualization literacy and learn what are good and bad visualization designs. For example, what visual encodings are effective for which type of data? What color palettes are appropriate for a given situation? Keep exercising by criticizing the work you see on the web, TV, in news articles, etc.

- What is the data set? What is it telling me?
- Is it misleading?
- Does it make data easier to understand?
- Analyze design choices: color, shape, layout, etc. Is there anything you like in particular? Did the work violate any known guidelines? If so, is there a good reason?
- What can be improved?
- How would you make it better?

When creating your own piece, it can be tempting to try a technique that looks fancy. Don't limit yourself by selecting how to visualize data beforehand (e.g. I want to make this a tree map) without knowing what you are visualizing. Start from data, not techniques. Figure out what you want to communicate to the audience. Keep it simple and pay attention to details. Avoid design choices that can mislead the user. Then keep iterating. Get feedback and improve your design.

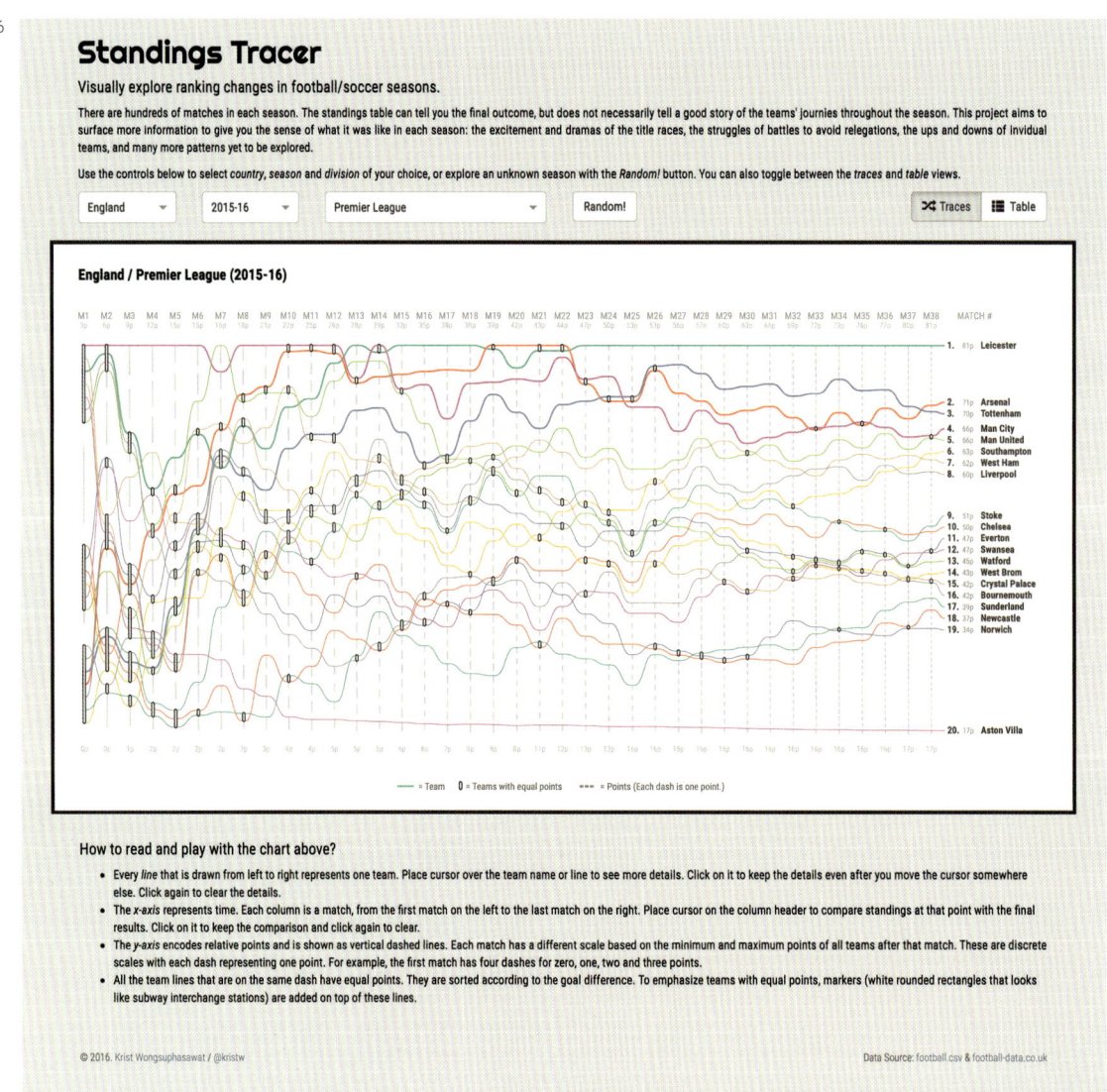

6

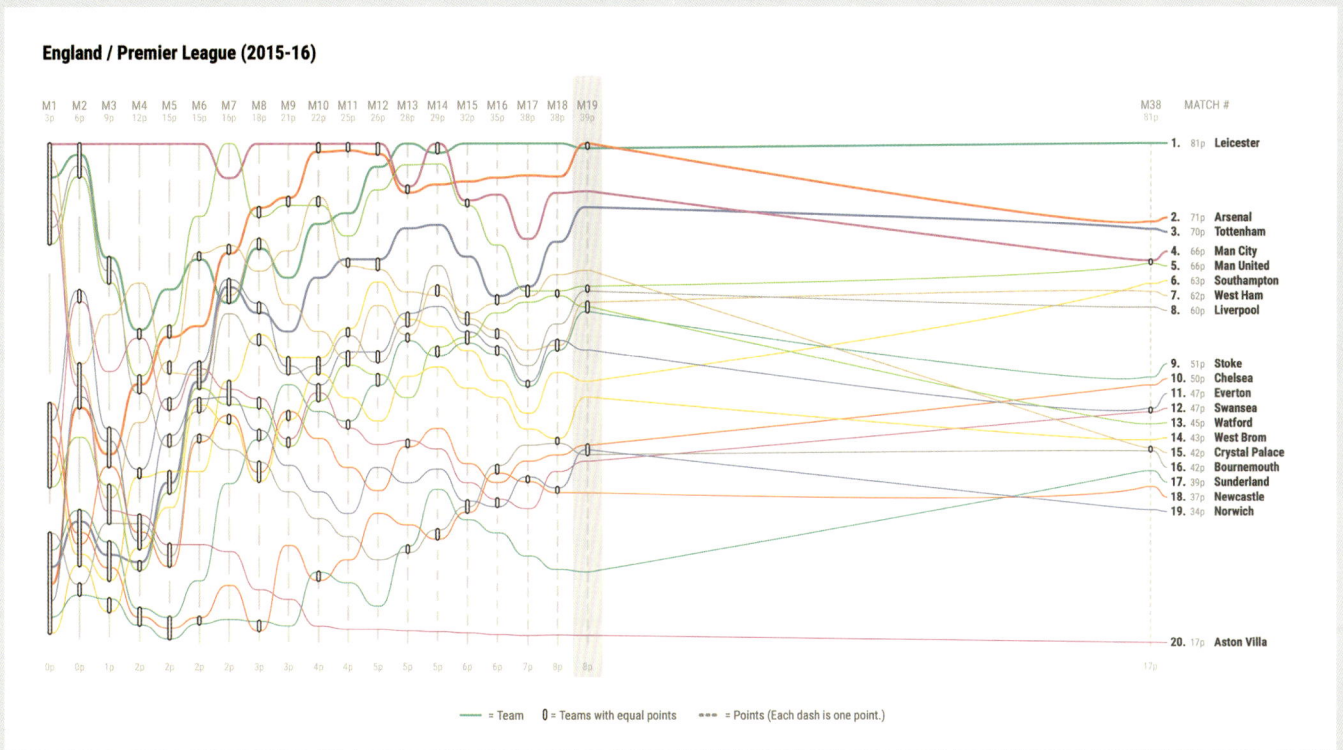

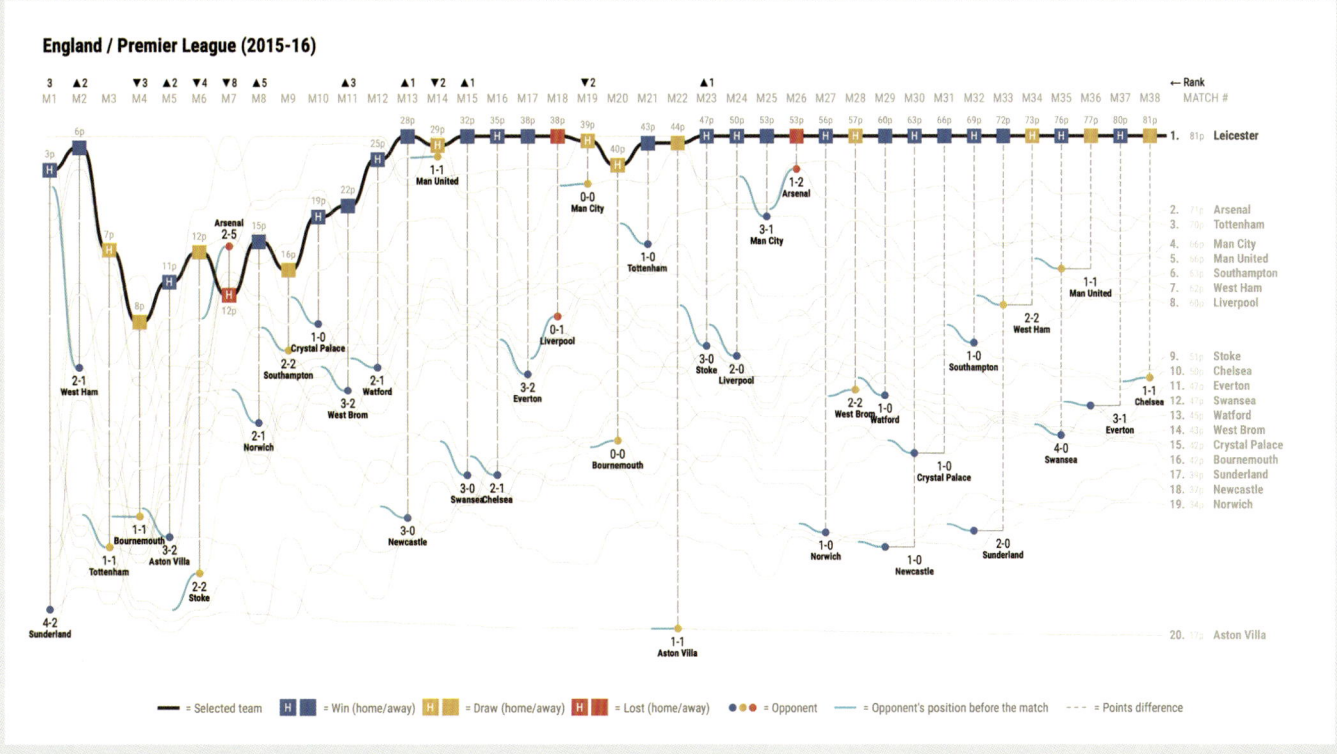

[6–8] Standings Tracer

Credit: Krist Wongsuphasawat
Completion: 2016
Interactive link: kristw.github.io/standings-tracer

Standings tables are commonly used to display the final outcome of a football season, but it does not tell the teams' journeys throughout the season well. To provide a more completed picture, each team is visualized as a line based on accumulated points over time. The most special thing about this work is how the *y*-axis works. It is not a continuous axis, but split into multiple blocks based on the possible points. For example, the first match day has four blocks based on possible points 0, 1, 2, and 3. If two teams have equal points, they are placed within the same block, ordered by goal difference and spaced out vertically to avoid overlap.

Each match day also has its own *y*-axis with a different number of blocks based on points accumulated by the teams at that time. This approach untangles the lines and reveals the gap between teams during the season really well. In addition, users can click on each team to reveal its opponents and results match by match. They can also click on any match day to compare the ranking at that time and the end of the season.

Carlo Zapponi

[Q] What do you think about data visualization/infographics?

[A] What I like about working in the field of data visualization is that every project is a mix of science and art, where both the parts contribute to the whole.

[Q] What kind of design methods do you commonly use?

[A] Data visualization inherits most of the practice from user-experience design, statistical analysis, and software development. Two of the methods I always use are understanding the audience and prototyping. Designing for newspaper readers is different. Attention time is a concern, and showing the interesting part of the story is the key. In the newsroom, where the pace is fast, we need to quickly transform ideas and validate them with the reporters through quick prototyping.

[Q] What kind of design elements do you commonly use?

[A] Data visualizations are user interfaces for reading and interacting with data. At the core of the interface there are usually one or more charts. Each type of chart is suited to displaying different types of data and to telling different types of stories; at the same time each design element of the interface is used to explore the data.

The data and the stories you want to tell determine the graphs you use. It's a combination of elements that brings the visualization to a level of clarity and refinement that makes it understandable. It's a blend of type of charts, use of colors and scales, layers of interactivity, and appropriate wording. All the elements have to work together in a seamless manner to help the reader.

The shapes and visual elements follow the story you are telling, the design, and ultimately the data. In some cases, the shapes can represent the element you are depicting based on their real nature (circles can be meteorites) and in other cases it can be more abstract (lines connecting dots can be traces of elements being moved around). The visual elements you decide to use are extremely important because they can facilitate the understanding of the topic and make the readers feel closer to the stories, and could trigger their interest into digging more deeply into the layers of the visual representation of the data.

Carlo Zapponi works at *The Guardian* (London) in the visual team as a data visualization designer. He specializes in data visualization, HCI, interaction design, UI experience, wire frames, and rapid prototyping. He likes to get his hands dirty with code, data, and wires, and is passionate about everything that mixes creativity, technology, and people.

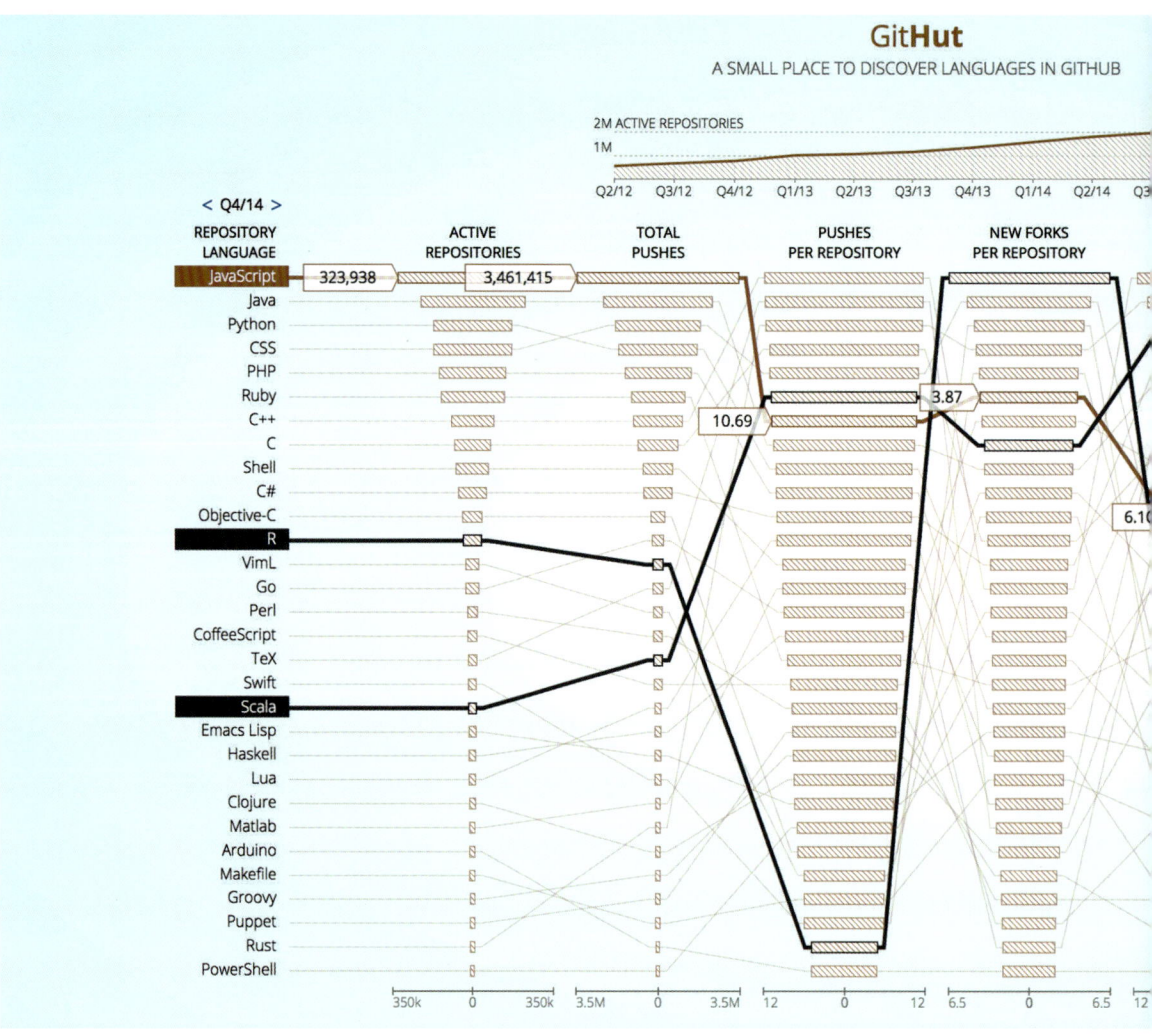

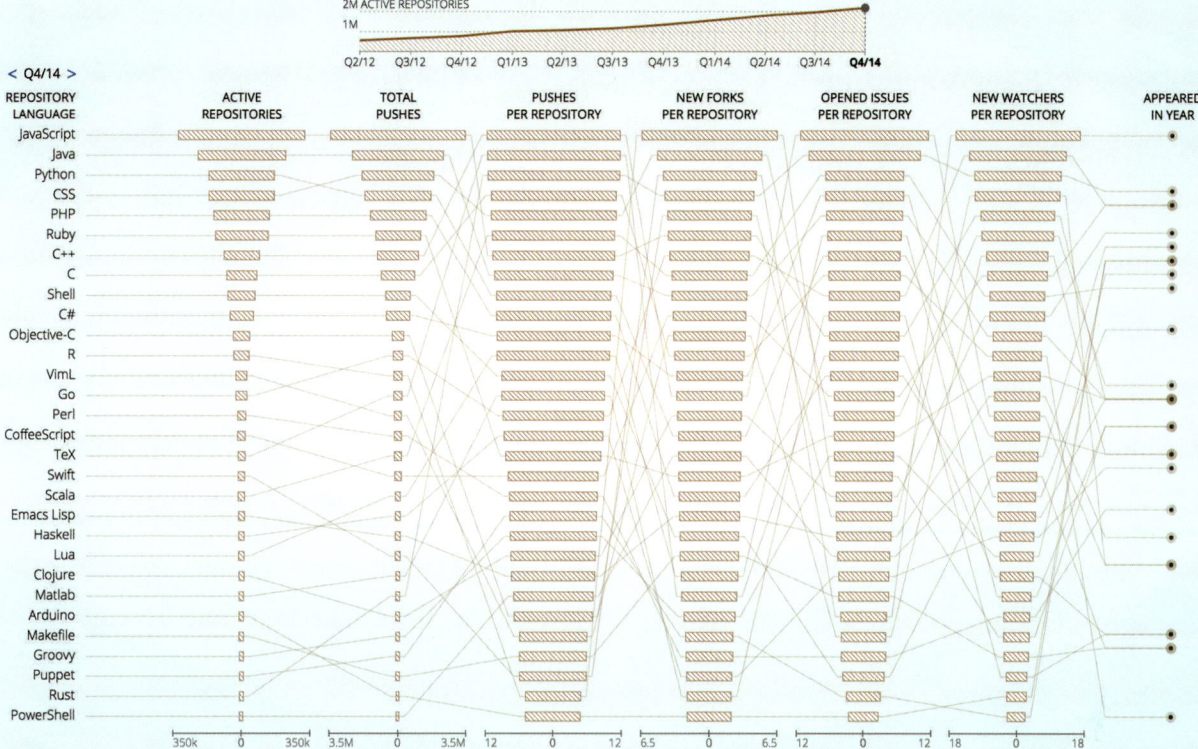

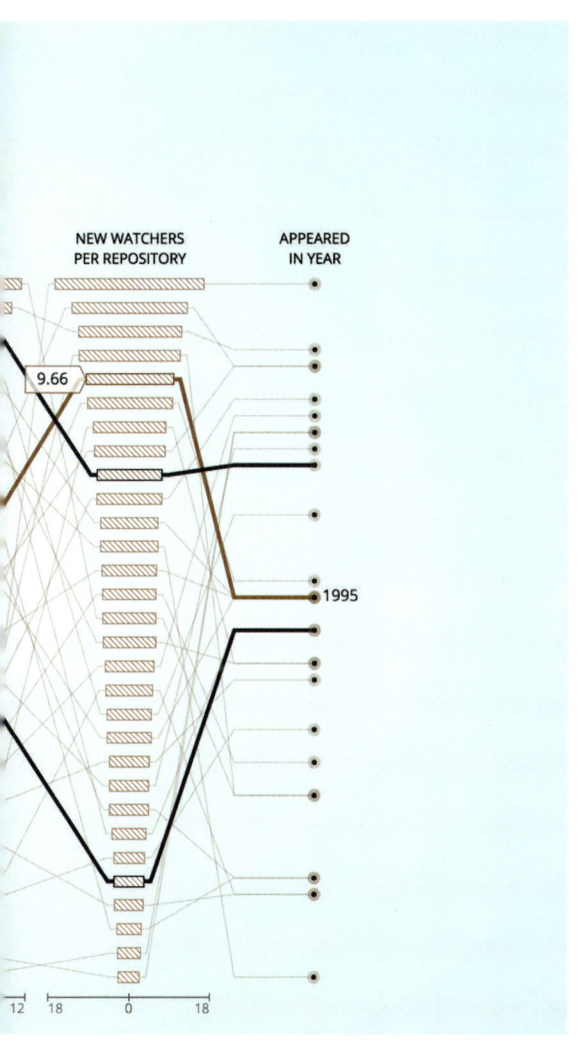

[1–2] Githut

Credit: Carlo Zapponi
Completion: 2014
Interactive link: www.githut.info

Githut is a visualization of the universe of programming languages used across the repositories hosted on GitHub. Programming languages are not simply the tool people use to create programs but also the instruments used to code and decode creativity. By observing the history of languages we can enjoy the quest of humankind for a better way to solve problems, to facilitate collaboration between people, and to reuse the effort of others. Githut uses a ranked parallel coordinates plot to show the use of languages and a series of line charts to show how it has changed in the last few years.

[3–4] Bolides

Credit: Carlo Zapponi
Completion: 2013
Interactive link: www.bolid.es

Bolides is a representation of all the known meteorites that have hit the Earth based on the data from the Meteoritical Society. The project approaches the data by providing a more emotional experience inspired by the world of video gaming and mixing it with a more analytical interactive layer. The design focuses on those meteorites that were witnessed when falling and hitting the ground—as of 2016, there were 1150 witnessed meteorites out of the 45,000 total recorded. The witnessed meteorites tend to be concentrated in the areas with high human population density such as Europe, Japan, and northern India.

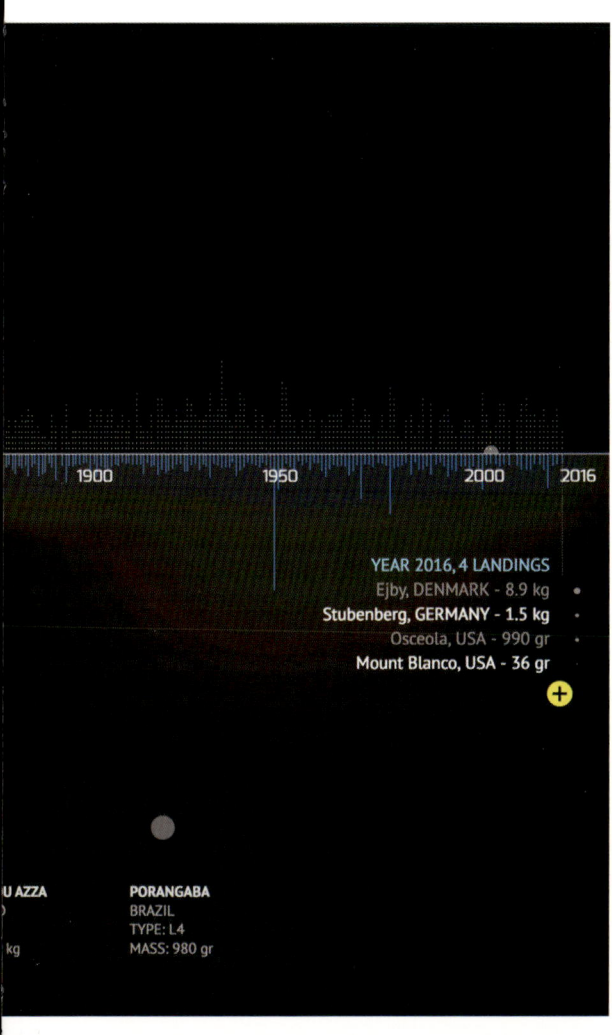

[Q] Where are your works applied?

[A] My projects are usually interactive visualizations for the web.

[Q] How do you turn boring and complex data into something interesting and understandable?

[A] I don't think data can be really boring, as every data set hides an exciting side. A viable approach to unlocking complexity is to start by presenting the data as a whole with explanatory texts and annotations, and later present smaller contextualized stories to help the reader to gain more insights and to ease the effort of exploring the data.

[Q] What is your suggestion for beginners?

[A] Don't be afraid to experiment with novel forms of visualization and at the same time do not be afraid to use bar charts and line charts. They might not look fancy or innovative, but they often show the data in the right way.

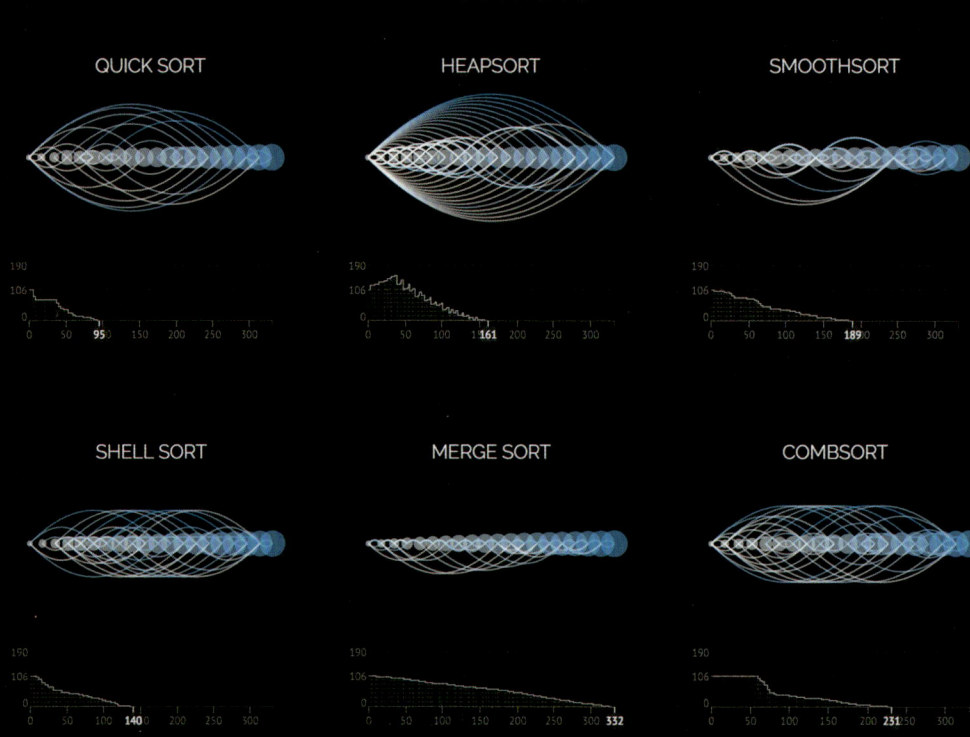

[5–7] Sorting

Credit: Carlo Zapponi
Completion: 2014
Interactive link: www.sorting.at

Ordering a sequence of items is one of the pillars of computer science. Sorting is a visualization of the most famous sorting algorithms. The project provides two standpoints to look at these algorithms. One is more artistic with the goal of creating unique visual representations that expose visual patterns. The other side is a walk-through that guides the reader step by step along the process of ordering a list of integer numbers.

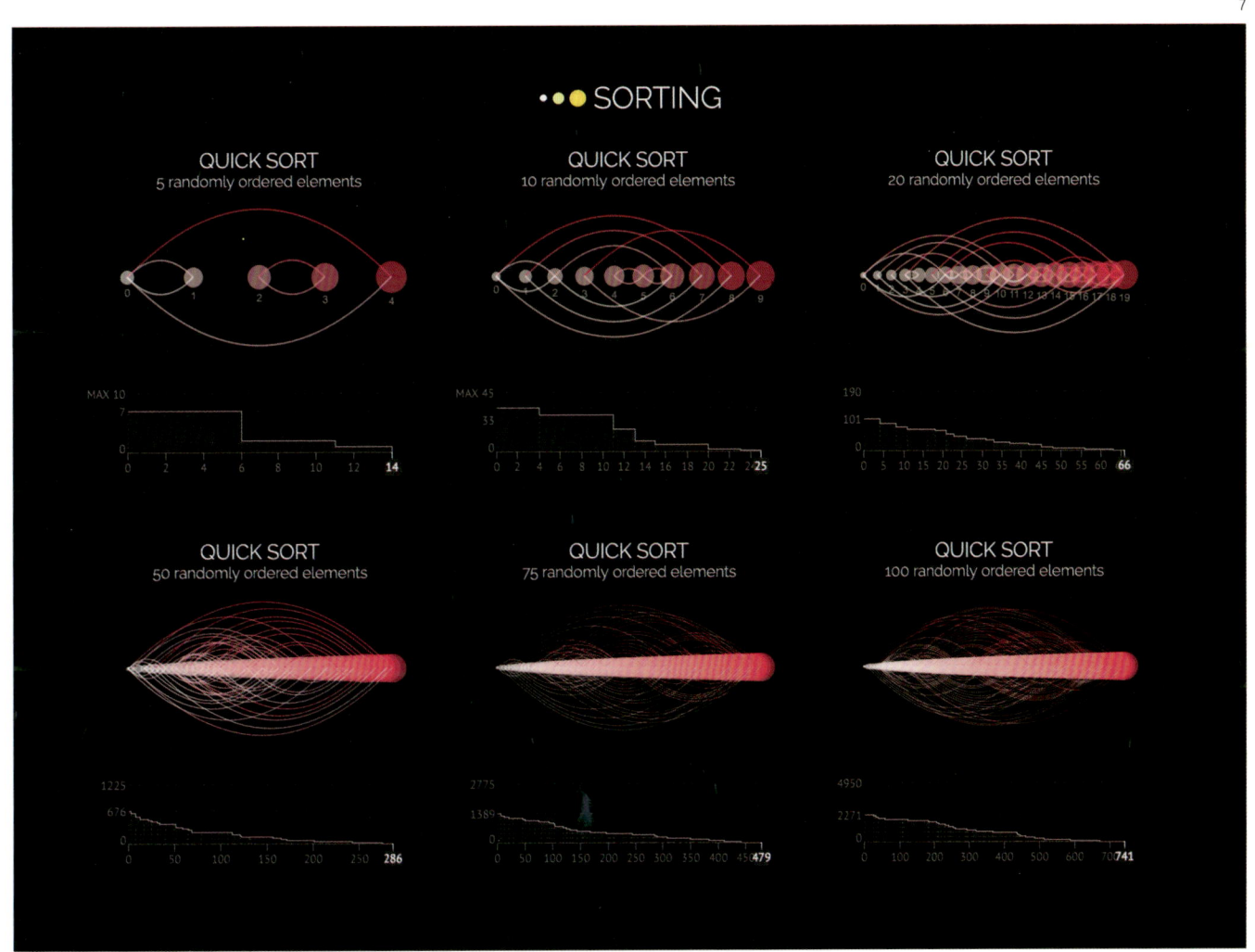

Index

▶ **Albrecht, Kim**
kimalbrecht.com

P13 Science Path
P14 Culturegraphy
P17 Untangling Tennis

▶ **Andrews, RJ**
www.infowetrust.com

P19 Endangered Safari
P20 Characters by the Numbers
P20 Creative Routines

▶ **Attus, Adriano**
adriano.attus.it

P22 Greece's Economic Challenges
P25 Shanghai Stock Exchange
P25 A Map of Mortgages in the First Nine Months of 2015
P26 The Identity Card of Young Europeans
P27 Law-making Activity in Italy

▶ **Braun, Steven**
www.stevenbraun.com

P29 IN/EFFLUX: Visualizing Snell Library Statistics
P31 Niki Segnit's *The Flavor Thesaurus*
P33 Passing the Beat: Crossover Artists in the US, UK, and Japan
P35 Throat Tones: Vowels and Pitch in the Music of Sia and Adele

▶ **Bremer, Nadieh**
www.visualcinnamon.com

P37 Olympic Feathers
P38 Traffic Accidents vs Influential Factors
P40 Switching Between Phone Brands
P43 The Top 10 Baby Names in the US Since 1880

▶ **Carli, Luis**
luiscarli.com

P45 Urban Villages
P46 Confederations Cup
P49 Wood Changes

▶ **Carlson, Chelsea**
chelseacarlson.com

P51 11 Days Deactivated
P51 Slacking off at Work
P52 The Rise and Fall of Airlines
P53 The Past, Present, and Future of Big Data Revenue

▶ **Castagnaviz, Sabina**
www.behance.net/scastagnaviz

P54 The Social Housing
P56 Technology in the Classroom
P57 The Scenery
P59 Our History: 140 Years of News

▶ **Chiang, Meng Chih**
mengchih.com

P61 A Stranger to Words
P65 Infographics for Match History

▶ **Cloudred**
www.cloudred.com

P67 An Interactive Visualization of NYC Street Trees
P69 Shakespeare at the Delacorte Theater

▶ **Dataveyes**
dataveyes.com

P71 Metropolitain
P73 News
P75 My Neighborhood

▶ **Duhalde, Marcelo**
marceloduhalde.com

P77 Scores from the East
P77 Experienced Coaches
P78 From Outside the Box
P78 Waiting in the Row

▶ **Farach, Antonio**
www.behance.net/antoniofarachdo5c

P81 Venues and Schedule
P82 Road to the Finals
P82 Gulf Cup 21 Match Analysis

▶ **Galocha, Artur**
www.arturgv.com

P84 The History of the World Cup
P87 Our Group
P87 Germany and Argentina in the World Cups
P89 The Blue Team

▶ **Garreton, Manuela**
diatomea.co

P91 Drawing Well-being
P92 Map8
P95 Music Score

▶ Guerra, Stefania
www.behance.net/stegue88e47f

P97   What Is Drinking Water Made of, Besides Water
P99   The More the Merrier?
P101 Surfing in Italy

▶ Hahn+Zimmermann
hahn-zimmermann.ch

P103 Infographics for Hochparterre
P105 Educational Pathways
P106 Summa cum Laude
P109 *Die Zeit* Infographics
P111 Swisscom Publication

▶ Heyday
www.heyday.ch

P115 Energy Consumption and Development in Switzerland
P117 Global Human Mobility

▶ Interactive Things
www.interactivethings.com

P119 Global Trade Africa
P123 Galaxy of Covers
P124 The Unified Hour

▶ JESS3
jess3.com

P127 HLN Social Index
P129 Sports Poll Poster, Spring 2014 Update

▶ LaTigre
latigre.net

P131 Viv
P131 Follow the Money
P132 Global Report 2013
P134 Love vs Desire
P134 *Elephant Magazine* #25 & #26

▶ Lopes, Susana
visualoop.com

P138 IRS: Tax with New Rules and Deadlines
P140 World Nuclear Power
P142 Oil Prices Going Down
P142 XXI Government: Which Universities Trained More Ministers

▶ Mauro, Massimiliano
www.behance.net/massimilianomauro

P144 Europe Is Gay-Friendly?
P147 The Russian Roulette of Public Health

▶ Ortiz, Santiago
moebio.com

P149 The Iliad: Gods, Achaeans and Troyans
P151 History Words Flow
P153 Visualization Resources Network
P154 Twitter Network
P156 Ross Spiral

▶ Pellegrini, Valerio
www.behance.net/valeriopellegrini

P159 The Rise and Fall of the UK's Biggest Spammer
P161 Pantheon
P161 FBI's Most Wanted
P162 The Quality of Life in Europe
P163 Auditel
P164 100 Most Valuable Brands
P165 Pasta

▶ Periscopic
www.periscopic.com

P167 Growing Hope
P169 A Model of Breast Cancer Causation
P171 A World of Terror

▶ Piccolomini, Sara
sarapiccolomini.com

P173 Box Office Cinema of Italia
P174 Freedom in Countries
P176 Who Does the Housework?
P176 The Numbers of Culture in Italy
P179 The Black Data of Piemonte
P180 World Ice-Creams Consumption

▶ Pitch Interactive
pitchinteractive.com

P183 Presidential Debates Search Interest Tool
P184 Montpellier
P184 Disease Squeeze
P186 Tech Executive Compensation
P186 An Unprecedented Drought

▶ **Raconteur Media**
raconteur.net

P189 Supply Chain Strategies
P189 The Insight Economy
P191 Future of Outsourcing
P191 Workplace Pensions

▶ **Rowett, Matthew**
matthewrowett.com

P193 The Effects of Spanking Children
P195 War on Terror
P197 Where Do Your Earnings and Taxes Really Go?

▶ **Signal Noise**
signal-noise.co.uk

P198 Data Breaches
P200 String Theories 1
P202 String Theories 2
P202 Rings of Fire
P205 Transfer Window

▶ **South China Morning Post**
www.scmp.com

P206 Measuring the Rule of Law
P209 Silver City
P209 Storm Watch
P210 The Cost of a Family in Hong Kong
P210 The Sum of the Parts

▶ **Stefaner, Moritz**
truth-and-beauty.net

P213 Müsli Ingredient Network
P215 Wahlland
P217 OECD Regional Well-being
P218 OECD Better Life Index
P220 Selfiecity
P222 Stadtbilder

▶ **Swain, Duncan**
beyondwordsstudio.com

P225 Kew Gardens—Full of Spice
P226 Sweet Tweets
P228 Good Country Index

▶ **The Design Surgery**
www.thedesignsurgery.co.uk

P231 Trading Strategies
P231 Cardiovascular Health
P232 Powering the Future
P232 Business Outsourcing

▶ **Torre, Roxana**
www.torre.nl

P235 Migration in the Netherlands
P237 How Healthy Is the Web
P239 How Cities Are Governed

▶ **Tulp, Jan Willem**
tulpinteractive.com

P240 Edible or Medical
P243 Flavor Connection
P245 Goldilocks

▶ **Warriner, Gemma**
gemmawarriner.com

P248 Twenty-Fifty

▶ **Wongsuphasawat, Krist**
kristw.yellowpigz.com

P251 The History of European Cup and UEFA Champions League Finals
P252 UEFA Champions League
P255 Standings Tracer

▶ **Zapponi, Carlo**
www.makinguse.com

P257 Githut
P258 Bolides
P261 Sorting